25.00

D1420938

DICTIONARY OF COMPUTING & INFORMATION TECHNOLOGY

English–German

DICTIONARY OF

COMPUTING
& INFORMATION TECHNOLOGY

English–German

S.M.H. Collin
Eva Torkar
Rupert Livesey

PETER COLLIN PUBLISHING

First published in Great Britain 1991
by Peter Collin Publishing Ltd
8 The Causeway, Teddington, Middlesex, TW11 0HE

British Library Cataloguing-in-Publication Data

Collin, S.M.H.
English – German dictionary of computing and information
technology.
  I. Title   II. Torkar, Eva
  433.0285

  ISBN 0-948549-20-3

Computer processing by Compulexis, Charlton-on-Otmoor, Oxford
Text computer typeset by Systemset, Stotfold, Hertfordshire

Printed in Germany

Vorwort

Das PONS Fachwörterbuch Datenverarbeitung enthält einen etwa 5000 Stichwörter und Wendungen umfassenden Basiswortschatz aus allen Bereichen der Datenverarbeitung. Aufgenommen sind Ausdrücke aus den Teilgebieten Hardware, Software, Peripheriegeräte, Netzwerke, Programmierung und Computeranwendungen wie z. B. Desktop-Publishing. Darüber hinaus werden wichtige Termini der Drucktechnik, der Kommunikationswissenschaften, des Fernmeldewesens sowie weiterer angrenzender Fachgebiete berücksichtigt.

Die Stichwörter und Wendungen werden in leicht verständlichem Englisch erklärt, um den Bedürfnissen des Fremdsprachenlerners Rechnung zu tragen. Der Definitionswortschatz beschränkt sich im wesentlichen auf die als Stichwörter aufgenommenen Termini – nur etwa 500 zusätzliche Wörter werden verwendet.

Den Bedeutungserklärungen folgen jeweils die deutschen Entsprechungen. Die Übersetzer waren dabei bestrebt, die Sprachwirklichkeit zu dokumentieren, auch wenn diese in vielen Fällen den englischen Ausdruck einer deutschen Lehnübersetzung oder Lehnbedeutung vorzieht. Bei der Übertragung ins Deutsche wurde auch der Tatsache Rechnung getragen, daß es für Fachtermini aus der EDV teilweise DIN-normierte Übersetzungen gibt.

Anhand zahlreicher englischer Beispiele wird die Verwendung der Stichwörter und Wendungen im Kontext aufgezeigt.

Bei jedem Stichwort ist die Wortklasse vermerkt. Wörtern, die bestimmte grammatikalische Probleme aufwerfen, sind kurze Erklärungen ("Notes"), beispielsweise mit Angaben zu unregelmäßigen Verb- oder Pluralformen, Konstruktionen oder sonstigen nützlichen Hinweisen beigefügt.

Das Wörterbuch enthält eine Vielzahl von Zitaten aus einem breiten Spektrum englischsprachiger Fachzeitschriften und Magazine. Sie zeigen dem Wörterbuchbenutzer typische, authentische Verwendungszusammenhänge für das jeweilige Stichwort auf. Dort, wo dies sachlich wichtig oder sinnvoll erscheint, folgen nach den Stichwortartikeln Kurzkommentare, beispielsweise zu neuen Entwicklungen, Programmiersprachen oder Anwendungen.

Im zweiten Teil des Wörterbuchs sind die übersetzten deutschen Fachtermini noch einmal mit ihren englischen Entsprechungen in einem alphabetischen Register aufgelistet. Das bietet den Vorteil, daß das Nachschlagen von Wörtern und Wendungen sowohl ausgehend vom Englischen als auch vom Deutschen erfolgen kann. Damit vereinigt das PONS Fachwörterbuch Datenverarbeitung die Vorzüge eines einsprachigen Erklärungswörterbuchs mit denen eines zweisprachigen Nachschlagewerks.

Der Anhang enthält Abbildungen zu Computer und Peripheriegeräten, zeigt die Architektur von Ein- und Mehrplatzsystemen und beschreibt die Zentraleinheit. Darüber hinaus sind ASCII- und EBCDIC-Tabellen sowie eine Darstellung einer RS-232-Schnittstelle enthalten, und Unterschiede verschiedener Programmiersprachen werden anhand eines Beispiels verdeutlicht.

Preface

The ENGLISH-GERMAN DICTIONARY OF COMPUTING AND INFORMATION TECHNOLOGY contains some 5000 English words and phrases with their German equivalents. The subject matter includes the areas of hardware, software, peripherals, networks and programming as well as many applications in which computers are used, such as desktop publishing, graphics, electronics and telecommunications.

The words and phrases are clearly defined in simple English and only 500 words are used in the definitions which do not appear in the dictionary as main words. Many examples are given to show how the words are used in normal contexts and some entries have simple grammar notes to remind the user of irregular verbs or plural forms, constructions used with particular words and other useful points.

General comments about special items of interest, complex ideas or hardware or software applications are given in separate boxes. Quotations from a wide range of magazines and journals are given to show how the words are used in real text.

In the second part of the dictionary a Glossary lists the translated German terms in alphabetical order, together with their English equivalents, thus enabling the user to refer to words both in English and in German.

The Supplement contains diagrams of computers and peripherals, describing the architecture of single and multi-user computer systems and a central processing unit. The ASCII and EBCDIC codes and SI measurements are listed and the RS-232 interface is described, along with examples of different programming languages and other information useful for computing and information technology studies.

Englisch-Deutsches
Wörterbuch

Aa

A = AMPERE base SI unit of electrical current; defined as the current flowing through an impedance of one ohm which has a voltage of one volt across it **A(mpere)**

A hexadecimal equivalent to decimal number 10 **A**

A-bus *noun* main internal bus in a microprocessor **Hauptübertragungsweg**

A programming language (APL) *noun* high-level programming language used for scientific and mathematical work **anwendungsorientierte Programmiersprache**

◊ **A1, A2, A3, A4, A5** *noun* ISO recommended international standard sizes of paper *or* sizes of screen **A1, A2, A3, A4, A5;** *you must photocopy the spreadsheet on A3 paper; we must order some more A4 headed notepaper; a standard 300 d.p.i. black and white A4 monitor* ⟿ APPENDIX

A to D *or* **A/D** = ANALOG TO DIGITAL changing a signal from an analog form to a digitally coded form **Analog-digital-Umwandlung; A to D converter** = (analog to digital converter) device used to convert an analog input to a digital output form which can be understood by a computer **Analog-digital-Umsetzer;** *the speech signal was first passed through an A to D converter before being analysed;* opposite is DIGITAL TO ANALOG

abbreviation *noun* short form of a word *or* command *or* instruction **Abkürzung;** *within the text, the abbreviation proc is used instead of processor;* **abbreviated addressing** *or* **abb. add.** = use of a smaller computer address word than normal which provides faster address decoding operations **Kurzadressierung**

abend *noun* = ABNORMAL END unexpected stoppage of a program being run, due to a fault *or* error *or* power failure **abnormales Ende;** *an interrupt from a faulty printer caused an abend;* **abend recovery program** = software that will reload a program (or system software) and restart it at the point where the abend occurred **Wiederanlaufprogramm nach abnormalem Ende;** *if a fault occurs, data loss will be* minimized due to the improved abend recovery program

aberration *noun*
(a) distortion of a light beam *or* image due to defects in the optical system **Aberration**
(b) distortion of a television picture caused by a corrupt signal *or* incorrect adjustment **Aberration;** *see also* SPHERICAL

abnormal *adjective* not normal **anormal;** *its abnormal for two consecutive disk drives to break down; abnormal error;* **abnormal end** *or* **abend** *or* **abnormal termination** = unexpected stoppage of a program being run, caused by a fault *or* error *or* power failure **anormaler Abbruch**

◊ **abnormally** *adverb* not as normal *or* not as usual **anormal;** *the signal is abnormally weak; the error rate with this disk is abnormally high*

abort *verb* to end a process (when a malfunction occurs), by switching the computer off manually *or* by an internal feature **abbrechen;** *the program was aborted by pressing the red button; abort the program before it erases any more files; see also* RESET

above-the-line costs *plural noun* variable costs involved in making TV films (such as scriptwriters, actors, sets, etc.) as opposed to below-the-line costs (film crew, technicians, etc.) **Kosten über dem Strich**

absolute address *or* **actual address** *or* **machine address** *noun*
(a) computer storage address that directly, without any modification, accesses a location *or* device **absolute Adresse;** *compare* INDEXED ADDRESS *program execution is slightly faster if you code only with absolute addresses*
(b) computer storage address that can only access one location **absolute Adresse; absolute addressing** = locating a data word in memory by the use of its absolute address **absolute Adressierung; absolute assembler** = type of assembly language program designed to produce code which uses only absolute addresses and values **absoluter Assemblierer; absolute code** = binary code which directly operates the

central processing unit, using only absolute addresses and values (this is the final form of a program after a compiler *or* assembler pass) **absoluter Code;** *see also* OBJECT CODE; **absolute instruction** = instruction which completely describes the operation to be performed (no other data is required) **endgültiger Maschinenbefehl; absolute loader** = program that loads a section of code into main memory **Ladeprogramm für absolute Programme; absolute maximum rating** = maximum values or limits of a system **absolute Maximumwerte; absolute program** = computer program written in absolute code **absolutes Programm; absolute value** = size *or* value of a number, regardless of its sign **Absolutwert;** *the absolute value of -62.34 is 62.34; an absolute value of the input is generated*

absorb *verb* to take in (light *or* liquid) **absorbieren, aufsaugen**

◊ **absorptance** *noun* percentage of light that is absorbed by a material instead of reflecting it **Absorptionskonstante;** NOTE: the opposite is **reflectance**

◊ **absorption** *noun* power loss of a signal when travelling through a medium, due to its absorptance **Absorption; absorption filter** = filter that blocks certain colours of light **Absorptionsfilter**

abstract
1 *noun* short version of a book *or* article **Kurzdarstellung, Zusammenfassung;** *in our library, abstracts are gathered together in separate volumes allowing an easy and rapid search for a particular subject*
2 *verb*
(a) to remove something from something **entwenden**
(b) to make a summary of an article **zusammenfassen**

AC = ALTERNATING CURRENT electric current whose value varies with time in a regular, sinusoidal way **Wechselstrom**

COMMENT: the mains electricity supply uses alternating current to minimize transmission power loss, with a frequency of 50Hz in U.K., 60Hz in the USA

ACC *noun* = ACCUMULATOR most important internal CPU storage register, containing the data word that is to be processed **Akkumulator(register)**

acceleration time *noun*
(a) time taken for a disk drive to spin a disk at the correct speed, from rest

Beschleunigungszeit; *allow for acceleration time in the access time*
(b) total time between an access instruction being issued (to a peripheral) and the data being transferred **Anlaufzeit**

accent *noun* small sign placed on *or* above a printed *or* written character to show that it is pronounced in a different way **Akzent; acute accent** = accent above a character, which slopes upwards to the right **Akut; circumflex accent** = accent above a character, shaped like an upside down 'v' **Zirkumflex; grave accent** = accent above a character, which slopes upwards to the left **Gravis;** *see also* CEDILLA, TILDE, UMLAUT
◊ **accented** *adjective* (letter) with an accent on it **(Buchstabe) mit Akzent, betont**

accept *verb*
(a) to agree to do something **annehmen, akzeptieren;** *he accepted the quoted price for printing; she has accepted our terms; he did not accept the programming job he was offered*
(b) to take something which is being offered **annehmen, akzeptieren;** *the laser printer will accept a card as small as a business card; the multi-disk reader will accept 3.5 inch disks as well as 5.25 inch formats;* **call accept signal** = signal sent by a device showing that it is willing to accept (caller's) data **Rufannahmesignal**
◊ **acceptable** *adjective* which can be accepted **annehmbar, akzeptabel;** *the error rate was very low, and is acceptable; for the price, the scratched case is acceptable*
◊ **acceptance** *noun* action of accepting something **Abnahme; acceptance angle** = angle of total field of view of a lens *or* optic fibres **Einfangwinkel;** *a light beam at an angle greater than the acceptance angle of the lens will not be transmitted;* **acceptance sampling** = testing a small random part of a batch to see if the whole batch is up to standard **Qualitätskontrolle mittels Stichprobe; acceptance test** *or* **testing** = method of checking that a piece of equipment will perform as required *or* will reach required standards **Abnahmeprüfung**

access
1 *noun* being allowed to use a computer and read *or* alter files stored in it (this is usually controlled by a security device such as a password) **Zugriff, Zugang; to have access to something** = to be able to get *or* examine *or* reach something **Zugang zu etwas haben;** *to have access to a file of data; he has access to numerous sensitive files;* **to bar access to a system** = to prevent a person from using a system **Zugang zu einem System verwehren;** *after he was discovered hacking,*

he was barred access to the system; **access arm** = mechanical device in a disk drive used to position the read/write head over the correct track on a disk **(Platten)zugriffsarm;** *the access arm moves to the parking region during transport;* **access charge** = cost due when logging onto a system *or* viewing special pages on a bulletin board **Zugriffsgebühr; access code** = series of characters *or* symbols that must be entered to identify a user before access to a computer is permitted **Zugriffscode;** *see also* PASSWORD; **access line** = permanently connected communications line between a terminal and a computer **Anschlußleitung; access method** = means used for the internal transfer of data between memory and display *or* peripheral devices (differences in the methods used is often the cause of compatibility problems) **Zugriffsmethode; access point** = test point on a circuit board *or* in software, allowing an engineer to check signals *or* data **Zugriffspunkt; direct access storage device (DASD)** = storage medium whose memory locations can be directly read *or* written to **Direktzugriffsspeicher; direct memory access (DMA)** = direct, rapid link between a peripheral and a computer's main memory which avoids the use of accessing routines for each item of data required **direkter Speicherzugriff; disk access** = operations required to read from or write to a magnetic disk, including device selection, sector and track address, movement of read/write head to the correct location and access the location on disk **Plattenzugriff; disk access management** = regulating the users who can access stored data **Plattenzugriffsverwaltung; instantaneous access** = storage that has virtually no access time delay, such as access to RAM **unmittelbarer Zugriff;** *the instantaneous access of the RAM disk was welcome;* **parallel access** = data transfer between two devices with a number of bits (usually one byte wide) being sent simultaneously **paralleler Zugriff; public access terminal** = terminal which can be used by anyone to access a computer **Datenstation mit allgemeiner Zugriffsberechtigung; random access** = ability to access immediately memory locations in any order **wahlfreier Zugriff; sequential access** = method of retrieving data from a storage device by starting at the beginning of the medium (such as tape) and reading each record until the required data is found **sequentieller Zugriff; serial access** = one item of data accessed by reading through all the data in a list until the correct one is found **serieller Zugriff**

2 *verb* to call up (data) which is stored in a computer; to obtain data from a storage device **zugreifen auf;** *she accessed the employee's file stored on the computer*

◊ **access control** *noun* security device (such as a password) that only allows selected users to use a computer system *or* read files **Zugriffskontrolle**

COMMENT: a good access control system should allow valid users to gain access and operate the computer easily with the minimum of checks, whilst barring entry to hackers *or* unauthorized users

◊ **accessible** *adjective* which can be reached *or* accessed **zugänglich;** *details of customers are easily accessible from the main computer files*

◊ **access time** *noun*
(a) total time which a storage device takes between the moment the data is requested and the data being returned **Zugriffszeit;** *the access time of this dynamic RAM chip is around 200nS we have faster versions if your system clock is running faster*
(b) length of time required to find a file *or* program, either in main memory *or* a secondary memory source **Ansprechzeit**

accessions *plural noun* new books which are added to a library **Neuerwerbungen; accession number** = serial number used in a library indexing system **Signatur**

accessory *noun* useful device which is attached to *or* used with another **Zubehör(teil);** *the printer comes with several accessories, such as a soundproof hood; this popular home computer has a large range of accessories*

accidental *adjective* which happens by accident **zufällig;** *always keep backup copies in case of accidental damage to the master file*

accordion fold *or* **fanfold** *noun* method of folding continuous paper, one sheet in one direction, the next sheet in the opposite direction, allowing the paper to be fed into a printer continuously with no action on the part of the user **Zickzackfaltung**

accumulate *verb* to gather several things together over a period of time **summieren, aufrechnen, anhäufen;** *we have gradually accumulated a large databank of names and addresses*

◊ **accumulator** *or* **ACC (register)** *noun* most important internal CPU storage register, containing the data word that is to be processed **Akkumulator(register);**

accumulator shift instruction = command to shift the contents of an accumulator left *or* right by one bit **Befehl zur Stellenverschiebung im Akkumulator**

accurate *adjective* correct; without any errors **genau, akkurat;** *the printed bar code has to be accurate to within a thousandth of a micron*

◊ **accurately** *adverb* correctly *or* with no errors **genau, akkurat;** *the OCR had difficulty in reading the new font accurately; the error was caused because the data had not been accurately keyed*

◊ **accuracy** *noun* total number of bits used to define a number in a computer, the more bits allocated the more accurate the definition **Genauigkeit**

> COMMENT: most high level languages allow numbers to be represented in a more accurate form by using two or more words to store the number

acetate *noun* sheet of transparent plastic used for making overlays **Azetat;** *the graphs were plotted on acetate, for use on an overhead projector*

achieve *verb* to succeed in doing something **leisten, erreichen;** *the hardware designers are trying to achieve compatibility between all the components of the system*

achromatic *adjective* (an optical device) that has been corrected for chromatic aberration **achromatisch**

ACIA = ASYNCHRONOUS COMMUNICATIONS INTERFACE ADAPTER circuit that allows a computer to transmit and receive serial data using asynchronous access **asynchroner Kommunikationsschnittstellenanschluß**

ACK = ACKNOWLEDGE *the printer generates an ACK signal when it has received data*

Ackerman's function *noun* recursive function used to test the ability of a compiler to cope with recursion **Ackermann-Funktion**

acknowledge
1 *noun* signal that is sent from a receiver to indicate that a transmitted message has been received and that it is ready for the next one **positive Rückmeldung**
2 *verb* (i) to tell a sender that a message *or* letter has been received; (ii) to send a signal from a receiver to show that a transmitted

message has been received **(i) & (ii) bestätigen; acknowledge character** = special code sent by a receiver to indicate to the transmitter that the message has been correctly received **Quittungszeichen**

◊ **acknowledgements** *noun* text printed at the beginning of a book, where the author *or* publisher thanks people who have helped **Danksagung, Anerkennung**

acoustic *adjective* referring to sound **akustisch; acoustic hood** = soundproof hood placed over a printer to reduce the noise **Schallschluckhaube;** *the acoustic hood allows us to speak and print in the same room;* **acoustic delay line** = original data storage method that delays data (in the form of sound pulses) as it travels across a medium **akustische Verzögerungsleitung; acoustic store** *or* **acoustic memory** = (old) regenerative memory that uses an acoustic delay line **akustischer Speicher**

◊ **acoustic coupler** *noun* device that connects to a telephone handset, converting binary computer data into sound signals to allow data to be transmitted down a telephone line **Akustikkoppler;** *I use an acoustic coupler with my lap-top computer*

> COMMENT: the acoustic coupler also converts back from sound signals to digital signals when receiving messages; it is basically the same as a modem but uses a loudspeaker on which a handset is placed to send the signals rather than direct connection to the phone line. It is portable, and clips over both ends of a normal telephone handset; it can be used even in a public phone booth

◊ **acoustical feedback** *noun* distortion in an audio signal, due to a part of an amplified signal being picked up by the microphone and amplified again until the amplifier is overloaded **akustische Rückmeldung**

◊ **acoustics** *noun* study and science of sound waves **Akustik**

acquisition *noun* accepting *or* capturing *or* collecting information **Erwerb; data acquisition** = gathering data about a subject **Datenerfassung**

ACR = AUDIO CASSETTE RECORDER; **ACR interface** = interface which allows a cassette recorder to be linked to a computer **Schnittstelle zu einem Kassettenrekorder**

acronym *noun* abbreviation, formed from various letters, which makes up a word which can be pronounced **Akronym;** *the acronym FORTRAN means Formula*

Translator; the acronym RAM means Random Access Memory

actinic light *noun* light which is able to cause chemical change in a material, such as film **aktinisches Licht**

action *noun*
(a) thing which has been done **Tat, Aktion;** *action has been taken to repair the fault;* **to take action** = to do something **Schritte unternehmen, etwas tun; action cycle** = complete set of actions involved in one operation (including reading data, processing, storing results, etc.) **Aktionszyklus; action message** = prompt given to inform the user that an action *or* input is required **Aktionsnachricht**
(b) movement **Aktion, Bewegung; action field** = area to be photographed by a camera **Aktionsfeld; action frame** = camera field of view where the filmed action is taking place **Aktionsrahmen; action shot** = still photograph showing action taking place (such as a person running) **Schnappschuß**

◊ **activate** *verb* to start a process *or* to make a device start working **aktivieren, einschalten;** *pressing CR activates the printer*

◊ **active** *adjective* busy *or* working *or* being used **aktiv, wirksam; active device** = electronic component that requires electrical power to operate and provides gain *or* a logical function **Aktivvorrichtung;** *compare with* PASSIVE DEVICE; **active file** = file which is being worked on **aktive Datei; active star** = network consisting of a central point with nodes branching out, in which a central processor controls and routes all messages between devices **sternförmiges Netzwerk; active state** = electronic state in which an action occurs **aktiver Status; active window** = area of display screen in which you are currently working **aktives Fenster;** *see also* WINDOW

◊ **activity** *noun*
(a) being active *or* busy **Tätigkeit, Aktivität; activity loading** = method of organizing disk contents so that the most often accessed files *or* programs can be loaded quickly **LRU-(Speicher)methode; activity ratio** = number of files currently in use compared to the total stored **Bewegungshäufigkeit**
(b) **activities** = jobs *or* tasks which are being performed on a computer **Tätigkeiten, Bewegungen**

actual address *or* **absolute address** *noun* computer storage address that directly, without any modification, accesses a location *or* device **absolute**

Adresse, tatsächliche Adresse; *compare with* INDEXED ADDRESS; **actual code** = binary code which directly operates the central processing unit, using only absolute addresses and values (this is the final form of a program after a compiler *or* assembler pass) **absoluter Code; actual instruction** = the resulting instruction executed after the modification of an original instruction **endgültiger Maschinenbefehl**

actuator *noun* mechanical device that can be controlled by an external signal (such as the read/write head in a disk drive) **Bestätigungsschaltstück**

ACU = AUTOMATIC CALLING UNIT device which allows a computer to call stations *or* dial telephone numbers automatically **automatische Anrufeinrichtung**

acuity *noun*
(a) ability of the eye to define between shades and shapes of an object **(Seh)schärfe**
(b) ability of the ear to detect frequency *or* volume changes **(Hör)schärfe**

acutance *noun* ability of a lens to produce clear edges **Randschärfe**

acute *adjective*
(a) very sharp *or* clear **scharf, spitz**
(b) **acute accent** = accent above a character, which slopes upwards to the right **Akut**

AD = ASSISTANT DIRECTOR, ASSOCIATE DIRECTOR

A/D *or* **A to D** = ANALOG TO DIGITAL change a signal from an analog form to a digitally coded form **Analog-Digital-Umwandlung**

ADA *noun* high-level programming language that is used mainly in military, industrial and scientific fields of computing **ADA (Programmiersprache)**

adapt *verb* to change to fit **anpassen;** *can this computer be adapted to take 5.25 inch disks?*

◊ **adapter** *or* **adaptor** *noun* device that allows two *or* more incompatible devices to be connected together **Adapter;** *the cable adapter allows attachment of the scanner to the SCSI interface; the cable to connect the scanner to the adapter is included in the package;* **adapter card** = add-on interface board that allows incompatible devices to communicate **Anschlußkarte; adapter plug** = plug which allows devices with different plugs (two-pin, three-pin, etc.) to be fitted into the same socket **Zwischenstecker; data adapter unit** = device that interfaces a CPU to one or more communications channels **Datenadapter, Ferndatensteuereinheit**

◊ **adaptation** *noun* ability of a device to adjust its sensitivity range according to various situations **Anpassungsfähigkeit;** *the adaptation of the eye to respond to different levels of brightness*

◊ **adaptive channel allocation** *noun* providing communications channels according to demand rather than a fixed allocation **adaptive Kanalzuordnung; adaptive routing** = ability of a system to change its communications routes according to various events *or* situations such as line failure **adaptiver Leitweg; adaptive systems** = ability of a system to alter its responses and processes according to inputs *or* events *or* situations **anpassungsfähige Systeme**

adaptor *see* ADAPTER

ADC *noun* = ANALOG TO DIGITAL CONVERTER device used to convert analog input to a digital output form, that can be understood by a computer **Analog-Digital-Umsetzer**

add *verb*
(a) to put figures together to make a total **addieren, hinzufügen;** *in the spreadsheet each column should be added to make a subtotal;* **add time** = period of time taken to perform one addition operation (either of a CPU *or* adder) **Additionszeit; add register** = register which is an adder **Additionsregister**
(b) to put things together to form a larger group **zusammenfügen;** *the software house has added a new management package to its range of products; adding or deleting material from the text is easy using function keys*

◊ **added entry** *noun* secondary file entry in a library catalogue **zusätzlicher/sekundärer Eintrag**

◊ **addend** *noun* number added to the augend in an addition **Summand**

◊ **adder** *noun* device *or* routine that provides the sum of two or more (digital *or* analog) inputs **Addiereinrichtung; adder-subtractor** = device that can either add or subtract **Addier-/Subtrahiereinrichtung; full adder** *or* **three input adder** = binary addition circuit which can produce the sum of two inputs, and can also accept a carry input, producing a carry output if necessary **Volladdierer; half adder** *or* **two input adder** = binary addition circuit which can produce the sum of two inputs and a carry output if necessary, but will not accept a carry input

Halbaddierer; parallel adder = a number of full adders arranged in parallel to add two words at once **Paralleladdierer; serial adder** = one bit full adder used to add two words one bit at a time **Serienaddierer**

COMMENT: a parallel adder takes one clock cycle to add two words, a serial adder takes a time equal to the number of bits in a word

◊ **add-in** *noun & adjective* (something) which is added **Zusatz; Zusatz-;** *the first method is to use a page description language, the second is to use an add-in processor card; can you explain the add-in card method? processing is much faster with add-in cards*

◊ **addition** *noun & adjective* arithmetic operation that produces the sum of an addend and augend **Addition; zusätzlich, Zusatz-, zusatz-; addition record** = record with changes used to update a master record *or* file **Zusatzdatensatz; addition time** = time an adder takes to carry out an add operation **Additionszeit; addition without carry** = addition operation without any carry bits *or* words **Addition ohne Übertrag;** *same as* EXOR FUNCTION; **destructive addition** = addition operation in which the result is stored in the location of one of the operands used in the sum, so overwriting it **löschende Addition**

◊ **additional** *adjective* which is added *or* which is extra **zusätzlich;** *can we add three additional workstations to the network?*

◊ **additive colour mixing** *noun* mixing different coloured lights to produce the colour which is wanted **additives Farbmischen**

◊ **add-on** *noun & adjective* piece of software *or* hardware that is added to a computer system to improve its performance **Zusatz; Zusatz-;** *the add-on hard disk will boost the computer's storage capabilities; the new add-on board allows colour graphics to be displayed*

address
1 *noun*
(a) details of number, street and town where an office is or a person lives **Adresse;** *my business address and phone number are printed on the card;* **cable address** = short address for sending cables **Telegrammadresse; home address** = address of a house or flat where someone lives **Privatadresse;** *please send the documents to my home address;* **address list** = list of addresses **Adressenliste;** *we keep an address list of two thousand businesses in Europe*
(b) number allowing a central processing unit to reference a physical location in a storage medium in a computer system

Adresse; *each separate memory word has its own unique address; this is the address at which the data starts;* **absolute address** *or* **actual address** *or* **direct address** = (i) computer storage address (within a CPU's address range) that directly, without any modification, accesses a location *or* device; (ii) computer storage address that can only access one location **(i) & (ii) absolute Adresse; address access time** = total time which a storage device takes between the moment the data is requested and the data being returned **Adressenzugriffszeit; address bus** = physical connection that carries the address data in parallel form from the central processing unit to external devices **Adreßbus; address computation** = operation on address data (in an instruction) **Adreßrechnung; address decoder** = logical circuit that will produce a signal when a certain address *or* range is placed on the address bus **Adressendecodierer; address field** *or* **operand field** = part of a computer instruction that contains the location of the operand **Adreßfeld; address format** = rules defining the way the operands, data and addresses are arranged in an instruction **Adreßformat; address mapping** = virtual address translated to an absolute real address **Adreßabbild; address mark** = special code on a disk that indicates the start of sector location data **Adreßmarke; address modification** = changing the address field, so that it can refer to a different location **Adreßänderung, Adreßmodifikation; address register** = register in a computer that is able to store all the bits that make up an address which can then be processed as a single unit (in small micros, the address register is usually made up of two data bytes) **Adressenregister;** *see also* MAR; **address space** = total number of possible locations that can be directly addressed by the program *or* CPU **Adreßraum; address strobe** = signal (pulse) that indicates that a valid address is on the address bus **Adreßimpulseingang; address track** = track on a magnetic disk containing the addresses of files, etc., stored on other tracks **Adressenspur; address word** = computer word, usually made up, in a small micro, of two data words that contain the address data **Adreßwort; base address** = initial address in a program used as a reference for others **Grund-, Bezugs-, Basisadresse; initial address** = address at which the first location of a program is stored **Anfangsadresse; machine address** = storage address that directly, without any modification, accesses a location *or* device **Maschinenadresse, absolute Adresse; relative address** = location specified in relation to a reference (address) **relative Adresse**

2 *verb*
(a) to write the details of an address on an envelope, etc. **adressieren;** *to address a letter or a parcel; please address your reply to the manager; a letter addressed to the managing director; an incorrectly addressed package*
(b) to put the location data onto an address bus to identify which word in memory *or* storage device is to be accessed **adressieren;** *a larger address word increases the amount of memory a computer can address*

◊ **addressability** *noun* the control available over pixels on screen **Adressierbarkeit**

◊ **addressable** *adjective* which can be addressed **adressierbar;** *all the 5Mb of RAM is addressable;* **addressable cursor** = cursor which can be programmed to be placed in a certain position **adressierbarer Positionsanzeiger/Cursor;** **addressable terminal** = terminal that will only accept data if it has the correct address and identification number in the message header **adressierbare Datenstation, adressierbarer Terminal**

◊ **addressee** *noun* person to whom a letter *or* package *or* communication is addressed **Adressat/-in, Empfänger/-in**

◊ **addressing** *noun* process of accessing a location in memory **Adressierung; absolute addressing** = locating a data word stored in memory, by the use of its absolute address **absolute Adressierung; abbreviated addressing** = use of a smaller address word than normal, which provides faster address decoding operations **Kurzadressierung; bit addressing** = selecting a register and examining one bit within it **Bitadressierung; deferred addressing** = indirect addressing where the location accessed contains the address of the operand to be processed **indirekte/ausgesetzte Adressierung; direct addressing** = method of addressing where the storage location address given in the instruction is the location to be used **direkte Adressierung; immediate addressing** = accessing data immediately because it is held in the address field itself **unmittelbare Adressierung; indexed addressing** = addressing mode, in which the storage location to be accessed is made up of a start (base) address and an offset (index) word, which is then added to it to give the address to be used **indizierte Adressierung; indirect addressing** = way of addressing data, where the first instruction refers to an address which contains a second address **indirekte Adressierung; addressing capacity** = largest location that a certain program *or* CPU can directly address, without special features (such as virtual memory *or* memory banks) **Adressierkapazität; addressing level** = zero-level: operand is the address part of the instruction; first-level: operand stored at the address of the instruction; second-level: operand stored at the address given in the in-struction **Adressierebene**; **addressing method** = manner in which a section of memory is located **Adressiermethode**; **addressing mode** = way in which a location is addressed, either sequential, indexed, direct, etc **Adressierungsart**

◊ **addressing machine** *noun* machine which puts addresses on envelopes automatically **Adressiermaschine**

adjacent *adjective* which is near *or* next to something **benachbart, angrenzend**; *the address is stored adjacent to the customer name field*

adjust *verb* to change something to fit new conditions *or* so that it works better **einstellen, einrichten, justieren, abstimmen**; *you can adjust the brightness and contrast by turning a knob*

◊ **adjustment** *noun* slight change made to something so that it works better **Angleichung, Abstimmung**; *the brightness needs adjustment; I think the joystick needs adjustment as it sometimes gets stuck*

administrator *noun* control *or* supervisor *or* executive software *or* person **Verwalter, Administrator**; **data administrator** = control section of a database management system **Datenverwalter**; **database administrator (DBA)** = person in charge of running and maintaining a database system **Datenbankverwalter**

ADP = AUTOMATIC DATA PROCESSING data processing done by a computer **automatische Datenverarbeitung**

advance *verb* to move forward; to make something move forward **vorwärtsbewegen**; *the paper is advanced by turning this knob; advance the cursor two spaces along the line*

◊ **advanced** *adjective* more complicated *or* more difficult to learn **erweitert, fortgeschritten; advanced version** = program with more complex features for use by an experienced user **erweiterte Version**

adventure game *noun* game played on a computer, where the user pretends to be a hero in an imaginary land and has to get through various dangerous situations, fight monsters, etc. **Abenteuerspiel**

aerial
1 *noun* device for receiving *or* sending radio transmissions by converting electromagnetic impulses into electrical signals and vice-versa **Antenne; aerial cable** = wire stretched between poles which acts as an aerial **Luftkabel**
2 *adjective* in the air **Luft-, luft-; aerial image** = a view from high above a scene **Luftbild, Luftansicht**

affect *verb* to touch *or* to influence *or* to change something **beeinflussen, sich auswirken auf**; *changes in voltage will affect the way the computer functions*

affiliate *verb* to connect *or* join with **angliedern**
◊ **affiliated** *adjective* connected with *or* owned by another company **angegliedert**; *one of our affiliated companies*

affirmative *adjective* meaning "yes" **bejahend, positiv, affirmativ; the answer was in the affirmative** = the answer was "yes" **die Antwort war positiv; affirmative acknowledgement** = acknowledge signal from the receiver that it has accepted the message and is ready for the next one **positive Rückmeldung**

AFNOR *in France* Association Française de Normalisation (the French standards organization) **französische Normenorganisation**

afterglow *see* PERSISTENCE

AGC = AUTOMATIC GAIN CONTROL electronic device that provides a constant amplitude output signal from a varying input signal by changing its gain **automatische Verstärkungsregelung**

agenda *noun* list of things to be discussed at a meeting **Tagesordnung**; *the conference agenda or the agenda of the conference; after two hours we were still discussing the first item on the agenda; the secretary put finance at the top of the agenda; the chairman wants two items removed from or taken off the agenda;* **agenda item** = topic on an agenda to be discussed **Tagesordnungspunkt, TOP**

aggregate *noun* **data aggregate** = collection of items of data that are related **Datenverbund**

AI = ARTIFICIAL INTELLIGENCE the design and development of computer programs that attempt to imitate human intelligence and decision-making functions, providing basic reasoning and other human characteristics **künstliche Intelligenz;** *see also* EXPERT SYSTEM, IKBS

A & I = ABSTRACTING AND INDEXING making summaries and indexes for articles and books **Kurzfassungen und Register machen**

aid
1 *noun* help **Hilfe, Unterstützung;** *the computer is a great aid to rapid processing of large amounts of information;* **diagnostic aid** = hardware *or* software device that helps find faults **Diagnostikhilfe**
2 *verb* to help **helfen, unterstützen;** *industrial design is aided by computers; see also* COMPUTER-AIDED

air gap *noun* narrow gap between a recording *or* playback head and the magnetic medium **Luftspalt**
◊ **air circuit breaker** *noun* mechanical device that has an electrical *or* manual switched circuit isolator **Luftschalter**

alarm *noun* ringing or other sound which warns of a danger **Warnsignal, Fehlersignalisierung;** *all staff must leave the building if the alarm sounds; an alarm rings when the printer has run out of paper*

albumen plate *noun* photographic plate, with a light-sensitive coating **Albumin**

ALC = AUTOMATIC LEVEL CONTROL *see* AGC

algebra *noun* use of letters in certain mathematical operations to represent unknown numbers *or* a range of possible numbers **Algebra; Boolean algebra** = rules set down to define, simplify and manipulate logical functions, based on statements that are true or false **Boolesche Algebra**

ALGOL = ALGORITHMIC LANGUAGE high level programming language using algorithmic methods for mathematical and technical applications **algorithmische Programmiersprache**

algorithm *noun* rules used to define *or* perform a specific task *or* to solve a specific problem **Algorithmus**
◊ **algorithmic** *adjective* expressed using algorithms **algorithmisch; algorithmic language** = computer language designed to

process and express algorithms, such as ALGOL **algorithmische Sprache**

QUOTE image processing algorithms are step by step procedures for performing image processing operations
Byte
QUOTE the steps are: acquiring a digitized image, developing an algorithm to process it, processing the image, modifying the algorithm until you are satisfied with the result
Byte
QUOTE the complex algorithms needed for geometrical calculations make heavy demands on the processor
PC Business World

alien *adjective* different *or* not fitting the usual system **fremd, anders; alien disk** = disk formatted on another system *or* containing data in a format which is in a form that cannot be read *or* understood **anders formatierte Diskette; alien disk reader** = add-on device which allows a computer to access data on disks from other computers *or* systems **Leser für anders formatierte Disketten;** *when you have an alien disk select the multi-disk option to allow you to turn the disk drive into an alien disk reader*

align *verb*
(a) to make sure that the characters to be printed are spaced and levelled correctly **justieren, ausrichten**
(b) to ensure that a read/write head is correctly positioned over the recording medium **ausrichten**
◊ **aligner** *noun* device used to make sure that the paper is straight in a printer **Ausrichtungstransportbahn, Zeilen(ein)richter, Justierschiene**
◊ **aligning edge** *noun* edge of an optical character recognition system used to position a document **Führungskante**
◊ **alignment** *noun* correct spacing and levelling of printed characters **Ausrichtung; in alignment** = correctly aligned **richtig ausgerichtet; out of alignment** = not aligned correctly **nicht richtig ausgerichtet; alignment pin** = peg that fits in a hole to ensure that two devices are correctly aligned **Ausrichtungsnadel**

allocate *verb* to divide (a period of time *or* a piece of work) in various ways and share it out between users **zuteilen;** *the operating system allocated most of main memory to the spreadsheet program*
◊ **allocation** *noun* dividing something in various ways **Zuteilung;** *allocation of time or capital to a project;* **allocation routine** = short program that divides the memory resources of a system between the software and peripherals that use it **Zuteilungsroutine; dynamic allocation** = system where

resources are allocated during a program run, rather than being determined in advance **dynamische Zuteilung; band allocation** = range of frequencies allocated to various users *or* for various purposes **Bandzuteilung;** *the new band allocation means we will have more channels*

allophone *noun* smallest unit of sound from which speech can be formed **Allophon**

alpha beta technique *noun* (free structure) technique used in artificial intelligence for solving game and strategy problems **Alpha-Beta-Technik**

alpha radiation *noun* naturally occurring radiation *α*-**Strahlen; alpha-particle** = emitted alpha radiation particle *α*-**Teilchen; alpha-particle sensitivity** = problem experienced by certain (MOS) memory devices exposed to alpha radiation, causing loss of stored charge (data) **Empfindlichkeit/Sensibilität für** *α*-**Teilchen**

alpha wrap *noun* method used for feeding tape into a helical scan video recorder to make sure the alignment is correct **Alphawindung**

alphabet *noun* the 26 letters used to make words **Alphabet**
◊ **alphabetic character (set)** *noun* characters (capitals and small letters) that make up the alphabet **Buchstabe; alphabetic string** = string that only contains alphabetic characters **Buchstabenkette**
◊ **alphabetical order** *noun* arrangement of records (such as files, index cards) in the order of the letters of the alphabet (A,B,C,D, etc.) **alphabetische Reihenfolge**
◊ **alphabetically** *adverb* in alphabetical order **alphabetisch;** *the files are arranged alphabetically under the customer's name*
◊ **alphabetize** *verb* to put into alphabetical order **alphabetisch ordnen;** *enter the bibliographical information and alphabetize it*

alphageometric *adjective* (set of codes) that instruct a teletext terminal to display various graphics patterns *or* characters **alphageometrisch**

alphameric *(US)* = ALPHANUMERIC

alphamosaic *adjective* (character set) used in teletext to provide alphanumeric and graphics characters **Alphamosaik-, alphamosaik(-)**

alphanumeric *adjective* **alphanumeric characters** *or* **alphanumerics** = roman letters and arabic numerals (and other signs such as punctuation marks) **alphanumerische Zeichen; alphanumeric data** = data that represents the letters of the alphabet and the arabic numerals **alphanumerische Daten; alphanumeric display** = display device able to show characters as well as numbers **alphanumerische Anzeige; alphanumeric keyboard** = keyboard containing character keys as well as numerical keys **alphanumerische Tastatur; alphanumeric operand** = operand which can contain alphanumeric characters, such as a string **alphanumerischer Operand; alphanumeric string** = series of alphanumeric characters that are manipulated and treated as a single unit **alphanumerische Zeichenkette**

QUOTE geometrical data takes up more storage space than alphanumeric data
PC Business World

alphaphotographic *adjective* which represents pictures using predefined graphics characters, for teletext services **alphafotografisch**
◊ **alphasort** *verb* to sort data into alphabetical order **alphabetisch ordnen**

alter *verb* to change **ändern, abändern;** *to alter the terms of a contract; the program specifications have just been altered*
◊ **alterable** *adjective* which can be altered **veränderbar;** *see* EAPROM, EAROM
◊ **alteration** *noun* change which has been made **Änderung;** *the agreement was signed without any alterations; the new version of the software has many alterations and improvements*

alternate
1 *verb* to change from one state to another and back, over and over again **wechseln, alternieren**
2 *adjective* which change from one to another **abwechselnd, alternierend; alternate mode** = application for multi-user use, where two operators can access and share a single file at the same time **Ausweichmodus, Alternativmodus; alternate route** = backup path in a communications system, used in case of a fault *or* breakdown **Alternativweg, Ausweichleitweg**
◊ **alternately** *adverb* switching from one to the other **abwechselnd, alternierend**
◊ **alternation** *noun* logical function that produces a true output if any input is true **Wechsel**
◊ **alternating current** *or* **AC** *noun* electric current whose value varies with time in a

regular, sinusoidal way (changing direction of flow each half cycle) **Wechselstrom**

◊ **alternator** *noun* device which produces an alternating current **Wechselstromgenerator, Lichtmaschine**

alternative
1 *noun* thing which can be done instead of another **Alternative, andere Wahl, Ausweichmöglichkeit;** *what is the alternative to re-keying all the data?;* **we have no alternative** = there is nothing else we can do **wir haben keine andere Wahl**
2 *adjective* other *or* which can take the place of something **alternativ; alternative denial** = logical function whose output is false if all inputs are true and true if any input is false **NAND-Funktion**

ALU = ARITHMETIC LOGIC UNIT section of the CPU that performs all arithmetic and logical functions **Rechenwerk im CPU**

AM = AMPLITUDE MODULATION

A-MAC low bandwidth variation of MAC **A-MAC**

ambient *adjective* normal background (conditions) **umgebend, im Hintergrund; ambient noise level** = normal background noise level **Hintergrundgeräusch;** *the ambient noise level in the office is greater than in the library;* **ambient temperature** = normal average temperature of the air around a device **Umgebungstemperatur**

ambiguous *adjective* which has two possible meanings **zweideutig, mehrdeutig, uneindeutig; ambiguous filename** = filename which is not unique to a single file, making it difficult to locate the file **uneindeutiger Dateiname**

◊ **ambiguity** *noun* something which is not clearly defined **Zwei-, Mehrdeutigkeit; ambiguity error** = error due to incorrect selection of ambiguous data **Fehler aufgrund von Uneindeutigkeit**

ambisonics *noun* recording more than one audio signal to give the effect of being surrounded by sound **umgebender Schall**

AMM = ANALOG MULTIMETER multimeter that uses a graduated scale and a moving needle as a readout for voltage, current and impedance levels **Analogmultimeter;** *compare with* DMM

amendment record *noun* record containing new information used to update a master record *or* file **Änderungssatz**

American National Standards Institute (ANSI) organization which specifies computer and software standards including those of high-level programming languages **amerikanische Organisation zur Erstellung von Industrienormen**

American Standard Code for Information Interchange (ASCII) code which represents alphanumeric characters as binary codes **ASCII-Code**

amount
1 *noun* quantity of data *or* paper, etc. **Menge;** *what is the largest amount of data which can be processed in one hour?*
2 *verb* **to amount to** = to make a total of **sich belaufen auf, betragen;** *the total keyboarded characters amount to ten million*

amp *or* **ampere (A)** *noun* base SI unit of electrical current; defined as the current flowing through an impedance of one ohm which has a voltage of one volt across it **Ampere**
NOTE: used with figures: **a 13-amp fuse**

ampersand *noun* printing sign (&) which means "and" **Und-Zeichen (&)**

amplifier *noun* electronic circuit that magnifies the power of a signal **Verstärker; audio amplifier** = domestic amplifier that handles frequencies in the human hearing range **Tonverstärker; low noise amplifier** = high-quality amplifier placed very close to a receiving aerial to amplify the received signals before they are corrupted by noise **rauscharmer Verstärker; amplifier class** = way of classifying the design of amplifiers meant for different jobs **Verstärkerklasse**

◊ **amplification** *noun* the output-to-input signal strength ratio **Verstärkung;** *increase the amplification of the input signal; the amplification is so high, the signal is distorting*

◊ **amplify** *verb* to magnify a signal power *or* amplitude **verstärken;** *the received signal needs to be amplified before it can be processed;* **amplified telephone** = system to allow hands-off telephone conversations **lautverstärktes Telefon**

amplitude *noun* strength *or* size of a signal **Amplitude; amplitude distortion** = distortion of a signal due to uneven (non-linear) amplification (high levels amplified less than low) **Amplitudenverzerrung; amplitude modulation (AM)** = system that varies the amplitude of a constant carrier according to an external signal **Amplitudenmodulation; amplitude quantization** = conversion of an analog signal to a numerical representation **(Amplituden-)Quantisierung**

analog *or* **analogue** *noun* representation and measurement of numerical data by continuously variable physical quantities, such as the size of electrical voltages **Entsprechung, Analog-;** *compare with* DIGITAL; **analog channel** = communications line that carries analog signals such as speech **Analogkanal; analog computer** = computer which processes data in analog form (that is, data which is represented by a continuously varying signal - as opposed to digital data) **Analogrechner; analog gate** = logic gate whose output is proportional to an input signal **Analogschaltelement; analog input card** = all circuitry on one PCB required for amplifying and converting analog input signals to a digital form **analoge Eingabekarte; analog multimeter** = multimeter that uses a graduated scale and a moving needle as a readout for voltage, current and impedance levels **Analogmultimeter;** *compare with* DMM; **analog output card** = all circuitry on one PCB required to convert digital output data from a computer to an analog form **analoge Ausgabekarte; analog recording** = storing signals in their natural form without conversion to digital form **Analogaufzeichnung; analog representation** = value *or* variable in analog form **Analogdarstellung; analog signal** = continuously varying signal **analoges Signal; analog to digital (A to D** *or* **A/D)** = change a signal from an analog form to a digitally coded form **Analog-Digital-Umwandlung; analog to digital converter (ADC** *or* **A to D converter)** = device used to convert an analog input signal to a digital output form, that can be understood by a computer **Analog-Digital-Umsetzer; digital to analog converter (DAC** *or* **D to A converter)** = circuit that outputs an analog signal that is proportional to the input digital number, and so converts a digital input to an analog form **Digital-Analog-Umsetzer**

> COMMENT: a DAC allows the computer to work outside the computer's environment, controlling machines, producing sound *or* speech, etc.; an ADC allows real-world signals to be processed by a computer

analyse *or* **analyze** *verb* to examine in detail **analysieren, kritisch untersuchen;** *to*

analyse a computer printout; to analyse the market potential for a new computer

◊ **analysis** *noun* detailed examination and report **Analyse, Untersuchung;** *market analysis; sales analysis; to carry out an analysis of the market potential; to write an analysis of the sales position;* **cost analysis** = examination in advance of the costs of a new product **Kostenanalyse; data analysis** = to extract information and results from data **Datenanalyse, Datenauswertung; systems analysis** = analysing a process *or* system to see if it could be more efficiently carried out by computer **Systemanalyse;** NOTE: plural is **analyses**

◊ **analyst** *noun* person who carries out an analysis of a problem **Analytiker/-in; systems analyst** = person who specializes in systems analysis **Systemanalytiker**

◊ **analyzer** *noun* electronic test equipment that displays various features of a signal **Analysator; frequency analyzer** = test equipment that displays the amplitudes of the various frequency components of a signal **Frequenzanalysator**

anamorphic image *noun* image which has been distorted in one direction **Verzeichnung**

ANAPROP = ANOMALOUS PROPAGATION distortion of transmitted television signals due to atmospheric conditions **verzerrte Übertragung**

anastigmat *noun* lens *or* optical device that has been corrected for astigmatism **anastigmatische Linse**

ancestral file *noun* system of backing up files (son to father to grandfather file), where the son is the current working file **Dateivorfahre**

ancillary equipment *noun* equipment which is used to make a task easier, but which is not absolutely necessary **Zusatzgeräte**

AND *or* **coincidence function** *noun* logical function whose output is true if both its inputs are true **UND-Funktion; AND** *or* **coincidence gate** *or* **circuit** *or* **element** = electronic gate that performs a logical AND function on electrical signals **UND-Schaltung; AND** *or* **coincidence operation** = processing two or more input signals, outputting their AND function **UND-Verknüpfung**

COMMENT: if both inputs are 1, results of the AND will be 1; if one of the input digits is 0, then AND will produce a 0

anechoic *adjective* (room) that produces no echoes, used for testing audio equipment **schalltot, echofrei**

angle *noun* measure of the change in direction, usually as the distance turned from a reference line **Winkel; wide-angle lens** = lens which has a large acceptance angle **Weitwinkelobjektiv**

angstrom *noun* unit of measurement equal to one thousand millionth of a metre **Ångström**

animate *verb* to make a series of drawings which, when filmed, will create moving images **beleben, (Film) animieren**
◊ **animation** *noun* drawing images on film, especially using a computer to create moving graphical images, such as cartoons **Animation**

annotation *noun* comment *or* note in a program which explains how the program is to be used **Bemerkung, Anmerkung; annotation symbol** = symbol used when making flowcharts, to allow comments to be added **Zeichen für eine Anmerkung**

annunciator *noun & adjective* signal that can be heard *or* seen that is used to attract attention **Signalgeber(-)**

anode *noun* positive electrical terminal of a device **Anode**

anomalistic period *noun* time taken for a satellite to travel between consecutive maximum points in its orbit **anomalistischer Zeitraum**

ANSI *(US)* = AMERICAN NATIONAL STANDARDS INSTITUTE organization which specifies computer and software standards, including those of high-level programming languages **amerikanische Organisation zur Erstellung von Industrienormen**

answer
1 *noun* reply *or* letter *or* conversation coming after someone has written or spoken **Antwort;** *I am writing in answer to your letter of October 6th; my letter got no answer or there was no answer to my letter; I tried to phone his office but there was no answer*
2 *verb*
(a) to speak *or* write after someone has spoken or written to you **antworten; to answer a letter** = to write a letter in reply to a letter which you have received **einen Brief beantworten; to answer the telephone** = to lift the telephone when it rings and listen to what the caller is saying **das Telefon abnehmen**
(b) to reply to a signal and set up a communications link **beantworten;** *the first modem originates the call and the second answers it;* **answer back** = signal sent by the receiving end of a communications system to identify itself *or* to transmit a message **Antwort; answer time** = time taken for a receiving device to respond to a signal **Beantwortungszeit**
◊ **answering** *noun* **answering machine** = machine which answers the telephone automatically when someone is not in the office **automatischer Anrufbeantworter; answering service** = office which answers the telephone and takes messages for someone *or* for a company **Anrufbeantworterbüro**
◊ **answerphone** *noun* cassette recorder attached to a telephone, which plays a prerecorded message and records messages from people dialling the number **automatischer Anrufbeantworter**

antenna *noun* aerial *or* device for receiving *or* sending radio transmissions by converting electromagnetic impulses into electrical signals and vice-versa **Antenne; antenna array** = series of small transmitting *or* receiving elements connected in parallel, that make up a complex antenna **Antennengruppierung; antenna gain** = transmitted signal power increase due to using a certain type of antenna **Antennenverstärkung**

anti- *prefix* meaning against **anti-, gegen-, wider-; anticoincidence circuit** *or* **function** = logical function whose output is true if either (of 2) inputs is true, and false if both inputs are the same **Antivalenzglied**
◊ **anti-tinkle suppression** *noun (in a modem)* switch which prevents other telephones on a line ringing when a modem dials out **Unterdrückung des Telefonklingelns**

APD = AVALANCHE PHOTODIODE

aperture *noun* opening in a device that allows a certain amount of light *or* a signal to pass through it **Öffnung; aperture card** = method of storing microfilmed information with a card sur-round, that can contain punched information **Filmlochkarte; aperture illumination** = pattern generated from an aperture antenna **Aperturflächenausleuchtung; aperture mask** = mask used in colour televisions *or* monitors to keep the red, green and blue beams separate **Schattenmaske**

APL = A PROGRAMMING LANGUAGE high-level programming language used in scientific and mathematical work **anwendungsorientierte Programmiersprache**

apochromatic lens *noun* optical lens that has been corrected for chromatic aberration **apochromatische Linse (gegen Farbabweichungen)**

apogee *noun* point in a satellite's orbit where it is at its maximum distance from the earth **Apogäum, erdfernster Punkt**

apostrophe *noun* printing sign ('), which generally indicates that a letter is missing *or* used in ('s), to indicate possession **Apostroph**
NOTE: **computer's** can mean 'belonging to a computer' *or* 'the computer is': **the computer's casing is blue; the computer's broken and has to be repaired.** Note that this is different from **it's** = 'it is' as opposed to **its** = 'belonging to it': **it's easy to program; you cannot edit a disk when its write protect tag is closed**

append *verb* to add data to an existing file *or* record **anhängen, anfügen, ketten**
◊ **appendix** *noun* section at the back of a book, containing additional information **Anhang, Ergänzung;** *for further details see the appendices; a complete list is printed in the appendix*
NOTE: plural is **appendices**

appliance *noun* machine, especially one used in the home **Gerät, Vorrichtung;** *all electrical appliances should be properly earthed*
◊ **appliance computer** *noun* ready to run computer system that can be bought in a shop, taken home and used immediately for a particular purpose **gebrauchsfertiger Computer;** *see also* TURNKEY

application *noun*
(a) asking for something, usually in writing **Antrag;** *application for an account on the system;* **application form** = form to be filled in when applying **Antragsformular;** *to fill in an application (form) for an account on the system*

(b) task which a computer performs *or* problem which a computer solves (as opposed to an operating system which is the way in which a computer works) **Anwendung; application layer** = top layer in an ISO/OSI network, which requests a transmission (from a users program) **anwendungsbezogene Schicht; application orientated language** = programming language that provides functions that allow the user to solve certain application problems **anwendungsbezogene Sprache; applications package** = set of computer programs and manuals that cover all aspects of a particular task (such as payroll, stock control, tax, etc.) **Anwendungsprogrammpaket; applications software** *or* **applications program** = programs which are used by a user to make the computer do what is required, designed to allow a particular task to be performed **Anwendungsprogramm;** *the multi-window editor is used to create and edit applications programs;* **applications specific integrated circuits (ASIC)** = specially designed ICs for one particular function *or* to special specifications **integrierte Schaltkreise für bestimmte Funktionen; applications terminal** = terminal (such as at a sales desk) which is specially configured to carry out certain tasks **anwendungsorientierte Datenstation**

> QUOTE they have announced a fourth generation application development tool which allows users of PCs and PC networks to exchange data with mainframe databases
> *Minicomputer News*

apply *verb*
(a) to ask for something, usually in writing **etwas beantragen, sich bewerben**
(b) to affect *or* to touch **betreffen;** *this formula applies only to data received after the interrupt signal*

appoint *verb* to choose someone for a job **einstellen, ernennen;** *to appoint James Smith (to the post of) manager; we have appointed a new computer services manager* NOTE: you appoint a person **to** a job
◊ **appointee** *noun* person who is appointed to a job **Ernannte(r)**
◊ **appointment** *noun*
(a) arrangement to meet **Termin, Verabredung;** *to make or to fix an appointment for two o'clock; to make an appointment with someone for two o'clock; he was late for his appointment; she had to cancel her appointment;* **appointments book** = desk diary in which appointments are noted **Terminkalender**
(b) being appointed to a job **Ernennung; on his appointment as manager** = when he was

made manager **bei seiner Ernennung zum Manager; letter of appointment** = letter in which someone is appointed to a job **Ernennungsschreiben** (c) job **Stelle; staff appointment** = job on the staff **Anstellung; computer appointments vacant** = list (in a newspaper) of jobs which are available in the computer industry **freie Stellen in der Computerindustrie**

approve verb
(a) **to approve of** = to think something is good **gutheißen, billigen**; *the new graphics monitor was approved by the safety council before being sold; I approve of the new editor - much easier to use*
(b) to agree to something **zustimmen**; *to approve the terms of a contract; the software has to be approved by the board; an approved modem should carry a label with a green circle and the words "Approved by...."*
◊ **approval** *noun*
(a) agreement that something can be used **Billigung, Zustimmung, Einverständnis**; *a BABT approval is needed for modems;* **certificate of approval** = document showing that an item has been approved officially **Anerkennungsurkunde, Genehmigungszertifikat**
(b) **on approval** = sale where the buyer only pays for goods if they are satisfactory **auf Probe, zur Ansicht**; *to buy a photocopier on approval*
NOTE: no plural

approximate adjective
not exact, but almost correct **annähernd**; *we have made an approximate calculation of the time needed for keyboarding*
◊ **approximately** *adverb* almost correctly **annähernd**; *processing time is approximately 10% lower than during the previous quarter*
◊ **approximating** *adjective* which is nearly correct **annähernd**; *using approximating A to D*
◊ **approximation** *noun* rough calculation **(An)näherung(swert)**; *approximation of keyboarding time; the final figure is only an approximation;* **approximation error** = error caused by rounding off a real number **Näherungsfehler**

APT = AUTOMATICALLY PROGRAMMED TOOLS programming language used to control numerically controlled machines **Programmiersprache**

Arabic *adjective* **Arabic numbers** *or* **figures** = figures such as 1, 2, 3, 4, etc. (as opposed to the Roman numerals I, II, III. IV, etc.) **arabische Zahlen**; *the page numbers are written in Arabic figures*

arbitration noun
bus arbitration = protocol and control of transmission over a bus that ensures fair usage by several users **Buszuteilung**

arcade game noun
computer game played on a machine in a public place **öffentliches Computerspiel**

archetype noun
document *or* book that illustrates the styles of a particular time and subject **Archetyp**

architecture noun
layout and interconnection of a computer's internal hardware and the logical relationships between CPU, memory and I/O devices **Aufbau, Architektur; onion skin architecture** = design of a computer system in layers, according to function *or* priority **Zwiebelschalenarchitektur**; *the onion skin architecture of this computer is made up of a kernel at the centre, an operating system, a low-level language and then the user's programs*

archive
1 *noun* storage of data over a long period **Archiv; archive file** = file containing data which is out of date, but which is kept for future reference **Archivdatei**
2 *verb* to put data in storage **archivieren; archived copy** = copy kept in storage **Archivkopie**
◊ **archival quality** *noun* length of time that a copy can be stored before it becomes illegible **Archivierungsqualität**

QUOTE on-line archiving is also used to keep down the interruption needed for archiving to seconds
Computer News

area noun
(a) measurement of the space taken up by something (calculated by multiplying the length by the width) **Bereich**; *the area of this office is 3,400 square feet; we are looking for a shop with a sales area of about 100 square metres;* **type area** = space on a page which is taken up by printed characters **Satzspiegel; area composition** = organizing and setting up pages before photocomposition **Layout**
(b) section of memory *or* code that is reserved for a certain purpose **Speicherbereich; area search** = search for specific data within a certain section of memory *or* files **Bereichssuche; image area** = region of a display screen in which characters can be displayed **Bildbereich; input area** = section of main memory that holds data transferred from backing store until it is processed **Eingabebereich**

(c) part of a country *or* town **Gebiet;** *his sales area is the centre of the town; he finds it difficult to cover all his area in a week;* **area code** = part of a telephone number that allows the exchange to identify the part of the country required **Vorwahl;** *the area code for London is 071;* **area exchange** = central point in a part of a country where telephone calls are directed to their correct destination inside the area *or* to another exchange **Telefonvermittlungsstelle**

◊ **area manager** *noun* manager who deals with a certain part of the country **Gebietsleiter**

argue *verb* to discuss something about which you do not agree **diskutieren, argumentieren;** *they argued over or about the design of the cover; we spent hours arguing with the managing director about the layout of the new factory* NOTE: you argue **with** someone **about** *or* **over** something

◊ **argument** *noun*
(a) discussing something without agreeing **Auseinandersetzung;** *they got into an argument with the customs officials over the documents; he was sacked after an argument with the managing director*
(b) variable acted upon by an operator *or* function **Parameter;** *see also* OPERAND

arithmetic *noun* concerned with mathematical functions such as addition, subtraction, division and multiplication **Arithmetik; arithmetic capability** = ability of a device to perform mathematical functions **arithmetische Fähigkeit; arithmetic check** = further arithmetic operation carried out to ensure that a result is correct **Rechenprüfung; arithmetic functions** = calculations carried out on numbers, such as addition, subtraction, multiplication, division **arithmetische Funktionen; arithmetic instruction** = program instruction in which the operator defines the arithmetic operation to be carried out **Rechenbefehl;** *compare with* LOGICAL INSTRUCTION; **arithmetic logic unit (ALU)** *or* **arithmetic unit** = hardware section of a CPU that performs all the mathematical and logical functions **Rechenwerk im CPU; arithmetic operation** = mathematical function carried out on data **Rechenoperation; arithmetic operators** = symbol which indicates an arithmetic function (such as + for addition, x for multiplication) **Rechenzeichen; arithmetic register** = memory location which stores operands **Rechenregister; arithmetic shift** = word *or* data moved one bit to the left *or* right inside a register, losing the bit shifted off the end **arithmetische Stellenverschiebung;** *compare with* LOGICAL SHIFT; **external arithmetic** = arithmetic performed by a coprocessor **extern ausgeführte Rechnung; internal arithmetic** = arithmetic performed by the ALU **im Rechenwerk ausgeführte Rechnung**

arm
1 *noun* **access arm** = mechanical device in a disk drive used to position the read/write head over the correct track on a disk **(Platten)zugriffsarm**
2 *verb* (i) to prepare a device *or* machine *or* routine for action *or* inputs; (ii) to define which interrupt lines are active **(i) & (ii) vorbereiten; armed interrupt** = interrupt line which has been made active (using an interrupt mask) **absichtliche Unterbrechung**

array *noun* ordered structure containing individually accessible elements referenced by numbers, used to store tables *or* sets of related data **Anordnung, Feldgruppe; alphanumeric array** = array whose elements are letters and numbers **alphanumerische Feldgruppe; array bounds** = limits to the number of elements which can be stored in an array **Grenzen der Strukturgröße; array dimension** = number of elements in an array, given as rows and columns **Matrixdimension; array element** = one individual piece of data within an array **Matrixelement; array processor** = computer that can act upon several arrays of data simultaneously, for very fast mathematical applications **Vektorenrechner;** *the array processor allows the array that contains the screen image to be rotated with one simple command;* **string array** = array whose elements can be strings (of alphanumeric characters) **Anordnung einer Zeichenkette; three-dimensional array** = array made up of a number of two dimensional arrays, arranged in parallel, giving rows, columns and depth **dreidimensionale Matrix; two-dimensional array** = ordered structure whose elements are arranged as a table (of rows and columns **zweidimensionale Matrix**

arsenide *see* GALLIUM ARSENIDE

article *noun*
(a) section of a newspaper *or* magazine **Artikel;** *he wrote an article about the user group for the local newspaper*
(b) section of an agreement **Artikel, Paragraph;** *see article 8 of the contract*

artificial intelligence (AI) *noun* the design and device of computer programs that attempt to imitate human intelligence and decision making functions, providing basic reasoning and other human characteristics **künstliche Intelligenz**

artwork *noun* graphical work *or* images which are to be printed **Reprovorlage;** *the artwork has been sent for filming*
NOTE: no plural

ASA American Standards Association **ASA (amerikanische Normeninstitution); ASA exposure index =** one standard method used to code the sensitivity of film **Filmempfindlichkeitsangabe**

ascender *noun* part of a character that rises above the main line of printed characters (as the 'tail' of a 'b', 'd', etc.) **Oberlänge**

ASCII = AMERICAN STANDARD CODE FOR INFORMATION INTERCHANGE code which represents alphanumeric characters in binary code **ASCII-Code; ASCII character** = character which is in the ASCII list of codes **ASCII-Zeichen; ASCII file =** stored file containing only ASCII coded character data **ASCII-Datei;** *use a word processor or other program that generates a standard ASCII file;* **ASCII keyboard =** keyboard which gives all the ASCII characters **ASCII-Tastatur;** NOTE: when speaking say "as-key"

ASIC = APPLICATION SPECIFIC INTEGRATED CIRCUITS specially designed ICs for one particular function *or* to special specifications **integrierte Schaltkreise für bestimmte Funktionen**

aspect *noun* way in which something appears **Erscheinung, Aussehen, Aspekt; aspect card =** card containing information on documents in an information retrieval system **Aspektkarte; aspect ratio =** ratio of the width to the height of pixel shapes **Längen- und Seitenverhältnis; aspect system =** method of storing and indexing documents in a retrieval system **Aspektsystem**

ASR = AUTOMATIC SEND/RECEIVE device *or* terminal that can transmit *or* receive information **automatischer Sender/Empfänger;** *compare* KSR

COMMENT: an ASR terminal can input information via a keyboard or via a tape cassette or paper tape. It can receive information and store it in internal memory or on tape

assemble *verb*
(a) to put a hardware *or* software product together from various smaller parts **zusammensetzen;** *the parts for the disk drive are made in Japan and assembled in France*
(b) to translate assembly code into machine code **assemblieren, umwandeln;** *there is a short wait during which time the program is assembled into object code; syntax errors spotted whilst the source program is being assembled*
(c) to insert specific library routines *or* macros *or* parameters into a program **assemblieren**

◊ **assembler (program)** *noun* assembly program *or* program which converts a program written in assembly language into machine code **Assemblerprogramm; absolute assembler =** type of assembly language program designed to produce code which uses only absolute addresses and values **absoluter Assemblierer; assembler error messages =** messages produced by an assembler program that indicate that errors have been found in the source code **Assemblierer-Fehlermeldungen; cross-assembler =** assembler that produces machine-code code for one computer while running on another **Kreuzassemblierer; single-pass assembler =** object code produced in one run through the assembler of the source program **Assemblierer mit einem Durchlauf; two-pass assembler =** assembler that converts an assembly language program into machine code in two passes, the first pass stores symbolic addresses, the second converts them to absolute addresses **Assemblierer mit zwei Durchläufen**

◊ **assembly** *noun*
(a) putting an item together from various parts **Montage;** *there are no assembly instructions to show you how to put the computer together;* **assembly plant =** factory where units are put together from parts made in other factories **Montagewerk**
(b) converting a program into machine code **Umwandlung; assembly code =** mnemonics which are used to represent machine code instructions in an assembler program **Umwandlungscode; assembly language** *or* **assembler language =** programming language used to code information which will then be converted to machine code **Assembliersprache; assembly listing =** display of an assembly program ordered according to memory location **Assemblerliste; assembly (language) program =** number of assembly code instructions which perform a task **Assemblerprogramm; assembly routine** *or* **system =** *see* ASSEMBLER; **assembly time =** (i) time taken by an assembler program to translate a program; (ii) period during which an assembler is converting a program from assembly language into machine code **(i) & (ii) Umwandlungszeit**

assertion *noun* (i) program statement of a fact *or* rule; (ii) fact that is true *or* defined as being true **(i) Behauptung; (ii) Beteuerung**

assign *verb*
(a) to give a computer *or* someone a job of work **anweisen;** *he was assigned the job of checking the sales figures; two PCs have been assigned to outputting the labels*
(b) (i) to set a variable equal to a string of characters *or* numbers; (ii) to reserve part of a computer system for use while a program is running **(i) zuordnen; (ii) freihalten; assigned frequency** = frequency reserved for one user *or* application **zugeordnete Frequenz**

◇ **assignment** *noun*
(a) transfer of a property *or* of a right **Übertragung, Übereignung, Abtretung;** *assignment of a copyright*
(b) particular job of work **Aufgabe;** *he was appointed managing director with the assignment to improve the company's profits; the oil team is on an assignment in the North Sea*
(c) setting a variable equal to a string of characters *or* a value **Zuordnung; assignment statement** = basic programming command that sets a variable equal to a value *or* string *or* character **Zuordnungsanweisung**

◇ **assignor** *noun* person who assigns something to someone **An-, Zuweiser; Abtretende(r); Zedent**

assist *verb* to help **helfen, assistieren;** *can you assist the stock controller in counting the stock? he assists me with my income tax returns* NOTE: you assist someone **in** doing something or **with** something

◇ **assistance** *noun* help **Hilfe, Unterstützung; financial assistance** = help in the form of money **finanzielle Unterstützung;** NOTE: no plural

◇ **assistant** *noun* person who helps *or* an ordinary employee **Assistent/-in; personal assistant** = secretary who also helps the boss in various ways **persönlicher Assistent; shop assistant** = person who serves the customers in a shop **Bedienung, Verkäufer/-in; assistant manager** = person who helps a manager **stellvertretender Manager**

associate
1 *adjective* linked **zugehörig, verbunden, assoziiert; associate company** = company which is partly owned by another **Teilhaberfirma, Beteiligungsgesellschaft**
2 *noun* person who works in the same business as someone **Kollege, Partner;** *she is a business associate of mine*

◇ **associational editing** *noun* way of editing a film *or* video so as to present together scenes which are similar to others **Assoziativschnitt**

◇ **associative addressing** *or* **content-addressable addressing** *noun* location addressed by its contents rather than its address **Assoziativadressierung; associative processor** = processor that uses associative storage **Assoziativprozessor; associative memory** *or* **storage** *or* **content-addressable storage** = method of data retrieval that uses part of the data rather than an address to locate the data **Assoziativspeicher; associative storage register** = register that is located by its contents rather than a name *or* address **Assoziativspeicherregister**

astable multivibrator *noun* electronic current that repeatedly switches an output between two voltage levels **astabiler/instabiler Multivibrator**

asterisk *noun* graphical symbol (*) used in programming as a sign for multiplication **Stern(chen) (*)**

astigmatism *noun* optical lens disorder which prevents the light beams from converging properly **Astigmatismus**

async *(informal)* = ASYNCHRONOUS

asynchronous *adjective* serial data *or* equipment which does not depend on being synchronized with another piece of equipment **asynchron; asynchronous access** = communications using handshaking to synchronize data transmission **asynchroner Zugriff; asynchronous communications** = data transmission between devices that is not synchronized to a clock, but is transmitted when ready **asynchrone Übertragung; asynchronous communications interface adapter (ACIA)** = circuit that allows a computer to transmit and receive serial data using asynchronous access **asynchroner Kommunikationsschnittstellenanschluß; asynchronous computer** = (i) computer that changes from one operation to the next according to signals received when the process is finished; (ii) computer in which a process starts on the arrival of signals *or* data, rather than on a clock pulse **(i) & (ii) Asynchronrechner; asynchronous mode** = terminal linked to another piece of equipment in a way where the two need not be synchronized **Asynchronübertragung; asynchronous port** = connection to a computer allowing asynchronous data access **Asynchronanschluß;** *since asynchronous ports are used no special hardware is required;* **asynchronous**

transmission = data transmission that uses handshaking signals rather than clock signals to synchronize data pulses **asynchrone Übertragung**

QUOTE each channel handles two forms of communication: asynchronous communication is mainly for transferring data between computers and peripheral devices, while character communication is for data transfer between computers

Electronics & Power

ATC = AUTHORIZATION TO COPY software publisher granting the user the permission to make a certain number of copies of a program **Kopiergenehmigung**

ATE = AUTOMATIC TEST EQUIPMENT computer controlled testing facilities, that can check a complex circuit *or* PCB for faults *or* problems **automatische Prüfeinrichtung**

ATM = AUTOMATED TELLER MACHINE

atmosphere *noun* gas which surrounds the earth **Atmosphäre**
◊ **atmospheric** *adjective* referring to the atmosphere **atmosphärisch; atmospheric absorption** = energy loss of a radio signal due to atmospheric conditions causing dispersion of the signal **atmosphärische Absorption; atmospheric conditions** = state of the atmosphere (including clouds, pressures, etc.) **atmosphärische Bedingungen**

atom *noun*
(a) smallest particle of an element that has the same properties as the element **Atom**
(b) value *or* string that cannot be reduced to a simpler form **Atom**
◊ **atomic** *adjective* referring to atoms **Atom-; atomic clock** = very accurate clock which uses changes in energy of atoms as a reference **Atomuhr**

attach *verb* to fasten *or* to link **anschließen, befestigen; attached processor** = separate microprocessor in a system that performs certain functions under the control of a central processor **Anschlußprozessor**
◊ **attachment** *noun* device which is attached to a machine for a special purpose **Anschluß, Zusatzgerät;** *there is a special single sheet feed attachment*

attack *noun* start of a sound **Einsatz; attack envelope** = shape of the initial section of a signal **Anfangskurve**

attend *verb* to be present at **anwesend sein**

◊ **attend to** *verb* to give careful thought to (something) and deal with it **Beachtung schenken, sich kummern um;** *attend to this fault first - its the worst*
◊ **attended operation** *noun* process which has an operator standing by in case of problems **überwachter Ablauf**
◊ **attention** *noun* giving careful thought, especially to processing a particular section of a program **Aufmerksamkeit; Abruf, Unterbrechung;** *this routine requires the attention of the processor every minute;* **attention interruption** = interrupt signal that requests the attention of the processor **Abrufunterbrechung, Achtung Unterbrechung; attention key** = key on a terminal that sends an interrupt signal to the processor **Unterbrechungstaste, Abruftaste**

attenuate *verb* to reduce the strength *or* size of peaks (of a signal) **abschwächen, dämpfen**
◊ **attenuation** *noun* reduction of a signal as it passes through a medium **Abschwächung, Dämpfung**

attribute *noun* (i) field entry in a file; (ii) information concerning the display *or* presentation of information **(i) Eintrag; (ii) Attribut;** *this attribute controls the colour of the screen;* **screen attributes** = variables defining the shape, size and colour of text *or* graphics displayed **Bildschirmattribute**

auctioneering device *noun* device that will select the maximum *or* minimum signal from a number of input signals **Vorrichtung zum Auswählen der Extremsignale**

audible *adjective* which can be heard **hörbar, akustisch;** *the printer makes an audible signal when it runs out of paper*

audience *noun* people who watch a TV programme *or* listen to a radio programme **Publikum; Zuschauer; Zuhörer; audience rating** = rating of a programme by calculating the number of people who have watched it **Einschaltquote**

audio *adjective & noun* referring to sound *or* to things which can be heard **audio-, Ton-; audio active** = system used in a learning laboratory, where the student can hear and respond to questions **audioaktiv; audio cassette** = reel of magnetic recording tape in a small protective casing inserted into a cassette recorder (for recording music *or* voice *or* data) **Tonkassette; audio compressor** = circuit that limits the maximum level of a signal by attenuating any peaks **Ton(frequenz)kompressor;** **audio**

conferencing *see* TELECONFERENCING; **audio frequency** = frequency within the audio range that a human can hear **Tonfrequenz; audio range** = frequency range between 50-20000Hz **Ton(frequenz)bereich; audio response unit** = speech synthesizer that allows a computer to speak responses to requests **Sprachausgabeeinheit; audio slide** = photographic slide that has magnetic tape along an edge allowing sound to be recorded **Diapositiv mit Tonspur**

◇ **audiovisual (AV)** *adjective* which uses sound and images **audiovisuell; audiovisual aids** = equipment used in teaching, which includes both sound and pictures **audiovisuelle Hilfsmittel**

audit *noun* noting tasks carried out by a computer **Protokoll, Revision; audit trail** = recording details of use of a system by noting transactions carried out (used for checking on illegal use *or* to trace a malfunction) **Buchungskontrolle**

augend *noun (in an addition)* the number to which another number, the addend, is added to produce the sum **Augend, erster Summand**

augment *verb* to increase **vermehren, vergrößern, erweitern; augmented addressing** = producing a usable address word from two shorter words **erweiterte Adressierung**

◇ **augmenter** *noun* value added to another **Summand**

aural *adjective* by ear **aural, Hör-, hör-**

authentic *adjective* which is true **echt, authentisch**

◇ **authenticate** *verb* to say that something is true *or* genuine **bestätigen, authentifizieren**

◇ **authentication** *noun* making sure that something is authentic **Bestätigung, Authentifizierung; authentication of messages** = using special codes to identify the sender of messages, so that the messages can be recognized as being genuine **Echtheitsbestätigung von Meldungen**

author *noun* person who wrote a program **Verfasser, Autor; author language** = programming language used to write CAL and training programs **Verfassersprache; authoring system** = computer system that is able to run an author language **Verfassersystem**

authority *noun* power to do something **Berechtigung, Vollmacht, Befugnis;** *he has no authority to delete your account;* **authority**

file *or* **list** = list of special terms used by people compiling a database and also by the users of the database **Benutzerdatei**

authorize *verb*
(a) to give permission for something to be done **genehmigen;** *to authorize the purchase of a new computer system*
(b) to give someone the authority to do something **berechtigen, autorisieren, ermächtigen**

◇ **authorization** *noun*
(a) permission *or* power to do something **Berechtigung; authorization to copy (ATC)** = software publisher granting the user the permission to make a certain number of copies of a program **Kopiergenehmigung**

> COMMENT: some companies have introduced ATC schemes which allow users of certain software to make duplicates of the companies' programs for a fee

(b) giving a user permission to access a system **Zugriffsberechtigung; authorization code** = code used to restrict access to a computer system to authorized users only **Berechtigungscode;** NOTE: no plural

◇ **authorized** *adjective* permitted **berechtigt, autorisiert; authorized user** = person who is allowed to access a system **berechtigter Benutzer**

auto *adjective & prefix* automatic *or* which works without the user needing to act **auto-, automatisch; auto advance** = paper in a printer that is automatically moved forward to the next line at the end of a line **automatischer Zeilenvorschub; auto-answer** = (modem) that will automatically answer a telephone when called **automatische Anrufbeantwortung; auto-baud scanning** circuit that can automatically sense and select the correct baud rate for a line **automatische Baud-Abtastung; auto boot** = computer system that will initiate a boot-up procedure when it is switched on **automatischer Urlader; auto-dial** = to dial a number automatically using stored data **selbstwählen; auto-login** *or* **auto-logon** = phone number, password and user's number transmitted when requested by a remote system to automate logon **automatische Anmeldung;** *see also* LOGIN, LOGON; **auto-redial** = (modem) that dials a telephone number again if engaged, until it replies **automatische Wählwiederholung; auto repeat** = facility where a character is automatically repeated if the key is kept pressed down **Dauerfunktion; auto restart** = computer that can initialize and reload its operating system if there is a fault *or* power failure *or* at switch on **automatischer**

Wiederanlauf; auto start = facility to load a program automatically when the computer is switched on **automatischer Start; auto stop** = feature of a tape player which stops when it has reached the end of a tape **Tonträger-Endabschaltung; auto verify** = verification procedure carried out automatically, as soon as the data has been saved **Selbstprüfung**

QUOTE expansion accessories include auto-dial and auto-answer
Electronic & Wireless World

automate *verb* to install machines to do work previously done by people **automatisieren; automated office** = office where many of the tasks are done by machines **automatisiertes Büro; automated teller machine (ATM)** = *(US)* automatic telling machine *or* machine linked to a main computer that allows cash to be taken out of a bank account when a special card is inserted and special instructions given **Geldausgabeautomat**

◇ **automation** *noun* use of machines to do work with very little supervision by people **Automatisierung**
NOTE: no plural

automatic *noun & adjective* (machine) which works by itself, without being worked by an operator **Automat; automatisch; automatic calling unit (ACU)** = device which allows a computer to call telephone numbers automatically **automatische Anrufeinrichtung; automatic carriage return** = system where the cursor automatically returns to the beginning of a new line when it reaches the end of the previous one **automatischer Wagenrücklauf; automatic checking** = error detection and validation check carried out automatically on received data **Selbstprüfung, automatische Prüfung; automatic data capture** = system where data is automatically recorded in a computer system, as it is input **automatische Datenaufzeichnung; automatic data processing (ADP)** = data processing done by a computer **automatische Datenverarbeitung; automatic decimal adjustment** = process of lining up all the decimal points in a column of figures **automatische Dezimalstellenausrichtung; automatic error correction** = correction of received data, using error detection and correction codes **automatische Fehlerkorrektur; automatic error detection** = use of an (alphanumeric) code, such as a gray code, that will allow any errors to be detected **automatische Fehlererkennung; automatic gain control (AGC)** = electronic device that provides a constant amplitude

output signal from a varying input signal, by changing its gain **Aussteuerungsautomatik; automatic letter writing** = writing of form letters (using a wordprocessor) **automatisches Briefschreiben; automatic loader** = short program (usually in ROM) that will boot up a system and load a program **automatisches Ladeprogramm; automatic message accounting** = system of logging telephone calls automatically so that details of them can be given to the user **automatische Anrufaufzeichnung; automatic programming** = process of producing an optimum (operating) system for a particular process **automatisches Programmieren; automatic repeat** = facility where a character is automatically repeated if the key is kept pressed down **Dauerfunktion; automatic sequencing** = ability of a computer to execute a number of programs *or* tasks without extra commands **automatische Programmsteuerung; automatic telephone exchange** = telephone exchange operated by a computer rather than a human operator **computergesteuertes Fernsprechamt; automatic telling machine** *or* *(US)* **automated teller machine (ATM)** = machine which allows money to be taken out of a bank account when a special card is inserted and special instructions given **Geldausgabeautomat; automatic test equipment (ATE)** = computer controlled testing facilities, that can check a complex circuit *or* PCB for faults *or* problems **automatische Prüfeinrichtung; automatic vending machine** = machine which provides drinks, cigarettes, etc., when money is put in **Automat**

◇ **automatically** *adverb* (machine) working without a person giving instructions **automatisch;** *the statements are sent out automatically; addresses are typed in automatically; a demand note is sent automatically when payment is late; the compiler automatically corrected the syntax errors; a SBC automatically limits the movement of the machine; the program is run automatically when the computer is switched on*

automation *see* AUTOMATE

autopositive *noun* photographic process that produces a positive image without a negative stage **Umkehrentwicklung**

auxiliary *adjective* which helps **Hilfs-, zusätzlich;** *the computer room has an auxiliary power supply in case there is a mains failure;* **auxiliary equipment** = backup *or* secondary equipment in case of a breakdown **Hilfs-, Zusatzgeräte; auxiliary processor** = extra, specialized processor, such as an array *or* numerical processor that can work with a main CPU to increase execution speed **Hilfsprozessor; auxiliary storage** *or* **memory** *or* **store** = any data storage medium (such a magnetic tape *or* floppy disk) that is not the main high speed computer storage (RAM) **Hilfsspeicher;** *disk drives and magnetic tape are auxiliary storage on this machine*

AV = AUDIOVISUAL

available *adjective* which can be obtained *or* bought **verfügbar;** *available in all branches; item no longer available; items available to order only;* **available light** = light which is present at a place where photographs are being taken, without needing additional artificial light **vorhandenes Licht, Tageslicht; available list** = list of unallocated memory and resources in a system **Liste freier Speicherplätze; available point** = smallest single unit *or* point of a display whose colour and brightness can be controlled **benutzbarer Punkt; available power** = maximum electrical *or* processing power that a system can deliver **Richt(leistungs)wirkungsgrad; available time** = time during which a system may be used **verfügbare Benutzerzeit**
◇ **availability** *noun* being easily obtained **Verfügbarkeit;** *the availability of the latest software package is very good;* **offer subject to availability** = the offer is valid only if the goods are available **solange Vorrat reicht** NOTE: no plural

avalanche *noun* one action starting a number of other actions **Lawine;** *there was an avalanche of errors after I pressed the wrong key;* **avalanche photodiode (APD)** = photodiode able to detect very low light levels (one photon received produces several electrons) **Lawinendiode, Avalanche-Diode**

average
1 *noun* number calculated by adding together several figures and dividing by the number of figures added **Durchschnitt;** *the average for the last three months or the last three months' average; sales average or average of sales;* **weighted average** = average which is calculated taking several factors into account, giving some more value than others **gewichteter Durchschnitt, Bewertungsdurchschnitt; on an average** = in general **durchschnittlich;** *we sell, on an average, five computers a day*
2 *adjective* middle (figure) **durchschnittlich;** *average cost per unit; average price; average*

sales per representative; **average access time** = the average time taken between a request being sent and data being returned from a memory device **mittlere Zugriffszeit; average delay** = average time that a user must wait when trying to access a communication network **mittlere Verzögerung;** *see also* MEAN *the average delay increases at nine-thirty when everyone tries to log-in*
3 *verb* to produce as an average figure **den Durchschnitt ermitteln**
◇ **average out** *verb* to come to a figure as an average **durchschnittlich betragen;** *it averages out at 120 dpi*

axis *noun* (i) line around which something turns; (ii) reference line which is the basis for coordinates on a graph **(i) Achse; (ii) Koordinate(nachse);** *the CAD package allows an axis to be placed anywhere;* **horizontal axis** = reference line used for horizontal coordinates on a graph **x-Achse, Abszisse(nachse); vertical axis** = reference line used for vertical coordinates on a graph **y-Achse, Ordinate(nachse)** NOTE: plural is **axes**

azerty keyboard *noun* method of arranging the keys on a keyboard where the first line begins AZERTY (used mainly in Europe) **AZERTY-Tastatur;** *compare* QWERTY

azimuth *noun* angle of a tape head to a reference (such as a tape plane) **Azimut, Richtungswinkel; azimuth alignment** = correct horizontal angle of a tape head to the magnetic tape **Justieren des Richtungswinkels;** *azimuth alignment is adjusted with this small screw; azimuth alignment might not be correct for tape recorded on a different machine*

Bb

B hexadecimal equivalent to decimal number 11 **B**

babble *noun* crosstalk *or* noise from other sources which interferes with a signal **Nebensprechen**

BABT = BRITISH APPROVAL BOARD FOR TELECOMMUNICATIONS; **BABT approval** = official approval for a device to be connected to the public telephone system **britische Telekommunikationsgenehmigung**

back

1 *noun* opposite side to the front **Rückseite;** *there is a wide range of connectors at the back of the main unit*
2 *verb* to help **unterstützen; battery-backed =** (volatile storage device) that has a battery backup **batterieunterstützt;** *the RAM disk card has the option to be battery-backed; battery-backed CMOS memory replaces a disk drive in this portable*

back-end processor *noun* special purpose auxiliary processor **Nachschaltrechner**

background *noun*

(a) past work *or* experience **Hintergrund, Werdegang;** *his background is in the computer industry; the company is looking for someone with a background of success in the electronics industry; what is his background or do you know anything about his background?*
(b) part of a picture which is behind the main object of interest **Hintergrund;** *the new graphics processor chip can handle background, foreground and sprite movement independently;* **background colour =** colour of a computer screen display (characters and graphics are normally displayed in a different foreground colour) **Hintergrundfarbe;** *white background colour with black characters is less stressful for the eyes;* **background noise =** noise which is present along with the required signal **Nebengeräusch;** *the other machines around this device will produce a lot of background noise; the modem is sensitive to background noise;* **background projection** *or* **back projection =** film projected onto the back of a screen, in front of which further action is filmed **Hintergrundprojektion**
(c) system in a computer where low-priority work can be done in the intervals when very important work is not being done **Hintergrundprogrammbetrieb; background job =** low priority task **Hintergrundjob; background printing =** printing from a computer while it is processing another task **Nebenherdrucken;** *background printing can be carried out whilst you are editing another document;* **background program =** computer program with a very low priority **Hintergrundprogramm; background task =** process executed at any time by the computer system, not normally noticed by the user **Hintergrundtask**

◊ **background processing** *noun*

(a) low priority job which is executed when there are no higher priority activities for the computer to attend to **nachrangige Verarbeitung**
(b) process which does not use the on-line capabilities of a system **Hintergrundverarbeitung**
NOTE: opposite is **foreground**

backing *noun* **backing store** *or* **storage** *or* **memory =** permanent storage medium onto which data can be recorded before being processed by the computer *or* after processing for later retrieval **Hilfs-, Zusatzspeicher;** *by adding another disk drive, I will increase the backing store capabilities; paper tape is one of the slowest access backing stores; compare with* MAIN MEMORY

backlog *noun* work *or* tasks that have yet to be processed **Rückstand;** *the programmers can't deal with the backlog of programming work; the queue was too short for the backlog of tasks waiting to be processed*
NOTE: no plural

back number *noun* old copy of a journal *or* periodical **alte Ausgabe**

back pack *noun* lightweight television recording equipment which the cameraman carries on his back when filming **Rucksack**

backplane *noun* part of the body of a computer which holds the circuit boards, buses and expansion connectors (the backplane does not provide any processing functions) **gedruckte Rückwandverdrahtung, Rückwandplatine;** *see* MOTHERBOARD, RACK

back projection *noun* background projection *or* film projected onto the back of a screen, in front of which further action is filmed **Hintergrundprojektion**

backscatter *noun* reflected *or* scattered radio wave travelling in the opposite direction to the original signal **Rückstreuung**

backspace *noun* movement of a cursor *or* printhead back by one character **Rückwärtsschritt; backspace character =** code that causes a backspace action in a display device **Rücksetzungszeichen; backspace key =** key which moves the cursor back one space **Rücktaste;** *if you make a mistake entering data, use the backspace key to correct it*

backtrack *verb* to carry out list processing in reverse, starting with the goal and working towards the proofs **zurückverfolgen**

back up *verb*
(a) to make a copy of a file *or* data *or* disk **sichern;** *the company accounts were backed up on disk as a protection against fire damage; the program enables users to back up hard disk files with a single command*
(b) to help **unterstützen;** *he brought along a file of documents to back up his claim; the printout backed up his argument for a new system*

◊ **backup** *adjective & noun*
(a) helping **unterstützend; Sicherung;** *we offer a free backup service to customers;* **battery backup** = use of a battery to provide power to a volatile device (RAM chip) to retain data after a computer has been switched off **Batteriesicherung**
(b) backup *or* **backup file** *or* **backup copy** = copy of a file *or* set of data kept for security against errors in the original *or* master copy **Sicherungskopie; backup copy** = copy of a computer disk to be kept in case the original disk is damaged **Sicherungskopie;** *the most recent backup copy is kept in the safe;* **backup procedure** = method of making backup copies of files **Datensicherungsprozedur; memory backup capacitor** = very high capacitance (small) device that can provide power for volatile RAM chips for up to two weeks (used instead of a battery) **Sicherungskondensatorspeicher**

QUOTE the system backs up at the rate of 2.5Mb per minute
Microcomputer News
QUOTE the previous version is retained, but its extension is changed to .BAK indicating that it's a back-up
Personal Computer World

Backus-Naur-Form (BNF) system of writing and expressing the syntax of a programming language **Backus-Naur-Form**

backward *or* **backwards** *adjective & adverb* towards the back *or* in the opposite direction **rückwärts; backward channel** = channel from the receiver to transmitter allowing the receiver to send control and handshaking signals **Hilfskanal; backward error correction** = correction of errors which are detected by the receiver and a signal is sent to the transmitter to request a re-transmission of the data **rückwärtige Fehlerkorrektur; backward mode** = negative displacement from an origin **Rückwärtsmodus; backward recovery** = data retrieval from a system that has crashed

Wiederherstellungsverfahren; backwards supervision = data transmission controlled by the receiver **Rückwärtssteuerung**

COMMENT: backward recovery is carried out by passing the semi-processed data from the crashed computer through a routine that reverses the effects of the main program to return the original data

bad break *noun* wrong hyphenation of a word at the end of a line of text **falsche Silbentrennung**

◊ **bad copy** *noun* illegible *or* badly edited manuscript which the typesetter will not accept **schlechtes Manuskript**

◊ **bad sector** *noun* sector which has been wrongly formatted *or* which contains an error *or* fault and is unable to be correctly written to or read from **fehlerhafter Sektor;** *you will probably receive error messages when you copy files that are stored on bad sectors on a disk*

badge reader *noun* machine that reads data from an identification badge **Ausweisleser;** *a badge reader makes sure that only authorized personnel can gain access to a computer room*

baffle *noun* sections of material placed in a loudspeaker, used to prevent unwanted internal resonating frequencies **Resonanzwand**

bag *noun* number of elements in no particular order **Beutel**

balance
1 *noun*
(a) placing of text and graphics on a page in an attractive way **Ausgewogenheit;** *the dtp package allows the user to see if the overall page balance is correct*
(b) positioning of musical instruments so that they may be recorded to their best advantage **Ausgeglichenheit**
(c) amplitude control of left and right audio signals in a stereo system **Ausgewogenheit; balance stripe** = thin magnetic stripe on a cine film on the opposite side to the sound track, so that the whole film will lie flat when played back **Ausgleichsstreifen**
2 *verb* to plan something so that two parts are equal **ausgleichen, ausbalancieren; balanced circuit** = electronic circuit that presents a correct load to a communications line (the correct load is usually equal to the impedance of a line element) **ausgeglichener Stromkreis;** *you must use a balanced circuit at the end of the*

line to prevent signal reflections; **balanced error** = the probability of any error occurring (from a number of errors) is the same for all errors **symmetrischer Fehler; balanced line** = communications line that is terminated at each end with a balanced circuit, preventing signal reflections **symmetrische Leitung**

band *noun*
(a) range of frequencies between two limits **Band; base band** = frequency range of a signal before it is processed *or* transmitted **Basisband;** *voice base band ranges from 20Hz to 15KHz;* **base band modem** = communications circuit that transmits an unmodulated (base band) signal over a short distance **Gleichstrom-Datenübertragungseinrichtung für niedrige Sendespannung;** *do not use a base band modem with a normal phone line;* **base band local area network** = LAN using unmodulated signals transmitted over coaxial cable, often using a CSMA/CD protocol **Basisbandnetz**
(b) group of tracks on a magnetic disk **Band**

◇ **banding** *noun* **elastic banding** = method of defining the limits of an image on the computer screen by stretching a boundary round it **elastische Grenzen;** *elastic banding is much easier to control with a mouse*

◇ **bandlimited** *adjective* (signal) whose frequency range has been limited to one band **bandbegrenzt**

◇ **bandpass filter** *noun* circuit that allows a certain band of frequencies to pass while stopping any that are higher *or* lower **Bandfilter, Bandpaß;** *compare with* LOW PASS, HIGH PASS

◇ **band printer** *noun* printer in which the characters are located along a movable steel belt **Banddrucker**

◇ **bandwidth** *noun* the limits of frequencies used **Bandbreite;** *telephone bandwidth is 3100 Hz*

bank *noun* collection of similar devices **Bank;** *a bank of minicomputers process all the raw data;* **bank switching** = selection of a particular memory bank from a group **Bankauswahl; memory bank** = collection of electronic memory devices connected together to form one large area of memory **Speicherbank;** *an add-on card has a 128KB memory bank made up of 16 chips; see also* DATABANK

COMMENT: memory banks are used to expand the main memory of a CPU (often above the addressing range of the CPU) by having a number of memory chips arranged into banks. Each bank operates over the same address range but is selected independently by a special code

banner *noun (in printing)* heading *or* title extending to the width of a page **Balkenüberschrift; banner headlines** = large headlines on a newspaper running across the width of the page **Schlagzeilen**

bar
1 *noun* thick line *or* block of colour **Strich, Balken**
2 *verb* to stop someone from doing something **verbieten, ausschließen; to bar entry to a file** = to stop someone accessing a file **den Zugang zu einer Datei verwehren**
◇ **bar chart** *or* **bar graph** *noun* graph on which values are represented as vertical *or* horizontal bars **Balkendiagramm**

◇ **bar code** *or (US)* **bar graphics** *noun* data represented as a series of printed stripes of varying widths **Streifencode; bar-code reader** *or* **optical scanner** = optical device that reads data from a bar code **optischer Leser, optischer Abtaster**

COMMENT: bar codes are found on most goods and their packages; the width and position of the stripes is sensed by a light pen *or* optical wand and provides information about the goods, such as price, stock quantities, etc.

◇ **bar printer** *noun* printer in which the characters are on arms which strike the paper to print characters **Stabdrucker;** *see also* DAISY WHEEL

barrel *noun* conducting post in a terminal **Tonne**
◇ **barrel distortion** *noun* optical lens distortion causing sides of objects to appear curved **Tonnenverzeichnung**
◇ **barrel printer** *noun* type of printer where characters are located around a rotating barrel **Typenwalzendrucker**

barrier box *noun* device that electrically isolates equipment from a telephone line to prevent damage **Isoliersteg**

baryta paper *noun* coated matt paper used to produce final high quality proofs before printing **Barytpapier**

base
1 *noun*
(a) lowest *or* first position **Basis**

(b) collection of files used as a reference **Basisdateien;** *see* DATABASE
(c) place where a company has its main office or factory *or* place where a businessman has his office **Hauptquartier, Sitz, Standort;** *the company has its base in London and branches in all European countries*
(d) initial *or* original position **Grundposition; base address** = initial address in a program used as a reference for others **Grund-, Bezugs-, Basisadresse; base addressing** = relative addressing **relative Adressierung; base band** = frequency range of a signal before it is processed *or* transmitted **Basisband; base band modem** = communications circuit that transmits an unmodulated (base band) signal over a short range **Gleichstrom-Datenübertragungseinrichtung für niedrige Sendespannung; base band local area network** = LAN for very short distances, in which devices use a base band modem **Basisbandnetz; base language** = assembly language **Assembliersprache; base line** = reference line used when printing to locate characters correctly **(Schrift)grundlinie; base register** = register in a CPU (not usually in small computers) that contains the address of the start of a program **Bezugs-, Basisregister**
(e) (notation) referring to a number system **Basis; base 2** = binary number system (using the two digits 0 and 1) **binäres Zahlensystem; base 8** = octal number system (using the eight digits 0 - 7) **oktales Zahlensystem; base 10** = decimal number system (using the ten digits 0 - 9) **dezimales Zahlensystem; base 16** = hexadecimal number system (using the six digits 0 - 9 and six letters A - F) **hexadezimales Zahlensystem**
2 *verb*
(a) to start to calculate from a position **ausgehen von;** *we based our calculations on the basic keyboarding rate;* **based on** = calculating from **ausgehend von;** *based on last year's figures; the price is based on estimates of keyboarding costs*
(b) to set up a company *or* a person in a place **stationieren, seinen Sitz haben;** *the European manager is based in our London office; a London-based system serves the whole country*

BASIC = BEGINNER'S ALL-PURPOSE SYMBOLIC INSTRUCTION CODE high-level programming language for developing programs in a conversational way, providing an easy introduction to computer programming **BASIC**

◊ **basic** *adjective* normal *or* from which everything starts **grundlegend;** *the basic architechture is the same for all models in this range;* **basic code** = binary code which directly operates the CPU, using only absolute addresses and values (this is the final form of a program after a compiler *or* assembler pass) **Grundcode; basic control system satellite (BCS)** = system that runs dedicated programs *or* tasks for a central computer, controlled using interrupt signals **Satellit für Grundsteuerungssysteme; basic input/output operating system (BIOS)** = system routines that interface between high-level program instructions and the system peripherals to control the input and output to various standard devices, this often includes controlling the screen, keyboard and disk drives **BIOS (Ein-/Ausgabesystem des Betriebssystems); basic instruction** = unmodified program instruction which is processed to obtain the instruction to be executed **Grundbefehl; basic mode link control** = standardized control of transmission links using special codes **Verfahren der (Daten)übertragungssteuerung; basic operating system (BOS)** = software that controls the basic, low-level running of the hardware and file management **BOS (Basisbetriebssystem); basic telecommunications access method (BTAM)** = method to provide access (read *or* write operations) to a remote device **BTAM-Zugriffsmethode; basic weight** = weight of printing paper per 500 sheets **Basisgewicht**

◊ **basically** *adverb* seen from the point from which everything starts **im Grunde, im wesentlichen;** *the acoustic coupler is basically the same as a modem*

◊ **basis** *noun* point *or* number from which calculations are made **Basis;** *we calculated keyboarding costs on the basis of 5,500 keystrokes per hour*

bass *noun & adjective* low sound *or* sound with a low frequency **Baß(-); bass signal** = audio signals in the frequency range below 100Hz **Baßsignal; bass control** = knob used to vary the strength of the bass frequencies in an audio signal **Tiefenregler; bass driver** *or* **speaker** = large loudspeaker able to produce low frequency sounds **Baßlautsprecher; bass response** = characteristics of a circuit *or* device to bass signals **Baßwiedergabe**

batch
1 *noun*
(a) group of items which are made at one time **Stapel;** *the last batch of disk drives are faulty*

(b) (i) group of documents which are processed at the same time; (ii) group of tasks *or* amount of data to be processed as a single unit **(i) Stapel; (ii) Stapelverarbeitung;** *today's batch of orders; we deal with the orders in batches of fifty;* **batch file** = stored file containing a sequence of system commands, used instead of typing them in **Stapelverarbeitungsdatei, Batchdatei;** *this batch file is used to save time and effort when carrying out a routine task;* **(processing data in) batch mode** = (processing the data) in related groups in one machine run **(Daten im) Stapelbetrieb/Batchbetrieb (verarbeiten); batch region** = memory area where the operating system executes batch programs **Stapel-, Batchregion; batch system** = system that executes batch files **Stapelverarbeitungssystem; batch total** = sum of a number of batches of data, used for error checking, validation or to provide useful information **Zwischensumme pro Stapel**

2 *verb*

(a) to put data *or* tasks together in groups **stapeln; batched communication** = high-speed transmission of large blocks of data without requiring an acknowledgement from the receiver for each data item **Stapelübertragung**

(b) to put items together in groups **stapeln**

◇ **batch number** *noun* reference number attached to a batch **Bearbeitungs-, Stapelnummer**

◇ **batch processor** *noun* system able to process groups of tasks **Stapelverarbeiter; batch processing** = system of data processing where information is collected into batches before being processed by the computer in one machine run **stapelweise Verarbeitung, Batch-Betrieb**

COMMENT: batch processing is the opposite to interactive processing (where the user gives instructions and receives an immediate response)

battery *noun* chemical device that produces electrical current **Batterie; battery backup** = use of a battery to provide power to volatile storage devices (RAM chips) to retain data after a computer has been switched off **Batteriesicherung; battery-backed** = (volatile storage device) that has a battery backup **mit Batterie abgesichert; battery voltage level** = size of voltage being provided by a battery **Spannungsebene der Batterie**

baud *or* **baud rate** *noun* measure of the number of signal changes transmitted per second **Baudrate;** *the baud rate of the binary*

signal was 300 bits per second; a modem with auto-baud scanner can automatically sense at which baud rate it should operate; **baud rate generator** = device that produces various timing signals to synchronize data at different baud rates **Baudratengenerator; split baud rate** = modem which receives data at one baud rate but transmits data at another **geteilte Baudrate;** *the viewdata modem uses a 1200/75 split baud rate; see also* SCANNING

COMMENT: baud rate is often considered the same as bits per second, but in fact it depends on the protocol used and the error checking (300 baud is roughly equivalent to 30 characters per second using standard error checking)

baudot code *noun* five-bit character transmission code, used mainly in teletypewriters **Baudot-Code**

B box *noun* register in a CPU (not usually in small computers) that contains the address of the start of a program **B-Register, Indexregister**

BBS = BULLETIN BOARD SYSTEM information and message database accessible by modem and computer link **Schwarzes-Brett-System**

BCC = BLOCK CHARACTER CHECK error detection method for blocks of transmitted data **Blockdatenprüfung**

BCD = BINARY CODED DECIMAL representation of single decimal digits as a pattern of four binary digits **binär codierte Dezimalzahl;** *the BCD representation of decimal 8 is 1000;* **BCD adder** = full adder able to add two four-bit BCD words **Addierer für binär codierte Dezimalzahlen**

BCH code = BOSE-CHANDHURI-HOCQUENGHEM CODE

BCPL *noun* high level programming language **BCPL (Programmiersprache)**

BCS

(a) = BRITISH COMPUTER SOCIETY

(b) = BASIC CONTROL SYSTEM (SATELLITE)

bead *noun* small section of a program that is used for a single task **Perle**

beam *noun* narrow radiated stream of waves *or* particles **Strahl;** *the LASER* produces a thin beam of light; **beam deflection** = change in beam direction **Strahlenablenkung**; a magnetic field is used for beam deflection in a CRT; **beam diversity** = using a single frequency communications band for two different sets of data **Frequenzbandaufteilung**; **beam splitter** = device to redirect a part of a beam **Strahlenteiler**; **beam width** = maximum size of a transmission beam which should not be exceeded if a constant received power is to maintained **Strahlenbreite**

beard noun blank section between bottom of a character and the type face limit **Fleisch**

beep
1 noun audible warning noise **Piepton, akustisches Signal**; the printer will make a beep when it runs out of paper
2 verb to make a beep **piepsen**; the computer beeped when the wrong key was hit; see also BLEEP

beginning noun first part **Anfang**; **beginning of file (bof)** = character or symbol that shows the start of a valid section of data **Dateianfang**; **beginning of information mark (bim)** = symbol indicating the start of a data stream stored on a disk drive or tape **Informationsanfangsmarke**; **beginning of tape (bot) marker** = section of material that marks the start of the recording area of a reel of magnetic tape **Bandanfangsmarke**

Beginner's All-Purpose Symbolic Instruction Code (BASIC) noun high-level programming language for developing programs in a conversational way, providing an easy introduction to computer programming **BASIC (Programmiersprache)**

bel noun unit used when expressing ratio of signal power in logarithmic form (P bels = Log (A/B) where A and B are signal power) **Bel**

bell character noun control code which causes a machine to produce an audible signal **Klingel**

below-the-line adjective **below-the-line expenditure** = exceptional payments which are separated from a company's normal accounts **Sonderausgaben, außerordentliche Aufwendungen**; **below-the-line costs** = costs of crew and technicians used in making a TV programme (as opposed to scriptwriters, actors, etc., who are above-the-line costs) **Kosten unter dem Strich**

benchmark noun
(a) point in an index which is important, and can be used to compare with other figures **Vergleichspunkt**
(b) program used to test the performance of software or hardware or a system **Test-, Referenzprogramm**; the magazine gave the new program's benchmark test results
◊ **benchmark problem** noun task or problem used to test and evaluate the performance of hardware or software **Leistungsvergleichsaufgabe**
◊ **benchmarking** noun testing a system or program with a benchmark **mit einem Referenzprogramm testen**

COMMENT: the same task or program is given to different systems and their results and speeds of working are compared

Bernoulli box noun high capacity storage system using exchangeable 20MB cartridges **Bernoulli-Box**

QUOTE I use a pair of Bernoulli boxes for back up and simply do a disk-to-disk copy
PC Business World

best fit noun (i) (something) which is the nearest match to a requirement; (ii) function that selects the smallest free space in main memory for a requested virtual page (i) **höchstpassend**; (ii) **Best Fit**

bias noun
(a) electrical reference level **Vorspannung**
(b) high frequency signal added to recorded information to minimize noise and distortion (the high frequency is removed on playback) **Vormagnetisierung**
(c) deviation of statistical results from a reference level **asymmetrischer Fehlerbereich**
◊ **biased** adjective which has a bias **voreingenommen, befangen**; **biased data** = data or records which point to one conclusion **tendenziöse Daten**; **biased exponent** = value of the exponent in a floating point number **kodierter Exponent**

bibliographic or **bibliographical** adjective referring to books or to bibliographies **bibliographisch**; **bibliographical information** = information about a book (name of author, number of pages, ISBN, etc.) which is used for library cataloguing **bibliographische Information**
◊ **bibliography** noun
(a) list of documents and books which are relevant to a certain subject **Bibliographie, Literaturverzeichnis**; he printed a bibliography at the end of each chapter
(b) catalogue of books **Bibliographie**

inch (bpi) = number of bits that can be recorded per inch of recording medium **Bits pro Inch; bits per second (bps)** = measure of the number of binary digits transmitted every second **Bits pro Sekunde; check bit** = one bit of a binary word that is used to provide a parity check **Prüfbit; mask bit** = one bit (in a mask) used to select the required bit from a word or string **Maskenbit; sign bit** = single bit that indicates if a binary number is positive or negative (usually 0 = positive, 1 = negative) **Vorzeichenbit;** see also BYTE

◊ **bit-map** verb to define events or data using an array of single bits; (this can be an image or graphics or a table of devices in use, etc.) **als (digitales) Muster speichern; bit-mapped graphics** = image whose individual pixels can be controlled by changing the value of its stored bit (one is on, zero is off; in colour displays, more than one bit is used to provide control for the three colours - Red, Green, Blue) **als digitales Muster gespeicherte Graphik**

QUOTE it became possible to store more than one bit per pixel
Practical Computing
QUOTE the expansion cards fit into the PC's expansion slot and convert bit-mapped screen images to video signals
Publish
QUOTE it is easy to turn any page into a bit-mapped graphic
PC Business World
QUOTE microcomputers invariably use raster-scan cathode ray tube displays, and frequently use a bit-map to store graphic images
Soft

black adjective with no colour **schwarz; black and white** = use of shades of grey to represent colours on a monitor or display **schwarz-weiß; black box** = device that performs a function without the user knowing how **Black Box; black crush** = conversion of a television picture to one with no tones, only black or white **Schattenschwärzung; black level** = level of a TV signal that produces no luminescence on screen **Schwarzpegel**

◊ **blackout** or **black out** noun complete loss of electrical power **Gesamtausfall;** compare with BROWN-OUT

◊ **black writer** noun printer where toner sticks to the points hit by the laser beam when the image drum is scanned **spezieller Laserdrucker;** compare WHITE WRITER

COMMENT: a black writer produces sharp edges and graphics, but large areas of black are muddy

blank
1 adjective empty or with nothing written

on it **leer; blank character** = character code that prints a space **Leerzeichen; blank instruction** = program instruction which does nothing **leere Anweisung; blank tape** or **blank disk** = magnetic tape or disk that does not have data stored on it **leeres Band; leere Platte; blank string** = (i) empty string; (ii) string containing spaces **(i) leere Zeichenfolge; (ii) Zeichenfolge aus Leerzeichen**
2 noun space on a form which has to be completed **(Text)lücke;** fill in the blanks and insert the form into the OCR

◊ **blanking** noun preventing a television signal from reaching the scanning beam on its return trace **Austasten; blanking interval** = time taken for the scanning beam in a TV to return from the end of a picture at the bottom right of the screen to top left **Austastlücke; blanking pulse** = electrical signal used to start the blanking of a TV signal **Leerimpuls**

blanket agreement noun agreement which covers many items **Pauschalabmachung; blanket cylinder** = rubber coated cylinder in a offset lithographic printing machine that transfers ink from the image plate to the paper **Gummituchzylinder**

◊ **blanketing** see JAMMING

blast verb
(a) to write data into a programmable ROM device **einbrennen**
(b) to free sections of previously allocated memory or resources **Bereiche freimachen**

◊ **blast-through alphanumerics** noun characters that can be displayed on a videotext terminal when it is in graphics mode **Zeichen, die im Graphikmodus sichtbar gemacht werden können**

bleed
1 noun line of printing that runs off the edge of the paper **angeschnittener Satzspiegel**
2 verb **the photo is bled off** = the photograph is printed so that the image runs off the edge of the page **das Foto ist angeschnitten**

bleep
1 noun audible warning noise **Piepton;** the printer will make a bleep when it runs out of paper
2 verb to make a bleep **piepsen;** see also BEEP

◊ **bleeper** noun device which bleeps (often used to mean radio pager) **Piepser;** the doctor's bleeper began to ring, and he went to the telephone; he is in the factory *somewhere - we'll try to find him on his bleeper*

blind *adjective* which will not respond to certain codes **blind, tot**

◊ **blind dialling** *noun* ability of a modem to dial out even if the line appears dead, used on certain private lines **blindes Anwählen; blind keyboard** = keyboard whose output is not displayed but is stored directly on magnetic tape *or* disk **unsichtbar schreibende Tastatur**

B-line counter *noun* address register that is added to a reference address to provide the location to be accessed **Zusatzadreßregister**

blinking *noun* flashing effect caused by varying the intensity of a displayed character **Blinken**

blister pack *noun* type of packing where the item for sale is covered with a thin plastic sheet sealed to a card backing **Schrumpffolienverpackung**

block
1 *noun*
(a) (i) series of items grouped together; (ii) number of stored records treated as a single unit **(i) & (ii) Satz, Block; block character check (BCC)** = error detection method for blocks of transmitted data **Blockzeichenprüfung; block code** = error detection and correction code for block data transmission **Blockcode; block compaction** = *see* COMPRESS, COMPACT; **block copy** = to duplicate a block of data to another section of memory **kopieren eines Blocks; block error rate** = number of blocks of data that contain errors compared with the total number transmitted **Blockfehlerhäufigkeit; block header** = information at the start of a file describing content organization or characteristics **Blockkopf; block ignore character** = symbol at the start of a block indicating that it contains corrupt data **Blockignorierungszeichen; block input processing** = input system that requires a whole error-free block to be received before it is processed **Blockeingabeverarbeitung; block length** = number of bytes of data in a block **Blocklänge; block list** = list of the blocks and records as they are organized in a file **Blockliste; block mark** = code that indicates the end of a block **Blockmarke; block operation** = process carried out on a block of data **Blockoperation; block parity** = parity error check on a block of data

Blockprüfung; block retrieval = accessing blocks of data stored in memory **Blockzugriff; block synchronization** = correct timing of start, stop and message bits according to a predefined protocol **Blocksynchronisierung; block transfer** = moving large numbers of records around in memory **Blockübertragung, Blocktransfer; building block** = self-contained unit that can be joined to others to form a system **Baustein; data block** = all the data required for *or* from a process **Datenblock; end of block (EOB)** = code which indicates that the last byte of a block of data has been sent **Ende des (Datenübertragungs)blocks; (inter)block gap (IBG)** = space between two blocks of stored data **Blockzwischenraum**
(b) wide printed bar **Blockade (in Form einer Linie); block diagram** = graphical representation of a system *or* program operation **Blockdiagramm**
(c) block capitals *or* block letters = capital letters (such as A,B,C) **Großbuchstaben, Blockschrift;** *write your name and address in block letters*
2 *verb*
(a) to stop something taking place **aufhalten, stoppen, blockieren;** *the system manager blocked his request for more CPU time*
(b) to block in = to sketch roughly the main items of a design **andeuten, skizzieren**

◊ **blocking factor** *noun* number of records in a block **Blockungsfaktor**

bloom *noun* bright spot on the screen of a faulty television **Überstrahlen**

bloop *verb* to pass a magnet over a tape to erase signals which are not needed **Fehler löschen**

blow *verb* to program a PROM device with data **einen Festwertspeicher programmieren**

blueprint *noun* copy of an original set of specifications *or* design in graphical form **Blaupause**

◊ **blue-ribbon program** *noun* perfect program that runs first time, with no errors *or* bugs **erstklassiges Programm**

blur
1 *noun* image where the edges *or* colours are not clear **verschwommenes Bild; Schmitz**
2 *verb* to make the edges *or* colours of an image fuzzy **verwackeln;** *the image becomes blurred when you turn the focus knob*

bn = BILLION

BNF = BACKUS-NAUR-FORM system of writing and expressing the syntax of a programming language **Backus-Naur-Form**

board *noun*
(a) flat insulation material on which electronic components are mounted and connected **Platine; bus board** = PCB containing conducting paths for all the computer signals (for the address, data and control buses) **Buskarte; daughter board** = add-on board that connects to a system motherboard **Erweiterungsplatine; expansion board** *or* **add on board** = printed circuit board that is connected to a system to increase its functions *or* performance **Erweiterungsplatine; motherboard** = main printed circuit board of a system, containing most of the components and connectors for expansion boards, etc. **Hauptplatine; printed circuit board (PCB)** = flat insulating material that has conducting tracks of metal printed *or* etched onto its surface, which complete a circuit when components are mounted on it **gedruckte Schaltkarte**
(b) people who run a company *or* group *or* society **Aufsichtsrat, Beirat, Firmenvorstand, Kommission; editorial board** = group of editors **Redaktionsausschuß**

◊ **bulletin board system (BBS)** *noun* information and message database accessible by modem and computer link **Schwarzes-Brett-System**

> QUOTE both models can be expanded to the current maximum of the terminals by adding further serial interface boards
> *Micro Decision*

body *noun* main section of text in a document **Text(körper); body size** = length of a section of text from top to bottom in points **Schriftspiegel; body type** = main style of type used in a text, as opposed to the style of type used for headings, notes, etc. **Text-, Grundschrift**

bof = BEGINNING OF FILE character *or* symbol that shows the start of a valid section of data **Dateianfang**

boilerplate *noun* final document that has been put together using standard sections of text held in a word processor **Schriftsatz (aus Standardtexten)**

◊ **boilerplating** *noun* putting together a final document out of various standard sections of text **Herstellung eines Schriftsatzes (aus Standardtexten)**

bold *noun & adjective* **bold face** = thicker and darker form of a typeface **Fettdruck; (fett)**

bomb
1 *verb (of software) informal* to fail **abstürzen;** *the program bombed, and we lost all the data; the system can bomb if you set up several desk accessories or memory-resident programs at the same time*
2 *noun* **logic bomb** = section of code that performs various unpleasant functions such as system crash when a number of conditions are true (the logic bomb is installed by unpleasant hackers *or* very annoyed programmers) **programmierte Zeitbombe;** *the system programmer installed a logic bomb when they made him redundant*

bond paper *noun* heavy grade writing paper **Bankpost-, Bondpapier**

book
1 *noun*
(a) set of sheets of paper attached together **Buch;** *they can print books up to 96 pages; the book is available in paperback and hard cover*
(b) **cheque book** = book of new cheques **Scheckbuch; phone book** *or* **telephone book** = book which lists names of people *or* companies with their addresses and telephone numbers **Telefonbuch**
2 *verb* to order *or* to reserve something **buchen;** *to book a room in a hotel or a table at a restaurant or a ticket on a plane; I booked a table for 7.45*

◊ **booklet** *noun* small book with a paper cover **Broschüre**

◊ **bookseller** *noun* person who sells books **Buchhändler**

◊ **bookshop** *noun* shop which sells books **Buchhandlung**

◊ **bookstall** *noun* small open bookshop (as in a railway station) **Bücherstand**

◊ **bookstore** *noun (US)* bookshop **Buchhandlung**

◊ **bookwork** *noun*
(a) keeping of financial records **Buchführungsarbeit**
(b) printing and binding of books **Buchproduktion**
NOTE: no plural

Boolean algebra *or* **logic** *noun* rules set down to define, simplify and manipulate logical functions, based on statements which are true or false **Boolesche Algebra;** *see* AND, NOT, OR

◊ **Boolean connective** *noun* symbol *or* character in a Boolean operation that describes the action to be performed on the operands **Boolescher Operator**

◊ **Boolean operation** *noun* logical operation on a number of operands, conforming to Boolean algebra rules **Boolesche Operation; Boolean operation table** = table showing two binary words (operands), the operation and the result **Tabelle der Booleschen Operationen; Boolean operator** = logical operator such as AND, OR etc. **Boolescher Operator; monadic Boolean operation** = logical operation on only one word, such as NOT **monadische oder einstellige Boolesche Operation; dyadic Boolean operation** = logical operation producing a result from two words, such as AND **dyadische oder zweistellige Boolesche Operation; Boolean value** = one of two values, either true or false **Boolescher Wert; Boolean variable** = binary word in which each bit represents true or false, using the digits 1 or 0 **Boolesche Variable**

boom
1 *noun*
(a) piece of metal which supports a microphone *or* antenna **Galgen**
(b) time when sales *or* production *or* business activity are increasing **Aufschwung, Boom; boom industry** = industry which is expanding rapidly **Aufschwungindustrie; the boom years** = years when there is a boom **die Jahre des Aufschwungs**
2 *verb* to expand *or* to do well in business **einen Aufschwung nehmen;** *sales are booming; a booming industry or company; technology is a booming sector of the economy*

boost
1 *noun* help received **Auftrieb;** *the prize was a real boost; the new model gave a boost to the sales figures*
2 *verb* to make something increase **anheben, verstärken;** *the extra hard disk will boost our storage capacity by 25Mb*

boot *verb* to execute a set of instructions automatically in order to reach a required state **laden**
◊ **boot up** *or* **booting** *noun* automatic execution of a set of instructions usually held in ROM when a computer is switched on **Laden**
◊ **bootleg** *noun* illegal copy of recorded material **Raubkopie**
◊ **bootstrap (loader)** *noun* set of instructions that are executed by the computer before a program is loaded, usually to load the operating system once

the computer is switched on **Urlader;** *compare* LOADER

> QUOTE the digital signal processor includes special on-chip bootstrap hardware to allow easy loading of user programs into the program RAM
> *Electronics & Wireless World*

booth *noun* small place for one person to stand *or* sit **Kabine; telephone booth** = soundproof cabin with a public telephone in it **Telefonzelle; ticket booth** = place outdoors where a person sells tickets **Kartenhäuschen**

border *noun* area around printed *or* displayed text **Umgrenzung**

borrow *verb*
(a) to take something (such as money *or* a library book) from someone for a time, returning it at the end of the period **entleihen;** *he borrowed £1,000 from the bank; she borrowed a book on computer construction*
(b) operation in certain arithmetic processes, such as subtraction from a smaller number **borgen**
◊ **borrower** *noun* person who borrows **Entleiher;** *borrowers from the library are allowed to keep books for two weeks*

BOS = BASIC OPERATING SYSTEM software that controls the basic, low-level running of the hardware and file management **BOS (Basisbetriebssystem)**

Bose-Chandhuri-Hocquenghem code (BCH) *noun* error correcting code **Bose-Chandhuri-Hocquenghem-Code**

bot *or* **BOT** = BEGINNING OF TAPE; **BOT marker** = section of material that marks the start of the recording area of magnetic tape **Bandanfang**

bottom space *noun* blank lines at the bottom of a page of printed text **Fußsteg**
◊ **bottom up method** *noun* combining low-level instructions to form a high-level instruction (which can then be further combined) **Bottom-Up-Verfahren**

bounce *noun* (error) multiple key contact caused by a faulty switch **Prellen; de-bounce** = preventing a single touch on a key producing multiple key contact **entprellen**

boundary *noun* limits of something **Grenzen; boundary protection** = preventing any program writing into a reserved area of memory **Grenzenschutz; boundary**

punctuation = punctuation which marks the beginning *or* end of a file **Grenzmarkierung; boundary register** = register in a multi-user system that contains the addresses for the limits of one user's memory allocation **Grenzenregister**

bounds *noun* limits *or* area in which one can operate **Grenzen; array bounds** = limits to the number of elements which can be given in an array **Matrixgrenzen**

box *noun*
(a) cardboard *or* wood *or* plastic container **Kasten;** *the goods were sent in thin cardboard boxes; the keyboard is packed in plastic foam before being put into the box;* **black box** = device that performs a function without the user knowing how **Black Box**
(b) box number = reference number used in a post office or an advertisement to avoid giving an address **Postfachnummer;** *please reply to Box No. 209; our address is: P.O. Box 74209, Edinburgh*
(c) cash box = metal box for keeping cash **Geldkassette; letter box** *or* **mail box** = place where incoming mail is put **Briefkasten; call box** = outdoor telephone booth **Telefonzelle**
(d) square of ruled lines round a text *or* illustration **Kasten;** *the comments and quotations are printed in boxes*
◊ **boxed** *adjective* put in a box *or* sold in a box **verpackt (in einer Schachtel); boxed set** = set of items sold together in a box **in einer Schachtel verpacktes Set**
◊ **box in** *verb* to surround a section of text with ruled lines **(mit einem Kasten) einrahmen**

BPI *or* **bpi** = BITS PER INCH number of bits that can be recorded per inch of recording medium **Bits pro Inch**

BPS *or* **bps** = BITS PER SECOND number of bits that can be transmitted per second **Bits pro Sekunde;** *their transmission rate is 60,000 bits per second (bps) through a parallel connection*

bracket
1 *noun* printing sign to show that an instruction *or* operations are to be separated **Klammer; round brackets** *or* **square brackets** = different types of bracket ( ), [ ] **runde Klammern ; eckige Klammern**
2 *verb* **to bracket together** = to print brackets round several items to show that they are treated in the same way and separated from the rest of the text **einklammern**
◊ **bracketed** *adjective* (characters) joined together with small lines between serif and main part **eingeklammert**

◊ **bracketing** *noun* photographing the same scene with different exposures to make sure there is one good picture **Belichtungsreihe**

Braille *noun* system of writing using raised dots on the paper to indicate letters, which allows a blind person to read by passing his fingers over the page **Blindenschrift;** *she was reading a Braille book; the book has been published in Braille;* **Braille marks** = raised patterns on equipment *or* in books to permit identification by touch **Blindenschrift**

branch
1 *noun*
(a) possible path *or* jump from one instruction to another **Programmzweig, Verzweigung; branch instruction** = conditional program instruction that provides the location of the next instruction in the program (if a condition is met) **Verzweigungsbefehl; program branch** = one or more paths that can be followed after a conditional statement **Programmzweig**
(b) line linking one or more devices to the main network **Verzweigung;** *the faulty station is on this branch*
2 *verb* to jump from one section of a program to another **verzweigen**
◊ **branchpoint** *noun* point in a program where a branch can take place **Verzweigungspunkt**

COMMENT: in BASIC, the instruction GOTO makes the system jump to the line indicated; this is an unconditional branch. The instruction IF...THEN is a conditional branch, because the jump will only take place if the condition is met

brand *noun* make of product, which can be recognized by a name *or* by a design **Marke;** *the number one brand of magnetic tape; the company is developing a new brand of screen cleaner;* **brand name** = name of a brand **Markenname; brand image** = idea of a product which is associated with the brand name **Markenimage, Markenprofil; own brand** = name of a store which is used on products which are specially packed for that store **Geschäftsname als Markenbezeichnung**
◊ **branded** *adjective* **branded goods** = goods sold under brand names **Markenartikel**
◊ **brand new** *adjective* quite new *or* very new **brandneu**

breach *noun* failure to carry out the terms of an agreement **Verletzung, Verstoß;**

breach of contract = failing to do something which is in a contract **Vertragsbruch; the company is in breach of contract** = it has failed to carry out the duties of the contract **die Firma ist vertragsbrüchig geworden; breach of warranty** = supplying goods which do not meet the standards of the warranty applied to them **Verletzung der Gewährleistung**

breadboard noun solderless connection board that allows prototypes of electronic circuits to be constructed quickly and easily **Brettschaltung**

break
1 noun action or key pressed to stop a program execution **Unterbrechung**
2 verb
(a) to fail to carry out the duties of an agreement **brechen;** the company has broken the agreement
(b) to decipher a difficult code **knacken;** he finally broke the cipher system NOTE: **breaking - broke - has broken**

◊ **break down** verb to stop working because of mechanical failure **ausfallen;** the modem has broken down; what do you do when your line printer breaks down?

◊ **breakdown** noun stopping work because of mechanical failure **Ausfall;** we cannot communicate with our New York office because of the breakdown of the telex lines

◊ **breaker** noun **circuit breaker** = device which protects equipment by cutting off the electrical supply **Stromkreisunterbrecher**

◊ **breakpoint** noun symbol inserted into a program which stops its execution at that point to allow registers, variables and memory locations to be examined (used when debugging a program) **bedingter Programmstop; breakpoint instruction** or **halt** = halt command inserted in a program to stop execution temporarily, allowing the programmer to examine data and registers while debugging a program **Stopbefehl; breakpoint symbol** = special character used to provide a breakpoint in a program (the debugging program allows breakpoint symbols to be inserted, it then executes the program until it reaches one, then halts) **Programmstopsignal**

◊ **breakup** noun loss or distortion of a signal **Verlust**

breezeway noun signal used to separate the colour information from the horizontal synchronizing pulse in a television signal **getrenntes Schalten von Ton und Bild**

B register noun (i) address register that is added to a reference address to provide the location to be accessed; (ii) register used to extend the accumulator in multiplication and division operations **(i) Zusatzadreßregister; (ii) B-Register**

bridge or **bridging product** noun
(a) matching communications equipment that makes sure that power losses are kept to a minimum **Brücke**
(b) hardware or software that allows parts of an old system to be used on a new system **Überbrückung;** a bridging product is available for companies with both generations of machines

◊ **bridgeware** noun hardware or software used to make the transfer from one computer system to another easier (by changing file format, translation etc.) **Bridgeware**

◊ **bridging** noun to use bridgeware to help transfer programs, data files etc., to another system **Überbrückung**

brightness noun luminance of an object which can be seen **Helligkeit;** a control knob allows you to adjust brightness and contrast; the brightness of the monitor can hurt the eyes; **brightness range** = variation of reflected light intensity **Helligkeitsbereich**

QUOTE there is a brightness control on the front panel
Micro Decision

brilliant adjective very bright and shining (light or colour) **brilliant;** the background colour is a brilliant red; he used brilliant white for the highlights

◊ **brilliance** noun the luminance of an object as seen in a picture **Brillianz**

British Standards Institute (BSI) organization that monitors design and safety standards in the UK **Britisches Normeninstitut**

broadband noun transmission channel whose bandwidth is greater than a voice channel (allowing faster data transmission) **Breitband; broadband radio** = radio communications link using a broadband channel **Breitbandradio**

broadcast
1 noun data or voice transmission to many receivers **Rundspruch; broadcast homes** = homes with at least one TV or radio receiver **Haushalt mit Radio- und/oder Fernsehgerät; broadcast network** = network for sending data to a number of receivers **Rundspruchnetz; broadcast satellite technique** = method of providing greatest channel bandwidth for a geostationary satellite **Rundfunksatellitentechnik**

2 *verb* to distribute information over a wide area *or* audience **senden, ausstrahlen;** *he broadcast the latest news over the radio or over the WAN;* **broadcasting station** = radio station that transmits received signals to other stations **Rundfunksendestelle**

broadsheet *noun* uncut sheet of paper *or* paper which has printing on one side only **einseitig bedrucktes Blatt, Einblattdruck**

broadside *noun (US)* publicity leaflet **Flugblatt**

brochure *noun* publicity booklet **Broschüre;** *we sent off for a brochure about holidays in Greece or about*

bromide *or* **bromide print** *noun*
(a) positive photographic print from a negative *or* the finished product from a phototypesetting machine **Bromidsilberdruck;** *in 24 hours we had bromides ready to film* **(b)** lithographic plate used for proofing **Bromidsilberplatte**

brown-out *noun* power failure (low voltage level rather than no voltage level) **Spannungsabfall;** *see also* BLACK-OUT

browse *verb* to search through and access database material without permission **(unerlaubt) durchsuchen**

brute force method *noun* problem-solving method which depends on computer power rather than elegant programming techniques **Methode der rohen Gewalt**

BSC = BINARY SYNCHRONOUS COMMUNICATIONS (old) standard for medium/high speed data communication links **binär-synchrone Übertragungssteuerung**

BSI = BRITISH STANDARDS INSTITUTE

BTAM = BASIC TELECOMMUNICATIONS ACCESS METHOD method to provide access (read *or* write operations) to a remote device **BTAM-Zugriffsmethode**

bubble memory *noun* method of storing binary data using the magnetic properties of certain materials, allowing very large amounts of data to be stored in primary memory **Blasenspeicher; bubble memory cassette** = bubble memory device on a removable cartridge that can be inserted into a controller card (like an audio cassette) to provide high capacity, high speed, removable memory **Blasenspeicherkassette**

◊ **bubble sort** *noun* sorting method which repeatedly exchanges various pairs of data items until they are in order **Bubblesort (einfaches Sortierverfahren)**

bucket *noun* storage area containing data for an application **Sammelfeld**

buckling *noun* distortion and bending of a film due to heat *or* dryness **Wölbung**

buffer
1 *noun*
(a) (circuit) that isolates and protects a system from damaging inputs from circuits *or* peripherals **Puffer;** *see also* DRIVER **(b)** temporary storage area for data waiting to be processed **Zwischenspeicher; buffer register** = temporary storage for data read from *or* being written to main memory **Pufferregister; buffer size** = total number of characters that can be held in a buffer **Puffergröße; data buffer** = temporary storage location for data received by a device that is not yet ready to process it **Datenpuffer; dynamic** *or* **elastic buffer** = buffer whose size varies with demand **elastischer Puffer; I/O buffer** = temporary storage area for data waiting to be input *or* output **Ein- /Ausgabepuffer**
2 *verb* using a temporary storage area to hold data until the processor *or* device is ready to deal with it **zwischenspeichern; buffered input/output** = use of a temporary storage area on input *or* output ports to allow slow peripherals to operate with a fast CPU **zwischengespeicherte Ein- /Ausgabe; buffered memory** = feature that allows instructions *or* data to be entered before the device has finished processing **Pufferspeicher; buffering** = using buffers to provide a link between slow and fast devices **Pufferung; double buffering** = two buffers working together so that one can be read while the other is accepting data **doppelte Pufferung**

COMMENT: buffers allow two parts of a computer system to work at different speeds (i.e. a high-speed central processing unit and a slower line printer)

QUOTE the speed is enhanced by the 8K RAM printer buffer included
QUOTE the software allocates a portion of cache as a print buffer to restore program control faster after sending data to the printer
Which PC?

bug

1 *noun (informal)*
(a) error in a computer program which makes it run incorrectly **Programm-, Softwarefehler;** *(informal)* **Mucken; bug patches** = (temporary) correction made to a program; small correction made to software by a user on the instructions of the software publisher **Ausmerzung von Softwarefehlern;** *see also* DEBUG
(b) hidden microphone which records conversations secretly **Wanze**
2 *verb* to hide a microphone to allow conversations to be recorded secretly **verwanzen;** *the conference room was bugged*
◊ **buggy** *noun* small computer-controlled vehicle **computergesteuertes Fahrzeug**

building block *noun* self-contained unit that can be joined to others to form a system **Baustein**

built-in *adjective* (special feature) that is already included in a system **eingebaut;** *the built-in adapter card makes it fully IBM compatible; the computer has a built-in hard disk;* **built-in check** = error detection and validation check carried out automatically on received data **automatische Selbstprüfung; built-in function** = special function already implemented in a program **eingebaute Standardfunktion**

◊ **built into** *adjective* feature that is already a physical part of a system **fest eingebaut;** *there are communications ports built into all modems*
NOTE: opposite is **add on**

bulk *noun* large quantity of something **große Mengen; in bulk** = in large quantities **in großen Mengen; bulk erase** = to erase a complete magnetic disk *or* tape in one action **vollständig löschen; bulk storage medium** = medium that is able to store large amounts of data in a convenient size and form **Massenspeichermedium;** *magnetic tape is a reliable bulk storage medium;* **bulk update terminal** = device used by an information provider to prepare videotext pages off-line, then transmit them rapidly to the main computer **Aktualisierungsdatenstation für große Datenmengen**

bulletin board system (BBS) *noun*

information and message database accessible by modem and computer link **Schwarzes-Brett-System**

bullet *noun*
(a) solid area of typeset tone indicating the required image intensity **Blockade (als Maß der Farbintensität)**

(b) method of indicating an important section of text by the use of a large dot on the page **kreisförmige Blockade, großer Punkt**

bundle *noun* number of optic fibres gathered together **(Leitungs)bündel**
◊ **bundled software** *noun* programs included in the price of a computer hardware package **im Kaufpreis inbegriffene Software**

bureau *noun* office which specializes in keyboarding data *or* processing batches of data for other small companies **Büro;** *the company offers a number of bureau services, such as printing and data collection; our data manipulation is handled by a bureau;* **information bureau** = office which gives information **Informationsbüro; word-processing bureau** = office which specializes in word-processing **Textverarbeitungsbüro;** *we farm out the office typing to a local bureau*
NOTE: the plural is **bureaux**

burner *noun* device which burns in programs onto PROM chips **Brenner**
◊ **burn-in** *noun* heat test for electronic components **Einbrennen, Voraltern**
◊ **burn in** *verb*
(a) to mark a (television *or* monitor) screen after displaying a high brightness image for too long **einbrennen**
(b) to write data into a PROM chip **einbrennen**
◊ **burn out** *noun* excess heat *or* incorrect use that causes an electronic circuit *or* device to fail **Ausbrennen**

burst *noun* short isolated sequence of transmitted signals **geschlossener Übertragungsblock; burst mode** = data transmission using intermittent bursts of data **Stoßbetrieb; error burst** = group of several consecutive errors (in a transmission) **Fehlerhäufung**

burster *noun* machine used to separate the sheets of continuous fanfold paper **Vereinzelungsmaschine**

bus *noun*

(a) communication link consisting of a set of leads *or* wires which connects different parts of a computer hardware system, and over which data is transmitted and received by various circuits in the system **Übertragungsweg, Bus; address bus** = bus carrying address data between a CPU and a memory device **Adreßbus; bi-directional bus** = data *or* control lines that can carry signals travelling in two directions **zweiseitig**

gerichteter Übertragungsweg; **bus address lines** = wires, each of which carries one bit of an address word **Adreßbusleitung; bus arbitration** = protocol and control of transmission over a bus that ensures fair usage by several users **Buszuteilung; bus board** = PCB containing conducting paths for all the computer signals **Busplatine; bus control lines** = wires, each of which carries one bit of a control word **Bussteuerungsleitung; bus data lines** = wires, each of which carries one bit of a data word **Busdatenübertragungsleitung; bus driver** = high power transistors *or* amplifier that can provide enough power to transmit signals to a number of devices **Bustreiber; bus master** = data source that controls the bus whilst transmitting (bus master status moves between sending stations) **Bushauptkontrolle; bus network** = network of computers where the machines are connected to a central bus unit which transmits the messages it receives **Busnetzwerk; bus slave** = data sink which receives data from a bus master **Busnebenstelle; bus structure** = way in which buses are organized, whether serial, parallel, bidirectional, etc. **Busstruktur; control bus** = bus carrying control signals between a CPU and other circuits **Steuerbus; daisy chain bus** = one communications bus that joins one device to the next, each device being able to receive *or* transmit *or* modify data as it passes through to the next device in line **verkettete Busstruktur; data bus** = bus carrying data between a CPU and memory and peripheral devices **Datenübertragungsweg; dual bus system** = way of linking different parts of a system which keeps the memory bus separate from the input/output bus **doppeltes Übertragungswegsystem; input/output data bus (I/O bus)** = links allowing data and control transfer between a CPU and external peripherals **Ein-/Ausgabedatenbus; memory bus** = bus carrying address data between a CPU and memory devices **Speicherbus**
(b) central source of information which supplies several devices **Hauptverbindung, Sammelschiene**

business *noun*
(a) work in buying *or* selling **Geschäft;** *business is expanding; business is slow; he does a good business in repairing computers; what's your line of business?;*

business computer = powerful small computer which is programmed for special business tasks **Geschäftscomputer; business efficiency exhibition** = exhibition which shows products (computers, word-processors) which help a business to be efficient **anwendungsorientierte Fachausstellung; business system** *or* **business package** = set of programs adapted for business use (such as payroll, invoicing, customers file, etc.) **Programmpaket für geschäftlichen Gebrauch**
(b) commercial company **Geschäft;** *he owns a small computer repair business; she runs a business from her home; he set up in business as an computer consultant;* **business address** = details of number, street and town where a company is located **Geschäftsadresse; business card** = card showing a businessman's name and the name and address of the company he works for **Visitenkarte; business equipment** = machines used in an office **Büroausstattung**
NOTE: no plural for (a); (b) has the plural **businesses**

busy *adjective*
(a) (i) occupied in doing something *or* in working; (ii) electrical signal indicating that a device is not ready to receive data **(i) beschäftigt; (ii) belegt, besetzt;** *when the busy line goes low, the printer will accept more data;* **the line is busy** = the telephone line is being used **die Leitung ist besetzt**
(b) distracting *or* detailed (background to a film shot) **unruhig**

buzz
1 *noun* sound like a loud hum **Summen**
2 *verb* to make a loud hum **summen**
◊ **buzzer** *noun* electrical device which makes a loud hum **Summer**
◊ **buzzword** *noun* (*informal*) word which is popular among a certain group of people **Jargon**

bypass *noun* alternative route around a component *or* device, so that it is not used **Nebenweg;** *there is an automatic bypass around any faulty equipment*

byte *noun* group of bits *or* binary digits (usually eight) which a computer operates on as a single unit **Byte; byte address** = location of data bytes in memory **Byteadresse; byte machine** = variable word length computer **Rechner mit variabler Wortlänge; byte manipulation** = moving, editing and changing the contents of a byte **Bytemanipulation; byte serial transmission** *or* **mode** = transmission of bytes of data sequentially, the individual bits of which can be sent in a serial *or* parallel way **byteserielle Übertragung**

> QUOTE if you can find a way of packing two eight-bit values into a single byte, you save substantial amounts of RAM or disk space
> *Practical Computing*

Cc

C high level programming language developed mainly for writing structured systems programs **C**

> QUOTE these days a lot of commercial software is written in C
> *PC Business World*

C hexadecimal number equivalent to decimal 12 **C**

cable
1 *noun*
(a) flexible conducting electrical *or* optical link **Kabel**; **cable television** *or* **cable TV** = television system where signals are broadcast to viewers' homes over cables **Kabelfernsehen**; **cable TV relay station** = receiving station which retransmits received television signals to a terminal point (where they are then distributed by cable to viewers' homes) **Relaisstation für Kabelfernsehen**; *see also* CATV
(b) telegram *or* message sent by telegraph **Telegramm**; *he sent a cable to his office asking for more money;* **cable address** = specially short address for sending cables **Telegrammadresse**
2 *verb* to send a message *or* money by telegraph **telegraphieren**; *he cabled his office to ask them to send more money; the office cabled him £1,000 to cover his expenses*

◊ **cablegram** *noun* telegram *or* message sent by telegraph **Telegramm**

◊ **cabling** *noun* cable (as a material) **Kabel**; *using high-quality cabling will allow the user to achieve very high data transfer rates; cabling costs up to £1 a foot*
NOTE: no plural

cache
1 *noun* **cache memory** = section of high-speed memory which stores data that the computer can access quickly **Cache-Speicher (schneller Pufferspeicher)**; *file access time is much quicker if the most frequently used data is stored in cache memory;* **instruction cache** = section of high-speed memory which stores the next few instructions to be executed by a processor (to speed up operation) **Befehlsschnellspeicher**
2 *verb* to file *or* store in a cache **gesondert verarbeiten**; *this program can cache any size font*

> QUOTE the first range of 5.25 inch Winchester disk drives to feature inbuilt cache
> *Minicomputer News*
> QUOTE a serious user might also want a tape streamer and cache memory
> *PC Business World*

CAD = COMPUTER AIDED DESIGN *or* COMPUTER ASSISTED DESIGN the use of a computer and graphics terminal to help a designer in his work **computergestützte Entwurf und Konstruktion (CAD)**; *all our engineers design on CAD workstations;* **CAD/CAM** = CAD/COMPUTER AIDED MANUFACTURE interaction between computers used for designing and those for manufacturing a product **computergestützte Entwurf und Fertigung (CAD/CAM)**

> QUOTE CAD software is memory-intensive
> *PC Business World*

CAI = COMPUTER AIDED INSTRUCTION *or* COMPUTER ASSISTED INSTRUCTION use of a computer to assist pupils in learning a subject **computergestützter Unterricht**

CAL = COMPUTER AIDED LEARNING *or* COMPUTER ASSISTED LEARNING use of a computer to assist pupils in learning a subject **computergestütztes Lernen**

calculate *verb*
(a) to find the answer to a problem using numbers **kalkulieren, berechnen**; *the DP manager calculated the rate for keyboarding; you need to calculate the remaining disk space*
(b) to estimate **schätzen**; *I calculate that we have six months' stock left*

◊ **calculation** *noun* answer to a problem in mathematics **Kalkulation, Berechnung**; **rough calculation** = approximate answer **grobe Berechnung**; *I made some rough calculations on the back of an envelope; according to my calculations, we have six months' stock left*

◊ **calculator** *noun* electronic machine which works out the answers to numerical problems **Rechenmaschine**; *my pocket calculator needs a new battery; he worked out the discount on his calculator*

calibration *noun* comparing the signal from an input with a known scale to provide a standardized reading **Eichung**

call
1 *noun* conversation (between people or machines) on the telephone **Anruf; local call** = call to a number on the same exchange **Ortsgespräch; trunk call** *or* **long-distance call** = call to a number in a different zone *or* area **Ferngespräch; person-to-person call** = call where you ask the operator to connect you with a named person **vorangemeldetes Gespräch zu bestimmten Personen; transferred charge call** *or* *(US)* **collect call** = call where the person receiving the call agrees to pay for it **Rückgespräch; to make a call** = to dial and speak to someone on the telephone **telefonieren; to take a call** = to answer the telephone **das Telefon abnehmen; to log calls** = to note all details of telephone calls made **Anrufe aufzeichnen**
2 *verb*
(a) to transfer control to a separate program *or* routine from a main program **aufrufen;** *after an input is received, the first function is called up; the subroutine call instruction should be at this point;* **call instruction** = programming instruction that directs control to a routine (after saving the program counter contents to show the return instruction where to return to in the main program) **Aufrufbefehl**
(b) to try to contact another user by telephone **anrufen;** *I'll call you at your office tomorrow;* **call accepted signal** = signal sent by device meaning willing to accept caller's data **Rufannahme; call control signal** = signal necessary to establish and end a call **Verbindungssteuerungssignal; call diverter** = device that on receiving a call, contacts another point and re-routes the call **Anrufablenker; call duration** = length of time spent between starting and ending a call **Anrufdauer;** *call duration depends on the complexity of the transaction; charges are related to call duration;* **call forwarding** = automatic redirection of calls to another user *or* station **Anrufumleitung;** *we are having all calls forwarded from the office to home;* **called party** = person *or* station to which a call is made **angerufene Seite**
◊ **call box** *noun* outdoor telephone booth **Telefonzelle**
◊ **caller** *noun* person who telephones *or* requests a call **Anrufer**
◊ **call in** *verb* to telephone to make contact **anrufen;** *we ask the representatives to call in every Friday to report the weeks' sales*
◊ **calling** *noun* signal to request attention, sent from a terminal *or* device to the main computer **Anruf; calling sequence** = series of program commands required to direct execution to or back from a subroutine **Aufruffolge von Unterprogrammen**
◊ **call up** *verb* to ask for information from a backing store to be displayed **abrufen;** *all the customers addresses were called up; call up the previous file*

callier effect *noun* scattering of light as it passes through one *or* more lenses **Callier-Effekt**

calligraphy *noun* art of handwriting **Kalligraphie**

CAM
(a) = COMPUTER AIDED MANUFACTURE *or* COMPUTER ASSISTED MANUFACTURING use of a computer to control machinery *or* assist in a manufacturing process **computergestützte Fertigung (CAM)**
(b) = CONTENT ADDRESSABLE MEMORY memory that is addressed and accessed by its contents rather than a location **Assoziativspeicher**

Cambridge ring *noun* local area networking standard used for connecting several devices and computers together in a ring with simple cable links **Cambridge-Netz**

cameo *noun*
(a) reverse characters, that is, white on a black background **invertierte Zeichen**
(b) front-lit subject filmed in front of a dark background **Hell-auf-dunkel-Bild, Aufnahme vor neutralem Hintergrund**

camera *noun* (i) photographic device that transfers a scene onto a piece of film, usually via a lens; (ii) device that transforms a scene into electronic signals that can be displayed on a television **(i) Fotoapparat; (ii) Filmkamera; camera chain** = pieces of equipment necessary to operate a television camera **Kameraaggregat; camera-ready copy (crc)** = final text *or* graphics ready to be photographed before printing **reproreife Vorlage**

cancel *verb* to stop a process *or* instruction before it has been fully executed **stornieren, abbrechen; cancel character** = control code used to indicate that the last data transmitted was incorrect **Ungültigkeitszeichen;** *the software automatically sends a cancel character after any error;* **cancel page** = extra printed page inserted into a book to take the place of a page with errors on it **Ersatz- und Ergänzungsblatt**
◊ **cancellation** *noun* action of stopping a process which has been started **Stornierung**

candela *noun* SI unit of measurement of light intensity **Candela, neue Kerze (NK)** ⇨ APPENDIX

canonical schema *noun* model of a database that is independent of hardware *or* software available **kanonisches Schema**

capability *noun* being able to do something **Leistungsfähigkeit;** *resolution capabilities; electronic mail capabilities;* **capability list** = list of operations that can be carried out **Leistungsliste**

◇ **capable** *adjective* able to do something **leistungsfähig;** *that is the highest speed that this printer is capable of; the software is capable of far more complex functions* NOTE: a device is capable **of** something

capacitance *noun* ability of a component to store electrical charge **Kapazität**

◇ **capacitative** *or* **capacititive** *adjective* something which has capacitance **kapazitiv**

◇ **capacitor** *noun* electronic component that can store charge **Kondensator; capacitor microphone** = microphone that uses variations in capacitance due to sound pressure to generate an electrical signal **Kondensatormikrophon; ceramic capacitors** = general purpose, non-polar small capacitors made from ceramic materials **Keramikkondensatoren; electrolytic capacitors** = polar, high-capacitance devices made in a variety of materials **elektrolytische Kondensatoren; non-electrolytic capacitors** = non-polar, low-capacitance devices made from a variety of materials **nicht-elektrolytische Kondensatoren; variable capacitor** = device whose capacitance can be varied over a small range, used for tuning purposes **variabler Kondensator; capacitor storage** = device using capacititive properties of a material to store data **Kondensatorspeicher; memory backup capacitor** = very high-capacitance, small device that can provide power for volatile RAM chips for up to two weeks (used instead of a battery) **Speicherkondensator;** *see also* BATTERY BACKUP

capacity *noun*
(a) amount which can be produced *or* amount of work which can be done **Leistungsvermögen;** *industrial or manufacturing or production capacity;* **channel capacity** = maximum rate for data transmission over a channel **Kanalkapazität; to work at full capacity** = to do as much work as possible **mit voller Kapazität arbeiten; to use up spare** *or* **excess capacity** = to make use of time *or* space which is not fully used **Restkapazitäten ausnutzen**

(b) amount of storage space available in a system *or* on a disk **Kapazität; storage capacity** = space available for storage **Speicherkapazität;** *total storage capacity is now 3Mb*

capitals *or* (*informal*) **caps** *noun* large form of letters (A,B,C,D, etc.) as opposed to lower case (a,b,c,d, etc.) **Großbuchstaben;** *the word BASIC is always written in caps;* **caps lock** = key on a keyboard *or* typewriter that allows all characters to be entered as capitals **Feststelltaste;** *the LED lights up when caps lock is pressed*

capstan *noun* device in a tape player which ensures that the tape moves at a constant speed **Capstan, Tonrolle**

caption *noun* note *or* explanation above, below or next to a picture *or* diagram **Bildüberschrift, Bildunterschrift, Bilderläuterung;** *the captions are printed in italics*

capture
1 *noun* **data capture** = action of obtaining data (either by keyboarding *or* by scanning or often automatically from a recording device *or* peripheral) **Datenerfassung;** *data capture starts when an interrupt is received* **2** *verb* to take data into a computer system **Daten erfassen, eingeben;** *the software allows captured images to be edited; scanners usually capture images at a resolution of 300 dots per inch (dpi)*

QUOTE images can then be captured, stored, manipulated and displayed
Electronics & Wireless World

carbon *noun*
(a) carbon paper **Kohlepapier;** *you forgot to put a carbon in the typewriter*
(b) carbon copy **Durchschlag;** *make a top copy and two carbons; see also* NCR

◇ **carbon copy** *noun* copy made with carbon paper **Durchschlag;** *give me the original, and file the carbon copy*

◇ **carbonless** *adjective* which makes a copy without using carbon paper **selbstdurchschreibend;** *our representatives use carbonless order pads;* **carbonless paper** = paper that transfers writing without carbon paper **selbstdurchschreibendes Papier**

◇ **carbon microphone** *noun* microphone that uses changes of resistance in carbon granules due to sound pressure to produce a signal **Kohlemikrophon**

◇ **carbon paper** *noun* thin paper with a coating of ink on one side, used to make copies in a typewriter *or* printer **Kohlepapier**

◇ **carbon ribbon** *noun* thin plastic ribbon, coated with black ink, used in printers **Karbonband;** *compare* FIBRE RIBBON

◇ **carbon set** *noun* forms with carbon paper attached **Formulare mit Kohlepapier**

◇ **carbon tissue** *noun* light-sensitive material used to transfer an image to the printing plate of a photogravure process **Pigmentpapier**

card *noun*
(a) stiff paper **Karton;** *we have printed the instructions on thick white card* NOTE: no plural
(b) small piece of stiff paper *or* plastic **Karte; cash card** = plastic card containing the owner's details on a magnetic stripe, used to obtain money from a cash dispenser **Bargeldkarte; charge card** = plastic card which allows you to buy goods and pay for them later **Kreditkarte; credit card** = plastic card which allows you to borrow money *or* to buy goods without paying for them immediately **Kreditkarte; filing card** = card with information written on it, used to classify information in correct order **Karteikarte; index card** = card used to make a card index **Karteikarte; punched card** = card with holes punched in it that represent data **Lochkarte; smart card** = plastic card with a memory and microprocessor device embedded in it, so that it can be used for electronic funds transfer *or* for identification of the user **Chip-Karte;** *smart cards reduce fraud; future smart cards could contain an image of the users fingerprint for identification*
(c) card code = combination of punched holes that represent characters on a punched card **Lochkartencode; card column** = line of punched information about one character, parallel to the shorter side of the card **Lochkartenspalte; card feed** = device which draws punched cards into a reader automatically **Kartenzuführung; card field** = part of a card column reserved for one type of data **Lochkartenfeld; card format** = way in which columns and rows are arranged to represent data fields *or* characters in a punched card **Kartenformat; card image** = section of memory that contains an exact representation of the information on a card **Dualkartenverarbeitung; card loader** = short program that transfers data from a punched card into main memory **Kartenlader; card punch (CP)** = machine that punches the holes in punched cards **Kartenlocher; card reader** *or* **punched card reader** = device that transforms data on a punched card to a form that can be

recognized by the computer **Lochkartenleser; card row** = punch positions parallel to the longer edge of a card **Kartenzeile**
(d) sheet of insulating material on which electronic components can be mounted **Platine; card cage** = metal supporting frame for circuit boards **Platinengehäuse; card edge connector** = series of metal tracks ending at the edge and on the surface of a card, allowing it to be plugged into an edge connector to provide electrical contact (for data transmission, etc.) **Kartenrandverbindung; card extender** = card containing only conducting tracks, inserted between a motherboard connector and an expansion card, allowing the expansion card to be worked on and examined easily, outside the card cage **Platinenerweiterung; expansion card** *or* **expansion board** = printed circuit board that is connected to a system (expansion connector) to increase its functions *or* performance **Erweiterungsplatine; hard card** = board containing a hard disk drive and the required interfacing electronics, which can be slotted into a system (expansion connector) **Festplattenlaufwerksplatine; card frame** *or* **card chassis** = frame containing a motherboard into which printed circuit boards can be plugged to provide a flexible system **Kartenchassis**

◇ **cardboard** *noun* thick stiff brown paper **Pappe, Karton; cardboard box** = box made of cardboard **Pappkarton;** NOTE: no plural

◇ **card index** *noun* series of cards with information written on them, kept in special order so that the information can be found easily **Kartei; card-index file** = information kept on filing cards **Katalogdatei**

◇ **card-index** *verb* to put information onto a card index **katalogisieren**

◇ **card-indexing** *noun* putting information onto a card index **Katalogisierung;** *no one can understand her card-indexing system*

QUOTE this card does not occupy system memory space and provides fifty functions including programmable character sets
Computing Today

cardioid response *noun* heart shaped response curve of an antenna *or* microphone when a signal source is moved around it **herzförmige Empfangscharakteristik**

caret mark *or* **sign** *noun* proofreading symbol to indicate that something has to be inserted in the text **Caret-Zeichen, Auslassungszeichen**

carriage *noun* mechanical section of a typewriter *or* printer that correctly feeds *or* moves the paper that is being printed **Vorschub; carriage control** = codes that control the movements of a printer carriage **Vorschubsteuerung;** *carriage control codes can be used to move the paper forward two lines between each line of text;* **carriage return (CR)** = signal *or* key to move to the beginning of the next line of print *or* display **Wagenrücklauf(taste);** *the carriage return key is badly placed for touch-typists*

carrier *noun*
(a) substance that holds the ink for photocopying *or* printing processes **Träger**
(b) device that holds a section of microfilm **Träger**
(c) continuous high frequency waveform that can be modulated by a signal **Trägerschwingung;** *he's not using a modem - there's no carrier signal on the line;* **carrier sense multiple access - collision detection (CSMA-CD)** = network communications protocol that prevents two sources transmitting at the same time by waiting for a quiet moment, then attempting to transmit **CSMA/CD (Verfahren zum Schutz, daß mehrere Sender in einem Netz nicht gleichzeitig senden); carrier signalling** = simple data transmission (by switching on and off a carrier signal according to binary data) **Trägersignal; carrier system** = method of transmitting several different signals on one channel by using different carrier frequencies **Trägerfrequenzsystem; carrier telegraphy** = method of transmitting telegraph signals via a carrier signal **Trägerfrequenztelegraphie; carrier wave** = waveform used as a carrier **Trägerschwingung; data carrier** = (i) any device *or* medium capable of storing data; (ii) a waveform used as a carrier for data signals **(i) Datenträger; (ii) Datenschwingungsträger; data carrier detect (DCD)** = RS232C signal from a modem to a computer, indicating a carrier wave is being received **Empfangssignal eines Datenschwingungsträgers;** *the call is stopped if the software does not receive a DCD signal from the modem*

carry
1 *noun* (extra) digit due to an addition result being greater than the number base used **Übertrag;** *when 5 and 7 are added, there is an answer of 2 and a carry which is put in the next column, giving 12;* **carry bit** *or* **flag** = indicator that a carry has occurred **Übertragsbit; carry complete signal** = signal from an adder circuit indicating that all carry operations have been completed „**Übertragung beendet"-Signal; carry look**

ahead = high speed adder that can predict if a carry will be generated by a sum and add it in, removing the delay found in an adder with ripple-through carry **Parallelübertrag; carry time** = period of time taken to transfer a carry digit to the next higher digit position **Übertragszeit; cascade carry** = carry generated in an adder from an input carry signal **Kaskadenübertrag; end-around carry** = most significant digit (the carry) is added into the least significant place (used in BCD arithmetic) **Übertrag des Überlaufs in die niedere Stelle; high speed carry** = when a carry into an adder results in a carry out, all produced in one operation **Schnellübertrag; partial carry** = temporary storage of all carries generated in parallel adders, rather than a direct transfer **Teilübertrag; ripple-through carry** = carry generated by a carry in to an adder **Schnellübertrag**
2 *verb* to move (something) from one place to another **hinübertragen;** *the fibre optic link carried all the data; the information-carrying abilities of this link are very good*

cartesian coordinates *noun* positional system that uses two axes at right angles to represent a point which is located with two numbers, giving a position on each **kartesische Koordinaten**

◊ **cartesian structure** *noun* data structure whose size is fixed and the elements are in (a linear) order **kartesische Struktur;** *compare with* AXIS, POLAR COORDINATES

cartridge *noun* removable cassette, containing a disk *or* tape *or* program *or* data (usually stored in ROM) **Kassette; data cartridge** = cartridge that contains stored data **Datenregister; disk cartridge** = removable hard disk **Plattenkassette; ROM cartridge** = sealed module (with electrical connections) which can be plugged into a computer and contains data *or* extra programs stored in a ROM chip **ROM-Kassette;** *the portable computer has no disk drives, but has a slot for ROM cartridges;* **tape cartridge** = cassette box containing magnetic tape **Magnetbandkassette; cartridge drive** = drive which uses a disk *or* tape in a cartridge **Cartridge-Laufwerk, Magnetbandkassettenlaufwerk; cartridge fonts** = ROM cartridge which can be plugged into a printer, providing a choice of new typefaces, but still limited to the typefaces and styles included in the cartridge **auswechselbare Zeichensätze;** *compare* RESIDENT FONTS; **cartridge ribbon** = printer ribbon in a closed cartridge **Kassettenfarbband**

◊ **cartridge paper** *noun* good quality white paper for drawing *or* printing **Zeichenpapier**

cascade carry *noun* carry generated in an adder from an input carry signal **Kaskadenübertrag**

◊ **cascade connection** *noun* number of devices *or* circuits arranged in series, the output of one driving the input of the next **Kaskadenverbindung**

◊ **cascade control** *noun* multiple control units, each controlling the next **Kaskadensteuerung**

case
1 *noun*
(a) protective container for a device *or* circuit **Gehäuse**
(b) box containing metal characters used in composing **Setzkasten; upper case** *or* **lower case** = capital letters *or* ordinary letters **Großbuchstaben; Kleinbuchstaben;** *he corrected the word "coMputer", replacing the upper case M with a lower case letter;* **case change** = key used to change from upper to lower case on a keyboard **Umschalttaste**
(c) cardboard cover for a book **Buchdecke;** *the library edition has a case and jacket; have you remembered to order the blocking for the spine of the case?;* **case binding** = stiff cardboard cover **fester Einband**
(d) cardboard *or* wooden box for packing and carrying goods **Schachtel, Kiste; packing case** = large wooden box for carrying items which can be easily broken **Kiste**
2 *verb*
(a) to bind a book in a stiff cardboard cover **fest binden; cased book** = book with a hard cover **fest gebundenes Buch**
(b) to pack in a case **in eine Kiste packen**

◊ **case-making machine** *noun* machine for cutting the cardboard which forms the cover of a book **Buchdeckenmaschine**

casing *noun* solid protective box in which a computer *or* delicate equipment is housed **Gehäuse**

cassette *noun* hard container used to store and protect magnetic tape **Kassette;** *you must back up the information from the computer onto a cassette;* **audio cassette** = small cassette containing a reel of narrow magnetic tape on which audio signal can be recorded (used to store data in small home computers) **Tonkassette; data cassette** = special high-quality tape for storing data **Datenkassette; video cassette** = large cassette containing a reel of wide magnetic tape on which video data can be recorded **Videokassette; cassette recorder** = machine to transfer audio signals onto magnetic tape **Kassettenrekorder; cassette tape** =

narrow reel of magnetic tape housed in a solid case for protection **Tonbandkassette**

COMMENT: using cassette tape allows data to be stored for future retrieval; it is used instead of a disk system on small computers or as a slow, serial access, high-capacity back-up medium for large systems

caster machine *noun* machine that produces metal type **Gießmaschine**

◊ **cast off**
1 *noun* amount of space required to print a text in a certain font **geschätzter Satzumfang**
2 *verb* to calculate the amount of space needed to print a text in a certain font **Satzumfang schätzen**

◊ **casting off** *noun* calculating the amount of space required to print text in a certain font **Schätzen des Satzumfangs**

CAT
(a) = COMPUTER AIDED *or* ASSISTED TRAINING use of a computer to demonstrate to and assist pupils in learning a skill **computergestütztes Training**
(b) = COMPUTER AIDED *or* ASSISTED TESTING use of a computer to test equipment *or* programs to find any faults **computergestütztes Prüfen**

catalogue
1 *noun* list of contents *or* items in order **Katalog; disk catalogue** *or* **directory** = list of files stored on a magnetic disk **Plattenverzeichnis;** *the entry in the disk catalogue is removed when the file is deleted*
2 *verb* to make a catalogue of items stored **katalogisieren;** *all the terminals were catalogued, with their location, call sign and attribute table*

◊ **cataloguer** *noun* person who makes a catalogue **Katalogisierer**

catastrophe *noun* serious fault, error *or* breakdown of equipment, usually leading to serious damage and shutdown of a system **Katastrophe**

◊ **catastrophic error** *noun* error that causes a program to crash *or* files to be accidentally erased **schlimmer Fehler; catastrophic failure** = complete system failure *or* crash **Totalausfall**

catena *noun* (i) number of items in a chained list; (ii) series of characters in a word **(i) Zahl der Kettenglieder; (ii) Kette**

◊ **catenate** *verb* to join together two or more sets of data **verketten**

cathode *noun* negative electrical terminal of a device *or* battery **Kathode**; NOTE: opposite is **anode**

◇ **cathode ray tube (CRT)** *noun* device used for displaying characters *or* figures *or* graphical information, similar to a TV set **Kathodenstrahlröhre, Bildröhre; cathode ray tube storage** = a cathode ray tube with a long persistence phosphor screen coating that retains an image for a long time **Bildröhrenspeicher**; NOTE: CRT is now often used to mean 'monitor'

COMMENT: cathode ray tubes are used in television sets, computer monitors and VDUs; a CRT consists of a vacuum tube, one end of which is flat and coated with phosphor, the other end containing an electron beam source. Characters *or* graphics are visible when the controllable electron beam strikes the phosphor causing it to glow

CATV = COMMUNITY ANTENNA TELEVISION cable television system using a single aerial to pick up television signals and then distribute them over a wide area via cable **Kabelfernsehen**

CB = CITIZENS BAND RADIO cheap popular system of radio communications, usually between vehicles **CB (Citizen-Band, Jedermannfunk)**

C band *noun* microwave communications frequency range of 3.9 - 6.2GHz **C-Band**

CBL = COMPUTER BASED LEARNING learning mainly using a computer **computergestütztes Lernen**

CBMS = COMPUTER BASED MESSAGE SYSTEM use of a computer system to allow users to send and receive messages from other users (usually in-house) **computergestütztes Nachrichtensystem**; *see also* BBS

CBT = COMPUTER BASED TRAINING use of a computer system to train students **computergestütztes Training**

CBX = COMPUTERIZED BRANCH EXCHANGE

CCD = CHARGE COUPLED DEVICE; **CCD memory** = capacitors used (with MOS transistors) to store data, allowing either serial or random access **ladungsgekoppelter Speicher**

CCITT = COMITE CONSULTATIF INTERNATIONAL TELEGRAPHIQUE ET TELEPHONIQUE

CCP = COMMAND CONSOLE PROCESSOR software which interfaces between a user's terminal and system BIOS **CCP (Teil des Betriebssystems, der direkt mit dem Anwender kommuniziert, bei CP/M)**

CCTV = CLOSED CIRCUIT TELEVISION

CCU = COMMUNICATIONS CONTROL UNIT

CD = COMPACT DISK; **CD-ROM** = COMPACT DISK-READ ONLY MEMORY small plastic disk that is used as a high capacity ROM device, data is stored in binary form as holes etched on the surface which are then read by a laser **CD-ROM**

cedilla *noun* accent under a letter c, used in certain languages to change the pronunciation **Cedille**

cell *noun*
(a) single function *or* number in a spreadsheet program **Zelle; cell reference variable** = register that contains the reference locating a certain cell that is being operated on **Zellreferenzvariable**
(b) single memory location, capable of storing a data word, accessed by an individual address **Zelle; cell phone** mobile telephone system that uses a network of stations to cover a large area **Zelltelefon**

◇ **cellular** *adjective* **cellular radio** = radio telephone linked to a main telephone system, which uses a network of stations, each covering a certain area, to provide a service over a large area (the radio is switched from one station to another as it moves from area to area) **Zellradio; cellular service** = changing from one transceiver station to another as a cellular radio *or* cell phone user moves from area to area **Zelltelefon-Fernsprechdienst**

cellar *noun* temporary storage for data *or* registers *or* tasks, in which items are added and retrieved from the same end of the list in a LIFO order **Keller**

centi- *prefix* meaning one hundred *or* one hundredth **zenti-; centimetre** = one hundredth of a metre **Zentimeter**

central *adjective* in the middle **zentral, Haupt-, haupt-; central computer** = HOST COMPUTER; **central memory (CM)** = area of memory whose locations can be directly and immediately addressed by the CPU **Zentralspeicher; central processing element (CPE)** = short (2, 4 or 8 bit) word length module that can be used to produce large word CPUs using bit slice techniques **Zentralverarbeitungseinheit; central processing unit (CPU)** or **central processor** = group of circuits which perform the basic functions of a computer, made up of three parts: the control unit, the arithmetic and logic unit and the input/output unit **Zentraleinheit (CPU); central terminal** = terminal which controls the communications between a central or host computer and remote terminals **Hauptterminal**

◊ **centralized** adjective which is located in a central position **zentralisiert; centralized data processing** = data processing facilities located in a centralized place that can be accessed by other users **zentrale Datenverarbeitung; centralized computer network** = network with processing power provided by a central computer **zentrales Computernetz**

centre or (US) **center**
1 noun point in the middle of something **Mittelpunkt; centre holes** = location holes punched along the centre of paper tape **Vorschublöcher; centre operator** = person who looks after central computer operations **Rechenzentrumsoperator; centre sprocket feed** = centre (sprocket) holes that line up with coding hole positions on punched tape **Stachelbandführung**
2 verb
(a) to align the read/write head correctly on a magnetic disk or tape **zentrieren**
(b) to place a piece of text in the centre of the paper or display screen **zentrieren**; which key do you press to centre the heading?

◊ **centering** noun action of putting text in the centre of the screen **Zentrierung**; centering of headings is easily done, using this function key

Centronics interface noun parallel printer interface devised by Centronics Inc **Centronics-Schnittstelle**

CEPT standard noun videotex character standard defined by the Conference of European Post Telephone and Telegraph **CEPT-Norm**

ceramic adjective made from baked clay **keramisch;** see CAPACITOR

CGA = COLOUR GRAPHICS ADAPTER popular microcomputer medium-

resolution colour display system **Farbgraphikadapter;** see also EGA

chad noun waste material produced from holes punched in tape or card **Stanzrückstand; chadded** or **chadless tape** = punched tape that retains chad by not punching holes through fully **Schuppenstreifen**

chain
1 noun (i) series of files or data items linked sequentially; (ii) series of instructions to be executed sequentially **(i) Kette; (ii) Kettenbefehl; chain code** = series of words, each word being derived (usually shifted by one bit) from the previous word **geketteter Code; chain delivery mechanism** = mechanical system to move paper from machine to machine **Kettenliefermethode; chain list** = list of data with each piece of information providing an address for the next consecutive item in the list **gekettete Liste; chain printer** = printer whose characters are located on a continuous belt **Kettendrucker; command chain** = list of commands (in a file) executed sequentially by a batch mode system **Befehlskette; daisy chain** = method of connecting equipment with a single cable passing from one machine or device to the next (rather than separate cables to each device) **Verkettung; daisy chain bus** = one communications bus that joins one device to the next, each device being able to receive or transmit or modify data as it passes through to the next device in line **verkettete Busstruktur**
2 verb to link files or data items in series by storing a pointer to the next file or item at each entry **(ver)ketten;** more than 1,000 articles or chapters can be chained together when printing; see also CATENA; **chained** or **threaded file** = file in which an entry will contain data and an address to the next entry that has the same data content (allowing rapid retrieval of all identical data records) **gekettete Datei; chained list** = list in which each element contains data and an address to the next element in the list **gekettete Liste; chained record** = data record in a chained file **geketteter Satz; daisy-chain** = to connect equipment using the daisy chain method **verketten;** daisy-chaining saves a lot of cable

◊ **chaining** noun execution of a very large program by executing small segments of it at a time, this allows programs larger than memory capacity to be run **Ketten; chaining search** = search of a file of elements arranged in a chained list **Suche in verknüpfter Liste; data chaining** = storing one record that holds the address of the next in the list **Daten(adreß)kettung**

change *verb* to make something different; to use one thing instead of another **austauschen, verändern; change dump** = printout of locations where data has been changed **Speicherauszug der Änderungen; change file** = file containing records that are to be used to update a master file **Änderungsdatei; change record** = record containing new data which is to be used to update a master record **Änderungssatz; change tape** = (magnetic) tape containing recent changes *or* transactions to records which is used to update a master file **Änderungsband**

◊ **change over** *verb* to switch from one computer system to another **überwechseln**

◊ **changer** *noun* device which changes one thing for another **Umwandler; gender changer** = two connectors, used to change a female connector to a male one (or vice-versa) **Geschlechtsumwandler;** *you can interconnect all these peripherals with just two cables and a gender changer;* **record changer** = device on a turntable which allows records to be changed automatically **Plattenwechsler**

channel
1 *noun*
(a) physical connection between two points that allows data to be transmitted (such as a link between a CPU and a peripheral) **Kanal; channel adapter** = interfacing device allowing different channels to be inter-connected **Kanalanschluß; channel bank** = collection of a number of channels, and circuits to switch between them **Kanalbank; channel capacity** = maximum rate of data transmission over a channel **Kanalkapazität; channel command** = instruction to a channel *or* control unit, providing control information such as data selection *or* routes **Kanalbefehl; channel group** = collection of twelve channels, treated as one group in a multiplexing system **Kanalgruppe; channel isolation** = separation of channels measured as the amount of crosstalk between two channels (low crosstalk is due to good channel isolation) **Isolationseinrichtung für Kanäle; channel overload** = transmission of data at a rate greater than the channel capacity **Kanalüberlastung; channel synchronizer** = interface between a central computer and peripherals, providing a channel, channel command interpretation and status signals from the peripherals **Kanalsynchronisierer; channel queue** = (i) queue of requests to use a channel; (ii) queue of data that has yet to be sent over a channel **(i) & (ii) Kanalwarteschlange; channel-to-channel connection** = direct link between the main I/O channels of two computers, allowing

high speed data transfer **Kanal-zu-Kanal-Verbindung;** data channel = communications link able to carry data signals **Datenkanal; dedicated channel** = communications channel reserved for a special purpose **dedizierter Kanal; I/O channel** = link between a processor and peripheral allowing data transfer **Ein-/Ausgabekanal**
(b) way in which information *or* goods are passed from one place to another **Weg; to go through the official channels** = to deal with government officials (especially when making a request) **den Dienstweg gehen; to open up new channels of communication** = to find new ways of communicating with someone **neue Nachrichtenverbindungen erschließen; distribution channels** *or* **channels of distribution** = ways of sending goods from the manufacturer for sale in shops **Verteilungskanäle**
2 *verb* to send signals *or* data via a particular path **leiten**

◊ **channelling** *noun* protective pipe containing cables *or* wires **Kanalisierung**

chapter *noun*
(a) section of a main program that can be executed in its own right, without the rest of the main program being required **Kapitel**
(b) sequence of frames on a video disk **Kapitel; chapter stop** = code at the end of a video disk chapter that enables rapid location of a particular chapter **Kapitelende**
(c) section of a book *or* document **Kapitel; chapter heading** = special heading at the beginning of each printed chapter **Kapitelüberschrift;** *chapter headings are in 12 point bold*

character *noun* graphical symbol which appears as a printed *or* displayed mark, such as one of the letters of the alphabet, a number or a punctuation mark **Zeichen; alphanumeric characters** = roman letters and arabic numerals (and other signs such as punctuation marks) **alphanumerische Zeichen; cancel character** = control code used to indicate that the last data transmitted was incorrect **Ungültigkeitszeichen; character assembly** = method of designing characters with pixels on a computer screen **Zeichenrasterung; character blink** = character whose intensity is switched on and off (as an indicator) **blinkendes Zeichen; character block** = the pattern of dots that will make up a character on a screen *or* printer **Zeichenblock; character byte** = byte of data containing the character code and any error check bits **Zeichenbyte; character check** = check to ensure that a character code protocol and format are correct

Zeichenprüfung; **character code** = system where each character is represented by a unique number **Zeichencode;** *the ASCII code is the most frequently used character coding system;* **character density** = number of characters that can be stored *or* displayed per unit area **Zeichendichte; character display** = device that displays data in alphanumeric form **(alphanumerische) Zeichenanzeige; character fill** = writing one character to every location within an area of memory (for clearing and resetting the memory) **mit Zeichen füllen; character generator** = ROM that provides the display circuits with a pattern of dots which represent the character (block) **Zeichengenerator;** *the ROM used as a character generator can be changed to provide different fonts;* **character key** = word processor control used to process text one character at a time **Zeichentaste; character machine** = computer in which the number of bits which make up a word is variable, and varies according to the type of data **Computer mit variabler Wortlänge; character orientated** = computer that addresses character locations rather than words **zeichenorientiert; character printer** = device that prints characters one at a time **Zeichendrucker;** *a daisy wheel printer is a character printer;* **character recognition** = system that optically reads written *or* printed characters into a computer, using various algorithms to ensure that characters are correctly recognized **Zeichenerkennung;** *see also* OCR; **character repertoire** = list of all the characters that can be displayed *or* printed **Zeichenvorrat; character representation** = combination of bits used for each character code **Zeichendarstellung; character rounding** = making a displayed character more pleasant to look at (within the limits of pixel size) by making sharp corners and edges smooth **Zeichenrundungen; character set** = list of all the characters that can be displayed *or* printed **Zeichensatz; character skew** = angle of a character in comparison to its correct position **Zeichenneigung; character string** = storage allocated for a series of alphanumeric characters **Zeichenfolge;** *compare with* NUMERIC STRING; **characters per inch (cpi)** = number of printed characters which fit within the space of one inch **Zeichen pro Inch;** *you can select 10 or 12 cpi with the green button;* **characters per second (cps)** = number of characters which are transmitted *or* printed per second **Zeichen pro Sekunde; character stuffing** = addition of blank characters to a file to increase its length to a preset size **Leerzeichenfüllung; check character** = additional character inserted into transmitted data to serve as an error detection check, its value is dependent on the text **Prüfzeichen; device control character** = special code sent in a transmission to a device to instruct it to perform a special function **Gerätesteuerzeichen**

◊ **characteristic**
1 *noun*
(a) value of exponent in a floating point number **Gleitpunktexponent;** *the floating point number 1.345 x 10³ , has a characteristic of 3;* **characteristic overflow** = exponent value of a floating point number that is greater than the maximum allowable **charakteristischer Überlauf**
(b) measurements *or* properties of a component **Merkmal**
2 *adjective* which is typical *or* special **charakteristisch;** *this fault is characteristic of this make and model of personal computer;* **characteristic curve** = response curve of an electronic component *or* circuit **charakteristische Kurve**

QUOTE the screen displays very sharp and stable characters, each cell occupying an 8 by 11 dot matrix
Computing Today

charge *noun* (i) a quantity of electricity; (ii) the number of *or* excess of *or* lack of electrons in a material *or* component **(i) & (ii) Ladung; charge-coupled device (CCD)** = electronic device operated by charge **ladungsgekoppelter Elektronikbaustein; charge-coupled device memory** = capacitors used (with MOS transistors) to store data, allowing serial and random access **ladungsgekoppelter Speicher; electric charge** = a number of atoms that are charged (due to an excess *or* deficiency of electrons) **elektrische Ladung**
2 *verb* to supply a device with an electric charge **laden; battery charging** = to replenish the charge stored in a re-chargeable battery **Batterieaufladen**
◊ **chargeable** *adjective* which can be charged **aufladbar; re-chargeable battery** = battery that can be used to supply power, and then have its charge replenished **wiederaufladbare Batterie;** *a re-chargeable battery is used for RAM back-up when the system is switched off*

chart *noun* diagram showing information as a series of lines *or* blocks, etc. **Abbildung, Diagramm; bar chart** = graph on which values are represented as vertical *or* horizontal bars of different heights *or* lengths **Balkendiagramm; flowchart** = diagram showing the arrangement of various work processes as a series of stages **Flußdiagramm;** *a flowchart is the first step to a well designed program;* **logical chart** = graphical representation of logic elements,

chart 50 **chord**

steps, decisions and interconnections in a system **Logikplan; pie chart** = diagram where ratios are shown as slices of a circle **Kreisdiagramm;** *the memory allocation is shown on this pie chart;* **chart recorder** = mechanical device that records input values by drawing lines on a moving reel of paper **Kreisblattschreiber**

chassis *noun* metal frame that houses the circuit boards together with the wiring and sockets required in a computer system *or* other equipment **Gehäuse;** *see also* RACK

check
1 *noun*
(a) act of making sure that something is correct **Prüfung; character check** = check to ensure that a character code protocol and format are correct **Zeichenprüfung; check bit** = one bit of a binary word that is used to provide a parity check **Prüfbit; check character** = additional character inserted into transmitted text to serve as an (error detection) check for the text, its value is dependent on the text **Prüfzeichen; check digit** *or* **number** = additional digit inserted into transmitted text to monitor and correct errors **Prüfzahl; check indicator** = hardware *or* software device that shows that received text is not correct and a check has failed **Prüfanzeiger; check key** = series of characters derived from a text used to check for and correct errors **Prüfzeichen; check point** = point in a program where data and program status can be recorded *or* displayed **Prüfpunkt; check point dump** = printout of data and program status at a check point **Speicherauszug des Programmstops; check register** = temporary storage for received data before it is checked against the same data received via another path *or* method **Prüfregister; check total** = CHECKSUM; **desk check** = dry run of a program **Probelauf**
(b) short fault *or* pause in a process (that does not stop the process) **Kurzunterbrechung; data check** = error in reading data due to a fault with the magnetic medium **Datenstop**
2 *verb* to examine *or* to make sure than something is in good working order **prüfen;** *the separate parts of the system were all checked for faults before being packaged;* **he checked the computer printout against the invoices** = he examined the printout and the invoices to see if the figures were the same **er verglich die Computerausdrucke mit den Rechnungen**

◊ **checkerboarding** *noun* (virtual page) memory organization that has resulted in odd pages *or* spread-out pages *or* segments of memory being filled, wasting memory by leaving unusable gaps in between **spezielle Speicherorganisation**

◊ **checking** *noun* examination **Überprüfung;** *the maintenance engineer found some defects whilst checking the equipment;* **checking program** = software that finds errors in program *or* data syntax, format and coding **Prüfprogramm, Diagnoseprogramm; self-checking code** = error detection code **Fehlererkennungscode;** NOTE: no plural

◊ **checksum** *or* **check total** *noun* program which checks that data is correct, by summing it and comparing the sum with a stored value **Kontrollsumme;** *the data must be corrupted if the checksum is different*

chemical
1 *adjective* referring to the interaction of substances **chemisch; chemical reaction** = interaction between two substances *or* elements **chemische Reaktion**
2 *noun* product resulting from the interaction of other substances *or* elements **Chemikalie**

chip *noun* device consisting of a small piece of a crystal of a semiconductor onto which are etched *or* manufactured (by doping) a number of components such as transistors, resistors and capacitors, which together perform a function **Chip; chip architecture** = design and layout of components on a chip **Chip-Architektur; chip card** = plastic card with a memory and microprocessor device embedded in it, so that it can be used for electronic funds transfer *or* identification of a user **Chip-Karte; chip count** = number of chips on a PCB *or* in a device **Chip-Anzahl;** *it's no good, the chip count is still too high;* **chip select line** = connection to a chip that will enable it to function when a signal is present **Chip-Verbindungsstelle;** *the data strobe line is connected to the latch chip select line;* **chip set** = chips which together will carry out a function **Chip-Satz; diagnostic chip** = chip that contains circuits to carry out tests on circuits *or* other chips **Diagnosechip;** *they are carrying out research on diagnostic chips to test computers that contain processors;* **single chip computer** = complete simple computer including CPU, memory and input/output ports on one chip **Einzelchipcomputer; sound chip** = device that will generate a sound *or* tune **Tonteil**

chop *see* BINARY

chord keying *noun* action of pressing two *or* more keys at the same time to perform a function **gleichzeitiges Drücken mehrerer Tasten;** *to access the second* *window, press control and F2; shift and character delete keys will delete a line of text*

chroma *noun* colour hue and saturation measure **Farbenreinheit, Farbenintensität; chroma control** = circuit in a TV that alters the colour saturation **Farbkontrolle; chroma detector** = television circuit that checks whether a signal is monochrome *or* colour **Farbdetektor**

◊ **chromatic** *adjective* referring to colours **Farb-, farb-, chromatisch; chromatic aberration** = optical lens that affects and focuses different colours in different ways **chromatische Abweichung, Farbabweichung, Farbaberration; chromatic dispersion** = uneven refraction index across an optic fibre causing signal distortion **chromatische Dispersion**

◊ **chromaticity** *noun* quality of light according to its most prominent colour and purity **Chromatizität**

◊ **chrominance signal** *noun* section of a colour monitor signal containing colour hue and saturation information **Farbsignal**

chronological order *noun* arrangement of records *or* files according to their dates **chronologische Anordnung**

CIM
(a) = COMPUTER INPUT FROM MICROFILM coordinated use of microfilm for computer data storage and the method of reading the data **CIM (Dateneingabe von Mikrofilm)**
(b) = COMPUTER INTEGRATED MANUFACTURE use of computers in every aspect of design and manufacturing **computerintegrierte Fertigung**

cine- *prefix* meaning moving pictures *or* film **Film-; cine camera** = camera that records motion pictures onto a roll of film **Filmkamera; cine orientated image** = data *or* graphics on a microfilm where the image is at right angles to the long edge of the roll of film **Zeilenanordnung quer (bei Mikrofilmen)**

◊ **cinema** *noun*
(a) the cinema = making of films for showing to the public **das Filmen**
(b) building where films are shown to the public **Kino**

◊ **cinematography** *noun* (i) motion picture photography; (ii) effects giving impression of motion **(i) Filmen; (ii) Cinematographie**

cipher *noun* system of transforming a message into an unreadable form with a secret key (the message can be read normally after it has passed through the cipher a second time) **Verschlüsselung;** always use a secure cipher when sending data over a telephone line; **cipher key** = secret sequence of characters used with a cipher system to provide a unique ciphertext **Chiffrierschlüssel; cipher system** = formula used to transform text into a secret form **Verschlüsselungssystem; public key cipher** = cipher that uses a public key to encrypt messages and a secret key to decrypt them (conventional ciphers use one secret key to encrypt and decrypt messages) **Verschlüsselungssystem mit bekanntem Chiffrierschlüssel; ciphertext** = data output from a cipher **verschlüsselter Text;** NOTE: opposite is **plaintext**

CIR = CURRENT INSTRUCTION REGISTER CPU register that stores the instruction that is currently being executed **aktuelles Befehlsregister**

circuit *noun* connection between electronic components that perform a function **Schaltung, Stromkreis; circuit board** *or* **card** = insulating board used to hold components which are then connected together (electrically) to form a circuit **Schaltkarte; circuit breaker** = device which protects equipment by cutting off the electrical supply when conditions are abnormal **Stromkreisunterbrecher; circuit capacity** = information-carrying capacity of a particular circuit **Leistungsvermögen eines Stromkreises; circuit diagram** = graphical description of a circuit **Schaltbild;** *the CAD program will plot the circuit diagram rapidly;* **circuit grade** = ability of a communication channel to carry information (the grades are: wideband, voice, subvoice and telegraph) **Übertragungsmöglichkeiten eines Nachrichtenkanals; circuit noise level** = amplitude of noise in a circuit compared to a reference level **Leitungsgeräuschpegel; circuit switched network** = communications network in which each link can be linked to another at a switching centre **Durchschaltnetz; circuit switching** = communications circuit established on demand and held until no longer required **Leitungsvermittlung; data circuit** = circuit which allows bi-directional data communications **Datenverbindung; decision circuit** = logical circuit that operates on binary inputs, producing an output according to the function set in hardware **Entscheidungsschaltung; digital circuit** = electronic circuit that operates on digital information providing logical functions *or* switching **Digitalschaltung; logic circuit** = electronic circuit made up of various logical gates, such as AND, OR and EXOR **logische Schaltung; printed circuit board**

(PCB) = flat insulating material that has conducting tracks of metal printed *or* etched onto its surface, which complete a circuit when components are mounted on it **gedruckte Schaltkarte**

◊ **circuitry** *noun* collection of circuits **Schaltlogik;** *the circuitry is still too complex* NOTE: no plural

circular

1 *adjective* which goes round in a circle **kreisförmig; circular buffer** = computer-based queue that uses two markers, for top and bottom of the line of stored items (the markers move as items are read from *or* written to the stack) **Rundpuffer; circular file** = a data file that has no visible beginning *or* end, each item points to the location of the next item with the last pointing back to the first **Runddatei; circular list** = list in which each element contains data and an address to the next element in the list with the last item pointing back to the first **Kreisliste; circular orbit** = orbit of a satellite that is always at a constant distance from the centre of the earth **Kreisumlaufbahn; circular shift** = rotation of bits in a word with the previous last bit inserted in the first bit position **Rundverschiebung; circular waveguide** = microwave beam carrying a channel, of circular cross-section, allowing high frequencies to be carried **Rundhohlleiter**

◊ **circulate** *verb*
(a) to go round in a circle, and return to the first point **kreisen**
(b) to send information to **in Umlauf bringen;** *they circulated the new list of prices to all their customers*

◊ **circulating** *adjective* which is moving about freely **zirkulierend; circulating register** = shift register whose output is fed back to its input to form a closed loop **Kreislaufregister; circulating storage** = storage device that maintains stored data as a series of pulses, that move along the length of the medium, being regenerated and re-input when they reach the end **Umlaufspeicher**

> COMMENT: circulating storage devices are not often used now, being slow (serial access) and bulky: typical devices are acoustic or mercury delay lines

◊ **circulation** *noun*
(a) movement **Umlauf;** *the company is trying to improve the circulation of information between departments*
(b) *(of a newspaper)* number of copies sold **Auflage(nziffer);** *what is the circulation of this computer magazine? specialized paper with a circulation of over 10,000*

circumflex *noun* printed accent (like a small 'v' printed upside down) placed above a letter, which may change the pronunciation *or* distinguish the letter from others **Zirkumflex**

CISC COMPLEX INSTRUCTION SET COMPUTER CPU design whose instruction set contains a number of long, complex instructions, that makes program writing easier, but reduces execution speed **konventioneller Rechner;** *compare with* RISC

citizens band radio (CB) *noun* cheap popular system of radio communications, usually between vehicles **Citizen-Band, Jedermannfunk (CB)**

cladding *noun* protective material surrounding a conducting core **Verkleidung;** *if the cladding is chipped, the fibre-optic cable will not functon well*

clamp *verb* to find the voltage of a signal **klemmen**

clapper *noun* mechanical part of a dot matrix printer that drives the printing needles onto the ribbon to print a character on the paper **Nadeldruckwerk**

clarity *noun* being clear **Klarheit;** *the atmospheric conditions affect the clarity of the signal*

classify *verb* to put into classes *or* under various headings **klassifizieren;** *the diagnostic printouts have been classified under T for test results;* **classified directory** = book which lists businesses grouped under various headings (such as computer shops *or* newsagents) **Branchenverzeichnis**

◊ **classification** *noun* way of putting into classes **Klassifizierung**

clean

1 *adjective* not dirty *or* with no errors *or* with no programs **sauber, gereinigt;** *I'll have to start again - I just erased the only clean file;* **clean copy** = copy which is ready for keyboarding, and does not have many changes on it **Reinkopie; clean machine** = computer that contains only the minimum of ROM based code to boot its system from disk, any languages required must be loaded in **Computer mit minimalem ROM-basiertem Code; clean page** = page (of memory) that has not been changed since it was read **unveränderte Speicherseite; clean proof** = proof without any corrections **Reinkopie**

2 *verb* to make something clean **reinigen;
data cleaning** = to remove errors from data
Datenreinigung; head cleaning disk = special
disk which will clean dirt from the
read/write head **Kopfreinigungsplatte;** *use a
head cleaning disk every week; write errors
occur if you do not use a head cleaning kit
regularly;* **screen cleaning kit** = liquids and
cloth which remove any static and dirt
from a VDU screen
Bildschirmreinigungsausrüstung

clear

1 *adjective* easily understood **klar
verständlich;** *the program manual is not
clear on copying files; the booklet gives clear
instructions how to connect the different
parts of the system; he made it clear that the
system will only work on IBM-compatible
hardware*
2 *verb*
(a) to wipe out *or* erase *or* set to zero a
computer file *or* variable *or* section of
memory **löschen;** *type CLS to clear the
screen; all arrays are cleared each time the
program is run; to clear an area of memory;
to clear the data register*
(b) to release a communications link when
transmissions have finished **freigeben; clear
to send (CTS)** = RS232C signal that a line *or*
device is ready for data transmission
sendebereit

◊ **clearance** *noun* authority to access a file
Berechtigung; *you do not have the required
clearance for this processor*

click

1 *noun*
(a) short duration sound, often used to
indicate that a key has been pressed **Klicken**
(b) pressing a key *or* button on a keyboard
Klicken; *you move through text and graphics
with a click of the button*
2 *verb* to press a key *or* a button on a
keyboard *or* the mouse **drücken;** *use the
mouse to enlarge a frame by clicking inside
its border*

clip

1 *noun* short piece of (live) film **Clip;** *there
was a clip of the disaster on the news*
2 *verb*
(a) to attach papers together with a wire
heften; *the corrections are clipped to the
computer printout*
(b) to cut out with scissors **ausschneiden;
clipping service** = service which cuts out
references to someone in newspapers *or*
magazines and sends them to him
Presseausschnittdienst
(c) to remove the peaks of a waveform
kappen; *the voltage signal was clipped to
prevent excess signal level*

clock *noun*
(a) machine which shows the time **Uhr;** *the
micro has a built-in clock; the time is shown
by the clock in the corner of the screen;*
digital clock = clock which shows the time
using numbers (as 12:05) **Digitaluhr**
(b) circuit that generates pulses used to
synchronize equipment **Taktgeber; clock
cycle** = time period between two
consecutive clock pulses **Taktzyklus; clock
pulse** = regular pulse used for timing *or*
synchronizing purposes **Taktsignal; clock
rate** = number of pulses that a clock
generates every second **Taktgeberrate; clock
track** = line of marks on a disk *or* tape which
provides data about the read head location
Taktspur; main clock = clock signal that
synchronizes all the components in a
system **Haupttaktgeber; programmable clock**
= circuit whose frequency can be set by the
user **programmgesteuerter Zeittaktgeber**
2 *verb* to synchronize signals *or* circuits with
a clock pulse **takten; clocked signals** =
signals that are synchronized with a clock
pulse **Synchronsignale**

clone *noun* computer *or* circuit that
behaves in the same way as the original it
was copied from **Klon;** *they have copied our
new personal computer and brought out a
cheaper clone; higher performance clones
are available for all the models in our range*

close *verb* to shut down access to a file *or*
disk drive **schließen; close file** = to execute a
computer instruction to shut down access
to a stored file **Datei schließen; closed loop** =
number of computer instructions that are
repeated **Schleife ohne Ausgang; closed
subroutine** = number of computer
instructions in a program that can be called
at any time, with control being returned on
completion to the next instruction in the
main program **abgeschlossenes
Unterprogramm; closed user group (CUG)** =
to restrict the entry to a database *or* bulletin
board *or* system (about or on a certain topic
or subject) to certain known and registered
users, usually by means of a password
geschlossener Benutzerkreis; *see also* USER
GROUP

◊ **close up** *verb* to move pieces of type *or*
typeset words closer together **aufschließen;**
*if we close up the lines, we should save a
page*

◊ **close-up** *noun* photograph taken very
close to the subject **Nahaufnahme**

cluster *noun* number of terminals *or*
stations *or* devices *or* memory locations
grouped together in one place, controlled
by a cluster controller **Mehrfachdatenstation;
cluster controller** = central computer that

controls communications to a cluster of devices *or* memory locations **Gruppensteuereinheit**

◊ **clustering** *noun* series of elements, occurring in a sequential line within a hash table **Gruppierung**

QUOTE cluster controllers are available with 8 or 16 channels
Microcomputer News
QUOTE these include IBM networking and clustering hardware and software
Personal Computer World

CM = CENTRAL MEMORY area of memory whose locations can be directly and immediately addressed by the CPU **Zentralspeicher**

C-MAC new direct-broadcast TV standard using time division multiplexing for signals **C-MAC**

CMI = COMPUTER MANAGED INSTRUCTION

CML = COMPUTER MANAGED LEARNING

CMOS = COMPLEMENTARY METAL OXIDE SEMICONDUCTOR integrated circuit design and construction method (using a pair of complementary p- and n-type transistors) **CMOS (Halbleiterelement; Kombination von PMOS- und NMOS-Technik)**

COMMENT: the final package uses very low power but is relatively slow and sensitive to static electricity as compared to TTL integrated circuits; their main use is in portable computers where battery power is being used

CNC = COMPUTER NUMERIC CONTROL machine operated automatically by computer **CNC (computergestützte, numerische Werkzeugmaschinensteuerung);** *see also* NUMERICAL CONTROL

coalesce *verb* to merge two or more files **vereinigen**

coat *verb* to cover with a layer (of clay, paint or varnish) **beschichten, überziehen; coated paper** = paper which has been covered with a layer of clay to make it shiny **gestrichenes Papier**

◊ **coating** *noun* material covering something **Überzug; Streichmasse;** *paper which has a coating of clay*

co-axial cable *noun* cable made up of a central core, surrounded by an insulating layer then a second shielding conductor **Koaxialkabel**

COMMENT: co-axial cable is used for high frequency, low loss applications such as TV aerials

COBOL = COMMON ORDINARY BUSINESS ORIENTED LANGUAGE programming language mainly used in business applications **COBOL**

code
1 *noun*
(a) rules used to convert instructions *or* data from one form to another **Code; code conversion** = rules used to change characters coded in one form, to another **Codeumsetzung**
(b) sequence of computer instructions **Code; chain code** = series of words, each word being derived (usually shifted by one bit) from the previous word **Kettencode; code area** = section of main memory in which program instructions are stored **Befehlsbereich; code line** = one written *or* displayed computer program instruction **Codierzeile; computer** *or* **machine code** = programming language that consists of commands in binary code that can be directly understood by the central processing unit, without the need for translation **Maschinencode; direct** *or* **one-level** *or* **specific code** = binary code which directly operates the central processing unit, using only absolute addresses and values (this is the final form of a program after a compiler *or* assembler pass) **Direktcode; macro code** = one word that is used to represent a number of instructions, simplifying program writing **Makrocode; object code** = (i) binary code which directly operates a CPU; (ii) program code after it has been translated, compiled or assembled (into machine code) **(i) & (ii) Objektcode; optimum code** = coding system that provides the fastest access and retrieval time for stored data items **optimale Codierung; source code** = set of codes (as a program) written by the programmer which cannot be directly executed by the computer, but have to be translated into an object code program by a compiler *or* assembler *or* interpreter **Quellcode; symbolic code** = instruction that is in mnemonic form rather than machine code **symbolischer Code**
(c) system of signs *or* numbers *or* letters which mean something **Code; area code** = numbers which indicate an area for telephoning **Ortsnetzkennzahl, Vorwahl;** *what is the code for Edinburgh?;* **bar code** = data represented as a series of printed stripes of

varying widths **Balkencode; bar-code reader** = optical device that reads data from a bar code **Balkencodeleser; code element** = voltage *or* signal used to represent binary digits **Codeelement; cyclic code** = coding system in which the binary representation of decimal numbers changes by only one bit at a time from one number to the next **zyklischer Code; device code** = unique identification and selection code for a peripheral **Gerätekennung; error code** = code that indicates that a particular type of error has occurred **Fehlercode; error correcting code** = coding system that allows bit errors occurring during transmission to be rapidly corrected by logical deduction methods **Fehlerkorrekturcode; error detecting code** = coding system that allows bit errors occurring during transmission to be detected, but is not complex enough to correct them **Fehlererkennungscode; escape codes** = transmitted code sequence which informs the receiver that all following characters represent control actions **ESC-Codes (Codeumschaltung); international dialling code** = numbers used for dialling to another country **Auslandsvorwahl, Internationale Vorwahl; machine-readable codes** = sets of signs *or* letters (such as bar codes *or* post codes) which can be read by computers **maschinenlesbare Codes; post code** *or (US)* **zip code** = letters and numbers used to indicate a town *or* street in an address on an envelope **Postleitzahl; punched code** = combination of holes that represent characters in a punched card **Lochkartencode; self-checking code** = error detecting code **Fehlererkennungscode; stock code** = numbers and letters which refer to an item of stock **Lager-, Warencode**
2 *verb*
(a) to convert instructions *or* data into another form **umsetzen**
(b) to write a program in a programming language **codieren**
◊ **coder** *noun* device which encodes a signal **Codierer**
◊ **coding** *noun* act of putting a code on something **Codieren; coding sheet** *or* **coding form** = special printed sheet used by programmers to write instructions for coding a certain type of program **Programmschema**

CODEC = CODER/DECODER device which codes a signal being sent *or* decodes a signal received (used in many advanced PABX systems) **Codierer/Decodierer**

coercivity *noun* magnetic field required to remove any flux saturation effects from a material **Koerzitivkraft**

coherent *adjective* referring to waveforms which are all in phase **zusammenhängend, kohärent;** *the laser produces coherent light;* **coherent bundle** = number of optical fibres, grouped together so that they are all the same length and produce coherent signals from either end **kohärentes Bündel**

coil *noun* number of turns of wire **Spule, Rolle;** *an inductor is made from a coil of wire*

coincidence circuit *or* **element** *noun* electronic circuit that produces an output signal when two inputs occur simultaneously *or* two binary words are equal **Koinzidenzschaltung, UND-Schaltung;** *see also* AND

cold *adjective*
(a) not hot **kalt;** *the machines work badly in cold weather*
(b) without being prepared **unvorbereitet; cold fault** = computer fault *or* error that occurs as soon as it is switched on **Kaltfehler; cold standby** = backup system that will allow the equipment to continue running, but with the loss of any volatile data **Cold-Standby-System;** *compare with* HOT, WARM STANDBY; **cold start** = switching on a computer *or* to run a program from its original start point **Kaltstart;** *compare* WARM START

collate *verb* (i) to compare and put items in order; (ii) to put signatures in order for sewing and binding **(i) sortieren; (ii) zusammentragen; collating marks** = marks printed on the spine of a signature so that the binder can see if they have been collated in correct order **Flattermarken; collating sequence** = (i) characters ordered according to their codes; (ii) order in which signatures are stacked for binding **(i) Kollationierungsfolge; (ii) Reihenfolge der Lagen**
◊ **collator** *noun* (i) software that collates data; (ii) device that collates punched cards **(i) Sortierer; (ii) Kartenmischer**

collect *verb* to receive *or* capture data **erfassen; data collection** = act of receiving data from various sources (either directly from a data capture device *or* from a cartridge) and inserting correctly in order into a database **Datenerfassung; data collection platform** = station that transmits collected data to a central point (usually via satellite) **Datenerfassungsstation**
◊ **collect transfer** *verb* to load a register with bits from a number of different locations **sammelnd laden**

collision detection *noun* the detecting and reporting of the coincidence of two actions *or* events **Zusammenstoßerkennung; carrier sense multiple access-collision detection (CSMA-CD)** = network communications protocol that prevents two sources transmitting at the same time by waiting for a quiet moment on the channel, then attempting to transmit **Verfahren zum Schutz davor, daß nicht mehrere Sender in einem Netz gleichzeitig senden (CSMA/CD)**

colon *noun* printing sign (:), which shows a break in a string of words **Doppelpunkt; semi-colon** = printed sign (;) which marks the end of a program line *or* statement in some languages (such as C and Pascal) **Strichpunkt**

colophon *noun* design *or* symbol *or* company name, used on a printed item to show who are the publisher and the printer **Signet**

colour *noun* sensation sensed by the eye, due to its response to various frequencies of light **Farbe; colour balance** = TV control adjustment to provide a pleasant image *or* various frequencies of light in a signal **Farbabstimmung; colour burst** = part of a TV signal used to provide information about the hue of the colour **Farberkennungssignal; colour cell** = smallest area on a CRT screen that can display colour information **Farbzelle; colour decoder** = device which converts colour burst and picture signals so that they can be displayed on a screen **Farbdecodierer; colour display** = display device able to represent characters *or* graphics in colour **Farbbildschirm; colour encoder** = device that produces a standard TV signal from separate Red, Green and Blue signals **Farbcodierer; colour graphics adapter (CGA)** = popular microcomputer colour display system **Farbgraphikadapter;** *see also* EGA; **colour monitor** = screen that has a demodulator which shows information in colour **Farbmonitor;** *the colour monitor is great for games;* **colour saturation** = purity of a colour signal **Farbsättigung; colour separation** = process by which colours are separated into their primary colours **Farbauszug; colour shift** = (unwanted) change in colour **Farbverschiebung; colour temperature** = method of standardizing the colour of a body (at a certain temperature) **Farbtemperatur; colour transparency** = transparent positive film in colour, which can be used to project on a screen *or* to make film for printing **Diapositiv, Farbdia**

column *noun*
(a) series of characters, printed one under the other **Spalte;** *to add up a column of figures; put the total at the bottom of the column;* **card column** = line of punched information about one character, parallel to the shorter side of the card **Lochkartenspalte; column parity** = parity check on every punched card *or* tape column **Spaltenparitätsprüfung; 80-column printer** = printer which has a maximum line width of 80 characters **80-Spalten-Drucker;** *an 80-column printer is included in the price*
(b) section of printed words in a newspaper *or* magazine **Kolumne, Spalte; column-centimetre** = space in centimetres in a newspaper column, used for calculating charges for advertising **Kolumnenzentimeter**

◇ **columnar** *adjective* in columns **in Spalten, spaltenweise; columnar graph** = graph on which values are shown as vertical *or* horizontal bars **Tabelle, Säulendiagramm; columnar working** = showing information in columns **in Tabellen arbeiten**

COM = COMPUTER OUTPUT ON MICROFILM recording the output from a computer directly onto microfilm **COM (Datenausgabe auf Mikrofilm)**

coma *noun* lens aberration **Koma**

COMAL = COMMON ALGORITHMIC LANGUAGE structured programming language similar to BASIC **COMAL (Programmiersprache)**

combine *verb* to join together **verbinden; combined head** = transducer that can read and write data from the surface of a magnetic storage medium, such as a floppy disk **kombinierter Lese-/Schreibkopf; combined station** = high-level data link control station that processes commands and responses **Hybridstation; combined symbol matching (CSM)** = efficient optical character recognition system **CSM (wirkungsvolles optisches Zeichenerkennungssystem)**

◇ **combination** *noun* several things which are joined together; series of numbers which open a lock **Kombination**

◇ **combinational** *adjective* which combines a number of separate elements **verbindend; combinational circuit** =

electronic circuit consisting of a number of connected components **Schaltnetz; combinational logic** = logic function made up from a number of separate logic gates **Kombinatorik**

comma *noun* printed *or* written sign (,) which indicates a small break in the sense of a sentence **Komma; inverted commas** = printing sign (" ") which marks the beginning and end of a quotation **Anführungszeichen**

command *noun*
(a) electrical pulse *or* signal that will start *or* stop a process **Befehl**
(b) word *or* phrase which is recognized by a computer system and starts *or* terminates an action **Befehl;** *interrupt command; the command to execute the program is RUN;* **channel command** = instruction to a channel *or* control unit, providing control actions such as data filtering *or* routes **Kanalbefehl; command code** = binary code that starts *or* stops an instruction *or* action in a CPU **Befehlscode; command console processor (CCP)** = software interface between a user's terminal and the BIOS **CCP (Teil des Betriebssystems, der direkt mit dem Anwender kommuniziert, bei CP/M); command control language** = programming language that allows equipment to be easily controlled **Befehlssteuersprache; command-driven program** = program which requires the user to enter instructions at every stage **befehlsgetriebenes Programm; command file** = sequence of frequently used commands stored in a file **Befehlsdatei; command file processor** = execution of a user's command file, allowing the user to create a customized simple operating environment *or* to carry out a series of frequently used commands **Befehlsdateiprozessor; command interface** = cue and prompts used by a program to inform and accept from a user required inputs (this can be user-friendly such as a WIMP environment, or not so friendly, such as a question mark) **Kommandoschnittstelle; command language** = programming language made up of procedures for various tasks, that can be called up by a series of commands **Kommandosprache; command line** = program line that contains a command instruction **Befehlszeile; command prompt** = symbol displayed to indicate a command is expected **Befehlseingabeformat; command register** = register that stores the instruction to be carried out *or* that is being processed **Befehlsregister; command window** = area of a screen where commands are entered **Befehlsfenster;** *the user can define the size of the command window;* **dot command** = method of writing instructions,

with a full stop followed by the command, used mainly for embedded commands in a word-processing system **Punktbefehl; embedded command** = printer control command, such as indicating that text should be in italics, inserted into test and used by a word-processor when formatting text **eingebetteter Befehl**

comment *noun* helpful notes in a program to guide the user **Kommentar;** *the lack of comments is annoying; BASIC allows comments to be written after a REM instruction;* **comment field** = section of a command line in an assembly language program that is not executed but provides notes and comments **Kommentarfeld**
◊ **commentary** *noun* spoken information which describes a film **Kommentar**

commercial *noun* advertising film on TV **Werbung, Werbespot**

common *adjective*
(a) which happens very often **häufig;** *this is a common fault with this printer model*
(b) belonging to several different people *or* programs *or* to everyone **gemeinsam; common carrier** = (i) firm which carries goods *or* passengers, and which anyone can use; (ii) company which can provide information services to the public (i) **öffentliches Transportunternehmen;** (ii) **Informationsbüro; common channel signalling** = one channel used as a communications link to a number of devices *or* circuits **Zeichengabe mit gemeinsamem Zeichenkanal; common business orientated language (COBOL)** = programming language mainly used in business applications **verbreitetste problemorientierte Programmiersprache für kaufmännische Anwendungen (COBOL); common hardware** = hardware items that can be used for a variety of tasks **Mehrzweckhardware; common language** = data *or* program instructions in a standardized form that can be understood by other processors *or* compilers/interpreters **einheitliche Maschinensprache; common mode noise** = external noise on all power and ground lines **asymmetrische Störung; common pricing** = illegal fixing of prices by several businesses so that they all charge the same price **Preisabsprache; common software** = useful (routines) that can be used by any program **Mehrzwecksoftware; common storage area** = memory *or* storage area used by more than one program **allgemeiner Speicherbereich;** *the file server memory is mainly common storage area, with a section reserved for the operating system*

communicate *verb* to pass information to someone **kommunizieren, übertragen;** *he finds it impossible to communicate with his staff; communicating with head office has been quicker since we installed the telex;* **communicating word processor** = word processor workstation which is able to transmit and receive data **Textfernverarbeiter**

communication *noun*
(a) passing of information **Nachrichtenverbindung;** *communication with the head office has been made easier by the telex*
(b) communications = process by which data is transmitted and received, by means of telephones, satellites, radio or any medium capable of carrying signals **DFV, Datenfernverarbeitung; communications buffer** = terminal *or* modem that is able to store transmitted data **DFV-Puffer; communications channel** = physical link over which data can be transmitted **Schaltbrücke; communications computer** = computer used to control data transmission in a network **Netzsteuerungscomputer; communications control unit** = electronic device that controls data transmission and routes in a network **Netzsteuerungseinheit; communications executive** = main set of programs that ensure that protocol, format and device and line handlers are correct for the type of device *or* line in use **DFV-Hauptsteuerprogramm; communications interface adapter** = electronic circuit that allows a computer to communicate with a modem **DFV-Schnittstellenanschluß; communications link** = physical path that joins a transmitter to a receiver **DFV-Verbindungsweg; communications link control** = processor that provides various handshaking and error detection functions for a number of links between devices **Steuerelement für DFV-Verbindungswege; communications network** = group of devices such as terminals and printers that are interconnected with a central computer, allowing the rapid and simple transfer of data **DFV-Netz; communications network processor** = processor that provides various interfacing and management (buffering *or* code conversion) between a computer and communications link control **DFV-Netz-Prozessor; communications port** = connection allowing a device to communicate **DFV-Anschluß; communications satellite** = satellite used for channelling radio *or* television *or* data signals from one point on the earth to another **DFV-Satellit; communications scanner** = line monitoring equipment to check for data request signals **DFV-Abtaster; data communications** = transmission and reception of data rather than speech *or* images **Datenfernverarbeitung, DFV; data communications buffer** = buffer on a receiver that allows a slow peripheral to accept data from a fast peripheral, without slowing either down **DFV-Puffer; data communications equipment (DCE)** = equipment (such as a modem) which receives *or* transmits data **Datenübertragungseinrichtung**

QUOTE it requires no additional hardware, other than a communications board in the PC
Electronics & Power

community *noun* group of people living *or* working in the same place **Gemeinschaft; the local business community** = the business people living and working in the area **Geschäftsleute am Ort**

◊ **community antenna television (CATV)** *noun* cable television system using a single aerial to pick up television signals and then distribute them over a wide area via cable **Kabelfernsehen**

compact
1 *adjective* (thing) which does not take up much space **kompakt; compact cassette** = magnetic recording tape contained inside a standard plastic box, used in home personal computers for data storage **Kompaktkassette; compact code** = minimum number of program instructions required for a task **Kompaktcode; compact disk (CD)** = small plastic disk that contains audio signals in digital form etched onto the surface **CD (Compact Disk); compact disk player** = machine that reads the digital data from a CD and converts it back to its original form **CD-Spieler; compact disk ROM** = small plastic disk that is used as a high capacity ROM device, data is stored in binary form as holes etched on the surface which are then read by a laser **CD-ROM;** *the compact disk ROM can store as much data as a dozen hard disks;* **compacting algorithm** = formula for reducing the amount of space required by text **Komprimierungsalgorithmus**
2 *verb* to reduce the space taken by something **komprimieren; data compacting** = reducing the storage space taken by data by coding it in a more efficient way **Datenkomprimierung**

companding = COMPRESSING AND EXPANDING two processes which reduce *or* compact data before transmission *or* storage then restore packed data to its original form **Kompandierung**

⋄ **compandor** *noun* = COMPRESSOR/EXPANDER device used for companding signals **Kompandierer**

compare *verb* to check the differences between two pieces of information **vergleichen**

⋄ **compare with** *verb* to put two things together to see how they differ **vergleichen mit**

⋄ **comparable** *adjective* which can be compared **vergleichbar;** *the two sets of figures are not comparable*

⋄ **comparator** *noun* logical device whose output is true if there is a difference between two inputs **Vergleicher**

⋄ **comparison** *noun* way of comparing **Vergleich; there is no comparison between speeds of the two processors** = one of the two is much faster than the other **es ist kein Vergleich zwischen den Geschwindigkeiten der beiden Prozessoren**

compatible

1 *adjective* (two hardware *or* software devices) that function correctly together **kompatibel;** *is the hardware IBM-compatible?*
2 *noun* hardware *or* software device that functions correctly with other equipment *or* is a clone **kompatible Hardware od Software;** *this computer is much cheaper than the other compatibles*

⋄ **compatibility** *noun (of two hardware or software devices)* ability to function together **Kompatibilität**

COMMENT: by conforming to the standards of another manufacturer *or* organization, compatibility of hardware *or* software allows programs *or* hardware to be interchanged with no modifications

QUOTE the compatibles bring computing to the masses
PC Business World
QUOTE low-cost compatibles have begun to find homes as terminals on LANS
Minicomputer News
QUOTE it is a fairly standard feature on most low-cost PC compatibles
Which PC?
QUOTE check for software compatibility before choosing a display or graphics adapter
PC Business World
QUOTE this was the only piece of software I found that wouldn't work, but it does show that there is no such thing as a totally compatible PC clone
Personal Computer World

compile *verb* to convert a high level language program into a machine code program that can be executed by itself **übersetzen, kompilieren;** *compiling takes a long time with this old version; debug your program, then compile it; compiled BASIC programs run much faster than the intrpretor version;* **compile and go** = computer program not requiring operator interaction that will load, compile and execute a high level language program **kompilieren und verarbeiten; compile phase** = the time during a program run, when the instructions are compiled **Kompilierphase**

⋄ **compilation** *noun* translation of an encoded source program into machine readable code **Kompilierung; compilation error** = syntax error found during compilation **Kompilierfehler;** *compilation errors result in the job being aborted;* **compilation time** = length of time it takes for a computer to compile a program **Kompilierzeit;** *compare with* DECOMPILATION

⋄ **compiler (program)** *noun* piece of software that converts an encoded program into a machine code program **Kompilierer;** *the new compiler has an in-built editor; this compiler produces a more efficient program;* **compiler diagnostics** = features in a compiler that help the programmer to find any faults **Kompilirerdiagnostik; compiler language** = high level language (such as C, Pascal) that will convert a source program that follows the language syntax into a machine code version, then run it **Kompilirersprache; cross-compiler** = assembler *or* compiler that compiles programs for one computer whilst running on another **Kreuzkompilierer;** *compare with* INTERPRETER *we can use the cross-compiler to develop the software before the new system arrives;* **language compiler** = software that converts an encoded source program into another (machine code) form **Sprachkompilierer**

complement

1 *noun* (i) inversion of a binary digit; (ii) result after subtracting a number from one less than the radix **(i) & (ii) Komplement;** *the complement is found by changing the 1's to 0's and 0's to 1's;* **one's complement** = inversion of a binary digit **Einerkomplement; nine's complement** = decimal complement (equivalent to binary one's complement) formed by subtracting each digit in the number from nine **Neunerkomplement; ten's complement** = formed by adding one to the nine's complement of the number **Zehnerkomplement; two's complement** = formed by adding one to the one's complement of a number **Zweierkomplement**
2 *verb* to invert a binary digit **komplementieren; complemented** = (binary

digit) that has had a complement performed **komplementiert**

◊ **complementary** *adjective* (two things) that complete each other *or* that go well together **komplementär; complementary colours** = two colours that when optically combined produce white **Komplementärfarben; complementary operation** = logical operation that results in the logical NOT of a function **negierte Operation**

◊ **complementary metal oxide semiconductor (CMOS)** *noun* integrated circuit design and construction method (using a pair of complementary p- and n-type transistors) **Halbleiterelement, Kombination aus PMOS- und NMOS-Technik**

◊ **complementation** *noun* number system used to represent positive and negative numbers **Komplementbildung**

complete
1 *adjective*
(a) finished *or* all ready **abgeschlossen, fertig;** *the spelling check is complete; when this job is complete, the next in the queue is processed*
(b) requiring nothing else (in order to function) **vollständig; complete operation** = operation that retrieves the necessary operands from memory, performs the operation, returns the results and operands to memory and reads the next instruction to be processed **vollständige Operation**
2 *verb* to finish a task **beenden;** *when you have completed the keyboarding, pass the text through the spelling checker*

◊ **completion** *noun* time when something is complete **Abschluß;** *completion date for the new software package is November 15th*

complex *adjective* very complicated *or* difficult to understand **komplex;** *the complex mathematical formula was difficult to solve; the controller must work hard to operate this complex network;* **complex instruction set computer (CISC)** = CPU design whose instruction set contains a number of long, complex instructions, that makes programming easier, but reduces execution speed **konventioneller Rechner;** *compare* REDUCED INSTRUCTION SET COMPUTER

◊ **complexity** *noun* being complicated **Komplexität; complexity measure** = measure of the system resources used in an operation *or* job **Komplexitätsmaß**

complicated *adjective* with many different parts *or* difficult to understand **kompliziert;** *this program is very*

complicated; the computer design is more complicated than necessary

component *noun* (i) piece of machinery *or* section which will be put into a final product; (ii) electronic device that affects an electrical signal **(i) Teilbauelement; (ii) Komponente; component density** = number of electronic components per unit area on a PCB **Komponentendichte;** *component density increases with production expertise; component density is so high on this motherboard, that no expansion connectors could be fitted;* **component error** = error introduced by a malfunctioning device *or* component rather than incorrect programming **Komponentenfehler**

compose *verb* to arrange the required type, in the correct order, prior to printing **setzen; composing room** = room in a typesetters *or* in a newspaper, where the text is composed by compositors **Setzraum, Setzerei**

◊ **composition** *noun* creating typeset text, either using metal type *or* by keyboarding on a computer typesetter **Setzen; composition size** = printing type size **Typengröße**

◊ **compositor** *noun* person who sets up the required type prior to printing **Setzer; electronic compositor** = computer that allows a user to easily arrange text on screen before it is electronically typeset **elektronische Setzmaschine**

composite circuit *noun* electronic circuit made up of a number of smaller circuits and components **kombinierter Schaltkreis**

◊ **composite video signal** *noun* single television signal containing synchronizing pulse and video signal in a modulated form **Farbmischsignal**

compound *adjective* **compound logical element** = logical circuit *or* function that produces an output from a number of inputs **zusammengesetztes logisches Element; compound statement** = a number of program instructions in one line of program **zusammengesetzte Anweisung;** *the debugger cannot handle compound statements*

compress *verb* to squeeze something to fit into a smaller space **verdichten, komprimieren;** *use the archiving program to compress the file*

◊ **compression** *noun* varying the gain of a device depending on input level to maintain an output signal within certain limits **Verdichtung, Komprimierung; data compression** = means of reducing the size of blocks of data by removing spaces, empty sections and unused material **Datenverdichtung**

◊ **compressor** *noun* (i) electronic circuit which compresses a signal; (ii) (program *or* device) that provides data compression **(i) Verdichter; (ii) Verdichtungsprogramm; audio compressor** = circuit which limits the maximum signal level **Tonkompressor**

comptometer *noun* machine which counts automatically **automatische Zählmaschine**

compute *verb* to calculate *or* to do calculations **berechnen;** *connect charges were computed on an hourly rate*

◊ **computable** *adjective* which can be calculated **berechenbar**

◊ **computation** *noun* calculation **Berechnung**

◊ **computational** *adjective* referring to computation **Rechen-; computational error** = mistake made in calculating **Rechenfehler**

computer *noun*

(a) machine that receives *or* stores *or* processes data very quickly according to a stored program **Computer, Rechner; analog computer** = computer which processes data in analog form (that is data which is represented by a continuously variable signal - as opposed to digital data) **Analogrechner; business computer** = powerful small computer which is programmed for special business uses **Geschäftscomputer; digital computer** = computer which processes data in digital form (that is data represented in discrete form) **Digitalrechner; mainframe computer** = large scale powerful computer system that can handle high capacity memory and backing storage devices as well as a number of operators simultaneously **Großrechner; microcomputer** *or* **micro** = complete small-scale, cheap, low-power computer system based around a microprocessor chip and having limited memory capacity **Mikrocomputer; minicomputer** *or* **mini** = small computer with a greater range of instructions and processing power than a microcomputer, but not able to compete with the speed or data handling capacity of a mainframe computer **Minicomputer; personal computer (PC)** *or* **home computer** = small computer which can be used in the home, in which the various sections (screen, keyboard, disk drives, processing unit, memory etc.) are in one or two small compact cases **Personalcomputer (PC); single**

board computer (sbc) = micro *or* mini computer whose components are all located on a single printed circuit board **Einzelplatinencomputer, Minicomputer; single chip computer** = complete simple computer, including CPU, memory and I/O ports on one chip **Einzelchipcomputer; supercomputer** = very powerful mainframe computer used for high speed mathematical tasks **Großrechner**

(b) computer animation = making a series of computer-generated images displayed in sequence to emulate motion **Computeranimation; computer applications** = the tasks and uses that a computer can carry out in a particular field *or* job **Computeranwendungen; computer architecture** = (i) layout and interconnection of a computer's internal hardware and the logical relationships between CPU, memory and I/O devices; (ii) way in which the CPU, terminals, printers and network connections are arranged **(i) & (ii) Computerarchitektur; computer bureau** = office which offers to do work on its computers for companies which do not have their own computers **Computerbüro; computer code** = programming language that consists of commands in binary code that can be directly understood by the central processing unit, without the need for translation **Computercode; computer conferencing** = connecting a number of computers *or* terminals together to allow a group of users to communicate **Computerkonferenz; computer crime** = theft, fraud or other crimes involving computers **Computerkriminalität; computer dating** = use of a computer to match single people who may want to get married **computerisierte Heiratsvermittlung; computer department** = department in a company which manages the company's computers **Computerabteilung; computer engineer** = person who maintains *or* programs *or* designs computer equipment **Computeringenieur; computer error** = mistake made by a computer **Computerfehler; computer file** = section of information on a computer (such as the payroll, list of addresses, customer accounts) **Computerdatei; computer graphics** = information represented graphically on a computer display **Computergraphik; computer image processing** = analysis of information in an image, usually by electronic means *or* using a computer, also used for recognition of objects in an image **computergestützte Bildverarbeitung; computer independent language** = programming language that will operate on any computer that has a correct compiler *or* interpreter **computerunabhängige Programmiersprache;**

computer input from microfilm (CIM) = use of microfilm for computer data storage, and the method of reading the data **Dateneingabe von Mikrofilm; computer language** = language (formed of figures *or* characters) used to communicate with a computer **Maschinensprache; computer listing** = printout of a list of items taken from data stored in a computer **Computerausdruck; computer literacy** = understanding the basic principles of computers, related expressions and concepts, and being able to use computers for programming *or* applications **Computerfachkenntnis; computer-literate** = (person) able to understand how to use a computer, the expressions and concepts used **computersachverständig;** *the managing director is simply not computer-literate;* **computer logic** = way in which the various sections of the CPU, memory and I/O are arranged (in hardware) **Computerlogik; computer mail** *or* **electronic mail** = messages sent between users of a bulletin board *or* network **elektronische Post; computer manager** = person in charge of a computer department **Computerverwalter; computer network** = number of computers, terminals and peripherals connected together to allow communications between each other **Computernetz; computer numeric control (CNC)** = control of a machine by computer **computergestützte, numerische Werkzeugmaschinensteuerung (CNC); computer office system** = computer and related peripherals used for office tasks (filing, word processing, etc.) **Computerbürosystem; computer operator** = person who operates a computer **Computerbediener; computer organization** *see* COMPUTER ARCHITECTURE; **computer output** = data *or* information produced after processing by a computer **Computerausgabe; computer output on microfilm (COM)** = information output from a computer, stored directly onto microfilm **Ausgabe auf Mikrofilm; computer power** = measure of speed and capacity of a computer (several tests exist, such as FLOPS *or* benchmark timings) **Computerstärke, Computerleistung; computer program** = series of instructions to a computer, telling it to do a particular piece of work **Computerprogramm;** *the user cannot write a computer program with this system;* **computer programmer** = person who writes computer programs **Programmierer; computer run** = action of processing instructions in a program by a computer **Computer-Programmlauf; computer science** = scientific study of computers, the organization of hardware and development of software **Informatik; computer services** = work using a computer, done by a

computer bureau **Computerservice; computer system** = a central processor with storage and associated peripherals that make up a working computer **Rechensystem; computer time** = time when a computer is being used (paid for at an hourly rate) **Rechenzeit;** *running all those sales reports costs a lot in computer time;* **computer word** = number of bits that make up a standard word within a CPU (usually 8,16 *or* 32 bits long) **Maschinenwort**

◊ **computer generations** *noun* way of defining the advances in the field of computing **Computergenerationen**

COMMENT: the development of computers has been divided into a series of "generations": *first generation:* computers constructed using valves having limited storage; *second generation:* computers where transistors were used in construction; *third generation:* use of integrated circuits in construction; *fourth generation:* most often used at present, using low cost memory and IC packages; *fifth generation:* future computers using very fast processors, large memory and allowing human input/output

computer- *prefix* referring to a computer **Computer-, computer-; computer-based learning (CBL)** = learning mainly using a computer **computergestütztes Lernen; computer-based message system (CBMS)** = use of a computer system to allow users to send and receive messages from other users (usually in-house) **computergestütztes Nachrichtensystem; computer-based training (CBT)** = use of a computer system to train students **computergestütztes Training; computer-generated** = which has been generated by a computer **computergeneriert;** *computer-generated graphics;* **computer-integrated manufacturing (CIM)** = coordinated use of computers in every aspect of design and manufacturing **computerintegrierte Fertigung; computer-integrated systems** = coordinated use of computers and other related equipment in a process **computerintegrierte Systeme;** *this firm is a very well-known supplier of computer-integrated systems which allow both batch pagination of very long documents with alteration of individual pages;* **computer-managed instruction (CMI)** = using a computer to assist students in learning a subject **computergestützter Unterricht; computer-managed learning (CML)** = using a computer to teach students and assess their progress **computergestütztes Lernen**

◊ **computer-aided** *or* **computer-assisted** *adjective* which uses a computer to make the work easier **computergestützt; computer-**

aided or **assisted design (CAD)** = the use of computer and graphics terminal to help a designer in his work **computergestützte Entwurf und Konstruktion (CAD); computer-aided** or **assisted engineering (CAE)** = use of a computer to help an engineer solve problems or calculate design or product specifications **computergestütztes Konstruieren; computer-aided** or **assisted instruction (CAI)** = use of a computer to assist pupils in learning a subject **computergestützter Unterricht (CAI); computer-aided** or **assisted learning (CAL)** = use of a computer to assist pupils to learn a subject **computergestütztes Lernen (CAL); computer-aided** or **assisted manufacture (CAM)** = use of a computer to control machinery or to assist in a manufacturing process **computergestützte Fertigung (CAM); computer-aided** or **assisted testing (CAT)** = use of a computer to test equipment or programs to find any faults **computergestütztes Prüfen (CAT); computer-aided** or **assisted training (CAT)** = use of a computer to demonstrate to and assist pupils in learning a skill **computergestütztes Training**

◊ **computer-readable** adjective which can be read and understood by a computer **computerlesbar;** computer-readable codes

computerize verb to change from a manual system to one using computers **computerisieren, auf EDV umstellen;** our stock control has been completely computerized; they operate a computerized invoicing system

◊ **computerization** noun action of introducing a computer system or of changing from a manual to a computer system **Computerisierung, Umstellung auf EDV;** computerization of the financial sector is proceeding very fast

computing adjective & noun referring to computers or work done on computers **Rechen-; Computing; computing power** = measure of speed and ability of a computer to perform calculations **Rechenstärke; computing speed** = speed at which a computer calculates **Rechengeschwindigkeit**

concatenate verb to join together two or more sets of data **verketten; concatenated data set** = more than one file or set of data joined together to produce one set **verkettete Dateien**

conceal verb to hide or not display information or graphics from a user **verbergen;** the hidden lines are concealed from view with this algorithm

concentrate verb (i) to focus a beam onto a narrow point; (ii) to combine a number of lines or circuits or data to take up less space **(i) konzentrieren; (ii) komprimieren;** to concentrate a beam of light on a lens; the concentrated data was transmitted cheaply

◊ **concentrator** noun device which combines intermittent data from various telephone lines and sends it along a single line in one go **Konzentrator**

concertina fold noun accordion fold or method of folding continuous paper, one sheet in one direction, the next sheet in the opposite direction, allowing the paper to be fed into a printer continuously with no action on the part of the user **Zickzackfaltung**

concurrent adjective almost simultaneous (actions or sets) **gleichzeitig ablaufend;** each concurrent process has its own window; three transputers provide concurrent processing cababilities for the entire department; **concurrent operating system** = operating system software that allows several programs or activities to be processed at the same time **Parallelbetriebssystem; concurrent programming** = running several programs apparently simultaneously, achieved by executing small sections from each program in turn **mehrere Programme gleichzeitig laufen lassen**

◊ **concurrently** adverb running at almost the same time **gleichzeitig ablaufend;** see also SISD, SIMD, MISD, MIMD the four categories for processors

condenser lens noun optical device, usually made of glass, that concentrates a beam of light onto a certain area **Sammellinse**

condition
1 noun (i) state of a circuit or device or register; (ii) series of requirements that have to be met before an action can occur **(i) Zustand; (ii) Bedingung; condition code register** = register that contains the state of the CPU after the execution of the last instruction **Anzeigeregister;** see also FLAG; **error condition** = state that is entered if an attempt is made to operate on data containing errors **Fehlerbedingung**
2 verb to modify data that is to be transmitted so as to meet set parameters **in die richtige Form bringen;** condition the raw data to a standard format
◊ **conditional** adjective
(a) provided that certain things take place **vorbehaltlich**

(b) (process) which is dependent on the result of another **bedingt; conditional breakpoint** = breakpoint inserted, after which the programmer can jump to one of a number of sections, depending on data *or* program status **bedingter Programmstop; conditional jump** *or* **branch** *or* **transfer** = programming instruction that provides a jump to a section of a program if a certain condition is met **bedingte(r) Sprung od Verzweigung od Übertragung;** *the conditional branch will select routine one if the response is yes and routine two if no;* **conditional statement** = program instruction that will redirect program control according to the outcome of an event **bedingte Anweisung**

conduct *verb* to allow an electrical current to flow through a material **leiten;** *to conduct electricity; copper conducts well*
◇ **conduction** *noun* ability of a material to conduct **Leitfähigkeit;** *the conduction of electricity by gold contacts*
◇ **conductive** *adjective* referring to the ability of a material to conduct **leitfähig**
◇ **conductor** *noun* substance (such as a metal) which conducts electricity **Leiter;** *copper is a good conductor of electricity; see also* SEMICONDUCTOR

conduit *noun* protective pipe *or* channel for wires *or* cables **Kabelrohr;** *the cables from each terminal are channelled to the computer centre by metal conduit*

cone *noun* moving section in most loudspeakers **Konus (Teil der Membran)**

conference *noun* meeting of people to discuss problems **Besprechung, Konferenz; to be in conference** = to be in a meeting **in einer Besprechung sein; conference phone** = telephone so arranged that several people can speak into it from around a table **Konferenztelefon; conference room** = room where small meetings can take place **Konferenzraum; conference call** = telephone call which connects together three or more telephone lines allowing each person *or* device to communicate with all the others **Konferenzschaltung; press conference** = meeting where newspaper and TV reporters are invited to hear news of a new product *or* a change of management, etc. **Pressekonferenz**
◇ **conferencing** *noun* teleconferencing *or* holding a meeting of people in different places, using the telephones to allow each person to communicate with the others **Telekonferenz; computer conferencing** = connecting a number of computers *or* terminals together to allow a group of users

to communicate **Computerkonferenz;** *the multi-user BBS has a computer conferencing facility*

confidence level *noun* likelihood that a number will lie within a range of values **statistische Sicherheit, Aussagewahrscheinlichkeit**

configure *verb* to select hardware, software and interconnections to make up a special system **konfigurieren;** *this terminal has been configured to display graphics; you only have to configure the PC once - when you first buy it*
◇ **configuration** *noun* way in which the hardware and software of a computer system are planned and set up **Konfiguration; configuration state** = state of a computer that allows it *or* the system *or* a program to be configured **Konfigurationszustand**
◇ **configured-in** = device whose configuration state indicates it is ready and available for use **konfiguriert; configured-off** *or* **configured out** = device whose configuration state indicates it is not available for use **nicht konfiguriert**

QUOTE the machine uses RAM to store system configuration information
PC Business World
QUOTE several configuration files are provided to assign memory to the program, depending on the available RAM on your system
PC Business World
QUOTE users can configure four of the eight ports to handle links at speeds of 64K bit/sec
Computer News
QUOTE if you modify a program with the editor, or with a word-processor specified in the configuration file, it will know that the program has changed and will execute the new one accordingly
PC Business World

conform *verb* to work according to set rules **entsprechen;** *the software will not run if it does not conform to the operating system standards*

congestion *noun* state that occurs when communication *or* processing demands are greater than the capacity of a system **Besetztzustand, Überlastung**

conjunct *noun* one of the variables in an logical AND function **Variable in der logischen UND-Funktion**
◇ **conjunction** *noun* logical function whose output is true if all inputs are true **UND-Funktion**

connect *verb* to link together two points in a circuit *or* communications network verbinden; **connect time** = length of time a user is logged onto an interactive system **Dauer der Verbindung**

◊ **connection** *noun* link *or* something which joins **Verbindung**; **parallel connection** = connector on a computer allowing parallel data to be transferred **Parallelverbindung**; *their transmission rate is 60,000 bps through parallel connection*

◊ **connector** *noun* physical device with a number of metal contacts that allow devices to be easily linked together **Anschluß(stecker)**; *the connector at the end of the cable will fit any standard serial port*; **card edge connector** = series of metal tracks ending at the edge and on the surface of a circuit board, allowing it to be plugged into an edge connector to provide electrical path (for data transmission, etc.) **Kartenrandverbindung**; *see also* FEMALE, MALE

connective *noun* symbol between two operands that describes the operation to be performed **Bindewort**

conscious error *noun* operator error that is immediately spotted, but cannot be prevented in time **bewußter Fehler**

consecutive *adjective* following one after another **aufeinanderfolgend**; *the computer ran three consecutive files*

◊ **consecutively** *adverb* one after the other **aufeinanderfolgend**; *the sections of the program run consecutively*

console *noun* unit (keyboard and VDU, and usually a printer) which allows an operator to communicate with a computer system **Konsole**; *the console consists of input device such as a keyboard, and an output device such as a printer or CRT*

constant
1 *noun* item of data, whose value does not change (as opposed to a variable) **Konstante**
2 *adjective* which does not change **konstant**; *the disk drive motor spins at a constant velocity*; **constant length field** = data field that always contains the same number of characters **Datenfeld mit konstanter Länge**; **constant ratio code** = character representation code that has a constant number of binary ones per word length **gleichgewichteter Code**

construct *verb* to build *or* to make (a device *or* a system) **errichten**
◊ **construction** *noun* building *or* making of a system **Errichtung**; *construction of the prototype is advancing rapidly; construction*

techniques have changed over the past few years

consult *verb* to ask an expert for advice **um Rat fragen**; *he consulted the maintenance manager about the disk fault*
◊ **consultancy** *noun* act of giving specialist advice **Beratung**; *a consultancy firm; he offers a consultancy service*
◊ **consultant** *noun* specialist who gives advice **Berater/-in**; *they called in a computer consultant to advise them on the system design*
◊ **consulting** *adjective* person who gives specialist advice **beratend**; *a consulting engineer*

consumables *plural noun* small cheap extra items required in the day-to-day running of a computer system (such as paper and printer ribbons) **Verbrauchsgüter**; *put all the printer leads and paper with the other consumables*

contact
1 *noun* section of a switch *or* connector that provides an electrical path when it touches another conductor **Kontakt**; *the circuit is not working because the contact is dirty*; **contact bounce** = *see* BOUNCE, DE-BOUNCE
2 *verb* to try to call a user *or* device in a network **aufrufen**
◊ **contact printing** *noun* photographic printing process in which the negative touches the light-sensitive paper **Kontaktdruck**

contain *verb* to hold something inside **enthalten**; *each carton contains two computers and their peripherals; we have lost a file containing important documents*

content *noun* the ideas inside a letter *or* other document **Inhalt, Gehalt**
◊ **contents** *plural noun*
(a) things contained *or* what is inside something **Inhalt**; *the contents of the bottle poured out onto the computer keyboard; the customs officials inspected the contents of the box*; **the contents of the letter** = the words written in the letter **der Inhalt des Briefes**
(b) list of items in a file **Inhalt**
◊ **content-addressable** *adjective* **content-addressable file** *or* **location** = method of storing data in which each item may be individually accessed **Assoziativdatei**; **content-addressable memory (CAM)** *or* **associative storage** = method of data retrieval which uses part of the data rather than an address to locate the data **Assoziativspeicher (CAM)**

contention *noun* situation that occurs when two or more devices are trying to communicate with the same piece of equipment **Konkurrenzbetrieb; contention bus** = communication control system in which a device must wait for a free moment before transmitting data **Konkurrenzbus; contention delay** = length of time spent waiting for equipment to become free for use **Verzögerung durch Konkurrenzbetrieb**

context *noun* words and phrases among which a word is used **Zusammenhang, Kontext;** *the example shows how the word is used in context*

contiguous *adjective* which touches the thing next to it **angrenzend; contiguous file** = file stored in a series of adjacent disk sectors **angrenzende Datei; contiguous graphics** = graphic cells *or* characters that touch each other **zusammenhängende Graphik;** *most display units do not provide contiguous graphics: their characters have a small space on each side to improve legibility*

contingency plan *noun* secondary plan *or* equipment that will be used if the first fails to work **Plan für unvorhersehbare Zwischenfälle**

continue *verb* to go on doing something *or* to do something which you were doing earlier **fortsetzen**

◇ **continual** *adjective* which happens again and again **ständig;** *the continual system breakdowns have slowed down the processing*

◇ **continually** *adverb* again and again **ständig**

◇ **continuation** *noun* act of continuing **Fortsetzung; continuation page** = page *or* screen of text that follows on from a main page **Folge-, Fortsetzungsseite**

◇ **continuity** *noun*
(a) clear conduction path between two points **Kontinuität**
(b) checking that the details of one scene in a film continue into the next scene to be shown, even if the two have been shot at different times **Anschluß**

◇ **continuous** *adjective* with no end *or* with no breaks; which goes on without stopping **andauernd, kontinuierlich; continuous data stream** = high speed serial data transmission, in which data words are not synchronized, but follow on immediately from each other **kontinuierlicher Datenstrom; continuous feed** = device which feeds continuous stationery into a printer

Endlospapiereinzug; continuous loop = endless piece of recording *or* projection tape **Dauerschleife; continuous signal** = analog (continuously variable) signal **Dauerkennzeichen; continuous stationery** = paper made as one long sheet, used in computer printers **Endlospapier; continuous wave** = high frequency waveform that can be modulated to carry data **kontinuierliche Schwingung;** *see also* CARRIER

◇ **continuously** *adverb* without stopping **ohne Unterbrechung;** *the printer overheated after working continuously for five hours*

contrast
1 *noun*
(a) difference between black and white **Kontrast;** *the control allows you to adjust brightness and contrast;* **contrast enhancement filter** = special filter put over a monitor to increase contrast and prevent eye-strain **Kontrastverstärkungsfilter**
(b) control knob on a display that alters the difference between black and white tones **Kontrasteinstellung**
2 *verb* to examine the differences between two sets of information **gegenüberstellen, kontrastieren;** *the old data was contrasted with the latest information*

◇ **contrasting** *adjective* which show a sharp difference **kontrastierend, Kontrast-;** *a cover design in contrasting colours*

control
1 *verb* to be in charge of something *or* to make sure that something is kept in check **steuern; controlled vocabulary** = set of terms *or* words used in an indexing language **Regelvokabular;** NOTE: **controlling - controlled**
2 *noun*
(a) restricting *or* checking something *or* making sure that something is kept in check **Kontrolle; control computer** = dedicated computer used to control a process *or* piece of equipment **Kontrollrechner; control total** = result of summing certain fields in a computer file to provide error detection **Kontrollsumme; out of control** = not kept in check **außer Kontrolle**
(b) (i) section of a computer *or* device that carries out instructions and processes signals, etc.; (ii) conditional program statements **(i) Steuerung; (ii) bedingte Anweisungen; control statement** = program instruction that redirects a program (to another branch etc.) **Steueranweisung; control unit (CU)** = section of central processor that selects and executes instructions **Steuereinheit; control word** = word that defines the actions (in a particular process) that are to be followed **Steuerwort; device control character** =

special code sent in a transmission to a device to instruct it to perform a special function **Gerätesteuerzeichen; line control =** special code used to control a communications link **Übertragungssteuerung**

(c) (i) key on a computer keyboard which sends a control character; (ii) data which controls something **(i) CTRL-Taste; (ii) Steuerdaten; control block =** reserved area of computer memory that contains control data **Steuerblock; control bus =** set of connections to a microcomputer that carry the control signals between CPU, memory and input/output devices **Steuerbus; control cards =** in a punched card system, the first cards which contain the processor control instructions **Steuerkarten; control character =** special character that provides a control sequence rather than a alphanumeric character **Steuerzeichen; control cycle =** events required to retrieve, decode and execute an instruction stored in memory **Steuerzyklus; control data =** data that controls the actions of a device **Steuerdaten; control driven =** computer architecture where instructions are executed once a control sequence has been received **steuerungsgetrieben; control field =** storage area for control instructions **Kontrollfeld; control instruction =** program instruction that controls the actions of a device **Steuerbefehl;** *the next control instruction will switch to italics;* **control language =** commands that describe the identification of and resources required by a job that a computer has to process **(Job)kontrollsprache; control memory** *or* **ROM =** memory which decodes control instructions into microinstructions which operate the computer *or* microcontroller **Mikroprogrammspeicher; control mode =** state of a device in which control signals can be received to select options *or* functions **Steuermodus; control panel =** main computer system control switches and status indicators **Bedienerkonsole; control program/monitor** *or* **control program for microcomputers (CP/M) =** old-fashioned but still popular operating system for microcomputers **Betriebssystem für Mikrocomputer mit 8-Bit-System (CP/M); control register =** storage location only used for control data **Steuerregister; control signals =** electrical signals transmitted to control the actions of a circuit **Steuerungssignale; control sequence =** (series of) codes containing a control character and various arguments, used to carry out a process *or* change mode in a device **Steuerungsablauf; control statement =** program instruction that directs a CPU to provide controlling actions *or* controls the operation of the CPU **Steueranweisung;**

control token = special sequence of bits transmitted over a LAN to provide control actions **Steuerkennzeichen, Steuertoken; control transfer =** redirection of the CPU when a jump *or* call instruction is encountered **Steuerungsübergabe**

(d) control group = small group which is used to check a sample group **Kontroll-, Vergleichsgruppe; control systems =** systems used to check that a computer system is working correctly **Kontrollsysteme**

◊ **controllable** *adjective* which can be controlled **kontrollierbar**

◊ **controller** *noun* hardware *or* software device that controls a peripheral (such as a printer) *or* monitors and directs the data transmission over a local area network **Regler; display controller =** device that accepts character *or* graphical codes and instructions, and converts them into dot-matrix patterns that are displayed on a screen **Bildschirmregler; printer's controller =** main device in a printer that translates output from the computer into printing instructions **Druckerregler;** *see also* DEVICE DRIVER

QUOTE a printer's controller is the brains of the machine. It translates the signals coming from your computer into printing instructions that result in a hard copy of your electronic document
Publish
QUOTE there are seven print control characters which can be placed in a document
Personal Computer World

---

convention *noun* well-known standards *or* rules which are followed, allowing hardware *or* software compatibility **Richtlinien, Konvention**

conversational (mode) *noun* computer system that provides immediate responses to a user's input **Dialogbetrieb;** *see also* INTERACTIVE MODE *compare with* BATCH MODE

conversion *noun* change from one system to another **Umsetzung; conversion equipment =** device that will convert data from one format to another (suitable for another system) without changing the content **Umsetzer; conversion tables** *or* **translation tables =** list of source codes *or* statements and their equivalent in another language *or* form **Übersetzungstabellen;** *conversion tables may be created and used in conjunction with the customer's data to convert it to our systems codes;* **conversion program =** (i) program that converts programs written for one computer into a suitable form for another; (ii) program that converts data format, coding, etc. for use in another program **(i)** & **(ii)** Konvertierungsprogramm

◇ **convert** *verb* to change one thing into another **umsetzen, konvertieren**

◇ **convertibility** *noun* ability to be changed **Konvertierbarkeit**

◇ **convertible** *adjective* which can be converted **konvertierbar**

◇ **converter** *or* **convertor** *noun* device *or* program that translates data from one form to another **Konverter, Umsetzer;** *the convertor allowed the old data to be used on the new system;* **analog to digital converter (ADC)** = device used to convert an analog signal to a digital output form, that can be understood by a computer **Analog-Digital-Umsetzer; digital to analog converter (DAC)** = circuit that outputs an analog signal that is proportional to the input digital number **Digital-Analog-Umsetzer**

convey *verb* to carry *or* import information **vermitteln, klar machen;** *the chart conveyed the sales problem graphically*

◇ **conveyor** *noun* method of carrying paper using a moving belt **Förderband**

coordinate
1 *noun* **coordinates** = values used to locate a point on a graph *or* map **Koordinaten; coordinate graph** = means of displaying one point on a graph, using two values referring to axes which are usually at right angles to each other **Koordinatenbild; polar coordinates** = use of a distance and a direction to locate a point **Polarkoordinaten; rectangular coordinates** = two numbers referring to distances along axes at right angles from an origin **rechtwinklige Koordinaten**
2 *verb* to organize complex tasks, so that they fit together efficiently **koordinieren, aufeinander abstimmen;** *she has to coordinate the keyboarding of several parts of a file in six different locations*

◇ **coordination** *noun* organizing complex tasks; synchronizing two *or* more processes **Koordinierung**

copier = COPYING MACHINE, PHOTOCOPIER

copper *noun* red-coloured soft metal, a good conductor of electricity, used in wires and as connecting tracks on PCBs **Kupfer**

◇ **copperplate printing** *noun* printing method that uses a copper plate on which the image is etched **Kupferdruck**

coprocessor *noun* extra, specialized processor, such as an array *or* numerical processor that can work with a main CPU to increase execution speed **Co-, Zusatzprozessor; graphics coprocessor** = high speed display adapter that is dedicated to graphics operations such as line drawing, plotting, etc. **Graphik-Coprozessor; maths coprocessor** = dedicated processor that provides results to mathematical operations much faster than the ALU section of a CPU **Rechen-Coprozessor**

copy
1 *noun*
(a) document which looks the same as another; duplicate of an original **Kopie; file copy** = copy of a document which is filed in an office for reference **Dateikopie**
(b) document **Exemplar; clean copy** = copy which is ready for keyboarding and does not have many changes to it **Reinkopie; fair copy** *or* **final copy** = document which is written *or* typed with no changes *or* mistakes **Reinschrift; hard copy** = printout of text *or* data which is stored in a computer **(Computer)ausdruck; rough copy** = draft of a program which, it is expected, will have changes made to it before it is complete **Rohprogramm; top copy** = first *or* top sheet of a document which is typed with carbon copies **Original**
(c) text of material ready to be keyboarded **Text;** *Tuesday is the last date for copy for the advertisement;* **copy reader** = person who checks copy before printing **Korrekturleser**
(d) a book *or* a newspaper **Ausgabe, Exemplar;** *I kept yesterday's copy of "The Times"; I read it in the office copy of "Fortune"; where is my copy of the telephone directory?*
2 *verb* to make a second document which is like the first; to duplicate original data **kopieren;** *he copied all the personnel files at night and took them home; there is a memory resident utility which copies the latest files onto backing store every 40 minutes*

◇ **copier** *or* **copying machine** *noun* machine which makes copies of documents **Kopiergerät**

◇ **copy protect** *noun (& verb)* switch to prevent copies of a disk being made **Kopierschutz; (kopiergeschützt);** *the program is not copy protected*

◇ **copy protection** *noun* preventing copies being made **Kopierschutz;** *a hard disk may crash because of copy protection; the new program will come without copy protection*

copyright
1 *noun* legal right (lasting for fifty years after the death of an artist whose work has been published) which a writer *or*

programmer has in his own work, allowing him not to have it copied without the payment of royalties **Urheberrecht; Copyright Act** = Act of Parliament making copyright legal, and controlling the copying of copyright material **Urheberrechtsgesetz; work which is out of copyright** = work by a writer, etc., who has been dead for fifty years, and which anyone can publish **freigewordenes/nicht mehr urheberrechtlich geschütztes Werk; work still in copyright** = work by a living writer, or by a writer who has not been dead for fifty years **urheberrechtlich geschütztes Werk; infringement of copyright** or **copyright infringement** = act of illegally copying a work which is in copyright **Verletzung des Urheberrechts; copyright notice** = note in a book showing who owns the copyright and the date of ownership **Urheberrechtsvermerk; copyright owner** = person who owns the copyright in a work **Urheber/-in**
2 verb to state the copyright of a written work by printing a copyright notice and publishing the work **urheberrechtlich schützen**
3 adjective covered by the laws of copyright **urheberrechtlich geschützt;** it is illegal to take copies of a copyright work

◊ **copyrighted** adjective in copyright **urheberrechtlich geschützt**

CORAL = COMMON REAL-TIME APPLICATIONS LANGUAGE computer programming language used in a real-time system **CORAL (Programmiersprache)**

cord noun wire used to connect a device to a socket **Kabel**

◊ **cordless telephone** noun telephone which is not connected to a line by a cord, but which uses a radio link **drahtloses Telefon**

core noun
(a) central conducting section of a cable **Kern**
(b) core memory or **store** = (i) central memory of a computer; (ii) non-volatile magnetic storage method used in old computers **(i) Hauptspeicher; (ii) Magnetkernspeicher; core program** = computer program stored in core memory **Kernprogramm**

coresident adjective (two or more programs) stored in main memory at the same time **co-resident**

coroutine noun section of a program or procedure that can pass data and control to

another coroutine then halt itself **Co-Routine**

correct
1 adjective accurate or right **richtig**
2 verb to remove mistakes from something **korrigieren; error correcting code** = coding system that allows bit errors occurring during transmission to be rapidly corrected by logical deduction methods rather than retransmission **Fehlerkorrekturcode**

◊ **correction** noun making something correct; change which makes something correct **Korrektur**

◊ **corrective maintenance** noun actions to trace, find and repair a fault after it has occurred **fehlerbedingte Wartung**

correspond verb
(a) to correspond with someone = to write letters to someone **mit jdm korrespondieren**
(b) to correspond with something = to fit or to match something **einer Sache entsprechen, mit etwas übereinstimmen**

◊ **correspondence** noun
(a) letters and messages sent from one person to another **Korrespondenz, Schreibwechsel; business correspondence** = letters concerned with a business **Geschäftskorrespondenz; to be in correspondence with someone** = to write letters to someone and receive letters back **mit jdm in Briefwechsel stehen; correspondence print quality** = quality of print from a computer printer that is acceptable for business letters (that is daisy-wheel rather than dot-matrix printing) **Korrespondenzfähigkeit;** NOTE: no plural
(b) way in which something fits in with something **Entsprechung**

◊ **correspondent** noun
(a) person who writes letters **Briefschreiber**
(b) journalist who writes articles for a newspaper on specialist subjects **Korrespondent/-in;** the computer correspondent; the "Times" business correspondent; he is the Paris correspondent of the "Telegraph"

corrupt
1 adjective data or program that contains errors **fehlerhaft**
2 verb to introduce errors into data or a program **verfälschen, verstümmeln;** power loss during disk access can corrupt the data

◊ **corruption** noun data corruption = errors introduced into data, due to noise or faulty equipment **Datenverfälschung;** acoustic couplers suffer from data corruption more than the direct connect form of modem;

data corruption on the disk has made one file unreadable

coulomb *noun* SI unit of electrical charge **Coulomb** ⇨ APPENDIX

COMMENT: a coulomb is measured as the amount of charge flowing in a conductor when one amp of current is present for one second
---

count *verb* to make a total of a number of items **zählen**

◇ **counting perforator** *noun* paper tape punch, used in typesetting, that keeps a record of the characters, their widths, etc., to allow justification operations **Zählperforator**

counter *noun* (i) device which counts; (ii) register *or* variable whose contents are increased *or* decreased by a set amount every time an action occurs **(i) & (ii) Zähler;** *the loop will repeat itself until the counter reaches 100; the number of items changed are recorded with the counter;* **instruction** *or* **program counter** = register in a CPU that contains the location of the next instruction to be processed **Befehlszähler**

counter- *prefix* against **gegen-**

◇ **counterprogramming** *noun* running a popular TV programme at the same time as another station is running a popular series, to try to steal viewers **ein Konkurrenzprogramm senden**

couple *verb* to join together **verbinden, koppeln;** *the two systems are coupled together*

◇ **coupler** *noun* mechanical device used to connect three or more conductors **Koppler; acoustic coupler** = device that connects to a telephone handset, converting binary computer data into sound signals to allow it to be transmitted down a telephone line **Akustikkoppler**

coverage *noun* size of the potential audience capable of receiving a broadcast **Erfassungsbereich; press coverage** *or* **media coverage** = reports about something in the newspapers *or* on TV, etc. **Berichterstattung;** *the company had good media coverage for the launch of its new model*

CP = CARD PUNCH

cpi = CHARACTERS PER INCH

CP/M = CONTROL PROGRAM/MONITOR popular operating system for microcomputers **CP/M**

CPM = CRITICAL PATH METHOD

cps = CHARACTERS PER SECOND number of characters printed *or* processed every second **Zeichen pro Sekunde**

CPU = CENTRAL PROCESSING UNIT group of circuits which perform the basic functions of a computer made up of three parts, the control unit, the arithmetic and logic unit and the input/output unit **CPU; CPU cycle** = period of time taken to fetch and execute an instruction (usually a simple ADD instruction) used as a measure of computer speed **CPU-Zyklus; CPU elements** = main sections that make up a CPU, including ALU, control unit, I/O bus, memory and various registers **CPU-Teile; CPU handshaking** = interfacing signals between a CPU and a peripheral *or* I/O device **CPU-Quittungsbetrieb; CPU time** = total period of time that a CPU is used to actually process instructions **CPU-Zeit**

COMMENT: in a file handling program CPU time might be minimal, since data retrieval (from disk) would account for a large part of the program run; in a mathematical program, the CPU time could be much higher in proportion to the total run time
---

CR = CARRIAGE RETURN, CARD READER

crash
1 *noun* failure of a component *or* a bug in a program during a run, which halts and prevents further use of the system **Absturz, Programmabbruch; disk crash** = fault caused by the read/write head touching the surface of the disk **Plattenabsturz**
2 *verb (of a computer or program)* to come to an sudden stop **abstürzen;** *the disk head has crashed and the data may have been lost*

◇ **crash-protected** *adjective* (disk) which uses a head protection *or* data corruption protection system **absturzgesichert;** *if the disk is crash-protected, you will never lose your data*

COMMENT: it is sometimes possible to recover data from a crashed hard disk before reformatting, if the crash was caused by a bad sector on the disk rather than contact between the r/w head and disk surface
---

crawl *noun* mechanical device that moves television *or* film titles down in front of a camera, to give the impression that they are moving up the screen **Crawl-Effekt**

CRC = CAMERA-READY COPY, CYCLIC REDUNDANCY CHECK

create *verb* to make **erstellen;** *a new file was created on disk to store the document; move to the CREATE NEW FILE instruction on the menu*

credit *noun*
(a) time given to a customer before he has to pay **(Kunden)kredit;** *they have asked for six months' credit;* **credit card** = plastic card which allows the owner to borrow money and buy goods without paying for them immediately **Kreditkarte**
(b) money received and placed in an account *or* in the balance sheet **Kredit**
(c) **credits** = text at the end of a film, giving the names of the actors *or* technical staff **Nachspann**

crew *noun* group of technical staff who work together (as on filming a TV programme, recording an outside broadcast, etc.) **Team; camera crew** = group of people who man a TV camera **Kamerateam;** *the camera crew had to film all day in the snow*

crippled leapfrog test *noun* standard leapfrog test that uses a single memory location rather than a changing location **Teilprüfung im Bocksprungprogramm**

criterion *noun* specification that has to be met **Kriterium**
NOTE: plural is **criteria**

critical fusion frequency *noun* the rate of display of frames of graphics *or* text that makes them appear continuous **kritische Fusionsfrequenz; critical path analysis** = the definition of tasks *or* jobs and the time each requires arranged in order to achieve certain goals **Analyse des kritischen Weges;** NOTE: also called PERT (Program Evaluation and Review Techniques) **critical path method (CPM)** = use of analysis and projection of each critical step in a large project to help a management team **CPM Methode der Netzplantechnik); critical resource** = resource that can only be used by one process at a time **kritische Betriebsmittel**

CR/LF = CARRIAGE RETURN/LINE FEED

cropping *noun* removal of areas of artwork *or* of a photograph which are not needed **Beschneiden;** *the photographs can be edited by cropping, sizing, touching up, etc.*

cross- *prefix* running from one side to another **Quer-; cross fade** = to fade out one signal while bringing in another **ausblenden; cross modulation** = two *or* more modulated signals on one channel interfering with each other **Quermodulation**

◊ **cross-assembler** *noun* assembler that produces machine-code code for one computer whilst running on another **Kreuzassemblierer**

◊ **cross-check** *noun* validation of an answer by using a different method of calculation **Gegenprobe**

◊ **cross-compiler** assembler *or* compiler that compiles programs for one computer whilst running on another **Kreuzkompilierer**

COMMENT: cross-compilers and assemblers are used to compile programs for micros, but are run on larger computers to make the operation faster

◊ **cross-reference generator** *noun* section of an assembler *or* compiler *or* interpreter that provides a list of program labels, variables *or* constants with their location within the program **Verweisgenerator**

crossfire *noun see* CROSSTALK

◊ **crossover** *noun* change from one system to another **Umstellung;** *the crossover to computerized file indexing was difficult*

◊ **cross-reference**
1 *noun* reference in a document to another part of the document **Querverweis**
2 *verb* to make a reference to another part of the document **einen Querverweis machen;** *the SI units are cross-referenced to the appendix*

◊ **cross-section** *noun* view of a material *or* object cut across its centre **Querschnitt;** *the cross-section of the optical fibre showed the problem*

◊ **crosstalk** *noun* interference in one channel due to another nearby channel *or* signal (caused by badly isolated signals) **Nebensprechen;** *the crosstalk was so bad, the signal was unreadable*

CRT = CATHODE RAY TUBE device used for displaying characters *or* figures *or* graphical information, similar to a TV set **Kathodenstrahlröhre, Bildröhre**

COMMENT: cathode ray tubes are used in television sets, computer monitors and VDUs; a CRT consists of a vacuum tube, one end of which is flat and coated with phosphor, the other end containing an electron beam source. Characters *or* graphics are visible when the controllable electron beam strikes the phosphor causing it to glow

cruncher, crunching *see* NUMBER

crushing *noun* reduced contrast range on a TV image due to a fault **Kompression**

cryogenic memory *noun* storage medium operating at very low temperatures (4°K) to use the superconductive properties of a material **supraleitender Speicher**

cryptanalysis *noun* study and methods of breaking ciphers **Kryptoanalyse**

cryptography *noun* study of encryption and decryption methods and techniques **Kryptographie**

◇ **cryptographic** *adjective* referring to cryptography **kryptographisch; cryptographic algorithm =** rules used to encipher and decipher data **Chiffrieralgorithmus; cryptographic key =** number *or* code that is used with a cipher algorithm to personalize the encryption and decryption of data **Chiffrierschlüssel**

crystal *noun* small slice of quartz crystal which vibrates at a certain frequency, used as a very accurate clock signal for computer *or* other high precision timing applications **Kristall; liquid crystal display (LCD) =** liquid crystals, that turn black when a voltage is applied, used in many watch, calculator and digital displays **Flüssigkristallanzeige (LCD); crystal microphone =** microphone that uses a piece of piezoelectric crystal which produces a signal when sound waves distort it **piezoelektrisches Mikrophon; crystal oscillator =** small piece of crystal that resonates at a certain frequency when a voltage is applied across it; this can be used as a high precision clock **Quarzoszillator**

CSDC = CIRCUIT SWITCHED DIGITAL CIRCUITRY

CSM = COMBINED SYMBOL MATCHING effecient optical character recognition system **CSM (wirkungsvolles optisches Zeichenerkennungssystem)**

CSMA-CD = CARRIER SENSE MULTIPLE ACCESS-COLLISION DETECTION

CTR *or* **CTRL** = CONTROL control key *or* key on a computer terminal that sends a control character to the computer when pressed **CTRL-Taste**

CTS = CLEAR TO SEND RS232C signal that a line *or* device is ready for data transmission **sendebereit**

CU = CONTROL UNIT

cue *noun* prompt *or* message displayed on a screen to remind the user that an input is expected **Aufruf**

CUG = CLOSED USER GROUP to restrict the entry to a database *or* bulletin board system (on a certain topic *or* subject) to certain known and registered users usually by means of a password **geschlossener Benutzerkreis**

cumulative index *noun* index made up from several different indexes **Kumulativindex**

current
1 *adjective* referring to the present time **aktuell; current address =** address being used (accessed) at this time **aktuelle Adresse; current address register (CAR) =** CPU register that stores the address that is currently being accessed **aktuelles Adreßregister; current instruction register (CIR) =** CPU register that stores the instruction that is currently being executed **aktuelles Befehlsregister**
2 *noun* movement of charge-carrying particles in a conductor **(elektrischer) Strom; direct current (DC) =** constant value electrical current that flows in one direction **Gleichstrom; alternating current (AC) =** electrical current whose value varies with time in a regular sinusoidal way (changing direction of flow each half cycle) **Wechselstrom**

COMMENT: mains electricity provides a 240v AC supply at 50Hz in the U.K. and 110v at 60Hz in the USA

cursor *noun* marker on a display device which shows where the next character will appear **Cursor, Positionsanzeiger; cursor control keys =** keys on a keyboard that allow the cursor to be moved in different directions **Cursortasten; cursor home =** movement of the cursor to the top left hand corner of the screen **Cursorausgangsstellung;**

cursor pad = group of cursor control keys **Cursortasten; addressable cursor** = cursor whose position on the screen can be defined by a program **adressierbarer Cursor**

COMMENT: cursors can take several forms, such as a square of bright light, a bright underline or a flashing light

---

QUOTE above the cursor pad are the insert and delete keys, which when shifted produce clear and home respectively
Computing Today
QUOTE further quick cursor movements are available for editing by combining one of the arrow keys with the control function
Personal Computer World

---

customer *noun* person who buys *or* uses a computer system *or* any peripherals **Kunde/Kundin; customer engineering** = maintenance and repair of a customer's equipment **technischer Außendienst; customer service department** = department which deals with customers and their complaints and orders **Kundendienst(abteilung)**

◊ **custom-built** *adjective* made specially for one customer **kundenspezifisch, auf Bestellung angefertigt**

◊ **custom ROM (PROM)** *noun* ROM produced (usually in small numbers) by a manufacturer to suit a customer's requirements **kundenspezifischer ROM (PROM)**

◊ **customize** *verb* to modify a system to the customer's requirements **individuell anpassen;** *we used customized computer terminals*

cut
1 *noun* removing a piece from a file *or* text; piece removed from a file *or* text **Kürzen; Kürzung;** *the editors have asked for cuts in the first chapter*
2 *verb*
(a) to divide something into parts, using scissors *or* knife *or* guillotine **schneiden; cut in notes** = printed notes in the outer edge of a paragraph of a page **eingezogene Marginalien; cut sheet feeder** mechanism that automatically feeds single sheets of paper into a printer **automatischer Einzelblatteinzug**
(b) to remove pieces of text *or* file to make it shorter **kürzen;** *the author was asked to cut his manuscript to 250 pages* NOTE: **cuts - cutting - has cut**

◊ **cut and paste** *noun* action of taking pieces of text from one point and inserting them at another (often used in dtp packages for easy page editing) **Textumstellung**

◊ **cut off** *verb*
(a) to remove part of something **abschneiden;** *six metres of paper were cut off the reel*
(b) to stop something flowing **unterbrechen;** *the electricity supply was cut off*

◊ **cutoff frequency** *noun* frequency at which the response of a device drops off **Grenzfrequenz; cutoff point** = point at which (something) stops **Unterbrechungspunkt**

◊ **cutting** *noun* action of cutting **Schneiden; cutting room** = room in a film studio where the unedited film is cut and joined together **Schneideraum; press cuttings** = pieces cut from newspapers *or* magazines which refer to someone *or* to a company **Zeitungsausschnitte**

CWP = COMMUNICATING WORD PROCESSOR

cybernetics *noun* study of the mechanics of human *or* electronic machine movements, and the way in which electronic devices can be made to work and imitate human actions **Kybernetik**

cycle
1 *noun* (i) period of time when something leaves its original position and then returns to it; (ii) one completed operation in a repeated process **(i) & (ii) Zyklus; action cycle** = all the steps required to carry out a process *or* operation on data, (such as reading, processing, output and storage) **Aktionszyklus; clock cycle** = period of time between two consecutive clock pulses **Taktzyklus; cycle availability** = period of time in a cycle, during which data can be accessed *or* transmitted **Zyklusverfügbarkeit; cycle count** = number of times a cycle has been repeated **Gangzahl; cycle index** = number of times a series of instructions have been *or* have to be repeated **Schleifenindex; cycle shift** = to shift a pattern of bits within a word, with the bit(s) that are shifted off the end being inserted at the beginning of the word **zyklische Stellenverschiebung; cycle stealing** = memory access operation by a peripheral that halts a CPU for one *or* more clock cycles whilst data is being transferred from memory to the device **direkter Speicherzugriff; cycle time** = time between start and stop of an operation, especially between addressing a memory location and receiving the data, and then ending the operation **Zykluszeit;** *compare* ADDRESS TIME
2 *verb* to repeat an operation *or* series of instructions until instructed to stop **immer wieder ausführen**

◊ **cyclic** *adjective* (operation) that is repeated regularly **zyklisch; cyclic access** =

access to stored information that can only occur at a certain point in a cycle **zyklischer Zugriff; cyclic check** = error detection method that uses *or* examines a bit of data every n bits (one bit examined then n bits transmitted, then another bit examined, etc.) **zyklische Fehlerprüfung; cyclic code** *see* GRAY CODE; **cyclic decimal code** = cyclic code that refers to decimal digits **zyklischer Dezimalcode; cyclic redundancy check (CRC)** = error detection code for transmitted data **zyklische Blockprüfung, CRC-Prüfung; cyclic shift** = rotation of bits in a word with the previous last bit inserted in the first bit position **zyklische Bitverschiebung**

cylinder *noun* the tracks in a multi-disk device that can be accessed without moving the read/write head **Zylinder**

cypher = CIPHER

Dd

D hexadecimal figure equivalent to decimal number 13 **D**

3D = THREE-DIMENSIONAL

QUOTE the software can create 3D images using data from a scanner or photographs from an electronic microscope
PC Business World

DAC *or* **D/A converter** = DIGITAL TO ANALOG CONVERTER circuit that outputs an analog number that is proportional to the input digital signal, and so converts a digital input to an analog form **Digital-Analog-Umsetzer;** *speech is output from the computer via a D/A converter; the D/A converter on the output port controls the analog machine*

COMMENT: a D/A converter allows the computer to work outside the computer environment, by driving a machine, imitating speech, etc.

DAD = DIGITAL AUDIO DISK method of recording sound by converting and storing signals in a digital form on magnetic disk **digitale Tonplatte**

dagger *noun* printing sign (†) used to mark a special word **Kreuz; double dagger** =

printing sign (‡) used to give a second reference level **Doppelkreuz**

daisy chain *noun* method of connecting equipment with a single cable passing from one machine *or* device to the next (rather than separate cables to each device) **Verkettung; daisy chain bus** = communications bus that joins one device to the next, each device being able to receive *or* transmit *or* modify data as it passes through to the next device in line **verkettete Busstruktur; daisy chain interrupt** = line joining all the interrupt outputs of a number of devices to a CPU **verkettete Unterbrechungsleitung; daisy chain recursion** = subroutines in a program that call another in the series, (the first routine calls the second routine which calls the third routine, etc.) **verkettete Rekursion**

◊ **daisy-chain** *verb* to connect equipment using the daisy chain method **verketten**

QUOTE you can often daisy-chain cards or plug them into expansion boxes
Byte

daisy-wheel *noun* wheel-shaped printing head, with characters on the end of spokes, used in a serial printer **Typenrad; daisy-wheel printer** *or* **daisy-wheel typewriter** = serial character printer *or* typewriter with characters arranged on interchangeable wheels **Typenraddrucker; Typenradschreibmaschine;** *a daisy-wheel printer produces much better quality text than a dot-matrix, but is slower*

DAMA = DEMAND ASSIGNED MULTIPLE ACCESS

damage
1 *noun* harm done to things **Schaden; to suffer damage** = to be harmed **Schaden erleiden; to cause damage** = to harm something **Schaden zufügen;** *the breakdown of the electricity supply caused damage estimated at £100,000* NOTE: no plural
2 *verb* to harm **beschädigen;** *the faulty read/write head appears to have damaged the disks; the hard disk was damaged when it was dropped*

◊ **damaged** *adjective* which has suffered damage *or* which has been harmed **beschädigt;** *is it possible to repair the damaged files?*

D to A converter = DIGITAL TO ANALOG CONVERTER circuit that outputs an analog signal that is proportional to an input digital number **Digital-Analog-Umsetzer**

dark current *noun* amount of electrical current that flows in an optoelectrical device when there is no light falling on it **Dunkelstrom**

◊ **dark trace tube** *noun* CRT with a dark image on a bright background **Dunkelschriftröhre**

darkroom *noun* special room with no light, where photographic film can be developed **Dunkelkammer**

DASD = DIRECT ACCESS STORAGE DEVICE storage medium whose memory locations can be directly read *or* written to **Direktzugriffsspeicher**

dash *noun* short line in printing **Gedankenstrich; em dash** *or* **em rule** = line as long as an em, used to separate one section of text from another **Gedankenstrich von zwei Gevierten, Trennstrich; en dash** *or* **en rule** = line as long as an en, used to link two words or parts of words **Gedankenstrich von einem Geviert, Bindestrich**

DAT = DIGITAL AUDIO TAPE method of recording sound by converting and storing signals in a digital form on magnetic tape **digitales Tonband;** *DAT produces a very high quality sound*

data *noun* collection of facts made up of numbers, characters and symbols, stored on a computer in such a way that it can be processed by the computer **Daten;** *programs act upon data files; data is input at one of several workstations; the company stores data on customers in its main computer file; a user needs a password to access data;* **raw data** = (i) pieces of information which have not been input into a computer system; (ii) data (in a databank) which has to be processed to provide information to the user; (iii) unprocessed data **(i)-(iii) Ursprungsdaten; data above voice (DAV)** = data transmission in a frequency range above that of the human voice **Datenübertragung über Sprachfrequenz; data access management** = regulating the users who can access stored data **Datenzugriffsverwaltung; data acquisition** = gathering data about a subject **Datenerfassung; data adapter unit** = device that interfaces a CPU to one or more communications channels **Datenanschlußeinheit; data administrator** = control section of a database management system **Datenverwalter; data aggregate** = collection of items of data that are related **Datengruppierung; data analysis** = extracting information and results from data

Datenanalyse; data area = amount of storage space that contains data (rather than instructions) **Datenbereich; databank** = collection of data (usually on one theme) **Datenbank; data block** = all the data required for *or* from a process **Datenblock; data break** = memory access operation by a peripheral that halts a CPU for one or more cycles whilst data is being transferred from memory to the device **Datenunterbrechung; data buffer** = temporary storage location for data received by a device that is not yet ready to accept it **Datenpuffer; data bus** = bus carrying the data between a CPU and memory and peripheral devices **Datenübertragungsweg; data capture** = act of obtaining data (either by keyboarding or by scanning, or often automatically from a recording device *or* peripheral) **Datenerfassung; data carrier** = (i) any device *or* medium capable of storing data; (ii) a waveform used as a carrier for data signals **(i) & (ii) Datenträger; data carrier detect (DCD)** = RS232C signal from a modem to a computer indicating a carrier wave is being received **Datenempfangssignal;** *the call is stopped if the software does not receive a DCD signal from the modem;* **data cartridge** = cartridge that contains stored data **Datenregister; data chaining** = one stored record that holds the address of the next in the list **Datenadreßkettung; data channel** = communication link able to carry data signals **Datenkanal; data check** = error in reading data due to a fault with the magnetic medium **Datenstop data circuit** = circuit which allows bi-directional data communications **Datenverbindung;**

data cleaning = removing errors from data **Datenkorrektur; data collection** = act of receiving data from various sources (either directly from a data capture device *or* from a cartridge) and inserting correctly in order into a database **Datenerfassung; data collection platform** = station that transmits collected data to a central point (usually via satellite) **Datenerfassungsstation; data communications** = transmission and reception of data rather than speech *or* images **Datenaustausch; data communications buffer** = buffer on a receiver that allows a slow peripheral to accept data from a fast computer, without slowing either down **Datenaustauschpuffer; data communications equipment (DCE)** = equipment (such as a modem) which receives *or* transmits data **Datenaustauschgerät; data communications network** = number of computers, terminals, operators and storage units connected together to allow data transmission between devices *or* files *or* users **Datenkommunikationsnetzwerk; data compacting** = reducing the space taken by data by coding it in a more efficient way **Datenverdichtung;** *all the files were stored on one disk with this new data compacting routine;* **data compression** = means of reducing size of data by removing spaces, empty sections and unused material from the blocks of data **Datenverdichtung;** *scanners use a technique called data compression which manages to reduce, even by a third, the storage required;* **data concentrator** = data which combines intermittent data from various lines and sends it along a single line in one go **Datenkonzentrator; data connection** = link which joins two devices and allows data transmission **Datenverbindung; data control** = data management to and from a database *or* processing system **Datenverwaltung; data corruption** = errors introduced into data due to noise *or* faulty equipment **Datenkorruption;** *data corruption occurs each time the motor is switched on;* **data delimiter** = special symbol *or* character that marks the end of a file *or* data item **Datenbegrenzungszeichen; data description language (DDL)** = part of database system software which describes the structure of the system and data **Datenbeschreibungssprache; data dictionary/directory (DD/D)** = software which gives a list of types and forms of data contained in a database **Datenwörterbuch, Feldnamenerklärung; data division** = part of a (COBOL) program giving full definitions of the data types and structures **Datenteil; data-driven** = (computer architecture) in which instructions are executed, once the relevant data has been received **datengesteuert; data element** *see* DATA ITEM; **data element chain** = more than one data element treated as a single element **Datenelementkette; data encryption** = encrypting data using a cipher system **Datenverschlüsselung; data encryption standard (DES)** = standard for a block data cipher system **Datenverschlüsselungsnorm; data entry** = method of entering data into a system (usually using a keyboard but also direct from disks after data preparation) **Datenerfassung, Dateneingabe; data error** = error due to incorrect *or* illegal data **Datenfehler; data field** = part of a computer instruction that contains the location of the data **Datenfeld; data file** = file with data in it (as opposed to a program file) **Datei;** *the data file has to be analysed;* **data flow** = movement of data through a system **Datenfluß; data flowchart** = diagram used to describe a computer *or* data processing system **Datenflußplan;** *the data flowchart allowed us to improve throughput, by using a better structure;* **data flow diagram (DFD)** = diagram used to describe the movement of data through a system

Datenflußdiagramm; data format = rules defining the way in which data is stored *or* transmitted **Datenformat; data hierarchy** = data structure organized hierarchically **Datenhierarchie; data highway** = bus carrying data signals between a CPU and peripherals **Datenübertragungsweg;** *see also* BUS; **data independence** = structure of a database which can be changed without affecting what the user sees **Datenunabhängigkeit; data input** = data transferred into a computer (from an I/O port or peripheral) **Dateneingabe; data input bus (DIB)** = bus used when transferring data from one section of a computer to another, such as between memory and CPU **Dateneingabebus; data integrity** = protection of data against damage *or* errors **Datensicherheit; data in voice (DIV)** = digital data transmission in place of a voice channel **Datenübertragung auf Sprachfrequenz; data item** = one unit of data such as the quantity of items in stock, a person's name, age or occupation **Datenfeld;**

data level = position of a data item within a database structure **Datenebene; data link** = connection between two devices to allow the transmission of data **Datenübertragungsabschnitt; data link control** = protocol and rules used to define the way in which data is transmitted *or* received **Datenleitungssteuerung; data link layer** = one layer in the ISO/OSI defined network that sends packets of data to the next link and deals with error correction **Sicherungsschicht; data logging** = automatic data collection **Datenerfassung; data management** = maintenance and upkeep of a database **Datenpflege; data manipulation language (DML)** = database software that allows the user to access, store and change data **Datenbehandlungssprache; data medium** = medium which allows data to be stored *or* displayed (such as a VDU *or* magnetic disk *or* screen) **Datenträger; data migration** = data transfer (by a user's instruction) from an on-line device to an off-line device **Datenumlagerung; data name** = group of characters used to identify one item of data **Datenname;** *problems occur if an ambiguous data name is chosen;* **data network** = networking system which transmits data **Datennetz; data origination** = conversion of data from its original form to one which can be read by a computer **Datenerstellung; data path** = bus *or* connections over which data is transmitted **Datenweg; data pointer** = register containing the location of the next item of data **Datenzeiger; data preparation** = conversion of data into a machine-readable form (usually by keyboarding) before data entry **Datenvorbereitung; data processing (DP** *or* **dp)** = selecting and operating on data to produce useful information; sorting *or* organizing data files **Datenverarbeitung; data processing manager** = person who runs a computer department **Datenverarbeitungsmanager; data protection** = means of making sure that data is private and secure **Datensicherung; data rate** = maximum rate at which data is processed *or* transmitted in a synchronous system, usually equal to the system clock rate **Datenübertragungsgeschwindigkeit; data record** = one record containing data for use with a program **Datensatz; data reduction** = production of compact, useful data from raw data **Datenverdichtung; data register** = area within a CPU used to store data temporarily before it is processed **Datenregister; data reliability** = measure of the number of data words with errors compared to the total number of words **Datenzuverlässigkeit; data retrieval** = process of searching, selecting and reading data from a stored file **Datenwiedergewinnung; data routing** = defining the path to be taken by a message in a network **Datenleitweg; data security** = protection of data against corruption *or* unauthorized users **Datensicherung; data services** = public services (such as the telephone system) which allow data to be transmitted **Datenservice; data set ready (DSR)** = signal from a device that is ready to accept data, this signal occurs after a DTR signal is received **Betriebsbereitschaft; data signals** = electrical *or* optical pulses *or* waveforms that represent binary data **Datensignale; data signalling rate** = total amount of data that is transmitted through a system per second **Datenübertragungsgeschwindigkeit; data sink** = device in a data terminal which receives data **Datensenke; data source** = device in a data terminal which sends data **Datenquelle; data station** = point that contains a data terminal and a data circuit **Datenstation; data storage** = medium able to store large quantities of data **Datenspeicher;** *see also* BACKING STORE; **data stream** = data transmitted serially one bit *or* character at a time **Datenstrom; data strobe** = signal (in the control bus) that indicates that valid data is on the data bus **Datenimpulseingang, Datenstrobe; data structure** = number of related items that are treated as one by the computer (in an address book record, the name, address and telephone number form separate entries which would be processed as one by the computer) **Datenstruktur; data switching exchange** = device used to direct and switch data between lines **Datenaustauschvermittlung; data tablet** *see* GRAPHICS TABLET; **data terminal** = device that is able to display and transmit *or* receive data **Datenstation;** *a printer is a data*

terminal for computer output; **data terminal equipment (DTE)** = device at which a communications path starts *or* finishes **Datenendeinrichtung; data terminal ready (DTR)** = signal from a device that indicates that it is ready to send data **Betriebsbereit-Signal; data transaction** = one complete operation on data **Datenbewegung; data transfer rate** = rate at which data is moved from one point to another **Datenübertragungsgeschwindigkeit, Transfergeschwindigkeit; data translation** = conversion of data from one system format to another **Datenumsetzung; data transmission** = process of sending data from one location to another over a data link **Datenübertragung; data type** = sort of data which can be stored in a register (such as string, number, etc.) **Datentyp; data under voice (DUV)** = data transmission in a frequency range lower than that of a human voice **Datenübertragung unter Sprachfrequenz; data validation** = process of checking data for errors and relevance in a situation **Datenprüfung; data vetting** = process of checking data as it is input for errors and validity **Datenprüfung; data word** = piece of data stored as a single word **Datenwort; data word length** = number of bits that make up a word in a computer **Datenwortlänge; master data** = reference data which is stored in a master file **Hauptdaten; optical data link** = connection between two devices to allow the transmission of data using light (either line-of-sight or using fibre optics) **optische Datenverbindung; variable data** = data which can be modified, and is not write protected **variable Daten**

COMMENT: Data is different from information in that it is facts stored in machine-readable form. When the facts are processed by the computer into a form which can be understood by people, the data becomes information

◊ **databank** *noun* (i) large amount of data stored in a structured form; (ii) personal records stored in a computer **(i) & (ii) Datenbank**

◊ **database** *noun* integrated collection of files of data stored in a structured form in a large memory, which can be accessed by one or more users at different terminals **Datenbank; database administrator (DBA)** = person in charge of running and maintaining a database system **Datenbankverwalter; database language** = series of languages, such as data description language, that make up a database management system **Datenbanksprache; database machine** = hardware and software combination designed for the rapid processing of

database information **Datenbankmaschine;
database management system (DBMS)** *or*
database manager = series of programs that
allow the user to create and modify
databases easily
**Datenbankverwaltungssystem; database
mapping** = description of the way in which
the records and fields in a database are
related **Datenbankaufgliederung; database
schema** = way in which a database is
organized and structured
Datenbankschema; database system = series
of programs that allows the user to create,
modify, manage and use a database (often
includes features such as a report writer *or*
graphical output of data) **Datenbanksystem;
on-line database** = interactive search,
retrieve and update of database records
using an on-line terminal **Datenbank mit
Direktanschluß**

◇ **datagram** *noun* packet of information in
a packet switching system that contains its
destination address and route **Datagramm**

◇ **dataline** *noun* one line of broadcast TV
signal that contains the teletext signals and
data (usually transmitted at the start of the
image and identified with a special code)
Datenleitung

◇ **dataplex** *noun* multiplexing of data
signals **Datenmultiplexmethode**

◇ **dataset** *noun* *(US)* modem **Modem;
dataset ready (DSR)** = RS232C signal from
a modem to a computer indicating it is
ready for use **Betriebsbereitschaftssignal**

QUOTE data compression is the art of squeezing
more and more information into fewer and fewer
bytes
Practical Computing
QUOTE a database is a file of individual records
of information which are stored in some kind of
sequential order
Which PC?

date
1 *noun* number of day, month and year
Datum; *I have received your message of
yesterday's date; the date of creation for the
file was the 10th of June*
2 *verb* to put a date on a document **datieren**

◇ **out of date** *adjective & adverb* old-
fashioned **veraltet;** *their computer system is
years out of date; they are still using out-of-
date equipment*

◇ **up to date** *adjective & adverb* current *or*
recent *or* modern **auf dem neuesten Stand;** *an
up-to-date computer system;* **to bring** *or* **keep
something up to date** = to add the latest
information to something **etwas auf den
neuesten Stand bringen/halten;** *we spend a lot
of time keeping our files up to date* NOTE:
when used as adjectives before a noun, out-of-date
and up-to-date are hyphenated

daughter board *noun* add-on board
that connects to a system mother board
Tochterplatine

DAV = DATA ABOVE VOICE

db *see* DECIBEL

DBA = DATABASE ADMINISTRATOR
person in charge of running and
maintaining a database system
Datenbankverwalter

DBMS = DATABASE MANAGEMENT
SYSTEM series of programs that allow the
user to create and modify databases
Datenbankverwaltungssystem

DC = DIRECT CURRENT; **DC signalling** =
method of communications using pulses of
current over a wire circuit, like a telegraph
system **Gleichstromsignal**

DCD = DATA CARRIER DETECT RS232C
signal from a modem to a computer
indicating a carrier is being received
Datenempfangssignal

DCE = DATA COMMUNICATIONS
EQUIPMENT

DD = DOUBLE DENSITY

DDC = DIRECT DIGITAL CONTROL
machine operated automatically by
machine **direkte digitale Regelung**

DD/D = DATA DICTIONARY/DIRECTORY
software which gives a list of types and
forms of data contained in a database
Datenwörterbuch, Feldnamenerklärung

DDE = DIRECT DATA ENTRY keying in
data directly onto magnetic tape *or* disk
direkte Dateneingabe

DDL = DATA DESCRIPTION LANGUAGE
*many of DDL's advantages come from the
fact that it is a second generation language*

DDP = DISTRIBUTED DATA PROCESSING
operations to derive information from data
which is kept in different places **verteilte
Datenverarbeitung**

dead *adjective*
(a) not working; (computer *or* piece of
equipment) that does not function **tot; dead
halt** *or* **drop dead halt** = program instruction
from the user *or* an error, that causes the

program to stop without allowing recovery **Unterbrechungshalt;** *the manual does not say what to do if a dead halt occurs;* **dead keys =** keys on a keyboard that cause a function rather than a character to occur, such as the shift key **Tot-, Funktionstasten; dead matter =** type that has been used for printing and is no longer required **Ablegesatz; dead time =** period of time between two events, in which nothing happens, to ensure that they do not interfere with each other **Totzeit, Verlustzeit;** *efficient job management minimises dead time*

(b) (room *or* space) that has no acoustical reverberation **schalldicht**

◇ **deaden** *verb* to make a sound *or* colour less sharp **dämpfen;** *acoustic hoods are used to deaden the noise of printers*

◇ **deadline** *noun* date by which something has to be done **Termin, Stichtag; to meet a deadline =** to finish something in time **den Termin einhalten;** *we've missed our October 1st deadline*

◇ **deadlock** *noun* situation when two users want to access two resources at the same time, one resource is assigned to each user but neither can use the other **gegenseitiges Sperren**

◇ **deadly embrace** *noun* = DEADLOCK

deal
1 *noun* business agreement *or* contract **Geschäft, Abmachung; package deal =** agreement where several different items are agreed at the same time **Pauschalangebot;** *they agreed a package deal, which involves the development of software, customizing hardware and training of staff*
2 *verb* **to deal with =** to organize **sich befassen mit, erledigen;** *leave it to the DP manager - he'll deal with it*

◇ **dealer** *noun* person who buys and sells **Händler;** *always buy hardware from a recognized dealer*

deallocate *verb* to free resources previously allocated to a job *or* process *or* peripheral **freigeben;** *when a reset button is pressed all resources are deallocated*

debit *noun* bit transmission rate that is twice the baud rate **Bitübertragungsgeschwindigkeit**

deblock *verb* to return a stored block of data to its original form (of individual records) **entblocken**

de-bounce *noun* preventing a single touch on a key giving multiple key contact **entprellen; de-bounce circuit =** electronic circuit that prevents a key contact producing more than one signal when pressed **Entprellungsstromkreis**

debug *verb* to test a program and locate and correct any faults *or* errors **korrigieren, bereinigen (Programmfehler);** *they spent weeks debugging the system; debugging takes up more time than construction;* **debugged program =** software that works correctly and in which all the mistakes have been removed *or* corrected **korrigiertes Programm**

◇ **debugger** *noun* software that helps a programmer find faults *or* errors in a program **Debugger, Fehlersuchprogramm**

> QUOTE the debug monitor makes development and testing very easy
> *Electronics & Wireless World*

decade *noun* ten items *or* events **Dekade; decade counter =** electronic device able to count actions *or* events from 0-9 before resetting to zero and starting again **Dekadenzähler**

decay
1 *noun* rate at which the electronic impulse *or* the amplitude of a signal fades away **Signalabfall; decay time =** time taken for an impulse to fade **Signalabfallzeit**
2 *verb* to decrease gradually in amplitude *or* size **abfallen, abnehmen;** *the signal decayed rapidly*

decentralized computer network *noun* network where the control is shared between several computers **dezentralisiertes Computernetz**

◇ **decentralized data processing** *noun* data processing and storage carried out at each location rather than in one central location **dezentralisierte Datenverarbeitung**

deci- *prefix* meaning one tenth of a number **dezi-, Dezi-**

◇ **decibel** *noun* unit of measurement of noise **Dezibel (dB); decibel meter =** signal power measuring device **Dezibelmeter**

decile *noun* one of a series of nine figures below which one tenth *or* several tenths of the total fall **Dezile, Zehntelwert**

decimal (notation) *noun* arithmetic and number representation using the decimal system **dezimale (Zahlendarstellung); correct to three places of decimals =** correct to three figures after the decimal point (e.g. 3.485) **auf drei Dezimalstellen genau berechnet; decimal point =** dot which indicates the division between the whole unit digits and the smaller (fractional) parts of a decimal number (such as 4.75) **Dezimalstelle; decimal system** = number system using the digits 0 - 9 **Dezimalsystem; decimal tabbing** = adjusting a column of numbers so that the decimal points are vertically aligned **mit Dezimaltabulator einrichten; decimal tab key** = key for entering decimal numbers (using a word processor) so that the decimal points are automatically vertically aligned **Dezimaltabulatortaste; decimal-to-binary conversion** = converting a decimal (base ten) number into a binary (base two) number **Dezimal-binär-Umwandlung**

◊ **decimalization** *noun* changing to a decimal system **Dezimalisierung**

◊ **decimalize** *verb* to change to a decimal system **dezimalisieren**

decimonic ringing *noun* selecting one telephone by sending a certain ringing frequency **dezimonisches Läuten**

decipher *verb* to convert an encrypted *or* encoded message (ciphertext) into the original message (plaintext) **entschlüsseln**

decision *noun* making up one's mind to do something **Entscheidung, Entschluß;** *to come to a decision or to reach a decision;* **decision box** = graphical symbol used in a flowchart to indicate that a decision is to be made and a branch *or* path *or* action carried out according to the result **Blockdiagrammsymbol: Entscheidung; decision circuit *or* element** = logical circuit that operates on binary inputs, providing an output according to the operation **Verknüpfungsglied; decision** *or* **discrimination instruction** = conditional program instruction that directs control by providing the location of the next instruction to be executed if a condition is met **logische Entscheidung; decision support system** = suite of programs that help a manager reach decisions using previous decisions, information and other databases **Entscheidungsunterstützungssystem; decision table** = chart which shows the relationships between certain variables and actions available when various conditions are met **Entscheidungstabelle; decision tree** = graphical representation of a decision table showing possible paths and actions if different conditions are met **Entscheidungsbaum**

deck *noun*
(a) **tape deck** = drive for magnetic tape **Bandlaufwerk**

(b) **pile of punched cards Lochkartensatz**

deckle edge *noun* rough edge of paper made by hand **Büttenrand**

declare *verb* to define a computer program variable *or* to set a variable equal to a number **benennen;** *he declared at the start of the program that X was equal to nine*

◊ **declaration** *or* **declarative statement** *noun* statement within a program that informs the compiler *or* interpreter of the form, type and size of a particular element, constant *or* variable **Vereinbarung; procedure declaration** = to write and declare the variable types used and (if any) the routine name and location **Prozedurvereinbarung**

decode *verb* to translate encoded data back to its original form **entschlüsseln**

◊ **decoder** *noun* program *or* device used to convert data into another form **Decodierer; instruction decoder** = hardware that converts a machine-code instruction (in binary form) into actions **Befehlsdecodierer**

◊ **decoding** *noun* converting encoded data back into its original form **Entschlüsselung**

decollate *verb* to separate continuous stationery into single sheets; to split two-part *or* three-part stationery into its separate parts (and remove the carbon paper) **trennen**

◊ **decollator** *noun* machine used to separate continuous stationery into single sheets *or* to split 2-part or 3-part stationery into separate parts **Trennmaschine**

decompilation *noun* conversion of a compiled program in object code into a source language **Rückumsetzung;** *fast incremental compilation and decompilation*

decrease
1 *noun* fall *or* reduction **Verminderung, Abfall;** *decrease in price; decrease in value; decrease in sales; sales show a 10% decrease on last year*
2 *verb* to fall *or* to become less **abnehmen, nachlassen;** *sales are decreasing; the value of the pound has decreased by 5%*

decrement *verb* to subtract a set number from a variable **Dekrement;** *the register contents were decremented until they reached zero*

decrypt *verb* to convert encrypted data back into its original form **entschlüsseln;**

decryption is done using hardware to increase speed

◊ **decryption** *noun* converting of encrypted data back into its original form **Entschlüsselung**

> QUOTE typically a file is encrypted using a password key and decrypted using the same key. A design fault of many systems means the use of the wrong password for decryption results in double and often irretrievable encryption
> *PC Business World*

dedicated *adjective* (program *or* procedure *or* system) reserved for a particular use **ausschließlich zugeordnet, dediziert;** *there's only one dedicated graphics workstation in this network;* **dedicated channel** = communications line reserved for a special purpose **dedizierter Kanal; dedicated computer** = computer which is only used for a single special purpose **dedizierter Computer; dedicated line** = telephone line used only for data communications **festgeschaltete Leitung; dedicated logic** = logical function implemented in hardware designed (usually for only one task *or* circuit **dedizierte Logik;** *the dedicated logic should have a knowledge of micro-based hardware and dedicated logic; the dedicated logic cuts down the chip count;* **dedicated word processor** = computer which has been configured specially for word processing and which cannot run any other programs **dedizierter Textverarbeitungscomputer**

> QUOTE the server should reduce networking costs by using standard networking cable instead of dedicated links
> *PC Business World*

deduct *verb* to remove something from a total **abziehen**

default *noun* predefined course of action *or* value that is assumed unless the operator alters it **Vorgabe; default drive** = disk drive that is accessed first in a multi-disk system (to try and load the operating system or a program) **Standardlaufwerk;** *the operating system allows the user to select the default drive;* **default option** = preset value *or* option that is to be used if no other value has been specified **Standardannahme; default rate** = baud rate (in a modem) that is used if no other is selected **vorgegebene Schrittgeschwindigkeit; default response** = value which is used if the user does not enter new data **Standardwert; default value** = value which is automatically used by the computer if no other value has been specified **Standardvorgabe;** *screen width has a default value of 80*

defect *noun* something which is wrong *or* which stops a machine from working properly **Fehler;** *a computer defect or a defect in the computer*

◊ **defective** *adjective* faulty *or* not working properly **defekt;** *the machine broke down because of a defective cooling system*

◊ **defect skipping** *noun* means of identifying and labelling defective magnetic tracks during manufacture so that they will not be used, instead pointing to the next good track to be used **fehlerhaftes Springen**

defensive computing *noun* method of programming that takes into account any problems *or* errors that might occur **defensives Programmieren**

deferred addressing *noun* indirect addressing, where the location accessed contains the address of the operand to be processed **indirekte/ausgesetzte Adressierung**

define *verb* (i) to assign a value to a variable; (ii) to assign the characteristics of processes *or* data to something **(i) definieren; (ii) zuweisen;** *all the variables were defined at initialization*

◊ **definition** *noun* (i) ability of a screen to display fine detail; (ii) value *or* formula assigned to a variable *or* label **(i) Auflösung; (ii) Zuweisung; macro definition** = description (in a program *or* to a system) of the structure, function and instructions that make up a macro operation **Makrodefinition**

deflect *verb* to change the direction of an object *or* beam **ablenken**

◊ **deflection** *noun* **deflection yoke** = magnetic coils around a cathode ray tube used to control the position of the picture beam on the screen **Ablenkjoch**

defocus *verb* to move the point of focus of an optical system from an object, so that it appears out of focus **defokussieren**

degauss *verb* to remove unwanted magnetic fields and effects from magnetic tape, disks *or* read/write heads **entmagnetisieren;** *the r/w heads have to be degaussed each week to ensure optimum performance*

◊ **degausser** *noun* device used to remove unwanted magnetic fields from a disk *or* tape *or* recording head **Entmagnetisierungsgerät**

degradation *noun*
(a) loss of picture *or* signal quality **Verschlechterung; image degradation** = loss of picture contrast and quality due to signal distortion *or* bad copying of a video signal **Bildverschlechterung**
(b) loss of processing capacity because of a malfunction **Verschlechterung; graceful degradation** = allowing some parts of a system to continue to function after a part has broken down **kontrollierter Leistungsrückgang**

delay
1 *noun* time when something is later than planned **Verspätung, Verzögerung;** *there was a delay of thirty seconds before the printer started printing; we are sorry for the delay in supplying your order, but the computer was not working;* **delay distortion** = signal corruption due to echoes **Laufzeitverzerrung; delay equalizer** = electronic circuit used to compensate for delays caused by a communications line **Laufzeitentzerrer; delay line** = device that causes a signal to take a certain time in crossing it **Verzögerungsleitung; delay line store** = (old) method of storing serial data as sound *or* pulses in a delay line, the data being constantly read, regenerated and fed back into the input **Laufzeitspeicher; delay vector** = time that a message will take to pass from one packet switching network node to another **Verzögerungsvektor**
2 *verb* to cause something to have a delay **aufhalten**

delete *verb*
(a) to cut out words in a document **streichen**
(b) to remove text *or* data from a storage device **löschen;** *the word-processor allows us to delete the whole file by pressing this key;* **delete character** = special code used to indicate data *or* text to be removed **Löschzeichen**

◊ **deletion** *noun* (i) making a cut in a document; (ii) text removed from a document **(i) & (ii) Streichung;** *the editors asked the author to make several deletions in the last chapter;* **deletion record** = record containing new data which is to be used to update *or* delete data in a master record **Löschsatz**

COMMENT: when you delete a file, you are not actually erasing it but you are making its space on disk available for another file by instructing the operating system to ignore the file by inserting a special code in the file header and deleting the entry from the directory

delimit *verb* to set up the size of data using delimiters **begrenzen**

◊ **delimiter** *noun* (i) character *or* symbol used to indicate to a language *or* program the start *or* end of data *or* a record *or* information; (ii) the boundary between an instruction and its argument **(i) Begrenzungssymbol; (ii) Abgrenzung**

delta *noun* type of connection used to connect the three wires in a 3-phase electrical supply **Dreieckschaltung; delta clock** = clock that provides timing pulses to synchronize a system, and will restart (with an interrupt signal) a computer *or* circuit that has had an error *or* entered an endless loop *or* faulty state **Delta-Uhr; delta-delta** = connection between a delta source and load **Delta-Delta-Verbindung; delta modulation** = differential pulse coded modulation that uses only one bit per sample **Deltamodulation; delta routing** = means of directing data around a packet switching network **Dreiecksleitweg**

demagnetize *verb* to remove stray *or* unwanted magnetic fields from a disk *or* tape *or* recording head **entmagnetisieren**

◊ **demagnetizer** *noun* device which demagnetizes something **Entmagnetisierer;** *he used the demagnetizer to degauss the tape heads*

demand
1 *noun* asking for something to be done **Bitte, Forderung; demand assigned multiple access (DAMA)** = means of switching in circuits as and when they are required **bedarfsbestimmter Mehrfachzugriff; demand multiplexing** = time division multiplexing method which allocates time segments to signals according to demand **bedarfsmäßige Multiplexmethode; demand paging** = system software that retrieves pages in a virtual memory system from backing store when it is required **Seitenabrufmethode; demand processing** = processing data when it appears, rather than waiting **unmittelbare Verarbeitung; demand reading/writing** = direct data transfer between a processor and storage **unmittelbares Lesen/Schreiben; demand staging** = moving files *or* data from a secondary storage device to a fast access device when required by a database program **bedarfsmäßiges Einspeichern**
2 *verb* to ask for something and expect to get it **fordern;** *she demanded her money back; the suppliers are demanding immediate payment*

demarcation *noun* showing the difference between two areas **Abgrenzung;**

demarcation strip = device that electrically isolates equipment from a telephone line (to prevent damage) **Demarkationsstreifen**

democratic network *noun* synchronized network where each station has equal priority **gleichberechtigtes Netz**

demodulation *noun* recovery of the original signal from a received modulated carrier wave **Demodulation**

◊ **demodulator** *noun* circuit that recovers a signal from a modulated carrier wave **Demodulator**

demonstrate *verb* to show how something works **vorführen;** *he demonstrated the file management program*

◊ **demonstration** *noun* act of showing how something works **Vorführung; demonstration model** = piece of equipment in a shop, used to show customers how the equipment works **Vorführgerät**

demultiplex *verb* to split one channel into the original signals that were combined at source **entmultiplexieren**

◊ **demultiplexor** *noun* device that separates out the original multiplexed signals from one channel **Entmultiplexor**

denary notation *noun* number system in base ten, using the digits 0 to 9 **Dezimaldarstellung**

denial *noun* **alternative denial** = logical function whose output is false if all inputs are true, and true if any input is false **NAND-Funktion; joint denial** = logical function whose output is false if any input is true **NOR-Funktion**

dense index *noun* database index containing an address *or* entry for every item *or* entry in the database **Gesamtindex; dense list** = list that has no free space for new records **vollständige Liste**

◊ **densitometer** *noun* photographic device used to measure the density of a photograph **Dichtemesser, Densitometer**

◊ **density** *noun*
(a) amount of light that a photographic negative blocks **Dichte**
(b) darkness of a printed image *or* text **Schwärzungsgrad; density dial** = knob that controls the density of a printed image **Schwärzungsskala;** *when fading occurs, turn the density dial on the printer to full black*
(c) amount of data that can be packed into a space on a disk *or* tape **Speicherkapazität;**

double density = system to double the storage capacity of a disk drive by doubling the number of bits which can be put on the disk surface **doppelte Speicherkapazität; double density disk (DD)** = disk that can store two bits of data per unit area compared to a standard disk, using a modified write process **Platte mit doppelter Speicherkapazität; packing** *or* **recording density** = number of bits that can be stored in a unit area on a magnetic disk *or* tape **Zeichendichte; single density disk (SD)** = standard magnetic disk able to store data **Platte mit einfacher Speicherkapazität**

COMMENT: scanner software produces various shades of grey by using different densities *or* arrangements of black and white dots and/or different sized dots

QUOTE diode lasers with shorter wavelengths will make doubling of the bit and track densities possible
Byte

deny access *verb* to refuse access to a circuit *or* system for reasons of workload *or* security **den Zugriff verwehren**

dependent *adjective* which is variable because of something **abhängig;** *a process which is dependent on the result of another process; the output is dependent on the physical state of the link;* **machine dependent** = not standardized *or* which cannot be used on hardware *or* software from a different manufacturer without modification **maschinenabhängig**

deposit
1 *noun* thin layer of a substance which is put on a surface **Schicht**
2 *verb*
(a) to print out the contents of all *or* a selected area of memory **darlegen**
(b) to coat a surface with a thin layer of a substance **mit einer Schicht überziehen**
(c) to write data into a register *or* storage location **ablegen**

◊ **deposition** *noun* process by which a surface (of a semiconductor) is coated with a thin layer of a substance **Überzugsverfahren**

depth of field *noun* amount of a scene that will be in focus when photographed with a certain aperture setting **Tiefenbereich; depth of focus** = position of film behind a camera lens that will result in a sharp image **Tiefenschärfe**

deque *noun* = DOUBLE-ENDED QUEUE queue in which new items can be added to either end **nach beiden Seiten offene Warteschlange**

derive *verb* to come from **sich ableiten von; derived indexing** = library index entries produced only from material in the book *or* document **abgeleitete Indizierung; derived sound** = sound signal produced by mixing the left and right hand channels of a stereo signal **monophones Tonsignal**

◊ **derivation graph** *noun* structure within a global database that provides information on the rules and paths used to reach any element *or* item of data **Ableitungsgraph**

DES = DATA ENCRYPTION STANDARD standardized popular cipher system for data encryption **Datenverschlüsselungsnorm**

descender *noun* part of a character that goes below the line (such as the 'tail' of a 'g' or 'p') **Unterlänge;** *compare* ASCENDER

de-scramble *verb* to reassemble an original message *or* signal from its scrambled form **entschlüsseln**

◊ **de-scrambler** *noun* device which changes a scrambled message back to its original, clear form **Decodierer**

describe *verb* to say what someone *or* something is like **beschreiben;** *the leaflet describes the services the company can offer; the specifications are described in greater detail at the back of the manual*

◊ **description** *noun* words which show what something is like **Beschreibung; description list** = list of data items and their attributes **Erklärungsliste; data description language (DDL)** = part of a database system which describes the structure of the system and data **Datenbeschreibungssprache; page description programming language** = programming language that accepts commands to define the size, position and typestyle for text *or* graphics on a page **Seitenbeschreibungssprache**

◊ **descriptor** *noun* code used to identify a filename *or* program name *or* pass code to a file **Beschreiber, Deskriptor**

design
1 *noun* planning *or* drawing of a product before it is built *or* manufactured **Entwurf; circuit design** = layout of components and interconnections in a circuit **Schaltungsentwurf; industrial design** = design of products made by machines (such as cars and refrigerators) **Industriedesign; product design** = design of products

Produktdesign; design department = department in a large company which designs the company's products *or* its advertising **Designabteilung; Werbeabteilung; design parameters** = specifications for the design of a product **Designparameter; design studio** = independent firm which specializes in creating designs **Designstudio, Grafikerbüro**
2 *verb* to plan *or* to draw something before it is built *or* manufactured **entwerfen;** *he designed a new chip factory; she designs typefaces*

◊ **designer** *noun* person who designs **Designer/-in;** *she is the designer of the new computer*

desk *noun* writing table in an office, usually with drawers for stationery **Schreibtisch;** *desk diary; desk drawer; desk light;* **desk check** = dry run of a program **Probelauf**

◊ **desktop** *adjective* which sits on top of a desk; which can be done on a desk **Tisch-; desktop computer (system)** = small microcomputer system that can be placed on a desk **Tischcomputer; desktop publishing (DTP)** = design, layout and printing of documents using special software, a small computer and a printer **Desktop Publishing, Publizieren am Schreibtisch**

QUOTE desktop publishing or the ability to produce high-quality publications using a minicomputer, essentially boils down to combining words and images on pages
Byte

despool *verb* to print out spooled files **übertragen**

despotic network *noun* network synchronized and controlled by one single clock **zwangssynchronisiertes Netz**

de-spun antenna *noun* satellite aerial that always points to the same place on the earth **raumfeste Antenne**

destination *noun* place to which something is sent *or* to which something is going; location to which a data is sent **Bestimmungsort**

destructive addition *noun* addition operation in which the result is stored in the location of one of the operands used in the sum, so overwriting it **Überschreibung**

◊ **destructive cursor** *noun* cursor that erases the text as it moves over it **löschender Cursor;** *reading the screen becomes difficult without a destructive cursor;* **destructive read** = read operation in which the stored data is erased as it is retrieved **löschendes Lesen; destructive readout** = form of storage medium that loses its data after it has been read **löschendes Auslesen**

detail

1 *noun* small part of a description **Detail; detail file** = file containing records that are to be used to update a master file **Detaildatei; in detail** = giving many particulars **im Detail;** *the catalogue lists all the products in detail;* **detail paper** = thin transparent paper used for layouts and tracing **Pauspapier**

2 *verb* to list in detail **genau auflisten;** *the catalogue details the shipping arrangements for customers; the terms of the licence are detailed in the contract*

◇ **detailed** *adjective* in detail **im Detail; detailed account** = account which lists every item **detaillierte Aufzeichnung/Rechnung**

detect *verb* to sense something (usually something very slight) **erkennen, aufdecken;** *the equipment can detect faint signals from the transducer;* **detected error** = error noticed during a program run, but not corrected **erkannter Fehler; error detecting code** = coding system that allows errors occurring during transmission to be detected, but is not complex enough to correct the errors **Fehlererkennungscode**

◇ **detection** *noun* process of detecting something **Erkennung;** *the detection of the cause of the fault is proving difficult*

◇ **detector** *noun* device which can detect **Detektor; metal detector** = device which can sense hidden metal objects **Metalldetektor**

deterministic *adjective* (result of a process) that depends on the initial state and inputs **deterministisch**

develop *verb*

a) to plan and produce **entwickeln;** *to develop a new product*

b) to apply a chemical process to photographic film and paper to produce an image **entwickeln**

◇ **developer** *noun*

a) property developer = person who plans and builds a group of new houses *or* new factories **Immobilienmakler, Erschließer; software developer** = person *or* company which writes software **Software-Entwickler**

b) chemical solution used to develop exposed film **Entwickler(flüssigkeit)**

◇ **development** *noun* planning the production of a new product **Entwicklung; research and development** = investigating new products and techniques **Forschung und Entwicklung; development software** = suite of programs that help a programmer write, edit, compile and debug new software **Programmentwicklungssoftware; development time** = amount of time required to develop a new product **Entwicklungszeit**

device *noun* small useful machine *or* piece of equipment **Bauelement, Gerät; device character control** = device control using various characters *or* special combinations to instruct the device **Gerätezeichensteuerung; device code** = unique identification and selection code for each peripheral **Gerätekennung; device control (character)** = special code sent in a transmission to a device to instruct it to perform a special function **Gerätesteuerzeichen; device driver** = program *or* routine used to interface and manage an I/O device *or* peripheral **Gerätetreiber; device flag** = one bit in a device status word, used to show the state of one device **Gerätekennung; device independent** = programming technique that results in a program that is able to run with any peripheral hardware **geräteunabhängig; device priority** = the importance of a peripheral device assigned by the user *or* central computer which dictates the order in which the CPU will serve an interrupt signal from it **Einheitenvorrangliste;** *the master console has a higher device priority than the printers and other terminals;* **device queue** = list of requests from users *or* programs to use a device **Warteschlange; device status word (DSW)** = data word transmitted from the device that contains information about its current status **Einheitenstatuswort;** *this routine checks the device status word and will not transmit data if the busy bit is set;* **I/O device** = peripheral (such as a terminal) which can be used for inputting or outputting data to a processor **Ein-/Ausgabeeinheit; output device** = device (such as a monitor *or* printer) which allows information to be displayed **Ausgabegerät**

devise *verb* to plan *or* build a system **sich ausdenken;** *they devised a cheap method of avoiding the problem*

Dewey decimal classification *noun* library cataloguing system using classes and subclasses that are arranged in groups of ten **Deweysche Dezimalklassifikation**

DFD = DATA FLOW DIAGRAM diagram used to describe the movement of data through a system **Datenflußdiagramm**

D-type flip-flop *noun* flip-flop device with one input and two outputs **Einheit mit bistabiler Schaltung**

diacritic *noun* accent above *or* below a letter **diakritisches Zeichen**

diagnose *verb* to find the cause and effect of a fault in hardware or error in software **diagnostizieren**
◇ **diagnosis** *noun* finding of a fault *or* discovering the cause of a fault (results of diagnosing faulty hardware or software) **Diagnose**

diagnostic
1 *noun* **diagnostic aid** = hardware *or* software device that helps to find faults **Diagnosehilfsmittel; diagnostic chip** = chip that contains circuits to carry out tests on other circuits *or* chips **Diagnosechip; diagnostic message** = message that appears to explain the type, location and probable cause of a software error *or* hardware failure **Diagnosemeldung; diagnostic program** = software that helps find faults in a computer system **Diagnoseprogramm; diagnostic routine** = routine in a program which helps to find faults in a computer system **Diagnostikprogramm; diagnostic test** = means of locating faults in hardware and software by test circuits *or* programs **Diagnosetest; self-diagnostic** = computer that runs a series of diagnostic programs (usually when the computer is switched on) to ensure that all circuits, memory and peripherals are working correctly **selbstdiagnostizierend**
◇ **diagnostics** *noun* functions *or* tests that help a user find faults in hardware *or* software **Diagnostik; compiler diagnostics** = function in a compiler that helps a programmer find faults in the program code **Kompilirerdiagnostik;** *thorough compiler diagnostics make debugging easy;* **error diagnostics** = information and system messages displayed when an error is detected to help a user debug and correct it **Fehlerdiagnose**

QUOTE the implementation of on-line diagnostic devices that measure key observable parameters
Byte
QUOTE to check for any hardware problems, a diagnostic disk is provided
Personal Computer World

diagonal cut *noun* method of joining two pieces of film *or* magnetic tape together by cutting the ends at an angle so making the join less obvious **Schrägschnitt**

diagram *noun* drawing which shows something as a plan *or* a map **Diagramm; flow diagram** = diagram showing the arrangement of work processes in a series **Flußdiagramm**
◇ **diagrammatic** *adjective* **in diagrammatic form** = in the form of a diagram **diagrammatisch, in einem Schaubild dargestellt;** *the chart showed the sales pattern in diagrammatic form*
◇ **diagramatically** *adverb* using a diagram **diagrammatisch;** *the chart shows the sales pattern diagramatically*

dial
1 *verb* to call a telephone number on a telephone **wählen;** *to dial a number; to dial the operator; he dialled the code for the USA; you can dial New York direct from London;* **to dial direct** = to contact a phone number without asking the operator to do it for you **durchwählen; auto-dial** = modem that can automatically dial a number (under the control of a computer) **Selbstwähler; to dial into** = to call a telephone number, which has a modem and computer at the other end **anwählen;** *with the right access code it is possible to dial into a customer's computer to extract the files needed for the report* NOTE: GB English is **dialling - dialled,** but US spelling is **dialing - dialed**
2 *noun* (i) circular mechanical device which is turned to select something; (ii) round face on an instrument, with numbers which indicate something (such as the time on a clock) **(i) Rundskala, Wählscheibe; (ii) Zifferblatt;** *to tune into the radio station, turn the dial;* **dial conference** = facility on a private exchange that allows one user to call a number of different extensions for a teleconference **Telekonferenzschaltung; dial pulse** = pulse-coded signals transmitted to represent numbers dialled **Wählimpuls; dial tone** = sound made by a telephone that indicates that the telephone system is ready for a number to be dialled **Wählton, Freizeichen; dial-in modem** = auto-answer modem that can be called at any time **Einwählmodem; density dial** = knob that controls the density of a printed image **Schwärzungsskala;** *if the text fades, turn the density dial on the printer to full black*
◇ **dialling** *noun* act of calling a telephone number **Wählen; dialling code** = special series of numbers which you use to make a call to another town *or* country **Vorwahl; dialling tone** = sound made by a telephone that indicates that the telephone system is ready for a number to be dialled **Wählton, Freizeichen; international direct dialling (IDD)** = calling telephone numbers in other countries direct **internationale Durchwahl**

dialect *noun* slight variation of a standard language **Dialekt**; *this manufacturer's dialect of BASIC is a little different to the one I'm used to*

dialogue *noun* speech *or* speaking to another person; communication between devices such as computers **Dialog; dialogue box** = on-screen message from a program to the user **Programmeldung**

diameter *noun* distance across a round object **Durchmesser**

DIANE = DIRECT INFORMATION ACCESS NETWORK FOR EUROPE services offered over the Euronet network **DIANE (direktes Informationsanschaltnetz für Europa)**

diaphragm *noun*
a) mechanical device in a camera that varies the aperture size **Membran**
b) moving part in a loudspeaker *or* microphone **Membran**; *the diaphragm in the microphone picks up sound waves*

diapositive *noun* positive transparency **Diapositiv**

diary *noun* book in which you can write notes *or* appointments for each day of the week **Terminkalender; diary management** = part of an office computer program, which records schedules and appointments **Terminverwaltung**

diascope *noun* slide projector *or* device that projects slide images onto a screen **Diaprojektor**

diazo (process) *noun* method for copying documents (using sensitized paper exposed to the original) **Diazokopie**

DIB = DATA INPUT BUS bus used when transferring data from one section of a computer to another, such as between memory and CPU **Dateneingabebus**

dibit *noun* digit made up of two binary bits **Dibit**

dichotomizing search *noun* fast search method for use on ordered lists of data (the search key is compared with the data in the middle of the list and one half is discarded, this is repeated with the half remaining until only one data item remains) **eliminierende Suche, Einstichverfahren**

dichroic *noun* chemical coating on the surface of a lens **Dichroise**

dictate *verb* to say something to someone who then writes down your words **diktieren**; *to dictate a letter to a secretary; he was dictating orders into his pocket dictating machine*; **dictating machine** = small tape recorder that is used to record notes *or* letters dictated by someone, which a secretary can play back and type out the text **Diktiergerät**

◇ **dictation** *noun* act of dictating **Diktat; to take dictation** = to write down what someone is saying **ein Diktat aufnehmen; dictation speed** = number of words per minute which a secretary can write down in shorthand **Diktiertempo; Silbenzahl pro Minute**

dictionary *noun* (i) book which lists words and meanings; (ii) data management structure which allows files to be referenced and sorted; (iii) part of a spelling checker program: the list of correctly spelled words against which the program checks a text **(i) Wörterbuch; (ii) Verzeichnis; (iii) Wörterbuch**

dielectric *noun* insulating material that allows an electric field to pass, but not an electric current **Dielektrikum, Nichtleiter**

differ *verb* not to be the same as something else **sich unterscheiden**; *the two products differ considerably - one has an external hard disk, the other has internal hard disk and external magnetic tape drive*

◇ **difference** *noun* way in which two things are not the same **Unterschied**; *what is the difference between these two products? differences in price or price differences;* **symmetric difference** = logical function whose output is true if either of the inputs is true, and false if both inputs are the same **symmetrische Differenz**

◇ **different** *adjective* not the same **anders, unterschiedlich**; *our product range is quite different in design from the Japanese models; we offer ten models each in six different colours*

◇ **differential** *adjective* which shows a difference **verschieden; differential PCM** = DIFFERENTIAL PULSE CODED MODULATION pulse coded modulation that uses the difference in size of a sample value and the previous one, requiring fewer bits when transmitting **Differentialpulscodemodulation**

diffuse *verb* to move *or* insert something over an area *or* through a substance **diffundieren**; *the smoke from the faulty machine rapidly diffused through the building; the chemical was diffused into the substrate*

◇ **diffusion** *noun* means of transferring doping materials into an integrated circuit substrate **Diffusion**

digipulse telephone *noun* push button telephone dialling method using coded pulses **Tastentelefon**

digit *noun* symbol *or* character which represents an integer that is smaller than the radix of the number base used **Ziffer**; *a phone number with eight digits or an eight-digit phone number; the decimal digit 8; the decimal number system uses the digits 0123456789;* **check digit** = additional digit inserted into transmitted text to monitor and correct errors **Prüfziffer**; **digit place** *or* **position** = position of a digit within a number **Ziffernstelle**; *see also* RADIX

◇ **digital** *adjective* which represents data *or* physical quantities in numerical form (especially using a binary system in computer related devices) **digital**; **digital audio disk (DAD)** = method of recording sound by converting and storing signals in a digital form on magnetic disk, providing very high quality reproduction **digitale Tonplatte**; *see also* COMPACT DISK; **digital audio tape (DAT)** = method of recording sound by converting and storing signals in a digital form on magnetic tape, providing very high quality reproduction **digitales Tonband**; **digital cassette** = high quality magnetic tape housed in a standard size cassette with write protect tabs, and a standard format leader **Digitalkassette**; **digital circuit** = electronic circuit that operates on digital information providing logical functions *or* switching **digitaler Stromkreis**; **digital clock** = clock which shows the time as a series of digits (such as 12:22:04) **Digitaluhr**; **digital computer** = computer which processes data in digital form (that is data represented in discrete digital form) **Digitalrechner**; *compare* ANALOG; **digital data** = data represented in (usually binary) numerical form **digitale Daten**; **digital logic** = applying Boolean algebra to hardware circuits **digitale Logik**; **digital multimeter (DMM)** = multimeter that uses a digital readout (giving better clarity than an AMM) **digitales Multimeter**; **digital optical recording (DOR)** = recording signals in binary form as small holes in the surface of an optical *or* compact disk which can then be read by laser **digitale optische Aufzeichnung**; **digital output** = computer output in digital form **Digitalausgabe**; *compare with* ANALOG OUTPUT; **digital plotter** = plotter whose pen position is controllable in discrete steps, so that drawings in the computer can be output graphically **digitaler Plotter**; **digital read-out** = data displayed in numerical form, such as numbers on an LCD in a calculator **digitale Sichtanzeige**; **digital recording** = conversion of sound signals into a digital form and storing them on magnetic disk *or* tape usually in binary form **Digitalaufnahme**; **digital representation** = data *or* quantities represented using discrete quantities (digits) **digitale Darstellung**; **digital resolution** = smallest number that can be represented with one digit, the value assigned to the least significant bit of a word *or* number **digitale Auflösung**; **digital signal** = electric signal that has only a number of possible states, as opposed to analog signals which are continuously variable **digitales Signal**; **digital signalling** = control and dialling codes sent down a (telephone line) in digital form **digitale Signalisierung**; **digital signature** = unique identification code sent by a terminal *or* device in digital form **digitale Signatur**; **digital speech** *see* SPEECH SYNTHESIS; **digital system** = system that deals with digital signals **Digitalsystem**; **digital switching** = operating communications connections and switches only by use of digital signals **digitale Vermittlung**; **digital to analog converter** *or* **D to A converter (DAC)** = circuit that converts a digital signal to an analog one (the analog signal is proportional to an input binary number) **Digital-Analog-Umsetzer**; **digital transmission system** = communications achieved by converting analog signals to a digital form then modulating and transmitting this (the signal is then converted back to analog form at the receiver) **digitales Übertragungssystem**

◇ **digitally** *adverb* (quantity represented) in digital form **digital**; *the machine takes digitally recorded data and generates an image*

digitize *verb* to change analog movement *or* signals into a digital form which can be processed by computers, etc. **digitalisieren**; *we can digitize your signature to allow it to be printed with any laser printer;* **digitized photograph** = image *or* photograph that has been scanned to produce an analog signal which is then converted to digital form and stored *or* displayed on a computer **digitalisierte photographische Aufnahme**; **digitizing pad** = sensitive surface that translates the position of a pen into numerical form, so that drawings can be entered into a computer **Digitalisierblock**

> **digitizer** *noun* analog to digital converter *or* device which converts an analog movement *or* signal to a digital one which can be understood by a computer **Digitalisierer**

DIL = DUAL-IN-LINE PACKAGE standard layout for integrated circuit packages using two parallel rows of connecting pins along each side **DIL-Gehäuse, Doppelreihengehäuse**

dimension *noun* measurement of size **Dimension, Ausmaß;** *the dimensions of the computer are small enough for it to fit into a case*

> **dimensioning** *noun* definition of the size of something (usually an array *or* matrix) **Dimensionierung;** *array dimensioning occurs at this line*

diminished radix complement *noun* number representation in which each digit of the number is subtracted from one less than the radix **B1-Komplement;** *see also* ONE'S, NINE'S COMPLEMENT

DIN = DEUTSCHE INDUSTRIENORM German industry standards organization **DIN (deutsche Industrienorm)**

diode *noun* electronic component that allows an electrical current to pass in one direction and not the other **Diode; light-emitting diode (LED)** = semiconductor diode that emits light when a current is applied (used in clock and calculator displays, and as an indicator) **lichtaussendende Diode**

diopter *or* **dioptre** *noun* unit of measurement for the power of an optical lens **Dioptrie; diopter lens** = optical device that is placed in front of a standard camera lens when close up shots are required **Nahlinse**

DIP = DUAL-IN-LINE PACKAGE standard layout for integrated circuit packages using two parallel rows of connecting pins along each side **DIL-Gehäuse, Doppelreihengehäuse**

diplex *noun* simultaneous transmission of two signals over the same line **Diplex**

dipole *noun* (i) material *or* molecule *or* object that has two potentials, one end positive and the other negative, due to electron displacement from an applied electric field; (ii) short straight radio aerial

that receives a signal from a central connector **(i) Dipol; (ii) Dipolantenne**

direct

1 *verb* to manage *or* to organize **leiten; directed scan** = file *or* array search method in which a starting point and a direction of scan is provided, either up *or* down from the starting point (an address *or* record number) **gerichtete Suchmethode**
2 *adjective* straight *or* with no processing *or* going in a straight way **direkt; direct access** = storage and retrieval of data without the need to read other data first **Direktzugriff; direct (access) address** = ABSOLUTE ADDRESS; **direct access storage device (DASD)** = storage medium whose memory locations can be directly read *or* written to **Direktzugriffsspeicher; direct addressing** = method of addressing where the storage location address given in the instruction is the location to be used **direkte Adressierung; direct broadcast satellite (DBS)** = TV and radio signal broadcast over a wide area from an earth station via a satellite, received with a dish aerial **direktstrahlender Satellit; direct change-over** = switching from one computer to another in one go **Direktumschaltung; direct code** = binary code which directly operates the CPU, using only absolute addresses and values **Direktcode; direct coding** = program instructions written in absolute code **direkte Codierung; direct connect** = (modem) which plugs straight into the standard square telephone socket **Direktanschluß; direct current (DC)** = constant value electric current that flows in one direction **Gleichstrom; direct data entry (DDE)** = keying in data directly onto a magnetic disk *or* tape **direkte Dateneingabe; direct dialling** = calling a telephone number without passing through an internal exchange **Durchwählen; direct digital control (DDC)** = machine operated automatically by computer **direkte Digitalsteuerung; direct image film** = photographic film that produces a positive image **Umkehrfilm; direct impression** = use of a typewriter to compose a piece of text that is to be printed **Direktsatz; direct information access network for Europe (DIANE)** = services offered over the Euronet network **DIANE (direktes Informationsanschaltnetz für Europa); direct-insert routine** *or* **subroutine** = routine which can be directly copied (inserted) into a larger routine *or* program without the need for a call instruction **offenes Programm od Unterprogramm; direct instruction** = program command that contains an operand and the code for the operation to be carried out **Direktanweisung; direct inward dialling** = automatic routing of telephone calls in a private exchange **Durchwahl; direct mail** =

selling a product by sending publicity material to possible customers through the post **Direktwerbung; Direktversand;** *these calculators are only sold by direct mail; the company runs a successful direct-mail operation;* **direct-mail advertising** = advertising by sending leaflets to people through the post **Direktwerbung; direct memory access (DMA)** = direct, rapid link between a peripheral and a computer's main memory which avoids the use of accessing routines for each item of data required **direkter Speicherzugriff;** *direct memory access transfer between the main memory and the second processor;* **direct memory access channel** = high speed data transfer link **direkter Speicherzugriffskanal; direct mode** = typing in a command which is executed once return is pressed **Direktmodus; direct outward dialling** = automatic access to a telephone network form a private exchange **Amtswahl; direct page register** = register that provides memory page access data when a CPU is carrying out a direct memory access, to allow access to any part of memory **direktes Seitenregister; direct reference address** = virtual address that can only be altered by indexing **direkte Bezugsadresse; direct transfer** = bit for bit copy of the contents of one register into another register (including any status bits, etc.) **Direktübertragung**
3 *adverb* straight *or* with no third party involved **direkt; to dial direct** = to contact a phone number yourself without asking the operator to do it for you **durchwählen;** *you can dial New York direct from London if you want*

◊ **direction** *noun*
(a) organizing *or* managing **Leitung;** *he took over the direction of a software distribution group*
(b) directions for use = instructions showing how to use something **Gebrauchsanweisung;** NOTE: no plural for (a)

◊ **directional** *adjective* which points in a certain direction **gerichtet; directional antenna** = aerial that transmits *or* receives signals from a single direction **Richtantenne; directional pattern** = chart of the response of an aerial *or* microphone to signals from various directions **Richtdiagramm**

◊ **directive** *noun* programming instruction used to control the language translator, compiler, etc. **Übersetzungsanweisung**

◊ **directly** *adverb*
(a) immediately **sofort**
(b) straight *or* with no third party involved **direkt;** *we deal directly with the manufacturer, without using a wholesaler*

◊ **director** *noun*
(a) person appointed by the shareholders to help run a company **Direktor/-in; managing**

director = director who is in charge of the whole company **geschäftsführender Direktor; board of directors** = all the directors of a company **Vorstand; Aufsichtsrat**
(b) person who is in charge of a project, an official institute, etc. **Leiter/-in;** *the director of the government computer research institute; she was appointed director of the organization*
(c) person who controls the filming of a film *or* TV programme **Regisseur/-in; casting director** = person in charge of choosing the actors for a film *or* TV programme **(Rollen)besetzungsdirektor; lighting director** = person in charge of lighting in a film *or* TV studio **Beleuchtungstechniker; technical director** = person in charge of the technical equipment (especially the cameras) in a TV studio **technischer Direktor/Leiter, Studioleiter**

directory *noun*
(a) list of people *or* businesses with information about their addresses and telephone numbers **Adreßbuch; Telefonbuch; classified directory** = list of businesses grouped under various headings, such as computer shops *or* newsagents **Branchenverzeichnis; commercial directory** *or* **trade directory** = book which lists all the businesses and business people in a town **Handelsadreßbuch, Firmenverzeichnis; street directory** = list of people living in a street map of a town which lists all the streets in alphabetical order in an index **Adreßbuch, Straßenverzeichnis, Stadtplan; telephone directory** = book which lists all people and businesses in alphabetical order with their phone numbers **Telefonbuch;** *to look up a number in the telephone directory; his number is in the London directory*
(b) disk directory = list of names and information about files in a backing storage device **Plattenverzeichnis;** *the disk directory shows file name, date and time of creation* **directory routing** = means of directing messages in a packet switching network by a list of preferred routes at each node **Verzeichnisleitweg**

dirty bit *noun* flag bit set by memory-resident programs (a utility *or* the operating system) to indicate that they have already been loaded into main memory **Kennbit**

disable *verb* to prevent a device *or* function from operating **ausschalten, sperren;** *he disabled the keyboard to prevent anyone changing the data;* **disable interrupt** = command to the CPU to ignore any interrupt signals **unwirksame Unterbrechung**

disarm *verb* to prevent an interrupt having any effect **desaktivieren; disarmed state** = state of an interrupt that has been disabled, and cannot accept a signal **Desaktivierung**

disassemble *verb* to translate machine code instructions back into assembly language mnemonics **rückassemblieren**
◇ **disassembler** *noun* software that translates a machine code program back into an assembly language form **Rückassemblierer, Disassembler**

disaster dump *noun* program and data dump just before *or* caused by a fatal error *or* system crash **Programm- und Datennotausdruck**

disc = DISK
NOTE: disc is the more usual spelling in the USA

discard *verb* to throw out something which is not needed **verwerfen**

disclose *verb* to reveal details of something which were supposed to be secret **enthüllen**
◇ **disclosure** *noun* act of telling details about something **Offenlegung**

disconnect *verb* to unplug *or* break a connection between two devices **trennen, abschalten;** *do not forget to disconnect the cable before moving the printer*

discrete *adjective* (values *or* events *or* energy *or* data) which occurs in small individual units **diskret;** *the data word is made up of discrete bits*

discretionary *adjective* which can be used if wanted *or* not used if not wanted **benutzerbestimmbar; discretionary hyphen** *or* **soft hyphen** = hyphen which is inserted to show that a word is broken (as at the end of a line), but which is not present when the word is written normally **weiches Trennungszeichen**

discrimination instruction *noun* conditional program instruction that directs control by providing the location of the next instruction to be executed (if a condition is met) **logische Entscheidung;** *see also* BRANCH, JUMP, CALL

dish aerial *noun* circular concave directional aerial used to pick up long distance transmissions **Parabolantenne;** *we use a dish aerial to receive signals from the satellite*

disjointed *adjective* (set of information *or* data) that has no common subject **unzusammenhängend**

disjunction *noun* logical function that produces a true output if any input is true **Disjunktion**
◇ **disjunctive search** *noun* search for data items that match at least one of a number of keys **disjunktive Suche**

disk *noun* flat circular plate coated with a substance that is capable of being magnetized (data is stored on this by magnetizing selective sections to represent binary digits) **Platte; backup disk** = disk which contains a copy of the information from other disks, as a security precaution **Datensicherungsplatte; disk access** = operations required to read from or write to a magnetic disk, including device selection, sector and track address, movement of read/write head to the correct location, access location on disk **Plattenzugriff; disk-based (operating system)** = (operating system) held on floppy *or* hard disk **auf Platten basierend; disk cartridge** = protective case containing a removable hard disk **Plattenkassette; disk controller** = IC *or* circuits used to translate a request for data by the CPU into control signals for the disk drive (including motor control and access arm movement) **Plattensteuereinheit; disk-controller card** = add-on card that contains all the electronics and connectors to interface a disk drive to a CPU **Plattensteuereinheitskarte; disk crash** = fault caused by the read/write head touching the surface of the disk **Plattenabsturz; disk drive** = device that spins a magnetic disk and controls the position of the read/write head **Plattenlaufwerk; disk file** = number of related records *or* data items stored under one name on disk **Plattendatei; disk formatting** = initial setting up of a blank disk with track and sector markers and other control information **Plattenformatierung; disk index holes** = holes around the hub of a disk that provide rotational information to a disk controller *or* number of holes providing sector location indicators on a hard-sectored disk **Plattenindexlöcher; disk map** = display of the organization of data on a disk **Plattendarstellung; disk operating system (DOS)** = section of the operating system software that controls disk and file management **DOS, Plattenbetriebssystem; MS disk operating system** *or* **Microsoft DOS (MS-DOS)** = popular DOS for microcomputers **MS-DOS; disk pack** = number of disks on a single hub, each with its own read/write head **Plattenstapel; disk sector** = smallest area on a magnetic disk that can be addressed by a computer **Plattensektor; disk storage** = using disks as a backing store **Plattenspeicher; disk track** = one of a series of (thin) concentric rings on a magnetic disk, which the read/write head accesses and along which data is stored in separate sectors **Plattenspur; disk unit** = disk drive **Platteneinheit; fixed disk** = magnetic disk which cannot be removed from the disk drive **Festplatte; floppy disk** = small disk for storing information which can be removed from a computer **Diskette; hard disk** = solid disk which will store a large amount of computer information in a sealed case, and cannot usually be removed from the computer **Festplatte; optical disk** = disk which contains binary data in the form of small holes which are read by a laser beam (also called WORM (write one, read many) when used on computers) **optische Platte; Winchester disk** = hard disk with a large storage capacity sealed in a computer **Winchesterplatte**

> COMMENT: the disk surface is divided into tracks and sectors which can be accessed individually; magnetic tapes cannot be accessed in this way

◊ **diskette** *noun* light, flexible disk that can store data in a magnetic form, used in most personal computers **Diskette**

◊ **diskless** *adjective* which does not use disks for data storage **plattenlos;** *diskless system; they want to create a diskless workstation*

disorderly close-down *noun* system crash that did not provide enough warning to carry out an orderly close-down **unplanmäßiger Abschluß**

dispatch *or* **despatch** *noun* action of sending material *or* information *or* messages to a location **Senden**

dispenser *noun* device which gives out something **Spender, Automat; cash dispenser** = device which gives money when a card is inserted and special instructions keyed in **Bargeldautomat**

dispersion *noun*
(a) separation of a beam of light into its different wavelengths **Dispersion, Streuung**
(b) logical function whose output is false if all inputs are true, and true if any input is false **NAND-Funktion**

displacement *noun* offset used in an indexed address **Distanz(adresse)**

display

1 *noun* device on which information *or* images can be presented visually **Datensichtgerät, Bildschirm; display adapter** = device which allows information in a computer to be displayed on a CRT (the adapter interfaces with both the computer and CRT) **Bildschirmanschluß; display attribute** = variable which defines the shape *or* size *or* colour of text *or* graphics displayed **Bildschirmvariable; display character** = graphical symbol which appears as a printed *or* displayed item, such as one of the letters of the alphabet *or* a number **Zeichen auf dem Bildschirm; display character generator** = ROM that provides the display circuits with a pattern of dots which form the character **Zeichengenerator; display colour** = colour of characters in a (videotext) display system **Bildschirmfarbe; display controller** = device that accepts character *or* graphics codes and instructions, and converts them into dot-matrix patterns that are displayed on a screen **Bildschirmsteuereinheit; display format** = number of characters that can be displayed on a screen, given as row and column lengths **Bildschirmformat; display highlights** = emphasis of certain words *or* paragraphs by changing character display colour **Intensivanzeige; display line** = horizontal printing positions for characters in a line of text **Bildzeile; display mode** = way of referring to the character set to be used, usually graphics *or* alphanumerics **Anzeigemodus; display processor** = processor that changes data to a format suitable for a display controller **Bildschirmprozessor; display register** = register that contains character *or* control *or* graphical data that is to be displayed **Anzeigeregister; display resolution** = number of pixels per unit area that a display can clearly show **Bildschirmauflösung; display screen** = the physical part of a Visual Display Unit *or* terminal *or* monitor, which allows the user to see characters *or* graphics (usually a Cathode Ray Tube, but sometimes LCD *or* LED displays are used) **Bildschirm; display scrolling** = movement of a screenful of information up or down one line or pixel at a time **Bildschirmblättern; display size** = character size greater than 14 points, used in composition and headlines rather than normal text **Bildschirmgröße; display space** = memory *or* amount of screen available to show graphics *or* text **Darstellungsfläche; display unit** = computer terminal *or* piece of equipment that is capable of showing data

· information, usually by means of CRT **ildschirm; gas discharge** or **plasma** or **lectroluminescent display** = flat **ghtweight** display screen that is made up **f** two flat pieces of glass covered with a **rid** of conductors, separated by a thin **ayer** of gas which luminesces when a point **f** the grid is selected by two electrical **gnals Plasmabildschirm;** see also VISUAL **ISPLAY UNIT**

verb to show information **anzeigen;** the **ustomer's** details were displayed on the **reen;** by keying HELP, the screen will **splay** the options available to the user

QUOTE the review machine also came with a monochrome display card plugged into one of the expansion slots
Personal Computer World

istant adjective which is located some **ay** away **entfernt;** the distant printers are **nnected** with cables

istinguish verb to tell the difference **tween** two things **unterscheiden;** the OCR **as** difficulty in distinguishing certain **haracters**

istort verb to introduce unwanted **ifferences** between a signal input and **utput** from a device **verzerren**

◊ **distortion** noun unwanted differences in signal before and after it has passed **rough** a piece of equipment **Verzerrung; istortion optics** = special photographic **ns** used to produce a distorted image for **ecial** effects **Verzerrungsobjektiv; image istortion** = fault in an optical lens causing **e** image to be distorted **Bildverzerrung**

istribute verb
a) to send out data or information to users **a** network or system **verteilen; distributed daptive routing** = directing messages in a **acket** network switching system by an **xchange** of information between nodes **erteilte adaptive Verkehrslenkung; istributed database system** = data system **here** the data is kept on different disks in **ifferent** places **verteiltes Datenbanksystem; istributed data processing (DDP)** = **perations** to derive information from data **hich** is kept in different places **verteilte atenverarbeitung; distributed file system** = **ystem** that uses files stored in more than **ne** location or backing store but are **rocessed** at a central point **verteiltes ateisystem; distributed intelligence** = **ecentralized** system in which a number of **nall** micros or mini-computers carry out a **et** of fixed (tasks rather than one large **omputer**) **verteilte Intelligenz; distributed**

(data) processing = system of processing in a large organization with many small computers at different workstations instead of one central computer **verteilte Datenverarbeitung; distributed system** = computer system which uses more than one processor in different locations, all connected to a central computer **Verbundsystem**

◊ **distribution** noun act of sending information out, especially via a network **Verteilung; distribution network** see LAN, WAN; **distribution point** = point from which cable television or telephone signals are split up from a main line and sent to individual users' homes **Verzweigungseinrichtung**

dittogram noun printing error caused by repeating the same letter twice **Dittographie**

DIV = DATA IN VOICE digital satellite data transmission in place of a voice channel **Datenübertragung auf Sprachfrequenz**

divergence noun failure of light or particle beams to meet at a certain point **Abweichung, Divergenz**

diversity noun coming from more than one source; being aimed at more than one use **Vielfalt; beam diversity** = using a single frequency communications band for two different sets of data **Frequenzbandaufteilung**

diverter noun circuit or device that redirects a message or signal from one path or route to another **Umleiter; call diverter** = device which, on receiving a telephone call, contacts another point and re-routes the call **Anrufumleiter**

divide verb
(a) to divide a number by four = to find out how many fours can be contained in the other number **eine Zahl durch vier teilen;** twenty-one divided by three gives seven
(b) to cut or to split into parts **trennen;** in the hyphenation program, long words are automatically divided at the end of lines

◊ **divider** noun **frequency divider** = circuit which divides the frequency of a signal by a certain amount to change the pitch **Frequenzteiler**

◊ **division** noun act of dividing **Division; Trennung**

dividend noun operand that is divided by a divisor in a division operation **Dividend**

COMMENT: the dividend is divided by the divisor to form the quotient and a remainder

divisor *noun* operand used to divide a dividend in a division operation **Divisor**

DMA = DIRECT MEMORY ACCESS direct rapid link between a peripheral and a computer's main memory, which avoids the use of accessing routines for each item of data read **direkter Speicherzugriff; DMA controller** = interface IC that controls high-speed data transfer between a high-speed peripheral and main memory, usually the controller will also halt *or* cycle steal from the CPU **direkte Speicherzugriffssteuerung; DMA cycle stealing** = CPU allowing the DMA controller to send data over the bus during clock cycles when it performs internal *or* NOP instructions **DMA-Zyklusraub**

DML = DATA MANIPULATION LANGUAGE

DMM = DIGITAL MULTIMETER

do-nothing (instruction) *noun* programming instruction that does not carry out any action (except increasing the program counter to the next instruction address **Leerbefehl**

docket *noun (US)* record of an official proceeding **(Vorgehens)erklärung**

document
1 *noun* piece of paper with writing on it *or* file containing text **Schriftstück, Beleg; document assembly** *or* **document merge** = creating a new file by combining two or more sections *or* complete documents **Zusammenstellung eines Schriftstücks; document processing** = processing of documents (such as invoices) by a computer **Belegbearbeitung; document reader** = device which converts written *or* typed information to a form that a computer can understand and process **Belegleser; document recovery** = program which allows a document which has been accidentally deleted to be recovered **Belegwiederherstellung; document retrieval system** = information storage and retrieval system that contains complete documents rather than just quotes *or* references **System zum Dokumentenretrieval**
2 *verb* to write a description of a process **beschreiben**
◇ **documentation** *noun*

(a) all documents referring to somethin **Dokumentation;** *please send a documentation concerning the product*
(b) information, notes and diagrams tha describe the function, use and operation o a piece of hardware *or* softwar **(Programm)unterlagen**
NOTE: no plural

dollar sign *noun* printed *or* writte character (\$) used in some languages t identify a variable as a string typ **Dollarzeichen**

domain *noun* **public domain** information *or* program which belongs t and is available to the public **Gemeingu program which is in the public domain** program which is not copyrighted **nich urheberrechtlich geschütztes Programm**

domestic *adjective* referring to the hom market *or* the market of the country wher the business is based **Inlands-, Binnen-domestic consumption** = consumption o the home market **Inlandskonsum; domesti market** = market in the country where company is based **Binnenmarkt;** *they produc goods for the domestic market;* **domesti production** = production of goods fo domestic consumption **Binnenproduktion domestic satellite** = satellite used fo television *or* radio transmission, rathe than research *or* military application **Radio- und Fernsehsatellit**

dongle *noun* coded circuit *or* chip that ha to be present in a system before a piece o copyright software will run **Dongle, Key**

dope *verb* to introduce a dopant into substance **dotieren**
◇ **dopant** *noun* chemical substance that i diffused *or* implanted onto the substrate o a chip during manufacture, to provide i with n- or p-type properties **Dotierungssto**
◇ **doped** *adjective* (chip) which has had dopant added **dotiert**
◇ **doping** *noun* adding of dopant to a chi **Dotierung**

DOR = DIGITAL OPTICAL READIN recording signals in binary form as sma holes in the surface of an optical *or* compac disk which can then be read by lase **digitales optisches Lesen**

DOS = DISK OPERATING SYSTEM sectio of the operating system software, tha controls the disk and file access **DOS Plattenbetriebssystem;** *boot up the DOS afte you switch on the PC*

lot *noun* small round spot **Punkt; dot command** = method of writing instructions with a full stop followed by the command, sed mainly for embedded commands in word-processor systems **Punktbefehl; dot matrix** = forming characters by use of dots inside a rectangular matrix **Punktmatrix; ots per inch** *or* **d.p.i.** *or* **dpi** = standard method used to describe the resolution capabilities of a page printer *or* scanner **unkte pro Inch;** *some laser printers offer igh resolution printing: 400 dpi*

◇ **dot-matrix printer** *noun* printer in which he characters are made up by a series of losely spaced dots (it produces a page line y line; a dot-matrix printer can be used ither for printing using a ribbon *or* for normal *or* electrostatic printing) **Matrixdrucker**

QUOTE the characters are formed from an array of dots like in a dot-matrix printer, except that much higher resolution is used
Practical Computing

double *adjective* twice; twice as large; twice the size **doppelt; double buffering** = use of two buffers, allowing one to be read while the other is being written to **doppelte Pufferung; double dagger** = typeset character used as a second reference mark **Doppelkreuz; double density** = system to double the storage capacity of a disk drive by doubling the number of bits which can be put on the disk surface **doppelte Speicherkapazität; double-density disk** = disk that can store two bits of data per unit area, compared to a standard disk **Platte mit doppelter Speicherkapazität; double document** = error in photographing documents for microfilm, where the same image appears consecutively **Doublette, Doppelbild; double ended queue (deque)** = queue in which new items can be added to either end **nach beiden Seiten offene Warteschlange; double exposure** = two images exposed on the same piece of photographic film, usually used for special effects **Doppelbelichtung; double-length** *or* **double precision arithmetic** = use of two data words to store a number, providing greater precision **Rechnen mit doppelter Stellenzahl; double sideband** = modulation technique whose frequency spectrum contains two modulated signals above and below the unmodulated carrier frequency **Zweiseitenbandübertragung; double sideband suppressed carrier (DSBSC)** = modulation technique that uses two modulated signal sidebands but no carrier signal **Zweiseitenbandübertragung mit unterdrückter Trägerwelle; double-sided disk** = disk which can store information on both sides **beidseitig beschreibbare Platte; double-sided**

disk drive = disk drive which can access data on double-sided disks **doppelseitiges Plattenlaufwerk; double-sided printed circuit board** = circuit board with conducting tracks on both sides **beidseitig gedruckte Schaltkarte; double word** = two bytes of data handled as one word, often used for address data **Doppelwort**

doublet *or* **diad** *noun* word made up of two bits **Diade, Zwei-Bit-Byte**

down *adverb (of computers or programs)* not working **ausgefallen;** *the computer system went down twice during the afternoon;* **down stroke** = wide heavy section of a character written with an ink pen **Abstrich; down time** = period of time during which a computer system is not working *or* usable **Ausfallzeit;** (NOTE: opposite is **up**)

download *verb* (i) to load a program *or* section of data from a remote computer via a telephone line; (ii) to load data from a mainframe to a small computer; (iii) to send printer font data stored on a disk to a printer (where it will be stored in temporary memory *or* RAM) **(i) fernladen; (ii) hinunterladen; (iii) Zeichensätze laden;** *there is no charge for downloading public domain software from the BBS*

◇ **downloadable** *adjective* which can be downloaded **fernladbar, hinunterladbar; downloadable fonts** = fonts *or* typefaces stored on a disk, which can be downloaded *or* sent to a printer and stored in temporary memory *or* RAM **zusätzlich ladbare Zeichensätze, Download-Fonts**

downward *adjective* towards a lower position **abwärts; downward compatibility** = ability of a complex computer system to work with a simple computer **Abwärtskompatibilität;** *the mainframe is downward compatible with the micro*

dp *or* **DP** = DATA PROCESSING operating on data to produce useful information *or* to sort and organize data files **DV, Datenverarbeitung**

d.p.i. *or* **dpi** = DOTS PER INCH standard method used to describe the resolution capabilities of a dot-matrix *or* laser printer *or* scanner **Punkte pro Inch;** *a 300 d.p.i. black and white A4 monitor; a 300 dpi image scanner*

COMMENT: 300 d.p.i. is the normal industry standard for a laser printer

DPM = DATA PROCESSING MANAGER

draft

1 *noun* rough copy of a document before errors have been corrected **Entwurf; draft printing** = low quality, high speed printing **Drucken mit geringerer Druckqualität**
2 *verb* to make a rough copy *or* drawing **einen Entwurf machen, entwerfen;** *he drafted out the details of the program on a piece of paper*

drag *verb* to move (a mouse) with a control key pressed, so moving an image on screen **(ver)schieben;** *you can enlarge a frame by clicking inside its border and dragging to the position wanted*

> QUOTE press the mouse button and drag the mouse: this produces a dotted rectangle on the screen
> QUOTE you can easily enlarge the frame by dragging from any of the eight black rectangles round the border, showing that it is selected
> *Desktop Publishing*

drain

1 *noun* electrical current provided by a battery *or* power supply; connection to a FET **Drain(strom)** ⇨ APPENDIX
2 *verb* to remove *or* decrease power *or* energy from a device such as a battery **Strom entnehmen**

DRAM = DYNAMIC RANDOM ACCESS MEMORY

> QUOTE cheap bulk memory systems are always built from DRAMs
> *Electronics & Power*

D-region *noun* section of the ionosphere 50-90km above the earth's surface **D-Schicht der Ionosphäre;** *the D-region is the main cause of attenuation in transmitted radio signals*

drift *noun* changes in the characteristics of a circuit with time *or* changing temperature **Drift, Abwanderung**

drive

1 *noun* part of a computer which operates a tape *or* disk **Laufwerk; disk drive** = device which spins a magnetic disk and controls the position of the read/write head **Plattenlaufwerk; tape drive** = mechanism that carries magnetic tape over the drive heads **Bandlaufwerk**
2 *verb* to make a tape *or* disk work **antreiben;** *the disk is driven by a motor*
◊ **driven** *adjective* operated by something **angetrieben; control driven** = computer architecture where instructions are executed once a control sequence has been received **kontrollgesteuert; event-driven** = computer program *or* process where each step of the execution relies on external actions **ereignisgesteuert**

◊ **driver** *or* **handler** *noun* program *or* routine used to interface and manage an input/output device *or* other peripheral **Treiber; printer driver** = dedicated software that controls and formats users' commands ready for a printer **Drucker-Treiber**

DRO = DESTRUCTIVE READOUT form of storage medium that loses its data after it has been read **löschendes Auslesen**

drop *noun* fall to a lower position **abfallen, hinunterfallen; drop cap** = first letter in a sentence, printed in a larger typeface than the rest of the sentence **Initiale (in einer großen Schriftgröße); drop dead halt** *or* **dead halt** = program instruction from the user *or* an error that causes the program to stop without allowing recovery **von außen herbeigeführte Programmunterbrechung; drop line** = cable television line, running from a feeder cable to a users home **Stichleitung**
◊ **drop in** *noun* small piece of dirt that is on a disk *or* tape surface, which does not allow data to be recorded on that section **Störsignal**
◊ **drop out** *noun*
(a) failure of a small piece of tape *or* disk to be correctly magnetized for the accurate storage of data
(b) loss of transmitted signals due to attenuation *or* noise **Signalausfall**

drum *noun* early type of magnetic computer storage **Trommelspeicher, magnetic drum** = cylindrical magnetic storage device **Magnettrommelspeicher; drum plotter** = computer output device that consists of a movable pen and a piece of paper around a drum that can be rotated, creating patterns and text when both are moved in various ways **Trommelplotter**

dry cell *noun* battery that cannot be recharged **Trockenelement;** *compare with* RECHARGEABLE BATTERY
◊ **dry circuit** *noun* voice signal transmitting circuit that contains no DC signals *or* levels **trockener Schaltkreis**
◊ **dry contact** *noun* faulty electrical connection, often causing an intermittent fault **trockener Kontakt**
◊ **dry joint** *noun* faulty *or* badly made electrical connection **trockene Verbindung**
◊ **dry run** *noun* running a program with test data to check everything works **Probelauf**

DSBSC = DOUBLE SIDEBAND SUPPRESSED CARRIER

DSE = DATA SWITCHING EXCHANGE

DSR = DATA SET READY signal from a device that it is ready to accept data, this signal occurs after a DTR signal is received **Betriebsbereitschaft (zum Empfang)**

DSW = DEVICE STATUS WORD data word transmitted from a device that contains information about its current status **Einheitenstatuswort**

DTE = DATA TERMINAL EQUIPMENT device at which a communications path starts or finishes **Datenendeinrichtung**

DTMF = DUAL TONE, MULTIFREQUENCY communication signalling system, using two different frequencies to transmit binary data **Mehrfrequenzwahlverfahren**

DTP = DESKTOP PUBLISHING the design, layout and printing of documents using special software, a desktop computer and a printer **Desktop Publishing, Publizieren am Schreibtisch**

DTR = DATA TERMINAL READY signal from a device that indicates that it is ready to send data **Betriebsbereitschaft (zum Senden)**

dual *adjective* using two or a pair **doppelt; dual channel** = two separate audio recording paths, as found in stereo equipment **Zweikanalsystem; dual clocking** = multiplexed data, each set of data is available and valid on a different clock pulse or edge **doppelte Taktgabe; dual column** = two separate parallel lists of information **Doppelreihe; dual-in-line package (DIL or DIP)** = standard layout for integrated circuit packages using two parallel rows of connecting pins along each edge **Doppelreihengehäuse, DIL-Gehäuse; dual port memory** = memory with two sets of data and memory lines to allow communications between CPUs **Dual-Port-Speicher; dual processor** = computer system with two processors for faster program execution **Dualprozessor(system); dual systems** = two computer systems, working in parallel on the same data, with the same instructions, to ensure high reliability **Doppelsystem; dual tone, multifrequency (DTMF)** = communication signalling system using two different frequencies to transmit binary data **Mehrfrequenzwahlverfahren**

dub *verb* to add sound to a film after the film has been shot (usually to add a sound version in another language) **synchronisieren; dubbed sound** = sound effects added after the film has been shot **einsynchronisierter Toneffekt; Untermalung**

◇ **dubbing** *noun* action of adding sound to a film after the film has been shot **Synchronisation**

duct *noun* pipe containing cables, providing a tidy and protective surrounding for a group of cables **Kabelkanal**

dumb terminal *noun* peripheral that can only transmit and receive data from a computer, but is not capable of processing data **nichtprogrammierbare Datenstation;** *compare* INTELLIGENT TERMINAL

dummy *noun* imitation product to test the reaction of potential customers to its design **Versuchsmuster; dummy instruction** = instruction in a program that is only there to satisfy language syntax or to make up a block length **leere Anweisung; dummy variable** = variable set up to satisfy the syntax of a language, but which is replaced when the program is executed **Scheinvariable**

dump
1 *noun* (i) data which has been copied from one device to another for storage; (ii) *(US)* printout of the contents of all or selected data in memory **(i) Sicherungskopie; (ii) Speicherauszug; binary dump** = sections of memory dumped onto another medium or printed out in binary form **binärer Speicherauszug; change dump** = printout of all the locations whose contents have been changed during a program run **Speicherauszug der Änderungen; dump and restart** = software that will stop a program execution, dump any relevant data or program status then restart the program **ausgeben und neu anfangen; dump point** = point in a program where the program and its data are saved onto backing store to minimize the effects of any future faults **Speicherauszugspunkt; screen dump** = outputting the text or graphics displayed on a screen to a printer **Bildschirmausdruck**
2 *verb* to move data from one device or storage area to another **kopieren;** *the account results were dumped to the backup disk*

duodecimal number system *noun*
number system with a radix of twelve
Duodezimalsystem

duplex *noun*
(a) photographic paper that is light
sensitive on both sides **Duplexpapier**
(b) simultaneous transmission of two
signals on one line **Duplexübertragung;**
duplex circuit = electronic circuit used to
transmit data in two directions
simultaneously **Gegenverkehrsverbindung;**
duplex computer = two identical computer
systems used in an on-line application,
with one used as a backup in case of failure
of the other **Duplexsystem; duplex operation**
= transmission of data in two directions
simultaneously **Duplexbetrieb;** *see also*
HALF-DUPLEX, FULL DUPLEX, SIMPLEX

duplicate
1 *noun* copy **Duplikat, Zweitschrift, Kopie;** *he
sent me the duplicate of the contract;*
duplicate receipt *or* **duplicate of a receipt** =
copy of a receipt **Quittungsduplikat; in
duplicate** = with a copy **in doppelter
Ausfertigung; receipt in duplicate** = two
copies of a receipt **Quittung in doppelter
Ausfertigung;** *to print an invoice in duplicate*
2 *verb* to copy **kopieren; to duplicate a letter**
= to make a copy of a letter **einen Brief
kopieren**
◊ **duplicating** *noun* copying **Kopieren;
duplicating machine** = machine which
makes copies of documents **Kopierer;
duplicating paper** = special paper to be used
in a duplicating machine **Kopierpapier**
◊ **duplication** *noun* copying of documents
Vervielfältigung; duplication of work = work
which is done twice without being
necessary **Arbeitswiederholung**
◊ **duplicator** *noun* machine which
produces multiple copies from a master
Vervielfältiger; duplicator paper = absorbent
paper used in a duplicator **Umdruckpapier**

durable *adjective* which will not be
destroyed easily **dauerhaft;** *durable cartridge*

duration *noun* length of time for which
something lasts **Dauer; pulse duration
modulation (PDM)** = pulse modulation
where the pulse width depends on the input
signal **Impulsdauermodulation**

dustcover *noun* protective cover for a
machine **Abdeckhaube**

duty-rated *adjective* referring to the
maximum number of operations which a
device can perform in a set time to a
certain specification **bezogen auf die
Nutzleistung**

DUV = DATA UNDER VOICE data
transmission in a frequency range *or*
channel lower than that of a human voice
Datenübertragung unter Sprachfrequenz

dyadic operation *noun* binary
operation using two binary operands
dyadische Operation

dynamic *adjective* referring to data which
can change with time **dynamisch; dynamic
allocation** = system where resources are
allocated during a program run, rather than
being determined in advance **dynamische
Zuteilung; dynamic buffer** = buffer whose
size varies with demand **dynamische Puffer;
dynamic data structure** = structure of a data
management system which can be changed
or adapted **dynamische Datenstruktur;
dynamic dump** = dump that is carried out
periodically during a program run
**dynamischer Speicherauszug; dynamic
memory** *or* **dynamic RAM** = random access
memory that requires its contents to be
updated regularly **dynamischer Speicher;
dynamic microphone** = microphone using a
coil that moves and induces a voltage
according to sound pressure **dynamisches
Mikrophon; dynamic multiplexing** = time
division multiplexing method which
allocates time segments to signals
according to demand **dynamische
Multiplexmethode; dynamic range** = range of
softest to loudest sounds that a device *or*
instrument can produce **Lautstärkeumfang,
Aussteuerbereich; dynamic relocation
(program)** = program that is moved from
one section of memory to another during
its run-time without affecting it *or* its data
dynamische Verschiebung; dynamic stop =
stop in a process where the system tells the
user that some action must be taken before
the processing will continue **bedingter
Programmstop; dynamic storage allocation** =
to allocate memory to a program when it
needs it rather than reserving a block
before it has run **dynamische
Speicherplatzzuordnung; dynamically
redefinable character set** = computer *or*
videotext character set that can be changed
when required **dynamisch neu definierbarer
Zeichensatz; dynamic subroutine** =
subroutine whose function must be defined
each time it is called **dynamisches
Unterprogramm;** *compare* STATIC

Ee

E hexadecimal number equivalent to decimal number 14 **E**

EAN = EUROPEAN ARTICLE NUMBER numbering system for bar codes (European version of UPC) **EAN (Europäische Artikelnummer bei Streifencodes)**

EAPROM = ELECTRICALLY ALTERABLE PROGRAMMABLE READ-ONLY MEMORY version of EAROM which can be programmed **EAPROM (elektrisch veränderbarer, programmierbarer Festwertspeicher)**

EAROM = ELECTRICALLY ALTERABLE READ-ONLY MEMORY

earth
1 *noun*
(a) the planet on which we live **Erde; earth coverage** = area of the earth's surface able to pick up a satellite's transmissions **Empfangsbereich; earth station** = dish antenna and circuitry used to communicate with a satellite **Bodenstation**
(b) connection in a circuit representing zero potential **Erde;** *all loose wires should be tied to earth;* **earth wire** = connecting wire between an electrical device and the earth, representing zero potential **Erdung**
2 *verb* to connect an electrical device to the earth **erden;** *all appliances must be earthed*
NOTE: US English is **ground**

easy-to-use *adjective* that is simple to understand and operate **einfach zu benutzen**

QUOTE it is a really easy-to-use, menu-driven program that allows you to produce presentation quality graphics with little or no training
Soft

EAX = ELECTRONIC AUTOMATIC EXCHANGE

EBCDIC = EXTENDED BINARY CODED DECIMAL INTERCHANGE CODE eight bit binary character coding system **EBCDIC-Code**

EBNF = EXTENDED BACKUS-NAUR FORM more flexible way of defining the syntax of a language **EBNF (erweiterte Backus-Naur-Form);** *see also* BNF

EBR = ELECTRON BEAM RECORDING (i) production of microfilm images by means of an electron beam; (ii) recording the output from a computer directly onto microfilm using an electron beam **(i) & (ii) Elektronenstrahlaufzeichnung(smethode)**

echo
1 *noun* return of a signal back to the source from which it was transmitted **Echo; echo chamber** = acoustic *or* electronic device used to increase the echo of a sound **Hallraum; echo check** = each character received at a terminal is returned to the transmitter and checked to ensure accurate data transmission **Echoprüfung; echo suppressor** = device used on long-distance speech lines to prevent echoing effects **Echosperre**
2 *verb* to return a received signal along the same transmission path **widerhallen**

ECL = EMITTER COUPLED LOGIC high-speed logic circuit design using the emitters of the transistors as output connections to other stages **emittergekoppelte Logik**

ECMA = EUROPEAN COMPUTER MANUFACTURERS ASSOCIATION; **ECMA symbols** = standard set of symbols used to draw flowcharts **Normen der ECMA (Zusammenschluß europäischer Computerhersteller)**

EDAC = ERROR DETECTION AND CORRECTION forward error correction system for data communications **Fehlererkennung und -korrektur**

edge *noun* side of a flat object *or* signal *or* clock pulse **Kante, Rand; edge board** *or* **card** = printed circuit board that has a series of contact strips along one edge allowing it to be inserted into an edge connector **gedruckte Schaltungen; edge connector** = long connector with a slot containing metal contacts to allow it to make electrical contact with an edge card **Randstecker; edge detection** = algorithm and routines used in image recognition to define the edges of an object **Randauswertung; edge notched card** = paper card which has punched holes along an edge to represent data **Kerblochkarte; edge-triggered** = process *or* circuit which is clocked *or* synchronized by the changing level (edge) of a clock signal rather than the level itself **taktflankengesteuert**

edit *verb* to change, correct and modify text *or* programs **aufbereiten, edieren; edit commands** = sequence of characters or keys that must be pressed to accomplish a function in an editor **EDIT-Befehle; edit key** = key that starts a function that makes an editor easier to use **EDIT-Taste;** *there are several special edit keys - this one will reformat the text;* **edit window** = area of the screen in which the user can display and edit text *or* graphics **EDIT-Fenster; editing plan** = detailed plan of how a film *or* TV programme is to be edited before being shown **Schnittliste; editing run** = processing to check that new data meets certain requirements before actually analysing the data and its implications **Aufbereitungslauf; editing symbol** = character on microfilm to aid positioning, cutting and editing of the frames **Aufbereitungssymbol; editing terms** = command words and instruction sequences used when editing **EDIT-Befehle; linkage editing** = combining separate programs together, and standardizing the calls and references within them **Binderprogramm, Linkage Editierung**

◊ **edition** *noun* all the copies of a book *or* newspaper printed at one time **Auflage;** *the second edition has had some changes to the text; did you see the late edition of the evening paper?*

◊ **editor** *noun*
(a) person who edits a film *or* book **Editor, Herausgeber**
(b) editor program = software that allows the user to select sections of a file and alter, delete or add to them **EDITOR, Textaufbereitungsprogramm;** · **line editor** = software in which only one line of a source program can be edited at a time **Zeilen-Editor; text editor** = piece of software used to enter and correct text *or* modify programs under development **Text-Editor**
(c) person in charge of a newspaper *or* a section of a newspaper **Chefredakteur;** *the editor of "The Times"; the paper's computer editor*

◊ **editorial**
1 *adjective* referring to an editor *or* to editing **redaktionell, Redaktions-; editorial processing centre** = number of small publishers that share a single computer to provide cheaper computing power **Redaktionstextverarbeitungszentrale**
2 *noun* main article in a newspaper, written by the editor **Leitartikel**

QUOTE an object orientated graphics editor enables you to add text to graphics
Byte
QUOTE while it has many formatting facilities, it does not include an editor with which to create the template for the report
Personal Computer World

EDP = ELECTRONIC DATA PROCESSING data processing using computers and electronic devices **EDV; EDP capability** =

word processor that is able to carry out certain data processing functions **Leistungen eines Datenverarbeitungssystems;** NOTE: EDP is more common in US English

EDS = EXCHANGEABLE DISK STORAGE disk drive using removable disk pack (as opposed to a fixed disk) **auswechselbarer Plattenspeicher**

educational *adjective* referring to education; which is used to teach **Bildungs-, Erziehungs-, Lehr-; educational TV** = television programme that is in some way educational **Bildungsprogramm (im Fernsehen)**

EEPROM = ELECTRICALLY ERASABLE PROGRAMMABLE READ-ONLY MEMORY

EEROM = ELECTRICALLY ERASABLE READ-ONLY MEMORY

QUOTE conventional EEPROM requires two transistors to store each bit of data
Electronics & Power

effective *adjective* which can be used to produce a certain result **effektiv, wirkungsvoll; effective address** = address resulting from the modification of an address **effektive Adresse; effective bandwidth** = usable frequency range of a system **effektive Bandbreite; effective instruction** = the resulting instruction executed after the modification of an original instruction **endgültiger Befehl; effective search speed** = rate of finding a particular section of information from a storage device **tatsächliche Suchgeschwindigkeit; effective throughput** = average throughput of a processor **effektive Verarbeitungsmenge**

◊ **effective aperture** *noun*
(a) received signal power at the output of an aerial **effektive Apertur**
(b) lens aperture after taking into account camera faults and lens defects **effektive Öffnung**

COMMENT: the effective aperture is measured as the ratio of focal length of the lens to the diameter of the diaphragm

efficient *adjective* which works well **leistungsfähig;** *the program is highly efficient at sorting files*

◊ **efficiently** *adverb* in an efficient way **leistungsfähig;** *the word-processing package has produced a series of labelled letters very efficiently*

◇ **efficiency** *noun* working well **Leistungsfähigkeit**; *he is doubtful about the efficiency of the new networking system*

EFT = ELECTRONIC FUNDS TRANSFER (SYSTEM) system where computers are used to transmit money to and from banks **elektronischer Zahlungsverkehr**

◇ **EFTPOS** = ELECTRONIC FUNDS TRANSFER POINT-OF-SALE terminal at a POS that is linked to a central computer which automatically transfers money from the customer's account to the shop's **elektronische Kasse**

EGA = ENHANCED GRAPHICS ADAPTER popular microcomputer high-resolution colour display standardized system **EGA (erweiterte Graphikkarte)**

QUOTE although the video BIOS services are enhanced by adding an EGA card, the DOS functions are not
.EXE

EHF = EXTREMELY HIGH FREQUENCY radio frequencies from 30 - 300GHz **extremhohe) Frequenz zwischen 30GHz und 300GHz**

EIA = ELECTRONIC INDUSTRY ASSOCIATION; **EIA interface** = standard defining interface signals, transmission rate and power, usually used to connect terminals to modems **Schnittstellennorm des Elektronikindustrieverbandes**

eight-bit (system) *noun* referring to an (old) small, low cost, low power home computer in which the CPU can process eight-bit words **8-Bit-System; eight-bit byte or octet** = byte made up of eight binary digits **Acht-Bit-Byte, Oktett;** *compare with* SIXTEEN, THIRTY-TWO BIT

◇ **eight-inch disk** *noun* high-capacity floppy disk which is eight inches in diameter **8-Zoll-Diskette; eight-inch drive** = disk drive for a eight-inch disk **8-Zoll-Laufwerk**

◇ **eighty-track disk** *noun* disk formatted to contain eighty tracks **Platte mit 80 Spuren; eighty-column screen** = screen that can display eighty characters horizontally **80-Spalten-Bildschirm**

either-or operation *noun* logical function that produces a true output if any input is true **ODER-Funktion**

◇ **either-way operation** *noun* data transmission in one direction at a time over a bidirectional channel **wechselseitige Datenübermittlung**

elapsed time *noun* time taken by the user to carry out a task on a computer **Gesamtverarbeitungszeit**

elastic banding *noun* method of defining the limits of an image on a computer screen by stretching a boundary around it **elastische Grenzen**

◇ **elastic buffer** *noun* buffer size that changes according to demand **elastischer Puffer**

electret *noun* piece of dielectric that keeps an electronic charge after a voltage has been applied at manufacture **(Ferro)dielektrikum; electret microphone** = microphone using a section of dielectric as a transducer that provides an electric signal with varying sound pressure **Elektretmikrophon**

electric *adjective* worked by electricity **elektrisch; electric current** = mass movement of electric charge in a conductor **elektrischer Strom; electric charge** = a number of atoms that are charged (due to excess *or* deficiency of electrons) **elektrische Ladung; electric typewriter** = typewriter whose keys are switches which control motors and solenoids to perform all the functions **elektrische Schreibmaschine**

◇ **electrical** *adjective* referring to electricity **elektrisch, Elektro-;** *the engineers are trying to repair an electrical fault*

◇ **electrically** *adverb* referring to electricity **elektrisch;** *an electrically-powered motor;* **electrically alterable, programmable read-only memory (EAPROM)** = version of EAROM that can be programmed **EAPROM (elektrisch veränderbarer, programmierbarer Festwertspeicher); electrically alterable read-only memory (EAROM)** = read-only memory chip whose contents can be programmed by applying a certain voltage to a write pin, and can be erased by light *or* a reverse voltage **EAROM (elektrisch veränderbarer Festwertspeicher); electrically erasable programmable read-only memory (EEPROM)** = ROM storage chip which can be programmed and erased using an electrical signal **EEPROM (elektrisch löschbarer, programmierbarer Festwertspeicher); electrically erasable read-only memory (EEROM)** = EAROM memory chip whose contents can be programmed by applying a certain voltage to a write pin, and can be erased by light *or* a reverse voltage **EEROM (elektrisch löschbarer Festwertspeicher)**

electricity *noun* electric current used to provide light *or* heat *or* power **Elektrizität;** *the* *electricity was cut off, and the computers crashed; electricity prices are an important factor in the production costs*

electrode *noun* part of an electric circuit *or* device that collects, controls or emits electrons **Elektrode**

electrographic printer *noun see* ELECTROSTATIC PRINTER

electroluminescence *noun* light emitted from a phosphor dot when it is struck by an electron *or* charged particle **Elektrolumineszenz**

◊ **electroluminescing** *adjective* (object) which is emitting light due to electroluminescence **elektrolumineszierend**

◊ **electroluminescent** *adjective* capable of emitting light due to electroluminescence **elektrolumineszent**; *the screen coating is electroluminescent*; **electroluminescent display** = flat, lightweight display screen that is made up of two pieces of glass covered with a grid of conductors, separated by a thin layer of gas which luminesces when a point of the grid is selected by two electric signals **Elektrolumineszenzanzeige**

electromagnet *noun* device that consists of a core and a coil of wire that produces a magnetic field when current is passed through the coil **Elektromagnet**

◊ **electromagnetic** *adjective* generating a magnetic field *or* magnetic effect when supplied with electrical power **elektromagnetisch**; **electromagnetic interference** = corruption of data due to nearby electrically generated magnetic fields **elektromagnetische Störung**; **electromagnetic spectrum** = frequency range of electromagnetic radiation (from light to radio wave) **elektromagnetisches Spektrum**

◊ **electromagnetically** *adverb* working due to electromagnetic effects **elektromagnetisch**

◊ **electromagnetic radiation** *noun* energy wave consisting of electric and/or magnetic fields **elektromagnetische Strahlung**

COMMENT: electromagnetic radiation requires no medium to support it, travels approximately at the speed of light and can support frequency ranges from light to radio waves

electromechanical switching *noun* connection of two paths by an electrically operated switch *or* relay **elektromechanische Schaltung**

electromotive force (EMF) *noun* difference in electrical potential across a source of electric current **elektromotorische Kraft (EMK)**

electron *noun* elementary particle with an elementary negative charge **Elektron**; **electron beam** = stream of electrons **Elektronenstrahl**; **electron beam recording (EBR)** = (i) production of microfilm images by means of an electron beam; (ii) recording the output from a computer directly onto microfilm using an electron beam **(i) & (ii) Elektronenstrahlaufzeichnung(smethode)**; **electron gun** = electronic component that emits a large number of electrons (usually by heating a filament of metal) **Elektronenkanone**

COMMENT: mass of 9.109×10^{-31} kg, and charge of 1.602×10^{-19} C

electronic *adjective* referring to something which is controlled by *or* controls electron flow **elektronisch**; **electronic automatic exchange** = telephone routing system that uses electronic circuits to switch signals **elektronische Wählvermittlungsstelle**; **electronic blackboard** = means of transmitting handwritten text and diagrams over a telephone line **elektronische Anzeigetafel**; **electronic composition** = text manipulation by computer before typesetting **elektronischer Schriftsatz**; **electronic data processing (EDP)** = data processing using computers and electronic devices **elektronische Datenverarbeitung (EDV)**; **electronic data processing capability** = ability of a word processor to carry out certain data processing functions **Leistungen eines Datenverarbeitungssystems**; **electronic digital computer** = digital computer constructed with electronic components (the basic form uses a CPU, main memory, backing storage and input/output devices; these are all implemented with electronic components and integrated circuits) **elektronischer Digitalrechner**; **electronic editing** = video film editing using computers, image storage, etc., rather than physically cutting the tape **elektronische Redaktion**; **electronic engineer** = person who specializes in work on electronic devices **Elektronikingenieur**; **electronic industry association interface (EIA)** = standard defining interface signals, transmission rate and power usually used to connect terminals to modems **Schnittstellennorm des Elektronikindustrieverbandes**; **electronic filing** = system of storage of documents which can be easily retrieved **elektronisches**

Ablagesystem; **electronic funds transfer (EFT)** = using a computer to transfer money to and from banks **elektronischer Zahlungsverkehr; electronic funds transfer point of sale (EFTPOS)** = terminal at a POS that is linked to a central computer which automatically transfers money from the customer's account to the shop's **elektronische Kasse; electronic keyboard** = keyboard that generates characters electronically in response to a switch making contact when pressed, rather than by mechanical means **elektronische Tastatur; electronic lock** = security device, usually in the form of a password (used to protect a file or piece of equipment from unauthorized use) **elektronische Sperre; electronic mail** = sending and receiving messages over a telephone network, usually using a bulletin board **elektronische Post; electronic mailbox** = system for holding messages sent by electronic mail until the person to whom they were sent is ready to accept them **elektronischer Briefkasten; electronic money** = smart cards or phonecards, etc., which take the place of money **Plastikgeld; electronic news gathering (ENG)** = method of reporting news items for TV news programmes, where the reporter has a cameraman with a portable video camera which can transmit live pictures direct to the studio **elektronische Berichterstattung; electronic office** = office where all the work is done using computers, which store information, communicate with different workstations, etc. **elektronisches Büro; electronic pen** or **stylus** or **wand** = light pen or wand; stylus used to draw on a graphics tablet **Lichtgriffel, Lichtstift; electronic point-of-sale (EPOS)** = system that uses a computer terminal at a point-of-sale site for electronic funds transfer or stock control as well as product identification, etc. **elektronische Kasse; electronic publishing** = (i) use of desktop publishing packages and laser printers to produce printed matter; (ii) using computers to write and display information, such as viewdata **(i) elektronisches Publizieren; (ii) Bildschirmtextverfahren; electronic pulse** = short voltage pulse **elektronischer Impuls; electronic shopping** = system of shopping from the home, using computerized catalogues and paying by credit card, all by means of a home computer terminal **Teleshopping; electronic signature** = special code which identifies the sender of a coded message **elektronische Signatur; electronic smog** = excessive stray electromagnetic fields and static electricity generated by large numbers of electronic equipment (this can damage equipment or a person's health) **elektronischer Smog; electronic stylus** or **wand** see LIGHT PEN; **electronic switching system** = telephone routing using a computer system to control the line switching circuits **elektronisches Vermittlungssystem; electronic traffic** = data transmitted in the form of electronic pulses **elektronischer Datenverkehr; electronic typewriter** = typewriter using an electronic keyboard linked, via a buffer, to an electrically driven printing mechanism, also with the facility to send or receive character data from a computer **elektronische Schreibmaschine; electronic viewfinder** = miniature cathode ray tube in a television or video camera that allows the camera operator to see the images being recorded **elektronischer Sucher**

◊ **electronically** adverb referring to operations using electronic methods **elektronisch;** the text is electronically transmitted to an outside typesetter

◊ **electronics** noun science of applying the study of electrons and their properties to manufactured products, such as components, computers, calculators or telephones **Elektronik;** the electronics industry; an electronics specialist NOTE: takes a singular verb

> QUOTE electronic mail is a system which allows computer users to send information to each other via a central computer
>
> *Which PC?*
>
> QUOTE electronic publishing will be used for printing on paper, but it can be applied equally to data storage on a database, transmission via telecommunications or for use with visual presentation media such as AV slides or television
>
> *Electronic Publishing & Print Show*

electro-optic effect noun changes in the refractive index of a material due to a nearby electric field **elektrooptischer Effekt**

◊ **electrophotography** noun forming an image using electrical and optical effects **Elektrofotografie**

◊ **electrosensitive** adjective **electrosensitive paper** = metal-coated printing paper, which can display characters using localized heating with a special dot-matrix print head **elektrosensitives Papier; electrosensitive printing** = printing using electrosensitive paper **elektrosensitives Drucken**

◊ **electrostatic** adjective referring to devices using the properties of static electrical charge **elektrostatisch; electrostatic printer** = type of printer which forms an image on the paper by charging certain regions to provide character shapes, etc., and using ink with an opposite charge which sticks to the paper where required **elektrostatischer Drucker; electrostatic screen** = metal cage surrounding sensitive equipment (and connected to ground) to protect it from interference **elektrostatischer Schirm; electrostatic speaker** = loudspeaker containing two large charged plates, one flexible which moves when a signal is applied, creating sound signals **elektrostatischer Lautsprecher; electrostatic storage** = data stored in the form of small electric charged regions on a dielectric material **elektrostatischer Speicher**

◊ **electrostatically** *adverb* using properties of static charge **elektrostatisch**

◊ **electrothermal printer** *noun* printer that uses a printing head with a dot-matrix of heating elements to form characters on electrosensitive paper **Thermodrucker**

elegant *adjective* **elegant programming** = writing a well-structured program using the minimum number of instructions **elegantes Programmieren**

element *noun*
(a) small part of an object which is made up of many similar parts **Element; logic element** = gate *or* combination of gates **logisches Element, Verknüpfungsglied; picture element** *or* **pixel** = smallest single unit *or* point on a display whose colour *or* brightness can be controlled **Bildelement; signal element** = smallest basic unit used when transmitting digital data **Schritt**
(b) one number *or* cell of a matrix *or* array **Punkt; array element** = one individual piece of data within an array **Matrixelement**
(c) coil of resistive wire to which an electric current is applied to generate heat **Brennelement**
(d) substance in which all the atoms have the same number of electrons and charge **Element**

◊ **elementary** *adjective* made of many similar small sections *or* objects **elementar; elementary cable section** = model of the characteristics of a short length of transmission cable that can be applied to the whole length of cable **elementarer Kabelausschnitt**

ELF = EXTREMELY LOW FREQUENCY communications frequencies of less than 100Hz **Niederfrequenz (niedriger als 100Hz)**

eliminate *verb* to remove something completely **ausschließen, eliminieren;** *using a computer should eliminate all possibility of error in the address system; the spelling checker does not eliminate all spelling mistakes*

◊ **elimination** *noun* removing of something completely **Eliminierung; elimination factor** = during a search, the

section of data that is not used **Eliminierungsfaktor**

QUOTE pointing with the cursor and pressing the joystick button eliminates use of the keyboard almost entirely
Soft

elite *noun* typewriter typeface **Elite**

ellipse *noun* oval shaped; like an elongated circle **Ellipse**

◊ **elliptical orbit** *noun* path of a satellite around the earth that is in the shape of an ellipse **elliptische Umlaufbahn**

else rule *noun* program logical rule used with an IF-THEN instruction to provide an alternative if the IF-THEN condition is not met **ELSE-Regel;** *IF X=20 THEN PRINT 'X is 20' ELSE PRINT 'X not 20'*

ELT = ELECTRONIC TYPEWRITER

em *noun* space taken by an 'm' in a given typeface (equal to 12 point *or* pica) **Em; em quad** = space printed of a size equal to an em **Geviert (in der Größe eines m); em dash** *or* **em rule** = dash as long as an 'm', showing that words are separated **Em-Strich, Gedankenstrich; ems per hour** = rate of production of characters from a machine *or* operator **Ems pro Stunde;** *see also* EN

EM = END OF MEDIUM

E-mail *or* **email** = ELECTRONIC MAIL

QUOTE to collect telex messages from an e-mail system, you have to remember to dial the system and check whether there are any telex messages in your mailbox
Which PC?

embedded code *noun* sections *or* routines written in machine code, inserted into a high-level program to speed up *or* perform a special function **eingebetteter Code; embedded command** = printer command (such as indicating that text should be in italic) inserted into the text and used by a word-processing system when producing formatted printed text **eingebetteter Befehl; embedded computer** *or* **system** = dedicated computer controlling a machine; dedicated computer within a larger system that performs one fixed function **eingebettetes System**

emboldening *noun* making a word print in bold type **halbfettes Drucken**

embrace *see* DEADLY

emf = ELECTROMOTIVE FORCE

EMI = ELECTROMAGNETIC INTERFERENCE corruption of data due to nearby electrically generated magnetic fields **elektromagnetische Störung**

emission *noun* sending out (of a signal *or* radiation, etc.); *the emission of the electron beam; the receiver picked up the radio emission* **Emission**
◊ **emit** *verb* to send out **ausstrahlen, aussenden**
◊ **emitter** *noun* connection to a bipolar transistor **Emitter; emitter-coupled logic (ECL)** = *noun* high-speed logic circuit design using the emitters of the transistors as output connections to other stages **emittergekoppelte Logik**

empty *adjective* with nothing inside **leer; empty** *or* **null list** = list with no elements **Leerliste; empty medium** = blank but formatted storage medium that is ready to receive data **unbeschrifteter Datenträger; empty** *or* **null** *or* **void set** = reserved area for related data items, containing no data **leerer Bereich; empty slot** = (i) packet of data in a packet-switching LAN that is carrying no information; (ii) unused expansion edge connector on a motherboard **(i) freier Platz; (ii) freier Steckerplatz; empty** *or* **null string** = variable containing no characters **Leerstring**

emulate *verb* to copy *or* behave like something else **emulieren;** *laser printer which emulates a wide range of office printers*
◊ **emulation** *noun* behaviour by one computer *or* printer which is exactly the same as another, which allows the same programs to be run and the same data to be processed **Emulation; emulation facility** = feature of hardware *or* software which emulates another system **Emulationsfähigkeit**
◊ **emulator** *noun* software *or* hardware that allows a machine to behave like another **Emulator**

QUOTE full communications error checking built into the software ensures reliable file transfers and a terminal emulation facility enables a user's terminal to be used as if it were a terminal to the remote computer
Byte
QUOTE some application programs do not have the right drivers for a laser printer, so look out for laser printers which are able to emulate the more popular office printers
Publish

emulsion *noun* light-sensitive coating on photographic film *or* paper **Beschichtung,** **Emulsion; emulsion laser storage** = digital storage technique using a laser to expose lightsensitive material **Schicht-Laserspeicher**

en *noun* half the width of an em **En; en dash** *or* **en rule** = line as long as an en, showing that two words *or* parts of words are joined together **En-Strich, Bindestrich; en quad** = space that is half the width of an em quad space **Halbgeviert (in der Größe eines n);** *see also* EM

enable *verb*
(a) to allow something to happen **erlauben;** *a spooling program enables editing work to be carried out which printing is going on*
(b) to use an electronic signal to start a process *or* access a function (on a chip *or* circuit) **einschalten, aktivieren; enabling signal** = signal that starts a process *or* allows one to take place **Betriebsbereitschaftssignal**

encipher *verb* to convert plaintext into a secure coded form by means of a cipher system **verschlüsseln;** *our competitors cannot understand our files - they have all been enciphered*

enclose *verb* to surround with something; to put something inside something else **umgeben; beilegen**
◊ **enclosure** *noun* protective casing for equipment **Gehäuse**

encode *verb* to apply the rules of a code to a program *or* data **codieren**
◊ **encoder** *noun* device that can translate data from one format to another **Codeumsetzer; colour encoder** = device that produces a standard TV signal from separate Red, Green and Blue signals **Farbumsetzer**
◊ **encoding** *noun* translation of a message *or* text according to a coding system **Umsetzung; binary encoding** = representing a character *or* element with a unique combination *or* pattern of bits in a word **binäre Umsetzung; encoding format** = method of coding data stored on a magnetic disk (to avoid a series of similar bits) **Codierungsformat; magnetic encoding** = storage of binary data signals on a magnetic medium **magnetische Speicherung**

encrypt *verb* to convert plaintext to a secure coded form, using a cipher system **verschlüsseln;** *the encrypted text can be sent along ordinary telephone lines, and no one will be able to understand it*
◊ **encryption** *noun* conversion of plaintext to a secure coded form by means of a cipher

system **Verschlüsselung; data encryption standard (DES)** = standard for a block data cipher system **Datenverschlüsselungsnorm**

end

1 *noun*
(a) final point *or* last part **Ende**; *at the end of the data transmission;* **end product** = manufactured product, made at the end of a production process **Endprodukt**; *after six months' trial production, the end product is still not acceptable;* **in the end** = at last *or* after a lot of problems **schließlich**; *in the end the company had to pull out of the US market; in the end the company had to call in a consultant engineer*
(b) statement *or* character to indicate the last word of a source file **Ende; end about carry** = most significant digit is added into the least significant place (used in BCD arithmetic) **Endübertrag; end about shift** = data movement to the left *or* right in a word, the bits falling outside the word boundary are discarded and replaced with zeros **Ringschieben; end of address (EOA)** = transmitted code which indicates that address data has been sent **Adressenende; end of block (EOB)** = code which shows that the last byte of a block of data has been sent through a communications link **Blockende; end of data (EOD)** = code which shows that the end of a stored data file has been reached **Datenende; end of document** *or* **end of file (EOF)** = marker after the last record in a file **EOF, Dateiende; end of job (EOJ)** = code used in batch processing to show that a job has been finished **Jobende; end of medium (EM)** = code that indicates the end of usable physical medium **Datenträgerende; end of message (EOM)** = code used to separate the last character of one message from the first of another message **Nachrichtenende; end of page indicator** = indicator on a typewriter to show that a page is nearly finished **Seitenendeanzeiger; end of record (EOR)** = code used to show the end of a record **Satzende; end of run routine** = routine carried out before a program run finishes to perform certain system housekeeping functions **Ende der Laufroutine; end of tape** = code used to indicate the end of a magnetic tape **Bandende; end of text (EOT** *or* **ETX)** = code sent after last character of text **Textende; end of transmission (EOT)** = sequence of characters that indicate that all the data from a terminal *or* peripheral has been transmitted **Übertragungsende**
2 *verb* to finish *or* to stop something **beenden**

◊ **ending** *noun*
(a) action of coming to an end *or* of stopping something **Abschluß**

(b) end part of something **Ende; line endings** = last words on each line of text, which may be hyphenated **Zeilenenden**

◊ **endless** *adjective* with no end **endlos; endless loop** = continuous piece of recording tape *or* number of computer instructions that are continuously repeated **Endlosschleife**

◊ **end user** *noun* person who will use the device *or* program *or* product **Endverbraucher;** *the company is creating a computer with a specific end user in mind*

energy *noun*
(a) force *or* strength; ability of a body *or* object to do work **Energie**
(b) power from electricity *or* petrol, etc. **Energie;** *we try to save energy by switching off the lights when the rooms are empty; if you reduce the room temperature to eighteen degrees, you will save energy* NOTE: no plural for (b)

◊ **energy-saving** *adjective* which saves energy **energiesparend;** *the company is introducing energy-saving measures*

ENG = ELECTRONIC NEWS GATHERING

enhance *verb* to make better *or* clearer **verbessern, erweitern; enhanced dot matrix** = clearer character *or* graphics printout (using smaller dots and more dots per inch) **verbesserte Punktmatrix; enhanced graphics adapter (EGA)** = popular standardized system of high-resolution colour display for microcomputers **erweiterte Graphikkarte (EGA); enhanced graphics adapter screen** = high-resolution colour monitor that can display EGA system signals and graphics **EGA-Bildschirm; enhanced small device interface (ESDI)** = interface standard between a CPU and peripherals such as disk drives **erweiterte Kleingerätschnittstelle**

◊ **enhancement** *noun* add-on facility which improves the output *or* performance of equipment **Erweiterung**

◊ **enhancer** *noun* device *or* software which enhances a process *or* product **Erweiterer**

> QUOTE the typefaces are fairly rudimentary, especially if you are not using an enhanced graphics adapter screen
> *Desktop Publishing*

enlarge *verb* to make (a photograph) larger **vergrößern**

◊ **enlargement** *noun* making larger; a larger version of a photograph **Vergrößerung;** *an enlargement of the photograph was used to provide better detail*

ENQ = ENQUIRY

enquiry *noun* request for data *or* information from a device *or* database; accessing data in a computer memory without changing the data **An-, Aufforderung; enquiry character** = special control code that is a request for identification *or* status *or* data from a device **Stationsaufforderung**

ensure *verb* to make sure **sicherstellen;** *pushing the write-protect tab will ensure that the data on the disk cannot be erased*

enter *verb* to type in information on a terminal *or* keyboard **eingeben;** *to enter a name on a list; the data has been entered on data capture forms;* **enter key** = key pressed to indicate the end of an input *or* line of text **Eingabetaste**
◊ **entering** *noun* act of typing in data *or* writing items in a record **Eingabe**
NOTE: no plural

entity *noun* subject to which the data stored in a file *or* database refers **Dateneinheit**

entry *noun*
(a) single record *or* data about one action *or* object in a database *or* library **Eintrag**
(b) place where you can enter **Eingabe; Eingang; entry condition** = condition that must be satisfied before a routine can be entered **Eingabebedingung; entry instruction** = first instruction executed in a called subroutine **Einsprungbefehl; entry point** = address from which a program *or* subroutine is to be executed **Einsprungstelle; entry time** = point in time when a program *or* job *or* batch will be executed by the operating system scheduler **Eingabezeit**

enumerated type *noun* data storage *or* classification using numbers to represent chosen convenient labels **Numerierungstyp**

COMMENT: if 'man', 'horse', 'dog', 'cat' are the items of data, stored by the machine simply as 0, 1, 2, 3, they can still be referred to in the program as man, horse, etc., to make it easier for the user to recognize them

envelope *noun*
(a) flat paper cover for sending letters **(Brief)umschlag; air mail envelope** = very light envelope for air mail letters **Luftpostumschlag; window envelope** = envelope with a hole covered with film so that the address on the letter inside can be seen **Fensterumschlag; sealed** *or* **unsealed envelope** = envelope where the flap has been stuck down to close it *or* envelope

where the flap has been pushed into the back of the envelope **zugeklebter/offener Umschlag**
(b) variation of amplitude of a signal *or* sound with time **Hüllkurve; attack envelope** = shape of the initial section of a signal **Anfangskurve; envelope delay** *see* DELAY DISTORTION; **envelope detection** = technique of signal recovery from a modulated waveform **Hüllkurvengleichrichtung**
(c) transmitted byte of data containing error and control bits **Enveloppe**

environment *noun*
(a) condition in a computer system of all the registers and memory locations **Umgebung**
(b) surroundings *or* physical conditions **Umgebung**

QUOTE one of the advantages of working in a PC-based environment is the enormous range of software which can run on the same computer
ESL Newsletter

EOA = END OF ADDRESS

EOB = END OF BLOCK

EOD = END OF DATA

EOF = END OF FILE

EOJ = END OF JOB

EOM = END OF MESSAGE

EOR = END OF RECORD

EOT = END OF TEXT *or* TRANSMISSION

episcope *noun* projector that can display opaque material and documents onto a screen **Epidiaskop**

epitaxy *noun* method of depositing very thin layers of materials onto a base, for use in chip manufacture **Epitaxie**
◊ **epitaxial layer** *noun* very thin layer of material *or* doped semiconductor deposited onto a substrate base **epitaxiale Schicht**

EPOS = ELECTRONIC POINT-OF-SALE system that uses a computer terminal at a point-of-sale site for electronic funds transfer *or* stock control as well as product identification **elektronische Kasse**

EPROM *noun*
(a) = ELECTRICALLY PROGRAMMABLE READ-ONLY MEMORY

(b) = ERASABLE PROGRAMMABLE READ-ONLY MEMORY

QUOTE the densest EPROMs commercially available today are at the 1Mbit level
Electronics & Power

equal
1 *adjective* exactly the same **gleich**
2 *verb* to be the same as **gleichkommen;** *production this month has equalled our best month ever* NOTE: **equalling - equalled** but US: **equaling - equaled**

◊ **equality** *noun* logical function whose output is true if either of two inputs is true, and false if both inputs are the same **Gleichheit**

◊ **equalize** *verb* to make equal (to preset values) **gleichmachen, ausgleichen;** *the received signal was equalized to an optimum shape*

◊ **equalization** *noun* process of making a signal equal (to preset values) **Entzerrung**

◊ **equalizer** *noun* device which changes the amplitude of various parts of a signal according to preset values **Entzerrer; frequency equalizer** = device that changes the amplitude of various frequency components of a signal according to preset values **Frequenzentzerrer**

◊ **equally** *adverb* in the same way **gleich;** *they were both equally responsible for the successful launch of the new system*

equate *verb* to make the same as **gleichsetzen;** *the variable was equated to the input data*

◊ **equation** *noun* formula **Gleichung; machine equation** = formula which an analog computer has been programmed to solve **Maschinengleichung**

equator *noun* imaginary line running round the middle of the earth **Äquator**

◊ **equatorial orbit** *noun* satellite flight path that follows the earth's equator **äquatoriale Umlaufbahn**

equip *verb* to provide with machinery *or* equipment **ausstatten**

◊ **equipment** *noun* machinery and furniture required to make a factory *or* office work **Ausstattung, Anlage, Einrichtung;** *office equipment or business equipment; computer equipment supplier; office equipment catalogue;* **equipment failure** = hardware fault, rather than a software fault **Gerätefehler**
NOTE: no plural

equivalent *adjective* **to be equivalent to** = to have the same value as *or* to be the same as **gleichwertig sein;** *the total characters keyboarded so far is equivalent to one day's printing time*

◊ **equivalence** *noun*
(a) being equivalent **Gleichheit, Gleichwertigkeit**
(b) logical operation that is true if all the inputs are the same **Äquivalenz; equivalence function** *or* **operation** = (i) AND function; (ii) logical function whose output is true if both inputs are the same **(i) UND-Funktion; (ii) Äquivalenz-Funktion; equivalence gate** = gate which performs an equivalence function **Äquivalenzglied; non-equivalence function (NEQ)** = logical function where the output is true if the inputs are not the same, otherwise the output is false **Antivalenzfunktion**

COMMENT: output is 1 if both inputs are 1 or if both are 0; if the two inputs are different, the output is 0

erase *verb*
(a) to set all the digits in a storage area to zero **auf Null setzen**
(b) to remove any signal from a magnetic medium **löschen; erase head** = small magnet that clears a magnetic tape *or* disk of recorded signals **Löschkopf**

◊ **erase character** *noun* character which means do nothing **Nullzeichen**

◊ **erasable** *adjective* which can be erased **löschbar; erasable storage** *or* **erasable memory** = (i) storage medium that can be re-used; (ii) temporary storage **(i) löschbarer Speicher; (ii) Zwischenspeicher; erasable programmable read-only memory (EPROM)** = read-only memory chip that can be programmed by a voltage applied to a write pin and data applied to its output pins, usually erasable with ultraviolet light **löschbarer, programmierbarer Festwertspeicher (EPROM)**

◊ **eraser** *noun* device that erases the contents of an EPROM (usually using UV light) **Löscheinrichtung**

ERCC = ERROR CHECKING AND CORRECTING memory which checks and corrects errors **Fehlerprüfung und -korrektur**

E-region *or* **Heaviside-Kennelly layer** *noun* section of the ionosphere that is 90-150 km above the earth's surface **E-Schicht der Ionosphäre**

ergonomics *noun* study of people at work, and their working conditions, concerned with improving safety and making machines easy to use **Ergonomie, Arbeitswissenschaft**

◇ **ergonomist** *noun* scientist who studies people at work and tries to improve their working conditions **Ergonom**

EROM = ERASABLE READ-ONLY MEMORY *(same as EAROM)*

erratum *noun* correction on a separate slip of paper to an error *or* omission from a document **Erratum; Schreib-, Druckfehler** NOTE: plural is **errata**

error *noun* mistake due to an operator; mistake caused by a hardware *or* software fault; mistake in a program that prevents a program *or* system running correctly **Fehler;** *we made an error in calculating the total; the secretary must have made a typing error;* **an error** *or* **by error** = by mistake **aus Versehen; margin of error** = number of mistakes which are acceptable in a document *or* in a calculation **Fehlerspielraum; ambiguity error** = error due to an incorrect selection from ambiguous data **Mehrdeutigkeitsfehler; error burst** = group of several consecutive errors (in a transmission) **Fehlerhäufung; error checking code** = general term used to describe all error correcting and error detecting codes **Fehlerprüfcode; error code** = code that indicates that a particular type of error has occurred **Fehlercode; error condition** = state that is entered if an attempt is made to operate on data containing errors **Fehlerbedingung; error control** = routines that ensure that errors are minimised and any errors that occur are detected and dealt with rapidly **Fehlerüberwachung; error correcting code** = coding system that allows bit errors occurring during transmission to be rapidly corrected by logical deduction methods rather than re-transmission **Fehlerkorrekturcode;** *see also* GRAY CODE; **error correction** = hardware *or* software that can detect and correct an error in a transmission **Fehlerkorrektur; error detecting code** = coding system that allows errors occurring during transmission to be detected but is not complex enough to correct the errors **Fehlererkennungscode; error detection** = using special hardware *or* software to detect errors in a data entry *or* transmission, then usually ask for re-transmission **Fehlererkennung; error detection and correction (EDAC)** = forward error correction system for data communications **Fehlererkennung und -korrektur; error diagnosis** = finding the cause of an error **Fehlerdiagnose; error diagnostics** = information and system messages displayed when an error is

detected to help a user diagnose and correct an error **Fehlerdiagnostik; error handling** *or* **management** = routines and procedures that diagnose and correct errors *or* minimise the effects of errors, so that a system will run when an error is detected **Fehlerbehebung; error interrupts** = interrupt signals sent due to an error in hardware *or* software **Fehlerunterbrechungen; error logging** = recording errors that have occurred **Fehlererfassung;** *features of the program include error logging;* **error message** = report that an error has occurred **Fehlermeldung; error propagation** = one error causing another **Fehlerfortpflanzung; error rate** = (i) number of mistakes per thousand entries *or* per page; (ii) number of corrupt bits of data in relation to the total transmission length **(i) Fehlerhäufigkeit; (ii) Fehlerquote;** *the error rate is less than 1%;* **error recovery** = software *or* hardware that can continue after an error has occurred **Fehlerbehebung; error routine** = short routine within a main program that handles any errors when they occur **Fehlerroutine; error trapping** = detecting and correcting errors before they cause any problems **Fehlerbehebung; compilation error** = error occurring during program compilation time **Kompilierfehler; diagnostic error message** = explanatory line of text displayed when an error has been found **diagnostische Fehlermeldung; execution error** = error occurring during program execution, due to bad inputs *or* a faulty program **Ausführungsfehler; logical error** = fault in a program design causing incorrect branching *or* operation **logischer Fehler; permanent error** = error in a system which cannot be repaired **dauerhafter Fehler; quantization error** = error in converting an analog signal into a numerical form due to limited accuracy *or* a rapidly changing signal **Quantisierungsfehler; recoverable error** = error that does not cause complete system shut-down, and allows the user to restart the program **wiederherstellbarer Fehler; rejection error** = error by the scanner which is unable to read a character and leaves a blank **Rückweisungsfehler; scanning error** = error introduced while scanning an image **Abtastfehler;** *a wrinkled or torn page may be the cause of scanning errors;* **substitution error** = error made by a scanner which mistakes one character *or* letter for another **Substitutionsfehler; syntax error** = error resulting from incorrect use of programming language syntax **Syntaxfehler; transient read error** = error which can be recovered from (caused by bad data recording) **transienter Lesefehler; undetected error** = error which is not detected by a coding system **unentdeckter Fehler**

ESC escape character code *or* key on a computer **ESC-Taste**

escape character *noun* character used to represent an escape code **ESC-Zeichen, Codeumschaltung; escape codes** = transmitted code sequence which informs the receiver that all following characters represent control actions **ESC-Codes; escape key** = key on a keyboard which allows the user to enter escape codes to control the computer's basic modes *or* actions **ESC-Taste, Codeumschaltungstaste**
◊ **escapement** *noun* preset vertical movement of a sheet of paper in a printer *or* in a typewriter **Schrittschaltung**

ESDI = ENHANCED SMALL DEVICE INTERFACE interface standard between a CPU and peripherals such as disk drives **erweiterte Kleingerätschnittstelle**

ESS = ELECTRONIC SWITCHING SYSTEM

establish *verb* (i) to discover and prove something; (ii) to define the use *or* value of something **(i) erweisen; (ii) festsetzen;** *they established which component was faulty*

etch *verb* to use an acid to remove selected layers of metal from a metal printing plate *or* printed circuit board **ätzen; etch type** = type for printing produced from an etched plate **Ätztype**

ETV = EDUCATIONAL TELEVISION

ETX = END OF TEXT

Euronet *noun* telephone connected network, covering the EC countries, that provides access to each country's scientific and economic information **Euronet**

evaluate *verb* to calculate a value *or* a quantity **auswerten, bewerten**
◊ **evaluation** *noun* action of calculating a value *or* a quantity **Auswertung**
◊ **evaluative abstract** *noun* library abstract that contains details of the value and usefulness of the document **gewertete Kurzdarstellung**

even *adjective* (quantity *or* number) that is a multiple of two **gerade;** *the first three even numbers are 2, 4, 6;* **even parity (check)** = error checking method that only transmits an even number of binary ones in each word **Prüfung auf gerade Bitzahl;** *compare* ODD PARITY; **even working** = section of printed material in 16, 32 or 64 page format **Drucken ohne Restbogen**

event *noun* an action *or* activity **Ereignis, Anreiz**
◊ **event-driven** *adjective* (computer program *or* process) where each step of the execution relies on external actions **anreizgesteuert**

except *preposition & conjunction* not including **außer;** *all the text has been keyboarded, except the last ten pages;* **except gate** = logical function whose output is true if either (of two) inputs is true, and false if both inputs are the same **exklusiv-ODER-Gatter**
◊ **exception** *noun* thing which is different from all others **Ausnahme; exception dictionary** = store of words and their special word-break requirements, for word-processing and photocomposition **Ausnahmelexikon; exception report** = report which only gives items which do not fit in the general rule *or* pattern **Ausnahmebericht**
◊ **exceptional** *adjective* not usual *or* different **außergewöhnlich; exceptional items** = items in a balance sheet which do not appear there each year **Sonderposten**

excess *noun* too much of something **Überschuß; excess-3 code** = code in which decimal digits are represented by the binary equivalent of three greater than the number **3-Überschußcode, Stibitz-Code;** *the excess-3 code representation of 6 is 1001*
◊ **excessive** *adjective* too much *or* too large **überschüssig;** *the program used an excessive amount of memory to accomplish the job*

exchange
1 *noun*
(a) giving of one thing for another **Austausch; part exchange** = giving an old product as part of the payment for a new one **in Zahlung geben**
(b) telephone equipment required to connect incoming and outgoing calls **Telefonzentrale; exchange line** = LOCAL LOOP
2 *verb*
(a) to exchange one article for another = to give one thing in place of something else **einen Artikel gegen einen anderen umtauschen; exchange selection** = sorting method which repeatedly exchanges various pairs of data items until they are in order **Sortiermethode**

(b) to swap data between two locations **austauschen**

◇ **exchangeable** *adjective* which can be exchanged **austauschbar, auswechselbar; exchangeable disk storage (EDS)** = disk drive using a removable disk pack (as opposed to a fixed disk) **auswechselbarer Plattenspeicher**

exclamation mark *noun* printed *or* written sign (!), which shows surprise **Ausrufezeichen**

exclude *verb* to keep out *or* not to include **ausschließen;** *the interest charges have been excluded from the document; the password is supposed to exclude hackers from the database*

◇ **excluding** *preposition* not including **außer, ausgenommen;** *all salesmen, excluding those living in London, can stay at hotels during the sales conference*

◇ **exclusion** *noun*
(a) act of not including **Ausschluß, Ausschließung; exclusion clause** = section of an insurance policy *or* warranty which says which items are not covered **Ausschluß-, Freizeichnungsklausel**
(b) restriction of access to a telephone line *or* system **Ausschluß**

◇ **exclusive** *adjective* which excludes **ausschließlich; exclusive agreement** = agreement where a person is made sole agent for a product in a market **Exklusivvertrag, Alleinvertretungsvereinbarung; exclusive NOR (EXNOR)** = logical function whose output is true if all inputs are the same level, and false if any are different **exklusiv-NOR-Funktion; exclusive NOR gate** = electronic implementation of the EXNOR function **exklusiv-NOR-Gatter; exclusive OR (EXOR)** = logical function whose output is true if any input is true, and false if all the inputs are the same **exklusiv-ODER-Funktion; exclusive OR gate** = electronic implementation of the EXOR function **exklusiv-ODER-Gatter**

executable form *noun* program translated *or* compiled into a machine code form that a processor can execute **ausführbare Form**

execute *verb* to run *or* carry out a computer program *or* process **aktivieren, ausführen; execute cycle** = events required to fetch, decode and carry out an instruction stored in memory **Ausführungszyklus; execute mode** = state of a computer that is executing a program **Ausführungsmodus;** *compare with* DIRECT MODE; **execute phase** = section of the execute cycle when the instruction is carried out **Ausführungsphase; execute signal** = signal that steps the CPU through the execute cycle **Ausführungssignal; execute statement** = basic operating system command to start a program run **Ausführungsbestimmung; execute time** = EXECUTION TIME; **fetch-execute cycle** = EXECUTE CYCLE

◇ **execution** *noun* carrying out of a computer program *or* process **Verarbeitung, Ausführung; execution address** = location in memory at which the first instruction in a program is stored **Ausführungsadresse; execution cycle** = period of time during which the instruction is executed **Ausführungszyklus; execution error** = error detected while a program is being run **Ausführungsfehler; execution phase** = EXECUTE PHASE; **execution time** = (i) time taken to run *or* carry out a program *or* series of instructions; (ii) time taken for one execution cycle **(i) & (ii) Ausführungszeit**

QUOTE fast execution speed is the single most important feature of a compiler
.EXE

executive
1 *adjective* **executive producer** = person who organizes and arranges for the finance for a film *or* TV programme but does not play an active part in making the film **Produzent; executive program** *or* **supervisor program** = master program in a computer system that controls the execution of other programs **Supervisor; executive control program** = OPERATING SYSTEM; **executive instruction** = instruction used to control and execute programs under the control of an operating system **Ausführungsbefehl;** *see also* SUPERVISOR INSTRUCTION
2 *noun* person in a business who takes decisions (such as a manager *or* director) **leitende(r) Angestellte(r), Führungskraft; executive terminal** = terminal which is specially adapted for use by company executives **Datenstation der Firmenleitung**

exerciser *noun* tester for a device **Testgerät**

exhaustive search *noun* search through every record in a database **erschöpfende Suche**

exit *verb* to stop program execution *or* to leave a program and return control to the operating system *or* interpreter **beenden; exit point** = point in a subroutine where control is returned to the main program

Ausgangsstelle; *you have to exit to another editing system to add headlines*

exjunction *noun* logical function whose output is true if either (of two) inputs are true, and false if both inputs are the same **exklusiv-ODER-Funktion**

EXNOR = EXCLUSIVE NOR logical function whose output is true if all inputs are the same level, false if any are different **exklusiv-NOR-Funktion; EXNOR gate** = electronic implementation of the EXNOR function **exklusiv-NOR-Gatter;** *see also* NOR

EXOR = EXCLUSIVE OR logical function whose output is true if any input is true, and false if the all inputs are the same **exklusiv-ODER-Funktion; EXOR gate** = electronic implementation of the EXOR function **exklusiv-ODER-Gatter;** *see also* OR

expand *verb* to make larger **expandieren, vergrößern;** *if you want to hold so much data, you will have to expand the disk capacity*

◊ **expandable** *adjective* which can be expanded **expandierbar; expandable system** = computer system that is designed to be able to grow (in power *or* memory) by hardware *or* software additions **expandierbares System**

◊ **expander** *noun* **video expander** = device that stores one frame of a video image as it is slowly received over a voice grade communications link, with a video compressor used at the transmitting end **Videoexpander**

◊ **expansion** *noun* increase in computing power *or* storage size **Kapazitätsausweitung; expansion card** *or* **expansion board** = printed circuit board that is connected to a system to increase its functions *or* performance **Erweiterungsplatine; expansion slot** = connector inside a computer into which an expansion card can be plugged **Erweiterungsposition;** *insert the board in the expansion slot;* **macro expansion** = process in which a macro call is replaced with the instuctions in the macro **Makroumwandlung**

> QUOTE it can be attached to mast kinds of printer, and, if that is not enough, an expansion box can be fitted to the bus connector
> *Personal Computer World*

expert *noun* person who knows a lot about something **Sachverständige(r), Experte/Expertin;** *he is a computer expert; she is an expert in programming languages;* **expert system** = software that applies the knowledge, advice and rules defined by experts in a particular field to a user's data to help solve a problem **Expertensystem**

expire *verb* to come to an end *or* to be no longer valid **ungültig werden, ablaufen**

◊ **expiration** *noun* coming to an end **Verfall, Ablauf; expiration date** = (i) last date at which photographic film *or* paper can be used with good results; (ii) date when a computer file is no longer protected from deletion by the operating system **(i) Verfallsdatum; (ii) Dateiverfallsdatum**

explicit address *noun* address provided in two parts, one is the reference point, the other a displacement *or* index value **absolute Adresse**

exponent *noun* number indicating the power to which a base number is to be raised **Exponent; binary exponent** = one word that contains the sign and exponent of a binary number (expressed in exponent and mantissa form) **Binärexponent;** *see also* MANTISSA

◊ **exponentiation** *noun* raising a base number to a certain power **Potenzierung**

express *verb* to state *or* to describe **ausdrücken;** *express the formula in its simplest form; the computer structure was expressed graphically*

◊ **expression** *noun*
(a) mathematical formula *or* relationship **Ausdruck**
(b) definition of a value *or* variable in a program **Ausdruck**

extend *verb* to make longer **verlängern, erweitern; extended arithmetic element** = section of a CPU that provides hardware implementations of various mathematical functions **erweitertes Rechenelement; extended binary coded decimal interchange code (EBCDIC)** = 8-bit character coding system **EBCDIC-Code; extended BNF (EBNF)** = more flexible way of defining the syntax of a language **erweiterte Backus-Naur-Form; extending serial file** = file that can be added to *or* that has no maximum size **erweiterbare serielle Datei**

◊ **extensible** *adjective* which can be extended **erweiterbar; extensible language** = computer programming language that allows the user to add his own data types and commands **erweiterbare Sprache**

◊ **extension** *noun* making longer; thing which makes something longer **Verlängerung, Erweiterung; extension cable** = cable that allows a device located at some distance to be connected **Verlängerungskabel; extension memory** = storage which is located outside the main computer system but which can be accessed by the CPU **Nebenspeicher;**

extension tube = device that moves photographic lens away from the camera to allow close-up shots **Tele-Objektiv; filename extension** = additional information after a filename, indicating the type *or* use of the file **Extension beim Dateinamen**

◇ **extent** *noun* number of pages in a printed document, such as a book **Umfang;** *by adding the appendix, we will increase the page extent to*

external *adjective* outside a program *or* device **extern, außerhalb; external clock** = clock *or* synchronizing signal supplied from outside a device **externer Taktgeber; external data file** = file containing data for a program that is stored separately from it **externe Datei; external device** = (i) item of hardware (such as terminals, printers, etc.) which is attached to a main computer; (ii) any device that allows communications between the computer and itself, but which is not directly operated by the main computer **(i) Hardwareteil; (ii) Peripheriegerät; external disk drive** = device not built into the computer, but which is added to increase its storage capabilities **externes Plattenlaufwerk; external interrupt** = interrupt signal from a peripheral device indicating that attention is required **externe Unterbrechung; external label** = identifying piece of paper stuck to the outside of a device *or* disk **Aufkleber, Etikett; external memory** = memory which is located outside the main computer system confines but which can be accessed by the CPU **externer Speicher; external registers** = user's registers that are located in main memory rather than within the CPU **externe Register; external schema** = user's view of the structure of data *or* a program **externes Schema; external sort** = method of sorting which uses a file stored in secondary memory, such as a disk, as its data source and uses the disk as temporary memory during sorting **externe Sortierung; external storage** *or* **external store** = storage device which is located outside the main computer system but which can be accessed by the CPU **Zubringerspeicher**

extra
1 *adjective* added *or* which is more than usual **zusätzlich**
2 *noun*
(a) item which is additional to the package **ein Extra;** *the mouse and cabling are sold as extras*
(b) mark at the end of a telegraphic transmission, induced by noise **Störstrom; extra-terrestrial noise** = random noise coming from the air, space and planets **außerirdisches Rauschen**

◇ **extracode** *noun* short routines within the operating system that emulate a hardware function **Extracode**

extract *verb* to remove required data *or* information from a database **herausnehmen;** *we can extract the files required for typesetting;* **extract instruction** = instruction to select and read required data from a database *or* file **Ausblendbefehl**

◇ **extractor** *noun see* MASK

extrapolation *noun* process of predicting future quantities *or* trends by the analysis of current and past data **Extrapolation, Hochrechnung**

extremely *adverb* to a very high degree **besonders, äußerst; extremely high frequency (EHF)** = radio frequencies from 30-300GHz **extremhohe Frequenz (EHF); extremely low frequency (ELF)** = communication frequencies of less than 100Hz **Frequenz niedriger als 100Hz**

eyepiece *noun* camera viewfinder **Sucher**

◇ **eye-strain** *noun* pain in the eyes, caused by looking at bright lights *or* at a VDU for too long **Überanstrengung der Augen**

> QUOTE to minimize eye-strain, it is vital to have good lighting conditions with this LCD system
> *Personal Computer World*

Ff

F
(a) hexadecimal number equivalent to decimal number 15 **F**
(b) = FARAD

f = FEMTO- *prefix* equal to one thousandth of a million millionth (10^{-15}) **f**

face *see* TYPEFACE

facet *noun* one surface *or* plane **Facette**
◇ **faceted code** *noun* code which indicates various details of an item, by assigning each one a value **Facettencode**

facility *noun*
(a) being able to do something easily **Möglichkeit, Fazilität;** *we offer facilities for processing a customer's own disks*

(b) facilities = equipment *or* buildings which make it easy to do something **Einrichtungen, Möglichkeiten;** *storage facilities*
(c) communications path between two or more locations, with no ancillary line equipment **Verbindungsweg**
(d) *(US)* single large building **Betriebsanlage;** *we have opened our new data processing facility*

facsimile *noun* exact copy of an original **Faksimile; facsimile character generator** = means of displaying characters on a computer screen by copying preprogrammed images from memory **Faksimilezeichengenerator; facsimile copy** = exact copy of a document **Kopie; facsimile transmission (FAX)** = method of sending and receiving images in digital form over a telephone *or* radio link **Bildfunk, Bildtelegraphie (FAX)**

factor *noun*
(a) thing which is important *or* which has an influence on something else **Faktor; deciding factor** = most important factor which influences someone's decision **entscheidender Faktor;** *the deciding factor was the superb graphics;* **elimination factor** = during a search, the section of data that is not used **Eliminierungsfaktor**
(b) any number in a multiplication that is the operand **Faktor; by a factor of ten** = ten times **zehnmal, mit dem Faktor zehn**

◊ **factorial** *noun* the product of all the numbers below a number **Fakultät;** *example: 4 factorial (written 4!) = 1x2x3x4 = 24*

◊ **factorize** *verb* to break down a number into two whole numbers which when multiplied will give the original number **in Faktoren zerlegen;** *when factorized, 15 gives the factors 1, 15 or 3, 5*

factory *noun* building where products are manufactured **Fabrik;** *computer factory; they have opened a new components factory;* **factory price** *or* **price ex factory** = price not including transport from the maker's factory **Fabrikpreis, Preis ab Werk**

fade *verb (of radio or electrical signal)* to become less strong **schwächer werden, nachlassen;** *(of colour or photograph)* to become less dark **verblassen, verbleichen; to fade out** = to reduce the strength of an audio signal to create an effect **abblenden**

◊ **fading** *noun* (i) variation in strength of radio and television broadcast signals; (ii); *(of photograph or colour)* becoming less dark (i) **Schwund;** (ii) **Verblassen;** *when fading*

occurs turn the density dial on the printer to full black

fail *verb* not to do something which should be done; not to work properly **ausfallen, versäumen, versagen;** *the company failed to carry out routine maintenance of its equipment; the prototype disk drive failed its first test; a computer has failed if you turn on the power supply and nothing happens;* **fail safe system** = system that has a predetermined state it will go to if a main program *or* device fails, so avoiding a total catastrophe that a complete system shutdown would produce **ausfallsicheres System; fail soft system** = system that will still be partly operational even after a part of the system has failed **System mit reduziertem Betrieb;** *see also* GRACEFUL DEGRADATION

◊ **failure** *noun* breaking down *or* stopping; not doing something which should be done **Ausfall, Versäumnis; failure logging** = section of the operating system that automatically saves the present system states and relevant data when an error *or* fault is detected **Störungsaufzeichnung; failure rate** = number of a certain type of failure within a specified period of time **Ausfallrate; failure recovery** = resuming a process *or* program after a failure has occurred and has been corrected **Fehlerwiederherstellung; induced failure** = failure of a device due to external effects **induzierter Ausfall; mean time between failures (MTBF)** = average period of time that a piece of equipment will operate for between breakdowns **mittlerer Ausfallabstand; power failure** = loss of the electric power supply **Stromausfall;** *see also* BLACKOUT, BROWN OUT

> QUOTE if one processor system fails, the other takes recovery action on the database, before taking on the workload of the failed system
> *Computer News*

fall back *noun* special *or* temporary instructions *or* procedures *or* data used in the event of a fault *or* failure **Wiederholungsanlauf; fall back recovery** = resuming a program after a fault has been fixed, from the point at which fall back routines were called **Programmwiederaufnahme; fall back routines** = routines that are called *or* procedures which are executed by a user when a machine *or* system has failed **Wiederanlaufroutine**

false *adjective* (i) wrong; not true *or* not correct; (ii) a logical term, equal to binary 0, opposite of true (i) **falsch;** (ii) **FALSE; false code** = code that contains values not within specified limits **FALSE-Code; false drop** *or*

retrieval = unwanted files retrieved from a database through the use of incorrect search codes **falsches Wiederauffinden; false error** = error warning given when no error has occurred **falsche Fehlermeldung**

FAM = FAST ACCESS MEMORY

family *noun*
(a) range of different designs of a particular typeface **(Schriften)familie**
(b) range of machines from one manufacturer that are compatible with other products in the same line from the same manufacturer **Familie**

fan
1 *noun* (i) mechanism that circulates air for cooling; (ii) a spread of data items *or* devices **(i) Ventilator; (ii) Auffächerung;** *if the fan fails, the system will rapidly overheat* **2** *verb* (i) to cool a device by blowing air over it; (ii) to spread out a series of items *or* devices **(i) mit Luft kühlen; (ii) auffächern; fan antenna** = antenna whose elements are arranged in a semicircle **Fächerantenne; fan-in** = maximum number of inputs that a circuit *or* chip can deal with **Eingangslastfaktor; fan-out** = maximum number of outputs that a circuit *or* chip can drive without exceeding its power dissipation limit **Ausgangslastfaktor; fanning strip** = cable supporting insulated strip **Drahtführungskamm**

◊ **fanfold** *or* **accordion fold** *noun* method of folding continuous paper, one sheet in one direction, the next sheet in the opposite direction, allowing the paper to be stored conveniently and fed into a printer continuously **Zickzackfaltung**

> QUOTE a filtered fan maintains positive air pressure within the cabinet, to keep dust and dirt from entering
> *Personal Computer World*

farad (F) *noun* SI unit of capacitance, defined as coulombs over volts **Faraday** ⇨ APPENDIX

Faraday cage *noun* wire *or* metal screen, connected to ground, that completely encloses sensitive equipment to prevent any interference from stray electromagnetic radiation **Faradaykäfig**

far end *see* RECEIVING END

fascia plate *noun* front panel on a device **Frontplatte;** *the fascia plate on the disk drive of this model is smaller than those on other models*

fast *adjective*
(a) which moves quickly; which works quickly; (storage *or* peripheral device) that performs its functions very rapidly **schnell;** *fast program execution; this hard disk is fast, it has an access time of 28mS;* **fast access memory (FAM)** = storage locations that can be read from *or* written to very rapidly **Schnellzugriffsspeicher; fast core** = high speed, low access time working memory for a CPU **Schnellspeicher;** *the fast core is used as a scratchpad for all calculations in this system;* **fast line** = special telecommunications line which allows data to be transmitted at 48K *or* 96K baud rates **Schnelleitung; fast peripheral** = peripheral that communicates with the computer at very high speeds, limited only by the speed of the electronic circuits, as opposed to a slow peripheral such as a card reader, where mechanical movement determines speed **schnelles Peripheriegerät; fast time-scale** = operation in which the time-scale factor is less than one **Zeitraffung (b)** (photographic lens) with a very wide aperture; highly lightsensitive photographic film **lichtstark; hochempfindlich**

fatal error *noun* fault in a program *or* device that causes the system to crash **unkorrigierbarer Abbruchfehler**

father file *noun* backup of the previous version of a file **Vaterdatei;** *see also* GRANDFATHER, SON

fault *noun* situation where something has gone wrong with software *or* hardware, causing it to malfunction **Fehler;** *the technical staff are trying to correct a programming fault; we think there is a basic fault in the product design; see also* BUG, ERROR ; **fault detection** = (automatic) process which logically *or* mathematically determines that a fault exists in a circuit **Fehlerentdeckung; fault diagnosis** = process by which the cause of a fault is located **Fehlerdiagnose; fault location program** = routine that is part of a diagnostic program that identifies the cause of faulty data *or* equipment **Fehlerlokalisierungsprogramm; fault time** = period of time during which a computer system is not working *or* usable **Ausfallzeit; fault trace** = program that checks and records the occurrences of faults in a system **Fehlerprotokoll**

◊ **fault tolerance** *noun* ability of a system to continue functioning even when a fault has occurred **Fehlertoleranz**

◊ **fault-tolerant** *adjective* (system *or* device) that is able to continue functioning even when a fault occurs **fehlertolerant;** *they* *market a highly successful range of fault-tolerant minis*

◊ **faulty** *adjective* which does not work properly **fehlerhaft**; *there must be a faulty piece of equipment in the system; they traced the fault to a faulty cable;* **faulty sector** = sector of a magnetic disk that cannot be written to *or* read from correctly **fehlerhafter Sektor**

QUOTE before fault-tolerant systems, users had to rely on cold standby
QUOTE fault tolerance is usually associated with a system's reliability
Computer News

fax *or* **FAX** *noun & verb informal* = FACSIMILE COPY, FACSIMILE TRANSMISSION **(Tele)fax; (tele)faxen;** *we will send a fax of the design plan; I've faxed the documents to our New York office; the fax machine is next to the telephone switchboard*

QUOTE investment in a good modem and communications system could reduce your costs considerably on both courier and fax services
Which PC?

fd *or* **FD**
(a) = FULL DUPLEX data transmission down a channel in two directions simultaneously **Duplex**
(b) = FLOPPY DISK

fdc = FLOPPY DISK CONTROLLER

FDM = FREQUENCY DIVISION MULTIPLEXING transmission of several independent signals along a single channel achieved by shifting each signal up in frequency by a different amount **Frequenz-Multiplexmethode**

fdx *or* **FDX** = FULL DUPLEX

feasibility *noun* ability to be done **Durchführbarkeit;** *he has been asked to report on the feasibility of a project;* **feasibility report** = report saying if something can be done **Durchführbarkeitsbericht; feasibility study** = examination and report into the usefulness and cost of a new product that is being considered for purchase **Projektstudie; to carry out a feasibility study on a project** = to carry out an examination of costs and profits to see if the project should be started **eine Projektstudie durchführen**
NOTE: no plural

feature *noun* special function *or* ability *or* design of hardware *or* software **Einrichtung; key feature** = most important feature **Haupteinrichtung;** *the key features of this*

system are: 20Mb of formatted storage with an access time of 60ms

FEDS = FIXED AND EXCHANGEABLE DISK STORAGE magnetic disk storage system that contains some removable disks, such as floppy disks and some fixed *or* hard disk drives **System mit Festplatten und flexiblen Disketten**

feed
1 *noun* device which puts paper *or* tape into and through a machine, such as a printer *or* photocopier **Zuführung; continuous feed** = device which feeds in continuous computer stationery into a printer **Endlospapiereinzug; front feed** *or* **sheet feed attachment** = device which can be attached to a line printer to allow individual sheets of paper to be fed in automatically **Einzelblatteinzug; feed holes** = punched sprocket holes along the edge of continuous paper **Führungslöcher; feed horn** = microwave channelling device used to direct transmitted signals **Speisehornstrahler; feed reel** = reel of tape which is being fed into a machine **Rollenzuführung; paper feed** = mechanism which pulls paper through a printer **Papiertransport; sheet feed** = device which puts in one sheet at a time into a printer **Einzelblatteinzug; tractor feed** = method of feeding paper into a printer, sprocket wheels on the printer connect with sprocket holes on each edge of the paper **Papiertraktor**
2 *verb* to put paper into a machine *or* information into a computer **zuführen;** *this paper should be manually fed into the printer; data is fed into the computer* NOTE: **feeding - fed**

◊ **feedback** *noun*
(a) adding part of the output of a circuit to the input **Rückführung; feedback loop** = path from output to input by which feedback occurs **Rückführungsschleife; negative feedback** = subtraction of part of the output from a device from its input signal **negative Rückführung; positive feedback** = addition of part of the output from a device to its input **positive Rückführung;** *see also* ACOUSTICAL
(b) information from one source which can be used to modify something *or* provide a constructive criticism of something **Rückkopplung; Reaktion, Rückinformation;** *we are getting customer feedback on the new system; they asked the sales teams for feedback on the reception of the new model; have you any feedback from the sales force about the customers' reaction to the new model? ;* **feedback control** = information about the effects of a controlling signal on a machine *or* device, returned to the controlling computer **Rückführungskreis;** NOTE: no plural

COMMENT: negative or positive feedback can be accidental (when it may cause severe overloading of the circuit) or designed into the circuit to make it more stable

eeder *noun*
a) channel that carries signals from one **oint** to another **Zubringer; feeder cable =** (i) **nain** transmission line that carries signals **rom** a central point for distribution; (ii) **:able** from an antenna to a circuit **(i) :ubringerkabel; (ii) Verbindungskabel**
b) mechanism that automatically inserts **he** paper into a printer **automatischer *apierzuführer**

eevee *noun (US) informal* paycable *or* **orm** of cable TV where the viewer pays an **xtra** fee for extra channels **extra zu •ezahlendes Kabelfernsehen**

eint *noun* very light lines on writing **)aper Feinlinierung**

emale *adjective* **female connector = :onnector** with connecting sockets into **vhich** the pins *or* plugs of a male connector **:an** be inserted **Anschlußbuchse; female :ocket =** hole into which a pin *or* plug can be **nserted** to make a connection **Steckdose**

emto- (f) *prefix* equal to ten exponent **ninus** fifteen (10^{-15}) **Femto-; femto second = :housandth** of a picosecond **Femtosekunde**

:EP = FRONT END PROCESSOR **•rocessor** placed between an input source **ind** the central computer, whose function **s** to preprocess received data to relieve the **vorkload** of the main computer *'orschaltrechner*

erric oxide *or* **ferrite** *noun* substance **iron** oxide) used as tape *or* disk coating **hat** can be magnetized to store data *or* **ignals Eisenoxid**
◊ **ferrite core** *noun* small bead of magnetic **naterial** that can hold an electromagnetic **:harge,** used in (old) core memory *erritkern, Magnetkern*
◊ **ferromagnetic material** *noun* any ferrite **naterial** that can be magnetized *erromagnetisches Material*

:ET = FIELD EFFECT TRANSISTOR **lectronic** device that can act as a variable **urrent** flow control, an external signal **aries** the resistance of the device and **urrent** flow by changing the width of a **onducting** channel **Feldeffekttransistor**

fetch *noun* command that retrieves the next instruction from memory **Abruf; demand fetching =** virtual page management system in which the pages are selected as required **Abruf auf Anforderung; fetch cycle =** events that retrieve the next instruction to be executed from memory (by placing the program counter contents on the address bus) **Abrufzyklus; fetch-execute cycle =** events required to retrieve, decode and carry out an instruction stored in memory **Abruf-Ausführ-Zyklus; fetch instruction =** computer instruction to select and read the next instruction *or* data to be processed **Abrufbefehl; fetch phase =** section of the fetch-execute cycle that retrieves and decodes the instructions from memory **Abrufphase; fetch protect =** to restrict access to a section of memory **Lesesperre; fetch signal =** signal that steps the CPU through the fetch cycle **Abrufsignal**

FF
(a) = FORM FEED
(b) = FLIP-FLOP

fibre optics *noun* light transmission through thin strands of glass *or* plastic, which allows data to be transmitted **Faseroptik; fibre optic cable** *or* **connection =** fine strands of glass *or* plastic protected by a surrounding material, used for transmission of light signals **Lichtwellenleiterkabel;** *fibre optic connections enabling nodes up to one kilometre apart to be used*
◊ **fibre ribbon** *noun* fabric-based ribbon used in printers **Gewebeband**

fiche *see* MICROFICHE

fidelity *noun* ability of an audio system to reproduce sound correctly **Klangtreue; high fidelity system (hi fi) =** high-quality equipment for playing records *or* compact disks *or* tapes *or* for listening to the radio (tape recorder, turntable, amplifier and speakers) **Hi-Fi-Anlage;** *see also* HI FI

field *noun*
(a) area of force and energy distribution, caused by magnetic *or* electric energy sources **Feld; field effect transistor (FET) =** electronic device that can act as a variable current flow control, an external signal varies the resistance of the device and current flow by changing the width of a conducting channel **Feldeffekttransistor; field programmable device** *see* PLA; **field programming =** writing data into a PROM **Feldprogrammierung;** *see also* BLOW; **field strength =** amplitude of the magnetic *or*

electric field at one point in that field **Feldstärke**
(b) section containing individual data items in a record **Feld**; *the employee record has a field for age;* **address** *or* **operand field** = part of a computer instruction that contains the location of the operand **Adreßfeld od Operandenfeld; card field** = part of a card column reserved for one type of data *or* record **Lochkartenfeld; data field** = part of a computer instruction that contains the location of the data **Datenfeld; field label** = series of characters used to identify a field or its location **Feldkennung; field length** = number of characters that a field can contain **Feldlänge; field marker** *or* **separator** = code used to indicate the end of one field and the start of the next **Feldmarkierungszeichen, Trennzeichen; protected field** = storage *or* display area that cannot be altered by the user **geschütztes Feld**
(c) method of building up a picture on a television screen **Halbbild; field blanking** = interval when television signal field synchronizing pulses are transmitted **(Halb)bildaustastung; field frequency** = number of field scans per second **Feldfrequenz; field flyback** = return of electron beam to top left hand corner of a screen **Bildrücklauf; field sweep** = vertical electron beam movement over a television screen **(Halb)bildabtastung; field sync pulse** = pulse in a TV signal that makes sure that the receiver's field sweep is in sync **Bildsynchronisierpuls**
(d) section of an image that is available after the light has passed through the camera and lens **Feld**
(e) in the field = outside an office *or* factory **im Außendienst; field engineer** = engineer who does not work at one single company, but travels between customers carrying out maintenance on their computers **Außendiensttechniker; field sales manager** = manager in charge of a group of salesmen working in a particular area of the country **Außendienstverkaufsleiter; field tested** = product tested outside a company *or* research laboratory, in a real situation **praxisgetestet; field work** = examining the situation among several potential customers **Feldforschung, Außenarbeit**

◊ **fielding** *noun* arrangement of field allocations inside a record and file **Feldanordnung**

FIFO = FIRST IN FIRST OUT storage read/write method in which the first item stored is the first read **FIFO (zuerst Abgelegtes wird als erstes bearbeitet); FIFO memory** = memory using a FIFO access scheme **FIFO-Speichermethode;** *the two*

computers operate at different rates, but can transmit data using a FIFO memory; **FIFO queue** = temporary (queue) storage, in which the first item written to the queue is the first to be read **FIFO-Warteschlange;** *compare* LIFO

fifth generation computers *noun* next stage of computer system design using fast VLSI circuits and powerful programming languages to allow human interaction **Computer der fünften Generation**

figure *noun*
(a) printed line illustration in a book **Abbildung;** *see figure 10 for a chart of ASCII codes*
(b) printed number **Zahl; figures case** = characters in a telegraphic transmission that are mainly numbers *or* signs **Ziffern- und Zeichenfeld; figures shift** = (i) transmitted code that indicates to the receiver that all following characters should be read as upper case; (ii) mechanical switch which allows a typewriter to print *or* keyboard to produce special characters and symbols located on the same keys as the numbers **(i) & (ii) Zeichenumschaltung; in round figures** = not totally accurate, but correct to the nearest 10 or 100 **auf-, abgerundet;** *they have a workforce of 2,500 in round figures*

file
1 *noun*
(a) cardboard holder for documents, which can fit in the drawer of a filing cabinet **Aktenordner;** *put these letters in the customer file; look in the file marked "Scottish sales";* **box file** = cardboard box for holding documents **kastenförmiger Aktenordner**
(b) documents kept for reference **Akte; to place something on file** = to keep a record of something **etwas zu den Akten tun; to keep someone's name on file** = to keep someone's name on a list for reference **jdn in den Akten führen; file copy** = copy of a document which is kept for reference in an office **Aktenkopie; card-index file** = information kept on filing cards **Kartei**
(c) section of data on a computer (such as payroll, address list, customer accounts), in the form of individual records which may contain data, characters, digits *or* graphics **Datei; data file** = file containing data (as opposed to a program file) **Datei; disk file** = number of related records *or* data items stored under one name on disk **Plattendatei; distributed file system** = system that uses files stored in more than one location *or* backing store, but which are processed at a central point **verteiltes Dateisystem; file activity ratio** = ratio of the number of different records accessed within a file

compared to the total number in store **Bewegungshäufigkeit der Dateien; file cleanup** = tidying and removing out of date *or* unnecessary data from a file **Dateisäuberung; file collating** = putting the contents of a file into order **Dateisortierung; file control block** = list (in main memory) of files in use within the system **Dateiverwaltungsblock; file conversion** = change of format *or* structure of a file system, usually when using a new program *or* file handling routine **Dateiumsetzung; file creation** = writing file header information onto a disk and writing an entry into the directory **Dateierstellung; file deletion** = erasing a file from storage **Dateilöschung;** *see also* DELETE; **file descriptor** = code *or* series of characters used to identify a file **Dateibeschreibung; file directory** = list of names and information about files in a backing storage device **Dateiverzeichnis; file extent** = actual area *or* number of tracks required to store a file **Dateiumfang; file gap** = section of blank tape *or* disk that indicates the end of a file **Dateizwischenraum; file handling routine** = short computer program that manages the reading/writing and organization of stored files **Dateiverwaltungsroutine; file identification** = unique label *or* name used to identify and locate a file stored on baking store **Dateiname; file index** = sorted table of the main entries in a file, with their address, allowing the rapid location of entries **Datei-Index; file label** = character(s) used to identify a file **Dateikennsatz; file layout** = set of rules defining internal file structure **Dateiaufbau; file maintenance** = process of updating a file by changing, adding *or* deleting entries **Dateiwartung, Fortschreibung; file management (system)** = section of a DOS that allocates disk space to files, keeping track of the sections and their sector addresses **Dateiverwaltung(ssystem); file manager** = routines used to create, locate and maintain files on backing store **Dateiverwalter; file merger** = (i) to combine two data files, but still retaining an overall structure; (ii) one file created from more than one file written one after the other (no order preserved) **(i) & (ii) Mischen von Dateien; file name** = word used to identify a particular stored file **Dateiname; file organization** *see* FILE LAYOUT; **file processing** = applying a set of rules *or* search limits to a file, in order to update *or* find information **Dateiverarbeitung; file protection** = (i) software *or* physical device used to prevent any accidental deletion *or* modification of a file *or* its records; (i) **Dateischutz; (ii);** *see* FILE SECURITY; **file protect tab** = plastic tab on a disk which prevents accidental erasure of a file

Schreibschutz; file purge = erasing the contents of a file **Dateilöschung; file-recovery utility** = software that allows files that have been accidentally deleted *or* damaged to be read again **Dateiwiederherstellungsprogramm;** *a lost file cannot be found without a file-recovery utility;* **file security** = hardware *or* software organization of a computer system to protect users' files from unauthorized access **Dateischutz; file server** = small microcomputer and large backing store device that is used for the management and storage of a user's files in a net work **Controller für Speicherzugriff; file set** = number of related files treated as one unit **Dateimenge; file sort** = to put the contents of a file into order **Dateisortierung; file storage** = physical means of preserving data in a file, such as a disk drive *or* tape machine **Dateispeicherung; file store** = files that are available in main memory at any time **Dateispeicher; file structure** = way in which a (data) file is organized **Dateistruktur; file transfer** = moving a file from one area of memory to another *or* to another storage device **Dateitransfer; file update** = (i) recent changes *or* transactions to a file; (ii) new version of software which is sent to users of an existing version **(i) Fortschreibung; (ii) neueste Software-Version; file validation** = checking that a file is correct **Dateiprüfung; hidden file** = important system file which is not displayed in a directory and cannot normally be read by a user **versteckte Datei; indexed file** = sequential file with an index of all the entries and their addresses **indizierte Datei; inverted file** = file with an index entry for every data item **invertierte Datei; output file** = set of records that have been completely processed according to various parameters **Ausgabedatei; program file** = file containing a program rather than data **Programmdatei; text file** = file that contains text rather than digits *or* data **Textdatei; threaded file** = file in which an entry will contain data and an address to the next entry that contains the same data (allowing rapid retrieval of all identical entries) **gekettete Datei; transaction** *or* **change** *or* **detail** *or* **movement file** = file containing recent changes to records *or* transactions used to update a master file **Bewegungsdatei**

2 *verb* **to file documents** = to put documents in order so that they can be found easily **Dokumente ablegen;** *the correspondence is filed under "complaints"; he filed the new papers in chronological order*

◇ **filename** *noun* unique identification code allotted to a program **Dateiname; filename extension** = additional information after a filename, indicating the type *or* use of the file **Extension (Erweiterung) beim Dateinamen;** *the filename* *extension SYS indicates that this is a system file*

> QUOTE it allows users to back up or restore read-only security files and hidden system files independently
> *Minicomputer News*
> QUOTE the lost file, while inaccessible without a file-recovery utility, remains on disk until new information writes over it
> *Publish*
> QUOTE when the filename is entered at the prompt, the operating system looks in the file and executes any instructions stored there
> *PC User*

filing *noun* documents which have to be put in order **Ablage;** *there is a lot of filing to do at the end of the week; the manager looked through the week's filing to see what letters had been sent;* **filing basket** *or* **filing tray** = container kept on a desk for documents which have to be filed **Ablagekorb; filing cabinet** = metal box with several drawers for keeping files **Aktenschrank; filing card** = card with information written on it, used to classify information in the correct order **Karteikarte;** NOTE: no plural

◊ **filing system** *noun*
(a) way of putting documents in order for reference **Ablagesystem**
(b) software which organizes files **Software, die Dateien verwaltet**

fill *verb*
(a) to make something full **füllen;** *the screen was filled with flickering images*
(b) to put characters into gaps in a field so that there are no spaces left **auffüllen; fill character** = character added to a string of characters to make up a required length **Füllzeichen; filled cable** = cable which uses a substance to fill any gaps between outer and conductors, so preventing water getting in **ausgegossenes Kabel**
(c) to draw an enclosed area in one colour *or* shading **ausfüllen**

◊ **fill up** *verb* to make something completely full **voll machen;** *the disk was quickly filled up*

film
1 *noun*
(a) transparent strip of plastic, coated with a light-sensitive compound and used to produce photographs with the aid of a camera **Film; film advance** = (i) lever on a camera used to wind on a roll of film to the next frame; (ii) the distance the film in a phototypesetting machine has to move prior to the next line being set **(i) Filmtransporthebel; (ii) Filmtransport; film assembly** = correct arrangement of photographs *or* negatives prior to the

production of a printing plate **Bildanordnung; film base** = thin transparent roll of plastic used as a supporting material for photographic film **Filmträger; film chain** = all the necessary equipment needed when showing film *or* slides on television, such as a projector, TV camera and synchronizer **Filmvorführaggregat; film optical scanning device for input into computers (FOSDIC)** = storage device for computer data using microfilm **optische Filmleseeinheit; film pickup** = transmission of a motion picture film by television by electronically scanning each frame **Filmabtaster; film strip** = set of related images on a reel of film, usually for educational purposes **Filmstreifen; photographic film** = light-sensitive film used in a camera to record images **fotografischer Film**
(b) projection at high speed of a series of still images that creates the impression of movement **Film**
2 *verb* to expose a photographic film to light by means of a camera, and so to produce images **fotografieren**

◊ **filming** *noun* shooting of a cinema film *or* TV film **Drehen, Dreharbeiten;** *filming will start next week if the weather is fine*

◊ **filmsetting** *noun* photocomposition **Fotosatz**

filter
1 *noun*
(a) electronic circuit that allows certain frequencies to pass while stopping others **Filter; bandpass filter** = circuit that allows a certain band of frequencies to pass while stopping any that are higher or lower **Bandfilter; high pass filter** = circuit that allows frequencies above a certain limit to pass, but blocks those below that limit **Hochpaßfilter; low pass filter** = circuit that blocks signals above a certain frequency **Tiefpaßfilter**
(b) optical coloured glass, which stops certain frequencies of light **Filter; absorption filter** = filter that blocks certain colours **Absorptionsfilter; character enhancement filter** = filter placed over a monitor to increase contrast, and also to prevent eye-strain **Linienanhebungsfilter; filter factor** = indicator of the amount of light that an optical filter absorbs when light passes through it **Siebfaktor**
(c) pattern of binary digits used to select various bits from a binary word (a one in the filter retains that bit in the source word) **Filter**
2 *verb*
(a) to remove unwanted elements from a signal *or* file **glätten**
(b) to select various bits *or* records from a word *or* file **herausfiltrieren**

final *adjective* last *or* coming at the end of a period **letzte(r/s);** *to keyboard the final data files; to make the final changes to a document*

find
1 *verb* to get something back which has been lost **finden;** *it took a lot of time to find the faulty chip; the debugger found the error very quickly* NOTE: **finding - found**
2 *noun* command to locate a piece of information **Suchen; find and replace** = feature on a word-processor that allows certain words *or* sections of text to be located and replaced with others **Suchen und Ersetzen**

fine *adjective*
a) very thin *or* very small **fein;** *the engraving has some very fine lines*
b) excellent *or* of very high quality **fein**
◇ **fine tune** *verb* to adjust by small amounts the features *or* parameters of hardware *or* software to improve performance **fein abstimmen;** *fine-tuning improved the speed by ten per cent*

finish
1 *noun*
a) final appearance **Finish, Aussehen;** *the product has an attractive finish*
b) end of a process *or* function **Ende**
2 *verb*
a) to do something *or* to make something completely **beenden, abschließen;** *the order was finished in time; she finished all the keyboarding before lunch*
b) to come to an end **fertig sein, (be)enden, auslaufen;** *the contract is due to finish next month*
◇ **finished** *adjective* which has been completed **fertig; finished document** = document which is typed, and is ready to be printed **fertiges Schriftstück, Reinschrift; finished goods** = manufactured goods which are ready to be sold **Fertigerzeugnisse**

finite-precision numbers *noun* use of a fixed number of bits to represent numbers **Zahl mit endlicher Genauigkeit**

firmware *noun* computer program *or* data that is permanently stored in a hardware memory chip, such as a ROM *or* EPROM **Firmware;** *compare with* HARDWARE, SOFTWARE

first-level address *noun* computer storage address that directly, without any modification, accesses a location *or* device **Erstadresse**

◇ **first fit** *noun* routine *or* algorithm that selects the first, largest section of free memory in which to store a (virtual) page **First Fit**

◇ **first generation computer** *noun* original computer made with valve based electronic technology, started around 1951 **Computer der ersten Generation; first generation image** = master copy of an original image, text *or* document **erste Kopie; first in first out (FIFO)** = temporary queue where the first item stored is the first read **zuerst Abgelegtes wird zuerst bearbeitet (FIFO); first party release** = ending of a telephone connection as soon as either party puts his phone down *or* disconnects his modem **Auslösung einer Verbindung durch zuerst einhängenden Teilnehmer**

fisheye lens *noun* extremely wide angle photographic lens that has a field of view of 180 degrees and produces a distorted circular image **Fischauge**

fix
1 *noun* chemical stage in processing a film that sets permanently the developed image on a film *or* paper **Fixierung**
2 *verb*
(a) to make something permanent *or* to attach something permanently **festsetzen, fixieren;** *the computer is fixed to the workstation;* **fixed and exchangeable disk storage (FEDS)** = magnetic disk storage system that contains some removable disks, such as floppy disks and some fixed *or* hard disk drives **System mit Festplatten und flexiblen Disketten; fixed cycle operation** = (i) process in which each operation is allocated a certain, fixed time limit; (ii) actions within a process that are synchronized to a clock **(i) & (ii) Arbeitsweise mit festem Takt; fixed data** = data written to a file *or* screen for information *or* identification purposes and which cannot be altered by the user **Festdaten; fixed disk storage** = hard disk *or* magnetic disk which cannot be removed from the disk drive **Festplattenspeicher; fixed field** = area in a stored record that can only contain a certain amount of data **festes Feld; fixed head disk (drive)** = use of a separate immovable read/write head over each disk track making access time very short **Schnellzugriffsplatte(nlaufwerk); fixed-length record** = record whose size cannot be changed **Satz mit fester Länge; fixed-length word** = preset number of bits that make up a computer word **Wort mit fester Länge; fixed program computer** = (hardwired) computer program that cannot be altered and is run automatically **Festprogrammcomputer; fixed routing** = communications direction

routing that does not consider traffic *or* efficient paths **feste Verkehrslenkung; fixed word length** = computer whose word size (in bits) cannot be changed **feste Wortlänge**
(b) to mend **reparieren;** *the technicians are trying to fix the switchboard; can you fix the photocopier?*

◊ **fixed-point notation** *noun* number representation that retains the position of the digits and decimal points in the computer, so limiting the maximum manageable numbers **Festkommaschreibweise;** *storage of fixed point numbers has two bytes allocated for the whole number and one byte for the fraction part;* **fixed-point arithmetic** = arithmetic rules and methods using fixed-point numbers **Festkommarechnung;** *compare with* FLOATING POINT

flag

1 *noun* (i) way of showing the end of field *or* of indicating something special in a database; (ii) method of reporting the status of a register after a mathematical *or* logical operation **(i) Anzeiger; (ii) Flag;** *if the result is zero, the zero flag is set;* **carry flag** = indicator that a carry has occurred after a subtraction *or* addition **Übertragsanzeiger; device flag** = one bit in a device status word, used to show the state of a device **Geräteanzeiger; overflow bit** *or* **flag** = single bit in a word that is set to one (1) if a mathematical overflow has occurred **Überlaufanzeiger; zero flag** = indicator that the contents of a register *or* result is zero **Nullkennzeichnung; flag bit** = single bit of a word used as a flag for certain operations **Synchronisationszeichen; flag code** = code sequence which informs the receiver that following characters represent control actions **Steuerzeichenkennzeichnung; flag event** = process *or* state *or* condition that sets a flag **Ereignis zum Kennzeichen setzen; flag register** = register that contains the status and flag bits of a CPU **Kennzeichenregister; flag sequence** = sequence of codes sent on a packet switching network as identification of the start and finish of a frame of data **Blockbegrenzung**
2 *verb* to attract the attention of a program while it is running to provide a result *or* to report an action *or* to indicate something special **markieren**

◊ **flagging** *noun*
(a) putting an indicator against an item so that it can be found later **Markieren**
(b) picture distortion from a video recorder due to incorrect synchronization of tape playback head **Markierung**

flare *noun* unwanted light due to internal lens *or* camera reflections causing bright spots on a photographic film **Lichtreflexe**

◊ **flared** *adjective* image with unwanted bright spots *or* lines due to internal lens *or* camera reflections **reflektierend**

flash *verb* to switch a light on and off; to increase and lower the brightness of a cursor to provide an indicator **blinken; flash A/D** = parallel high speed A/D converter **Hochgeschwindigkeits-analog-digital-Umsetzer; flash card** = card containing indexing information photographed with a document **Indexkarte; flashing character** = character intensity that is switched on and off (as an indicator) **blinkendes Zeichen**

flat *adjective*
(a) lacking contrast (in an image *or* photograph) **kontrastarm**
(b) smooth (surface) **eben; flat file** = two-dimensional file of data items **Flachdatei; flat pack** = integrated circuit package whose leads extend horizontally, allowing the device to be mounted directly onto a PCB without the need for holes **Flachgehäuse**
(c) fixed *or* not changing **pauschal; flat rate** = set pricing rate that covers all the uses of a facility **Pauschaltarif**

◊ **flatbed** *noun* printing *or* scanning machine that holds the paper *or* image on a flat surface while processing **Flachbettgerät;** *scanners are either flatbed models or platen type, paper-fed models; paper cannot be rolled through flatbed scanners;* **flatbed plotter** = movable pen that draws diagrams under the control of a computer onto a flat piece of paper **Flachbettplotter; flatbed press** = mechanical printing machine where the inked printing plate lies flat on the bed of the machine **Flachbettpresse; flatbed transmitter** = device that keeps a document flat while it is being scanned before being transmitted by facsimile means **Flachbettscanner**

flex *noun* wire *or* cable used to connect an appliance to the mains electricity supply **Kabel**
NOTE: no plural: **a piece of flex**

flexible *adjective* which can be altered *or* changed **flexibel; flexible array** = array whose size and limits can be altered **flexible Feldgruppe; flexible disk** = FLOPPY DISK; **flexible disk cartridge** = FLOPPY DISK; **flexible machining system (FMS)** = computer numeric control (CNC) *or* control of a machine by a computer **flexibles Maschinensteuerungssystem;**

flexible manufacturing system (FMS) = use of CNC machines, robots and other automated devices in manufacturing **flexibles Fertigungssystem; flexible working hours** = system where workers can start *or* stop working at different hours of the morning *or* evening, provided that they work a certain number of hours per week **gleitende Arbeitszeit**

◊ **flexibility** *noun* ability of hardware *or* software *or* adapt to various conditions *or* tasks **Flexibilität**

flicker

noun
a) random variation of brightness in a television picture **Flimmern**
b) effect that occurs when a frame from a video disk is frozen and two different pictures are displayed alternately at high speed due to the incorrect field matching **Flimmern**
c) computer graphic image whose brightness alternates due to a low image refresh rate *or* signal corruption **Flimmern**
‡ *verb* to move very slightly **flimmern, flackern;** *the image flickers when the printer is switched on*

◊ **flicker-free** *adjective* (display) that does not flicker **flimmerfrei**

QUOTE the new 640 by 480 pixel standard, coupled with the flicker-free displays on the four new monitors and a maximum of 256 colours from a palette of more than quarter of a million
PC User

flier *noun* small advertising leaflet designed to encourage customers to ask for more information about a product *or* service **Hand-, Werbezettel**

flip-flop (FF) *noun* electronic circuit *or* chip whose output can be one of two states, which is determined by one or two inputs, can be used to store one bit of digital data **Flipflop, bistabile Schaltung; JK-flip-flop =** flip-flop device with two inputs (J and K) and two outputs whose states are always complementary and dependent on the inputs **JK-Flipflop** ⇨ APPENDIX **D-flip-flop =** flip-flop device with one input and two outputs **D-Flipflop**

flippy *noun* disk that is double-sided but used in a single-sided drive, so it has to be turned over to read the other side **Flippy (doppelseitig beschreibbare, umzudrehende Diskette)**

float *noun* addition of the origin address to all indexed *or* relative addresses to check the amount of memory a program will

require **Speicherauszug des gesamten Systems; float factor =** location in memory at which the first instruction of a program is stored **Startadresse; float relocate =** to convert floating addresses to absolute addresses **Umsetzung relativer in absolute Adressen**

◊ **floating** *adjective* not fixed; character which is separate from the character it should be attached to **fließend; floating accent =** method of printing an accent in text where the accent is separate from the letter above which it is printed (on a typewriter, an accented letter may need three keystrokes, one for the accent, then backspace, then key the letter) **gleitender Akzent; floating address =** location specified in relation to a reference address **symbolische Adresse; floating head =** FLYING HEAD; **floating point arithmetic =** arithmetic operations on floating point numbers **Fließkommaarithmetik; floating point (notation) =** numerical notation in which a fractional number is represented with a point after the first digit and a power of ten, so that any number can be stored in a standard form **Fließkommaschreibweise;** *the fixed number 56.47 in floating-point arithmetic would be 0.5647 and a power of 2;* **floating point number =** number represented using floating point notation **Fließkommazahl; floating point operation (FLOP) =** mathematical operation carried out on a floating point number **Fließkommaoperation; floating point processor =** specialized CPU that can process floating point numbers very rapidly **Fließkommaprozessor;** *the floating point processor speeds up the processing of the graphics software; this model includes a built-in floating point processor;* **floating symbolic address =** symbol *or* label that identifies a particular instruction *or* word, regardless of its location **symbolische Adresse; floating voltage =** voltage in a network *or* device that has no related ground *or* reference plane **Schwebspannung**

flooding *noun* rapid, reliable but not very efficient means of routing packet-switched data, in which each node sends the data received to each of its neighbours **paketvermittelte Datenübertragungsmethode**

FLOP = FLOATING POINT OPERATION; **FLOPs per second =** measure of computing power as the number of floating point operations that a computer can execute every second **Fließkommarechnungen pro Sekunde**

floppy disk *or* **floppy** *or* **FD** *noun* secondary storage device, in the form of a flat, circular flexible disk onto which data can be stored in a magnetic form (a floppy disk cannot store as much data as a hard disk, but is easily removed, and is protected by a flexible paper *or* plastic sleeve; **floppy disk controller (FDC)** = combination of hardware and software devices that control and manage the read/write operations of a disk drive from a computer **Diskettensteuerelemente; floppy disk sector** = smallest area on a magnetic (floppy) disk that can be individually addressed by a computer **Diskettensektor; floppy disk drive** *or* **unit** = disk drive for floppy disks and ancillary electronics as a separate assembly **Diskettenlaufwerk; floppy tape** *or* **tape streamer** = continuous loop of tape, used for backing storage **Band;** *see also* MICROFLOPPY

COMMENT: floppies are available in various sizes: the commonest are 3.5 inch, 5.25 inch and 8 inch. The size refers to the diameter of the disk inside the sleeve

flow

1 *noun* regular movement **Fluß;** *automatic text flow across pages; the device controls the copy flow; current flow is regulated by a resistor;* **flow control** = management of the flow of data into queues and buffers, to prevent spillage *or* lost data **Flußsteuerung 2** *verb* to move smoothly **fließen;** *work is flowing normally again after the breakdown of the printer;* **data flow** = movement of data through a system **Datenfluß**

◇ **flowchart** *or* **flow diagram**
1 *noun* chart which shows the arrangement of the steps in a process *or* program **Flußdiagramm; data flowchart** = diagram used to describe a computer *or* data processing system structure **Datenflußplan; flowchart symbols** = special symbols used to represent devices, decisions and operations in a flowchart **Sinnbild für Datenflußläufe; flowchart template** = plastic sheet with template symbols cut out, to allow symbols to be drawn quickly and clearly **Zeichenschablone; logical flowchart** = diagram showing where the logical decisions occur in a structure and their effects on program execution **logisches Flußdiagramm 2** *verb* to describe a process, its control and routes graphically **im Flußdiagramm darstellen; flow diagram** = FLOWCHART; **flow direction** = order in which events occurring a flowchart **Ablaufrichtung; flowline** = lines connecting flowchart symbols, showing the direction of flow within a flowchart **Ablauflinie**

fluctuate *verb* to move up and down **schwanken;** *the electric current fluctuates between 1 Amp and 1.3 Amp; fluctuating signal strength*

◇ **fluctuation** *noun* up and down movement **Schwankung;** *voltage fluctuations can affect the functioning of the computer system*

flush

1 *verb* to clear *or* erase all the contents of a queue, buffer, file or section of memory **löschen; flush buffers** = to erase any data remaining in a buffer, ready for a new job *or* after a job has been aborted **Speicher löschen 2** *adjective* level *or* in line with **auf gleicher Ebene, glatt beschnitten;** *the covers are trimmed flush with the pages;* **flush left** *or* **flush right** *see* JUSTIFY LEFT, JUSTIFY RIGHT

flutter *noun* fluctuations of tape speed due to mechanical *or* circuit problems, causing signal distortion **Gleichlaufschwankung, Jaulen;** *wow and flutter are common faults on cheap tape recorders*

fly *verb* to move through the air **fliegen; flying spot scan** = method of transferring a frame of film to television by scanning it with a light beam **Lichtpunktabtastung**

◇ **flyback** *noun* electron picture beam return from the end of a scan to the beginning of the next **Rücklauf**

flying head *noun* hard disk read/write head that is wing-shaped to fly just above the surface of the spinning disk **fliegender Lese-/Schreibkopf**

FM = FREQUENCY MODULATION

FMS = FLEXIBLE MACHINING SYSTEM, FLEXIBLE MANUFACTURING SYSTEM computer numeric control (CNC) *or* control of a machine by a computer **flexibles Maschinensteuerungssystem; flexibles Fertigungssystem**

FNP = FRONT END NETWORK PROCESSOR

f-number *noun* measurement of the amount of light that an optical lens can collect, measured as the ratio of focal length to maximum aperture **Blendenöffnungsverhältnis, Brennzahl**

focal length *noun* distance between the centre of an optical lens and the focusing plane, when the lens is focused at infinity **Brennweite**

focus
1 *noun* image *or* beam that is clear and well defined **Schärfe; the picture is out of focus** *or* **is not in focus** = the picture is not clear **das Bild ist unscharf**
2 *verb* to adjust the focal length of a lens *or* beam deflection system so that the image *or* beam is clear and well defined **scharfstellen;** *the camera is focused on the foreground; they adjusted the lens position so that the beam focused correctly*

fog *noun* effect on photographic material which has been accidentally exposed to unwanted light, causing a loss of picture contrast **(Grau)schleier**

fold *verb* to bend a flat thing, so that part of it is on top of the rest **falten;** *she folded the letter so that the address was clearly visible;* **accordion fold** *or* **fanfold** = method of folding continuous stationery, one sheet in one direction, the next sheet in the opposite direction **Zickzackfaltung**
◊ **-fold** *suffix* times **-fach; four-fold** = four times **vierfach**
◊ **folder** *noun* cardboard envelope for carrying papers **Aktendeckel;** *put all the documents in a folder for the chairman*
◊ **folding** *noun* hashing method (that generates an address by splitting the key into parts and adding them together) **Streuspeichermethode**
◊ **folding machine** *noun* machine which automatically folds sheets of paper **Falzmaschine**

folio
1 *noun* page with a number, especially two facing pages in an account book which have the same number **numerierte Seite**
2 *verb* to put a number on a page **paginieren**

font *or* **fount** *noun* set of characters all of the same style, size and typeface **Schriftart, Zeichensatz, Font; font change** = function on a computer to change the style of characters used on a display screen **Zeichensatzänderung; font disk** = (i) transparent disk that contains the master images of a particular font, used in a phototypesetting machine; (ii) magnetic disk that contains the data to drive a character generator to make up the various fonts on a computer display **(i) Schriftenplatte; (ii) Schriftdatenplatte; downloadable fonts** *or* **resident fonts** = fonts

or typefaces which are stored on a disk and can be downloaded to a printer and stored in temporary memory **verfügbare Zeichensätze**

QUOTE laser printers store fonts in several ways: as resident, cartridge and downloadable fonts
Desktop Publishing Today

foolscap *noun* large size of writing paper, longer than A4; *entspricht* **Kanzleipapier;** *the letter was on six sheets of foolscap;* **a foolscap envelope** = large envelope which takes foolscap paper **Umschlag für Kanzleipapier**
NOTE: no plural

foot *noun* bottom part **Fuß;** *he signed his name at the foot of the letter*
◊ **foot candle** *noun* amount of light illumination in one square foot when the incident flux is one lumen **Fußkerze (= 1 Lumen pro sq.ft.)**
◊ **footer** *or* **footing** *noun* message at the bottom of all the pages in a printed document (such as the page number) **Fußzeile**
◊ **footnote** *noun* note at the bottom of a page, which refers to the text above it, usually using a superior number as a reference **Fußnote**
◊ **footprint** *noun*
(a) area covered by a transmitting device such as a satellite *or* antenna **Erfassungsbereich**
(b) area that a computer takes up on a desk **Installationsfläche**

for-next loop *noun* loop or routine that is repeated until a condition no longer occurs **FOR-NEXT-Schleife;** *for X=1 to 5: print X: next X - this will print out 1 2 3 4 5*

forbid *verb* to say that something must not be done **verbieten;** *the contract forbids sale of the goods to the USA;* **forbidden character** *or* **combination** = bit combination in a computer word that is not allowed according to the rules defined by the programmer *or* system designer **verbotenes Zeichen; verbotene Zeichenkombination**
NOTE: **forbidding - forbade - forbidden**

force
1 *noun* strength **Kraft; to come into force** = to start to operate *or* work **in Kraft treten;** *the new regulations will come into force on January 1st*
2 *verb* to make someone do something **zwingen;** *competition has forced the company to lower its prices;* **forced page break** = embedded code which indicates a new page start **erzwungener Seitenumbruch**

foreground *noun*
(a) front part of an illustration (as opposed to the background) **Vordergrund; foreground colour** = colour of characters and text displayed on a screen **Vordergrundfarbe**
(b) high priority task done by a computer **Prioritätsaufgabe; foreground/background modes** = computer system in which two modes for program execution are possible: foreground mode for interactive user programs, background mode for housekeeping and other necessary system programs **Vorder-/Hintergrundmodus; foreground processing** *or* **foregrounding** = execution of high priority jobs *or* programs in a multitasking operating system **Vordergrundverarbeitung; foreground program** = high priority program in a multitasking system, whose results are usually visible to the user **Vordergrundprogramm, Prioritäts-, Vorrangprogramm;** *compare* BACKGROUND

forest *noun* number of interconnected data structure trees **Wald**

form
1 *noun*
(a) preprinted document with blank spaces where information can be entered **Vordruck, Formular**
(b) complete plate *or* block of type, ready for printing **Druckform**
(c) page of computer stationery **Formularseite; form feed** = command to a printer to move to the next sheet of paper **Formularvorschub; form flash** = text heading held in store and printed out at the same time as the text **Formulareinblendung; form handling equipment** = peripherals (such as decollator) which deal with output from a printer **Papiernachbereitungsmaschine; form letter** = standard letter into which personal details of each addressee are inserted, such as name, address and job **Formbrief; form mode** = display method on a data entry terminal, the form is displayed on the screen and the operator enters relevant details **Formularmodus; form overlay** = heading *or* other matter held in store and printed out at the same time as the text **Formmaske, Formschablone; form stop** = sensor on a printer which indicates when the paper has run out **Papierendesensor**
2 *verb* to create a shape; to construct **bilden;** *the system is formed of five separate modules*

format
1 *noun*
(a) size and shape of a book **Format;** *the printer can deal with all formats up to quarto*

(b) specific method of arranging text *or* data; way of arranging data on disk **Format; address format** = way in which address data is stored including which bits select pages, memory protect, etc. **Adreßformat; card format** = way in which columns and rows are arranged to represent data *or* characters in a punched card **Lochkartenformat; data format** = rules defining the way in which data is stored *or* transmitted **Datenformat; display format** = number of characters that can be displayed on a screen, given as row and column lengths **Anzeigeformat; format mode** = use of protected display fields on a screen to show a blank form *or* page which cannot be altered, but into which a user can enter information **Formatmodus; instruction format** = rules defining the way the operands, data and address are arranged in an instruction **Befehlsstruktur; local format storage** = format of a empty form *or* repeated page stored in a terminal rather than being repeatedly transmitted **Schablonenspeicherung; variable format** = changing method of arranging data *or* text within an area **variables Format**
(c) precise syntax of instructions and arguments **Format; symbolic-coding format** = assembly language instruction syntax, using a label, operation and operand fields **Format zur symbolischen Codierung**
(d) way of arranging a TV programme **Struktur; magazine format** = type of information programme which contains several different items linked together **Magazinformat**
2 *verb*
(a) to arrange text as it will appear in printed form on paper **anordnen;** *style sheets are used to format documents;* **formatted dump** = text *or* data printed in a certain format **formatisierter Speicherauszug**
(b) to format a disk = (i) to set up a blank disk so that it is ready for data, by writing control and track location information on it; (ii) to define the areas of a disk reserved for data and control **(i) & (ii) formatieren; disk formatting** = setting up a blank disk by writing control and track location information on it **Formatierung;** *disk formatting has to be done before you can use a new floppy disk*

◇ **formatter** *noun* hardware *or* software that arranges text *or* data according to certain rules **Formatisierungsprogramm; print formatter** = software that converts embedded codes and print commands to printer control signals **Druckformatierer; text formatter** = program that converts text to a new form *or* layout according to parameters *or* embedded codes (such as line width, page size, justification, etc.) **Textformatierer**

formula *noun* set of mathematical rules applied to solve a problem **Formel; formula portability** = feature in a spreadsheet program to find a value in a single cell from data in others, with the possibility of using the same formula in other cells **Werteaustauschbarkeit; formula translator** = FORTRAN
NOTE: plural is **formulae**

FORTH computer programming language mainly used in control applications **FORTH Programmiersprache)**

FORTRAN = FORMULA TRANSLATOR programming language developed in the first place for scientific use **FORTRAN Programmiersprache)**

forty-track disk *noun* floppy disk formatted to contain forty tracks of data **Diskette mit 40 Spuren**

forward
1 *adjective* moving in advance *or* in front **vorwärts; forward channel** = communications line containing data transmitted from the user to another party **Hauptvermittlungskanal; forward clearing** = switching telephone systems back to their clear state, starting from the point where the call was made and travelling forward towards the destination **Weitervermittlung; forward error correction** = method of detecting and correcting certain error conditions with the use of redundant codes **Vorwärtsfehlerkorrektur; forward reference** = reference to something which has not yet been established **Verweis nach vorne; forward scatter** = scattered sections of wave travelling in the same direction as the incident **Vorwärtsstreuung**
2 *verb* to pass a call on to another point **weitervermitteln**

◊ **forward mode** *noun* to add a number *or* index *or* displacement to an origin **Vorwärtsmodus**

FOSDIC = FILM OPTICAL SCANNING DEVICE FOR INPUT INTO COMPUTERS storage device for computer data using microfilm **optische Filmleseeinheit**

fount = FONT set of characters all of the same style, size and typeface **Schriftart, Zeichensatz**

four-address instruction *noun* program instruction which contains four addresses within its address field, usually the location of the two operands, the result and the location of the next instruction **Vieradreßbefehl; four-plus-one address** = instruction that contains the locations of four registers and the location of the next instruction **Vier-plus-eins-Adreßbefehl**

Fourier series *noun* mathematical representation of waveforms by a combination of fundamental and harmonic components of a frequency **Fourier-Serie**

fourth generation computers *noun* computer technology using LSI circuits, developed around 1970 and still in current use **Computer der vierten Generation; fourth generation languages** = languages that are user-friendly and have been designed with the non-expert in mind **Programmiersprachen der vierten Generation**

four-track recorder *noun* tape recorder that is able to record and play back four independent audio tracks at once **Vierspurrekorder**

fps = FRAMES PER SECOND

fraction *noun* (i) part of a whole unit, expressed as one figure above another (such as ½, ¾, etc.); (ii) mantissa of a floating point number **(i) Bruch; (ii) Mantisse (einer Fließkommazahl)**
◊ **fractional** *adjective* made of fractions; referring to fractions **gebrochen, Bruch-, bruch-;** *the root is the fractional power of a number;* **fractional part** = mantissa of a floating point number **Stellen hinter dem Komma einer Zahl**

fragmentation *noun* main memory allocation to a number of files, which has resulted in many small, free sections *or* fragments that are too small to be of any use, but waste a lot of space **Zerstückelung, Fragmentierung**

frame *noun*
(a) (i) space on magnetic tape for one character code; (ii) packet of transmitted data including control and route information **(i) Rahmen; (ii) Datenübertragungsblock; frame error** = error

due to a faulty bit within a frame on magnetic tape **Rahmenfehler**
(b) one complete television *or* photographic image **Rasterfeld; Einzelbild; video frame** = one image on a video film **Videoeinzelbild;** *with the image processor you can freeze a video frame;* **frame flyback** = electron beam return from the bottom right to the top left corner of the screen to start building up a new field **Rahmenrücklauf; frame frequency** = number of television frames transmitted per second **Bildfrequenz;** *in the UK the frame frequency is 25 fps;* **frame grabber** = high speed digital sampling circuit that stores a television picture frame in memory so that it can then be processed by a computer **Bild-Grabber; frame store** = digital storage of analog TV signals on disk **Bildspeicher;** *the image processor allows you to store a video frame in a built-in 8-bit frame store; the frame store can be used to display weather satellite pictures*

◊ **frames per second (fps)** *noun*
(a) speed of single frames of a motion picture through a projector *or* camera every second **Bilder pro Sekunde**
(b) number of television picture frames transmitted per second **Bilder pro Sekunde**

◊ **framing** *noun*
(a) positioning of a camera's field of view for a required image **Einstellung**
(b) synchronization of time division multiplexed frames of data **Bildlageeinstellung; framing bit** = sync bit *or* transmitted bit used to synchronize devices **Rahmenbit; framing code** = method of synchronizing a receiver with a broadcast teletext stream of data **Rahmencode**

◊ **framework** *noun* basic structure of a database *or* process *or* program **Grundstruktur;** *the program framework was designed first*

fraud *noun* making money by tricking people *or* by making them believe something which is not true **Betrug; computer fraud** = theft of data *or* dishonest use *or* other crimes involving computers **Computerkriminalität**

QUOTE the offences led to the arrest of nine teenagers who were all charged with computer fraud
Computer News

free
1 *adjective* available for use *or* not currently being used; (spare bytes) available on disk *or* in memory **frei; free indexing** = library entries having references to documents which the indexer considers useful, even if they do not appear in the text **freie Indizierung; free line** = telephone line that is not connected and so is available for use

freie Telefonleitung; **free running mode** = interactive computer mode that allows more than one user to have simultaneous use of a program **freier Durchlaufbetrieb; free space loss** = measure of the loss of transmitted signals from a satellite antenna to an earth station **Freiraumdämpfung; free space media** = empty space between a transmitter and a receiving aerial which is used for transmission **freier Raum; free wheeling** = transmission protocol where the computer transmitting receives no status signals from the receiver **Freilaufprotokoll**
2 *verb* to erase *or* remove *or* backup programs *or* files to provide space in memory **löschen**

◊ **freedom** *noun* being free to do something without restriction **Freiheit; freedom of information** = being able to examine computer records (referring both to government activities and to records kept about individuals) **Informationsfreiheit; freedom of the press** = being able to write and publish in a newspaper what you wish without being afraid of prosecution, provided that you do not break the law **Pressefreiheit; freedom of speech** = being able to say what you want without being afraid of prosecution, provided that you do not break the law **Redefreiheit**

◊ **freely** *adverb* with no restrictions **frei, unbeschränkt**

freeze *verb* **to freeze (frame)** = to stop and display a single frame from a film *or* TV *or* video disk *or* video tape machine **einfrieren;** *the image processor will freeze a single TV frame*

F-region section of the ionosphere that is 150 - 400Km from the earth's surface **F-Schicht der Ionosphäre**

frequency *noun* number of cycles *or* periods of a regular waveform that are repeated per second **Frequenz; frequency changer** = electronic circuit that shifts the frequency of a signal up *or* down **Frequenzverschieber; frequency divider** = electronic circuit that reduces the frequency of a signal by a multiple of two **Frequenzteiler; frequency division multiplexing (FDM)** = transmission of several independent signals along a single channel, achieved by shifting each signal up in frequency by a different amount **Frequenz-Multiplexmethode; frequency domain** = effects of a certain circuit on the frequency range of a signal **Frequenzebene; frequency modulation (FM)** = varying the frequency of a carrier waveform according to a signal amplitude **Frequenzmodulation**

(FM); frequency range = range of allowable frequencies, between two limits **Frequenzbereich; frequency response** = electronic circuit parameter given as the ratio of output to input signal amplitudes at various frequencies **Frequenzgang, Übertragungsbereich; frequency shift keying (FSK)** = transmission system using the translation of two state binary data into two different frequencies, one for on, one for off **Frequenzumtastung; frequency variation** = change of frequency of a signal from normal **Frequenzvariation; clock frequency** = frequency of the main clock that synchronizes a computer system **Taktfrequenz;** *the main clock frequency is 10MHz*

◊ **frequent** *adjective* which comes *or* goes *or* takes place often **häufig;** *we send frequent telexes to New York; how frequent are the planes to Birmingham?*

◊ **frequently** *adverb* often **häufig;** *the photocopier is frequently out of use; we telex our New York office very frequently - at least four times a day*

friction feed *noun* printer mechanism where the paper is advanced by holding it between two rollers (as opposed to tractor feed) **Friktionsantrieb**

FROM = FUSIBLE READ ONLY MEMORY

front *noun* part of something which faces away from the back **Vorderseite, Front;** *the disks are inserted in slots in the front of the terminal;* **front panel** = main computer system control switches and status indicators **vordere Verkleidungsplatte; front porch** = section of television signal between the line blanking pulse and the line sync pulse **vordere Schwarztreppe; front projection** = projection of background images onto a screen located behind a person **Aufprojektion**

◊ **front-end** *adjective* located at the start *or* most important point of a circuit *or* network **Eingangs-; front-end processor (FEP)** = processor placed between an input source and the central computer whose function is to preprocess received data to relieve the workload of the main computer **Vorschaltrechner; front-end system** = typesetting system, where text is keyboarded on a terminal directly connected to the typesetting computer **Vorverarbeitungssystem**

FSK = FREQUENCY SHIFT KEYING

full *adjective*
(a) with as much inside as possible **voll;** *the*
disk is full, so the material will have to be stored on another disk
(b) complete *or* including everything **vollständig; full adder** = binary addition circuit that can produce the sum of two inputs and can also accept a carry input, producing a carry output if necessary **Volladdierer; full duplex** = data transmission down a channel in two directions simultaneously **Duplex;** *see also* DUPLEX, HALF-DUPLEX, SIMPLEX; **full-frame time code** = standard method of counting video frames rather than using a time check signal for synchronization with music and effects **Zeitcode zum Zählen von Videovollbildern; full-size display** = large screen VDU which can display a whole page of text **Anzeige in voller Größe; full subtractor** = binary subtractor circuit that can produce the difference of two inputs and can also accept a carry input, producing a carry output if necessary **Subtrahierwerk**

◊ **fully** *adverb* completely **vollständig; fully connected network** = situation where each node in a network is connected with every other **vollverbundenes Netz; fully formed characters** = characters produced by a printer in a single action **Volltypen;** *a daisy wheel printer produces fully formed characters*

function
1 *noun*
(a) mathematical formula, where a result is dependent upon several other numbers **Funktion**
(b) sequence of computer program instructions in a main program that perform a certain task **Funktion; function digit** = code used to instruct a computer as to which function *or* branch in a program to follow **Funktionscode; function table** = list that gives the relationship between two sets of instructions *or* data **Funktionstabelle**
(c) special feature available on a computer *or* word-processor **Funktion;** *the word-processor had a spelling-checker function but no built-in text-editing function;* **function code** = printing codes that control an action rather than representing a character **Funktionscode**
2 *verb* to operate *or* perform correctly **funktionieren;** *the new system has not functioned properly since it was installed*

◊ **functional** *adjective* which refers to the way something works **Funktions-, funktions-; functional diagram** = drawing of the internal workings and processes of a machine *or* piece of software **Funktionsdiagramm; functional specification** = specification which defines the results which a program is expected to produce **Funktionsbeschreibung; functional unit** = hardware *or* software that works as it should **Funktionseinheit**

◊ **function key** *or* **programmable function key** *noun* key *or* switch that has been assigned a particular task *or* sequence of instructions **Funktionstaste;** *tags can be allocated to function keys; hitting F5 will put you into insert mode*

COMMENT: function keys often form a separate group of keys on the keyboard, and have specific functions attached to them. They may be labelled F1, F2, etc.

QUOTE they made it clear that the PC was to take its place as part of a much larger computing function that comprised of local area networks, wide area networks, small systems, distributed systems and mainframes
Minicomputer News
QUOTE if your computer has a MOD function, you will not need the function defined in line 3010
Computing Today
QUOTE the final set of keys are to be found above the main keyboard and comprise 5 function keys, which together with shift, give 10 user-defined keys
Computing Today

fundamental frequency *noun* most prominent frequency in a complex signal **Grundfrequenz**

COMMENT: almost all signals contain parts of other frequencies (harmonics) at lower amplitudes to the fundamental, which often causes distortion

fuse
1 *noun* electrical protection device consisting of a small piece of metal, which will melt when too much power passes through it **Sicherung; to blow a fuse** = to melt a fuse by passing too much current through it **eine Sicherung durchbrennen lassen**
2 *verb* to draw too much current, causing a fuse to melt **durchbrennen;** *when the air-conditioning was switched on, it fused the whole system*

◊ **fusible link** *noun* small link in a PLA that can be blown to program the device permanently **Sicherung, die durch Durchbrennen programmiert**

◊ **fusible read only memory (FROM)** *noun* PROM that is made up of a matrix of fusible links which are selectively blown to program it **FROM (spezielle ROMs, die durch den Einbau und das spätere Durchbrennen von Sicherungen programmiert werden)**

◊ **fusion** *noun* combining two hardware devices *or* programs *or* chemical substances to create a single form **Verschmelzung, Fusion**

fuzzy *noun* not clear **verschwommen;** *top quality paper will eliminate fuzzy characters;* **fuzzy logic** *or* **fuzzy theory** = type of logic applied to computer programming, which tries to replicate the reasoning methods of the human brain **verschwommene Theorie**

Gg

G = GIGA *prefix* meaning one thousand million **G; GHz** = gigahertz **GHz** ⇨ APPENDIX

COMMENT: in computing G refers to 2^{30}, equal to 1,073,741,824

GaAs = GALLIUM ARSENIDE

gain
1 *noun* increase *or* becoming larger; amount by which a signal amplitude is changed as it passes through a circuit, usually given as a ratio of output to input amplitude **Verstärkungsgrad; gain control** = variable control that sets the amount of gain a circuit *or* amplifier will provide **Verstärkungsregelung**
2 *verb* to obtain *or* to get **erhalten; to gain access to a file** = to be able to access a file **Zugang zu einer Datei erhalten;** *the user cannot gain access to the confidential information in the file without a password*

galactic noise *noun* random electrical noise which originates from planets and stars in space **galaktisches Rauschen**

gallium arsenide (GaAs) *noun* semiconductor compound, a new material for chip construction, that allows faster operation than silicon chips **GaAs (Galliumarsenid)**

galley proof *or* **slip** *noun* rough initial proof of a column *or* section of text, printed on a long piece of paper **Korrekturfahne**

game *noun* something which is played for enjoyment *or* relaxation **Spiel; computer game** = game played on a computer, using special software **Computerspiel; game paddle** = device held in the hand to move a cursor *or* graphics in a computer game **Steuerknüppel**

gamma *noun* (i) measure of the development of a photographic image, and so its contrast range; (ii) logarithm of the luminescence of the image on a TV screen, in relation to that of the original scene when filmed **(i) Kontrastgrad; (ii) Gamma**

ganged *adjective* mechanically linked (devices) that are operated by a single action **zusammengefaßt, gruppiert; ganged switch** = series of switches that operate on different parts of a circuit, but which are all switched by a single action **Gruppenschalter** *a ganged switch is used to select which data bus a printer will respond to*

gap *noun*
(a) space between recorded data **Spalt, Zwischenraum; block** *or* **interblock gap (IBG)** = blank magnetic tape between the end of one block of data and the start of the next in backing store **Blockzwischenraum; gap character** = an extra character added to a group of characters (for parity or another purpose, but not data *or* instructions) **Füllzeichen; gap digit** = an extra digit added to a group of data (for parity or another purpose, but not data *or* instructions) **Füllziffer; record gap** = blank section of magnetic tape between two consecutive records **Satzzwischenraum**
(b) space between a read head and the magnetic medium **Spalt; gap loss** = signal attenuation due to incorrect alignment of the read/write head with the storage medium **Signaldämpfung durch unkorrekte Lese-/Schreibkopfausrichtung; air** *or* **head gap** = narrow gap between a recording *or* playback head and the magnetic medium **Luftspalt**
(c) method of radio communications using a carrier signal that is switched on and off, as in a telegraphic system **Funkübertragungssystem**

garbage *noun*
(a) radio interference from adjacent channels **Funkstörung**
(b) data *or* information that is no longer required because it is out of date *or* contains errors **Abfall; garbage collection** = reorganization and removal of unwanted *or* out of date files and records; clearing a section of memory of a program *or* its data that is not in use **Speicherbereinigung; garbage in garbage out (GIGO)** = expression meaning that the accuracy and quality of information that is output depends on the quality of the input **GIGO (Unsinn rein Unsinn raus)**

COMMENT: GIGO is sometimes taken to mean "garbage in gospel out": i.e. that whatever wrong information is put into a computer, people will always believe that the output results are true

gas discharge display *or* **gas plasma display** *noun* flat, lightweight display screen that is made of two flat pieces of glass covered with a grid of conductors, separated by a thin layer of a gas which luminesces when one point of the grid is selected by two electric signals **Plasmabildschirm**

COMMENT: mainly used in modern portable computer displays, but the definition is not as good as in cathode ray tube displays

gate *noun*
(a) logical electronic switch whose output depends on the states of the inputs and the type of logical function implemented **Gatter; AND gate** = gate that performs a logical AND function **UND-Gatter; coincidence gate** = gate that produces a logical output depending on various input coincidences (an AND gate requires the coincidence in time of all logically true inputs) **Koinzidenzgatter; EXNOR gate** = electronic implementation of the EXNOR function **exklusiv-NOR-Gatter; EXOR gate** = electronic implementation of the EXOR function **exklusiv-ODER-Gatter; NAND gate** = electronic circuit that provides a NAND function **NAND-Gatter; negation** *or* **NOT gate** = single input gate whose output is equal to the logical inverse of the input **NICHT-Gatter; NOR gate** = electronic circuit which performs a NOR function **NOR-Gatter; OR gate** = electronic circuit that provides the OR function **ODER-Gatter; gate array** = number of interconnected logic gates built into an integrated circuit to perform a complex function **Gatteranordnung; gate delay** *or* **propagation time** = time taken for a gate to produce an output after it has received inputs **Schaltverzögerung; gate circuit** = electronic components that implement a logical function **Schaltkreis**
(b) connection pin of a FET device **Torschaltung**
(c) mechanical film *or* slide frame aligner in a camera *or* projector **Justiervorrichtung**

◇ **gateway** *noun* hard *or* software protocol translation device that allows users working in one network to access another **Verbindungsrechner**

gather *verb* to receive data from various sources (either directly from a data capture device or from a cartridge) and sort and insert in correct order into a database **sammeln; gather write** = to write a group of separate records as one block of data **sammelnd (auf)schreiben**

gauge
1 *noun* device which measures thickness *or* width **Meßlehre**
2 *verb* to measure the thickness *or* width of something **messen**

gender changer *noun (informal)* device for changing a female connection to a male or vice versa **Geschlechtsumwandler**

general *adjective*
(a) ordinary *or* not special **allgemein; general office** = main administrative office **Hauptbüro**
(b) dealing with everything **universal; general purpose computer** = computer whose processing power may be applied to many different sorts of applications, depending on its hardware *or* software instructions **Universalcomputer; general purpose interface bus (GPIB)** = standard for an interface bus between a computer and laboratory equipment **IEC-Bus, Universalschnittstellenbus; general purpose program** = program *or* device able to perform many different jobs *or* applications **Universalprogramm; general register** *or* **general purpose register (gpr)** = data register in a computer processing unit that can store items of data for many different mathematical *or* logical operations **Mehrzweckregister**

generate *verb* to use software *or* a device to produce codes *or* a program automatically **generieren, erzeugen;** *to generate an image from digitally recorded data; the graphics tablet generates a pair of co-ordinates each time the pen is moved;* **computer-generated** = produced using a computer **computergeneriert;** *they analyzed the computer-generated image;* **generated address** = location used by a program that has been produced by instructions within the program **errechnete Adresse; generated error** = error occurring due to inaccuracies in data used (such as a sum total error due to a series of numbers which are rounded up) **generierter Fehler**

◇ **generation** *noun*
(a) producing data *or* software *or* programs using a computer **Generierung;** *the computer is used in the generation of graphic images; code generation is automatic ;* **program generation** *see* GENERATOR
(b) state *or* age of the technology used in the design of a system **Generation; first**

generation = earliest type of technology **erste Generation; first generation computers** = original computers made with valve-based electronic technology, started around 1951 **Computer der ersten Generation; first generation image** = master copy of an original image, text *or* document **erste Kopie vom Original; second generation computers** = computers which used transistors instead of valves **Computer der zweiten Generation; third generation computers** = computers which used integrated circuits instead of transistors **Computer der dritten Generation; fourth generation computers** = computer technology using LSI circuits, developed around 1970 and still in current use **Computer der vierten Generation; fourth generation languages** = languages that are user-friendly and have been designed with the non-expert in mind **Computersprachen der vierten Generation; fifth generation computers** = next stage of computer system design using fast VLSI circuits and powerful programming languages to allow human interaction **Computer der fünften Generation**
(c) distance between a file and the original version, used when making backups **Generation;** *the father file is a first generation backup*

◇ **generator** *noun*
(a) (program) that generates new programs according to rules *or* specifications set out by the user **Generierungsprogramm**
(b) device which generates electricity **Generator;** *the computer centre has its own independent generator, in case of mains power failure*

> QUOTE vector and character generation are executed in hardware by a graphics display processor
> *Computing Today*

generic *adjective* (something) that is compatible with a whole family of hardware *or* software devices from one manufacturer **auswählbar**

genuine *adjective* real *or* correct **echt;** *authentication allows the system to recognize that a sender's message is genuine*

geometric distortion *noun* linear distortion of a television picture, which can be caused by video tape speed fluctuations **lineare Verzerrung**

geostationary satellite *noun* satellite which moves at the same velocity as the earth, so remains above the same area of the earth's surface, and appears stationary when viewed from the earth **geostationärer Satellit**

germanium *noun* semiconductor material, used as a substrate in some transistors instead of silicon **Germanium**

get *noun* instruction to obtain a record from a file *or* database **Holanweisung**

GHz = GIGAHERTZ

ghost *noun* effect on a television image where a weaker copy of the picture is displayed to one side of the main image, caused by signal reflections **Geisterbild; ghost cursor** = second cursor which can be used in some programs **Zusatzcursor**

gibberish *noun* useless and meaningless information **Unsinn**

giga- *or* **G** *prefix* meaning one thousand million **Giga** *or* **G; gigabyte** = 10^9 bytes **Gigabyte; gigahertz** = frequency of 10^9 Hertz **Gigahertz**

COMMENT: in computing giga refers to 2^{30}, which is equal to 1,073,741,824

GIGO = GARBAGE IN GARBAGE OUT expression meaning that the accuracy and quality of information that is output depends on the quality of the input **GIGO (Unsinn rein Unsinn raus)**

COMMENT: GIGO is sometimes taken to mean "garbage in gospel out": i.e. that whatever wrong information is put into a computer, people will always believe that the output results are true

GINO = GRAPHICAL INPUT OUTPUT graphical control routine written in FORTRAN **GINO**

GKS = GRAPHICS KERNEL SYSTEM standard for software command and functions describing graphical input/output to provide the same functions etc. on any type of hardware **Graphikkernsystem**

glare *noun* very bright light reflections, especially on a VDU screen **Blendung;** *the glare from the screen makes my eyes hurt* NOTE: no plural

glitch *noun (informal)* anything which causes the sudden unexpected failure of a computer *or* equipment **Störimpuls**

global *adjective* covering everything **global, umfassend; global exchange** = replace function which replaces one piece of text (such as a word) with another throughout a whole text **globale Austauschfunktion; global knowledge** = all the knowledge about one problem *or* task **globale Kenntnis; global search and replace** = word-processor search and replace function covering a complete file *or* document **globales Suchen und Ersetzen; global variable** = variable *or* number that can be accessed by any routine *or* structure in a program **globale Variable;** *compare* LOCAL VARIABLE

glossy
1 *adjective* shiny (paper) **glänzend, Glanz-;** *the illustrations are printed on glossy art paper*
2 *noun (informal)* **the glossies** = expensive magazines **die Hochglänzenden**

GND = GROUND electrical circuit connection to earth *or* to a point with a zero voltage level **Masse, Erde**

go ahead *noun* signal to indicate that a receiver *or* device is ready to accept information **Startsignal**

goal *noun* (i) aim *or* what you are trying to do; (ii) final state reached when a task has been finished *or* has produced satisfactory results **(i) & (ii) Ziel**

gofer *noun (US) informal* person who does all types of work in an office *or* studio, etc. **Mädchen für alles, Faktotum**

gold contacts *noun* electrical contacts, (usually for low-level signals) that are coated with gold to reduce the electrical resistance **Goldkontakte**

golf-ball *noun* metal ball with characters on its surface, which produces printed characters by striking a ribbon onto paper **Kugelkopf; golf-ball printer** = computer printer using a golf-ball as a printing head **Kugelkopfdrucker**

COMMENT: a golf-ball contains all the characters of a single typeface; to change the face, the ball is taken out and replaced by another. The main defect of a golf-ball typewriter when used as a printer, is that it is slower than a dot-matrix printer

gospel *see note at* GARBAGE

GOTO programming command which instructs a jump **Sprunganweisung**; *GOTO 105 instructs a jump to line 105*

COMMENT: GOTO statements are frowned upon by software experts since their use discourages set, structured programming techniques

GPIB = GENERAL PURPOSE INTERFACE BUS standard for an interface bus between a computer and laboratory equipment **IEC-Bus, Universalschnittstellenbus**

gpr = GENERAL PURPOSE REGISTER data register in a computer processing unit that can store items of data for many different mathematical *or* logical operations **Mehrzweckregister**

grab *verb* to take something and hold it **greifen, packen**
◊ **grabber** *noun* **frame grabber** = high speed digital sampling circuit that stores a TV picture in memory so that it can then be processed by a computer **Bild-Grabber**

QUOTE sometimes a program can grab all the available memory, even if it is not going to use it
Byte
QUOTE the frame grabber is distinguished by its ability to acquire a TV image in a single frame interval
Electronics & Wireless World

graceful degradation *noun* allowing some parts of a system to continue to function after a part has broken down **kontrollierter Leistungsrückgang**

grade *noun* level *or* rank **Grad, Niveau, (Güte)klasse**; *a top-grade computer expert;* **grade of service** = quality of telephone service at a given time, defined by the likelihood of a successful connection via a telephone network at its busiest time **Servicequalität**
◊ **graduated** *adjective* which has a scale *or* measurements marked on it **mit Maßeinteilung versehen**

grain *noun* spotted effect on fast photographic films due to the size of the light-sensitive silver halide crystals **Korn**

gram *or* **gramme** *noun* unit of measurement of weight, one thousandth of a kilogram **Gramm**; *the book is printed on 70 gram paper*
◊ **grammage** *noun* weight of paper, calculated as grams per square metre **Papiergewicht**
NOTE: usually shown as **gsm : 80 gsm paper**

grammatical error *noun* incorrect use of a computer programming language syntax **Syntaxfehler**
◊ **grammar** *noun* rules for the correct use of language **Grammatik**

grandfather file *noun* third most recent version of a backed up file, after father and son files **Großvaterdatei**; **grandfather cycle** = period in which the grandfather file is retrieved and updated to produce a new father file, the old father file becoming the new grandfather file **Großvaterzyklus**

granularity *noun* size of memory segments in a virtual memory system **Körnung**

graph *noun* diagram showing the relationship between two *or* more variables as a line *or* series of points **Diagramm, Graph**; **graph paper** = paper with many little squares, used for drawing graphs **Millimeterpapier**; **graph plotter** = printing device with a pen which takes data from a computer and plots it in graphic form **Plotter, Kurvenschreiber**
◊ **graphic** *adjective* (representation of information) in the form of pictures *or* plots instead of by text **graphisch, zeichnerisch**; **graphic data** = stored data that represents graphical information (when displayed on a screen) **graphische Daten**; **graphic display** = computer screen able to present graphical information **graphischer Bildschirm**; **graphic display resolution** = number of pixels that a computer is able to display on the screen **graphisches Auflösungsvermögen des Bildschirms**; **graphic language** = computer programming language with inbuilt commands that are useful when displaying graphics **Computersprache zum Programmieren von Graphiken**; *this graphic language can plot lines, circles and graphs with a single command*
◊ **graphical** *adjective* referring to something represented by graphics **graphisch**
◊ **graphically** *adverb* using pictures **graphisch**; *the sales figures are graphically represented as a pie chart*
◊ **graphics** *noun* pictures *or* lines which can be drawn on paper *or* on a screen to represent information **Graphik**; *graphics output such as bar charts, pie charts, line drawings, etc.;* **graphics art terminal** = typesetting terminal that is used with a phototypesetter **Graphikterminal für Fotosatz**; **graphics character** = preprogrammed shape that can be displayed on a non-graphical screen instead of a character, used extensively in videotext systems to display

simple pictures **graphisches Zeichen; graphics kernel system (GKS)** = standard for software command and functions describing graphical input/output to provide the same functions etc. on any type of hardware **Graphikkernsystem; graphics library** = number of routines stored in a library file that can be added to any user program to simplify the task of writing graphics programs **Graphikbibliothek; graphics light pen** = high-accuracy light pen used for drawing onto a graphics display screen **graphischer Lichtstift; graphics mode** = videotext terminal whose displayed characters are taken from a range of graphics characters instead of text **Graphikmodus; graphics pad** or **tablet** = flat device that allows a user to input graphical information into a computer by drawing on its surface **Graphikblock; graphics processor** = dedicated processor and memory used only to produce and control images on a display, to provide high speed graphics handling capabilities **Graphikprozessor; graphics software** = prewritten routines that perform standard graphics commands such as line drawing, plotting, etc., that can be called from within a program to simplify program writing **Graphiksoftware; graphics terminal** = special terminal with a high-resolution graphic display and graphics pad or other input device **Graphikterminal; graphics VDU** = special VDU which can display high-resolution or colour graphics as well as text **Graphik-VDU**

QUOTE one interesting feature of this model is graphics amplification, which permits graphic or text enlargement of up to 800 per cent
QUOTE the custom graphics chips can display an image that has 640 columns by 400 rows of 4-bit pixel
QUOTE several tools exist for manipulating image and graphical data: some were designed for graphics manipulation

Byte

gravure *see* PHOTOGRAVURE

Gray code *noun* coding system in which the binary representation of decimal numbers changes by only one bit at a time from one number to the next **Gray-Verschlüsselung**

COMMENT: used in communications systems to provide error detection facilities

green phosphor *noun* most commonly used phosphor for monochrome screen coating, which displays green characters on a black background **grüner Phosphor**

COMMENT: a new popular screen type is paper-white, using a white phosphor to display black characters on a white background

gremlin *noun (informal)* unexplained fault in a system **Maschinenteufelchen; line gremlin** = unexplained fault when data is lost during transmission **unerklärlicher Datenverlust**

grey scale *noun*
(a) shades of grey that are used to measure the correct exposure when filming **Grauskala**
(b) shades which are produced from displaying what should be colour information on a monochrome monitor **Grauschattierung, Grauwerte**

grid *noun* system of numbered squares used to help when drawing; matrix of lines at right angles allowing points to be easily plotted or located **Raster, Koordinatennetz**

grip
1 *noun* person who works on the stage in a film or TV studio **Bühnenarbeiter**
2 *verb* to hold something tightly **greifen**; *in friction feed, the paper is gripped by the rollers*

ground *noun*
(a) electrical circuit connection to earth or to a point with a zero voltage level **Masse, Erde**; NOTE: **ground** is more common in US English; the U.K. English is **earth**
(b) the earth's surface **Boden; ground absorption** = loss of transmitted power in radio waves that are near the ground **Absorptionsverlust; ground station** = equipment and antenna on the earth used to communicate with an orbiting satellite **Bodenfunkstelle**

group
1 *noun*
(a) set of computer records that contain related information **Verbund; group mark** or **marker** = code used to identify the start and end of a group of related records or items of data **Gruppenmarke, Trennungsmarke; group poll** = polling a number of devices at once **Gruppenaufruf, Gruppenabruf**
(b) six-character word used in telegraphic communications **Gruppe**
(c) single communications channel made up from a number of others that have been multiplexed together **Gruppe**
2 *verb* to bring several things together **gruppieren**

gsm *or* **g/m²** = GRAMS PER SQUARE METRE (PER SHEET) way of showing the weight of paper used in printing **Gramm pro Quadratmeter;** *the book is printed on 70 gsm coated paper*

guarantee *noun* legal document promising that a machine will work properly *or* that an item is of good quality **Garantie;** *the system is still under guarantee and will be repaired free of charge*

guard band *noun*
(a) frequency gap between two communication bands to prevent data corruption due to interference between each other **Schutzabstand**
(b) section of magnetic tape between two channels recorded on the same tape **Schutzabstand**
◊ **guard bit** *noun* one bit within a stored word that indicates to the computer whether it can be altered or if it is protected **Schutzbit**
◊ **guarding** *noun* joining a single sheet to a book *or* magazine **Einkleben eines Einsteckbogens**

guide bars *noun* special lines in a bar code that show the start and finish of the code **Leitlinien;** *the standard guide bars are two thin lines that are a little longer than the coding lines*

guillotine *noun* office machine for cutting paper **Papierschneidemaschine**

gulp *noun* a group of words, usually two bytes **Zwei-Byte-Wortgruppe;** *see also* BYTE, NIBBLE

gun *or* **electron gun** *noun* source of an electron beam located inside a cathode ray tube **Elektronenkanone**

COMMENT: black and white monitors have a single beam gun, while colour monitors contain three, one for each primary colour (Red, Green and Blue) used

gutter *noun* inside margin between two pages of type **Bundsteg**

Hh

hack *verb*
(a) to experiment and explore computer software and hardware **Hard- und Software untersuchen**
(b) to break into a computer system for criminal purposes **Hard- und Software illegal untersuchen**
◊ **hacker** *noun* person who hacks **Hacker**

QUOTE software manufacturers try more and more sophisticated methods to protect their programs and the hackers use equally clever methods to break into them
Electronics & Wireless World
QUOTE the hackers used their own software to break into the credit card centre
Computer News
QUOTE any computer linked to the system will be alerted if a hacker uses its code number
Practical Computing

halation *noun* photographic effect seen as a dark region with a very bright surround, caused by pointing the camera into the light **Lichthofbildung**

half *noun* one of two equal parts **Hälfte;** *half the data was lost in transmission; the second half of the program contains some errors;* **half adder** = binary adder that can produce the sum of two inputs, producing a carry output if necessary, but cannot accept a carry input **Halbaddierer; half duplex** = data transmission in one direction at a time over a bidirectional channel **Halbduplex(übertragung); half-duplex modem** = modem which works in one mode at a time (either transmitting *or* receiving) **Halbduplexmodem;** *some modems can operate in half-duplex mode if required; see also* DUPLEX; **half-height drive** = disk drive whose front is half the height of a standard drive (half height drives, usually 5.25 inches are now the norm on PCs) **halbhohes Laufwerk; half-intensity** = character *or* graphics display at half the usual display brightness **halbe Intensität; half space** = paper movement in a printer by a half the amount of a normal character **halber Abstand; half title** = first page of a book, with the title, but not the publisher's colophon *or* details of the author **Schmutztitel; half wave rectifier** = circuit that allows current to pass in one direction only **Einweggleichrichter; half word** = sequence of bits occupying half a standard computer word, but which can be accessed as a single unit **Halbwort**
◊ **halftone** *or* **half-tone** *noun*
(a) (i) continuous shading of a printed area; (ii) grey shade half way between white and black **(i) & (ii) Halbton; halftone process** *or* **half-toning** = making halftones from photographs **Autotypieverfahren**

(b) illustration made using the halftone process **Halbtonbild;** *the book is illustrated with twenty halftones*

halide *noun* silver compound that is used to provide a light-sensitive coating on photographic film and paper **(Silber)halogenid**

hall effect *noun* description of the effect of a magnetic field on electron flow **Halleffekt; hall effect switch** = solid state electronic switch operated by a magnetic field **Halleffektschalter**

halo *noun* photographic effect seen as a dark region with a very bright line around it, caused by pointing the camera into the light **Lichthof**

halt
1 *noun* computer instruction to stop a CPU carrying out any further instructions until restarted, or until the program is restarted, usually by external means (such as a reset button) **Halt, Stop; dead** *or* **drop-dead halt** = program instruction from the user *or* an error that causes the program to stop without allowing recovery **Unterbrechungshalt; halt instruction** = program instruction that causes a CPU to halt, suspending operations, usually until it is reset **Haltbefehl; programmed halt** = instruction within a program which when executed, halts the processor (to restart the program, a reset is usually required) **programmierter Halt; halt condition** = operating state reached when a CPU reaches a fault or faulty instruction *or* halt instruction *or* halt instruction in the program that is being run **Haltbedingung**
2 *verb* to stop **anhalten;** *hitting CTRL S will halt the program*

ham *noun* **radio ham** = private radio operator who works especially with a short-wave transceiver **Funkamateur**

◇ **Hamming code** *noun* coding system that uses check bits and checksums to detect and correct errors in transmitted data, mainly used in teletext systems **Hamming-Code; Hamming distance** = the number of digits that are different in two equal length words **Hamming-Abstand**

hand *noun* **hands off** = working system where: (i) the operator does not control the operation which is automatic; (ii) the operator does not need to touch the device in use **(i) & (ii) automatisches System; hands on** = working system where the operator controls the operations by keying

instructions on the keyboard **operatorbedientes System;** *the sales representatives have received hands-on experience of the new computer; the computer firm gives a two day hands-on training course;* **hand portable sets** *or* **handy talkies** *or* **HT's** = small low-range portable transceivers **Sprechfunkgeräte; hand receiver** = hand-held device containing all necessary electronics to allow reception of broadcast radio signals **Kofferradio; hand viewer** = hand-held magnifying lens with a mount to allow photographic slides to be viewed **Diabetrachter, Gucki**

◇ **hand-held** *adjective* which can be held in the hand **tragbar; hand-held computer** *or* **programmable** = very small computer which can be held in the hand, useful for basic information input, when a terminal is not available **Taschencomputer**

◇ **handler** *or* **driver** *noun* section of the operating system *or* program which controls a peripheral **Treiber**

◇ **hand off** *verb* to pass control of a communications channel from one transmitter to another **übergeben**

◇ **handset** *noun* telephone receiver, with both microphone and loudspeaker **Telefonhörer;** *see also* ACOUSTIC COUPLER

handshake *or* **handshaking** *noun* standardized signals between two devices to make sure that the system is working correctly, equipment is compatible and data transfer is correct (signals would include ready to receive, ready to transmit, data OK) **Quittungsbetrieb; full handshaking** = signals transmitted between two communicating devices indicating ready-to-transmit, ready-to-receive, received, transmitted, etc. **Vollquittungsbetrieb; handshake I/O control** = use of handshake signals meaning ready-to-send and ready-to-receive, that allow a computer to communicate with a slower peripheral **Ein-/Ausgabequittungsbetrieb**

handwriting *noun* words written by hand **Handschrift;** *the keyboarders are having difficulty in reading the author's handwriting*

◇ **handwritten** *adjective* written by hand, using a pen or pencil, not typed **handgeschrieben;** *the author sent in two hundred pages of handwritten manuscript*

QUOTE all acquisition, data reduction, processing, and memory circuitry is contained in the single hand-held unit
Byte
QUOTE if a line is free, the device waits another 400ms before reserving the line with a quick handshake process
Practical Computing

hang *verb* to enter an endless loop and not respond to further instruction **aufhängen**

◊ **hangover** *noun*
(a) effect on a TV screen where the previous image can still be seen when the next image appears **Auftreten von Fahnen**
(b) sudden tone change on a document that is transmitted over a fax machine as a gradual change, caused by equipment faults **Farbtonänderung**

◊ **hang up** *verb* to cut off a communications line **auflegen;** *after she had finished talking on the telephone, she hung up*

◊ **hangup** *noun* sudden stop of a working program (often due to the CPU executing an illegal instruction *or* entering an endless loop) **Abbruch**

hard *adjective*
(a) solid, as opposed to soft; (parts of a computer system) that cannot be programmed *or* altered **hart; hard card** = board containing a hard disk drive and the required interfacing electronics, which can be slotted into a system's expansion connector **Festplattenlaufwerksplatine; hard copy** = printed document *or* copy of information contained in a computer *or* system, in a form that is readable (as opposed to soft copy) **Hartkopie; hard copy interface** = serial *or* parallel interface used to transmit data between a computer and a printer **Druckerschnittstelle; hard disk** = rigid magnetic disk that is able to store many times more data than a floppy disk, and usually cannot be removed from the disk drive **Festplatte; hard disk drive** = unit used to store and retrieve data from a spinning hard disk (on the commands of a computer) **Festplattenlaufwerk; hard disk model** = model of computer with a hard disk **Festplattenmodell; hard error** = error which is permanent in a system **andauernder Fehler; hard failure** = fault (in hardware) that must be mended before a device will function correctly **Hardware-Fehler;** *the hard failure was due to a burnt-out chip*
(b) high contrast (photographic paper *or* film) **scharf, kontrastreich**

◊ **hardbound** *adjective* (book) with a hard cased cover, as opposed to a paperback **steif gebunden**

◊ **hardcover** *noun & adjective* version of a book with a cased binding (as opposed to paperback) **Hardcover(-);** *we printed 4,000 copies of the hardcover edition, and 10,000 of the paperback*

◊ **hard-sectoring** *noun* method of permanently formatting a disk, where each track is split into sectors, sometimes preformatted by a series of punched holes around the central hub, where each hole marks the start of a sector **Hartformatierung**

hardware *noun* physical units, components, integrated circuits, disks and mechanisms that make up a computer *or* its peripherals **Hardware, Maschinenausrüstung; hardware compatibility** = architecture of two different computers that allows one to run the programs of the other without changing any device drivers *or* memory locations, or the ability of one to use the add-on boards of the other **Hardwarekompatibilität; hardware configuration** = way in which the hardware of a computer system is connected together **Geräteanordnung; hardware interrupt** = interrupt signal generated by a piece of hardware rather than by software **Hardwareunterbrechung; hardware reliability** = ability of a piece of hardware to function normally over a period of time **Maschinenzuverlässigkeit; hardware security** = making a system secure by means of hardware (such as keys, cards, etc.) **Hardwaresicherheit;** NOTE: no plural *compare* SOFTWARE

> COMMENT: computer hardware can include the computer itself, the disks and disk drive, printer, VDU, etc.

hardwired connection *noun* permanent phone line connection, instead of a plug and socket **festverdrahtete Verbindung**

◊ **hardwired logic** *noun* logical function *or* program, which is built into the hardware, using electronic devices, such as gates, rather than in software **festverdrahtete Logik**

◊ **hardwired program** *noun* computer program built into the hardware, and which cannot be changed **festverdrahtetes Programm**

harmonic *noun* frequency of an order of magnitude greater *or* smaller than a fundamental **harmonische Oberschwingung; harmonic distortion** = unwanted harmonics produced by a non-linear circuit from an input signal **Klirrverzerrung; harmonic telephone ringer** = telephone that will only detect a certain range of ringing frequencies, this allows many telephones on a single line to be rung individually **harmonisches Telefonklingeln**

hartley *noun* unit of information, equal to 3.32 bits, or the probability of one state out of ten equally probable states **Hartley**

hash
1 *verb* to produce a unique number derived

from the entry itself, for each entry in a database **mit Hilfe der Streuspeichertechnik abbilden; hashing function** = algorithm used to produce a hash code for an entry and ensure that it is different from every other entry **Hash-Funktion (Algorithmus, um einen Hash-Code zu erzeugen)**

2 *noun*

(a) *see* HASHMARK

(b) **hash code** = coding system derived from the ASCII codes, where the code numbers for the first three letters are added up, giving a new number used as hash code **Hash-Code (Algorithmus zur Adreßberechnung); hash-code system** = coding system using hash codes **Hash-Code-System; hash index** = list of entries according to their hashed numbers **Hash-index; hash table** = list of all entries in a file with their hashed key address **Hash-Tabelle; hash total** = total of a number of hashed entries used for error detection **Kontrollsumme; hash value** = number arrived at after a key is hashed **Hash-Wert**

◇ **hashmark** *or* **hash mark** *noun* printed sign (#) used as a hard copy marker *or* as an indicator **Hash-Zeichen**

NOTE: in US usage (#) means number; # 32 = number 32 (apartment number in an address, paragraph number in a text, etc.). In computer usage, the pound sign (£) is often used in the US instead of the hash to avoid confusion

hazard *noun* fault in hardware due to incorrect signal timing **Gefahr; hazard-free implementation** = logical function design that has taken into account any hazards that could occur, and solved them **gefahrfreie Ausführung**

HD = HALF DUPLEX data transmission in one direction only, over a bidirectional channel **Halbduplex(übertragung)**

HDLC = HIGH LEVEL DATA LINK CONTROL

HDVS = HIGH DEFINITION VIDEO SYSTEM proposed new television format made up of 1 125 lines and requiring a wide screen and high bandwidth equipment to view it on, so limited at present to satellite and cable television installations **HD-Videosystem, hochauflösendes Videosystem**

HDX = HALF DUPLEX

head

1 *noun*

(a) **combined head** *or* **read/write head** = transducer that can read *or* write data from the surface of a magnetic storage medium, such as a floppy disk **Lese-/Schreibkopf;**

head alignment = (i) correct position of a tape *or* disk head in relation to the magnetic surface, to give the best performance and correct track location; (ii) location of the read head in the same position as the write head was (in relation to the magnetic medium) **(i) & (ii) Kopfausrichtung; head cleaning disk** = special disk which is used to clean the disk read/write heads **Kopfreinigungsdiskette; head crash** = component failure in a disk drive, where the head is allowed to hit the surface of the spinning disk, causing disk surface damage and data corruption **fehlerhafte Funktion des (Lese-/Schreib)kopfes; head demagnetizer** = device used to remove any stray magnetic effects that might have built up on the tape head **Kopfentmagnetisierer; head park** = to move the read/write head in a (hard) disk drive to a safe position, not over the disk, so that if the unit is knocked *or* jarred the head will not damage the disk surface **Kopfparken; head wheel** = wheel that keeps video tape in contact with the head **Kopfrad; disk head** = head which reads *or* writes on a floppy disk **Festkopf; flying head** = hard disk read/write head that uses a 'wing' to fly just over the surface of the spinning disk **fliegender Kopf; playback head** = transducer that reads signals recorded on a storage medium and usually converts them to an electrical signal **Hörkopf; read head** = transducer that can read data from a magnetic storage medium such as a floppy disk **Lesekopf; tape head** = head which reads *or* writes signals on a magnetic tape **Bandkopf; write head** = transducer that can write data onto a magnetic medium **Schreibkopf**

(b) data that indicates the start address of a list of items stored in memory **Kopf**

(c) top edge of a book *or* of a page **Kopf; head of form** = first line on a form *or* sheet of paper that can be printed on **oberste Zeile**

(d) start of a reel of recording tape *or* photographic film **Anfang**

(e) top part of a device, network *or* body **Kopf; head end** = interconnection equipment between an antenna and a cable television network **Kopfstelle**

2 *verb* to be the first item of data in a list **anführen;** *the queue was headed by my file*

◇ **header** *noun*

(a) in a local area network, a packet of data that is sent before a transmission to provide information on destination and routing **Vorsatz**

(b) information at the beginning of a list of data relating to the rest of the data **Kopfzeile, Anfangskennsatz; header block** = block of data at the beginning of a file containing data about file characteristics **Vorsatzblock; header card** = punched card

containing information about the rest of the cards in the set **Leitkarte; header label** = section of data at the beginning of a magnetic tape, that contains identification, format and control information **Anfangskennsatz; tape header** = identification information at the beginning of a tape **Bandvorsatz**
(c) words at the top of a page of a document (such as title, author's name, page number, etc.) **Kopfzeile, Spitzmarke;** *see also* FOOTER
◇ **heading** *noun*
(a) title *or* name of a document or file **Überschrift**
(b) header *or* words at the top of each page of a document (such as the title, the page numbers, etc.) **Kopfzeile, Spitzmarke**
◇ **headlife** *noun* length of time that a video *or* tape head can work before being serviced *or* replaced **Lebensdauer eines Kopfes**
◇ **headline** *noun* = HEADING
◇ **headset** *or* **headphones** *noun* small speakers with padding, worn over a person's ears (used for private listening, instead of loudspeakers) **Kopfhörer**
◇ **headword** *noun* main entry word in a printed dictionary **Stichwort**

heap *noun*
(a) temporary data storage area that allows random access **Freispeicher;** *compare with* STACK
(b) binary tree **binärer Baum**

heat sensitive paper *noun see* ELECTROSTATIC PRINTING

heat-sink *noun* metal device used to conduct heat away from an electronic component to prevent damage **Kühlkörper**

Heaviside-Kennelly layer *see* E-REGION

helical scan *noun* method of accessing data stored on video tape which is stored at an angle to the tape edge **Schrägspurverfahren**

helios noise *noun* noise originating from the sun that is picked up by an earthbased antenna when it points in the direction of the sun **Sonnenrauschen**

help *noun*
(a) thing which makes it easy to do something **Hilfe;** *he finds his word-processor a great help in the office; they need some help with their programming*
(b) function in a program *or* system that provides useful information about the

program in use **HILFE-Funktion;** *hit the HELP key if you want information about what to do next*

Hertz *noun* SI unit of frequency, defined as the number of cycles per second of time **Hertz**

COMMENT: Hertz rate is the frequency at which mains electricity is supplied to the consumer. The Hertz rate in the USA and Canada is 60; in Europe it is 50

heterodyne *noun* circuit producing two outputs equal to the sum and difference in frequency of two inputs **Überlagerung**

heterogeneous network *noun* computer network joining computers of many different types and makes **heterogenes Netz; heterogeneous multiplexing** = communications multiplexing system that can deal with channels with different transmission rates and protocols **heterogene Multiplexmethode**

heuristic *adjective* which learns from past experiences **heuristisch;** *a heuristic program learns from its previous actions and decisions*

hex *or* **hexadecimal notation** *noun* number system using base 16 and digits 0-9 and A-F **Hexadezimalschreibweise; hex dump** = display of a section of memory in hexadecimal form **hexadezimale Darstellung; hex pad** = keypad with keys for each hexadecimal digit **hexadezimale Tastatur**

HF = HIGH FREQUENCY radio communications range of frequencies from 3 - 30 MHz **Hochfrequenz**

hidden *adjective* which cannot be seen **versteckt, verborgen; hidden defect in a program** = defect which was not seen when the program was tested **verborgener Programmfehler; hidden files** = important system files which are not displayed in a directory listing and cannot normally be read by a user **verborgene Dateien;** *it allows users to backup or restore hidden system files independently;* **hidden lines** = lines which make up a three-dimensional object, but are obscured when displayed as a two-dimensional image **versteckte Linien; hidden line algorithm** = mathematical formula that removes hidden lines from a two-dimensional computer image of a 3-D object **Hidden-Line-Algorithmus; hidden line removal** = erasure of lines which should not be visible when looking at a two-dimensional image of a three-dimensional object **Entfernung verdeckter Linien**

hierarchy *noun* way in which objects *or* data *or* structures are organized, usually with the most important *or* highest priority *or* most general item at the top, then working down a tree structure **Hierarchie; data hierarchy** = data structure organized hierarchically **Datenhierarchie**

hierarchical classification *noun* library classification system where the list of subjects is divided down into more and more selective subsets **hierarchische Einteilung; hierarchical communications system** = network in which each branch has a number of separate minor branches dividing from it **hierarchisches Kommunikationssystem; hierarchical computer network** = method of allocating control and processing functions in a network to the computers which are most suited to the task **hierarchisches Computernetz; hierarchical database** = database in which records can be related to each other in a defined structure **hierarchische Datenbank; hierarchical directory** = directory listing of files on a disk, showing the main directory and its files, branches and any sub-directories **hierarchisches Verzeichnis**

hi fi *or* **hifi** = HIGH FIDELITY accurate reproduction of audio signals by equipment such as a record player and amplifier **Hi-Fi; a hi fi system *or* a hi fi** = equipment for playing records *or* compact disks *or* tapes *or* listening to the radio (including tape recorder, turntable, amplifier and speakers) **eine Hi-Fi-Anlage**

high *adjective*
(a) large *or* very great **hoch; high density storage** = very large number of bits stored per area of storage medium **Speicher mit hoher Dichte;** *a hard disk is a high density storage medium compared to paper tape;* **high fidelity** *or* **hifi** *or* **hi fi** = accurate reproduction of audio signals by equipment such as a record player and amplifier **High-Fidelity, Klangtreue; high frequency** = radio communications range of frequencies between 3-30 Mhz **Hochfrequenz; high-level data link control (HLDLC)** = ISO defined communications interface protocol which allows several computers to be linked **codeunabhängiges Steuerungsverfahren; high-level data link control station** = equipment and programs which correctly receive and transmit standard HLDLC data frames **Station für codeunabhängige Steuerungsverfahren; high-**

level (programming) language (HLL) = computer programming language that is easy to learn and allows the user to write programs using words and commands that are easy to understand and look like English words, the program is then translated into machine code, with one HLL command often representing a number of machine code instructions **höhere Programmiersprache;** *programmers should have a knowledge of high-level languages, particularly PASCAL; compare* LOW-LEVEL LANGUAGE; **high order** = (digit) with the greatest weighting within a number **(Ziffer) mit höchster Wertigkeit; high-order language** = HIGH-LEVEL LANGUAGE; **high pass filter** = circuit that allows frequencies above a certain limit to pass, while blocking those below that frequency limit **Hochpaßfilter; high performance equipment** = very good quality *or* high specification equipment **Hochleistungsausrüstung; high priority program** = program that is important *or* urgent and is processed before others **Programm mit hoher Priorität; high reduction** = reduction of text *or* graphics for use in micrographics, usually reduced by 30 to 60 times **starke Verkleinerung; high specification** *or* **high spec** = giving a high degree of accuracy *or* having a large number of features **hohe Spezifikation;** *high spec cabling needs to be very carefully handled;* **high speed carry** = single operation in which a carry into an adder results in a carry out **Schnellübertrag; high usage trunk** = main communications line that carries a large number of calls **Querleitung**
(b) logical high = equal to logic TRUE state or 1 **logischer Pegel H;** *compare* LOGICAL LOW; FALSE

◊ **highlight**
1 *noun* highlights = characters *or* symbols treated to make them stand out from the rest of the text, often by using bold type **Hervorhebungen**
2 *verb* to make part of the text stand out from the rest **hervorheben;** *the headings are highlighted in bold*

◊ **high-resolution** *or* **hi-res** *noun* ability to display *or* detect a very large number of pixels per unit area **hohe Auflösung;** *high-resolution graphics; this high-resolution monitor can display 640 x 320 pixels; the new hi-res optical scanner can detect 300 dots per inch*

◊ **high-speed** *adjective* which operates faster than normal data transmission *or* processing **Hochgeschwindigkeits-; high-speed duplicator** = machine that copies video *or* audio tapes by running them at a faster speed than normal **Hochgeschwindigkeitskopierer; high-speed**

skip = rapid movement in a printer to miss the perforations in continuous stationery **schneller Sprung**

◊ **highway** or **bus** noun communications link consisting of a set of leads or wires which connect different parts of a computer hardware system and over which data is transmitted and received by various circuits inside the system **Vielfachleitung; address highway** = physical connections that carry the address data in a parallel form between the central processing unit and memory or external devices **Adressenvielfachleitung; data highway** = bus carrying the data signals in parallel form between the central processing unit and memory or external devices **Datenvielfachleitung**

QUOTE they have proposed a standardized high-level language for importing image data into desktop publishing and other applications programs
QUOTE the computer is uniquely suited to image processing because of its high-resolution graphics
Byte

hill climbing noun method of achieving a goal in an expert system **Problemlösungsmethode in einem Expertensystem**

hi-res = HIGH RESOLUTION *hi-res graphics; this hi-res monitor can display 640 x 320 pixels; the new hi-res optical scanner can detect 300 dots per inch*

hiss noun high-frequency noise mixed with a signal **Nebengeräusch**

histogram noun graph on which values are represented as vertical or horizontal bars **Histogramm**

hit
1 noun successful match or search of a database **Treffer;** *there was a hit after just a few seconds; there are three hits for this search key;* **hit on the line** = short period of noise on a communications line, causing data corruption **Störung der Übertragungsleitung**
2 verb to press a key **anschlagen;** *to save the text, hit ESCAPE S*

QUOTE the cause of the data disaster is usually due to your finger hitting the wrong key
PC Business World

HLDLC = HIGH-LEVEL DATA LINK CONTROL

HLL = HIGH-LEVEL LANGUAGE

HMI = HUMAN-MACHINE INTERFACE facilities provided to improve the interaction betweeen a user and a computer system **Mensch-Maschine-Schnittstelle**

HOF = HEAD OF FORM

hold
1 noun synchronization timing pulse for a television time base signal **Halteimpuls**
2 verb to retain or keep a value or communications line or section of memory **anhalten; hold current** = amount of electrical current that has to be supplied to keep a device in its operating state, but not operating **Haltestrom; holding line** = boundary line indicating the limits of an area of artwork or tone **Haltelinie; holding loop** = section of program that loops until it is broken by some action, most often used when waiting for a response from the keyboard or a device **Warteschleife; holding time** = time spent by a communications circuit on call **Haltezeit**

◊ **holdup** noun (i) time period over which power will be supplied by a UPS; (ii) pause in a program or device due to a malfunction **(i) Aufrechterhaltung der Spannung durch eine USV (unterbrechungsfreie Stromversorgung); (ii) Verzögerung, Stockung**

COMMENT: the hold feature keeps the picture steady and central on the screen; some televisions have horizontal and vertical hold controls to allow the picture to be moved and set up according to various conditions

hole noun
(a) punched gap in a punched paper tape or card, representing data **Loch; index hole** = hole in the edge of a hard-sectored disk **Indexloch**
(b) method of describing the absence of an electron from an atomic structure **Defektelektron**

COMMENT: a hole may move, but in the opposite direction to the flow of electrons in a material; it is also considered to have a positive charge as compared to a electron. This concept is mostly used in semiconductor physics, where the bulk movement of holes and electrons in an electronic device are studied

Hollerith code noun coding system that uses punched holes in a card to represent characters and symbols, the system uses two sets of twelve rows to provide possible positions for each code **Hollerith-Code**

hologram *noun* imagined three-dimensional image produced by the interference pattern when a part of a coherent light beam is reflected from an object and mixed with the main beam **Hologramm**

◊ **holograph** *noun* handwritten manuscript, as written by the author using a pen *or* pencil, but not typed **handschriftliches Manuskript, Holographum**

◊ **holographic image** *noun* hologram of a three-dimensional object **Hologramm; holographic storage** = storage of data as a holographic image which is then read by a bank of photocells and a laser (a new storage medium with massive storage potential) **holographische Speicherung**

◊ **holography** *noun* science and study of holograms and their manufacture **Holographie**

home *noun*
a) place where a person lives **Zuhause; home banking** = method of examining and carrying out bank transactions via a terminal and modem in the user's home **Home-Banking (Abwicklung von Bankgeschäften durch Bildschirmtext); home computer** = microcomputer designed for home use, whose applications might include teaching, games, personal finance and word-processing **Heimcomputer**
b) starting point for printing on a screen, usually taken as the top left hand corner **Ausgangsstellung; home record** = first *or* initial data record in a file **Anfangssatz**

◊ **homing** *noun* location of the source of a transmitted signal *or* data item **Quellenfindung**

homogeneous computer network *noun* network made up of similar machines, that are compatible *or* from the same manufacturer **homogenes Computernetz; homogeneous multiplexing** = switching multiplexer system where all the channels contain data using the same protocol and transmission rate **homogene Multiplexmethode**

hood *noun* cover which protects something **Hülle, Haube; acoustic hood** = soundproof cover put over a line printer to cut down its noise **Schallschluckhaube**

hooking *noun* distortion of a video picture caused by tape head timing errors **Störung des Videobildes (am oberen Bildrand) hervorgerufen durch Zeitfehler**

hop *noun* direct transmission path, using the reflections from only the ionosphere,

not the earth, to propagate the signal from one point on the earth to another **Funkfeld**

hopper *noun* device which holds punched cards and feeds them into the reader **Kartenmagazin**

horizontal *adjective* lying flat *or* going from side to side, not up and down **horizontal; horizontal blanking** = prevention of a picture signal reaching a television beam during the time it contains no picture information on its return trace **Teilbildunterdrückung; horizontal check** = error detection method for transmitted data **Horizontalprüfung;** *see also* CYCLIC CHECK; **horizontal synchronization pulse** = pulse in a television broadcast signal that synchronizes the receiver sweep circuitry **Horizontalsynchronisationsimpuls; horizontal wraparound** = movement of a cursor on a computer display from the end of one line to the beginning of the next **Zeilenumlauf**

horn *noun* directional radio device with a wider open end leading to a narrow section, used for the reception and transmission of radio waves **Hornstrahler; feed horn** = microwave channelling device used to direct transmitted signals **Speisehornstrahler**

host *noun & adjective* **host adapter** = adapter which connects to a host computer **Adapter zum Hauptrechner;** *the cable to connect the scanner to the host adapter is included*

◊ **host computer** *noun*
(a) main controlling computer in a multi-user *or* distributed system **Hauptrechner**
(b) computer used to write and debug software for another computer, often using a cross compiler **Leitrechner**
(c) computer in a network that provides special services *or* programming languages to all users **Spezialcomputer**

> QUOTE you select fonts manually or through commands sent from the host computer along with the text
>
> *Byte*

hot chassis *noun* metal framework *or* case around a computer that is connected to a voltage supply rather than being earthed **nichtgeerdetes Gehäuse; hot frame** = very bright film frame caused by over exposure **heller Bildrahmen hervorgerufen durch Überbelichtung; hot metal composition** = old method of producing typeset pages from individual metal letters which were cast from hot liquid metal, now mainly replaced by phototypesetting **gegossener**

Hartbleisatz; **hot spot** = region of high brightness on a film *or* display screen **intensiver Lichtfleck**; **hot standby** = piece of hardware that is kept operational at all times and is used as backup in case of system failure **Hot-Standby-System (mitlaufendes Reservesystem)**; **hot type** = characters cast from hot liquid metal **Bleisatz**; **hot zone** = text area to the left of the right margin in a word-processed document (if a word does not fit in completely, a hyphen is automatically inserted) **Ausschließzone**

house
1 *noun* company (especially a publishing company) **Firma; Verlag**; *one of the biggest software houses in the US*; **house corrections** = printing *or* composition errors, caused by and corrected by the printers of a document **Hauskorrekturen**; **house style** = (i) style of spelling and layout, used by a publishing company in all its books; (ii) method *or* design of a company's products, used to identify them from the products of competitors **(i) Verlagsstil; (ii) Hausstil**
2 *verb* to put a device in a case **einbauen**; *the magnetic tape is housed in a solid plastic case*

◊ **housekeeping** *noun* tasks that have to be regularly carried out to maintain a computer system (checking backups, deleting unwanted files, etc.) **Systemverwaltung; housekeeping routine** = set of instructions executed once, at the start of a new program to carry out system actions such as clear memory, configure function keys or change screen display mode **Systemverwaltungsroutine**; *see also* IN-HOUSE

◊ **housing** *noun* solid case **Gehäuse**; *the computer housing was damaged when it fell on the floor*

howler *noun*
(a) buzzer that indicates to a telephone exchange operator that a user's telephone handset is not on the receiver **Summer**
(b) very bad and obvious mistake; *what a howler, no wonder your program won't work* **grober Schnitzer, ‚Hammer'**

HRG = HIGH RESOLUTION GRAPHICS ability to display a large number of pixels per unit area **Graphik mit hoher Auflösung**; *the HRG board can control up to 300 pixels per inch*

HT = HANDY TALKIES small portable transceivers **Sprechfunkgeräte**

hub *noun* central part of a disk, usually with a hole and ring which the disk drive grips to spin the disk **Wickelkern**

huffman code *noun* data compression code, where frequent characters occupy less bit space than less frequent ones **Huffman-Code**

hum *noun* low frequency electrical noise *or* interference on a signal **Brummen**

human-computer *or* **human-machine interface (HMI)** *noun* facilities provided to improve the interaction between a user and a computer system **Mensch-Maschine-Schnittstelle**

hunting *noun* process of searching out a data record in a file **Suchen**

hybrid circuit *noun* connection of a number of different electronic components such as integrated circuits, transistors, resistors and capacitors in a small package, which since the components are not contained in their own protective packages, requires far less space than the individual discrete components **Hybridschaltung; hybrid computer** = combination of analog and digital circuits in a computer system to achieve a particular goal **Hybridrechner; hybrid interface** = one-off interface between a computer and a piece of analog equipment **Hybridschnittstelle; hybrid system** = combination of analog and digital computers and equipment to provide an optimal system for a particular task **Hybridanlage**

hyphen *noun* printing sign (-) to show that a word has been split **Bindestrich, Trennungszeichen; soft** *or* **discretionary hyphen** = hyphen which is inserted when a word is split at the end of a line in word-processed text, but is not present when the word is written normally **weiches Trennungszeichen**

◊ **hyphenated** *adjective* written with a hyphen **mit Bindestrich geschrieben**; *the word 'high-level' is usually hyphenated*

◊ **hyphenation** *noun* splitting of a word (as at the end of a line, when the word is too long to fit) **Silben-, Worttrennung; hyphenation and justification** *or* **H & J** = justifying lines to a set width, splitting the long words correctly at the end of each line **Trennung und Randausgleich**; *an American hyphenation and justification program will not work with British English spellings*

hypo *abbreviation* photographic fixing solution **Hypo**

Hz = HERTZ

Ii

IAM = INTERMEDIATE ACCESS MEMORY memory storage that has an access time between that of main memory and a disk based system **Speicher mit mittlerer Zugriffszeit**

IAR = INSTRUCTION ADDRESS REGISTER register in a CPU that contains the location of the next instruction to be processed **Befehlsadreßregister**

IAS = IMMEDIATE ACCESS STORE high-speed main memory area in a computer system **Schnellspeicher**

IBG = INTERBLOCK GAP

IC = INTEGRATED CIRCUIT NOTE: plural is **ICs**

icand *noun* = MULTIPLICAND

icon *or* **ikon** *noun* graphic symbol *or* small picture displayed on screen, used in an interactive computer system to provide an easy way of identifying a function **ikonisches Zeichen, Piktogramm;** *the icon for the graphics program is a small picture of a palette; click twice over the wordprocessor icon - the picture of the typewriter*

ID = IDENTIFICATION; **ID card** = card which identifies a person **Kennkarte; Personalausweis; ID code** = password *or* word that identifies a user so that he can access a system **Identifizierungscode;** *after*

you wake up the system, you have to input your ID code then your password

IDA = INTEGRATED DIGITAL ACCESS

IDD = INTERNATIONAL DIRECT DIALLING

ideal *adjective* perfect *or* very good for something **ideal;** *she is the ideal designer for children's books;* **ideal format** = standard large format for photographic negatives, used mainly in professional equipment **Idealformat**

identical *adjective* exactly the same **identisch;** *the two systems use identical software; the performance of the two clones is identical*

identify *verb* to establish who someone is *or* what something is **identifizieren;** *the user has to identify himself to the system by using a password before access is allowed; the maintenance engineers have identified the cause of the system failure*

◇ **identification** *noun* procedure used by a host computer to establish the identity and nature of the calling computer *or* user (this could be for security and access restriction purposes *or* to provide transmission protocol information) **Identifikation; identification character** = single character sent to a host computer to establish the identity and location of a remote computer *or* terminal **Identifikationszeichen; identification division** = section of a COBOL program source code, in which the identifiers and formats for data and variables to be used within the program are declared **Erkennungsteil**

◇ **identifier** *noun* set of characters used to distinguish between different blocks of data *or* files **Kennzeichen, Name; identifier word** = word that is used as a block *or* file identifier **Kennwort**

◇ **identity** *noun* who someone *or* what something is **Identität; identity burst** = pattern of bits before the first block of data on a magnetic tape that identifies the tape format used **Identitätsblock; identity gate** *or* **element** = logical gate that provides a single output that is true if the inputs are both the same **Identitätsgatter; identity number** = unique number, used usually with a password to identify a user when logging into a system **Kennummer;** *don't forget to log in your identity number;* **identity operation** = logical function whose output is true only if all the operands are of the same value **Identitätsfunktion**

idiot tape *noun* tape containing unformatted text, which cannot be typeset until formatting data, such as justification, line width, and page size, has been added by a computer **nicht-justiertes Band**

idle *adjective* (machine *or* telephone line *or* device) which is not being used, but is ready and waiting to be used **bereit**; **idle character** = symbol *or* code that means 'do nothing' *or* a code that is transmitted when there is no data available for transmission at that time **Leerzeichen, Synchronisierzeichen**; **idle time** = period of time when a device is switched on but not doing anything **Leerlaufzeit**

IDP = INTEGRATED DATA PROCESSING

IEE *U.K.* = INSTITUTION OF ELECTRICAL ENGINEERS

IEEE *USA* = INSTITUTE OF ELECTRICAL AND ELECTRONIC ENGINEERS; **IEEE bus** = interface that conforms to IEEE standards **IEEE-Bus**; **IEEE-488** = interfacing standard as laid down by the IEEE, where only data and handshaking signals are used, mainly used in laboratories to connect computers to measuring equipment **IEEE-488-Norm**

ier *noun* = MULTIPLIER

IF *or* **if** = INTERMEDIATE FREQUENCY

IF statement *noun* computer programming statement, meaning do an action IF a condition is true (usually followed by THEN) **IF-Anweisung, WENN-Anweisung**; **IF-THEN-ELSE** = high-level programming language statement, meaning IF something cannot be done, THEN do this, or ELSE do that **IF-THEN-ELSE-Anweisung, WENN-DANN-SONST-Anweisung**

ignore *verb* not to recognize *or* not to do what someone says **übergehen**; *this command instructs the computer to ignore all punctuation*; **ignore character** = null *or* fill character **Ungültigkeitszeichen**

IH = INTERRUPT HANDLER

IIL = INTEGRATED INJECTION LOGIC

IKBS = INTELLIGENT KNOWLEDGE-BASED SYSTEM

ikon *or* **icon** *noun* graphic symbol *or* picture displayed on screen, used in an interactive computer system to provide an easy way of identifying a function **ikonisches Zeichen, Piktogramm**; *see also* ICON

ILF = INFRA LOW FREQUENCY

ILL = INTER-LIBRARY LOAN

illegal *adjective* which is not legal *or* which is against the law *or* against rules of syntax **illegal; unzulässig**; **illegal character** = invalid combination of bits in a computer word, according to preset rules **unzulässiges Zeichen**; **illegal instruction** = instruction code not within the repertoire of a language **unzulässiger Befehl**; **illegal operation** = instruction *or* process that does not follow the computer system's protocol *or* language syntax **unzulässige Operation**

◇ **illegally** *adverb* against the law *or* against rules **illegal; unzulässig**; *the company has been illegally copying copyright software*

illegible *adjective* which cannot be read **unleserlich**; *if the manuscript is illegible, send it back to the author to have it typed*

illiterate *adjective* (person) who cannot read **analphabetisch**; **computer illiterate** = person who does not understand computer-related expressions *or* operations **jemand, der sich mit Computern nicht auskennt**; *see also* LITERATE

QUOTE three years ago the number of people who were computer illiterate was much higher than today
Minicomputer News

illuminate *verb* to shine a light on something **beleuchten**; *the screen is illuminated by a low-power light*

◇ **illumination** *noun* lighting **Beleuchtung**; **aperture illumination** = pattern generated from an aperture antenna **Ausleuchtung**

◇ **illuminance** *noun* measurement of the amount of light that strikes a surface, measured in lux **Beleuchtungsstärke** ▷ APPENDIX

illustrate *verb* to add pictures to a text **illustrieren, bebildern**; *the book is illustrated in colour; the manual is illustrated with charts and pictures of the networking connections*

◇ **illustration** *noun* picture (in a book) **Illustration**; *the book has twenty-five pages of full-colour illustrations*

image *noun*

a) exact duplicate of an area of memory **Abbild**

b) copy of an original picture *or* design **Abbild; image area** = region of microfilm *or* display screen on which characters *or* designs can be displayed **Bildbereich; image carrier** = storage medium containing data that defines the typefaces used in a phototypesetter **Bildträger; image degradation** = picture contrast and quality loss due to signal distortion *or* bad copying of a video signal **Bildverschlechterung; image distortion** = optical lens fault causing an image to be distorted **Bildverzerrung; image enhancer** = electronic device that improves the clarity of an image **Vorrichtung zur Qualitätsverbesserung eines Bildes; image master** = data describing fonts and character shapes in a phototypesetter **Image Master; image plane** = region where the photographic film is located in a camera, where a sharp image of a scene is formed when the lens is correctly focused **Filmebene; image processing** = analysis of information contained in an image, usually by electronic means *or* using a computer which provide the analysis *or* recognition of objects in the image, etc. **Bildverarbeitung; image processor** = electronic *or* computer system used for image processing, and to extract information from the image **Bildverarbeiter; image retention** = time taken for a TV image to disappear after it has been displayed, caused by long persistence phosphor **Bildkonservierung; image scanner** = input device which converts documents *or* drawings *or* photographs into a digitized, machine-readable form **Bildabtaster; image sensor** = photoelectric device that produces a signal related to the amount of light falling on it (this scans horizontally over an image, reading in one line at a time) **Bildsensor; image stability** = ability of a display screen to provide a flicker-free picture **Bildbeständigkeit; image storage space** = region of memory in which a digitized image is stored **Bildspeicherplatz; image table** = two bit-mapped tables used to control input and output devices *or* processes **Bild(wiederholungs)speicher**

imaging *noun* technique for creating pictures on a screen (in medicine used to provide pictures of sections of the body, using scanners attached to computers) **Bildgestaltungstechnik; magnetic resonance imaging** = scanning technique, using magnetic fields and radio waves **Kernspintomographie; X-ray imaging** = showing X-ray pictures of the inside of part of the body on a screen **Röntgenbildprojektion auf dem Bildschirm**

immediate *adjective* which happens at once **sofort, schnell; immediate access store (IAS)** = high-speed main memory area in a computer system **Schnellspeicher; immediate addressing** = accessing data immediately because it is held in the address field of an instruction **unmittelbare Adressierung; immediate instruction** = computer instruction in which the operand is included within the instruction, rather than an address of the operand location **Direktbefehl; immediate mode** = mode in which a computer executes an instruction as soon as it is entered **Direktmodus; immediate operand** = operand which is fetched at the same time as the instruction (within an immediate addressing operation) **Direktoperand; immediate processing** = processing data when it appears, rather than waiting for a synchronizing clock pulse *or* time **unmittelbare Verarbeitung;** *compare with* BATCH

immunity *see* INTERFERENCE

impact *noun* hitting *or* striking something **Auftreffen, Auswirkung; impact printer** = printer that prints text and symbols by striking an ink ribbon onto paper with a metal character, such as a daisy-wheel printer (as opposed to a non-impact printer like a laser printer) **mechanischer Drucker;** *see also* DAISY-WHEEL PRINTER, DOT MATRIX PRINTER

impedance *noun* measurement of the effect an electrical circuit has on signal current magnitude and phase when a steady voltage is applied **Impedanz, Scheinwiderstand; impedance matching** = means of making the best signal power transfer between two circuits by making sure that their output and input impedances are the same as the transmission line **Scheinwiderstandsanpassung;** *impedance matching a transmitter and receiver minimizes power losses to transmitted signals;* **impedance mismatch** = situation where the impedance of the transmission *or* receiving end of a system does not match the other, resulting in loss of signal power (due to increased attenuation effects of the two different impedances) **fehlerhafte Scheinwiderstandsanpassung;** *see also* OHM

implant *verb* to fix deeply into something; to bond one substance into another chemically **implantieren;** *the dopant is implanted into the substrate*

implement *verb* to carry out *or* to put something into action **realisieren, implementieren**

◊ **implementation** *noun* version of something that works **Realisierung, Implementierung;** *the latest implementation of the software runs much faster*

implication *noun* logical operation that uses an IF-THEN structure, if A is true and if B is true this implies that the AND function of A and B will be true **Implikation**

implied addressing *noun* assembler instruction that operates on only one register (this is preset at manufacture and the user does not have to specify an address **Fortschaltungsadressierung;** *implied addressing for the accumulator is used in the instruction LDA,16*

import *verb*
(a) to bring goods into a country for sale **importieren**
(b) to bring something in from outside a system **zurückladen;** *you can import images from the CAD package into the DTP program;* **imported signal** = broadcast television signal from outside a normal reception area, that is routed into and distributed over a cable network **importiertes Signal**

◊ **importation** *noun* the act of importing something into a system from outside **Fremdübernahme**

QUOTE text and graphics importation from other systems is possible
Publish

impression *noun* number of books *or* documents printed all on the same printrun **Auflage; impression cylinder** = roller in a printing press that presses the sheets of paper against the inked type **Druckzylinder**

imprint *noun* publisher's *or* printer's name which appears on the title page *or* in the bibliographical details of a book **Impressum; imprint position** = on a sheet of paper, place where the next letter *or* symbol is to be printed **Andruckposition**

impulse *noun* (voltage) pulse which lasts a very short time **Impuls**

◊ **impulsive** *adjective* lasting a very short time **impulsiv; impulsive noise** = interference on a signal caused by short periods of noise **Impulsstörung**

inaccurate *adjective* not correct *or* wrong **falsch;** *he entered an inaccurate password*

◊ **inaccuracy** *noun* mistake *or* error **Fehler, Ungenauigkeit;** *the bibliography is full of inaccuracies*

inactive *adjective* not working *or* running **nicht aktiv**

in-band signalling *noun* use of a normal voice grade channel for data transmission **Imband-Signalisierung**

inbuilt *adjective* (feature *or* device) included in a system **eingebaut;** *this software has inbuilt error correction*

in camera process *noun* film processing which takes place inside the camera **Sofortbildentwicklung**

incandescence *noun* generation of light by heating a wire in an inert gas (as in a light bulb) **Weißglut**

◊ **incandescent** *adjective* shining because of heat produced in an inert gas **weißglühend;** *current passing through gas and heating a filament in a light bulb causes it to produce incandescent light*

inches-per-second (ips) way of showing the speed of tape past the read/write heads **Inches pro Sekunde**

in-circuit emulator *noun* (circuit) that emulates a device *or* integrated circuit and is inserted into a new or faulty circuit to test it working correctly **Emulationsadapter von eingebauten Schaltungen;** *this in-circuit emulator is used to test the floppy disk controller by emulating a disk drive*

inclined orbit *noun* orbit that is not polar *or* equatorial **geneigte Umlaufbahn**

inclusion *noun* logical operation that uses an IF-THEN structure, if A is true and if B is true this implies that the AND function of A and B will be true **Inklusion**

◊ **inclusive** *adjective* which counts something in with other things **inklusiv;** *prices are inclusive of VAT;* **inclusive OR** *see* OR

incoming *adjective* which is coming in from outside **ankommend; incoming message** = message received in a computer **eingehende Nachricht; incoming traffic** = amount of data *or* messages received **ankommender Verkehr**

ncompatible *adjective* not compatible *or* which cannot work together **nicht ompatibel;** *they tried to link the two systems, but found they were incompatible*

ncorrect *adjective* not correct *or* with mistakes **falsch;** *the input data was incorrect, so the output was also incorrect*
◇ **incorrectly** *adverb* not correctly *or* with mistakes **falsch;** *the data was incorrectly keyboarded*

ncrement
1 *noun*
a) addition of a set number, usually one, to a register, often for counting purposes **Zuwachs;** *an increment is added to the counter each time a pulse is detected*
b) value of the number added to a register **Inkrement;** *increase the increment to three*
2 *verb*
a) to add something *or* to increase a number **hochzählen;** *the counter is incremented each time an instruction is executed*
b) to move forward to the next location **inkrementieren**
c) to move a document *or* card forward to its next preset location for printing *or* reading **inkrementieren**
◇ **incremental computer** *noun* computer that stores variables as the difference between their actual value and an absolute initial value **Inkrementalrechner; incremental data** = data which represents the difference of a value from an original value **Inkrementdaten; incremental plotter** = graphical output device that can only move in small steps, with input data representing the difference between present position and the position required, so drawing lines and curves as a series of short straight lines **Stufenform-Plotter**

indent
1 *noun* space *or* series of spaces from the left margin, when starting a line of text **Einrückung, Einzug**
2 *verb* to start a line of text with a space in from the left margin **einrücken;** *the first line of the paragraph is indented two spaces*
◇ **indentation** *noun* leaving a space at the beginning of a line of text **Einrücken**

independent *adjective* free *or* not controlled by anyone **unabhängig**
◇ **independently** *adverb* freely *or* without being controlled *or* without being connected **unabhängig;** *in spooling, the printer is acting independently of the keyboard; the item is indexed independently*

indeterminate system *noun* system whose logical (output) state cannot be predicted **unbestimmtes System**

index
1 *noun*
(a) list of items in a computer memory, usually arranged alphabetically **Index; index build** = creation of an ordered list from the results of a database *or* file search **Indexerstellung; index page** = videotext page that tells the user the locations of other pages *or* areas of interest **Indexseite; index register** = computer address register that is added to a reference address to provide the location to be accessed **Indexregister**
(b) list of subjects covered in a book in alphabetical order (usually at the back of a book) **Register, Index**
(c) list of terms classified into groups *or* put in alphabetical order **Index, Stichwortverzeichnis; index card** = small card used for storing information **Karteikarte; index letter** *or* **index number** = letter *or* number which identifies an item in an index **Indexbuchstabe; Indexzahl**
(d) address to be used that is the result of an offset value added to a start location **Index;** *see* INDEXED ADDRESSING; **index value** = offset value added to an address to produce a usable address **Indexwert**
(e) guide marks along the edge of a piece of film *or* strip of microfilm **Index; index hole** = hole in the edge of a hand-sectored disk **Indexloch**
2 *verb*
(a) to write an index (for a book) **ein Register zusammenstellen;** *the book was sent out for indexing; the book has been badly indexed*
(b) to put marks against items, so that they will be selected and sorted to form an index **indizieren; indexed address** = address of the location to be accessed which is found in an index register **indizierte Adresse; indexed addressing** = method of addressing where the storage location is addressed with a start address and an offset word, which is added to give the destination address **indizierte Adressierung; indexed file** = sequential file with an index of all entries and their addresses **indizierte Datei; indexed instruction** = instruction that contains an origin and offset that are added to provide the location to be accessed **indizierter Befehl; indexed sequential access method (ISAM)** = data retrieval method using a list containing the address of each stored record, where the list is searched, then the record is retrieved from the address in the list **indexsequentielle Zugriffsmethode; indexed sequential storage** = method of storing records in a consecutive order, but

in such a way that they can be accessed rapidly **Speicher mit indexsequentiellem Zugriff**

◇ **indexer** *noun* person who writes an index **Person, die ein Register zusammenstellt**

◇ **indexing** *noun*
(a) use of indexed addressing methods in a computer **Spezialindizierung**
(b) process of building and sorting a list of records **Indizieren; indexing language =** language used in building library *or* book indexes **Indiziersprache**
(c) writing an index for a book **Registererstellung; computer indexing =** using a computer to compile an index for a book by selecting relevant words *or* items from the text **Registererstellung mit Hilfe eines Computers**

QUOTE in microcomputer implementations of COBOL, indexed files are usually based on some type of B-tree structure which allows rapid data retrieval based on the value of the key being used
PC-User

indicate *verb* to show **anzeigen**

◇ **indication** *noun* sign *or* thing which shows **Melder**

◇ **indicator** *noun* something which shows the state of a process, usually a light *or* buzzer **Anzeiger; indicator chart =** graphical representation of the location and use of indicator flags within a program **Anzeigerdiagramm; indicator flag =** register *or* single bit that indicates the state of the processor and its registers, such as a carry *or* overflow **Anzeigebit; indicator light =** light used to warn *or* to indicate the condition of equipment **Anzeigelicht**

indirect *adjective* not direct **indirekt; indirect addressing =** way of addressing data, where the first instruction refers to an address which contains a second address **indirekte Adressierung; indirect ray =** transmission path of a radio wave that does not take the shortest route, such as a reflection **indirekter Strahl**

individual
1 *noun* single person **Individuum, Einzelperson;** *each individual has his own password to access the system*
2 *adjective* single *or* belonging to a single person **individuell;** *the individual workstations are all linked to the mainframe*

induce *verb* (i) to generate an electrical current in a coil of wire by electromagnetic effects; (ii) to prove (something) mathematically **(i) induzieren; (ii) beweisen;**

induced failure = failure of a device due to external effects **induziertes Versagen; induced interference =** electrical noise on a signal due to induced signals from nearby electromagnetic sources **induzierte Störung**

◇ **inductance** *noun* measurement of the amount of energy a device can store in its magnetic field **Induktivität**

◇ **induction** *noun* (i) generation of an electrical current due to electromagnetic effects from a nearby source; (ii) mathematically proving a formula *or* fact **(i) Induktion; (ii) Beweis; induction coil =** transformer consisting of two nearby coils of insulated wire, one inducing a signal in the other; is often used either to isolate a signal supply from a some equipment *or* as a method of stepping up *or* down a voltage **Induktionsspule;** *see also* TRANSFORMER

◇ **inductive coordination** *noun* agreement between electrical power suppliers and communication providers on methods of reducing induced interference **Kooperation zum Abbau induzierter Störungen**

◇ **inductor** *noun* electrical component consisting of a coil of wire used to introduce inductance effects into a circuit (by storing energy in its magnetic field) **Spule**

inert *adjective* (chemical substance *or* gas) that does not react with other chemicals **inert, (reaktions)träge**

COMMENT: inert gas is used to protect a filament from oxidizing

inequivalence *noun* logical function where the output is true if the inputs are not the same, otherwise the output is false **Inäquivalenz-Funktion**

inference *noun*
(a) deduction of results from data according to certain rules **Inferenz, logisches Schließen; inference engine** *or* **machine =** set of rules used in an expert system to deduce goals *or* results from data **Regelsatz in einem Expertensystem**
(b) method of deducing a result about confidential information concerning an individual by using various data related to groups of people **Inferenz; inference control =** determining which information may be released without disclosing personal information about a single individual **Inferenzkontrolle**

inferior figures *noun* smaller numbers *or* characters that are printed slightly below normal characters, used in mathematical and chemical formulae **tiefgestellte Zahlen,**

ndizes; *see also* SUBSCRIPT, UPERSCRIPT, SUPERIOR
NOTE: used in formulae: CO_2

nfinite *adjective* with no end **unendlich; nfinite loop** = loop which has no exit except by ending the running of the program by switching off the machine *or* resetting) **Endlosschleife**
◊ **infinity** *noun*
a) very large incomprehensible quantity even bigger than the biggest you can think of **Unendlichkeit**
b) distance of an object from a viewer where beams of light from the object would be seen to be parallel (i.e. very far away) **nendlicheinstellung**

nfix notation *noun* method of computer programming syntax where operators are embedded inside operands (such as C - D or X + Y) **Infixschreibweise;** *compare with* PREFIX, POSTFIX NOTATION

nformatics *noun* science and study of ways and means of information processing and transmission **Informatik**
NOTE: no plural

nformation *noun*
a) knowledge presented to a person in a form which can be understood **Information**
b) data that has been processed *or* arranged to provide facts which have a meaning **nformation; information bearer channel** = communications channel that is able to carry control and message data, usually at a higher rate than a data only channel **nformationsträgerkanal; information content** = measurement of the amount of information conveyed by the transmission of a symbol *or* character, often measured in shannons **Informationsgehalt; information flow control** = regulation of access to certain information **Steuerung des nformationsflusses; information input** = information received from an input device **nformationseingabe; information line** = line running across the screen which gives the user information about the program running *or* the file being edited, etc. **nformationszeile; information management system** = computer program that allows information to be easily stored, retrieved, searched and updated **nformationsverwaltungssystem; information network** = number of databases linked together, usually by telephone lines and modems, allowing a large amount of data to be accessed by a wider group of users **atenbanknetz; information output** = display of information on an output device **nformationsausgabe; information processing** = organizing, processing and extracting information from data **Informationsverarbeitung; information processor** = machine that processes a received signal, according to a program, using stored information to provide an output (this is an example of a computer that is not dealing with mathematical functions) **informationsverarbeitende Maschine; information provider (IP)** = company *or* user that provides an information source for use in a videotext system (such as the company providing weather information *or* stock market reports) **Informationsanbieter; information rate** = amount of information content per character multiplied by the number of characters transmitted per second **mittlerer Informationsfluß; information retrieval (IR)** = locating quantities of data stored in a database and producing useful information from the data **Wiederauffinden von Informationen, Informationswiedergewinnung; information retrieval centre** = information search system, providing specific information from a database for a user **Zentrale für Informationsanbieter und Benutzer; information storage** = storing data in a form which allows it to be processed at a later date **Informationsspeicherung; information storage and retrieval (ISR)** = techniques involved in storing information and retrieving data from a store **Informationsspeicherung und -wiederauffindung; information structure** *see* DATA STRUCTURE; **information system** = computer system which provides information according to a user's requests **Informationssystem; information technology (IT)** = technology involved in acquiring, storing, processing and distributing information by electronic means (including radio, television, telephone, computers) **Informationstechnik; information theory** = formulae and mathematics concerned with data transmission equipment and signals **Informationstheorie; information transfer channel** = connection between a data transmitter and a receiver **Nachrichtenübertragungskanal;** *see also* DATA TERMINAL EQUIPMENT

QUOTE Information Technology is still too young to be an established discipline. However, the national and international IT research programmes are reasonably agreed that it comprises electronics, computing and telecommunications

Electronics and Power

infra- *prefix* meaning below *or* less than **Infra-, infra-; infra-low frequency (ILF)** = range of audio frequencies between 300Hz-3KHz **Frequenz zwischen 300Hz und 3KHz**

infrared *adjective* section of the electromagnetic radiation spectrum extending from visible red to microwaves **infrarot; infrared communications** = line of sight of communications path using a modulated infrared light beam rather than electrical signals down a cable **Infrarotnachrichtenübermittlung; infrared detector** = photoelectric cell that is sensitive to the infrared region of the electromagnetic spectrum **Infrarotdetektor; infrared photography** = type of photography that uses a special film which is sensitive to infrared radiation and so can be used in situations where the light level is very low **Infrarotfotografie; infrared sights** = camera and specialized optical equipment that can be used in situations where the light level is low, providing bright, enhanced images **Infrarotsichtgeräte**

◊ **infrasonic frequency** *noun* sound wave frequency that is in the range below that audible by the human ear **Infraschallfrequenz**

◊ **infrastructure** *noun* basic structure *or* basic services **Infrastruktur**

infringement *noun* breaking the law *or* a rule **Übertretung; copyright infringement** = illegally making a copy of a book *or* program which is in copyright **Verletzung des Urheberrechts**

inherent addressing *noun* instruction that contains all the data required for the address to be accessed with no further operation **Anfangsadressierung;** *compare with* EXTENDED, INDEXED

inherited error *noun* error that is the result of a fault in a previous process *or* action **mitgeschleppter Fehler**

inhibit *verb* to stop a process taking place *or* to prevent an integrated circuit *or* gate from operating, (by means of a signal *or* command) **sperren; inhibiting input** = one input of a gate which blocks the output signal **Sperreingang**

in-house *adverb & adjective* working inside a company **innerbetrieblich;** *all the data processing is done in-house; the in-house maintenance staff deal with all our equipment*

initial
1 *adjective* first *or* at the beginning **Anfangs-, initial address** = address at which the first instruction of a program is stored **Anfangsadresse; initial condition** = condition that must be satisfied before a

routine can be entered **Anfangsbedingung; initial error** = error in data that is the difference between the value of the data at the start of processing and its present actual value **Anfangsfehler; initial instructions** = routine that acts as an initial program loader **Startbefehle; initial program header** = small machine-code program usually stored in a read-only memory device that directs the CPU to load a larger program *or* operating system from store into main memory (such as a boot up routine that loads the operating system when a computer is switched on) **Startprogramm; initial program loader (IPL)** = short routine that loads a program (the operating system) from backing store into main memory **Urlader; initial value** = starting point (usually zero) set when initializing variables at the beginning of a program **Anfangswert**
2 *noun* first letter of a word, especially of a name **Anfangsbuchstabe, Initiale;** *what do the initials IBM stand for?*

◊ **initialization** *noun* process of initializing **Initialisierung;** *initialization is often carried out without the user knowing*

◊ **initialize** *verb* to set values *or* parameters *or* control lines to their initial values, to allow a program *or* process to be re-started **initialisieren**

injection laser *noun* solid state laser device used to transmit data as pulses of light down an optic fibre **Injektionslaser**

◊ **injection logic** *see* INTEGRATED

ink
1 *noun* dark liquid used to mark *or* write with **Tinte; ink-jet printer** = computer printer that produces characters by sending a stream of tiny drops of electrically charged ink onto the paper (the movement of the ink drops is controlled by an electric field; this is a non-impact printer with few moving parts) **Tintenstrahldrucker;** *colour ink-jet technology and thermal transfer technology compete with each other*
2 *verb* to draw lines on paper with a pen *or* using a plotter device **mit Tinte zeichnen/schreiben**

QUOTE ink-jet printers work by squirting a fine stream of ink onto the paper
Personal Computer World

inlay card *noun* identification card inside a tape *or* disk box **Begleitkarte**

inline
1 *noun* connection pins on a chip arranged in one or two rows **gereihte Anschlußstifte**

2 *adverb* way in which unsorted *or* unedited data is processed **schritthaltend; in-line program** = program that contains no loops **gestrecktes Programm; in-line processing** = processing data when it appears rather than waiting for a synchronizing *or* clock pulse **schritthaltende Verarbeitung**

inner loop *noun* loop contained inside another loop **Innenschleife;** *see also* NESTED LOOP

in phase *adverb*
(a) (two electrical signals) that have no phase difference between them, i.e. there is no delay *or* a delay of one complete cycle between them **phasengleich**
(b) synchronization of film frames and projector shutter timing **Projektorsynchronisation**

input (i/p *or* **I/P)**
1 *verb* to transfer data *or* information from outside a computer to its main memory **eingeben;** *the data was input via a modem* NOTE: **inputs - inputting - input**
2 *noun*
(a) action of inputting information **Eingeben**
(b) data *or* information that is transferred into a computer **Eingabe; input area** = section of main memory that holds data transferred from backing store until it is processed *or* distributed to other sections **Eingabespeicherbereich; input block** = block of data transferred to an input area **Eingabeblock; input buffer register** = temporary store for data from an input device before it is transferred to main *or* backing store **Eingabepufferregister; input device** = device such as a keyboard *or* bar code reader, which converts actions *or* information into a form which a computer can understand and transfers the data to the processor **Eingabegerät; input lead** = lead which connects an input device to a computer **Kabel zwischen Eingabegerät und Computer; input limited** = (program) which is not running as fast as it could due to limiting input rate from a slower peripheral **eingabebegrenzt; input mode** = computer which is receiving data **Eingabemodus; input port** = circuit *or* connector that allows a computer to receive data from other external devices **Eingabeanschluß; input register** = temporary store for data received at slow speeds from an I/O device, the data is then transferred at high speed to main memory **Eingaberegister; input routine** = set of instructions which control an I/O device and direct data received from it to the correct storage location **Eingabeprogramm; input section** = (i) input routine; (ii) input area **(i) Eingabeprogramm; (ii) Eingabespeicherbereich; input statement** = computer programming command that waits for data entry from a port *or* keyboard **Eingabeanweisung; input storage** *see* INPUT AREA; **input unit** = an input device **Eingabeeinheit; input work queue** = list of commands to be carried out in the order they were entered (or in order by priority) **Eingabewarteschlange**
(c) electrical signals which are applied to relevant circuits to perform the operation **Eingang**
◊ **input-bound** *or* **limited** *adjective* (program) which is not running as fast as it could due to limiting input rate from a slower peripheral **eingabebegrenzt**
◊ **input/output (I/O)** *noun* receiving *or* transmitting data between a computer and its peripherals, and other points outside the system **Ein-/Ausgabe; input/output buffer** = temporary storage area for data waiting to be output *or* data input **Ein-/Ausgabepuffer; input/output bus** = links allowing data and control signal transfer between a CPU and memory *or* peripheral devices **Ein-/Ausgabebus; input/output channel** = link between a processor and peripheral allowing data transfer **Ein-/Ausgabekanal; input/output control program** = monitoring and control of I/O operations and data flow by a section of the operating system *or* supervisory program **Ein-/Ausgabesteuerprogramm; input/output controller** = intelligent device that monitors, directs and controls data flow between a CPU and I/O devices **Ein-/Ausgabesteuereinheit; input/output device** *or* **unit** = peripheral (such as a terminal in a workstation) which can be used both for inputting and outputting data to a processor **Ein-/Ausgabeeinheit; input/output executive** = master program that controls all the I/O activities of a computer **Ein-/Ausgabesteuerprogramm; input/output instruction** = computer programming instruction that allows data to be input *or* output from a processor **Ein-/Ausgabebefehl; input/output interface** = circuit allowing controlled data input and output from a CPU, consisting usually of: input/output channel, parallel input/output port and a DMA interface **Ein-/Ausgabeschnittstelle; input/output interrupt** = interrupt signal from a peripheral device *or* to indicate that an input or output operation is required **Ein-/Ausgabeunterbrechung; input/output library** = set of routines that can be used by the programmer to help simplify input/output tasks (such as printer drivers *or* port control routines) **Ein-/Ausgabebibliothek; input/output port** = circuit *or* connector that provides an

input/output channel to another device **Ein-/Ausgabeanschluß;** *the joystick can be connected to the input/output port;* **input/output processor (IOP)** = processor that carries out input/output transfers for a CPU, including DMA and error correction facilities **Ein-/Ausgabeprozessor; input/output referencing** = use of labels to refer to specific input/output devices, the actual address of the device being inserted at run-time **Ein-/Ausgabebezugnahme; input/output register** = temporary store for data received from main memory before being transferred to an I/O device (or data from an I/O device to be stored in main memory or processed) **Ein-/Ausgaberegister; input/output request (IORQ)** = request signal from the CPU for data input or output **Ein-/Ausgabeanforderung; input/output status word** = word whose bits describe the state of peripheral devices (busy, free, etc.) **Ein-/Ausgabestatuswort; parallel input/output (PIO)** = data input or output from a computer **parallele Ein-/Ausgabe**

QUOTE inputs include raster scan files and ASCII files
Byte

inquiry *noun* (i) asking a question; (ii) accessing data held in a computer system **(i) Anfrage; (ii) Abfrage; inquiry character (ENQ)** = code transmitted by a computer to a remote terminal, asking for a response **Anfragecode; inquiry station** = terminal that is used to access and interrogate files stored on a remote computer **Abfragestation; inquiry/response** = interactive computer mode, in which a user's commands and enquiries are responded to very quickly **Frage-Antwort-System**

insert *verb*
(a) to put something into something **hineinstecken;** *first insert the system disk in the left slot*
(b) to add new text inside a word or sentence **einfügen; inserted subroutine** = series of instructions that are copied directly into the main program where a call instruction appears or where a user requires **eingefügtes Unterprogramm**

◊ **insertion loss** *noun* attenuation to a signal caused by adding a device into an existing channel or circuit **Einfügungsdämpfung**

◊ **insert mode** *noun* interactive computer mode used for editing and correcting documents **Einfügemodus**

COMMENT: this is a standard feature on most word-processing packages where the cursor is placed at the required point in the document and any characters typed will be added, with the existing text moving on as necessary

install *verb* to put a machine into an office or factory; to set up a new computer system to the user's requirements or to configure a new program to the existing system capabilities **installieren;** *the system is easy to install and simple to use*

◊ **installation** *noun*
(a) computer and equipment used for one type of work and processing **(Computer)anlage;** *the engineers are still testing the new installation*
(b) setting up a new computer system **Montage;** *the installation of the equipment took only a few hours*

instantaneous access *noun* extremely short access time to a random access device **Sofortzugriff**

instant replay *noun* feature found in video recording systems that allows the action that has just been recorded to be viewed immediately **Sofortwidergabe**

instruct *verb* to tell someone or a computer what to do **befehlen**

◊ **instruction** *noun* word used in a programming language that is understood by the computer to represent an action **Befehl;** *the instruction PRINT is used in this BASIC dialect as an operand to display the following data;* **absolute instruction** = instruction which completely describes the operation to be performed (i.e. no other data is required) **endgültiger Maschinenbefehl; arithmetic instruction** = instruction to perform an arithmetic operation on data rather than a logical function **Rechenbefehl; blank** or **null** or **dummy instruction** = instruction in a program that is only there to satisfy language syntax or to make up a block length **leere Anweisung; breakpoint instruction** = halt command inserted in a program to temporarily stop execution, allowing the programmer to examine data and registers whilst debugging a program **Stopbefehl; decision** *or* **discrimination instruction** = conditional program instruction that directs control by providing the location of the next instruction to be executed (if a condition is met) **logische Entscheidung; dummy instruction** = instruction in a program that is only there to satisfy language syntax *or to* make up a block length **leere Anweisung; executive instruction** = instruction used to control and execute programs under the control of an operating system **Ausführungsbefehl; four-address instruction** = program instruction which contains four addresses within its address field, usually the location of the two operands, the result and the location of the next instruction **Vieradreßbefehl; indexed instruction** = instruction that contains an origin and location of an offset that are added together to provide the address to be accessed **indizierter Befehl; input/output instruction** = computer programming instruction that allows data to be input *or* output from a processor **Ein-/Ausgabebefehl; jump instruction** = program command to end one set of instructions and direct the processor to another section of the program **Sprungbefehl; macro instruction** = one programming instruction that refers to a number of instructions within a routine *or* macro **Makrobefehl; no-op instruction** = instruction that does not carry out any functions, but increments the program counter **Befehl "keine Operation"; n-plus-one instruction** = instruction made up of a number (n) of addresses and one other address that is the location of the next instruction to be executed **n-plus-Eins-Befehl; supervisory instruction** = instruction used to control and execute programs under the control of an operating system **Überwachungsbefehl; three-address-instruction** = instruction format which contains the addresses of two operands and the location where the result is to be stored **Dreiadreßbefehl; two-address-instruction** = instruction format containing the locations of two operands, the result being stored in one of the operand locations **Zweiadreßbefehl; two-plus-one-address instruction** = instruction containing locations of two operands and an address for the storage of the result **Zwei-plus-Eins-Adreßbefehl; instruction address** = location of an instruction **Befehlsadresse; instruction address register (IAR)** register in a CPU that contains the location of the next

instruction to be processed **Befehlsadreßregister; instruction area** = section of memory that is used to store instructions **Befehls(speicher)bereich; instruction cache** = area of high-speed memory which stores the next few instructions to be executed by a processor **Befehlsschnellspeicher; instruction character** = special character that provides a control sequence rather than an alphanumeric character **Befehlszeichen; instruction codes** = set of symbols *or* codes that a CPU can directly understand and execute **Befehlscodes; instruction counter** *or* **instruction address register (IAR)** *or* **program counter** = register in a CPU that contains the location of the next instruction to be processed **Befehlszähler; Befehlsadreßregister; instruction cycle** = sequence of events and their timing that is involved when fetching and executing an instruction stored in memory **Befehlsablauf; instruction cycle time** = amount of time taken for one instruction cycle **Befehlsablaufzeit; instruction decoder** = program which decodes instructions in machine code **Befehlsdecodierer; instruction execution time** = time taken for a central processing unit to carry out a complete instruction **Befehlsausführungszeit; instruction format** = rules defining the way the operands, data and addresses are arranged in an instruction **Befehlsformat; instruction modification** = altering a part of an instruction (data *or* operator) so that it carries out a different function when next executed **Befehlsänderung; instruction pipelining** = beginning processing a second instruction while still processing the present one (this increases program speed of execution) **Pipeline-Verarbeitung der Befehle; instruction processor** = section of the central processing unit that decodes the instruction and performs the necessary arithmetic and logical functions **Befehlsprozessor; instruction register (IR)** = register in a central processing unit that stores an instruction during decoding and execution operations **Befehlsregister; instruction repertoire** *or* **set** = total number of instructions that a processor can recognize and execute **Befehlsvorrat; instruction storage** *see* INSTRUCTION AREA; **instruction word** = fixed set of characters used to initiate an instruction **Befehlswort;** *the manufacturers of this CPU have decided that JMP will be the instruction word to call the jump function*

COMMENT: in a high level language the instructions are translated by the compiler *or* interpreter to a form that is understood by the central processing unit

instrumentation *noun* equipment for testing, display or recording signals **Instrumentierung;** *we've improved the instrumentation on this model to keep you better informed of the machine's position*

insufficient *adjective* not enough **ungenügend;** *there is insufficient time to train the keyboarders properly*

insulate *verb* to prevent a voltage *or* energy from a conductor reaching another point by separating the two points with an insulation material **isolieren**
◊ **insulation material** *noun* substance that is very bad conductor, used to prevent a voltage *or* energy reaching a point **Isoliermaterial**
◊ **insulator** *noun* material that can insulate **Isolator**

integer *noun* mathematical term to describe a whole number (it may be positive *or* negative *or* zero) **ganze Zahl; double-precision integer** = two computer words used to store an integer **ganze Zahl doppelter Wortlänge; integer BASIC** = faster version of BASIC that uses only integer mathematics and cannot support fractions **BASIC-Version**
◊ **integral** *noun & adjective* add-on device *or* special feature that is already built into a system **eingebaut(e Einheit);** *the integral disk drives and modem reduced desk space*

> QUOTE an integral 7 inch amber display screen, two half-height disk drives and terminal emulation for easy interfacing with mainframes
> *Computing Today*

integrated *adjective* (system) that contains many peripherals grouped together in order to provide a neat, complete system **integriert; integrated database** = database that is able to provide information for varied requirements without any redundant data **integrierte Datenbank; integrated data processing (IDP)** = organizational method for the entry and retrieval of data to provide maximum efficiency **integrierte Datenverarbeitung; integrated device** = device that is part of another machine *or* device **integriertes Bauelement;** *our competitor's computer doesn't have an integrated disk drive like this model;* **integrated digital access (IDA)** = system where subscribers can make two telephone calls and be linked (from their office *or* home) to a database, and send material by fax, all at the same time **integrierter Digitalzugriff; integrated digital network** = communications network that uses digital signals to transmit data

integriertes Digitalnetz; integrated emulator = emulator program run within a multitasking operating system **integrierter Emulator; integrated injection logic (IIL)** = method of designing and constructing logical circuits on an integrated circuit to provide low power consumption with medium speed gates **IIL-Logik; integrated modem** = modem that is a internal part of the system **Einbaumodem; integrated office** = office environment in which all operations are carried out using a central computer (to store information, print, etc.) **im Rechnerverband arbeitendes Büro; integrated optical circuit** = optoelectronic circuit that can generate, detect and transmit light for communications over optical fibres **integrierter optischer Schaltkreis; integrated services digital network (ISDN)** = international digital communications network which can transmit sound, fax and data over the same channel **integriertes Sprach- und Datennetz (ISDN); integrated software** = software such as an operating system *or* word-processor that is stored in the computer system and has been tailored to the requirements of the system **integrierte Software**

◊ **integrated circuit (IC)** *noun* circuit where all the active and passive components are formed on one small piece of semiconductor, by means of etching and chemical processes **integrierter Schaltkreis (IC)**

◊ **integration** *noun* bringing several operations together **Integration;** *small scale integration (SSI); medium scale integration (MSI); large scale integration (LSI); very large scale integration (VLSI); super large scale integration (SLSI)*

> COMMENT: integrated circuits can be classified as follows: Small Scale Integration (SSI): 1 to 10 components per IC; Medium Scale Integration (MSI): 10 to 500 components per IC; Large Scale Integration (LSI): 500 to 10,000 components per IC; Very Large Scale Integration (VLSI): 10,000 to 100,000 components per IC; Super Large Scale Integration (SLCI): more than 100,000 components per IC

integrity *noun* reliability of data (when being processed *or* stored on disk) **Integrität, Vollständigkeit; integrity of a file** = the fact that a file that has been stored on disk is not corrupted *or* distorted in any way **Vollständigkeit einer Datei; the data in this file has integrity** = the data has not been corrupted **die Daten in dieser Datei sind vollständig**

QUOTE it is intended for use in applications demanding high data integrity, such as archival storage or permanent databases

Minicomputer News

intelligence *noun* (i) ability to reason; (ii) ability of a device to carry out processing *or* run a program **(i) & (ii) intelligenz; artificial intelligence (AI)** = the design of computer programs and systems that attempt to imitate human intelligence and decision-making functions, providing basic reasoning and human characteristics **künstliche Intelligenz**

◊ **intelligent** *noun (of a machine)* (program *or* device) that is capable of limited reasoning facilities, giving it human-like responses **intelligent; intelligent device** = peripheral device that contains a central processing unit allowing it to process data **intelligentes Gerät; intelligent knowledge-based system (IKBS)** *or* **expert system** = software that applies the knowledge, advice and rules defined by an expert in a particular field to a user's data to help solve a problem **intelligentes, wissensbasiertes System; Expertensystem (XPS); intelligent spacer** = facility on a word-processing system used to prevent words from being hyphenated *or* separated at the wrong point **intelligentes Trennprogramm; intelligent tutoring system** = computer-aided learning system that provides responsive and interactive teaching facilities for users **intelligentes Lernsystem; intelligent terminal** = computer terminal which contains a CPU and memory, usually with a facility to allow the user to program it independently of the main CPU **intelligente, frei programmierbare Datenstation;** NOTE: the opposite is **dumb terminal**

INTELSAT = INTERNATIONAL TELECOMMUNICATIONS SATELLITE ORGANIZATION international group that deals with the design, construction and allocation of space to various communications satellite projects **internationaler Fernmeldesatellit**

intensity *noun* measure of the strength of a signal *or* the brightness of a light source *or* the loudness of a noise **Intensität; Helligkeit; Lautstärke**

COMMENT: sound intensity is usually measured in decibels

inter- *prefix* meaning between **zwischen; interblock** = between blocks **zwischen Blöcken**

interact *verb (of two things)* to act on each other **aufeinander wirken**

◊ **interaction** *noun* action of two things on each other **Interaktion, Wechselwirkung**

◊ **interactive** *adjective* (system *or* piece of software) that allows communication between the user and the computer (in conversational mode) **interaktiv, im Dialogbetrieb; interactive cable television** = cable television system that allows the viewer to transmit signals such as program choice, teleshopping *or* answers to game questions back to the television transmission centre **dialogfähiges Kabelfernsehen; interactive debugging system** = software development tool that allows the user to run a program under test, set breakpoints, examine source and object code, examine registers and memory contents and trace the instruction execution **integriertes Dialogtestsystem; interactive graphics** = display system that is able to react to different inputs from the user **dialogfähige Graphikverarbeitung;** *the space invaders machine has great interactive graphics, the player controls the position of his spaceship on the screen with the joystick;* **interactive media** = communication between a group of people using different transmission means **interaktive Medien; interactive mode** *or* **processing** = computer mode that allows the user to enter commands *or* programs *or* data and receive immediate responses **(Verarbeitung im) Dialogbetrieb;** *see also* INQUIRY/RESPONSE; **interactive routine** = computer program that can accept data from an operator, process it and provide a real-time reaction to it **Dialogprogramm; interactive system** = system which provides an immediate response to the user's commands *or* programs *or* data **Dialogsystem; interactive terminal** = terminal in an interactive system which sends and receives information **dialogfähige Datenstation; interactive videotext** = viewdata service that allows the operator to select pages, display them, ask questions use a service such as teleshopping **Bildschirmtextsystem**

◊ **interactive video** *noun* system that uses a computer linked to a video disk player to provide processing power and real images *or* moving pictures **interaktives Videosystem**

COMMENT: this system is often used in teaching to ask a student questions, which if answered correctly will provide him with a filmed sequence from the videodisk

QUOTE soon pupils will be able to go shopping in a French town from the comfort of their classroom - carried to their destination by interactive video, a medium which combines the power of the computer with the audiovisual impact of video
Electronics & Power
QUOTE interactivity is a buzzword you've been hearing a lot lately. Resign yourself to it because you're going to be hearing a lot more of it
Music Technology

interblock gap (IBG) *noun* blank magnetic tape between the end of one block of data and the start of the next in backing store **Blockzwischenraum**

intercarrier noise *noun* interference caused by two different signal carriers getting mixed **Zwischenträgerrauschen;** *television intercarrier noise is noticed when the picture and the sound signal carriers clash*

interchange
1 *noun* exchange of one thing for another **Austausch;** *the machine allows document interchange between it and other machines without reformatting*
2 *verb* to exchange one thing for another **austauschen**

◊ **interchangeable** *adjective* which can be exchanged **austauschbar**

intercharacter spacing *noun* word-processor feature that provides variable spacing between words to create a justified line **variable Zeichenlücken**

intercom *noun* short-range voice communications system **(Gegen)sprechanlage**

COMMENT: used mainly in offices *or* in automatic door systems where room-to-room communication of voice signals is required

interconnect *verb* (*of several things*) to connect together **verbinden;** *a series of interconnected terminals*

◊ **interconnection** *noun*
(a) section of connecting material between two devices **Verbindung**
(b) connection between a telephone set and a telephone network **Verbindung**

interface
1 *noun* (i) point at which one computer system ends and another begins; (ii) circuit *or* device *or* port that allows two *or* more incompatible units to be linked together in a standard communication system,

allowing data to be transferred between them; (iii) section of a program which allows transmission of data to another program **(i)(ii)&(iii) Schnittstelle; EIA interface** = standard defining interface signals, transmission rate and power usually used to connect terminals to modems **EIA-Schnittstelle; general purpose interface adapter (GPIA)** = usually used to interface a processing unit to a IEEE-488 bus **Mehrzweckschnittstelle; general purpose interface bus (GPIB)** = standard for an interface bus between a computer and laboratory equipment **Mehrzweckschnittstellenbus (IEC-Bus); input/output interface** = circuit allowing controlled data input and output from a CPU, consisting usually of: input/output channel, parallel input/output port and a DMA interface **Ein-/Ausgabe-Schnittstelle; interface card** = add-on board that allows a computer to interface to certain equipment *or* conform to a certain standard **Schnittstellenkarte; interface message processor** = computer in a packet switching network that deals with the flow of data, acting as an interface processor **Schnittstellenprozessor in einem Schaltnetzwerk; interface processor** = computer that controls data transfer between a processor and a terminal *or* network **Schnittstellenprozessor; interface routines** = software that allows programs *or* data for one system to run on another **Schnittstellenprogramm; parallel interface** = computer circuit *or* connector that allows parallel data to be transmitted *or* received **parallele Schnittstelle;** NOTE: parallel interfaces are usually used to drive printers **serial interface** = circuit that converts parallel data in a computer to and from a serial form, allowing serial data to be transmitted to *or* received from other equipment **serielle Schnittstelle;** NOTE: the most common serial interface is RS232C
2 *verb* (i) to modify a device by adding a circuit *or* connector to allow it to conform to a standard communications system; (ii) to connect two or more incompatible devices together with a circuit, to allow them to communicate **(i) anpassen; (ii) zusammenschalten**

◊ **interfacing** *noun* hardware *or* software used to interface two computers *or* programs *or* devices **Anschlußteil**

interfere *verb* to interfere with something = to stop something working properly *or* to get in the way **etwas stören**

◊ **interference** *noun*
(a) unwanted addition of signals *or* noise to a transmitted signal **Störung**

b) effect seen when two signals are added, creating constructive interference when both signals are in phase *or* destructive interference when they are out of phase **Überlagerung; interference fading** = effect in radio reception when destructive interference occurs **Interferenzschwund; interference immunity** = ability of a system (i) to ignore interference signals; (ii) to function correctly even with interference **(i) & (ii) Störfestigkeit; interference pattern** = effect seen when light *or* radio *or* x-ray waves interact and produce destructive and constructive interference, causing patterns **Störmuster, Interferenzbild; constructive interference** = increase in peak and trough amplitude when two in phase signals are added **Verstärkung; destructive interference** = cancellation of peaks and troughs when two out of phase signals are added (if the signals are exactly out of phase, they completely cancel out each other) **Auslöschung; electromagnetic interference** = corruption of data due to nearby electrically generated magnetic fields **elektromagnetische Störung; induced interference** = electrical noise on a signal due to induced signals from nearby electromagnetic sources **induzierte Störung**

COMMENT: interference can be due to electrical noise (such as from a relay), natural galactic noise or two signals mixing due to insufficient insulation

nterior label *noun* identification label stored on a storage medium (magnetic tape *or* disk) rather than an exterior *or* physical label stuck to the case **Innenkennung**

nterlace *verb* to build up an image on a television screen using two passes, each displaying alternate lines **sich verflechten, ineinandergreifen**

COMMENT: this system uses two picture fields made up of alternate lines to reduce picture flicker effects

nterleaved *adjective*
a) (thin sheets of paper) which are stuck between the pages of a book **durchschossen;** *blank paper was interleaved with the newly printed text to prevent the ink running*
b) sections of two programs executed alternately to give the impression that they are running simultaneously **verzahnt**

◊ **interleaving** *noun*
a) processor dealing with slices *or* sections of processes alternately, so that they appear to be executed simultaneously **Verzahnung**

(b) addition of blank paper between printed sheets to prevent the ink from making other sheets dirty **Durchschießen**
(c) dividing data storage into sections so that each can be accessed separately **Überlappung**

QUOTE there are two separate 40-bit arrays on each card to allow interleaved operation, achieving data access every 170ns machine cycle
Minicomputer News

inter-library loan (ILL) *noun* lending of books *or* documents between from one library to another **Fernleihe**

interlinear spacing *noun (on a phototypesetter)* insertion of spaces between lines of text **Einrichten des Zeilenabstands**

interlock
1 *noun*
(a) security device which is part of the logon prompt and requires a password **Verriegelung**
(b) method of synchronizing audio tape with a video *or* filmed sequence (this can be achieved by using a frame counter *or* a timer *or* by running both audio and visual tapes on the same motor) **Synchronisierungsmechanismus; interlock projector** = film display machine that can also provide synchronized sound **Synchronisierungsprojektor**
2 *verb* to prevent a device from performing another task until the present one has been completed **verriegeln**

interlude *noun* small initial routine at the start of a program that carries out housekeeping tasks **Vorprogramm**

intermediate *adjective* which is at a stage between two others **Zwischen-, zwischen-; intermediate access memory (IAM)** = memory storage that has an access time between that of main memory and disk based systems **Hilfszugriffsspeicher; intermediate code** = code used by a computer *or* assembler during the translation of a high-level code to machine code **Zwischencode; intermediate file** = series of records that contain partially processed data, that will be used at a later date to complete that task **Zwischendatei; intermediate materials** = medium *or* format used for recording prior to the transfer to another format **Zwischenmedien;** *those slides, photographs, video and film are the intermediate materials to be mastered onto the video disk;* **intermediate storage** =

temporary area of memory for items that are currently being processed **Zwischenspeicher**

◇ **intermediate frequency (IF** or **if)** noun frequency in a radio receiver to which the incoming received signal is transformed **Zwischenfrequenz**

> COMMENT: this is to allow high frequency signals to be converted to a lower intermediate frequency so that they can be processed with standard components, rather than more expensive high-frequency versions

intermittent error noun error which apparently occurs randomly in a computer or communications system due to a program fault or noise **zeitweise auftretender Fehler**

> COMMENT: these errors are very difficult to trace and correct due to their apparent random appearance

internal adjective which is inside **intern; internal arithmetic** = arithmetic operations performed by the ALU **interner Rechenvorgang; internal character code** = representation of characters in a particular operating system **interner Zeichencode; internal format** = way in which data and instructions are represented within a CPU or backing store **internes Format; internal language** = language used in a computer system that is not under the direct control of the operator **interne Sprache**

> COMMENT: many compiled languages are translated to an internal language

◇ **internal memory** or **store** noun section of RAM and ROM to which the central processing unit is directly connected without the use of an interface (as in external memory devices such as disk drives) **interner Speicher**

◇ **internal sort** noun sorting program using only the main memory of a system **interne Sortierung**

◇ **internally stored program** noun computer program code that is stored in a ROM device in a computer system (and does not have to be loaded from backing store) **intern gespeichertes Programm**

international adjective referring to different countries **international; international direct dialling (IDD)** = system using an international dialling code that allow a user to telephone any country without going through an operator **internationale Durchwahl; international dialling code** = INTERNATIONAL PREFIX CODE; **international number** = digits to be dialled after the international prefix code to reach a subscriber in another country **internationale Nummer; international prefix code** = code number to be dialled at the start of a number to select another country's exchange system **internatonale Zugangskennzahl; international standard book number (ISBN)** = ten-digit identifying number allocated to every new book published **ISBN; international standard serial number (ISSN)** = identifying number allocated to every journal or magazine published **ISSN**

◇ **International Standards Organization (ISO)** noun organization which regulates standards for many types of product **internationale Normenorganisation; International Standards Organization Open System Interconnection (ISO/OSI)** = standardized ISO network design which is constructed in layered form, with each layer having a specific task, allowing different systems to communicate if they conform to the standard **ISO-Norm**

interpolation noun calculation of intermediate values between two points **Interpolierung**

interpret verb to translate what is said in one language into another **übersetzen, auswerten; interpreted language** = programming language that is executed by an interpreter **Übersetzersprache**

◇ **interpreter** noun software that is used to translate (at the time of execution) a user's high-level program into machine code **Übersetzer(programm), Interpretierer;** compare with COMPILER

> COMMENT: a compiler translates the high-level language into machine code and then executes it, rather than the real-time translation by an interpreter

◇ **interpretative** adjective **interpretative code** = code used with an interpretative program **Interpretiercode; interpretative program** = software that translates (at run-time) high level interpretative code into machine code instructions **Interpretierprogramm**

interrecord gap = INTERBLOCK GAP

interrogation noun asking questions **(Ab)frage; file interrogation** = questions asked to select various records or data items from a file **Dateiabfrage**

interrupt
1 verb to stop something happening while it

is happening **unterbrechen**

2 *noun*

(a) stopping of a transmission due to an action at the receiving end of a system **Unterbrechung**

(b) signal which diverts a central processing unit from one task to another which has higher priority, allowing the CPU to return to the first task later **Programmunterbrechung**; *this printer port design uses an interrupt line to let the CPU know it is ready to receive data;* **armed interrupt** = interrupt line which has been made active (using an interrupt mask) **absichtliche Unterbrechung; interrupt disable** = to disable an interrupt (by resetting a bit in the interrupt mask to zero) **eine Unterbrechung unmöglich machen; interrupt enable** = to arm an interrupt (by setting a bit in the interrupt mask) **eine Unterbrechung herbeiführen; interrupt handler (IH)** = software that accepts interrupt signals and acts on them (such as running a special routine *or* sending data to a peripheral) **Unterbrechungs-Steuerungsprogramm; interrupt level** = priority assigned to the interrupt from a peripheral **Unterbrechungsebene; interrupt line** = connection to a central processing unit from outside the system that allows external devices to use the CPU's interrupt facility **Unterbrechungsleitung; interrupt mask** = term in computer programming that selects which interrupt lines are to be activated **Unterbrechungsmaske; interrupt priorities** = deciding which interrupt is given highest priority **Unterbrechungsprioritäten;** *see also* NON-MASKABLE INTERRUPT; **interrupt request** = signal from a device that indicates to the CPU that it requires attention **Unterbrechungsanforderung; interrupt servicing** = carrying out some action when an interrupt is detected, such as running a routine **Unterbrechungsservice; interrupt signal** *see* INTERRUPT; **interrupt stacking** = storing interrupts in a queue and processing according to priority **Unterbrechungsschichtung; maskable interrupt** = interrupt line that can be disabled and ignored using an interrupt mask **maskierbare Unterbrechung; non-maskable interrupt (NMI)** = high priority interrupt signal that cannot be blocked and overrides all other commands **nichtmaskierbare Unterbrechung (mit höchster Priorität); polled interrupt** = interrupt signal determined by polling **Unterbrechung auf Abruf; transparent interrupt** = mode in which if an interrupt occurs, all machine and program states are saved, the interrupt is serviced then the system restores all previous states and continues normally **transparente Unterbrechung; vectored interrupt** = interrupt which directs the CPU to transfer to a particular location **zeigergesteuerte Unterbrechung**

intersection *noun* logical function whose output is only true if both its inputs are true **UND-Funktion; Schnittmenge**

interstation muting *noun* ability of a radio receiver to prevent the noise found between radio stations from being amplified and heard by the user **geräuschfreie Abstimmung**

interval *noun* short pause between two actions **Pause;** *there was an interval between pressing the key and the starting of the printout*

intervention *noun* acting to make a change in a system **Eingriff**

interword spacing *noun* variable spacing between words in a text, used to justify lines **variabler Wortzwischenraum**

intimate *noun* software that operates and interacts closely with hardware in a system **hardwaregeeichte Software**

intrinsic *adjective* pure (substance) which has had no other chemicals (such as dopants) added **spezifisch, rein;** *the base material for ICs is an intrinsic semiconductor which is then doped*

introduce *verb* to put something into something **einführen;** *errors were introduced into the text at keyboarding*

intrusion *noun* action by a telephone operator to allow both parties on each end of the telephone line to hear his *or* her message **Mitsprechanlage**

invalid *adjective* not valid **ungültig;** *he tried to use an invalid password; the message was that the instruction was invalid*

inverse *noun* changing the logical state of a signal *or* device to its logical opposite **Umkehrung, Gegenteil;** *the inverse of true is false; the inverse of 1 is 0;* **inverse video** = television effect created by swapping the background and foreground text display colours **invertiertes Videobild**

◇ **inversion** *noun* changing over the numbers in a binary word (one to zero, zero to one) **Umkehrung;** *the inversion of a binary digit takes place in one's complement*

◊ **invert** *verb* to change all binary ones to zeros and zeros to ones **umkehren; inverted commas** = printing sign (" ") which is usually used to indicate a quotation **Anführungszeichen; inverted file** = file with an index entry for all the data items **invertierte Datei**

◊ **inverter** *noun*
(a) logical gate that provides inversion facilities **Inverter**
(b) circuit used to provide alternating current supply from a DC battery source **Gleichstromumrichter; inverter (AC/DC)** = device which changes alternating current to direct current, or direct current to alternating current **Wechselrichter**

invitation *noun* action by a processor to contact another device to allow it to send a message **Aufruf; invitation to send (ITS)** = special character transmitted to indicate to a device that the host computer is willing to receive messages **Sendeaufruf**

◊ **invite** *verb* to ask someone to do something **aufrufen, auffordern**

invoke *verb* to start *or* run a program (often a memory resident utility) **aufrufen**

involve *verb* to have to do with; to include (something) in a process **betreffen;** *backing up involves copying current working files onto a separate storage disk*

I/O = INPUT/OUTPUT referring to the receiving *or* transmitting of data **Ein-/Ausgabe; I/O bound** = processor that is doing very little processing since its time is taken up reading *or* writing data from a I/O port **Ein-/Ausgabeabhängig; I/O buffer** = temporary storage area for data waiting to be input *or* output **Ein-/Ausgabepuffer; I/O bus** = links allowing data and control signal transfer between a CPU and memory *or* peripheral devices **Ein-/Ausgabebus; I/O channel** = link between a processor and peripheral, allowing data transfer **Ein-/Ausgabekanal; I/O device** = peripheral (such as a terminal in a workstation) which can be used for both inputting and outputting data to a processor **Ein-/Ausgabegerät; I/O file** = file whose contents have been *or* will be transferred from storage to a peripheral **Ein-/Ausgabedatei; I/O instruction** = computer programming instruction that allows data to be input *or* output from a processor **Ein-/Ausgabebefehl; I/O mapping**

= method of assigning a special address to each I/O port that does not use any memory locations **Ein-/Ausgabemapping;** *compare with* MEMORY MAPPING; **I/O port** = circuit *or* connector that provides an input/output channel from a CPU to another device **Ein-/Ausgabeanschlußstelle;** *see also* SERIAL PORT, PARALLEL PORT

ion *noun* charged particle **Ion**

COMMENT: an ion is an atom that has gained *or* lost an extra electron, producing a negative *or* positive ion

◊ **ionosphere** *noun* layer of charged particles surrounding the earth **Ionosphäre**

COMMENT: the ionosphere extends from 50km above the surface of the earth

IOP = INPUT/OUTPUT PROCESSOR

IORQ = INPUT/OUTPUT REQUEST

i/p *or* **I/P** = INPUT

ip = INFORMATION PROVIDER company *or* user that provides an information source for use in a videotext system **Informationsanbieter, Btx-Anbieter; ip terminal** = special visual display unit that allows users to create and edit videotext pages before sending to the main videotext page database **Btx-Datenstation**

IPL = INITIAL PROGRAM LOADER

ips = INCHES PER SECOND

IPSE = INTEGRATED PROJECT SUPPORT ENVIRONMENT

IR
(a) = INFORMATION RETRIEVAL
(b) = INDEX REGISTER
(c) = INSTRUCTION REGISTER
◊ **IRC** = INFORMATION RETRIEVAL CENTRE

irretrievable *adjective* which cannot be retrieved **nicht wiederauffindbar;** *the files are irretrievable since the computer crashed*

irreversible process *noun* process which, once carried out, cannot be reversed **irreversibler Prozeß**

IS = INDEXED SEQUENTIAL

ISAM = INDEXED SEQUENTIAL ACCESS METHOD

ISBN = INTERNATIONAL STANDARD BOOK NUMBER

ISDN = INTEGRATED SERVICES DIGITAL NETWORK

ISO = INTERNATIONAL STANDARDS ORGANIZATION; **ISO/OSI** = INTERNATIONAL STANDARDS ORGANIZATION OPEN SYSTEM INTERCONNECTION

isolate *verb* (i) to separate something from a system; (ii) to insulate (something) electrically **(i) trennen; (ii) isolieren; isolated adaptive routing** = method of controlling message transmission path **isolierte adaptive Verkehrslenkung; isolated location** = (hardware) storage location which cannot be directly accessed by a user's program, protecting it against accidental erasure **geschützter Speicherplatz**
◊ **isolation** *noun* being isolated **Isolation; isolation transformer** = transformer used to isolate equipment from direct connection with the mains electricity supply, in case of voltage spikes etc. **Trennübertrager**
◊ **isolator** *noun* device *or* material which isolates **Isolator**

isotropic *adjective* with the same properties in all dimensions and directions **isotrop; isotropic radiator** = antenna that transmits in all directions **Kugelantenne**

ISR = INFORMATION STORAGE AND RETRIEVAL

ISSN = INTERNATIONAL STANDARD SERIAL NUMBER

IT = INFORMATION TECHNOLOGY

italic *adjective & noun* type of character font in which the characters slope to the right **kursiv; Kursive;** *the headline is printed in italic and underlined;* **italics** = italic characters **Kursivschrift;** *all the footnotes are printed in italics; hit CTRL I to print the text in italics*

item *noun* single thing among many **Element, (Daten)feld;** *a data item can be a word or a series of figures or a record in a file;* **item size** = number of characters *or* digits in an item of data **Feldgröße**

iterate *or* **iterative routine** *noun* loop *or* series of instructions in a program which repeat over and over again until the program is completed **Iterationsschleife**
◊ **iteration** *noun* repeated application of a program to solve a problem **Iteration**
◊ **iterative process** *noun* process that is continuously repeated until a condition is met **iterative Operation**

ITS = INVITATION TO SEND

Jj

jack *noun* plug which consists of a single pin **Stecker, Buchse;** **data jack** = plug that allows a modem to be connected directly to the telephone system **Modembuchse**

jacket *noun* cover for a book *or* disk **Umschlag, Hülle;** *the book jacket has the author's name on it*

jam
1 *noun* process *or* mechanism which has stopped working due to a fault **Stau;** *a jam in the paper feed*
2 *verb*
(a) *(of a device)* to stop working because something is blocking the functioning **sich stauen;** *the recorder's not working because the tape is jammed in the motor; lightweight copier paper will feed without jamming*
(b) to prevent a transmission from being correctly received by transmitting a strong noise at the same frequency (often used to prevent unauthorized transmission) **stören;** *the TV signals are being jammed from that tower*

jar *verb* to give a sharp shock to a device **schlagen, stoßen;** *you can cause trouble by turning off or jarring the PC while the disk read heads are moving; hard disks are very sensitive to jarring*

JCL = JOB CONTROL LANGUAGE commands that describe the identification of and resources required by a job that a computer has to process **Jobkontrollsprache**

jet *see* INK-JET

jingle *noun* short easily-remembered tune used to advertise a product on television **Werbemelodie, Bimmeln, Jingle**

jitter *noun* fault where there is rapid small up-and-down movement of characters *or* pixels on a screen of image bits in a facsimile transmission **Flattern;** *looking at this screen jitter is giving me a headache*

JK-flip-flop *noun* flip-flop device with two inputs (J and K) and two complementary outputs that are dependent on the inputs **JK-Flipflop**

job *noun* task *or* number of tasks *or* work to be processed as a single unit **Job, Arbeitsauftrag;** *the next job to be processed is to sort all the records;* **job control file** = file which contains instructions in a JCL **Jobkontrolldatei; job control language (JCL)** = commands that describe the identification of and resources required by a job that a computer has to process **Jobbetriebssprache; job control program** = short program of job control instructions loaded before a particular application is run, that sets up the system as required by the application **Jobsteuerprogramm; job file** = file containing jobs *or* job names waiting to be processed **Jobdatei; job mix** = the jobs being executed at any one time in a system **Jobmischung; job number** = number which is given to a job in a queue, waiting to be processed **Jobnummer; job orientated language** = computer programming language that provides specialized instructions relating to job control tasks and processing **aufgabenorientierte Programmiersprache; job orientated terminal** = computer terminal designed for and used for a particular task **aufgabenorientierte Außenstation; job priority** = importance of a job compared to others **Jobpriorität; job processing** = to read in job control instructions from an input source and execute them **Jobverarbeitung; job queue** *or* **job stream** = number of tasks arranged in an order waiting to be processed in a multitasking *or* batch system **Jobwarteschlange; job scheduling** = arranging the order in which jobs are processed **Joborganisation; job statement control** = use of instructions and statements to control the actions of the operating system of a computer **Jobanweisungssteuerung; job step** *or* **stream** = one unit of processing involved in a task **Jobschritt; Jobfolge; remote job entry (RJE)** = use of an interactive user terminal to enter job control instructions **Jobferneingabe; stacked job control** = queue of job control instructions that are processed in the order in which they were received **sequentielle Jobbearbeitung**

◊ **jobbing printer** *noun* person who does small printing jobs, such as printing business cards **Akzidenzdrucker**

jog *verb* to advance a video tape by one frame at a time **Videoband um 1 Bild weiterstellen**

joggle *verb* to align a stack of punched cards *or* sheets of paper **rütteln**

join *verb*
(a) to put several things together **verbinden**
(b) to combine two or more pieces of information to produce a single unit of information **zusammenfügen; join files** = instruction to produce a new file consisting of one file added to the end of another **Dateien zusammenfügen**

(c) logical function that produces a true output if any input is true **ODER-Funktion**

joint denial *noun* logical function whose output is false if any input is true **NOR-Funktion**

journal *noun*
(a) record of all communications to and from a terminal **Protokoll; journal file** = stored record of every communication between a user and the central computer, used to help retrieve files after a system crash *or* fault **Protokolldatei**
(b) list of any changes *or* updates to a file **Protokoll;** *the modified records were added to the master file and noted in the journal*
(c) **learned journal** = specialized magazine **Fachzeitschrift**

◊ **journalist** *noun* person who writes for a newspaper **Journalist/-in**

joystick *noun* device that allows a user to move a cursor around the screen by moving an upright rod connected to an I/O port on the computer **Joystick, Steuerknüppel; joystick port** = circuit and connector used to interface a joystick with a computer **Joystickanschlußstelle;** *a joystick port is provided with the home computer*

> COMMENT: mostly used for computer games *or* CAD *or* desktop publishing packages

judder *noun* unwanted movement in a printing *or* facsimile machine that results in a distorted picture **Ungleichförmigkeit, Verwacklung**

jumbo chip *noun* integrated circuit made using the whole of a semiconductor wafer **Jumbochip;** *see also* WAFER SCALE INTEGRATION

> COMMENT: these devices are very new and proving rather difficult to manufacture without faults to any of the thousands of gates on the surface; when working, these devices will be extremely powerful

jump (instruction)
1 *noun* programming command to end one set of instructions and direct the processor to another section of the program **Sprungbefehl; conditional jump** = situation where the processor is directed to another section of the program only if a condition is met **bedingter Sprungbefehl; jump operation** = situation where the CPU is sent from the instruction it is currently executing to another point in the program

Sprungoperation; unconditional jump = instruction which transfers control from one point in the program to another, without requiring any condition to be met **unbedingter Sprungbefehl**
2 *verb*
(a) to direct a CPU to another section of a program **springen; jump on zero** = conditional jump executed if a flag *or* register is zero **Sprungbefehl bei Null**
(b) to miss a page *or* a line *or* a space when printing **überspringen;** *the typewriter jumped two lines; the paging system has jumped two folio numbers*

◇ **jumper** *noun* temporary wire connection on a circuit board **Brücke; jumper-selectable** = circuit *or* device whose options can be selected by positioning various wire connections **wählbare Brücke;** *the printer's typeface was jumper-selectable*

junction *noun*
(a) connection between wires *or* cables **Zusammenführung (von Leitungen); junction box** = small box where a number of wires can be interconnected **Verteilerkasten**
(b) region between two areas of semiconductor which have different doping levels (such as a p-type and n-type area), resulting in a potential difference between them **Zonenübergang; bipolar junction transistor (BJT)** = transistor constructed of 3 layers of alternating types of doped semiconductor (p-n-p *or* n-p-n), each layer having a terminal labelled as emitter, base and collector; usually the base controls the current flow between emitter and collector **bipolarer Sperrschichttransistor**

junk
1 *noun* information *or* hardware which is useless *or* out-of-date *or* non-functional **Unsinn, Schrott; junk mail** = form letters containing special offers *or* advertisements **Postwurfsendungen; space junk** = satellites and hardware that are out of action and no longer used, but are still in orbit in space **Weltraumabfall**
2 *verb* to get rid of a file; to make a file *or* piece of hardware redundant **löschen; to junk a file** = to erase *or* delete from storage a file that is no longer used **eine Datei löschen**

justify *verb*
(a) to change the spacing between words *or* characters in a document so that the left and right margins will be straight **ausschließen (der Zeile), Rand ausgleichen; justify inhibit** = to prevent a word processor justifying a document **das Ausschließen verbieten; justify margin** *see* LEFT *or* RIGHT JUSTIFY; **hyphenate and justify** = to break long words correctly

where they split at the ends of lines, so as to give a straight right margin **trennen und ausgleichen; left justify** = to print with a straight left-hand margin **linksbündig ausrichten; right justify** = to print with a straight right-hand margin **rechtsbündig ausrichten**
(b) to shift the contents of a computer register by a set amount **verschieben**

◇ **justification** *noun* moving data bits *or* characters to the left *or* right so that the lines have straight margins **Randausgleich; hyphenation and justification** *or* **H & J** = justifying lines to a set width, splitting the long words correctly at the end of each line **Trennung und Randausgleich;** *an American hyphenation and justification program will not work with British English spellings*

juxtaposition *noun* arranging *or* placing items next to or adjacent to each other **Nebeneinanderstellung**

Kk

K *prefix*
(a) = KILO symbol used to represent one thousand **k**
(b) symbol used to represent 1,024, equal to 2^{10} **K**

◇ **Kb** = KILOBIT measure of 1,024 bits **Kb**
◇ **KB** *or* **K byte** = KILOBYTE unit of measure for high capacity storage devices meaning 1,024 bytes **Kilobyte;** *the new disk drive has a 100KB capacity; the original PC cannot access more than 640K bytes of RAM*

COMMENT: 1,024 is the strict definition in computer or electronics applications, being equal to a convenient power of two; these abbreviations can also be taken to equal approximately one thousand, even in computing applications. 1KB is roughly equal to 1,000 output characters in a PC

Karnaugh map *noun* graphical representation of states and conditions in a logic circuit **Karnaugh-Diagramm;** *the prototype was checked for hazards with a Karnaugh map*

kernel *noun* basic essential instruction routines required as a basis for any operations in a computer system **Kernroutine; graphics kernel system (gks)** = number of basic commands required to illuminate in various shades and colours the pixels on a screen (these are then used to provide more complex functions such as line *or* shape plotting) **Graphikkernsystem**

> COMMENT: kernel routines are usually hidden from the user; they are used by the operating system for tasks such as loading a program or displaying text on a screen

kerning *noun* slight overlapping of certain printed character areas to prevent large spaces between them, giving a neater appearance **Kerning**

key

1 *noun*

(a) button on a keyboard that operates a switch **Taste;** *there are 64 keys on the keyboard;* **key click** = sound produced by a computer to allow the operator to know that the key he pressed has been registered **Anschlagsklicken; key force** = pressure required to close the switch in a key **Tastenwiderstand; key matrix** = design of interconnections between keys on a keyboard **Tastenmatrix; key number** = numeric code used to identify which key has been pressed **Tastennummer; key overlay** = paper placed over the keys on a keyboard describing their functions for a particular application **Tastenschablone;** *without the key overlay, I would never remember which function key does what;* **key punch** = machine used for punching data into punched cards by means of a keyboard **Kartenlocher; key rollover** = use of a buffer between the keyboard and computer to provide rapid key stroke storage for fast typists who hit several keys in rapid succession **überlappende Tastung; key strip** = piece of paper above certain keys used to remind the operator of their special functions **Tastenerklärungsstreifen; key travel** = distance a key has to be pressed before it registers **Tastenweg**

(b) *(names of keys)* **alphanumeric key** *or* **character key** = key which produces a character (letter *or* symbol *or* figure) **Zeichentaste; carriage return key** = key which moves a cursor *or* printhead to the beginning of the next line on screen *or* on a typewriter *or* in printing **Wagenrücklauftaste; function key** = key which has a specific task *or* sequence of instructions **Funktionstaste;** *tags can be allocated to function keys;* **shift key** = key which provides a second function for a key (usually by moving the output into upper case) **Umschalttaste**

(c) important object *or* group of characters in a computer system, used to represent an instruction *or* set of data **Schlüssel; key plate** = initial printing plate used when printing

colour images **Konturplatte, Klatsch; key terminal** = most important terminal in a computer system *or* one with the highest priority **Hauptdatenstation**

(d) special combination of numbers *or* characters that are used with a cipher to encrypt *or* decrypt a message **Schlüssel;** *type this key into the machine, that will decode the last message;* **key management** = selection, protection and safe transmission of cipher keys **Schlüsselverwaltung**

(e) identification code *or* word used for a stored record *or* data item **Schlüssel;** *we selected all the records with the word DISK in their keys;* **index key** = one field which is used to index a record **Indexschlüssel; key field** = field which identifies entries in a record **Schlüsselfeld; keyed sequential access method (KSAM)** = file structure that allows data to be accessed using key fields or key field content **sequentieller Zugriff in Schlüsselfolge**

2 *verb* **to key in** = to enter text *or* commands via a keyboard **eingeben;** *they keyed in the latest data*

◇ **keyboard**

1 *noun* number of keys fixed together in some order, used to enter information into a computer *or* to produce characters on a typewriter **Tastatur; keyboard to disk entry** = system where information entered on a keyboard is stored directly on to disk with no processing **Eingabe von der Tastatur direkt auf die Platte; ANSI keyboard** = standard for a keyboard that provides either upper case or upper and lower case characters on a typewriter style keyboard **ANSI-Tastatur; ASCII keyboard** = keyboard that provides a key for every ASCII code **ASCII-Tastatur; ASR keyboard** = communications console keyboard that has all the characters and punctuation keys and special control, send and receive keys **ASR-Tastatur; AZERTY keyboard** = non-English language key layout (the first six letters on the top left row of the keyboard being AZERTY) **AZERTY-Tastatur; interactive keyboard** = keyboard that helps to direct the user *or* prompts for an input by lighting up certain keys on the keyboard (under program control) **interaktive Tastatur; keyboard contact bounce** = multiple signals from a key pressed just once, due to a faulty switch and key bounce **Tastaturkontaktprellen; keyboard encoder** = way in which each key generates a unique word when pressed **Tastaturcodierer; keyboard layout** = way in which various function and character keys are arranged **Tastenanordnung; keyboard overlay** = paper placed over the keys on a keyboard describing their special functions for a particular application **Tastaturschablone; keyboard scan** = method for a computer to determine if a key has

been pressed by applying a voltage across each key switch (if the key is pressed a signal will be read by the computer) **Tastenabtaster; keyboard send/receive (KSR)** = terminal which has a keyboard and monitor, and is linked to a CPU **KSR (Datenstation mit Tastatur und seriellem Drucker mit Bildschirmfunktion); keyboard to disk entry** = system where information entered on a keyboard is stored directly onto disk with no processing **Eingabe von der Tastatur direkt auf die Platte; QWERTY keyboard** = standard English language key layout (the first six letters on the top left row of keys are QWERTY) **QWERTY-Tastatur; touch sensitive keyboard** = thin, flat membrane type keyboard whose keys are activated by touching the particular key, with no movement involved (often used for heavy duty or dirty environments where normal keys would not function correctly) **Folientastatur**
2 *verb* to enter information by using a keyboard **eingeben;** *it was cheaper to have the manuscript keyboarded by another company*

◇ **keyboarder** *noun* person who enters data via a keyboard **Dateneingeber**

◇ **keyboarding** *noun* action of entering data using a keyboard **Eingeben;** *the cost of keyboarding is calculated in keystrokes per hour*

◇ **keypad** *noun* group of special keys used for certain applications **Tastenblock;** *you can use the numeric keypad to enter the figures;* **hex keypad** = keypad with 16 keys (0-9 and A-F) for all the hexadecimal digits **hexadezimale Tastatur; numeric keypad** = set of ten keys with figures (0-9), included in most computer keyboards as a separate group, used for entering large amounts of data in numeric form **numerische Tastatur**

◇ **keystroke** *noun* action of pressing a key **Tastenanschlag;** *he keyboards at a rate of 3500 keystrokes per hour;* **keystroke count** = counting of each keystroke made, often used to calculate keyboarding costs **Anschlagzahl; keystroke verification** = check made on each key pressed to make sure it is valid for a particular application **Anschlagbestätigung**

◇ **key-to-disk** *noun* system where data is keyed in and stored directly on disk without any processing **Eingabe von der Tastatur direkt auf die Platte**

◇ **keyword** *noun* (i) command word used in a programming language to provide a function; (ii) important *or* informative word in a title *or* document that describes its contents; (iii) word which is relevant *or* important to a text **(i) Kennwort; (ii) & (iii) Schlüsselwort;** *the BASIC keyword PRINT will display text on the screen; computer is a*

keyword in IT; **keyword and context (KWAC)** = library index system using important words from the text and title as index entries **KWAC-Index; keyword in context (KWIC)** = library index system that uses keywords from the title *or* text of a book *or* document as an indexed entry, followed by the title *or* text it relates to **KWIC-Index; keyword out of context (KWOC)** = library index system that indexes book *or* document titles under any relevant keywords **KWOC-Index**

QUOTE where large orders are being placed over the telephone it is easy to key them into the micro
Micro Decision
QUOTE the new keyboard is almost unchanged, and features sixteen programmable function keys
Micro Decision
QUOTE it uses a six button keypad to select the devices and functions
Byte
QUOTE the main QWERTY typing area is in the centre of the keyboard with the 10 function keys on the left
Personal Computer World

kHz = KILOHERTZ unit of frequency measurement equal to one thousand Hertz **KHz;** *see also* HERTZ ⇨ APPENDIX

kill *verb* to erase a file *or* stop a program during execution **löschen, stoppen; kill file** = command to erase a stored file completely **Datei löschen; kill job** = command to halt a computer job while it is running **Stopbefehl**

kilo *prefix*
(a) meaning one thousand **Kilo-; kilobaud** = 1,000 bits per second **Kilobaud; kilohertz** *or* **KHz** = unit of frequency measurement equal to one thousand Hertz **Kilohertz** ⇨ APPENDIX **kilo instructions per second (KIPS)** = one thousand computer instructions processed every second, used as a measure of computer power **tausend Anweisungen pro Sekunde; kilo-ohm** = resistance of one thousand ohms **Kiloohm; kiloVolt-ampere output rating (KVA)** = method of measuring the power rating of a device **Anschlußwerte-Meßmethode; kilowatt** *or* **kW** = power measurement equal to one thousand watts **Kilowatt**
(b) meaning 1,024 units, equal to 2^{10} (used only in computer and electronics applications) **Kilo-; kilobit** *or* **Kb** = 1,024 bits of data **Kilobit; kilobyte** *or* **KB** *or* **Kbyte** = unit of measurement for high capacity storage devices meaning 1,024 bytes of data **Kilobyte; kiloword** *or* **KW** = unit of measurement of 1,024 computer words **Kilowort, KWort**

kimball tag *noun* coded card attached to a product in a shop, containing information about the product that is read by a scanner when the product is sold **Kimball-Etikett**

KIPS = KILO INSTRUCTIONS PER SECOND one thousand computer instructions processed every second, used as a measure of computer power **tausend Anweisungen pro Sekunde**

kludge *or* **kluge** *noun informal* (i) temporary correction made to a badly written *or* constructed piece of software *or* to a keyboarding error; (ii) hardware which should be used for demonstration purposes only **(i) Flickschusterei; (ii) Vorführgerät**
◊ **kluged** *adjective* temporarily repaired **zusammengeflickt**

knob *noun* round button (such as on a monitor), which can be turned to control some process **Knopf;** *turn the on/off knob; the brightness can be regulated by turning a knob at the back of the monitor*

knowledge *noun* what is known **Wissen; intelligent knowledge-based system (IKBS)** = software that applies the knowledge, advice and rules defined by experts in a particular subject, to a user's data to help solve a problem **intelligentes, wissensbasiertes System; knowledge-based system** = computer system that applies the stored reactions, instructions and knowledge of experts in a particular field to a problem **wissensbasiertes System;** *see also* EXPERT SYSTEM; **knowledge engineering** = designing and writing expert computer systems **Wissenstechnik**

KSR = KEYBOARD SEND/RECEIVE terminal which has a keyboard and monitor, and is linked to a CPU **KSR (Datenstation mit Tastatur und seriellem Drucker mit Bildschirmfunktion);** *compare with* ASR

KVA = KILOVOLT-AMPERE OUTPUT RATING

KW = KILOWORD

KWAC = KEYWORD AND CONTEXT library indexing system using important words from the text and title as indexed entries **KWAC-Index**
◊ **KWIC** = KEYWORD IN CONTEXT library indexing system that uses keywords from the title *or* text of a book *or* document as an indexed entry followed by the text it relates to **KWIC-Index**
◊ **KWOC** = KEYWORD OUT OF CONTEXT library indexing system that indexes books *or* document titles under any relevant keywords **KWOC-Index**

LI

label
1
(a) *noun* (i) word *or* other symbol used in a computer program to identify a routine *or* statement; (ii) character(s) used to identify a variable *or* piece of data *or* a file **(i) Bezeichnung, Marke; (ii) Kennung;** *BASIC uses many program labels such as line numbers;* **label field** = an item of data in a record that contains a label **Kennungsfeld; label record** = record containing identification for a stored file **Kennsatz**
(b) piece of paper *or* card attached to something to show instructions for use *or* an address **Hinweisschildchen; external label** = identifying piece of paper stuck to the outside of a device *or* disk **Etikett**
2 *verb* to print an address on a label **bezeichnen**
NOTE: **labelling - labelled** but US **labeling - labeled**
◊ **labelling** *noun* printing labels **Bezeichnen;** *the word-processor has a special utility allowing simple and rapid labelling*
NOTE: no plural

laboratory *noun* place where scientists work on research and development of new products **Labor;** *the new chip is being developed in the university laboratories*

lag *noun*
(a) time taken for a signal to pass through a circuit, such that the output is delayed compared to the input **Verzögerung;** *time lag is noticeable on international phone calls*
(b) time taken for an image to be no longer visible after it has been displayed on a CRT screen (this is caused by long persistence phosphor) **Kurzzeit-Nachleuchten**

laminate *verb* to cover a paper with a thin film of plastic, to give it a glossy look **beschichten, zellglasieren;** *the book has a laminated cover*

LAN *or* **lan** = LOCAL AREA NETWORK network where various terminals and equipment are all within a short distance of one another (at a maximum distance of about 500m, for example in the same building), and can be interconnected by cables **LAN, Lokalnetz; LAN server =** dedicated computer and backing storage facility used by terminals and operators of a LAN **LAN-Server, Lokalnetzbediener;** *compare* WAN

QUOTE since most of the LAN hardware is already present, the installation costs are only $50 per connection
Practical Computing

landline *noun* permanent direct link using cables laid in the ground between two points **Überlandleitung**

language *noun*
(a) spoken *or* written words which are used to communicate with other people **Sprache;** *he speaks several European languages;* **foreign language =** language which is spoken by people of another country **Fremdsprache**
(b) system of words *or* symbols which allows communication with computers (such as one that allows computer instructions to be entered as words which are easy to understand, and then translates them into machine code) **Programmiersprache; assembly language** *or* **assembler language =** programming language using mnemonics to code instructions which will then be converted to machine code **Assembliersprache; command language =** programming language made up of procedures for various tasks, that can be called up by a series of commands **Befehlssprache; control language =** commands that identify and describe the resources required by a job that a computer has to perform **(Job)steuerungssprache; graphic language =** computer programming language with inbuilt commands that are useful when displaying graphics **Programmiersprache zur Erstellung von Graphiken; high-level language (HLL) =** computer programming language that is easy to learn and allows the user to write programs using words and commands that are easy to understand and look like English words, the program is then translated into machine code, with one HLL instruction often representing more than one machine code instruction **höhere Programmiersprache; low-level language (LLL) =** language which is fast, but long and complex to program in, where each instruction represents a single machine code instruction **maschinenorientierte Programmiersprache; machine language =** programming language

that consists of commands in binary code form that can be directly understood by the CPU **Maschinensprache; programming language =** software that allows a user to enter a program in a certain language and then to execute it **Programmiersprache; query language =** language in a database management system that allows a database to be easily searched and queried **Abfragesprache; source language =** original language in which a program is written prior to processing by a computer **Ursprungssprache; language assembler =** program used to translate and assemble a source code program into a machine executable binary form **Sprachassemblierer; language compiler =** software that converts an encoded source program into another (machine code) form, and then executes it **Umsetzungsprogramm; language interpreter =** any program that takes each consecutive line of source program and translates it into another (machine code) language at run-time **Übersetzungsprogramm; language processor =** language translator from one language to machine code (there are three types of language processor: assembler, compiler and interpreter) **Sprachverarbeiter; language rules =** syntax and format for instructions and data items used in a particular language **Sprachregeln; language support environment =** hardware and software tools supplied to help the programmer write programs in a particular language **Programmierungshilfe; language translation =** using a computer to translate text from one language to another **Computerübersetzung; language translator =** program that converts code written in one language into equivalent instructions in another language **Übersetzungsprogramm**

COMMENT: There are three main types of computer languages: machine code, assembler and high-level language. The higher the level the language is, the easier it is to program and understand, but the slower it is to execute. The following are the commonest high-level languages: ADA, ALGOL, APL, BASIC, C, COBOL, COMAL, CORAL, FORTH, FORTRAN, LISP, LOGO, PASCAL, PL/1, POP-2, PROLOG. Assembly language uses mnemonics to represent machine code instructions; machine code is the basic binary patterns that instruct the processor to perform various tasks

lap *noun*
(a) a person's knees, when he is sitting down **Schoß;** *he placed the computer on his lap and keyboarded some orders while sitting in his car*

(b) overlap of printed colours which prevents any gaps showing **Überlappung**

◇ **lapheld computer** or **laptop computer** noun computer that is light enough to carry but not so small as to fit in a pocket, usually containing a screen, keyboard and disk drive **Laptop-Computer, Aktentaschencomputer**

QUOTE in our summary of seven laphelds we found features to admire in every machine
QUOTE the idea of a hard disk in a lapheld machine which runs on batteries is not brand new
PC Business World

lapel microphone noun small microphone that is pinned to someone's jacket **Ansteckmikrophon**

large-scale computer noun high-powered (large word size) computer system that can access high capacity memory and backing storage devices as well as multiple users **Großrechner**

◇ **large-scale integration (LSI)** noun integrated circuit with 500 to 10,000 components **Großintegration**

laser noun = LIGHT AMPLIFICATION BY STIMULATED EMISSION OF RADIATION device that produces coherent light of a single wavelength in a narrow beam, by exciting a material so that it emits photons of light **Laser; laser beam recording** = production of characters on a light-sensitive film by a laser beam controlled directly from a computer **Laserstrahlaufzeichnung; laser beam communications** = use of a modulated laser beam as a line-of-sight communications medium **Laserstrahlkommunikation; laser disk** = plastic disk containing binary data in the form of small etched dots that can be read by a laser, used to record high quality TV images or sound in digital form **Laserbildplatte; laser emulsion storage** = digital storage technique using a laser to expose light-sensitive material **Speicher mit Laserschicht; laser printer** = high-resolution computer printer that uses a laser source to print high-quality dot matrix character patterns on paper (these have a much higher resolution than normal printers, usually 300 dpi) **Laserdrucker; injection laser** = solid-state laser device used to transmit data as pulses of light down an optic fibre **Injektionslaser**

last in first out (LIFO) noun queue system that reads the last item stored, first **LIFO (zuletzt Abgelegtes wird als erstes bearbeitet);** *this computer stack uses a last in first out data retrieval method; compare with* FIRST IN FIRST OUT

latch
1 noun electronic component that maintains an output condition until it receives an input signal to change **elektronischer Schalter;** *see also* FLIP-FLOP
2 verb to set an output state **verriegeln;** *the output latched high until we reset the computer*

QUOTE other features of the device include a programmable latch bypass which allows any number of latches from 0 to 8 so that this device may be used as latched or combinatorial
Electronics & Power

latency noun time delay between the moment when an instruction is given to a computer and the execution of the instruction or return of a result (such as the delay between a request for data and the data being transferred from memory) **Wartezeit**

◇ **latent image** noun image formed before developing on light sensitive film after it has been exposed **latentes Bild**

lateral reversal noun creating the mirror image of a picture by swapping left and right **Kontern**

launch
1 noun (i) putting a new product on the market; (ii) putting a satellite in space **(i) Einführung, Lancierung; (ii) Abschuß;** *the launch of the new PC has been put back six months; the launch date for the network will be September*
2 verb (i) to put a new product on the market; (ii) to put a satellite in space **(i) einführen, lancieren; (ii) abschießen;** *the new PC was launched at the Personal Computer Show; launching costs for the computer range were calculated at $250,000*

◇ **launch amplifier** noun amplifier used to boost the television signals before they are transmitted over a cable network **Fernsehsignalverstärker**

◇ **launch vehicle** noun spacecraft used to transport a satellite from earth into space **Trägerrakete**

layer noun
(a) division of sections of space at certain distances from the earth into separate regions used for various radio communications (these are: D-Region from 50 - 90km above earth's surface, E-Region from 90 - 150km above earth's surface, F-Region from 150 - 400km above earth's surface) **Schicht**

(b) ISO/OSI standards defining the stages a message has to pass through when being transmitted from one computer to another over a network **Schicht; application layer =** the program that requests a transmission **Anwendungsschicht; data link layer =** layer that sends packets of data to the next link, and deals with error correction **Sicherungsschicht; network layer =** layer that decides on the routes to be used, the costs, etc. **Vermittlungsschicht; physical layer =** layer that defines the rules for bit rate, power, medium for transmission, etc. **Bitübertragungsschicht; presentation layer =** section that agrees on format, codes and request for start/end of a connection **Darstellungsschicht; session layer =** layer that makes the connection/disconnection between a transmitter and receiver **Sitzungsschicht; transport layer =** layer that checks and controls the quality of the connection **Transportschicht**

◇ **layered** *adjective* consisting of layers **geschichtet;** *the kernel has a layered structure according to user priority*

◇ **lay in** *verb* to synchronize a frame of film with the music *or* sound tracks **(Tonspur) anlegen**

◇ **layout** *noun*
(a) mock-up of a finished piece of printed work showing the positioning and sizes of text and graphics **Entwurf, Montage;** *the design team is working on the layouts for the new magazine*
(b) rules governing the data input and output from a computer **Aufbau**

◇ **lay out** *verb* to plan and design the positions and sizes of a piece of work to be printed **entwerfen;** *the designers have laid out the pages in A4 format*

LBR = LASER BEAM RECORDING producing characters on a light sensitive film by laser beam directly controlled from a computer **Laserstrahlaufzeichnung**

LC circuit *noun* simple inductor-capacitor circuit that acts as a filter *or* oscillator **LC-Oszillator**

LCD = LIQUID CRYSTAL DISPLAY liquid crystal that turns black when a voltage is applied, used in many watches, calculators and other small digital displays **LCD-Anzeige, Flüssigkristallanzeige**

QUOTE LCD screens can run for long periods on ordinary or rechargeable batteries
Micro Decision

LCP = LINK CONTROL PROCEDURE rules defining the transmission of data over a channel **Verbindungssteuerungsverfahren**

LDS = LOCAL DISTRIBUTION SERVICE TV signal relay station that transmits signals to another point from which they are distributed over cable **lokaler Verteilerservice**

lead *noun*
(a) electrical conducting wire **Netzkabel**
(b) thin piece of metal used to give extra space between lines of type before printing **Durchschuß**

◇ **lead in page** *noun* videotext page that directs the user to other pages of interest **Einführungsseite**

◇ **leader** *noun*
(a) section of magnetic tape *or* photographic film that contains no signal *or* images, used at the beginning of the reel for identification and to aid the tape machine to pick up the tape **(Streifen)vorspann; leader record =** initial record containing information (such as titles, format, etc.) about following records in a file **Vorlaufsatz**
(b) row of printed dots **Führungspunkte**

◇ **leading** *noun* extra space between lines of print **Durchschuß**

◇ **leading edge** *noun* first edge of a punched card that enters the card reader **Führungskante**

◇ **leading zero** *noun* zero digit used to pad out the beginning of a stored number **führende Null**

leaf *noun*
(a) page of a book (printed on both sides) **Blatt**
(b) final node in a data tree structure **Blatt**

◇ **leaflet** *noun* small publicity sheet (usually one page folded in half) **Hand-, Reklamezettel**

leak
1 *noun*
(a) loss of secret documents *or* a breach of security **Leck;** *a leak informed the press of our new designs*
(b) gradual loss of charge from a charged component due to imperfect insulation **undichte Stelle**
2 *verb*
(a) to provide secret information to unauthorized people **etwas durchsickern lassen, zuspielen;** *the details of our new software package have been leaked to the press*
(b) to lose electric charge gradually **entweichen;** *in this circuit, the capacitor charge leaks out at 10% per second*

◇ **leakage** *noun* loss of signal strength **Leck**

> QUOTE signal leakages in both directions can
> be a major problem in co-axial cable systems
> *Electronics & Wireless World*

leap-frog test *noun* memory location
test, in which a program skips from one
location to another random location,
writing data then reading and comparing
for faults, until all locations have been
tested **Bocksprungtest, sprungweise
Durchprüfung; crippled leap-frog test** =
standard leap-frog test that uses a single
memory location rather than a changing
location **Teilprüfung im Bocksprungprogramm**

learning curve *noun* the rate at which
someone can acquire knowledge about a
subject **Lernkurve**

lease
1 *noun* written contract for letting *or*
renting a piece of equipment for a period
against payment of a fee **Leasing-Vertrag**
2 *verb*
(a) to let *or* rent equipment for a period
mieten; *the company has a policy of only
using leased equipment;* **leased circuit** =
electronic circuit *or* communications
channel rented for a period **Mietleitung;
leased line** = communications channel,
such as a telephone line, which is rented for
the exclusive use of the subscriber
Mietleitung
(b) to use equipment for a time and pay a
fee **mieten;** *the company leases all its
computers*

least cost design *noun* best money-
saving use of space *or* components
Niedrigstkostenplan; *the budget is only
£1000, we need the least cost design for the
new circuit*

◊ **least recently used algorithm** *noun*
algorithm which finds the page of memory
that was last accessed before any other, and
erases it to make room for another page
**LRU-Algorithmus (am längsten nicht benutzter
Algorithmus)**

◊ **least significant digit (LSD)** *noun* digit
which occupies the right hand position in a
number and so carries the least power
(equal to the number radix raised to zero =
1) **niederwertigste Ziffer; least significant bit
(LSB)** = binary digit occupying the right
hand position of a word and carrying the
least power of two in the word (usually
equal to two raised to zero = 1)
niederwertigstes Bit

leaving files open *phrase* meaning that
a file has not been closed *or* does not
contain an end of text marker (this will

result in the loss of data since the text will
not have been saved) **Offenlassen von
Dateien**

LED = LIGHT EMITTING DIODE
semiconductor diode that emits light when
a current is applied **LED
(Leuchtdiodenanzeige)**

> COMMENT: LED displays are used to
> display small amounts of information, as
> in pocket calculators, watches, indicators,
> etc.

left justification *noun*
(a) shifting a binary number to the left
hand end of the word containing it
Stellenverschiebung nach links
(b) making the left hand margin of the text
even **Linksausrichtung, Linksbündigkeit**
◊ **left justify** *verb* printing command that
makes the left hand margin of the text even
linksbündig machen
◊ **left shift** *noun* left arithmetic shift by
one bit of data in a word, a binary number
is doubled for each left shift
Linksverschiebung

leg *noun* one possible path through a
routine **Zweig einer Schaltung**

legal *adjective* statement or instruction
that is acceptable within language syntax
rules **gültig**

legible *adjective* which can be read easily
lesbar; *the manuscript is written in pencil
and is hardly legible*
◊ **legibility** *noun* being able to be read
Lesbarkeit; *the keyboarders find the
manuscript lacks legibility*

length *noun* how long something is; the
number of data items in a variable *or* list
Länge; block length = number of records *or*
fields *or* characters in a block of data
Blocklänge; buffer length = number of data
items that can be stored in a buffer while
waiting for the processor to attend to them
Pufferlänge; field length = number of
characters stored in a field **Feldlänge; file
length** = number of characters *or* bytes in a
stored file **Dateilänge; length of filename** =
number of characters allowed for
identification of a file **Länge des
Dateinamens; line length** = number of
characters which can be displayed
horizontally on one line of a display (CRT
displays often use an 80 character line
length) **Zeilenlänge; record length** = total
number of characters contained in the
various fields within a stored record

Satzlänge; **register length** = number of bits that make up a register **Registerlänge**

lens *noun* shaped glass that changes the path of a light beam **Linse; concave lens** = lens that is thinner in the centre than at the edges, bending light out **konkave Linse; convex lens** = lens that is thicker in the centre than the edges, bending light in **konvexe Linse; lens speed** = the maximum aperture of a lens, relating to the amount of light that can enter the lens **Öffnungsverhältnis; lens stop** = lens aperture size **Blende**

letter *noun*
(a) piece of writing sent from one person to another *or* from a company to another, to give information, to send instructions, etc. **Brief; form letter** *or* **standard letter** = letter sent to several addressees by name without any change to the text **Formbrief**
(b) written *or* printed sign, which goes to make a word (such as A, B, C, etc.) **Buchstabe;** *his name was written in capital letters*

◊ **letterhead** *noun* name and address of a company printed at the top of the company's notepaper **Briefkopf;** *business forms and letterheads can now be designed on a PC*

◊ **letter-quality (LQ) printing** *noun* feature of some dot-matrix printers to provide characters of the same quality as a typewriter by using dots which are very close together **LQ (Schönschriftdruck); near-letter-quality (NLQ) printing** = printing by a dot-matrix printer that provides higher quality type, which is almost as good as a typewriter, by decreasing the space between the dots **NLQ (korrespondenzfähiges Schriftbild)**

QUOTE the printer offers reasonable speeds of printing in both draft and letter-quality modes
Which PC?

level *noun*
(a) strength *or* power of an electrical signal **Pegel;** *turn the sound level down, it's far too loud;* **sound pressure level (SPL)** = measurement of the magnitude of the pressure wave conveying sound **Schalldruckpegel**
(b) quantity of bits that make up a digital transmitted signal **Stufe; quatenary level quantization** = use of four bits of data in an A/D conversion process **quaternäre Stufenquantisierung**

lexical analysis *noun* stage in program translation when the compiling *or* translating software replaces program keywords with machine code instructions **lexikalische Analyse**

lexicographical order *noun* order of items, where the words are listed in the order of the letters of the alphabet, as in a dictionary **lexikographische Anordnung**

LF
(a) = LOW FREQUENCY range of audio frequencies between 5 - 300Hz *or* range of radio frequencies between 30 - 300KHz **Niederfrequenz**
(b) = LINE FEED

library *noun*
(a) collection of files *or* documents *or* books *or* records, etc., which can be consulted *or* borrowed by the public, usually kept in a public place **Bibliothek;** *the editors have checked all the references in the local library; a copy of each new book has to be deposited in the British Library; look up the bibliographical details in the library catalogue*
(b) collection of programs *or* books belonging to a person **Bibliothek;** *he has a large library of computer games;* **library function** = software routine that a user can insert into his program to provide the function with no effort **Bibliotheksfunktion; library program** = (i) number of specially written *or* relevant software routines, which a user can insert into his own program, saving time and effort; (ii) group of functions which a computer needs to refer to often, but which are not stored in main memory **(i) & (ii) Bibliotheksprogramm;** *the square root function is already in the library program;* **macro library** = number of useful, independent routines that can be incorporated into any program to ease program writing **Makrobibliothek; library routine** = prewritten routine that can be inserted into a main program and called up when required **Bibliotheksroutine; library subroutine** = tried and tested subroutine stored in a library, and which can be inserted into a user's program when required **Bibliotheks(unter)programm; library track** = one track on a magnetic disk *or* tape used to store information about the contents (such as titles, format and index data) **Hinweisspur**

◊ **librarian** *noun* person who works in a library **Bibliothekar/-in**

QUOTE a library of popular shapes and images is supplied
Practical Computing

licence *noun* permission given by one manufacturer to another manufacturer to make copies of his products against payment of a fee **Lizenz;** *the software is manufactured in this country under licence*

LIFO = LAST IN FIRST OUT queue system that reads the last item stored, first **LIFO (zuletzt Abgelegtes wird als erstes bearbeitet);** *this computer stack uses a LIFO data retrieval method; see also* FIFO

lifter *noun* mechanical device that lifts magnetic tape away from the heads when rewinding the tape **Anheber**

ligature *noun* two characters printed together to form a combined character *or* a short line connecting two characters **Ligatur**

light
1 *noun* perception of brightness due to electromagnetic effects in the frequency range 400 - 750 nm, which allows a person to see **Licht;** *the VDU should not be placed under a bright light;* **light conduit** = fibre optics used to transmit light from one place to another rather than for the transmission of data **Lichtleitung; light emitting diode (LED)** = semiconductor diode that emits light when a current is applied (used in calculators and clock displays and as indicators) **LED (lichtaussendende Diode); light guide** = fine strands of glass *or* plastic protected by a surrounding material, used for the transmission of light **Lichtwellenleiter; light pen** = computer accessory in the shape of a pen that contains a light-sensitive device that can detect pixels on a video screen (often used with suitable software to draw graphics on a screen *or* position a cursor) **Lichtstift; light pipe** = LIGHT GUIDE; **coherent light** = light beam in which all the waveforms are in phase **kohärentes Licht; visible light** = range of light colours that can be seen with the human eye **sichtbares Licht; ultra-violet light (UV light)** = electromagnetic radiation with wavelengths just greater than the visible spectrum, from 200 to 4,000 angstroms (often used to erase data from EPROMs) **ultraviolettes Licht (UV-Licht); infrared light (IR light)** = electromagnetic radiation just below visible red (often used for communications purposes such as remote control) **Infrarotlicht (IR-Licht).**
2 *adjective* not dark **hell; light face** = typeface with thin lines, which appears light on the page **magere Schrift**

◊ **light-sensitive** *adjective* which is sensitive to light **lichtempfindlich;** *the photograph is printed on light-sensitive paper;* **light-sensitive device** = device (such as a phototransistor) which is sensitive to

light, and produces a change in signal strength *or* resistance **Photozelle**

◊ **lightweight** *adjective* which is not heavy **leicht(gewichtig);** *a lightweight computer which can easily fit into a suitcase*

limits *noun* predefined maximum ranges for numbers in a computer **Grenzwerte**

◊ **limited distance modem** *noun* data transmission device with a very short range that sends pure digital data rather than a modulated carrier **Modem für begrenzte Entfernungen**

◊ **limiter** *noun* electronic circuit that prevents a signal from going above a certain level **Begrenzer**

◊ **limiting resolution** *noun* maximum number of lines that make up a television picture **Grenzauflösung**

line *noun*
(a) physical connection for data transmission (such as a cable between parts of a system *or* a telephone wire) **Leitung; access line** = permanently connected communications line between a terminal and a DSE **Anschlußleitung; fast line** = special communications link that allows data to be transmitted at 48K *or* 96K baud **Schnelleitung; line busy tone** = signal indicating that a telephone link cannot be made since the intended receiver is busy **Besetztzeichen; line communications** = signal transmission using a cable link *or* telegraph wire **drahtgebundene Übertragung; line control** = special codes used to control a communications channel **Übertragungssteuerung; line driver** = high power circuit and amplifier used to send signals over a long distance line without too much loss of signal **Kabeltreiber; line extender** = circuit used to boost a television signal **Nebenleitung; line impedance** = impedance of a communications line *or* cable (equipment should have a matching load to minimize power loss) **Leitungsimpedanz; line level** = amplitude of a signal transmitted over a cable **Leitungsstufe; line load** = number of messages transmitted over a line compared to the maximum capacity **Leitungsbelastung; line speed** = rate at which data is sent along a line **Übertragungsgeschwindigkeit; line switching** = communications line and circuit established on demand and held until no longer required **Durchschaltevermittlungstechnik; line transient** = large voltage spike on a line **Wanderwelle**
(b) single long thin mark drawn by a pen *or* printed on a surface **Linie, Strich;** *the printer has difficulty in reproducing very fine lines*

line art = black and white graphics, with no shades of grey **schwarz/weiß Graphik; line drawings** = drawings made of lines drawn by the artist **Strichzeichnungen;** *the book is illustrated with line drawings and halftones*

(c) one trace by the electron picture beam on a screen *or* monitor **Zeile; line blanking interval** = period of time when the picture beam is not displayed, this is during line flyback **Zeilenaustastlücke; line drive signal** = signal to start the scanning procedure in a television camera **Zeilentreibersignal; line flyback** = electron beam returning from the end of one line to the beginning of the next **Zeilenrücklauf; line frequency** = number of picture lines that are scanned per second **Zeilenfrequenz**

(d) row of characters (printed on a page *or* displayed on a computer screen *or* printer) **Zeile;** *each page has 52 lines of text; several lines of manuscript seem to have been missed by the keyboarder; can we insert an extra line of spacing between the paragraphs?;* **command line** = program line that contains a command **Kommandozeile; information line** = line running across the screen which gives the user information about the program being executed *or* the file being edited **Informationszeile; line editor** = piece of software that allows the operator to modify one line of text from a file at a time **Zeilen-Editor; line ending** = character which shows that a line has ended (instructed by pressing the carriage return key) **Zeilenende; line feed (LF)** = control on a printer *or* computer terminal that moves the cursor down by one line **Zeilenvorschub; line folding** = move a section of a long line of text onto the next row **Zeilenumbruch; line increment** = minimum distance between two lines of type, which can be as small as one eighteenth of a point **(kleinster) Zeilenschritt; line length** = number of characters contained in a displayed line (on a computer screen this is normally 80 haracters, on a printer often 132 characters) **Zeilenlänge; line spacing** = distance between two rows of characters **Zeilenabstand; lines per minute (LPM)** = number of lines printed by a line printer per minute **Zeilen pro Minute**

(e) series of characters received as a single input by a computer **Zeile; line input** = command to receive all characters including punctuation entered up to a carriage return code **Zeileneingabe**

(f) one row of commands *or* arguments in a computer program **Zeile; line number** = number that refers to a line of program code in a computer program **Zeilennummer**

COMMENT: the programming language will sort out the program into order according to line number

QUOTE straight lines are drawn by clicking the points on the screen where you would like the line to start and finish
Personal Computer World
QUOTE while pixel editing is handy for line art, most desktop scanners have trouble producing the shades of grey or half-tones found in black and white photography
Publish

line of sight *noun* clear transmission path for radio communications in a straight line **Sichtverbindung**

COMMENT: line of sight paths are used with a very directional transmission medium such as a laser beam rather than a uni-directional one such as radio

line printer *noun* device for printing draft quality information at high speeds, typical output is 200 to 3000 lines per minute **Zeilendrucker**

COMMENT: line printers print a whole line at a time, running from right to left and left to right, and are usually dot matrix printers with not very high quality print. Compare page printers, which print a whole page at a time

linear *adjective* (circuit output) that varies directly with the input signal so that the output to input characteristics are a straight line (in practice this is never achieved since all components have maximum and minimum output limits at which points the signal becomes distorted) **linear; linear array** = antenna whose elements lie in a straight line **Dipolzeilenantenne; linear function** = mathematical expression where the input is not raised to a power above one and contains no multiplications other than by a constant **lineare Funktion;** *the expression* $Y = 10 + 5X - 3W$ *is a linear function; the expression* $Y = (10 + 5X^2)$ *is not a linear function;* **linear integrated circuit** = electronic device whose output varies linearly with its input over a restricted range (device usually used to provide gain to an analog signal) **analoge integrierte Schaltung; linear list** = list that has no free space for new records within its structure **lineare Liste; linear program** = computer program that contains no loops *or* branches **lineares Programm; linear programming** = method of mathematically breaking down a problem so that it can be solved by computer **lineare Programmierung; linear**

search = search method which compares each item in a list with the search key until the correct entry is found (starting with the first item and working sequentially towards the end) **lineare Suche**

link

1 *noun*
(a) communications path *or* channel between two components *or* devices **Verbindungsstrecke;** *to transmit faster, you can use the direct link with the mainframe;* **data link layer** = ISO/OSI layer that sends packets of data to the next link, and deals with error correction **Sicherungsschicht; link control procedure (LCP)** = rules defining the transmission of data over a channel **Verbindungssteuerungsverfahren; link loss** = attenuation of signals transmitted over a link **Signaldämpfung; satellite link** = use of a satellite to allow the transmission of data from one point on earth to another **Satellitenstrecke**
(b) software routine that allows data transfer between incompatible programs **Verbindungsprogramm; link trials** = testing computer programs so as to see if each module works in conjunction with the others **Verbindungsüberprüfung**
2 *verb* to join *or* interface two pieces of software *or* hardware **verbinden;** *the two computers are linked;* **link files** = command to merge together a list of separate files **Dateien verschmelzen; linked list** = list of data where each entry carries the address of the next consecutive entry **verbundene Liste; linked subroutine** = number of computer instructions in a program that can be called at any time, with control being returned on completion to the next instruction in the main program **verbundenes Unterprogramm**

◊ **linkage** *noun* act of linking two things **Verbindung; linkage editing** = combining separate programs together, and standardizing the calls *or* references within them **Binderprogramm, Linkage Editierung; linkage software** = special software which links sections of program code with any library routines *or* other code **Programmverbindungssoftware;** *graphics and text are joined without linkage software*

◊ **linking** *noun* merging of a number of small programs together to enable them to run as one unit **Programmverbindung; linking loader** = short software routine that merges sections of programs to allow them to be run as one **Bindelader**

LIPS = LOGICAL INFERENCES PER SECOND standard for the measurement of processing power of an inference engine **logische Schlußfolgerungen pro Sekunde**

COMMENT: one inference often requires thousands of computer instructions

liquid crystal display (LCD) *noun*
liquid crystals that turn black when a voltage is applied, used in many watch, calculator and digital displays **Flüssigkristallanzeige (LCD)**

COMMENT: LCDs do not generate light and so cannot be seen in the dark without an external light source (as opposed to LEDs)

LISP = LIST PROCESSING high-level language used mainly in processing lists of instructions *or* data and in artificial intelligence work **LISP (Programmiersprache)**

list

1 *noun* series of ordered items of data **Liste; chained list** = list in which each element contains data and an address to the next element in the list **gekettete Liste; linear list** = list that has no free space for new records within its structure **lineare Liste; linked list** = list of data where each entry carries the address of the next consecutive entry **gekettete Liste; pushdown list** = temporary storage, in a LIFO format, for a list of items of data **Rückstelliste; reference list** = list of routines *or* instructions and their location within a program **Verweisliste; stop list** = list of words that are not to be used *or* are not significant for a file search **Liste der verbotenen Wörter; list processing** = (i) computation of a series of items of data such as adding *or* deleting *or* sorting *or* updating entries; (ii) LISP *or* a high-level language used mainly in processing lists of instructions *or* data, and in artificial intelligence work **(i) Listenbearbeitung; (ii) LISP (Programmiersprache)**
2 *verb* to print *or* display certain items of information **auflisten; to list a program** = to display a program line by line in correct order **ein Programm auflisten**

◊ **listing** *noun*
(a) program lines printed *or* displayed in an ordered way **Auflistung; computer listing** = printout of a list of items, taken from data stored in a computer **Computerauflistung; a program listing** = a printed copy of the lines of a program **eine (gedruckte) Programmauflistung; listing paper** = continuous stationery **Endlospapier**
(b) **listings** = series of information items (such as cinema times, etc.) listed in a newspaper **Programm**

literal *noun*
(a) (operand) computer instruction tha

contains the actual number *or* address to be used, rather than a label *or* its location **Literal**

(b) printing error when one character is replaced by another *or* when two characters are transposed **Druckfehler**

literate *adjective* (person) who can read and write **des Lesens und Schreibens kundig; computer-literate** = able to understand expressions relating to computers and how to use a computer **computersachverständig**

◊ **literacy** *noun* being able to read and write **Kenntnis des Lesens und Schreibens; computer literacy** = understanding the basic principles of computers, related expressions and being able to use computers for programming *or* applications **Fähigkeit, sich mit Computern auszukennen**

lith film *noun* high quality and contrast photographic film used in lithographic printing **lithographischer Film**

◊ **lithography** *or (informal)*

◊ **litho** *noun* **offset lithography** = printing process used for printing books, where the ink sticks to dry areas on the film and is transferred to rubber rollers from which it is printed on to the paper **Offsetlithographie**

◊ **lithographic** *adjective* referring to lithography **lithographisch; lithographic film** = LITH FILM

liveware *noun* the operators and users of a computer system (as opposed to the hardware and software) **EDV-Personal**

LLL = LOW-LEVEL LANGUAGE

load

1 *noun*

(a) job *or* piece of work to be done **Aufgabe, Belastung; load sharing** = use of more than one computer in a network to even out the work load on each processor **Belastungsverteilung; line load** = number of messages transmitted over a line compared to the maximum capacity of the line **Leitungsbelastung; work load** = number of tasks that a machine has to complete **Arbeitsbelastung**

(b) impedance presented to a line *or* device **Belastung; load life** = length of time an impedance can operate with a certain power before it is no longer usable **Lebensdauer bei Belastung; matched load** = load that is the same as the impedance of the transmission line *or* device connected to it **angepaßte Belastung**

2 *verb*

(a) to transfer a file *or* program from disk *or* tape to main memory **laden; scatter load** = loading sequential data into various non-continuous locations in memory **Streuladen; load and run** *or* **load and go** = computer program that is loaded into main memory and then starts to execute itself automatically **laden und automatisch laufen**

(b) to put a disk *or* tape into a computer, so that it can be run **laden**

(c) to place an impedance *or* device at the end of a line **belasten**

◊ **loading** *noun* action of transferring a file *or* program from disk to memory **Laden; loading can be a long process**

◊ **load point** *noun* start of a recording section in a reel of magnetic tape **Ladepunkt**

◊ **loader** *noun* program which loads another file *or* program into computer memory **Ladeprogramm; absolute loader** = program that loads a section of code into main memory **Ladeprogramm für absolute Programme;** *compare* BOOTSTRAP; **binary loader** = short section of program code that allows programs in binary form (such as object code from a linker *or* assembler) to be loaded into memory **binäres Ladeprogramm; card loader** = short program that transfers data from a punched card into main memory **Kartenlader; initial program loader (IPL)** = short routine that loads the first section of a program, after which it continues the loading process itself **Urlader**

lobe *noun* section of a response curve around an antenna *or* microphone **(Strahlungs)keule**

local *adjective & noun*

(a) (variable *or* argument) that is only used in a certain section of a computer program *or* structure **lokal, Lokal-, lokal-; local declaration** = assignment of a variable that is only valid in a section of a computer program *or* structure **lokale Erklärung; local memory** = high speed RAM that is used instead of a hardware device to store bit streams *or* patterns **Lokalspeicher; local variable** = variable which can only be accessed by certain routines in a certain section of a computer program **lokale Variable;** *compare* GLOBAL VARIABLE

(b) referring to a system with limited access **lokal;** *(of a terminal)* **on local** = not working with a CPU, but being used as a stand-alone terminal **stationärer Betrieb; local mode** = operating state of a computer terminal that does not receive messages **stationärer Betrieb**

◊ **local area network (LAN** or **lan)** noun network where various terminals and equipment are all a short distance from one another (at a maximum distance of about 500m, for example in the same building) and can be interconnected by cables **Lokalnetz (LAN);** compare with WAN; **local area network server** = dedicated computer and backing storage facility used by terminals and operators of a LAN **Lokalnetzserver, Lokalnetzbediener**

COMMENT: LANs use cables or optical fibre links; WANs use modems, radio and other long distance transmission methods

locate verb (i) to be situated; (ii) to find (i)**sich befinden; (ii) lokalisieren;** the computer is located in the main office building; have you managed to locate the programming fault?

◊ **location** noun
(a) number or absolute address which specifies the point in memory where a data word can be found and accessed **Speicherstelle**
(b) on location = filming in real situations, and not in the studio **vor Ort; location shots** = sections of a film which are shot on location **Außenaufnahmen**

lock verb to prevent access to a system or file **sperren; locking a file** = the action of preventing any further writing to a file **eine Datei sperren; to lock onto** = to synchronize an internal clock with a received signal **einstellen auf**

◊ **lockout** noun preventing a user sending messages over a network by continuously transmitting data **Aussperrung**

◊ **lock up** noun faulty operating state of computer that cannot be recovered from without switching off the power **Sperre**

COMMENT: this can be caused by an infinite program loop or a deadly embrace

log
1 noun record of computer processing operations **Protokoll**
2 verb to record a series of actions **protokollieren; to log in** or **log on** = to enter various identification data, such as a password, usually by means of a terminal, to the central computer before accessing a program or data (used as a means of making sure that only authorized users can access the computer system) **sich anmelden; automatic log on** = telephone number, password and user number transmitted when requested by a remote system to

automate logon **automatische Anmeldung; to log off** or **log out** = to enter a symbol or instruction at the end of a computing session to close all files and break the channel between the user's terminal and the main computer **sich abmelden;** NOTE: the verbs can be spelled **log on, log-on,** or **logon; log off, log-off** or **logoff**

◊ **logger** noun **call logger** = device which logs telephone calls (and notes the number called, the time when the call was made, and the length of the call) **Anrufaufzeichner**

◊ **logging** noun input of data into a system **Aufzeichnen; logging on** or **logging off** = process of opening or ending operations with a system **Anmelden; Abmelden; call logging** = system of monitoring telephone calls **Anrufaufzeichnung; error logging** = recording errors met **Fehlererfassung;** features of the program include error logging

QUOTE logging on and off from terminals is simple, requiring only a user name and password
QUOTE once the server is up and running it is possible for users to log-on
Micro Decision
QUOTE facilities for protection against hardware failure and software malfunction include log files
Computer News

logarithm noun mathematical operation that gives the power a number must be raised to, to give the required number **Logarithmus;** decimal logarithm of 1,000 is 3 (= 10 x 10 x 10)

◊ **logarithmic** adjective referring to variations in the logarithm of a scale **logarithmisch;** bel is a unit in the logarithmic scale; **logarithmic graph** = graph whose axes have a scale that is the logarithm of the linear measurement **logarithmische Darstellung**

logic noun
(a) science which deals with thought and reasoning **Logik; formal logic** = treatment of form and structure, ignoring content **formale Logik**
(b) mathematical treatment of formal logic operations such as AND, OR, etc., and their transformation into various circuits **Art der Schaltungstechnik;** see also BOOLEAN ALGEBRA; **logic map** = graphical representation of states and conditions in a logic circuit **logische Map; logic state** = one out of two possible levels in a digital circuit, the levels being 1 and 0 or TRUE and FALSE **logischer Zustand; logic state analyzer** = test equipment that displays the logic states of a number of components or circuits **Logikanalysator; logic symbol** = graphical symbol used to represent a type of logic function **logisches Symbol**

(c) system for deducing results from binary data **Logik; logic bomb** = section of code that performs various unpleasant functions such as system crash when a number of conditions are true (the logic bomb is installed by unpleasant hackers *or* very annoyed programmers) **programmierte Zeitbombe; logic level** = voltage used to represent a particular logic state (this is often five volts for a one and zero volts for a zero) **Logikpegel; logic operation** = computer operation *or* procedure in which a decision is made **logische Operation**
(d) components of a computer *or* digital system **Logik; sequential logic** = logic circuit whose output depends on the logic state of the previous inputs **sequentielle Logik; logic card** *or* **logic board** = printed circuit board containing binary logic gates rather than analog components **Schaltkreisplatine; logic circuit** = electronic circuit made up of various logical gates such as AND, OR and EXOR **logischer Schaltkreis; logic element** = gate *or* combination of logic gates **Verknüpfungsglied; logic flowchart** = graphical representation of logic elements, steps and decisions and the interconnections **logisches Flußdiagramm; logic gate** = electronic circuit that applies a logical operator to an input signal and produces an output **logisches Steuerelement; see also** GATE

◊ **logical** *adjective* that uses logic in its operation **logisch;** *logical reasoning can be simulated by an artificial intelligence machine;* **logical channel** = electronic circuit between a terminal and a network node in a packet switching system **logischer Kanal; logical chart** = graphical representation of logic elements, steps and decisions and their interconnections **logisches Diagramm; logical comparison** = function to see if two logic signals are the same **Identitätsvergleich; logical decision** = one of two paths chosen as a result of one of two possible answers to a question **logische Entscheidung; logical error** = fault in a program design causing incorrect branching *or* operations **logischer Fehler; logical expression** = function made up from a series of logical operators such as AND and OR **logischer Ausdruck; logical high** = equal to logic true state *or* 1 **logischer Pegel H; logical low** = equal to logic false state *or* 0 **logischer Pegel L; logical operator** = character *or* word that describes the logical action it will perform (the most common logical operators are AND, NOT, and OR) **logischer Operator; logical record** = unit of information ready for processing that is not necessarily the same as the original data item in storage, which might contain control data, etc. **logischer Satz; logical shift** = data movement to the left *or* right in a

word, the bits falling outside the word boundary are discarded, the free positions are filled with zeros **logisches Verschieben;** *compare with* ARITHMETIC SHIFT

◊ **logic-seeking** *adjective* (printer) that can print the required information with the minimum head movement, detecting ends of lines, justification commands, etc. **logisch(er Drucker)**

> QUOTE a reduction in the number of logic gates leads to faster operation and lower silicon costs
> QUOTE the removal of complex but infrequently used logic makes the core of the processor simpler and faster, so simple operations execute faster
>
> *Electronics & Power*

login = LOGGING IN

LOGO *noun* high-level programming language used mainly for educational purposes, with graphical commands that are easy to use **LOGO (Programmiersprache)**
◊ **logo** *noun* special printed set of characters *or* symbols used to identify a company *or* product **Logo**

logoff = LOG OFF, LOGGING OFF
◊ **logon** = LOG ON, LOGGING ON
◊ **logout** = LOGGING OUT

long haul network *noun* communications network between distant computers that usually uses the public telephone system **Überlandnetz**

long persistence phosphor *noun* television screen coating that retains the displayed image for a period of time longer than the refresh rate, reducing flicker effects **Bildschirmbeschichtung mit langer Nachleuchtdauer**

look ahead *noun* action by some CPUs to fetch instructions and examine them before they are executed (to speed up operations) **Vorgriff; carry look ahead** = high speed adder that can predict if a carry will be generated by a sum and add it in, removing the delay found in a ripple through carry adder **Addierer mit Parallelübertrag**
◊ **binary look-up** *noun* fast search method for use on ordered lists of data; the search key is compared with the data in the middle of the list and one half is discarded, this is repeated with remaining half until only one data item remains **binäre Abfragemethode**
◊ **look-up table** *or* **LUT** *noun* collection of stored results that can be accessed very rapidly by a program without the need to

calculate each result whenever needed **Nachschlagetabelle;** *lookup tables are preprogrammed then used in processing so saving calculations for each result required*

> QUOTE a lookup table changes a pixel's value based on the values in a table
>
> *Byte*

loop

1 *noun*
(a) procedure *or* series of instructions in a computer program that are performed again and again until a test shows that a specific condition has been met *or* until the program is completed **Schleife; closed loop** = computer control operation in which data is fed back from the output of the controlled device to the controlling loop **geschlossener Regelkreis; endless loop** *or* **infinite loop** = loop which has no end, except when the program is stopped **Endlosschleife; holding loop** = section of program that loops until it is broken by some action, most often used when waiting for a response from the keyboard or a device **Warteschleife; modification loop** = instructions within a loop that change other instructions *or* data within a program **Modifikationsschleife; nested loop** = loop contained inside another **Schleife in der Schleife; loop body** = main section of instructions within a loop that carry out the primary function rather than being used to enter *or* leave *or* setup the loop **Schleifenrumpf; loop check** = check that data has been correctly transmitted down a line by returning the data to the transmitter **Schleifenprüfung; loop counter** = register that contains the number of times a loop has been repeated **Schleifenzähler; loop program** = sequence of instructions that are repeated until a condition is met **Schleifenprogramm**
(b) (i) long piece of tape with the two ends joined; (ii) communications channel that is passed via all receivers and is terminated where it started from **(i) Schlaufe; (ii) Schleife; loop film** = endless piece of magnetic *or* photographic film that plays continuously **Endlosfilm**
(c) length of wire coiled in the shape of a circle **Schlinge; loop antenna** = aerial in the shape of a circle **Rahmenantenne; loop network** = communications network that consists of a ring of cable joining all terminals **Ringnetz**
2 *verb* to make a piece of wire *or* tape into a circle **eine Schlinge machen; looping program** = computer program that runs continuously **Schleifenprogramm**

lose *verb* not to have something any more **verlieren;** *we have lost the signal in the noise;*

all the current files were lost when the system crashed and we had no backup copies; **lost call** = telephone call that cannot be established **Verlustbelegung; lost time** = period of a transmitted facsimile signal when the image is being scanned, that contains no image data **Verlustzeit**

◊ **loss** *noun* the power of a signal that is lost when passing through a circuit **Dämpfung; Verlust**

loudness *noun* volume of a signal which you can hear **Lautstärke**

◊ **loudspeaker** *noun* electromagnetic construction that moves a paper cone according to an input signal so producing sound waves from an electrical input **Lautsprecher**

low frequency (LF) *noun* range of
audio frequencies between 5-300Hz *or* range of radio frequencies between 30-300kHz **Niederfrequenz; low pass filter** = electronic circuit that blocks signals above a certain frequency **Durchgangsfilter für niedrige Frequenzen; low-priority work** = task which is not particularly important **Aufgabe niedriger Priorität; low-resolution graphics** *or* **low-res graphics** = ability to display character-sized graphic blocks *or* preset shapes on a screen rather than using individual pixels **Graphik mit niedriger Auflösung;** *compare* HIGH-RESOLUTION; **low speed communications** = data transmission at less than 2400 bits per second **normale Übertragungsgeschwindigkeit**

◊ **lower case** *noun* small characters (such as a, b, c, as opposed to upper case A, B, C) **Kleinbuchstaben**

◊ **low-level language (LLL)** *noun* programming language similar to assembler and in which each instruction has a single equivalent machine code instruction (the language is particular to one system *or* computer) **maschinenorientierte Programmiersprache;** *see also* HIGH-LEVEL LANGUAGE

◊ **low-order digit** *noun* digit in the position within a number that represents the lowest weighting of the number base **niederwertiges Bit;** *the number 234156 has a low-order digit of 6*

◊ **low-res** *see* LOW-RESOLUTION

LPM = LINES PER MINUTE

LQ = LETTER QUALITY

LSB = LEAST SIGNIFICANT BIT binary digit occupying the right hand position of a word and carrying the least power of two in the word, usually equal to two raised to zero = 1 **niederwertigstes Bit**

LSD = LEAST SIGNIFICANT DIGIT digit which occupies the right hand position in a number and so carries least power (equal to the number radix raised to zero = 1) **niederwertigste Ziffer**

LSI = LARGE SCALE INTEGRATION system with between 500 and 10,000 circuits on a single IC **LSI (Großintegration)**

luggable *noun (informal)* personal computer that is just about portable and usually will not run off batteries (it is much heavier and less compact than a lap-top or true transportable machine) **Koffercomputer**

lumen *noun* SI unit of illumination, defined as the amount of flux emitted from a candela into an angle of one steradion **Lumen** ⇨ APPENDIX

luminance *noun* amount of light radiated from a source **Leuchtdichte; luminance signal** = part of television signal providing luminance data **Leuchtdichtsignal**

LUT LOOK-UP TABLE

QUOTE an image processing system can have three LUTs that map the image memory to the display device
Byte

lux *noun* SI unit of measurement of one lumen per square metre **Lux** ⇨ APPENDIX

Mm

m *prefix* = MILLI one thousandth **m**

M *prefix* = MEGA
(a) one million **M; Mbps** = MEGA BITS PER SECOND number of million bits transmitted every second **Mbps; MFLOPS** = MEGA FLOATING POINT OPERATIONS PER SECOND measure of computing power and speed, equal to one million floating point operations per second **Millionen Fließkommaoperationen pro Sekunde (MFLOPS)**
(b) symbol for 1,048,576, used only in computer and electronic related applications, equal to 2^{20} **M; Mbyte (MB)** = measurement of mass storage equal to

1,048,576 bytes **Mbyte (MB);** *the latest model has a 30Mbyte hard disk*

MAC
(a) = MULTIPLEXED ANALOG COMPONENTS standard television broadcast signal format **MAC**
(b) = MESSAGE AUTHENTICATION CODE special code transmitted at the same time as a message as proof of its authenticity **Nachrichtenberechtigungscode**

machine *noun*
(a) number of separate moving parts *or* components, acting together to carry out a process **Maschine; copying machine** *or* **duplicating machine** = machine which makes copies of documents **Kopiergerät; dictating machine** = recording machine which records what someone dictates, so that the text can be typed **Diktiergerät; machine proof** = proof of sheets of a book, taken from the printing machine **Maschinenabzug**
(b) computer *or* system *or* processor made of various components connected together to provide a function *or* perform a task **Computer; clean machine** = computer that contains only the minimum of ROM based code to boot its system from disk, any languages required must be loaded separately **Computer mit minimalem ROM-basiertem Code; source machine** = computer which can compile source code **Übersetzungsrechner; virtual machine** = simulated machine and its operations **virtuelle Maschine; machine address** = number *or* absolute address which specifies the point in memory where a data word can be found and accessed **Maschinenadresse, absolute Adresse; machine check** = fault caused by equipment failure **Maschinenprüfung; machine code** *or* **machine language** = programming language that consists of commands in binary code that can be directly understood by the central processing unit without the need for translation **Maschinencode; Maschinensprache; machine code format** = a machine code instruction is usually made up of 1,2 or 3 bytes for operand, data and address **Maschinencodeformat; machine code instruction** = instruction that directly controls the CPU and is recognized without the need for translation **Maschinencodebefehl; machine cycle** = minimum period of time taken by the CPU for the execution of an instruction **Maschinenzyklus; machine dependent** = not standardized *or* which cannot be used on hardware *or* software from a different manufacturer without modifications **maschinenabhängig; machine equation** =

formula which an analog computer has been programmed to solve **Maschinengleichung; machine independent** = (computer software) that can be run on any computer system **maschinenunabhängig; machine independent language** = programming language that can be translated and executed on any computer that has a suitable compiler **maschinenunabhängige Programmiersprache; machine instruction** = an instruction which can be recognized by a machine and is part of its limited set of commands **Maschinenbefehl; machine intelligence** = the design of computer programs and devices that attempt to imitate human intelligence and decision-making functions, providing basic reasoning and other human characteristics **künstliche Intelligenz; machine intimate** = software that operates and interacts closely with the hardware in a system **hardwarenah; machine language** = (i) the way in which machine code is written; (ii) MACHINE CODE (i) **Maschinensprache;** (ii) **Maschinencode; machine language compile** = to generate a machine code program from a HLL program by translating and assembling each HLL instruction **die Maschinensprache umsetzen; machine language programming** = slowest and most complex method of programming a CPU, but the fastest in execution, achieved by entering directly into RAM or ROM the binary representation for the machine code instructions to be carried out (rather than using an assembler with assembly language programs *or* a compiler with HLL programs) **Programmieren in Maschinensprache; machine-readable** = (commands *or* data) stored on a medium that can be directly input to the computer **maschinenlesbar;** *the disk stores data in machine-readable form;* **machine run** = action of processing instructions in a program by a computer **Computerlauf; machine translation** = computer system that is used to translate text and commands from one language and syntax to another **Maschinenübersetzung; machine word** = number of bits of data operated on simultaneously by a CPU in one machine cycle, often 8, 16 or 32 bits **Maschinenwort**

◇ **machinery** *noun* machines **Maschinerie**
NOTE: no plural

◇ **machining** *noun* making a product using a machine; printing the sheets of a book **maschinelle Fertigung; Druckgang**

◇ **machinist** *noun* person who works a machine **Maschinist/-in**

macro- *prefix* very large *or* applying to the whole system **Makro-**

◇ **macro** *noun* program routine *or* block of instructions identified by a single word *or* label **Makro; macro assembler** *or* **assembly program** = assembler program that is able to decode macro instructions **Makroassemblierer; macro call** = use of a label in an assembly language program to indicate to an assembler that the macro routine is to be inserted at that point **Makroaufruf; macro code** *or* **macro command** *or* **macro instruction** = one word that is used to represent a number of instructions simplifying program writing **Makrobefehl; macro definition** = description (in a program *or* to the operating system) of the structure, function and instructions that make up a macro operation **Makrodefinition; macro expansion** = process in which a macro call is replaced with the instruction in the macro **Makroauflösung; macro flowchart** = graphical representation of the logical steps, stages and actions within a routine **Makroflußdiagramm; macro language** = programming language that allows the programmer to define and use macro instructions **Makrosprache; macro programming** = writing a program using macro instructions *or* defining macro instructions **Makroprogrammierung**

◇ **macroelement** *noun* number of data items treated as one element **Makroelement**

◇ **macroinstruction** *noun* one programming instruction that refers to a number of instructions within a routine *or* macro **Makrobefehl**

magazine *noun*
(a) paper, usually with illustrations which comes out regularly, every month or every week **Zeitschrift;** *a weekly magazine; he edits a computer magazine*
(b) number of pages in a videotext system **Magazin**
(c) container for photographic film **Magazin**

magnet *noun* something that produces a magnetic field **Magnet**

◇ **magnetic** *adjective* which has a magnetic field associated with it **magnetisch; magnetic bubble memory** = method of storing large amounts of binary data as small magnetized areas in the medium (made of certain pure materials) **Magnetblasenspeicher; magnetic card** = plastic card with a strip of magnetic recording material on its surface, allowing data to be stored (used in automatic cash dispensers) **Magnetkarte; magnetic card reader** *or* **magnetic strip reader** = machine that can read data stored on a magnetic card **Magnetkartenleser; Magnetstreifenleser; magnetic cartridge** *or* **cassette** = small box containing a reel of magnetic tape and pick up reel **Magnetbandkassette; magnetic cell** = small piece of material whose magnetic field can be altered to represent the two states of binary data **Magnetzelle; magnetic core** = early main memory system for storing data in the first types of computer, each bit of data was stored in a magnetic cell **Magnetkern; magnetic disk** = flat circular piece of material coated with a substance, allowing signals and data to be stored magnetically **Magnetplatte;** *see also* FLOPPY DISK, HARD DISK; **magnetic disk unit** = computer peripheral made up of a disk drive and necessary control electronics **Magnetplatteneinheit; magnetic drum** = computer data storage peripheral that uses a coated cylinder to store data magnetically(not often used now) **Magnettrommelspeicher; magnetic encoding** = storage of (binary) data signals on a magnetic medium **magnetische Codierung; magnetic field** = description of the polarity and strength of magnetic effects at a point **Magnetfeld; magnetic flux** = measure of magnetic field strength per unit area **magnetischer Fluß; magnetic focusing** = use of magnetic field to focus a beam of electrons (in a television) **magnetische Fokussierung; magnetic head** = electromagnetic component that converts electrical signals into a magnetic field, allowing them to be stored on a magnetic medium **Magnetkopf; magnetic ink** = printing ink that contains a magnetic material, used in some character recognition systems **Magnettinte; magnetic ink character recognition (MICR)** = system that identifies characters by sensing the magnetic ink patterns (as used on bank cheques) **Magnetschrift-Zeichenerkennung; magnetic master** = original version of a recorded tape *or* disk **Original; magnetic material** *or* **medium** = substance that will retain a magnetic flux pattern after a magnetic field is removed **Magnetträger; magnetic media** = magnetic materials used to store signals, such as disk, tape, etc. **magnetische Medien; magnetic memory** *or* **store** = storage that uses a medium that can store data bits as magnetic field changes **Magnetspeicher; magnetic recording** = transferring an electrical signal onto a moving magnetic tape *or* disk by means of a magnetic field generated by a magnetic head **magnetische Aufzeichnung; magnetic screen** = metal screen used to prevent stray magnetic fields affecting electronic components **Magnetschirm; magnetic storm** = disturbance in the earth's magnetic fields affecting radio and cable communications **(erd)magnetischer Sturm; magnetic strip** = layer of magnetic material on the surface of a plastic card, used for recording data **Magnetstreifen; magnetic thin film storage** = high-speed access RAM device using a matrix of magnetic cells and a matrix of read/write heads to access them **Dünnschichtspeicher; magnetic transfer** = copy signals stored on one type of magnetic medium to another **magnetische Übertragung**

◇ **magnetic tape** *noun* narrow length of thin plastic coated with a magnetic material used to store signals magnetically **Magnetband; magnetic tape cartridge** *or* **cassette** = small box containing a reel of magnetic tape and a pick up reel, used in a cassette player *or* tape drive **Magnetbandkassette; magnetic tape encoder** = device that directly writes data entered at a keyboard onto magnetic tape **Magnetbandcodierer; magnetic tape reader** = machine that can read signals stored on magnetic tape and convert them to an electrical form that can be understood by a computer **Magnetbandleser; magnetic tape recorder** = device with a magnetic head, motor and circuitry to allow electrical signals to be recorded onto *or* played back from a magnetic tape **Magnetbandgerät; magnetic tape transport** = computer-controlled magnetic tape drive mechanism **Magnetbandtransport**

◇ **magnetize** *verb* to convert a material *or* object into a magnet **magnetisieren**

> COMMENT: magnetic tape is available on spools of between 200 and 800 metres. The tape is magnetized by the read/write head. Tape is a storage medium which only allows serial access, that is, all the tape has to be read until the required location is found (as opposed to disk storage, which can be accessed randomly)

magnify *verb* to make something appear larger **vergrößern;** *the photograph has been magnified 200 times*

◇ **magnification** *noun* amount by which something has been made to appear larger **Vergrößerung;** *the lens gives a magnification of 10 times*

magnitude *noun* level *or* strength of a signal *or* variable **Ausmaß; signal magnitude** = strength of an electrical current and voltage *or* power signal **Signalgröße**

mag tape *noun informal* = MAGNETIC TAPE

mail
1 *noun*
(a) system of sending letters and parcels from one place to another **Post**
(b) letters sent *or* received **Post**

(c) electronic messages to and from users of a bulletin board *or* network **Post; electronic mail** *or* **email** *or* **e-mail** = messages sent between users of a bulletin board *or* interconnecting network **elektronische Post, E-Mail**

2 *verb* to send something by post **mit der Post schicken;** *to mail a letter; we mailed our order last Wednesday*

◊ **mailbox** *or* **mail box** *noun* electronic storage space with an address in which a user's incoming messages are stored **Briefkasten**

◊ **mailing** *noun* sending something using the post **Verschicken;** *the mailing of publicity material;* **direct mailing** = sending of publicity material by post to possible buyers **Direktwerbung; mailing list** = list of names and addresses of people who might be interested in a product *or* list of names and addresses of members of a society **Adreßliste;** *his name is on our mailing list; to build up a mailing list;* **to buy a mailing list** = to pay a society, etc. money to buy the list of members so that you can use it to mail publicity material **eine Adreßliste erwerben; mailing piece** = leaflet suitable for sending by direct mail **Postwurfsendung, Mailer; mailing shot** = leaflets sent by mail to possible customers **Werbeprospekte**

◊ **mail-merge** *noun* word-processing program which allows a standard form letter to be printed out to a series of different names and addresses **Mailmerge**

main *adjective* most important **Haupt-; main beam** = direction of the central most powerful region of an antenna's transmission pattern **Hauptstrahl; main clock** = clock signal that synchronizes all the components in a system **Haupttaktgeber; main distributing frame** = racks of termination circuits for the cables in a telephone network **Hauptverteiler; main entry** = entry in a catalogue under which is contained the most important information about the document **Haupteintrag; main index** = more general index that directs the user gradually to more specific index areas **Generalindex; main memory** *or* **main storage** = fast access RAM whose locations can be directly and immediately addressed by the CPU **Hauptspeicher;** *the 16-bit system includes up to 3Mb of main memory;* **main routine** = section of instructions that make up the main part of a program (a program often consists of a main routine and several subroutines, which are called from the main routine) **Hauptprogramm**

◊ **mainframe (computer)** *noun* large-scale high power computer system that can handle high capacity memory and backing storage devices as well as a number of operators simultaneously **Großrechner; mainframe access** = using microcomputers to access a mainframe computer **Großrechnerzugang**

mains electricity *noun* normal domestic electricity supply to consumers **öffentliches Versorgungsnetz**

COMMENT: in UK this is 240 volts at 50Hz; in the USA, it is 120 volts at 60Hz

maintain *verb* to ensure a system is in good condition and functioning correctly **warten; well maintained** = well looked after **gut gewartet**

◊ **maintainability** *noun* the ability to have repairs carried out quickly and efficiently if a failure occurs **Wartbarkeit**

◊ **maintenance** *noun* (i) keeping a machine in good working condition; (ii) tasks carried out in order to keep a system running, such as repairing faults, replacing components, etc. **(i) Instandhaltung; (ii) Wartung; file maintenance** = process of updating a file by changing *or* adding *or* deleting entries **Dateiwartung; preventive maintenance** = regular inspection and cleaning of a system to prevent faults occurring **vorbeugende Wartung; maintenance contract** = arrangement with a repair company that provides regular checks and special repair prices in the event of a fault **Wartungsvertrag; maintenance routine** = software diagnostic tool used by an engineer during preventative maintenance operations **Wartungsroutine**

major cycle *noun* minimum access time of a mechanical storage device **Hauptzyklus**

majuscule *noun* capital letter **Großbuchstabe, Majuskel**

make-ready time *noun* time taken by a printer to prepare the machines and film for printing **Vorbereitungs-, Zurichtungszeit**

◊ **make up** *verb* to arrange type into the correct page formats before printing **umbrechen**

◊ **make up** *or* **makeup** *noun* arrangement and layout of type into correct page formats before printing **Umbruch;** *corrections after the page makeup are very expensive*

male connector *noun* plug with conducting pins that can be inserted into a female connector to provide an electrical connection **Stecker**

malfunction
noun *(of hardware or software)* not working correctly **Störung**; *the data was lost due to a software malfunction;* **malfunction routine** = software routine used to find and help diagnose the cause of an error or fault **Fehlererkennungsroutine**
verb not to work properly **nicht richtig funktionieren**; *some of the keys on the keyboard have started to malfunction*

◊ **malfunctioning** *noun* not working properly **Störung**

man machine interface (MMI) *noun* hardware and software designed to make it easier for users to communicate effectively with a machine **Mensch-Maschine-Schnittstelle**

◊ **man-made** *adjective* not natural, produced by man **künstlich; man-made noise** = electrical interference caused by machines *or* motors **technische Funktionsstörung**; *compare* GALACTIC NOISE

manage *verb* to direct *or* to be in charge of **leiten**

◊ **manageable** *adjective* which can be dealt with easily **zu bewältigen**; *processing problems which are still manageable; the problems are too large to be manageable; data should be split into manageable files*

◊ **management** *noun* directing *or* organizing (work *or* a business) **Leitung, Verwaltung; network management** = organization, planning, running and upkeep of a network **Netzführung; product management** = directing the making and selling of a product as an independent item **Produktmanagement; management information system (MIS)** = computer system that provides management staff with relevant, up-to-date information **Managementinformationssystem; management training** = training managers by making them study problems and work out ways of solving them **Managementtraining;** NOTE: no plural

◊ **manager** *noun*
(a) user-friendly front end software that allows easy access to operating system commands **benutzerfreundliche Zugangssoftware; file manager** = section of disk operating system that allocates disk space to files, keeping track of the file sections (if it has to be split) and their sector addresses **Dateimanager; queue manager** = software which orders tasks waiting to be processed **Warteschlangenverwaltung; records manager** = program which maintains records and can access and process them

Satzverwaltungssystem; text manager = facilities that allow text to be written, stored, retrieved, edited and printed **Textverwaltungssystem**
(b) head of a department in a company **Leiter/-in**; *a department manager; data processing manager; production manager*

◊ **managerial** *adjective* referring to managers **Management-**; *managerial staff*

manipulate *verb* to move, edit and change text *or* data **bearbeiten**; *an image processor that captures, displays and manipulates video images*

◊ **manipulation** *noun* moving *or* editing *or* changing text *or* data **Bearbeitung**; *the high-speed database management program allows the manipulation of very large amounts of data*

mantissa *noun* fractional part of a number **Mantisse**; *the mantissa of the number 45.897 is 0.897*

manual
1 *noun* document containing instructions about the operation of a system *or* piece of software **Handbuch**; *the manual is included with the system;* **installation manual** = booklet showing how a system should be installed **Installationshandbuch; instruction manual** = document describing how to use a system *or* software **Handbuch mit Anweisungen; user's manual** = booklet showing how a device *or* system should be used **Benutzerhandbuch**
2 *adjective* (work) done by hand; (process) carried out by the operator without the help of a machine **manuell, von Hand; manual data processing** = sorting and processing information without the help of a computer **manuelle Datenverarbeitung; manual entry** *or* **manual input** = act of entering data into a computer, by an operator via a keyboard **Eingeben von Hand**

◊ **manually** *adverb* done by hand, not automatically **manuell, von Hand**; *the paper has to be fed into the printer manually*

manufacture *verb* to make in a factory **herstellen**; *the company manufactures diskettes and magnetic tape*

◊ **manufacturer** *noun* company which manufactures a product **Hersteller**; *if the system develops a fault it should be returned to the manufacturer for checking; the manufacturer guarantees the system for 12 months*

manuscript *or* **MS** *noun* original draft copy of a book written *or* typed by the author **Manuskript**; *this manuscript was all written on computer*

map

1 *noun* diagram representing the internal layout of a computer's memory *or* communications regions **Abbild, Map; memory map** = diagram indicating the allocation of address ranges to various memory devices, such as RAM, ROM and memory-mapped input/output devices **Hauptspeicherabbild**

2 *verb* to retrieve data and display it as a map **abbilden; database mapping** = description of the way in which the records and fields in a database are related **Datenbankaufgliederung; I/O mapping** = method of assigning a special address to each (I/O) port in a microcomputer rather than a memory location **Ein-/Ausgabeadressierung; to map out** = to draw *or* set down the basic way in which something should be done **entwerfen; memory-mapped (input/output)** = allocation of addresses to a computer's input/output devices to allow them to be accessed as if they are a memory location **speicherorientiert(e Ein-/Ausgabe);** *a memory-mapped screen has an address allocated to each pixel allowing direct access to the screen by the CPU; see also* BIT-MAP, BIT-MAPPED

MAR = MEMORY ADDRESS REGISTER register within the CPU that contains the next location to be accessed **Speicheradreßregister**

marching display *noun* display device that contains a buffer to show the last few characters entered **wandernde Anzeige**

margin *noun*

(a) blank space around a section of printed text **Rand;** *when typing the contract leave wide margins; the left margin and right margin are the two sections of blank paper on either side of the page;* **to set the margin** = to define the size of a margin **den Rand setzen**

(b) extra time *or* space **Spielraum; safety margin** = time *or* space allowed for something to be safe **Sicherheitsspielraum; margin of error** = number of mistakes which are accepted in a document *or* in a calculation **Fehlerspanne**

◇ **margination** *noun* giving margins to a printed page **Marginierung, Umrandung**

mark

1 *noun*
(a) sign put on a page to show something **Zeichen; proof correction marks** = special

marks used to show changes to a proo **Korrekturzeichen**

(b) transmitted signal that represents logical one *or* true condition **Marke; marl hold** = continuously transmitted marl signal that indicates there are no message on the network **Freizeichensignal; marl space** = two-state transmission code using mark and a space (without a mark) a signals **Code bestehend aus einem Zeicher und einem Abstand**

2 *verb* to put a mark on somethin **kennzeichnen, markieren; mark block** = t put a block marker at the beginning anc end of a block of tex **Blockmarkierungszeichen setzen; markin interval** = time when a mark signal is bein carried out **Markierungszeit; mark sense** = t write characters with conductive *o* magnetic ink so that they are then machin readable **für Zeichenabfühlung lesbar macher mark sense device** *or* **reader** = device tha reads data from special cards containin conductive *or* magnetic mark **Markierungsleser; mark sensing card** = preprinted card with spaces for mark sens characters **Zeichenlochkarte**

◇ **marker** *noun*
(a) **marker pen** = coloured pen used t indicate *or* highlight sections of tex **Markierstift, Textmarker**
(b) code inserted in a file *or* text to indicat a special section **Markierung; block marker** = two markers inserted at the start anc finish of a section of data *or* text to indicat a special block which can then be moved o deleted *or* copied as a single uni **Blockmarkierungszeichen; field marker** = code used to indicate the end of one fiel and the start of the nex **Feldmarkierungszeichen; word marker** = symbol indicating the start of a word in variable word length machin **Wortmarkierungszeichen**

◇ **mark up** *verb* to prepare copy for th compositor to set, by showing on the cop the typeface to be used, the line width, anc other typesetting instruction **Satzanweisungen machen, auszeichnen**

MASER = MICROWAVE AMPLIFICATIO BY STIMULATED EMISSION OF RADIATIO low noise amplifier, formerly used fo microwave signals from satellites **Maser**

mask

1 *noun*
(a) integrated circuit layout stencil that i used to define the pattern to be etched o doped onto a slice of semiconducto

Schablone; *a mask or stencil is used to transfer the transistor design onto silicon*
(b) photographic device used to prevent light reaching selected areas of the film **Maske**
(c) pattern of binary digits used to select various bits from a binary word (a one in the mask retains that bit in the word) **Maske; mask bit** = one bit used to select the required bit from a word *or* string **Maskenbit; mask register** = storage location in a computer that contains the pattern of bits used as a mask **Maskenregister; interrupt mask** = data word in a computer that selects which interrupt lines are to be activated **Abbruchmaske**
2 *verb* to cover an area of (something) with (something) **maskieren; masked ROM** = read-only memory device that is programmed during manufacture, by depositing metal onto selected regions dictated by the shape of a mask **maskierter Festspeicher**

◇ **maskable** *adjective* which can be masked **maskierbar; maskable interrupt** = interrupt which can be activated by using an interrupt mask **maskierbare Unterbrechung; non-maskable interrupt (NMI)** = high priority interrupt signal that cannot be deactivated **nichtmaskierbare Unterbrechung (mit höchster Priorität)**

◇ **masking** *noun* operation used to select various bits in a word **Maskierung**

QUOTE the device features a maskable interrupt feature which reduces CPU overheads
Electronics & Power

mass media *noun* media which aim to reach a large public (such as television, radio, mass-market newspapers) **Massenmedien**

◇ **mass storage** *noun* storage and retrieval of large amounts of data **Massenspeicher; mass storage device** = computer backing store device that is able to store large amounts of data **Massenspeichereinheit;** *the hard disk is definitely a mass storage device;* **mass storage system** = data storage system that can hold more than one million million bits of data **Massenspeichersystem**

mast *noun* **radio mast** *or* **TV mast** = tall structure used to position an aerial above natural obstacles (such as houses, hills, etc.) **Mast**

master
1 *adjective (& noun)* main *or* most important **Haupt-, Leit-, Original-, Stamm-;** *the master computer controls everything else;* **master antenna television system (MATV)**
= single main receiving antenna that provides television signals to a number of nearby receivers **Gemeinschaftsantennenanlage; master card** = first punched card in a pack that provides information about the rest of the pack **Leitkarte; master clock** = timing signal to which all components in a system are synchronized **Haupttaktgeber; master computer** = computer in a multiprocessor system that controls the other processors and allocates jobs, etc. **Hauptrechner; master control program (MCP)** = software that controls the operations in a system **Steuerprogramm; master data** = reference data which is stored in a master file **Leitdaten; master disk** = (i) disk containing all the files for a task; (ii) disk containing the code for a computer's operating system that must be loaded before the system will operate (i) **Hauptplatte;** (ii) **Betriebssystemplatte; master file** = set of all the reference data required for an application, which is updated periodically **Stammdatei; master/master computer system** = system in which each processor is a master, dedicated to one task **Leitrechner(system); master program file** = magnetic medium which contains all the programs required for an application **Hauptprogrammdatei; master proof** = final proof of a section of text before it is printed **Korrekturbogen mit Preßrevision; master/slave computer system** = system with a master controlling computer and a slave that takes commands from the master **Computersystem, in dem der eine dem anderen übergeordnet ist; master tape** = magnetic tape which contains all the vital operating system routines, loaded once when the computer is switched on (by the initial program loader) **System-Urband; master terminal** = one terminal in a network that has priority over any other, used by the system manager to set up the system *or* carry out privileged commands **Hauptbedienerstation; image master** = data describing fonts and character shapes in a phototypesetter **Image Master**
2 *verb* to learn and understand a language *or* process **beherrschen;** *we mastered the new word-processor quite quickly; the user-friendly package is easier to master*

match *verb*
(a) to search through a database for a similar piece of information **vergleichen**
(b) to set a register *or* electrical impedance equal to another **abgleichen; matched load** = impedance of the same value as the cable across which it is connected, so minimizing signal reflections **angepaßte Belastung; matching transformer** = transformer used to connect and match two lines of differing

impedance, while isolating them electrically **Anpassungstransformator; impedance matching** = means of making the best signal power transfer between two circuits by making sure that their output and input impedances are the same **Scheinwiderstandsanpassung**

material *noun*
(a) substance which can be used to make a finished product **Material;** *gold is the ideal material for electrical connections;* **synthetic materials** = substances made as products of a chemical process **Kunststoffe; materials control** = system to check that a company has enough materials in stock to do its work **Materialsteuerung; materials handling** = storing and moving materials from one part of a factory to another in an efficient way **innerbetriebliches Transport- und Lagerwesen**
(b) **display material** = posters, photographs, etc., which can be used to attract attention to goods which are for sale **Ausstellungsmaterial**

mathematics *noun* study of the relationship between numbers, their manipulation and organization to (logically) prove facts and theories **Mathematik;** *see also* ALGEBRA
◇ **mathematical** *adjective* referring to mathematics **mathematisch; mathematical model** = representation of a system using mathematical ideas and formulae **mathematisches Modell; mathematical subroutines** = library routines that carry out standard mathematical functions, such as square root, logarithm, cosine, sine, etc. **mathematische Unterprogramme**

◇ **maths** *or (US)* **math** *informal* = MATHEMATICS; **maths chip** *or* **coprocessor** = dedicated IC that can be added to a system to carry out mathematical functions far more rapidly than a standard CPU, speeding up the execution of a program **mathematischer Zusatzprozessor**

matrix *noun*
(a) array of numbers *or* data items arranged in rows and columns **Matrix; matrix rotation** = swapping the rows with the columns in an array (equal to rotating by 90 degrees) **Matrixdrehung**
(b) array of connections between logic gates providing a number of possible logical functions **Matrix; key matrix** = way in which the keys of a keyboard are arranged as an array of connections **Schlüsselmatrix**
(c) pattern of the dots that make up a character on a computer screen *or* dot-matrix *or* laser printer **Matrix; matrix printer**

or **dot-matrix printer** = printer in which the characters are made up by a series of dots printed close together, producing a page line by line; a dot-matrix printer can be used either for printing using a ribbon or for thermal *or* electrostatic printing **Matrixdrucker; character matrix** = pattern of dots that makes up a displayed character **Zeichenmatrix**

matt *or* matte
1 *noun*
(a) addition of an image onto a film of a background **Aufprojektion, Mattaufnahme**
(b) mask used to prevent light reaching certain areas on a film **Lichthofschutzschicht**
2 *adjective* (print) which is not shiny **matt**

matter *noun*
(a) question *or* problem to be discussed **Angelegenheit, Sache, Thema; it is a matter of concern to the members of the committee** = the members of the committee are worried about it **es ist eine Angelegenheit, die den Mitgliedern des Kommittees Sorge macht;** *the most important matter on the agenda; we shall consider first the matter of last month's fall in prices*
(b) main section of text on a page as opposed to titles *or* headlines **Satzspiegel, Text; printed matter** = printed books, newspapers, publicity sheets, etc **Drucksache; publicity matter** = sheets *o* posters *or* leaflets used for publicity **Werbematerial**
NOTE: no plural for (b)

MATV = MASTER ANTENNA TELEVISION SYSTEM

maximum *adjective & noun* highest value
used *or* which is allowed **maximal, Höchst-, höchst-; Maximum; maximum capacity** = greatest amount of data that can be stored **Höchstleistungsgrenze; maximum reading** = greatest signal magnitude recorded **Vollaussteuerung; maximum transmission rate** = greatest number of data that can be transmitted every second **höchste Übertragungsgeschwindigkeit; maximum usable frequency** = highest signal frequency which can be used in a circuit without distortion **höchste Nutzfrequenz; maximum users** = greatest number of users that a system can support at any one time **höchstmögliche Benutzerzahl**

MB *or* **Mb** *or* **Mbyte** = MEGABYTE equal to 1,048,576 bytes of storage, equal to 2^{20} bytes **Mbyte**

◇ **Mbps** = MEGA BITS PER SECOND

MBR = MEMORY BUFFER REGISTER register in a CPU that temporarily buffers all inputs and outputs **Speicherpufferregister**

mC = MILLICOULOMB

MCP = MASTER CONTROL PROGRAM

MDR = MEMORY DATA REGISTER register in a CPU that holds data before it is processed *or* moved to a memory location **Speicherdatenregister**

mean
1 *noun & adjective* average value of a set of numbers *or* values **Mittelwert, Durchschnitt; Mittel-, mittlere(r,s), durchschnittlich; mean time between failures (MTBF)** = average period of time that a piece of equipment will operate between failures **mittlerer Ausfallabstand; mean time to failure (MTF)** = average period of time for which a device will operate (usually continuously) before failing **mittlere Lebensdauer; mean time to repair** = average period of time required to repair a faulty piece of equipment **mittlere Reparaturdauer**
2 *verb* to signify something **bedeuten;** *the message DISK FULL means that there is no more room on the disk for further data*

measure
1 *noun*
a) way of calculating size *or* quantity **Maß; square measure** = area in square feet *or* metres, calculated by multiplying width and length **Flächenmaß**
b) tape measure = long tape with centimetres *or* inches marked on it, used to measure how long something is **Bandmaß**
c) total width of a printed line of text shown in picas **Satzbreite**
d) type of action **Maßnahme, Vorkehrung; to take measures to prevent something happening** = to act to stop something happening **Vorkehrungen treffen, um etwas zu verhindern; safety measures** = actions to make sure that something is safe **Sicherheitsvorkehrungen**
2 *verb* to find out the size *or* quantity of something; to be of a certain size *or* quantity **messen**

◊ **measurement** *noun*
a) measurements = size **Maße;** *to write down the measurements of a package*
b) way of judging something **Maßstab;** *performance measurement or measurement*

of performance is carried out by running a benchmark program

mechanical *adjective* referring to machines **mechanisch; mechanical paper** = paper (such as newsprint) made from rough wood, which has not been processed **Holzschliffpapier**

◊ **mechanism** *noun* piece of machinery **Mechanismus;** *the printer mechanism is very simple; the drive mechanism appears to be faulty*

media
(a) means of communicating information to the public (such as television, radio, newspapers) **Medien;** *the product attracted a lot of interest in the media or a lot of media interest;* **media analysis** *or* **media research** = examining different types of media (such as the readers of newspapers, television viewers) to see which is best for advertising a certain type of product **Medienforschung; media coverage** = number of reports about an event *or* product in newspapers, magazines and on TV **Berichterstattung durch die Medien;** *we got good media coverage for the launch of the new model* NOTE: **media** is followed by a singular or plural verb
(b) *see* MEDIUM; **magnetic media** = magnetic materials used to store signals, such as disk, tape, etc. **magnetische Medien**

medium
1 *adjective* middle *or* average **Mittel-, mittel-;** *a medium-sized computer system*
2 *noun*
(a) way of doing something *or* means of doing something **Mittel; advertising medium** = type of advertisement (such as a TV commercial) **Werbeträger;** *the product was advertised through the medium of the trade press*
(b) storage medium = any physical material that can be used to store data for a computer application **Datenträger;** *data storage mediums such as paper tape, magnetic disk, magnetic tape, paper, card and microfiche are available;* **data medium** = medium which allows data to be stored *or* displayed such as magnetic disk *or* a VDU **Datenträger; empty medium** = blank but formatted storage medium that is ready to accept data **unbeschrifteter Datenträger; magnetic medium** *or* **material** = substance that will retain a magnetic flux pattern after a magnetic field is removed **Magnetträger;** NOTE: plural is **mediums** or **media**

◊ **medium frequency** *noun* radio frequency range between 300 to 3000KHz (often referred to as medium wave (MW), especially on radio receivers) **Mittelfrequenz**

◇ **medium lens** *noun* optical photographic lens that has a focal length near the standard for the film size **mittlere Linse**

◇ **medium scale integration (MSI)** *noun* integrated circuit with 10 to 500 components **mittlere Integrationstechnik**

◇ **medium speed** *noun* data communication speed between 2400 and 9600 bits per second **mittlere Geschwindigkeit**

COMMENT: medium speed transmission describes the maximum rate of transfer for a normal voice grade channel

◇ **medium wave (MW)** *see* MEDIUM FREQUENCY

meet *noun* logical function whose output is true if both inputs are true **UND/ODER-Funktion**

mega- *prefix*
(a) meaning one million **Mega-, mega-**; **megabits per second (Mbps)** = number of million bits transmitted every second **Megabits pro Sekunde**; **megaflops (MFLOPS)** measure of computing power and speed equal to one million floating point instructions per second **Millionen Fließkommaoperationen pro Sekunde (MFLOPS)**
(b) meaning 1,048,576 (equal to 2^{20}) and used only in computing and electronic related applications **Mega-, mega-**; **megabit (Mb)** = equal to 1,048,576 bits **Megabit**; **megabyte (MB)** equal to 1,048,576 bytes of storage **Megabyte (MB)**

QUOTE adding multiple megabytes of memory is a simple matter of plugging memory cards into the internal bus
Byte

member *noun* individual record *or* item in a field **Glied**

memomotion *noun* method of filming an action by taking one frame every few seconds **Memomotion**

memory *noun* storage space in a computer system *or* medium that is capable of retaining data *or* instructions **(Haupt)speicher**; **associative memory** = method of data retrieval that uses part of the data rather than an address to locate data **Assoziativspeicher**; **backing memory** = any data storage medium, such as a magnetic tape *or* floppy disk, that is not the main high speed memory **Zusatzspeicher**; **bootstrap memory** = permanent memory within a terminal *or* microcomputer, that allows a user to customize the attributes,

booting the system and loading programs **Urladerprogrammspeicher**; **bubble memory** = method of storing large amounts of binary data, as small magnetized areas in the medium (certain pure materials) **Blasenspeicher**; **cache memory** = section of high-speed memory which stores data that the CPU needs to access quickly **Cache-Speicher (schneller Pufferspeicher)**; **charge coupled device (CCD) memory** = volatile, low-cost, high-storage capability memory device **ladungsgekoppelter Speicher**; **content-addressable memory** = memory that is addressed and accessed by its contents rather than a location **Assoziativspeicher**; **control memory** = memory which decodes control instructions into microinstructions which operate the computer *or* microcontroller **Mikroprogrammspeicher**; **core memory** *or* **primary memory** = central fast-access memory which stores the programs and data currently in use **Kernspeicher**; **disk memory** = data stored on magnetic disk, not on tape **Plattenspeicher**; **dynamic memory** = random access memory that requires its contents to be updated regularly **dynamischer Speicher**; **external memory** = memory which is located outside the main computer system confines, but which can be accessed by the CPU **externer Speicher**; **fast access memory (FAM)** = storage locations that can be read from *or* written to very rapidly **Schnellzugriffsspeicher**; **FIFO memory** *or* **first in first out memory** = memory using a FIFO access scheme **FIFO-Speichermethode**; **internal memory** = storage available within and under the direct control of the main computer, such as main memory **Hauptspeicher**; **magnetic memory** = storage that uses a medium that can store data bits as magnetic field changes **Magnetspeicher**; **main memory** = fast access RAM whose locations can be directly and immediately addressed by a CPU **Zentralspeicher**; **nonvolatile memory** = storage medium that retains data even when power has been switched off **nichtflüchtiger Speicher**; **random access memory (RAM)** = memory that allows access to any location in any order without having to access the rest of memory **Direktzugriffsspeicher (RAM)**; **read only memory (ROM)** = memory device that has had data written into it at manufacture, which can only be read **Festspeicher (ROM)**; **scratchpad memory** = workspace or area of high-speed memory that is used for the temporary storage of data currently in use **Notizblockspeicher**; **serial memory** = storage whose locations can only be accessed in a serial way, locating one item requires a search through every location **Speicher mit seriellem Zugriff**; *magnetic tape is a high capacity serial memory*; **static memory** =

non-volatile memory that does not require refreshing **statischer Speicher; virtual memory** = system where the workspace is held in both backing store and memory at the same time **virtueller Speicher; volatile memory** = memory *or* storage medium which loses data stored in it when its power supply is switched off **flüchtiger Speicher; memory access time** = time delay between requesting access to a location and being able to do so **Speicherzugriffszeit; memory address register (MAR)** = register within the CPU that contains the address of the next location to be accessed **Speicheradreßregister; memory bank** = number of smaller storage devices connected together to form one large area of memory **Speicherbank; memory board** = printed circuit board containing memory chips **Speicherplatine; memory buffer register (MBR)** = register in a CPU that temporarily buffers all inputs and outputs **Speicherpufferregister; memory capacity** = number of bits *or* bytes that can be stored within a memory device **Speicherkapazität; memory cell** = smallest location that can be individually accessed **Speicherelement; memory chip** = electronic component that is able to store binary data **Speicherchip; memory cycle** = period of time from when the CPU reads *or* writes to a location and the action being performed **Operationszyklus; memory data register (MDR)** = register in a CPU which holds data before it is processed *or* moved to a memory location **Speicherdatenregister; memory diagnostic** = software routine that checks each memory location in main memory for faults **Speicherdiagnose; memory dump** = printout of all the contents of an area of memory **Speicherauszug; memory edit** = to change (selectively) the contents of various memory locations **Speicheraufbereitung; memory hierarchy** = the different types (capacity and access time) of memory available in a system **Speicherhierarchie; memory intensive** = software that uses large amounts of RAM or disk storage during run-time, such as programs whose entire code has to be in main memory during execution **speicherintensiv; memory management** = software that controls and regulates the flow and position in memory of files and data **Speicherverwaltung; memory map** = diagram indicating the allocation of address ranges to various devices such as RAM, ROM and memory-mapped input/output devices **Hauptspeicherabbild; memory-mapped** = with addresses allocated to a computer's input *or* output devices to allow them to be accessed as if they were a memory location **speicherorientiert;** *a memory-mapped screen has an address*

allocated to each pixel, allowing direct access to the screen by the CPU; **memory-mapped I/O** = an I/O port which can be accessed as if it were a memory location within the CPU's normal address range **speicherorientierte Ein-/Ausgabe; memory page** = one section of main store which is divided into pages, which contains data *or* programs **Speicherseite; memory protect** = feature on most storage systems to prevent the accidental overwriting of data **Speicherschutz; memory-resident** = (program) that is held permanently in memory **speicherresident;** *the system can bomb if you set up too many memory-resident programs at the same time;* **memory switching system** = system which communicates information, stores it in memory and then transmits it according to instructions **Speicherschaltersystem; memory workspace** = amount of extra memory required by a program to store data used during execution **Speicherarbeitsbereich**

◇ **memorize** *verb* to remember *or* to retain in the memory **sich erinnern**

QUOTE when a program is loaded into memory, some is used for the code, some for the permanent data, and some is reserved for the stack which grows and shrinks for function calls and local data
Personal Computer World

menu *noun* list of options *or* programs available to the user **Menü; menu-driven software** = program where commands *or* options are selected from a menu by the operator **menügesteuerte Software; menu selection** = choosing commands from a list of options presented to the operator **Auswahl; main menu** = list of primary options available **Hauptmenü; pop-up menu** *or* **pull-down menu** = menu of options that can be displayed at any time, usually overwriting any other text **Pulldown-Menü, Hervorholmenü;** *the pull-down menu is viewed by clicking over the icon at the top of the screen*

QUOTE when the operator is required to make a choice a menu is displayed
Micro Decision

mercury delay line *noun* (old) method of storing serial data as pulses in a length of mercury, the data was constantly read, regenerated and fed back into the input **Quecksilber-Verzögerungsleitung**

merge *verb* to combine two data files, but still retaining an overall order **mischen;** *the system automatically merges text and illustrations into the document;* **merge sort** = software application in which the sorted files are merged into a new file **mischendes Sortieren;** *see also* MAIL-MERGE

mesh *noun* any system with two *or* more possible paths at each interconnection **Vermaschung; mesh network** = method of connecting several machines together, where each pair of devices has two *or* more connections **vermaschtes Netz**

message *noun*
(a) information sent from one person to another **Nachricht**
(b) certain defined amount of information **Nachricht; message format** = predetermined rules defining the coding, size and speed of transmitted messages **Nachrichtenformat; message heading** = section of a message that contains routing and destination information **Nachrichtenkopf; message numbering** = identification of messages by allocating a number to each one **Nachrichtennumerierung; message routing** = selection of a suitable path between the source and destination of a message in a network **Nachrichtenvermittlung; message slot** = number of bits that can hold a message which circulates around a ring network **Nachrichtenschlitz; message switching** = storing, arranging and making up batches of convenient sizes of data to allow for their economical transmission over a network **Nachrichtenvermitteln; message text** = information that concerns the user at the destination without routing *or* network control data **Nachrichtentext**

metabit *noun* extra identifying bit for each data word **Metabit**

◊ **metacompilation** *noun* compiling a program that will compile other programs when executed **Metakompilierung**

◊ **metalanguage** *noun* language which describes a programming language **Metasprache**

metal oxide semiconductor (MOS) *noun* production and design method for a certain family of integrated circuits using patterns of metal conductors and oxide deposited onto a semiconductor **Metalloxid-Halbleiter; metal oxide semiconductor field effect transistor (MOSFET)** = high-powered and high-speed field effect transistor manufactured using MOS techniques **Feldeffekttransistor mit Metalloxid-Halbleiteraufbau; MOS-Transistor; complementary metal oxide semiconductor (CMOS)** = integrated circuit design and construction method, using a pair of complementary p- and n-type transistors **Halbleiterelement; Kombination von PMOS- und NMOS-Technik (CMOS)**

meter
1 *noun* device which counts *or* records something **Zähler;** *an electricity meter; a meter attached to the photocopier records the number of copies made; see also* MULTIMETER
2 *verb* to record and count **zählen;** *the calls from each office are metered by the call logger*

MF = MEDIUM FREQUENCY

MFLOPS = MEGA FLOATING POINT INSTRUCTIONS PER SECOND

MHz = MEGAHERTZ one million cycles per second **MHz**

MICR = MAGNETIC INK CHARACTER RECOGNITION system that identifies characters by sensing magnetic ink patterns (as used on bank cheques) **Magnetschrift-Zeichenerkennung**

micro *noun* = MICROCOMPUTER

micro- *prefix*
(a) meaning one millionth of a unit **Mikro-mikro-; micrometre** = one millionth of a metre **Mikrometer; microsecond** = one millionth of a second **Mikrosekunde**
(b) meaning very small **mikro; microcassette** = small format audio cassette used mainly in pocket dictating equipment **Mikrokassette; microchip** = circuit in which all the active and passive components are formed on one small piece of semiconductor, by means of etching and chemical processes **Mikrochip; microcircuit** = complex integrated circuit **Mikroschaltung; microcode** = ALU control instructions implemented as hardwired software **Mikrobefehlscode**

microcomputer *or* **micro** *noun* complete small-scale, cheap, low-power computer system based around a microprocessor chip and having limited memory capacity **Mikrocomputer; microcomputer architecture** = layout and interconnection of a microcomputer's internal hardware **Mikrocomputerarchitektur; microcomputer backplane** = main printed circuit board of a system, containing most of the components and connections for expansion boards, etc. **Mikrocomputer-Rückwandplatine; microcomputer bus** = main data, address and control buses in a microcomputer **Mikrocomputerbus;**

microcomputer development kit = basic computer based around a new CPU chip that allows hardware and software designers to experiment with the new device **Mikrocomputerentwicklungsbausatz; single-board microcomputer** = microcomputer whose components are all contained on a single printed circuit board **Einzelplatinenmikrocomputer**

◇ **microcomputing** *adjective* & *noun* referring to microcomputers and their use **Mikrocomputer-; Mikrocomputing;** *the microcomputing industry*

COMMENT: micros are particularly used as home computers *or* as small office computers

microcontroller *noun* small self-contained microcomputer for use in dedicated control applications **Mikrocontroller; single-chip microcontroller** = one integrated circuit that contains a CPU, I/O ports, RAM and often a basic programming language **Einchip-Mikrocontroller**

◇ **microcycle** *noun* unit of time (usually a multiple of the system clock period) used to give the execution time of instructions **Mikrozyklus**

◇ **microdevice** *noun* very small device, such as a microprocessor **Mikrogerät**

◇ **microelectronics** *noun* design and manufacture of electronic circuits with integrated circuits and chips **Mikroelektronik**

◇ **microfiche** *noun* sheet of text and graphics in highly reduced form on a photographic film **Mikrofiche**

◇ **microfilm**
1 *noun* reel of film containing a sequence of very small images used for document storage **Mikrofilm;** *we hold all our records on microfilm*
2 *verb* to take very small photographs **auf Mikrofilm aufnehmen;** *the 1985 records have been sent away for microfilming*

◇ **microfloppy** *noun* small size magnetic floppy disk (usually refers to 3.5 inch disks) **Mikrodiskette**

◇ **microform** *noun* medium used for storing information in microimage form **Mikroform**

◇ **micrographics** *noun* images and graphics stored as microimages **Mikrographie**

◇ **microimage** *noun* graphical image too small to be seen with the naked eye **Mikrobild**

◇ **microinstruction** *noun* one hardwired instruction (part of a microcode) that controls the actions of the ALU **Mikrobefehl**

◇ **micron** *noun* one millionth of a metre **Mikron**

◇ **microphone** *noun* device that converts sound waves into an electrical signal **Mikrophon; dynamic microphone** = microphone using a coil that moves and induces a voltage according to sound pressure **dynamisches Mikrophon; lapel microphone** = small microphone that is pinned to someone's jacket **Ansteckmikrophon; moving coil microphone** = microphone that uses a coil of wire moved by sound waves to generate an electrical signal **Tauchspulenmikrophon**

◇ **microphotography** *noun* photographic production of microimages (too small to be seen with the naked eye) **Mikrofotografie**

◇ **microprocessor** *noun* central processing unit elements, often contained on a single integrated circuit chip, which when combined with other memory and I/O chips will make up a microcomputer **Mikroprozessor; bit-slice microprocessor** = large word size CPU constructed by joining a number of smaller word size blocks **Slice-Mikroprozessor;** *the bit-slice microprocessor uses four 4-bit processors to make a 16-bit word processor;* **microprocessor addressing capabilities** = highest address that a CPU can directly address, without special features (this depends on the address word size - the bigger the word the greater the addressing capacity) **Mikroprozessor-Adreßleistungen; microprocessor architecture** = layout of the basic parts within a CPU (I/O, ALU, etc.) **Mikroprozessoraufbau; microprocessor chip** = integrated circuit that contains all the elements of a central processing unit, connected with other memory and I/O chips to make a microcomputer **Mikroprozessorchip; microprocessor unit (MPU)** = unit containing the main elements of a microprocessor **Mikroprozessor (MIP)**

◇ **microprogram** *noun* series of microinstructions **Mikroprogramm; microprogram assembly language** = each assembly language instruction of a computer is carried out by a microprogram **Mikroprogramm-Assembliersprache; microprogram counter** = register that stores the address of the next microinstruction to be carried out (the microprogram counter is the same as the memory address register) **Mikroprogrammzähler; microprogram instruction set** = complete set of basic microinstructions available in a CPU **Mikroprogramm-Befehlsvorrat; microprogram store** = storage device used to hold a microprogram **Mikroprogrammspeicher**

◇ **microprogramming** *noun* writing microcode using microinstructions **Mikroprogrammierung**

◇ **microsecond** *noun* one millionth of a second **Mikrosekunde**

◇ **microsequence** *noun* series of microinstructions **Mikrosequenz**

◇ **microwave** *noun* radio frequency range from 1 to 3000GHz **Mikrowelle; microwave communications link** = use of a microwave beam to transmit data between two points **Mikrowellenübertragung; microwave relay** = radiocommunications equipment used to receive microwave signals, then boost and retransmit them **Mikrowellenrelais; microwave transmission** = communication using modulated microwaves allowing high data rates, used for international telephone and satellite communications **Mikrowellenübertragung**

◇ **microwriter** *noun* portable keyboard and display, used for keyboarding when travelling **Mikroschreiber**

mid-user *noun* operator who retrieves relevant information from a database for a customer *or* end user **Vermittler**

middleware *noun* system software that has been customized by a dealer for a particular user **Middleware**

migration *noun* **data migration** = moving data between a high priority or on-line device to a low-priority or off-line device **Datenumlagerung**

milk disk *noun* disk used to transfer data from a small machine onto a larger computer, which provides greater processing power **Datenübertragungsplatte**

◇ **milking machine** *noun* portable machine which can accept data from different machines, then transfer it to another larger computer **Datenübertragungsmaschine**

milli- *prefix* meaning one thousandth **Milli-, milli-; milliampere** *or* **mA** = electrical current measure equal to one thousandth of an ampere **Milliampere, mA; millisecond** *or* **ms** = one thousandth of a second **Millisekunde, ms**

MIMD = MULTIPLE INSTRUCTION STREAM - MULTIPLE DATA STREAM architecture of a parallel processor that uses a number of ALUs and memory devices in parallel to provide high speed processing **Mehrfachbefehlsstrom - Mehrfachdatenstrom**

mini- *prefix* meaning small **Mini-, mini-; miniaturization** = making something very small **Miniaturisierung; minidisk** = magnetic disk smaller than the 5.25 inch standard, usually 3.5 inch **Miniplatte; minifloppy** = magnetic disk (usually refers to the 5.25 inch standard) **Minidiskette;** *(slang)* **miniwinny** = small Winchester hard disk **Mini-Winchesterplatte**

minicomputer *or* **mini** *noun* small computer, with a greater range of instructions and processing power than a microcomputer, but not able to compete with the speed *or* data handling capacity of a mainframe computer **Minicomputer**

minimal latency coding *see* MINIMUM ACCESS CODE

◇ **minimal tree** *noun* tree whose nodes are organized in the optimum way, providing maximum efficiency **Kleinstbaum**

minimum *noun* the smallest amount of something **Minimum; minimum access code** *or* **minimum delay code** = coding system that provides the fastest access and retrieval time for stored data items **Bestzeitcode; minimum weight routing** = method of optimizing the transmission path of a message through a network **optimaler Nachrichtenübertragungsleitweg**

◇ **minimize** *verb* to make as small as possible **minimieren;** *we minimized costs by cutting down the number of components*

minmax *noun* method used in artificial intelligence to solve problems **Minimax-Methode**

minuend *noun* number from which another is subtracted **Minuend**

minus *or* **minus sign** *noun* printed *or* written sign (like a small dash) to indicate subtraction *or* to show a negative value **Minuszeichen**

minuscule *noun* lower case printed character **Kleinbuchstabe, Minuskel**

MIPS = MILLION INSTRUCTIONS PER SECOND measure of computing power of a computer **Millionen Befehle pro Sekunde**

mirror
1 *noun* glass with a metal backing, which reflects an image **Spiegel; mirror image** = image produced that is equivalent to that which would be seen in a mirror **Spiegelbild**
2 *verb* to create an identical copy **spiegeln**

MIS = MANAGEMENT INFORMATION SYSTEM

MISD = MULTIPLE INSTRUCTION STREAM SINGLE DATA STREAM architecture of a parallel computer that has a single ALU and data bus with a number of control units **Mehrfachbefehlsstrom - Einfachdatenstrom**

mismatch *noun* situation occurring when two things are not correctly matched **Fehlanpassung; impedance mismatch** = situation where the impedance of the transmission *or* receiving end of a system does not match the other, resulting in loss of signal power **fehlerhafte Scheinwiderstandsanpassung**

mix
1 *noun* way in which different signals have been combined to form a single signal (usually audio) **Mischung**
2 *verb* to combine several separate signals into a single signal **mischen; to mix down** = to combine the signals from several sources such as a number of recorded audio tracks *or* instruments into a single signal **vermischen**
◇ **mixed highs** *noun* fine colour detail that is in monochrome in a TV signal **gemischte Höhen**
◇ **mixer** *noun* electronic circuit used to combine two *or* more separate signals into a single output **Mischer**
◇ **mixing** *noun*
(a) combining several audio signals into a single signal **Mischen; mixing studio** = room with audio mixers and sound processors used when recording music **Tonmischstudio**
(b) printing a line of text with several different typefaces **Typenmischung, Mischsatz**

MKS = METRE KILOGRAM SECOND widely used measurement system based on the metre, kilogram and second **mks-System**; *see also* SI UNITS

MMI = MAN MACHINE INTERFACE hardware and software designed to make it easier for users to communicate effectively with a machine **Mensch-Maschine-Schnittstelle**

mnemonic(s) *noun* shortened form of a word *or* function that is helpful as a reminder (such as INCA for increment register A) **Mnemonik; assembler mnemonics** *or* **mnemonic operation codes** = standard word abbreviations used when writing a program for a particular CPU in assembly language (such as LDA for load register A) **symbolische Operationsschlüssel**

mobile *adjective & noun* (i) which can move about; (ii); *informal* a travelling radio base such as a car transceiver **(i) beweglich; (ii) mobiler Funkempfänger; mobile earth terminal** = satellite communications equipment that is mobile **mobile Erdstation; mobile unit** = complete set of television filming and editing equipment carried in a vehicle (for outside broadcasts) **mobile Einheit; mobile radiophone** = radio telephone linked to a main telephone system, which uses a network of stations, each covering a certain area, to provide a service over a large area **mobiles Funktelefon**

mock-up *noun* model of a new product for testing *or* to show to possible customers **Attrappe**

mode *noun*
(a) way of doing something; method of operating a computer **Art und Weise; Betriebsart;** *when you want to type in text, press this function key which will put the terminal in its alphanumeric mode;* **burst mode** = data transmission using intermittent bursts of data **Stoßbetrieb; byte mode** = data transmitted one byte at a time **Byte-Modus; control mode** = state of a device in which control signals can be received to select options *or* functions **Steuermodus; deferred mode** = entering a command as a program line, then executing the program **verzögerter Modus; direct mode** = typing in a command which is executed once carriage return has been pressed **Direktmodus; execute mode** = command entered in direct mode to start a program run **Ausführungsmodus; form mode** = display method on a data entry terminal, the form is displayed on the screen and the operator enters relevant details **Formularmodus; input mode** = computer which is receiving data **Eingabemodus; insert mode** = interactive computer mode in which new text is entered within the previous text, which adjusts to make room for it **Einfügungsmodus; interactive mode** = computer that allows the user to enter commands *or* programs *or* data and receive an immediate response **Dialogbetrieb; noisy mode** = floating point arithmetic in which a digit other than a zero is deliberately added

in the least significant position during the normalization of a floating point number **Fließkommabetriebsart; replace mode =** interactive computer mode in which new text entered replaces any previous text **Überschreibmodus; sequential mode =** each instruction in a program is stored in consecutive locations **Sequenzmodus**
(b) number of paths taken by light when travelling down an optical fibre **Moden; mode dispersion =** loss of power in a light signal transmitted down an optic fibre due to dispersion from transmission paths that are not directly along the axis of the fibre **Modenstreuung;** *see* MONOMODE, MULTIMODE
(c) number that occurs most frequently in a series of samples **häufigster Wert**

◇ **modal** *adjective* referring to modes **modal**

QUOTE the printer gives print quality in three modes: high speed, data processing and letter-quality
Minicomputer News

model
1 *noun*
(a) small copy of something to show what it will look like when finished **Modell;** *he showed us a model of the new computer centre building*
(b) style *or* type of product; version of a product **Modell;** *the new model B has taken the place of model A; this is the latest model; the model on display is last year's; they are selling off the old models at half price;* **demonstration model =** piece of equipment used in demonstrations (and then sold cheaply) **Demonstrationsmodell**
2 *adjective* which is a perfect example to be copied **Modell-, modellhaft, Muster-, vorbildlich;** *a model agreement*
3 *verb* to make a computerized model of a new product *or* of the economic system, etc. **ein Modell erstellen;** NOTE: **modelling - modelled** but US **modeling - modeled**

◇ **modelling** *noun* creating computer models **Erstellen von Computermodellen**

modem *or* **MODEM** *noun* = MODULATOR/DEMODULATOR device that allows data to be sent over telephone lines by converting binary signals from a computer into analog sound signals which can be transmitted over a telephone line **Modem; dial-in modem =** auto-answer modem that can be called at any time to access a system **Modem bereit für ankommende Rufe;** *see also* STANDARD *compare with* ACOUSTIC COUPLER

COMMENT: the process of converting binary signals to analog is called "modulation". When the signal is received, another modem reverses the process (called "demodulation"). Both modems must be working according to the same standards

modify *verb* to change something *or* to make something fit a different use **abändern;** *the keyboard was modified for European users; we are running a modified version of the mail-merge system; the software will have to be modified to run on a small PC*

◇ **modification** *noun* change made to something **Abänderung;** *the modifications to the system allow it to be run as part of a LAN;* **modification loop =** instructions within a loop that changes other instructions *or* data within a program **Modifikationsschleife**

◇ **modified frequency modulation** *noun* method of frequency modulation used to record data onto a magnetic medium **modifizierte Frequenzmodulation**

◇ **modifier** *noun* programming instruction that alters the normal action of a command **Modifizierer**

modular *adjective* (method of constructing hardware *or* software products) by connecting several smaller blocks together to produce a customized product **nach dem Baukastenprinzip, modular; modular programming =** programming small individually written sections of computer code that can be made to fit into a structured program and can be called up from a main program **modulare Programmierung**

◇ **modularity** *noun* being made up from modules **Modularität;** *the modularity of the software or hardware allows the system to be changed*

◇ **modularization** *noun* designing programs from a set of standard modules **Modularisierung**

modulate *verb* to change a carrier wave so that it can carry data **modulieren; modulated signal =** constant frequency and amplitude carrier signal that is used in a modulated form to transmit data **moduliertes Signal; modulating signal =** signal to be transmitted that is used to modulate a carrier **Modulationssignal**

◇ **modulation** *noun* process of varying a carrier's amplitude *or* frequency *or* phase according to an applied signal **Modulation** ⊃ APPENDIX **amplitude modulation (AM) =** system that varies the amplitude of a constant carrier signal according to an external signal **Amplitudenmodulation (AM)**; **frequency modulation (FM)** = system that varies the frequency of a constant amplitude carrier signal according to an external signal **Frequenzmodulation (FM)**

◊ **modulator** *noun* electronic circuit that varies a carrier signal according to an applied signal **Modulator, Sender-Signalumsetzer**; **modulator/demodulator** = MODEM

module *noun*

(a) small section of a large program that can if required function independently as a program in its own right **Programmodul**
(b) self-contained piece of hardware that can be connected with other modules to form a new system **Baustein;** *a multifunction analog interface module includes analog to digital and digital to analog converters*

modulo arithmetic *noun* branch of

arithmetic that uses the remainder of one number when divided by another **Modulo-Arithmetik; modulo-N** = modulo arithmetic using base N **Modulo N; modulo-N check** = error detection test using the remainder from a modulo arithmetic operation on data **Modulo-N-Prüfung**

modulus *or* MOD *noun* the remainder

after the division of one number by another **Rest**; *7 mod 3 = 1*

momentary switch *noun* switch that

only conducts while it is being pressed **federnder Schalter, Taster**

monadic (Boolean) operator *noun*

logical operator with only one operand **monadischer Operator;** *the monadic operator NOT can be used here;* **monadic operation** = operation that uses one operand to produce one result **monadische Operation**

monitor

1 *noun*
(a) visual display unit used to display high quality text *or* graphics, generated by a computer **Monitor, Bildschirm; multi-scan** *or* **multi-sync monitor** = monitor which has circuitry to lock onto the required scanning frequency for any type of graphics card **Multiscan-Monitor; monitor unit** *see* VDU
(b) (i) loudspeaker used to listen to the sound signals produced during recording *or* mixing; (ii) TV screen in a TV studio control room, which shows the image being filmed by one of the cameras **(i) Kontrollautsprecher; (ii) Kontrollschirm**

(c) **monitor program** = computer program that allows basic commands to be entered to operate a system (such as load a program, examine the state of devices, etc.) **Monitorprogramm;** *see also* OPERATING SYSTEM; **firmware monitor** = monitor program that is resident in a ROM device, used to load in the operating system when a machine is switched on **residentes Festspeichermonitorprogramm**
(c) system that watches for faults *or* failures in a circuit **Überwachungssystem; power monitor** = circuit that shuts off the electricity supply if it is faulty *or* likely to damage equipment **Netzspannungsüberwachung**
2 *verb* (i) to check *or* to examine how something is working; (ii) to look after and supervise a process *or* experiment to make sure it is operating correctly **(i) & (ii) überwachen;** *he is monitoring the progress of the trainee programmers; the machine monitors each signal as it is sent out*

mono- *prefix* meaning single *or* one **mono-, ein-**

◊ **monoaural** *adjective* single audio channel presented to only one ear **einohrig**

◊ **monochrome** *adjective & noun* (image) in one colour, usually shades of grey and black and white **einfarbig, monochrom, schwarz/weiß; einfarbiges Bild; monochrome monitor** = computer monitor that displays text and graphics in black, white and shades of grey instead of colours **Schwarz/weiß-Monitor**

◊ **monolithic** *adjective* (integrated circuit) manufactured on a single crystal of semiconductor **monolithisch**

◊ **monomode fibre** *noun* optical fibre that only allows light to travel along its axis without any internal reflections, as the result of having a very fine core diameter **Monomode-Faser;** *see also* MODE

◊ **monophonic** *adjective* system where one audio signal is used to feed one *or* more loudspeakers **monophon;** *compare with* STEREOPHONIC

◊ **monoprogramming system** *noun* computer batch processing system that executes one program at a time **Einprogrammsystem;** *compare with* MULTIPROGRAMMING SYSTEM

◊ **monospacing** *noun* system of printing where each character occupies the same amount of space, as on a typewriter (as opposed to proportional spacing) **gleichbleibender Schaltschritt (Schriftart, bei der die Drucktypen die gleiche Dickte haben)**

◊ **monostable** *adjective & noun* (electronic circuit) that produces an output pulse for a predetermined period when it receives an input signal **monostabil(er Stromkreis)**

Monte Carlo method *noun* statistical analysis technique **Monte-Carlo-Methode**

Morse code *noun* system of signalling using only two symbols: dots and dashes **Morsealphabet; morse key** = switch used to send morse messages by hand **Morsetaste**

MOS = METAL OXIDE SEMICONDUCTOR production and design method for a certain family of integrated circuits using patterns of metal conductors and oxide deposited onto a semiconductor **MOS (Metalloid-Halbleiterelement);** *see also* MOSFET ; **MOS memory** = solid-state memory using MOSFETs to store binary data **MOS-Speicher; CMOS** = COMPLEMENTARY METAL OXIDE SEMICONDUCTOR integrated circuit design and construction method (using a pair of complementary p- and n- type transistors) **CMOS (Halbleiterelement; Kombination von PMOS- und NMOS-Technik)**

QUOTE integrated circuits fall into one of two distinct classes, based either on bipolar or metal oxide semiconductor (MOS) transistors
Electronics & Power

mosaic *noun* display character used in videotext systems that is made up of small dots **Mosaik**

MOSFET = METAL OXIDE SEMICONDUCTOR FIELD EFFECT TRANSISTOR high power and high speed field effect transistor manufactured using MOS techniques **Feldeffekttransistor mit Metalloxid-Halbleiteraufbau; MOS-Transistor**

most significant bit *or* **msb** *or* **MSB** *noun* bit in a word that represents the greatest value *or* weighting (usually the bit which is furthest to the left) **wichtigstes Bit;** *the most significant bit in an eight bit binary word represents 128 in decimal notation*

◇ **most significant character** *or* **most significant digit (MSD)** *noun* digit at the far left of a number, that represents the greatest power of the base **wichtigstes Zeichen; wichtigste Ziffer;** NOTE: the opposite is LSB, LSD

motherboard *noun* main printed circuit board of a system, containing most of the components and connections for expansion boards, etc. **Grundplatine**

motion picture *noun* projection at high speed of a series of still images that creates the impression of movement **Film**

motor *noun* electromagnetic machine that converts an electrical supply into (rotary) motion (by means of a magnetic field) **Motor**

mount *verb* to fix a device *or* a circuit onto a base **befestigen;** *the chips are mounted in sockets on the PCB*

mouse *noun* small hand-held input device moved on a flat surface to control the position of a cursor on the screen **Maus; mouse-driven** = (software) which uses a mouse rather than a keyboard for input **mausgesteuert; mouse driver** = program which converts data from a mouse to a standard form that can be used by any software **Maustreiber;** NOTE: the plural is **mice** or sometimes **mouses**

QUOTE a powerful new mouse-based editor:- you can cut, paste and copy with the mouse
Personal Computer World
QUOTE you can use a mouse to access pop-up menus and a keyboard for a word-processor
Byte

mouth *noun* open end of an antenna **(Trichter)öffnung**

M out of N code *noun* coding system providing error detection, each valid character which is N bits long must contain M binary "one" bits **Codiersystem**

move *verb* to change the place of something **bewegen; move block** = command which changes the place of a block of text identified by block markers **Blockbewegungsbefehl; moving coil microphone** = microphone which uses a coil of wire moved by sound waves to generate an electrical signal **Tauchspulenmikrophon**

◇ **movable** *adjective* which can be moved **beweglich; movable head disk** = magnetic disk head assembly that moves across the disk until the required track is reached **Platte mit beweglichem Kopf**

◇ **movement** *noun* changing the place of something **Bewegung; movement file** = file containing recent changes *or* transactions to records, which is then used to update a master file **Bewegungsdatei**

MPS = MICROPROCESSOR SYSTEM

MPU = MICROPROCESSOR UNIT

ms = MILLISECOND one thousandth of a second **ms**

MS = MANUSCRIPT
NOTE: plural is **MSS**

msb *or* **MSB** = MOST SIGNIFICANT BIT bit in a word that represents the greatest value *or* weight (usually the bit furthest to the left) **wichtigstes Bit**

MSD = MOST SIGNIFICANT DIGIT

MSI = MEDIUM SCALE INTEGRATION

M signal *noun* signal produced from the sum of left and right signals in a stereophonic system **M-Signal, Mittensignal**

MSX *noun* hardware and software standard for home computers that can use interchangeable software **MSX-Norm**

MTBF = MEAN TIME BETWEEN FAILURES average period of time that a piece of equipment will operate between failures **mittlerer Ausfallabstand**

MTF = MEAN TIME TO FAILURE average period of time for which a device will operate (usually continuously) before failing **mittlere Lebensdauer**

multi- *prefix* meaning many *or* more than one **mehrfach, Multi-, multi-**; *multimegabyte memory card; a multistandard unit;* **multi-access system** = computer system that allows several users to access one file *or* program at the same time **System mit mehrfachem Zugriff;** *see also* MULTI-USER; **multi-address** *or* **multi-address instruction** = instruction that contains more than one address (of data *or* locations *or* input/output) **Mehradreßbefehl**

◇ **multi-board computer** *noun* computer which has several integrated circuit boards connected to a mother board **Mehrplatinencomputer**

◇ **multiburst signal** *noun* television test signal **Multi-Burst-Signal**

◇ **multi-bus system** *noun* computer architecture that uses a high speed bus between CPU and main memory and a slower bus between CPU and other peripherals **Mehrbussystem**

◇ **multicasting** *noun* broadcasting to a number of receivers *or* nodes, with an address in each message to indicate the node required **Mehrfachausstrahlung**

◇ **multichannel** *adjective* with more than one channel **Mehrkanal-**

◇ **multicolour** *adjective* with several colours **mehrfarbig**

◇ **multidimensional** *adjective* with features in more than one dimension **mehrdimensional; multidimensional array** = number of arrays arranged in parallel, providing depth **mehrdimensionale Feldgruppe; multidimensional language** = programming language that can be represented in a number of ways **mehrdimensionale Programmiersprache**

◇ **multi-disk** *adjective* referring to several types of disk **Mehrplatten-; multi-disk option** = system that can have disk drives installed in a number of sizes **Mehrplatten-Option; multi-disk reader** = device which can read from various sizes and formats of disk **Mehrplatten-Leser**

◇ **multidrop circuit** *noun* network allowing communications between a number of terminals and a central computer, but not directly between terminals **Übertragungsleitung mit mehreren Stationen**

◇ **multifrequency** *noun* **dual tone, multifrequency (DTMF)** = communication signalling system using two different frequencies to transmit binary data **Mehrfrequenzwahlverfahren (MFV)**

◇ **multifunction** *adjective* which has several functions **Mehrfunktions-, multifunktional;** *a multifunction analog interface module includes analog to digital and digital to analog converters;* **multifunction card** = add-on circuit board that provides many features to upgrade a computer **Mehrfunktionskarteneinheit; multifunction workstation** = workstation where several tasks can be carried out **Mehrfunktionsdatenstation**

◇ **multifunctional** *adjective* which has several functions **Mehrfunktions-, multifunktional;** *a multifunctional scanner*

◇ **multilayer** *noun* printed circuit board that has several layers *or* interconnecting conduction tracks **Mehrschichtplatine**

◇ **multilevel** *adjective* (signal) with a number of possible values (quaternary signals have four levels) **mehrstufig**

◇ **multilink system** *noun* system where there is more than one connection between two points **Mehrfachverbindungssystem**

◇ **multimedia** *adjective* referring to several forms of media **multimedial; multimedia mail** = messages that can contain voice, sound, images or data **multimediale Post**

◇ **multimeter** *noun* testing equipment that provides an indication of the voltage *or* current *or* impedance at a point or of a component **Multimeter; analog multimeter (AMM)** = testing equipment using a moving needle to indicate voltage, current *or* impedance levels **Analogmultimeter;**

digital multimeter (DMM) = multimeter that uses a digital readout to indicate voltage, current *or* impedance levels **Digitalmultimeter**

◇ **multimode fibre** *noun* optical fibre that allows many different paths in addition to the direct straight path for light beams, causing pulse stretching and interference on reception of the signal **Multimode-Faser**

◇ **multi-part stationery** *noun* continuous stationery with two *or* more sheets together, either with carbons between *or* carbonless **Vordrucksatz**

◇ **multipass overlap** *noun* system of producing higher quality print from a dot matrix printer by repeating the line of characters but shifted slightly, so making the dots less noticeable **Mehrfachüberschreibung**

◇ **multiphase program** *noun* program that requires more than one fetch operation before execution is complete **Mehrphasenprogramm**

multiple *adjective* having many parts *or* acting in many ways **mehrfach**; **multiple access** *see* MULTI-ACCESS; **multiple address code** = instruction with more than one address for the operands, result and the location of the next instruction to be executed **Mehrfachzugriffscode**; *see also* THREE-PLUS-ONE; FOUR-PLUS-ONE ADDRESS; **multiple bus architecture** = computer architecture that uses a high speed bus between CPU and main memory and a slower bus between CPU and other peripherals **Mehrfachbusarchitektur**; **multiple instruction stream - multiple data stream (MIMD)** = architecture of a parallel processor that uses a number of ALUs and memories in parallel to provide high speed processing **Mehrfachbefehlsstrom - Mehrfachdatenstrom**; **multiple instruction stream - single data stream (MISD)** = architecture of a parallel computer that has a single ALU and data bus with a number of control units **Mehrfachbefehlsstrom - Einfachdatenstrom**; **multiple precision** = use of more than one byte of data for number storage to increase possible precision **Mehrfachgenauigkeit**

multiplex *verb* to combine several messages in the same transmission medium **vielfach ausnutzen; multiplexed analog components (MAC)** = standard television broadcast signal format **MAC; multiplexed bus** = one bus used to carry address, data and control signals at different times **Multiplexbus**

◇ **multiplexing** *noun* combining several messages in the same transmission medium **Multiplexmethode (Unterteilung eines Übertragungskanals in mehrere Kanäle); dynamic multiplexing** = multiplexing method which allocates time segments to signals according to demand **dynamische Multiplexmethode; homogeneous multiplexing** = switching multiplexor system where all the channels contain data using the same protocol and transmission rate **homogene Multiplexmethode; optical multiplexing** = sending several light beams down a single path *or* fibre **optisches Multiplexing**

◇ **multiplexor (MUX)** *noun* circuit that combines a number of inputs into a smaller number of outputs **Multiplexor;** *compare with* DEMULTIPLEXOR *a 4 to 1 multiplexor combines four inputs into a single output*

QUOTE the displays use BCD input signals and can be multiplexed to provide up to six digits
Electronics & Power

multiply *verb* to perform a multiplication of a number (the multiplier) **multiplizieren**

◇ **multiplicand** *noun* number which is multiplied by another number **Multiplikant**

◇ **multiplication** *noun* mathematical operation that adds one number to itself a number of times **Multiplikation;** *the multiplication of 5 and 3 = 15;* **multiplication sign** = printed *or* written sign (x) used to show that numbers are multiplied **Multiplikationszeichen**

◇ **multiplier** *noun* number which multiplies a multiplicand **Multiplikator**

multipoint *adjective* (connection) with several lines, attaching several terminals to a single line to a single computer **Mehrpunkt-**

◇ **multiprecision** *noun* use of more than one data word to represent numbers (increasing the range *or* precision possible) **Mehrfachgenauigkeit**

◇ **multiprocessing system** *noun* system where several processing units work together sharing the same memory **Simultanverarbeitungssystem**

◇ **multiprocessor** *noun* number of processing units acting together *or* separately but sharing the same area of memory **Mehrprozessorsystem; multiprocessor interleaving** = each processor in a multiprocessor system dealing with a section of one or more processes **Mehrprozessorenverschachtelung**

◇ **multi-programming** *noun* operating system used to execute more than one program apparently simultaneously (each program being executed a little at a time) **Mehrprogrammbetrieb**

◇ **multi-scan** *or* **multi-sync monitor** *noun* monitor which contains circuitry to lock onto the required scanning frequency of any type of graphics card **Multiscan-Monitor**

◇ **multi-statement line** *noun* line from a computer program that contains more than one instruction *or* statement **Mehrfachanweisungszeile**

◇ **multi-strike printer ribbon** *noun* inked ribbon in a printer that can be used more than once **mehrfach benutzbares Farbband**

multitasking *or* **multi-tasking** *noun* ability of a computer system to run two or more programs at the same time **Multitasking;** *the system is multi-user and multi-tasking;* **real-time multitasking =** executing several (real-time) tasks simultaneously without slowing the execution of any of the processors **Echtzeit-Multitasking**

COMMENT: few small systems are capable of simultaneous multitasking, since each program would require its own processor; this is overcome by allocating to each program an amount of processing time, executing each a little at a time so that they will appear to run simultaneously due to the speed of the processor and the relatively short gaps between programs

QUOTE this is a true multi-tasking system, meaning that several computer applications can be running at the same time
Which PC?
QUOTE page management programs are so greedy for memory that it is not a good idea to ask them to share RAM space with anything else, so the question of multi-tasking does not arise here
Desktop Publishing

multi-terminal system *noun* system where several terminals are linked to a single CPU **System mit mehreren Datenstationen**

◇ **multithread** *noun* program design using more than one logical path through it, each path being concurrently executed **Mehrpfadprogramm**

◇ **multi-user system** *noun* computer system that can support more than one user at a time **Mehrplatzsystem;** *the program runs on a standalone machine or a multi-user system*

◇ **multivibrator** *noun* electronic circuit that switches continuously between two output states, often used for clock generation **Multivibrator; astable multivibrator =** electronic circuit that repeatedly switches an output between two voltage levels **astabiler/instabiler Multivibrator**

◇ **multi-window editor** *noun* program used for creating and editing a number of applications programs independently, each in a separate window on screen at the same time **Mehrfenster-Editor**

mung up *verb (informal)* to distort data *or* to ruin a file **versauen**

Murray code *noun* code used for teleprinters that uses only 5 bits **Murray-Code**

mush *noun* distortion and loss of signal **Störung; mush area =** distortion and loss of signal due to two transmissions interfering **Störungsgebiet**

music chip *noun* integrated circuit capable of generating musical sounds and tunes **Musikchip; music synthesizer =** device able to generate musical notes which are similar to those made by musical instruments **Synthesizer**

muting *noun* **interstation muting =** ability of a radio receiver to prevent the noise found between radio stations from being amplified and heard by the user **geräuschfreie Abstimmung**

MUX = MULTIPLEXOR circuit that combines a number of inputs into a smaller number of outputs **Multiplexor;** *compare* DEMULTIPLEXOR

MW = MEDIUMWAVE

Nn

n *prefix* meaning nano- **n**

n-channel metal oxide semiconductor *noun* transistor design, with MOS techniques, that uses an n-type region for conduction **N-Kanal-Metalloxidhalbleiter**

N-key rollover *noun* facility on a keyboard where each keystroke (up to a maximum of N) is registered in sequence even if they are struck very fast **Tastatur mit überlappender Eingabe über mehr als 2 Tasten**

NAK = NEGATIVE ACKNOWLEDGEMENT

name *noun*
(a) word used to call a thing *or* a person **Name; brand name =** name of a particular make of product **Markenname; corporate name =** name of a large corporation **Firmenname;** *the company buys computer*

parts from several suppliers, and packages them together to make their own name product
(b) ordinary word used to identify an address in machine language **Name; file name** = word used to identify a particular stored file **Dateiname; program name** = identification name for a stored program file **Programmname; name table** *or* **symbol table** = list of reserved words *or* commands in a language and the addresses in the computer that refer to them **Namen-, Symboltabelle; variable name** = word used to identify a variable in a program **Variablenname**

NAND function *noun* logical function whose output is false if all inputs are true, and true if any input is false **NAND-Funktion; NAND gate** = electronic circuit that provides a NAND function **NAND-Gatter;** NOTE: the NAND function is equivalent to an AND function with a NOT function at the output

COMMENT: the output is 0 only if both inputs are 1; if one input is 1 and the other 0, or if both inputs are 0, then the output is 1

nano- *or* **n** *prefix* meaning one thousand millionth *or, (US)* one billionth **nano-;** *(US)* **ein milliardstel; nanocircuit** *or* **nanosecond circuit** = electronic and logic circuits that can respond to impulses within nanoseconds **Nanoschaltung; nanometre** *or* **nm** one thousand millionth of a metre **Nanometer; nanosecond** *or* **ns** = one thousand millionth of a second **Nanosekunde;** NOTE: US billion is the same as UK one thousand million (10 to the power of nine); UK billion is one million million (10 to the power of 10)

QUOTE the cache's internal RAM is accessed in under 70ns from address strobe to ready signal
Electronics & Power

narrative *noun* explanatory notes or comments to help a user operate a program **Erklärung**

◇ **narrative statement** *noun* statement which sets variables and allocates storage at the start of a program **erklärende Festlegung**

narrow band *noun* communication method that uses a bandwidth less than that of a voice channel **Schmalband; narrow band FM (NBFM)** = frequency modulation system using very small bandwidth (with only one pair of sidebands) **Schmalbandfrequenzmodulation;** *compare* WIDE BAND

National Television Standards Committee (NTSC) *noun* official body that defines television and video formats *or* standards used mainly in the USA and in Japan **NTSC;** *see also* VIDEO STANDARDS

COMMENT: NTSC standards are based on 525 horizontal lines and 60 frames per second

native *adjective* **native format** = first *or* basic format **Ursprungsformat**

natural *adjective* occurring in nature *or* not created artificially **natürlich; natural binary coded decimal (NBCD)** = representation of single decimal digits as a pattern of 4 bits **natürliche binärcodierte Dezimale; natural language** = language that is used *or* understood by humans **natürliche Sprache;** *the expert system can be programmed in a natural language*

QUOTE there are two main types of natural-language interface: those based on menus, and those where the user has to discover what questions the computer will respond to by trial and error
Electronics & Power

NBCD = NATURAL BINARY CODED DECIMAL

NBFM = NARROW BAND FREQUENCY MODULATION

NC = NUMERICAL CONTROL machine operated automatically by computer *or* circuits controlled by a stored program *or* data **NC (Computer, die zur numerischen Steuerung von Werkzeugmaschinen dienen)**

NCR paper = NO CARBON REQUIRED paper *see* CARBONLESS PAPER

NDR = NON DESTRUCTIVE READOUT display system that continues to display previous characters when new ones are displayed **nichtlöschendes Auslesen**

near letter-quality (NLQ) *noun* printing by a dot-matrix printer that provides higher quality type, which is almost as good as a typewriter, by decreasing the spaces between the dots **korrespondenzfähiges Schriftbild, NLQ Druckmodus;** *switch the printer to NLQ for these form letters*

needle *noun* tiny metal pin on a dot matrix printer which prints one of the dots **Nadel**

negate *verb* to reverse the sign of a number **negieren**; *if you negate 23.4 the result is -23.4*

◇ **negation** *noun* reversing the sign of a number (such as from 5 to -5) **Negierung**

◇ **negative**
‖ *adjective* meaning "no" **negativ; negative acknowledgement (NAK)** = signal sent by a receiver to indicate that data has been incorrectly *or* incompletely received **negative Rückmeldung; negative feedback** = loop around a circuit in which part of the output signal is subtracted from the input signal **negative Rückkopplung; negative number** = number which represents the number subtracted from zero, indicated by a minus sign in front of the number **negative Zahl; negative-true logic** = use of a lower voltage level to represent binary 1 than for binary 0 **negative Logik**
‖ *noun* normal photographic film where the colours are reversed (black is white and white is black) **Negativfilm; contact negative** = film which can be used to produce a print without any reduction *or* enlargement **Kontaktstreifen**

neither-nor function *noun* logical function whose output is false if any input is true **NOR-Funktion**

NEQ = NON-EQUIVALENCE; **NEQ function** = logical function where the output is true if the inputs are not the same, otherwise the output is false **Inäquivalenz-Funktion; NEQ gate** = electronic implementation of an NEQ function **Inäquivalenz-Gatter**

nest *verb* (i) to insert a subroutine within a program *or* another routine; (ii) to use a routine that calls itself recursively **(i) & (ii) verschachteln; nested loop** = loop inside another loop in the same program **verschachtelte Schleife; nested macrocall** = a macro called from within another macro **verschachtelter Makroaufruf; nesting level** = number of subroutines within a subroutine **verschachtelungsgrad; nesting store** = hardware stack (normally stacks are implemented with software) **Stapelspeicher**

network
noun any system made of a number of points *or* circuits that are interconnected **Netz; communications network** = group of devices such as terminals and printers that are interconnected with a central computer allowing the rapid and simple transfer of data **Nachrichtennetz; computer network** = shared use of a series of interconnected computers, peripherals and terminals

Computernetz; information network = number of databases linked together, usually using telephone lines and modems, allowing a large amount of data to be accessed by a wider number of users **Informationsnetz; local area network (LAN)** = network where the various terminals and equipment are all within a short distance of one another (at a maximum distance of 500m, for example in the same building) and can be interconnected by cables **Lokalnetz; long haul network** = communications network between distant computers that usually uses the public telephone system **Überlandnetz; radio** *or* **television network** = series of local radio *or* TV stations linked to a main central station **Funk- od Fernsehnetz; wide area network (WAN)** = network where the various terminals are far apart and linked by radio *or* satellite **Weitverkehrsnetz; network analysis** = study of messages, destinations and routes in a network to provide a better operation **Netzplantechnik; network architecture** = method in which a network is constructed, such as layers in an OSI system **Netzwerkarchitektur; network control program** = software that regulates the flow of and channels for data transmitted in a network **Netzwerksteuerprogramm; network controller** = network user responsible for allocating disk space, answering queries and solving problems from other users of the same network **Netzüberwacher; network database** = database structure in which data items can be linked together **Datenbanknetz; network diagram** = graphical representation describing the interconnections between points **Netzwerkplan; network hardware** = physical links, computers and control equipment that make up a network **Netzwerk-Hardware; network layer** = ISO/OSI standard layer that decides on the routes to be used, the costs, etc. **Vermittlungsschicht;** *see also* LAYER; **network management** = organization, planning, running and upkeep of a network **Netzführung; network processor** = signal multiplexer controlled by a microprocessor in a network **Netzwerkprozessor; network redundancy** = extra links between points allowing continued operation in the event of one failing **Netzwerkredundanz; network software** = software which is used to establish the link between a user's program and the network **Netzwerk-Software; network structure** = data structure that allows each node to be connected to any of the others **Netzstruktur; network timing** = signals that correctly synchronize the transmission of data **Netzsynchronisation;** *see also* BUS, MESH, PROTOCOL, RING, STAR, TOPOLOGY

2 *verb* to link points together in a network **vernetzen;** *they run a system of networked micros; the workstations have been networked together rather than used as standalone systems;* **networked TV programme** = programme which is broadcast (usually simultaneously) by all the stations in a TV network **vernetztes Fernsehprogramm**

◊ **networking** *noun*
(a) broadcasting a prime-time TV programme over several local stations at the same time **Netzwerkausstrahlung**
(b) (i) working *or* organization of a network; (ii) interconnecting two *or* more computers either in the same room *or* different buildings, in the same town *or* different towns, allowing them to exchange information (i) **Netzwerkbetrieb;** (ii) **Netzwerkverlegung; networking hardware** *or* **network hardware** = physical links, computers and control equipment that make up a network **Netzwerk-Hardware; networking software** *or* **network software** = software which is used to establish the link between a user's program and the network **Netzwerk-Software; networking specialist** = company *or* person who specializes in designing and setting up networks **Netzwerkspezialist;** *this computer firm is a UK networking specialist*

COMMENT: networking allows a machine with a floppy disk drive to use another PC's hard disk when both machines are linked by a cable and are using networking software

QUOTE the traditional way of operating networks involves having a network manager and training network users to familiarize themselves with a special set of new commands
Which PC?
QUOTE workstations are cheaper the more you buy, because they are usually networked and share resources
PC Business World

neutral *adjective* with no state *or* bias *or* voltage **neutral; neutral transmission** = (transmission) system in which a voltage pulse and zero volts represent the binary digits 1 and 0 **neutrale Übertragung**

new *adjective* recent *or* not old **neu;** *they have installed a new computer system; the new programmer does not seem as efficient as the old one;* **new (command)** = program command that clears main memory of the present program ready to accept a new program to be entered **NEW (zu Beginn einer neuen Programmeingabe); new line character** = character that moves a cursor *or* printhead to the beginning of the next line **Zeilenvorschubzeichen;** *see also* CARRIAGE RETURN (CR); LINEFEED (LF); **new technology** = electronic instruments which have recently been invented **neue Technologie**

◊ **news** *noun* information about things which have happened **Nachrichten;** *business news; financial news; financial markets were shocked by the news of the collapse of the computer company;* **news agency** = office which distributes news to newspapers and television companies **Nachrichtenagentur; news release** = sheet giving information about a new event which is sent to newspapers and TV and radio stations so that they can use it **Nachrichtenveröffentlichung;** *the company sent out a news release about the new managing director*

◊ **newsletter** *noun* **company newsletter** = printed sheet *or* small newspaper giving news about a company **Firmeninformationsblatt**

◊ **newsprint** *noun* mechanical paper used for printing newspapers **Zeitungspapier**
NOTE: no plural

next instruction register *noun* register in a CPU that contains the location where the next instruction to be executed is stored **Befehlsfolgeregister;** *see also* REGISTER

nexus *noun* connection point between units in a network **Verknüpfung**

nibble *or* **nybble** *noun* half the length of a standard byte **Vier-Bit-Byte**
NOTE: a nibble is normally 4 bits, but can vary according to different micros or people

nil pointer *noun* pointer used to indicate the end of a chained list of items **Nullanzeiger**

nine's complement *noun* decimal complement (equivalent to the binary one's complement) formed by subtracting each digit in the number from nine **Neunerkomplement;** *see also* TEN'S COMPLEMENT

n-level logic *noun* logic gate design in which no more than n gates occur in a series **n-stufige Logik**

NLQ = NEAR LETTER-QUALITY

NMI = NON-MASKABLE INTERRUPT

NMOS = N-CHANNEL METAL OXIDE SEMICONDUCTOR

no-address operation *noun* instruction which does not require an address within it **Anweisung ohne Adresse**
◇ **no op** *or* **no operation instruction** = NO OPERATION programming instruction which does nothing „**keine Operation**"

node *noun* interconnection point in a structure *or* network **Netzknoten;** *a tree is made of branches that connect together at nodes; this network has fibre optic connection with nodes up to one kilometre apart*

noise *noun* random signal present in addition to any wanted signal, caused by static, temperature, power supply, magnetic or electric fields and also from stars and the sun **Rauschen, Störungen; noise immunity** = ability of a circuit to ignore *or* filter out *or* be protected from noise **Störfestigkeit; noise margin** = maximum amplitude of noise that will affect a device, such as switch a logic gate **Störabstand; noise temperature** = temperature of a component for it to produce the same thermal noise as a source **Rauschtemperatur; galactic noise** = electrical noise which originates from planets and stars in space **galaktisches Rauschen; impulsive noise** = interference on a signal caused by short periods of noise **Impulsstörung; thermal noise** = background noise signal caused by temperature variations in components **thermisches Rauschen**
◇ **noisy mode** *noun* floating point arithmetic system, in which a digit other than a zero is deliberately added in the least significant position during the normalization of a floating point number **fließkommabetriebsart; noisy digit** = digit, usually not zero, added during the normalization of a floating point number when in noisy mode **Normierungsbit**

QUOTE the photographs were grainy, out of focus, and distorted by signal noise
Byte

nomenclature *noun* predefined system for assigning words and symbols to represent numbers or terms **Nomenklatur**

nomogram *or* **nomograph** *noun* graphical system for solving one value given two others **Nomogramm, Funktionsnetz**

non- *prefix* meaning not **nicht**
◇ **nonaligned** *adjective* two devices that are not correctly positioned in relation to each other, for optimum performance **nicht richtig ausgerichtet; nonaligned read head** = read head that is not in the same position

on a magnetic medium as the write head was, producing a loss of signal quality **nicht richtig ausgerichteter Lesekopf**
◇ **non-arithmetic shift** *see* LOGICAL SHIFT
◇ **noncompatibility** *noun* two or more pieces of hardware *or* software that cannot exchange data *or* use the same peripherals **fehlende Kompatibilität**
◇ **noncounting keyboard** *noun* entry keyboard on a phototypesetter that does not allow page format instructions to be entered **nicht zählende Tastatur**
◇ **non-destructive cursor** *noun* cursor on a display that does not erase characters already displayed as it passes over them **nichtlöschender Cursor;** *the screen quickly became unreadable when using a non-destructive cursor;* **non-destructive readout (NDR)** = display device that retains previous characters when displaying new characters **nichtlöschendes Auslesen; non-destructive test** = series of tests carried out on a piece of equipment without destroying it **nichtlöschender Test;** *I will carry out a number of non-destructive tests on your computer; if it passes, you can start using it again;* **non-scrollable** = part of the screen display which is always displayed (in a WP, the text can scroll whilst instructions, etc., are non-scrollable) **nicht umblätterbar;** *see also* STATUS LINE
◇ **non-equivalence function (NEQ)** *noun* logical function where the output is true if the inputs are not the same, otherwise the output is false **Antivalenzfunktion; non-equivalence gate** = electronic implementation of an NEQ function **Antivalenzglied**
◇ **nonerasable storage** *noun* storage medium that cannot be erased and re-used **nichtlöschbarer Speicher;** *paper tape is a nonerasable storage*
◇ **non-impact printer** *noun* printer (like an ink-jet printer) where the character form does not hit a ribbon onto the paper **nichtmechanischer Drucker; (Laserdrucker)**
◇ **nonlinear** *adjective* electronic circuit whose output does not change linearly in proportion to its input **nichtlinear**
◇ **non-maskable interrupt (NMI)** *noun* high priority interrupt signal that cannot be blocked by software and overrides other commands **nichtmaskierbare Unterbrechung**
◇ **non-operable instruction** *noun* instruction that does not carry out any function, but increments the program counter **nicht ausführbare Anweisung**
◇ **non-printing codes** *noun* codes that represent an action of the printer rather than a printed character **Druckanweisungscodes;** *the line width can be*

*set using one of the non-printing codes,
.LW, then a number*

◊ **non return to zero (NRZ)** *noun*
signalling system in which a positive
voltage represents one binary digit and a
negative voltage the other; representation
of binary data in which the signal changes
when the data changes state, and does not
return to zero volts after each bit of data
ohne Rückkehr zu Null

◊ **non-volatile** *adjective* **non-volatile
memory** *or* **non-volatile store** *or* **storage** =
storage medium *or* memory that retains
data even when the power has been
switched off **nichtflüchtiger Speicher;** *bubble
memory is a non-volatile storage; using
magnetic tape provides non-volatile
memory*
NOTE: opposite is **volatile**

COMMENT: disks (both hard and floppy)
and tapes are non-volatile memory stores;
solid-state memory, such as RAM chips are
volatile unless battery backed

no op = NO OPERATION programming
instruction which does nothing „**keine
Operation**"

NOR function *noun* logical function
whose output is false if either input is true
NOR-Funktion; NOR gate = electric circuit *or*
chip which performs a NOR function **NOR-
Gatter**

COMMENT: the output is 1 only if both
inputs are 0; if the two inputs are different
or if both are 1, the output is 0

normal *adjective* usual *or* which happens
regularly **normal;** *the normal procedure is for
backup copies to be made at the end of each
day's work;* **normal format** = standardized
format for data storage **Normalformat;
normal range** = expected range for a result
or number, any outside this range are errors
Normalbereich

◊ **normalize** *verb*
(a) to convert data into a form which can be
read by a particular computer system
normalisieren, standardisieren
(b) to convert characters into just capitals
or into just a lower case form **normalisieren**
(c) to store and represent numbers in a pre-
agreed form, usually to provide maximum
precision **normieren;** *all the new data has
been normalized to 10 decimal places;*
normalized form = floating point number
that has been normalized so that its
mantissa is within a certain range
Standardform

◊ **normalization** *noun* process of
normalizing data **Normalisierung,**

Standardisierung; normalization routine =
routine that normalizes a floating point
number and adds extra (noisy) digits in the
least significant position
Standardisierungsroutine

NOT function *noun* logical inverse
function where the output is true if the
input is false **NICHT-Funktion; NOT-AND** =
equivalent to the NAND function **NAND-
Funktion; NOT gate** = electronic circuit *or*
chip which performs a NOT function
NICHT-Gatter

COMMENT: if the input is 1, the output is 0;
if the input is 0, the output is 1

notation *noun* method of writing *or*
representing numbers **Schreibweise; binary
notation** = base two numerical system using
only the digits 0 and 1 **Binärschreibweise;
decimal notation** = number representation
in base 10, using the digits 0-9
Dezimalschreibweise; hexadecimal notation
= number system using base 16 and the
digits 0-9 and A-F **hexadezimale
Schreibweise; infix notation** = mathematical
syntax where operators are embedded
inside operands (such as C - D or X + Y)
Infixschreibweise; octal notation = number
system using base 8 and the digits 0-7 **oktale
Schreibweise; postfix notation** =
mathematical operations written in a
logical way, so that the operator appears
after the operands, this removes the need
for brackets **Postfixschreibweise;** *normal
notation: (x-y) + z, but using postfix
notation: xy - z +;* **prefix notation** =
mathematical operations written in a
logical way, so that the operator appears
before the operands, this removes the need
for brackets **Präfixschreibweise**

notched *see* EDGE NOTCHED CARD

notepad *noun* **screen notepad** = part of
the screen used to store information even
when the terminal is switched off
Bildschirmnotizblock

notice board *noun* (i) board fixed to a
wall where notices can be pinned up; (ii)
type of bulletin board on which messages to
all users can be left **(i) Schwarzes Brett; (ii)
Anschlagetafel**

n-plus-one address instruction
noun instruction made up of a number (n)
of addresses and one other address that is
the location of the next instruction **n-plus-
Eins-Adreßbefehl**

npn transistor *noun* bipolar transistor design using p-type semiconductor for the base and n-type for the collector and emitter **bipolarer Transistortyp;** *see also* TRANSISTOR, BIPOLAR

NRZ = NON RETURN TO ZERO

ns *abbreviation* nanosecond **ns**

NTSC = NATIONAL TELEVISION STANDARDS COMMITTEE official body that defines television and video formats *or* standards used mainly in the USA and in Japan **NTSC;** *see also* VIDEO STANDARDS

COMMENT: the NTSC standard is based on 525 horizontal lines and 60 frames per seconds

QUOTE the system has a composite video output port that conforms to the NTSC video specification
Byte

n-type material *or* **N-type material** *or* **n-type semiconductor** *noun* semiconductor that has been doped with a substance that provides extra electrons in the material, giving it an overall negative charge compared to the intrinsic semiconductor **Material vom N-Typ; N-Halbleiter;** *see also* NPN TRANSISTOR

null *noun* nothing **nichts; null character =** character which means nothing (usually code 0) **Nullzeichen; null instruction =** program instruction that does nothing **leere Anweisung; null list =** list which contains nothing **Leerliste; null modem =** emulator circuit that allows two pieces of equipment that normally require modems to communicate, to be connected together over a short distance **Nullmodem;** *this cable is configured as a null modem, which will allow me to connect these 2 computers together easily;* **null set =** set that only contains zeros **Nullsatz; null string =** string that contains no characters **Zeichenfolge der Länge Null**

QUOTE you have to connect the two RS232 ports together using a crossed cable, or null modem
PC Business World

number
1 *noun*
(a) representation of a quantity **Zahl; number cruncher =** dedicated processor used for high-speed calculations **Zahlenfresser', Supercomputer; number**

crunching = performing high-speed calculations **Zahlenfressen';** *a very powerful processor is needed for graphics applications which require extensive number crunching capabilities;* **number range =** set of allowable values **Zahlenbereich**
(b) written figure **Nummer;** *each piece of hardware has a production number; please note the reference number of your order;* **box number =** reference number used when asking for mail to be sent to a post office *or* to a newspaper, in reply to advertisements **Postfachnummer; check number =** number produced from data for parity *or* error detection **Prüfnummer**
2 *verb*
(a) to put a figure on a document **numerieren;** *the pages of the manual are numbered 1 to 395*
(b) to assign digits to a list of items in an ordered manner **durchnumerieren**

◊ **numeral** *noun* character *or* symbol which represents a number **Ziffer, Numeral; Arabic numerals =** figures written 1, 2, 3, 4, etc. **arabische Ziffern; Roman numerals =** figures written I, II, III, IV, etc. **römische Ziffern**

◊ **numeric** *adjective* (i) referring to numbers; (ii) (field, etc.) which contains only numbers **(i) & (ii) numerisch; numeric array =** array containing numbers **numerische Matrix; numeric character =** letter used in some notations to represent numbers (for example in hex the letters A-F are numeric characters) **numerisches Zeichen; numeric keypad =** set of ten keys with figures, included in most computer keyboards as a separate group, used for entering large amounts of data in numeric form **numerischer 10er-Block; numeric operand =** operand that only uses numerals **numerischer Operand; numeric pad =** numeric keypad **numerische Tastatur, numerischer 10er-Block; numeric punch =** punched hole in rows 0-9 of a punched card **numerische Lochung**

◊ **numerical** *adjective* referring to numbers **numerisch; numerical analysis =** study of ways of solving mathematical problems **numerische Analyse; numerical control (NC)** *or* **computer numerical control (CNC)** = machine operated automatically by computer *or* circuits controlled by stored data **NC (Computer, die zur numerische Steuerung von Werkzeugmaschinen dienen)**

nybble *or* **nibble** *noun (informal)* half the length of a standard byte **Vier-Bit-Byte** NOTE: a nybble is normally 4 bits, but can vary according to different micros

Oo

OA = OFFICE AUTOMATION

object *noun*
(a) variable used in an expert system within a reasoning operation **Objektvariable**
(b) data in a statement which is to be operated on by the operator **Objekt**; *see also* ARGUMENT, OPERAND; **object** *or* **object-orientated architecture** = structure where all files, outputs, etc., in a system are represented as objects **objektorientierter Aufbau**; **object code** = binary code which directly operates a central processing unit (a program code after it has been translated, compiled or assembled into machine code) **Objektcode, Maschinensprache**; **object computer** = computer system for which a program has been written and compiled **Programmablaufanlage**; **object deck** = punched cards that contain a program **Objektprogrammkartensatz**; **object language** = the language of a program after it has been translated **Maschinensprache**; *compare with* SOURCE LANGUAGE; **object program** = computer program in object code form, produced by a compiler *or* assembler **Zielprogramm**

◊ **objective** *noun*
(a) something which someone tries to do **Absicht, Ziel**
(b) optical lens nearest the object viewed **Objektiv**

obtain *verb* to get *or* to receive **erhalten**; *to obtain data from a storage device; a clear signal is obtained after filtering*

OCCAM computer programming language, used in large multiprocessor *or* multi-user systems **OCCAM (Programmiersprache)**

COMMENT: this is the development language for transputer systems

occur *verb* to happen *or* to take place **geschehen**; *data loss can occur because of power supply variations*

OCP = ORDER CODE PROCESSOR *(in a multiprocessor system)* a processor which decides and performs the arithmetic and logical operations according to the program code **OCP (Anweisungscodeprozessor)**

OCR
(a) = OPTICAL CHARACTER READER device which scans printed *or* written characters, recognizes them, and converts them into machine-readable form for processing in a computer **(maschineller) optischer Leser**
(b) = OPTICAL CHARACTER RECOGNITION process that allows printed *or* written characters to be recognized optically and converted into machine-readable code that can be input into a computer, using an optical character reader **(maschinelle) optische Zeichenerkennung**; **OCR font** = character design that can be easily read using an OCR reader **OCR-Zeichensatz**

COMMENT: there are two OCR fonts in common use: OCR-A, which is easy for scanners to read, and OCR-B, which is easier for people to read than the OCR-A font

octal (notation) *noun* number notation using base 8, with digits 0 to 7 **Oktalsystem**; **octal digit** = digit (0 to 7) used in the octal system **Oktalziffer**; **octal scale** = power of eight associated with each digit position in a number **Oktalskala**

COMMENT: in octal, the digits used are 0 to 7; so decimal 9 is octal 11

octave *noun* series of 8 musical notes, each a semitone higher than the previous one **Oktave**

octet *noun* a group of eight bits treated as one unit; word made up of eight bits **Oktett**; *see also* BYTE

odd *adjective* (number, such as 5 or 7) which cannot be divided by two **ungerade**; **odd-even check** = method of checking that transmitted binary data has not been corrupted **Paritätsprüfung**; **odd parity (check)** = error checking system in which any series of bits transmitted must have an odd number of binary ones **Prüfung auf ungerade Parität**; (NOTE: opposite is **even**)

OEM = ORIGINAL EQUIPMENT MANUFACTURER company which produces equipment using basic parts made by other manufacturers, and customizes the product for a particular application **Hersteller von Fremdfabrikaten**

off-cut *noun* scrap paper that is left when a sheet is trimmed to size **Beschnitt**

off hook *adverb* state of a telephone unit indicating to incoming calls that it is being used **Hörer abgehoben**
NOTE: opposite is **on hook**

office *noun* room *or* building where a company works *or* where business is done **Büro; office automation (OA)** = use of machines and computers to carry out normal office tasks **Textverarbeitung, Büroautomatisierung; office computer** = small computer (sometimes with a hard disk and several terminals) suitable for office use **Bürocomputer; office copier** = copying machine in an office **Bürokopierer; office equipment** = desks, typewriters, and other furniture and machines needed in an office **Büroausstattung; office of the future** = design of an office that is completely coordinated by a computer **Büro der Zukunft;** *see also* PAPERLESS OFFICE

off-line *adverb & adjective* (i) (processor *or* printer *or* terminal) that is not connected to a network *or* central computer (usually temporarily); (ii) (peripheral) connected to a network, but not available for use **(i) systemunabhängig, offline; (ii) offline;** *before changing the paper in the printer, switch it off-line;* **off-line printing** = printout operation that is not supervised by a computer **Offline-Drucken; off-line processing** processing by devices not under the control of a central computer **Offline-Verarbeitung**
NOTE: opposite is **on-line**

offprint *noun* section of a journal reprinted separately **Sonderdruck**

off screen *adverb* TV action that is taking place off the screen, outside the viewer's field of vision **außerhalb des Bildschirms**

offset
1 *noun*
a) offset lithography = printing process used for printing books, where the ink sticks to dry areas on the film and is transferred to rubber rollers from which it is printed on to the paper **Offsetlithographie; offset printing** = printing method that transfers the ink image to the paper via a second roller **Offsetdruck**
b) quantity added to a number *or* address to give a final number **Ausgleichszahl; offset value** *or* **offset word** = value to be added to a base address to provide a final indexed address **Relativzeigerwert**

ohm *noun* unit of measurement of electrical resistance **Ohm;** *this resistance has a value of 100 ohms;* **kilo-ohm** = one thousand ohms **Kiloohm** ⇨ APPENDIX
◇ **Ohm's Law** *noun* definition of one ohm as: one volt drop across a resistance of one

ohm when one amp of current is flowing **Ohmsches Gesetz**

O.K. used as a prompt in place of 'ready' in some systems **bereit-Signal**

omega wrap *noun* system of threading video tape around a video head **Omega-Wicklung**

COMMENT: the tape passes over most of the circular head and is held in place by two small rollers

omission factor *noun* number of relevant documents that were missed in a search **Vermißtenfaktor**

omnidirectional *adjective* device that can pick up signals from all directions **mit Kugel(charakteristik);** *omnidirectional aerial; omnidirectional microphone*

OMR
(a) = OPTICAL MARK READER device that can recognize marks *or* lines on a special form (such as on an order form *or* a reply to a questionnaire) and that inputs them into a computer **optischer Markierungsleser**
(b) = OPTICAL MARK RECOGNITION process that allows certain marks *or* lines on special forms (such as on an order form *or* a reply to a questionnaire) to be recognized by an optical mark reader, and input into a computer **optische Markierungserkennung**

on-board *adjective* (feature *or* circuit) which is contained on a motherboard *or* main PCB **auf der Platine**

QUOTE the electronic page is converted to a printer-readable video image by the on-board raster image processor
QUOTE the key intelligence features of these laser printers are emulation modes and on-board memory
Byte

on chip *noun* circuit constructed on a chip **Schaltung auf dem Chip**
◇ **on-chip** *adjective* (circuit) constructed on a chip **auf dem Chip;** *the processor uses on-chip bootstrap software to allow programs to be loaded rapidly*

one address computer *noun* computer structure whose machine code only uses one address at a time **Einadreßcomputer; one address instruction** = instruction made up of an operator and one address **Einadreßbefehl**

◊ **one element** *noun* logical function that produces a true output if any input is true **eingliedriges Element**

◊ **one for one** *noun* programming language, usually assembler, that produces one machine code instruction for each instruction *or* command word in the language **One-for-one (Assembliersprache)**

COMMENT: compilers and interpreters are usually used for translating high-level languages which use more than one machine code instruction for each high-level instruction

---

◊ **one-level address** *noun* storage address that directly, without any modification, accesses a location *or* device **direkte Adresse; one-level code** = binary code which directly operates the CPU, using only absolute addresses and values (this is the final form of a program after a compiler *or* assembler pass) **Direktcode; one-level store** = organization of storage in which each different type of storage device is treated as if it were the same **einschichtiger Speicher; one-level subroutine** = subroutine which does not call another subroutine during its execution **einstufiges Unterprogramm**

◊ **one's complement** *noun* inverse of a binary number **Einerkomplement**; *the one's complement of 10011 is 01100; see also* COMPLEMENT; TWO'S COMPLEMENT

◊ **one-pass assembler** *noun* assembler program that translates the source code in one action **Assemblierer mit einem Durchlauf;** *this new one-pass assembler is very quick in operation*

◊ **one-plus-one address** *noun* address format that provides the location of one register and the location of the next instruction **Eins-plus-Eins-Adresse**

◊ **one-time pad** *noun* coding system that uses a unique cipher key each time it is used **hochspezielles Codiersystem**

COMMENT: two identical pieces of paper with an encrypted alphabet printed on each one are used, one by the sender, one by the receiver; this is one of the most secure cipher systems

---

◊ **one to zero ratio** *noun* ratio between the amplitude of a binary one and zero output **Eins-zu-Null-Verhältnis**

on hook *adverb* state of a telephone unit indicating that it is not busy and can receive incoming calls **Hörer aufgelegt**

onion skin architecture *noun* design of a computer system in layers, according to function *or* priority **Zwiebelschalenarchitektur;** *the onion skin architecture of this computer is made up of a* kernel at the centre, an operating system, *a* low-level language and then the user's program

◊ **onion skin language** *noun* database manipulation language that can process hierarchical data structures **Zwiebelschalensprache**

on-line *adverb & adjective* (terminal *or* device) connected to and under the control of a central processor **im Dialogbetrieb online;** *the terminal is on-line to the mainframe;* **on-line database** = interactive search, retrieve and update of database records, with a terminal that is on-line **Online-Datenbank; on-line information retrieval** = system that allows an operator of an on-line terminal to access, search and display data held in a main computer **Online-Informationswiedergewinnung; on-line processing** = processing by device connected to and under the control of the central computer (the user remains in contact with the central computer while processing) **Online-Verarbeitung; on-line storage** = data storage equipment that is directly controlled by a computer **rechnerabhängiger Speicher; on-line system** = computer system that allows users who are on-line to transmit and receive information **Online-System, Dialogbetrieb; on-line transaction processing** = interactive processing in which a user enters commands and data on a terminal which is linked to a central computer, with results being displayed on the screen **Online-Transaktionsverarbeitung**

on-screen *adjective* (information) that is displayed on a computer screen rather than printed out **am Bildschirm**

◊ **on-site** *adjective* at the place where something is **am Einsatzort;** *the new model has an on-site upgrade facility*

on the fly *adverb* (to examine and modify data) during a program run without stopping the run **fliegend**

O/P *or* **o/p** = OUTPUT

opacity *noun* measure of how opaque an optical lens is **Lichtundurchlässigkeit, Opazität**
NOTE: opposite is **transmittance**

op amp = OPERATIONAL AMPLIFIER term for a versatile electronic component that provides amplification, integration, addition, subtraction and many other functions on signals depending on external components added **Operationsverstärker**

COMMENT: usually in the form of an 8 pin IC package with 2 inputs (inverting and non-inverting), output, power supply and other control functions

op code = OPERATION CODE part of the machine code instruction that defines the action to be performed **Operationscode, Operationsschlüssel**

QUOTE the subroutine at 3300 is used to find the op code corresponding to the byte whose hex value is in B

Computing Today

opaque *adjective* will not allow light to pass through it **undurchsichtig, opak;** *the screen is opaque - you cannot see through it;* **opaque projector** = device that is able to project an image of an opaque object **Epidiaskop**

open
adjective
(a) command to prepare a file before reading *or* writing actions can occur **eröffnet;** *you cannot access the data unless the file is open*
(b) not closed **offen; open access** = system where many workstations are available for anyone to use **offener Zugang; open code** = extra instructions required in a program that mainly uses macroinstructions **Open Code; open-ended program** = program designed to allow future expansion and easy modification **Programm mit offenem Ende; open loop** = control system whose input is free of feedback **offener Regelkreis;** *see also* FEEDBACK; **open reel** = magnetic tape on a reel that is not enclosed in a cartridge *or* cassette **offene Spule; open routine** = routine which can be inserted into a larger routine *or* program without using a call instruction **Open-Routine, Dateieröffnungsroutine; open subroutine** = code for a subroutine which is copied into memory whenever a call instruction is found, rather than executing a jump to the subroutine's address **offenes Interprogramm; open system** = system which is constructed in such a way that different operating systems can work together **offenes System; Open System Interconnection (OSI)** = standardized ISO network which is constructed in layered form, with each layer having a specific task, allowing different systems to communicate if they conform to the standard **Kommunikation offener Systeme (OSI);** *see also* ISO/OSI LAYERS, INTERNATIONAL
verb
(a) to take the cover off *or* to make a door

open **öffnen;** *open the disk drive door; open the top of the computer by lifting here*
(b) to prepare a file before accessing *or* editing *or* carrying out other transactions on stored records **eröffnen;** *you cannot access the data unless the file has been opened*

operand *noun* data (in a computer instruction) which is to be operated on by the operator **Rechengröße, Operand;** *in the instruction ADD 74, the operator ADD will add the operand 74 to the accumulator;* **immediate operand** = within an immediate addressing operation, the operand is fetched at the same time as the instruction **Direktoperand; literal operand** = actual number *or* address to be used rather than a label *or* its location **aktueller Operand; numeric operand** = operand that only contains numerals **numerischer Operand; operand field** = space allocated for an operand in a program instruction **Operandenfeld;** *see also* ARGUMENT, MACHINE-CODE INSTRUCTION

operate *verb* to work *or* to make a machine work **arbeiten, bedienen;** *do you know how to operate the telephone switchboard?;* **disk operating system (DOS)** = section of the operating system software that controls disk and file management **Betriebssystem; operating code (op code)** = part of the machine code instruction that defines the action to be performed **Operationsschlüssel; operating console** = terminal in an interactive system which sends and receives information **Bedienerkonsole; operating instructions** = commands and instructions used to operate a computer **Bedienungsanweisung; operating system (OS)** = software that controls the basic, low-level hardware operations, and file management, without the user having to operate it (the operating system is usually supplied with the computer as part of the bundled software or in ROM) **Betriebssystem; operating time** = total time required to carry out a task **Betriebszeit**

◊ **operation** *noun* working (of a machine) **Operation, Arbeitsgang; arithmetic operation** = mathematical function carried out on data **Rechenoperation; binary operation** = (i) operation on two operands; (ii) operation on an operand in binary form **(i) duale Operation; (ii) Binäroperation; block operation** = process carried out on a block of data **Blockoperation; Boolean operation** = logical operation on a number of operands, conforming to Boolean algebra rules **Boolesche Operation; complete operation** =

operation that retrieves the necessary operands from memory, performs the operation and returns the results and operands to memory, then reads the next instruction to be processed **vollständige Operation; dyadic Boolean operation** = logical operation that produces an output from two inputs **dyadische Boolesche Operation; no-address operation** = instruction which does not require an address within it **adreßfreie Operation; no-operation instruction (no-op)** = programming instruction which does nothing **Befehl: „keine Operation"; operation code (op code)** = part of a machine-code instruction that defines the action to be performed **Operationsschlüssel; operation cycle** = section of the machine cycle during which the instruction is executed **Operationszyklus;** *see also* FETCH-EXECUTE CYCLE, MACHINE CYCLE; **operation decoder** = hardware that converts a machine-code instruction (in binary form) into actions **Operationsumwandler; operation field** = part of an assembly language statement that contains the mnemonic or symbol for the op code **Operationsfeld; operation priority** = the sequence order in which the operations within a statement are carried out **Arbeitsgangpriorität; operation register** = register that contains the op code during its execution **Operationsregister; operation time** = period of time that an operation requires for its operation cycle **Operationszeit; operation trial** = series of tests to check programs and data preparation **Betriebsuntersuchung; operations manual** *see* INSTRUCTION MANUAL

◊ **operational** *adjective* which is working or which refers to the way a machine works **funktionsfähig; operational information** = information about the normal operations of a system **Betriebsinformation**

◊ **operational amplifier (op amp)** *noun* versatile electronic component that provides amplification, integration, addition, subtraction and many other functions on signals depending on external components added **Operationsverstärker**

COMMENT: usually in the form of an 8 pin IC package with 2 inputs (inverting and non-inverting) output, power supply and other control functions

operator *noun*
(a) person who makes a machine or process work **Bediener, Operator;** *the operator was sitting at his console;* **computer operator** = person who operates a computer **Computeroperator; operator's console** = input and output devices used by an operator to control a computer (usually consisting of a keyboard and VDU **Bedienerkonsole; operator precedence** = order in which a number of mathematica operations will be carried out **Operationenrangfolge; operator procedure** = set of actions that an operator has to carry out to work a machine or process **Vorgehensweise des Operatoren**
(b) character or symbol or word that define a function or operation **Operator;** *x is the multiplication operator;* **arithmetic operator** = symbol which indicates an arithmetic function (such as + for addition, x for multiplication) **Rechenzeichen**

op register *noun* register that contains the operating code for the instruction that is being executed **Operationsschlüsselregister**

optic fibres = OPTICAL FIBRES; **fibre optics** = using optical fibres (fine strands of glass or plastic protected by a surrounding material) for the transmission of light signals which can carry data **Faseroptik**

optical *adjective* referring to or making use of light **optisch;** *an optical reader uses a light beam to scan characters or patterns or lines;* **optical bar reader** or **bar code reader** o **optical wand** = optical device that reads data from a bar code **Balkencodeleser optical character reader (OCR)** = device which scans printed or written characters recognizes them, and converts them into machine-readable code for processing in a computer **optischer Zeichenleser; optical character recognition (OCR)** = process that allows printed or written characters to be recognized optically and converted into machine-readable code that can be input into a computer, using an optical character reader **optische Zeichenerkennung; optical communication system** = communication system using fibre optics **optisches Nachrichtenübertragungssystem; optical link** = connection between two devices to allow the transmission of data using light signals (either line-of-sight or optic fibre **optische Datenverbindung; optical disk** = disk that contains binary data in the form of small holes in the surface which are read with a laser beam **Laserplatte, VLP-Bildplatte** (NOTE: also called WORM (write once, read man' times, for computers) which can be programmee once, or compact disk (CD) and video disk which are programmed at manufacture) **optical fibre** = fine strand of glass or plastic protected by a surrounding material, that is used for the convenient transmission of light signals **Glasfaser; optical font** or **OCR font** = character design that can be easily read using an OCR reader **OCR-Zeichensatz; optical mark reader (OMR)** = device that can recognize marks or lines on a special forms (such as on an order form or a reply to a questionnaire) and convert them into a form a computer can process **optischer Markierungsleser; optical mark recognition (OMR)** = process that allows certain marks or lines on special forms (such as on an order form or a reply to a questionnaire) to be recognized by an optical mark reader, and input into a computer **optische Markierungserkennung; optical memory** = optical disks **Laserplatte, VLP-Bildplatte; optical scanner** = equipment that converts an image into electrical signals which can be stored in and displayed on a computer **optischer Abtaster, Scanner; optical storage** = data storage using mediums such as optical disk, etc. **optischer Speicher; optical transmission** = use of fibre optic cables, laser beams and other light sources to carry data, in the form of pulses of light **optische Übertragung; optical wand** = OPTICAL BAR READER

optimization noun making something work as efficiently as possible **Optimierung**

◇ **optimize** verb to make something work as efficiently as possible **optimieren; optimized code** = program that has been passed through an optimizer to remove any inefficient code or statements **Optimierungscode**

◇ **optimizer** noun program which adapts another program to run more efficiently **Optimierer**

optimum noun & adjective best possible **Optimum, optimal; optimum code** or **minimum access code** or **minimum delay code** = coding system that provides the fastest access and retrieval time for stored data items **Bestzeitcode**

option noun action which can be chosen **Auswahlmöglichkeit, Option;** there are usually four options along the top of the screen; the options available are described in the main menu

◇ **optional** adjective which can be chosen **wahlfrei;** the system comes with optional 3.5 or 5.25 disk drives

optoelectrical adjective which converts light to electrical signals or electrical signals into light **optoelektrisch**

◇ **optoelectronic** adjective (microelectronic component) that has optoelectrical properties **optoelektronisch**

◇ **optoelectronics** noun electronic components that can generate or detect light, such as phototransistors, light-emitting diodes **Optoelektronik**

OR function noun logical function that produces a true output if any input is true **ODER-Funktion; OR gate** = electronic implementation of the OR function **ODER-Gatter**

COMMENT: the result of the OR function will be 1 if either or both inputs is 1; if both inputs are 0, then the result is 0

orbit
1 noun path in space that a satellite follows around the earth **Umlaufbahn;** the satellite's orbit is 100km from the earth's surface; **elliptical orbit** = path of a satellite around the earth that is in the shape of an ellipse **elliptische Umlaufbahn; geostationary orbit** = satellite which moves at the same velocity as the earth, so remains above the same area of the earth's surface, and appears stationary when viewed from earth **geostationäre Umlaufbahn; polar orbit** = satellite flight path that goes over the earth's poles **polare Umlaufbahn**
2 verb to follow a path in space around the earth **umkreisen;** the weather satellite orbits the earth every four hours

order noun
(a) instruction **Anweisung, Befehl; order code** = operation code **Befehlscode; order code processor (OCP)** = (in a multiprocessor system) a processor which decodes and performs the arithmetic and logical operations according to the program code **Befehlscodeprozessor (OCP)**
(b) sorted according to a key **geordnet;** in alphabetical order; **ordered list** = list of data items which has been sorted into an order **geordnete Liste**
2 verb to direct or instruct **anweisen**

organize verb to arrange something so that it works efficiently **organisieren**
◇ **organization** noun
(a) way of arranging something so that it works efficiently **Organisation;** the chairman handles the organization of the sales force; the organization of the group is too centralized to be efficient; the organization of the head office into departments; **organization and methods** = examining how an office works, and suggesting how it can be made more efficient **Organisation und Durchführung; organization chart** = list of

people working in various departments, showing how a company *or* office is organized **Organigramm, Stellenbesetzungsplan**
(b) group of people which is arranged for efficient work **Organisation; a government organization** = official body, run by the government **eine staatliche Organisation; an employers' organization** = group of employers with similar interests **ein Arbeitgeberverband**
NOTE: no plural for (a)

◊ **organizational** *adjective* referring to the way in which something is organized **organisatorisch**

orientated *adjective* aimed towards **orientiert; problem-orientated language (POL)** = high-level programming language that allows caertain problems to be expressed easily **problemorientierte Programmiersprache**

◊ **orientation** *noun* direction *or* position of an object **Orientierung**

origin *noun*
(a) position on a display screen to which all coordinates are referenced, usually the top left hand corner of the screen **Anfang**
(b) location in memory at which the first instruction of a program is stored **Programmbeginn;** *see also* INDEXED

original
1 *adjective* used *or* made first **original;** *this is the original artwork for the advertisement*
2 *noun*
(a) first document, from which a copy is made **Original(vorlage);** *did you keep the original of the letter? the original document is too faint to photocopy well*
(b) (first) master data disk *or* photographic film *or* sound recording used, from which a copy can be made **Original**

◊ **original equipment manufacturer (OEM)** *noun* company which produces equipment using basic parts made by other manufacturers, and customizes the product for a particular application **Fremdhersteller;** *one OEM supplies the disk drive, another the monitor; he started in business as a manufacturer of PCs for the OEM market*

◊ **originate** *verb* to start *or* come from **stammen von;** *the data originated from the new computer*

◊ **origination** *noun* work involved in creating something **Herstellung, Anfertigung;** *the origination of the artwork will take several weeks*

orphan *noun* **orphan (line)** = last line of a section which falls at the top of a page and seems to be not connected with what goes before it **Schusterjunge;** *see also* WIDOW

ortho *or* **orthochromatic film** *noun* photographic black and white film that is not sensitive to red light **orthochromatischer Film**

orthogonal *adjective* (instruction) made up of independent parameters *or* parts **orthogonal**

OS = OPERATING SYSTEM software that controls the basic, low-level hardware operations, and file management, without the user having to operate it (the operating system is usually supplied with the computer as part of the bundled software in ROM) **Betriebssystem**

oscillator *noun* electronic circuit that produces a pulse *or* signal at a particular frequency **Oszillator**

oscilloscope *noun* electronic test equipment that displays on a CRT the size and shape of an electrical signal **Oszilloskop**

OSI = OPEN SYSTEM INTERCONNECTION *see also* ISO/OSI

out of band signalling *noun* transmission of signals outside the frequency limits of a normal voice channel **Außerbandsignalisierung**

◊ **out of phase** *adverb* situation where a waveform is delayed in comparison to another **phasenverschoben**

◊ **out of range** *adjective* (number *or* quantity) that is outside the limits of a system **außer Reichweite**

outage *noun* time during which a system is not operational **Ausfall**

outdent *verb* to move part of a line of text into the margin **ausrücken**
NOTE: opposite is **indent**

outlet *noun* connection *or* point in a circuit *or* network where a signal *or* data can be accessed **Ausgang**

outline *noun* the main features of something **Gliederung; outline flowchart** = flowchart of the main features, steps and decisions in a program *or* system **Gliederungsdiagramm**

output (o/p *or* **O/P)**
1 *noun*
(a) information *or* data that is transferred from a CPU *or* the main memory to another device such as a monitor *or* printer *or* secondary storage device **Ausgabe; computer output** = data *or* information produced after processing by a computer **Computerausgabe;** NOTE: opposite is **input**
(b) action of transferring the information *or* data from store to a user **Ausgabe; output area** *or* **block** = section of memory that contains data to be transferred to an output device **Ausgabebereich; output bound** *or* **limited** = processor that cannot function at normal speed because of a slower peripheral **ausgabegebunden; output buffer register** = temporary store for data that is waiting to be output **Ausgabe-Pufferregister; output device** = device (such as a monitor *or* printer) which allows information to be displayed **Ausgabegerät; output file** = set of records that have been completely processed according to various parameters **Ausgabedatei; output formatter** = (i) software used to format data *or* programs and output them) so that they are compatible with another sort of storage medium; (ii) part of a word processor program that formats text according to embedded commands **(i) & (ii) Ausgabeformatierer; output mode** = computer mode in which data is moved from internal storage *or* the CPU to external devices **Ausgabemodus; output register** = register that stores data to be output until the receiver is ready *or* the channel is free **Ausgaberegister; output stream** = communications channel carrying data output to a peripheral **Ausgabestrom; output port** = circuit and connector to allow a computer to output *or* transmit data to other devices *or* machines **Ausgabeanschlußpunkt;** *connect the printer to the printer output port;* **input/output (I/O)** = (i) receiving *or* transmitting of data between a computer and its peripherals and other points outside the system; (ii) all data received *or* transmitted by a computer **(i) & (ii) Ein-/Ausgabe;** *see also* INPUT
2 *verb* to transfer data from a computer to a monitor *or* printer **ausgeben;** *finished documents can be output to the laser printer* NOTE: **outputting - output**

OV = OVERFLOW

overflow *or* **OV** *noun*
(a) mathematical result that is greater than the limits of the computer's number

storage system **Überlauf; overflow bit** *or* **flag** *or* **indicator** = single bit in a word that is set to one (1) if a mathematical overflow has occurred **Überlaufbit; Überlaufanzeiger; overflow check** = examining an overflow flag to see if an overflow has occurred **Überlaufprüfung**
(b) situation in a network when the number of transmissions is greater than the line capacity and are transferred by another route **Kapazitätsüberschreitung**

overhead *noun*
(a) extra code that has to be stored to organize the program **Zusatzcode;** *the line numbers in a BASIC program are an overhead;* **overhead bit** = single bit used for error detection in a transmission **Zusatzbit; polling overhead** = amount of time spent by a computer calling and checking each terminal in a network **Sendeaufrufzeit**
(b) overhead projector = projector which projects an image of transparent artwork onto a screen **Tageslichtprojektor**

overheat *verb* to become too hot **überhitzen;** *the system may overheat if the room is not air-conditioned*

overink *verb* to put on too much ink when printing **zu stark einfärben;** *two signatures were spoilt by overinking*

overlap
1 *noun* two things where one covers part of the other *or* two sections of data that are placed on top of each other **überlappen; multipass overlap** = system of producing higher quality print from a dot matrix printer by repeating the line of characters but shifted slightly, so making the dots less noticeable (used to produce NLQ print) **Mehrfachüberschreibung**
2 *verb* to cover part of an item with another **überdecken**

overlay *noun*
(a) keyboard overlay = strip of paper that is placed above keys on a keyboard to indicate their function **Tastaturschablone**
(b) small section of a program that is larger than the main memory capacity of a computer, and is loaded into memory when required, so that main memory only contains the sections it requires to run a program **Überlagerung; form overlay** = heading *or* other matter held in store and printed out at the same time as the text **Formmaske, Formschablone; overlay manager** = system software that manages (during run-time) the loading and execution of sections of a program when they are

required **Overlay-Systemprogramm; overlay region** = area of main memory that can be used by the overlay manager to store the current section of the program being run **Überlagerungsbereich; overlay segments** = short sections of a long program that can be loaded into memory when required and executed **Überlagerungssegmente**

COMMENT: contrast with virtual memory management

◇ **overlay   network** *noun* two communications networks that have some common   interconnections **Überlagerungsnetz**

◇ **overlaying** *noun* putting an overlay into action **Überlagern**

overload *verb* to demand more than the device is capable of **überlasten;** *the computer is overloaded with that amount of processing;* **channel   overload   =** transmission of data at a rate greater than the channel capacity **Kanalüberlastung**

overmodulation *noun* situation where an amplitude modulated carrier signal is reduced to zero by excessive input signal **Übermodulation**

overpunching *noun* altering data on a paper tape by punching additional holes **Überlochung**

overscan *noun* period when the television picture beam is outside the screen limits **Nutzflächenüberschreitung**

overstrike *verb* to print on top of an existing character to produce a new one **überschreiben**

overtones *noun see* HARMONICS

overrun *verb* data that was missed by a receiver because it was not synchronized with the transmitter *or* because it operates at a slower speed than the transmitter and has no buffer **überlaufen**

overwrite *verb* to write data to a location (memory *or* tape *or* disk) and, in doing so, to destroy any data already contained in that location **überschreiben;** *the latest data input has overwritten the old information*

over-voltage protection *noun* safety device that prevents a power supply voltage exceeding certain specified limits **Überspannungsschutz**

oxide *noun* chemical compound of oxygen **Oxid; ferric oxide** = iron oxide used as a coating for magnetic disks and tapes **Eisenoxid; metal oxide semiconductors (MOS)** = production and design method for a certain family of integrated circuits using patterns of metal conductors and oxide deposited onto a semiconductor **Metalloxid-Halbleiterelemente;** *see also* MOSFET, CMOS

Pp

p = PICO-

PA = PUBLIC ADDRESS

p-channel *noun* section of semiconductor that is p-type **p-Kanal; p-channel MOS** = MOS transistor that conducts via a small region of p-type semiconductor **p-Kanal-MOS;** *see also* MOS, P-TYPE SEMICONDUCTOR

P-code *noun* intermediate code produced by a compiler that is ready for an interpreter to process, usually from PASCAL programs **p-Code**

PABX = PRIVATE AUTOMATIC BRANCH EXCHANGE

pack
1 *noun* number of punched cards or magnetic disks **Stapel; disk pack** = number of magnetic disks on a single spindle, either fixed or removable (from the drive) **Plattenstapel**
2 *verb*
(a) to put things into a container for selling *or* sending **packen;** *to pack goods into cartons; the diskettes are packed in plastic wrappers; the computer is packed in expanded polystyrene before being shipped*
(b) to store a quantity of data in a reduced form, often by representing several characters of data with one stored character **verdichten; packed decimal** = way of storing decimal digits in a small space by using only four bits for each digit **gepackte Dezimalzahl; packed format** = two binary coded decimal digits stored within one computer word *or* byte (usually achieved by removing the check *or* parity bit) **gepacktes   Format,   verdichtete Datenanordnung**
NOTE: opposite is **padding**

package *noun*
a) group of different items joined together in one deal **Komplex, Paket; package deal** = agreement where several different items are agreed at the same time **Pauschalangebot;** *we are offering a package deal which includes the whole office computer system, staff training and hardware maintenance*
b) applications package = set of computer programs and manuals that cover all aspects of a particular task (such as payroll, stock control, invoicing, etc.) **Anwendungssoftwarepaket; packaged** *or* **canned software** *or* **software package** = computer programs and manuals designed for a special purpose **Software-Paket;** *the computer is sold with accounting and word-processing packages*

◊ **packaging** *noun*
a) material used to protect goods which are being packed; attractive material used to wrap goods for display **Verpackung;** *airtight packaging; packaging material*
b) creating books for publishers **Packaging;**
NOTE: no plural

◊ **packager** *noun* person who creates a book for a publisher **Packager**

packet *noun* group of bits of uniform size which can be transmitted as a group, using a packet switched network **Datenpaket; packet assembler/disassembler (PAD)** = dedicated computer that converts serial data from asynchronous terminals to a form that can be transmitted along a packet switched (synchronous) network **Konzentrator, der Datenpakete zusammenstellt bzw. auseinandernimmt;** *the remote terminal is connected to a PAD device through which it accesses the host computer;* **packet switched data service** *or* **packet switched network (PSN)** = service which transmits data in packets of a set length **paketweiser Datenservice; Netz im Datenpaketbetrieb; packet switching** = method of sending messages *or* data in uniform-sized packets, and processing and routing packets rather than bit streams **Datenpaketvermittlung**

packing *noun*
a) action of putting goods into boxes and wrapping them for shipping **(Ver)packen;** *what is the cost of the packing? packing is included in the price*
b) putting large amounts of data into a small area of storage **Verdichtung; packing density** = amount of bits of data which can be stored in a unit area of a disk *or* tape **Zeichendichte; packing routine** = program which packs data into a small storage area **Verdichtungsprogramm**

(c) material used to protect goods **Verpackung(smaterial);** *packed in airtight packing;* **non-returnable packing** = packing which is to be thrown away when it has been used and not returned to the sender **Einwegverpackung**
NOTE: no plural

PAD = PACKET ASSEMBLER/DISASSEMBLER

pad
1 *noun* number of keys arranged together **Block; cursor pad** = group of cursor control keys **Cursortasten; keypad** = group of special keys used for certain applications **Tastatur; hex keypad** = set of sixteen keys, with all the figures (0-9, A-F) needed to enter hexadecimal numbers **hexadezimale Tastatur; numerical keypad** = set of ten keys with figures (0-9), included on most computer keyboards as a separate group, used for entering large amounts of data in numeric form **numerische Tastatur**
2 *verb* to fill out **stopfen, auffüllen; pad character** = extra character added to a string *or* packet *or* file until it is a required size **Auffüllzeichen**

◊ **padding** *noun* material (characters or digits) added to fill out a string *or* packet until it is the right length **Auffüllen**
NOTE: opposite is **packing**

paddle *noun* computer peripheral consisting of a knob *or* device which is turned to move a cursor *or* pointer on the screen **Konsole; game paddle** = device held in the hand to move a cursor *or* graphics in a computer game **Spielkonsole, Steuerknüppel**

page *noun*
(a) sheet of paper **Blatt**
(b) (i) one side of a printed sheet of paper in a book *or* newspaper *or* magazine *or* catalogue, etc.; (ii) text held on a computer monitor screen (which if printed out will fill a page of paper *or* which fills the screen) **(i) & (ii) Seite; page break** = (i) point at which a page ends and a new page starts (in continuous text); (ii) marker used when word-processing to show where a new page should start **(i) Seitenwechsel; (ii) Umbruch; page description language (PDL)** = software that controls a printer's actions to print a page of text to a particular format according to a user's instructions **Seitenbeschreibungssprache; page display** = showing on the screen a page of text as it will appear when printed out **Seitenanzeige; page length** = length of a page (in word-processing) **Seitenlänge; pages per minute (ppm)** = measurement of the speed of a

printer as the number of pages of text printed every minute **Seiten pro Minute; page printer** = printer which composes one page of text and then prints it rapidly **Blattschreiber**

(c) section of main store, which contains data *or* programs **Speicherseite; multiple base page** = multi-user system in which each user and the operating system have one page of main memory, which can then call up other pages within main memory **Gemeinschaftscomputersystem; page addressing** = main memory which has been split into blocks, with a unique address allocated to each block of memory which can then be called up and accessed individually, when required **Seitenadressierung(sspeicher); page boundary** = point where one page ends and the next starts **Seitengrenze; page protection** = software controls to ensure that pages are not overwritten by accident or copied into a reserved section of memory **Seitenschutz; page table** = list of all the pages and their locations within main memory, used by the operating system when accessing a page **Seitentabelle**

(d) one section of a main program which can be loaded into main memory when required **Seite**

2 *verb*

(a) to page someone = to try to find someone in a building (using a PA *or* radio pager) **jemanden ausrufen lassen;** *see also* RADIO PAGING

(b) to make up a text into pages **Seitenumbruch machen**

(c) to divide computer backing store into sections to allow long programs to be executed in a small main memory **umlagern**

◇ **pager** *noun* small device carried by someone, which allows him to be called from a central office, by using a radio signal **Piepser, Mobilfunk**

◇ **pagination** *noun* putting a text into pages; arrangement of pages in a book **Seitenumbruch, Paginierung**

◇ **paging** *noun* virtual memory technique that splits main memory into small blocks (pages) which are allocated an address and which can be called up when required **Aufteilung in Speicherseiten; paging algorithm** = formula by which the memory management allocates memory to pages, also covering the transfer from backing storage to main memory in the most efficient way **Algorithmus zur Aufteilung von Speicherseiten**

COMMENT: a virtual memory management system stores data as pages in memory to provide an apparently larger capacity main memory by storing unused pages in backing store, copying them into main memory only when required

paired register *noun* two basic word size registers used together as one large word size register (often used for storing address words) **gepaartes Register;** *the 8-bit CPU uses a paired register to provide a 16-bit address register*

PAL = PHASE ALTERNATING LINE standard that defines television and video formats, using 625 horizontal scan lines and 50 frames per second **PAL-System**

COMMENT: mainly used in Western Europe, Australia, some parts of the Middle East and Africa

palette *noun* range of colours which can be used (on a printer *or* computer display) **Palette**

QUOTE the colour palette option offer sixteen colours from a range of over four thousand
Electronics & Wireless World

PAM = PULSE AMPLITUDE MODULATION pulse modulation in which the height of the pulse varies with the input signal **PAM (Pulsamplitudenmodulation)** ⟶ APPENDIX

panel *noun* flat section of a casing with control knobs *or* sockets **Konsole;** *the socket is on the back panel;* **control panel** = panel with indicators and switches which allows an operator to monitor and control the actions of a computer *or* peripheral **Bedienerkonsole; front panel** = main computer system control switches and status indicators **vordere Verkleidungsplatte**

paper *noun* thin material used for making books *or* newspapers *or* stationery items **Papier;** *the book is printed on 80gsm paper; glossy paper is used for printing half-tones; bad quality paper gives too much show through;* **paper feed** = mechanism which pulls paper through a printer **Papiertransport;** *(US)* **paper slew** = PAPER THROW; **paper tape** = long strip of paper on which data can be recorded, usually in the form of punched holes **(ungelochter) Lochstreifen; paper tape feed** = method by which paper tape is passed into a machine **Lochstreifenzuführung; paper tape punch** = device which punches holes in paper tape to carry data **Lochstreifenstanzer; paper tape reader** = device which accepts punched aper tape and converts the punched information stored on it into signals which computer can process **Lochstreifenleser**; **aper throw** = rapid vertical movement of aper in a printer **schneller Papiervorschub**; **aper tray** = container used to hold paper to e fed into a printer **Papierbehälter; paper eight** = weight of paper used in printing usually measured in gsm or grams per quare metre) **Papiergewicht**

◊ **paperback** noun book which has a paper over **Paperback, Taschenbuch**; we are ublishing the book as a hardback and as a aperback

◊ **paperbound** adjective (book) bound vith a paper cover (as opposed to ardbound) **broschiert**

◊ **paper-fed** adjective (device) which is ctivated when paper is introduced into it urch **Papiereinschub aktiviert(es Gerät)** a aper-fed scanner

◊ **paperless** adjective without using paper hne Papier; **paperless office** = electronic ffice or office which uses computers and ther electronic devices for office tasks and voids the use of paper **computerisiertes üro**

arallel adjective (i) (computer system) in vhich two or more processors operate imultaneously on one or more items of lata; (ii) two or more bits of a word ransmitted over separate lines at the same ime **(i) simultan; (ii) parallel; parallel access** = lata transfer between two devices with a umber of bits (usually one byte wide) eing sent simultaneously **Parallelzugriff; arallel adder** = number of adders joined ogether in parallel, allowing several digits o be added at once **Paralleladdierer; parallel omputer** = computer with one or more ogic or arithmetic units, allowing parallel rocessing **Simultanrechner; parallel onnection** = transmission link that handles arallel data **Parallelschaltung;** their average ransmission rate is 60,000 bps through arallel connection; **parallel data ransmission** = transmission of bits of data imultaneously along a number of data nes **parallele Datenübertragung; parallel nput/output (PIO)** = data input or output rom a computer in a parallel form **parallele in-/Ausgabe; parallel input/output chip** = edicated integrated circuit that performs ll handshaking, buffering, etc., needed vhen transferring parallel data to and from CPU **paralleler Ein-/Ausgabe-Chip; parallel nput/parallel output (PIPO)** = device that an accept and transmit parallel data **arallele Eingabe/parallele Ausgabe; parallel nput/serial output (PISO)** = device that an accept parallel data and transmit serial lata **parallele Eingabe/serielle Ausgabe;**

parallel interface or **port** = circuit and connector that allows parallel data to be received or transmitted **paralleler Schnittstellenanschluß; parallel operation** = number of processes carried out simultaneously on a number of inputs **Parallelbetrieb; parallel port** see PARALLEL INTERFACE; **parallel priority system** = number of peripherals connected in parallel to one bus, if they require attention, they send their address and an interrupt signal, which is then processed by the computer according to device priority **paralleles Rangsystem; parallel printer** = printer that accepts character data in parallel form **Paralleldrucker; parallel processing** = computer operating on several tasks simultaneously **Simultanverarbeitung; parallel running** = running an old and a new computer system together to allow the new system to be checked before it becomes the only system used **Parallellauf; parallel search storage** = data retrieval from storage that uses part of the data other than an address to locate the data **Parallelabfragespeicher; parallel transfer** = data transfer between two devices with a number of bits (usually one byte wide) being sent simultaneously **Parallelübertragung; parallel transmission** = number of data lines carrying all the bits of a data word simultaneously **Parallelübergabe**

NOTE: opposite is **serial transmission**

parameter noun information which defines the limits or actions of something, such as a variable or routine or program **Parameter;** the X parameter defines the number of characters displayed across a screen; the size of the array is set with this parameter; **parameter-driven software** = software whose main functions can be modified and tailored to a user's needs by a number of variables **parametergesteuerte Software; parameter testing** = program to examine the parameters and set up the system or program accordingly **Parameterprüfung; parameter word** = data word that contains information defining the limits or actions of a routine or program **Parameterwort; physical parameter** = description of the size, weight, voltage or power of a system **physikalischer Parameter**

◊ **parametric (subroutine)** noun subroutine that uses parameters to define its limits or actions **parametrisches Unterprogramm**

◊ **parameterization** noun action of setting parameters for software **Parametrisierung**

parity noun being equal **Parität, Gleichheit; block parity** = parity check on a block of data **Blockparitätsprüfung; column parity** =

parity check on every punched card *or* tape column **Spaltenparitätsprüfung; even parity (check)** = error checking system in which any series of bits transmitted must have an even number of binary ones **Prüfen auf gerade Parität; odd parity (check)** = error checking system in which any series of bits transmitted must have an odd number of binary ones **Prüfung auf ungerade Parität; parity bit** = extra bit added to a data word as a parity checking device **Prüfbit; parity check** = method of checking (odd *or* even parity check) for errors and that transmitted binary data has not been corrupted **Paritätsprüfung; parity flag** = indicator that shows if data has passed a parity check or if data has odd or even parity **Paritätsanzeiger; parity interrupt** = interrupt signal from an error checking routine that indicates that received data has failed a parity check and is corrupt **Paritätsprüfungsabbruch; parity track** = one track on magnetic *or* paper tape that carries the parity bit **Prüfspur**

parsing *noun* operation to break down high-level language code into its element parts when translating into machine code **Parsing (Syntaxanalyse)**

part *noun*
(a) section of something **Teil; part page display** = display of only a section of a page, and not the whole page **Teilseitenanzeige**
(b) spare part = small piece of a machine which is needed to replace a piece which is broken *or* missing **Ersatzteil;** *the printer won't work - we need to get a spare part*
(c) one of a series **Teil; two part stationery** = stationery (invoices, receipts, etc.) with a top sheet and a copy sheet **Vordruck in zweifacher Ausführung; four-part invoice** = invoice with four sheets (a top sheet and three copies) **Rechnung in vierfacher Ausführung;** *see also* MULTI-PART

partial carry *noun* temporary storage of all carries generated by parallel adders rather than a direct transfer **Teilübertrag**
◊ **partial RAM** *noun* RAM chip in which only a certain area of the chip functions correctly, usually in newly released chips (partial RAM's can be used by employing more than one to make up the capacity of one fully functional chip) **Teil-RAM**

particle *noun* very small piece of matter **Teilchen**

partition
1 *noun* section of computer memory set aside as foreground *or* background memory

Arbeitsspeicherbereich; partitioned file = one file made up of several smaller sequentia files, each part can be accessed individually by the control program **untergliederte Date**
2 *verb* to divide a large file *or* block into several smaller units which can be accessee and handled more easily **aufteilen**

party line *or* **shared line** *noun* one telephone line shared by a number o subscribers **Gemeinschaftsleitung**

PASCAL high-level structure programming language used both or micros and for teaching programming **PASCAL (Programmiersprache)**

pass
1 *noun* (i) the execution of a loop, once; (ii single operation **(i) Durchlauf; (ii) Arbeitsgang single-pass assembler** = assembler program that translates the source code in one action **Assemblierer mit einem Durchlauf sorting pass** = single run through a list o items to put them into order **Sortierlauf**
2 *verb* action of moving the whole length o a magnetic tape over the read/write head **ablaufen**

password *noun* word *or* series o characters which identifies a user so that he can access a system **Kennwort, Paßwort;** *the user has to key in the password before he car access the database*

patch *noun* (temporary) correction made to a program; small correction made to software by the user, on the instructions o the software publisher **Korrektur**
◊ **patchboard** *noun* board with a number of sockets connected to devices, into which plugs can be inserted to connect othe devices *or* functions **Schalttafel**
◊ **patchcord** *noun* cord with a plug at each end, which is used to link sockets in a patchboard **steckbare Verbindungsleitung**

path *noun* possible route or sequence o events *or* instructions within the execution of a program **Pfad**

pattern *noun* series of regular lines o shapes which are repeated again and again **Struktur, Muster; pattern recognition** = algorithms *or* program functions that can identify a shape from a video camera, etc **Strukturerkennung**

◇ **patterned** *adjective* with patterns **strukturiert**

pay TV *noun* form of cable television, where the viewer pays for programs *or* channels watched **Fernsehen mit Extragebühr**
◇ **paycable** *noun (US)* form of cable television where the viewer pays an extra fee for extra channels **Kabelfernsehen mit Extragebühr**

PAX = PRIVATE AUTOMATIC EXCHANGE

PBX = PRIVATE BRANCH EXCHANGE

PC
(a) = PERSONAL COMPUTER low cost microcomputer intended mainly for home and light business use **PC (Personalcomputer); PC compatible** = computer that is compatible with another common make (usually the IBM PC) **PC-kompatibel**
(b) = PRINTED CIRCUIT (BOARD)
(c) = PROGRAM COUNTER

QUOTE in the UK, the company is known not for PCs but for PC printers
Which PC?

PCB = PRINTED CIRCUIT BOARD

PCM
(a) = PULSE CODE MODULATION pulse stream that carries data about a signal in binary form **PCM (Pulscodemodulation)** ⇨ APPENDIX *see also* PULSE AMPLITUDE, PULSE DURATION, PULSE POSITION
(b) = PLUG-COMPATIBLE MANUFACTURER company that produces add-on boards which are compatible with another manufacturer's computer **steckerkompatibler Anbieter**

PCU = PERIPHERAL CONTROL UNIT device that converts input and output signals and instructions to a form that a peripheral device will understand **periphere Steuereinheit**

PDL = PAGE DESCRIPTION LANGUAGE, PROGRAM DESIGN LANGUAGE

PDM = PULSE DURATION MODULATION pulse modulation system where the pulse width varies with the magnitude of the input signal **PDM (Pulsdauermodulation)** ⇨ APPENDIX

PDN = PUBLIC DATA NETWORK

peak
1 *noun* highest point; maximum value of a variable *or* signal **Spitze;** *keep the peak power below 60 watts or the amplifier will overheat; the marker on the thermometer shows the peak temperature for today;* **peak and trough** = maximum and minimum points of a waveform **Wellenberg und Wellental; peak period** = time of the day when most power is being used **Hauptbelastungszeit; time of peak demand** = time when something is being used most **Spitzenbedarfszeit; peak output** = highest output **Höchstleistung**
2 *verb* to reach the highest point **den Höchststand erreichen;** *the power peaked at 1,200 volts; sales peaked in January*

peek *noun* BASIC computer instruction that allows the user to read the contents of a memory location **PEEK-Anweisung (Blick in den Speicher);** *you need the instruction PEEK 1452 here to examine the contents of memory location 1452; compare* POKE

peg *verb* sudden swing of an analog meter to its maximum reading due to a large signal **ausschlagen;** *after he turned up the input level, the signal level meter was pegging on its maximum stop*

pel *see* PIXEL

pen *see* LIGHT PEN; **pen recorder** = peripheral which moves a pen over paper according to an input (a value or coordinate) **Tintenschreiber**

per *preposition*
(a) as per = according to **gemäß; as per sample** = as shown in the sample **gemäß dem Muster; as per specification** = according to the details given in the specification **wie angegeben**
(b) at a rate of; **per hour** *or* **per day** *or* **per week** *or* **per year** = for each hour *or* day *or* week *or* year **pro Stunde; pro Tag; pro Woche; pro Jahr**
(c) out of **von, pro;** *the rate of imperfect items is about twenty-five per thousand; the error rate has fallen to twelve per hundred*

◇ **per cent** *noun, adjective & adverb* out of each hundred *or* for each hundred **Prozent; prozentual; 10 per cent** = ten in every hundred **10 Prozent, 10 %;** *what is the increase per cent? fifty per cent of nothing is still nothing*

◇ **percentage** *noun* amount shown as part of one hundred **Prozentsatz; percentage increase** = increase calculated on the basis of a rate for one hundred **prozentualer Anstieg; percentage point** = one per cent **Prozentpunkt**

◊ **percentile** *noun* one of a series of ninety-nine figures below which a certain percentage of the total falls **Perzentil**

perfect

1 *adjective* completely correct *or* with no mistakes **perfekt, vollkommen;** *we check each batch to make sure it is perfect; she did a perfect typing test*
2 *verb* to make something which is completely correct **vervollkommnen;** *he perfected the process for making high grade steel*

◊ **perfect binding** *noun* method of binding paperback books, where the pages are trimmed at the spine, and glued to the cover **Klebebindung**

◊ **perfect bound** *adjective* (book, usually a paperback) bound without sewing, where the pages are trimmed at the spine and glued to the cover with strong glue **(Buch) mit Klebebindung**

◊ **perfectly** *adverb* with no mistakes *or* correctly **fehlerfrei, perfekt;** *she typed the letter perfectly*

◊ **perfector** *noun* printing machine that prints on both sides of a sheet of paper **Perfektor, Schön- und Widerdruckmaschine**

perforations *noun* line of very small holes in a sheet of paper *or* continuous stationery, to help when tearing **Perforationen**

◊ **perforated tape** *noun* paper tape *or* long strip of tape on which data can be recorded in the form of punched holes **Lochstreifen**

◊ **perforator** *noun* machine that punches holes in a paper tape **Locher**

perform *verb* to do well *or* badly **abschneiden, aus-, durchführen**

◊ **performance** *noun* way in which someone *or* something acts **Leistung(sniveau); as a measure of the system's performance** = as a way of judging if the system is working well **als Maßstab für das Leistungsniveau des Systems;** *in benchmarking, the performances of several systems or devices are tested against a standard benchmark;* **high performance** = high quality *or* high specification equipment **Hochleistung**

perigee *noun* point during the orbit of a satellite when it is closest to the earth **Perigäum, erdnächster Punkt**

period *noun*
(a) length of time **Zeitraum;** *for a period of time or for a period of months or for a six-year period; sales over a period of three months*

(b) *(US)* full stop *or* printing sign used at the end of a piece of text **Punkt**

◊ **periodic** *or* **periodical**
1 *adjective*
(a) from time to time **periodisch;** *a periodic review of the company's performance*
(b) **periodic** = (signal *or* event) that occurs regularly **regelmäßig;** *the clock signal is periodic*
2 *noun* **periodical** = magazine which comes out regularly **Zeitschrift, Periodika**

◊ **periodically** *adverb* from time to time **regelmäßig**

peripheral

1 *adjective* which is not essential *or* which is attached to something else **peripher, Zusatz-, zusatz-**
2 *noun* (i) item of hardware (such as terminals, printers, monitors, etc.) which is attached to a main computer system; (ii) any device that allows communication between a system and itself, but is not directly operated by the system **(i) Anschlußgerät; (ii) Peripheriegerät;** *peripherals such as disk drives or printers allow data transfer and are controlled by a system, but contain independent circuits for their operation* ; **fast peripheral** = peripheral that communicates with the computer at very high speeds, limited only by the speed of the electronic circuits **schnelles Peripheriegerät; slow peripheral** = peripheral such as a card reader, where mechanical movement determines speed **langsames Peripheriegerät; peripheral control unit (PCU)** = device that converts the input/output signals and instructions from a computer to a form and protocol which the peripheral will understand **periphere Steuereinheit; peripheral driver** = program *or* routine used to interface, manage and control an input/output device *or* peripheral **Treiberroutine; peripheral equipment** = (i) external devices that are used with a computer, such as a printer *or* scanner; (ii) (communications) equipment external to a central processor that provides extra features **(i) Anschlußgeräte; (ii) Peripheriegeräte; peripheral interface adapter (PIA)** = circuit that allows a computer to communicate with a peripheral by providing serial and parallel ports and other handshaking signals required to interface the peripheral **peripherer Schnittstellenadapter; peripheral limited** = CPU that cannot execute instructions at normal speed because of a slow peripheral **durch Peripheriegeräte in der Geschwindigkeit eingeschränkt; peripheral memory** = storage capacity available in a peripheral **peripherer Speicher; peripheral processing units (PPU)** = device used for

input, output or storage which is controlled by the CPU **Peripherietechnik; peripheral software driver** = short section of computer program that allows a user to access and control a peripheral easily **Gerätesteuerprogramm;** *same as* DEVICE DRIVER; **peripheral transfer** = movement of data between a CPU and peripheral **periphere Übertragung; peripheral unit** = (i) item of hardware (such as terminal, printer, monitor, etc.) which is attached to a main computer system; (ii) any device that allows communication between a system and itself, but is not operated only by the system **(i) Anschlußgerät; (ii) Peripheriegerät**

permanent *adjective* which will last for a very long time *or* for ever **dauerhaft, ständig; permanent dynamic memory** = storage medium which retains data even when power is removed **dynamischer Dauerspeicher; permanent error** = error in a system which cannot be mended **ständiger Fehler; permanent file** = data file that is stored in a backing storage device such as a disk drive **permanente Datei; permanent memory** = computer memory that retains data even when power is removed **Dauerspeicher;** *see also* NON-VOLATILE MEMORY

◊ **permanently** *adverb* done in a way which will last for a long time **dauerhaft, ständig;** *the production number is permanently engraved on the back of the computer casing*

permeability *noun* measure of the ratio of the magnetic flux in a material to the size of the generating field **magnetische Durchlässigkeit, Permeabilität**

permutation *noun* number of different ways in which something can be arranged **Permutation;** *the cipher system is very secure since there are so many possible permutations for the key*

persistence *noun* length of time that a CRT will continue to display an image after the picture beam has stopped tracing it on the screen **Nachleuchtdauer;** *slow scan rate monitors need long persistence phosphor to prevent the image flickering*

person *noun* human being **Person; person-to-person call** = telephone call placed through an operator, where the caller will only speak to a certain person **Gespräch mit namentlicher Voranmeldung**

◊ **personal** *adjective* referring to one person **persönlich; personal computer (PC)** = low-cost microcomputer intended mainly for home and light business use **Personalcomputer (PC); personal identification device (PID)** = device (such as a card) connected *or* inserted into a system to identify *or* provide authorization for a user **Kennkarte; personal identification number (PIN)** = unique sequence of digits that identifies a user to provide authorization to access a system (often used on automatic cash dispensers *or* with a PID *or* password to enter a system) **persönliche Identifikationsnummer**

◊ **personalize** *verb* to customize *or* to adapt a product specially for a certain user **individuell anfertigen**

PERT = PROGRAM EVALUATION AND REVIEW TECHNIQUE definition of tasks *or* jobs and the time each requires, arranged in order to achieve a goal **Netzplantechnik zur Terminüberwachung von komplexen Projekten**

petal printer = DAISY WHEEL PRINTER

pF = PICOFARAD unit of measurement of capacitance equal to one million millionth of a farad **Picofarad**

phantom ROM *noun* duplicate area of read-only memory that is accessed by a special code **Phantom-ROM**

phase
1 *noun*
(a) one part of a larger process **Phase; run phase** = period of time when a program is run **Ausführungsphase; compile phase** = period of time during which a program is compiled **Kompilierphase**
(b) delay between two similar waveforms **Phase; in phase** = two signals that have no time delay between them **phasengleich; out of phase** = one signal that has a time delay when compared to another **phasenverschoben; phase alternating line (PAL)** = method of providing colour information in a television signal, used in standard receivers in certain countries **PAL-System; phase angle** = measurement of the phase difference between two signals, where a phase angle of 0 degrees represents signals that are in phase **Phasenwinkel; phase equalizer** = circuit that introduces delays into signal paths to produce a phase angle of zero degrees **Phasenentzerrer; phase modulation** = modulation method in which the phase of a carrier signal varies with the input **Phasenmodulation**
2 *verb* **to phase in** *or* **to phase out** = to introduce something gradually *or* to reduce

something gradually **allmählich einführen; auslaufen lassen; phased change-over** = new device that is gradually introduced as the old one is used less and less **schrittweise Umstellung**

COMMENT: when two signals are in phase there is no time delay between them, when one is delayed they are said to be out of phase by a certain phase angle

phon _noun_ measure of sound equal to a one thousand Hertz signal at one decibel **Phon**

phone
1 _noun_ telephone _or_ machine used for speaking to someone over a long distance **Telefon;** _we had a new phone system installed last week;_ **house phone** _or_ **internal phone** = telephone for calling from one office to another **Haustelefon; by phone** = using the telephone **per Telefon; to be on the phone** = to be speaking to someone on the telephone **telefonieren;** _she has been on the phone all morning; he spoke to the manager on the phone;_ **card phone** = public telephone that accepts a phonecard instead of money **Kartentelefon; phone book** = book which lists names of people and companies with their addresses and phone numbers **Telefonbuch;** _look up his address in the phone book;_ **phone call** = speaking to someone on the phone **Telefonanruf; to make a phone call** = to speak to someone on the telephone **telefonieren; to answer the phone** _or_ **to take a phone call** = to reply to a call on the phone **das Telefon abnehmen; phonecard** = special plastic card which allows the user to use a card phone for a certain length of time **Telefonkarte; phone number** = set of figures for a particular telephone **Telefonnummer;** _he keeps a list of phone numbers in a little black book; the phone number is on the company notepaper; can you give me your phone number?_
2 _verb_ **to phone someone** = to call someone by telephone **jemanden anrufen;** _don't phone me, I'll phone you; his secretary phoned to say he would be late; he phoned the order through to the warehouse;_ **to phone for something** = to make a phone call to ask for something **wegen etwas anrufen; etwas telefonisch bestellen;** _he phoned for a taxi;_ **to phone about something** = to make a phone call to speak about something **wegen etwas anrufen;** _he phoned about the order for computer stationery_

◊ **phone back** _verb_ to reply by phone **zurückrufen;** _the chairman is in a meeting, can you phone back in about half an hour? Mr Smith called while you were out and asked if you would phone him back_

phoneme _noun_ single item of sound used in speech **Phonem;** _the phoneme "oo" is present in the words too and zoo_

◊ **phonetic** _adjective_ referring to phonetics **phonetisch;** _the pronunciation is indicated in phonetic script_

◊ **phonetics** _noun_ written symbols that are used to represent the correct pronunciation of a word **Phonetik**

phosphor _noun_ substance that produces light when excited by some form of energy, usually an electron beam, used for the coating inside a cathode ray tube **Phosphor;** _see_ TELEVISION; **phosphor coating** = thin layer of phosphor on the inside of a CRT screen **Phosphorbeschichtung; phosphor dots** = individual dots of red, green and blue phosphor on a colour CRT screen **Phosphorpunkte; phosphor efficiency** = measure of the amount of light produced in ratio to the energy received from an electron beam **Phosphorwirksamkeit; long persistence phosphor** = television screen coating that retains the displayed image for a period of time longer than the refresh rate, so reducing flicker effects **langleuchtender Phosphor**

COMMENT: a thin layer of phosphor is arranged in a pattern of small dots on the inside of a television screen which produces an image when scanned by the picture beam

phosphorescence _noun_ ability of a material to produce light when excited by some form of energy **Postlumineszenz, Phosphoreszenz**

photo
1 _prefix_ referring to light **Photo-, Foto-**
2 _abbreviation of_ PHOTOGRAPH

◊ **photocell** _noun_ electronic device that produces _or_ varies an electrical signal according to the amount of light shining on it **Photozelle**

◊ **photocomposition** _noun_ composition of typeset text direct onto film **Fotosatz**

◊ **photoconductivity** _noun_ material which varies its resistance according to the amount of light striking it **Photoleitfähigkeit**

◊ **photoconductor** _noun_ photocell whose resistance varies with the amount of light shining on it **Photoleiter**

◊ **photocopier** _noun_ machine which makes a copy of a document by photographing and printing it **Fotokopierer**

◊ **photocopy**
1 _noun_ copy of a document made by

photographing and printing it **Fotokopie;** *make six photocopies of the contract*
2 *verb* to make a copy of a document by photographing and printing it **fotokopieren;** *she photocopied the contract*

◊ **photocopying** *noun* making photocopies **Fotokopieren;** *photocopying costs are rising each year;* **photocopying bureau** = office which photocopies documents for companies which do not possess their own photocopiers **Fotokopierbüro; there is a mass of photocopying to be done** = there are many documents waiting to be photocopied **es gibt eine Menge zu fotokopieren**
NOTE: no plural

◊ **photodigital memory** *noun* computer memory system that uses a LASER to write data onto a piece of film which can then be read many times but not written to again **Laserspeicher;** NOTE: also called WORM (Write Once Read Many times memory)

◊ **photodiode** *noun* electronic component displaying the electrical properties of a diode but whose resistance varies with the amount of light that shines on it **Photodiode;** *see also* AVALANCHE

◊ **photoelectric** *adjective* (material) that generates an electrical signal when light shines on it **photoelektrisch; photoelectric cell** = component which produces *or* varies an electrical signal when a light shines on it **Photozelle;** *the photoelectric cell detects the amount of light passing through the liquid*

◊ **photoelectricity** *noun* production of an electrical signal from a material that has light shining on it **Photoelektrizität**

◊ **photoemission** *noun* material that emits electrons when light strikes it **Photoemission**

photograph *noun* image formed by light striking a light-sensitive surface, usually coated paper **Fotografie;** *colour photograph; black and white photograph; it's a photograph of the author; he took six photographs of the set; we will be using a colour photograph of the author on the back of the jacket*

◊ **photographic** *adjective* referring to photography *or* photographs **fotografisch;** *the copier makes a photographic reproduction of the printed page*

◊ **photographically** *adverb* using photography **fotografisch;** *the text film can be reproduced photographically*

◊ **photography** *noun* method of creating images by exposing light-sensitive paper to light, using a camera **Fotografie**

photogravure *noun* printing method in which the paper is pressed directly onto the etched printing plate **Foto-, Heliogravüre**

◊ **photolithography** *noun* printing using a lithographic printing plate formed photographically **Fotolithographie**

◊ **photomechanical transfer (PMT)** *noun* system for transferring line drawings and text onto film before printing **fotomechanische Übertragung**

◊ **photometry** *noun* study and measurement of light **Photometrie**

◊ **photon** *noun* packet of electromagnetic radiation **Photon**

◊ **photoprint** *noun (in typesetting)* final proof **druckfertige Vorlage**

◊ **photoresist** *noun* chemical *or* material that hardens into an etch resistant material when light is shone on it **Fotoresist, Fotolack;** *to make the PCB, coat the board with photoresist, place the opaque pattern above, expose, then develop and etch, leaving the conducting tracks;* **positive photoresist** = method of forming photographic images where exposed areas of photoresist are removed, used in making PCBs **positives Fotoresistverfahren**

◊ **photosensor** *noun* component *or* circuit that can produce a signal related to the amount of light striking it **Photosensor**

◊ **photostat**
1 *noun* type of photocopy **Fotokopie**
2 *verb* to make a photostat of a document **fotokopieren**

◊ **phototelegraphy** *noun* transmission of images over a telephone line **Bildtelegraphie;** *see also* FACSIMILE TRANSMISSION

◊ **phototext** *noun* characters and text that have been produced by a phototypesetter **Fotosatz**

◊ **phototransistor** *noun* electronic component that can detect light and amplify the generated signal *or* vary a supply according to light intensity **Phototransistor, Photozelle**

phototypesetter *noun* company which specializes in phototypesetting **Fotosetzer**

◊ **phototypesetting** *noun* method of typesetting that creates characters using a computer and exposing a sensitive film in front of a mask containing the required character shape **Fotosatz**

COMMENT: this is the method by which most new publications are typeset, superseding metal type, since it produces a good quality result in a shorter time

photovoltaic *adjective* which produces a voltage across a material due to light shining on it **photovoltaisch**

physical *adjective* solid *or* which can be touched **physisch, wirklich; physical database** = organization and structure of a stored database **physische Datenbank; physical layer** = the ISO/OSI defined network layer that defines rules for bit rate, power and medium for signal transmission **Bitübertragungsschicht;** *see also* LAYER

◊ **physical record** *noun*
(a) maximum unit of data that can be transmitted in a single operation **physischer Satz**
(b) all the information, including control data for one record stored in a computer system **physischer Satz**

PIA = PERIPHERAL INTERFACE ADAPTER circuit that allows a computer to communicate with a peripheral by providing serial and parallel ports and other handshaking signals required to interface the peripheral **peripherer Schnittstellenadapter**

pica *noun*
(a) method of measurement used in printing and typesetting (equal to twelve point type) **Pica**
(b) typeface used on a printer, giving ten characters to the inch **Pica**

pickup *noun* arm and cartridge used to playback music from a record **Tonarm**
◊ **pickup reel** *noun* empty reel used to take the tape as it is played from a full reel **Aufnahmespule**

pico- (p) *prefix* representing one million millionth of a unit **Pico-, pico-; picofarad (pF)** = measure of capacitance equal to one million millionth of a farad **Picofarad; picosecond (ps)** = one million millionth of a second **Picosekunde**

picture
1 *noun* printed *or* drawn image of an object or scene **Bild;** *this picture shows the new design;* **picture beam** = moving electron beam in a TV, that produces an image on the screen by illuminating the phosphor coating and by varying its intensity according to the received signal **Strahlstrom; picture element** *or* **pixel** = smallest single unit *or* point on a display whose colour *or* brightness can be controlled **Bildelement;** *see also* PIXEL; **picture phone** = communications system that allows sound and images of the user to be transmitted and received **Bildtelefon; picture processing** = analysis of information contained in an image, usually by computer *or* electronic methods, providing analysis *or* recognition of objects in the image **Bildverarbeitung; picture transmission** = transmission of images over a telephone line **Bildübertragung;** *see also* FACSIMILE TRANSMISSION
2 *verb* to visualize an object *or* scene **sich vorstellen;** *try to picture the layout before starting to draw it in*

PID = PERSONAL IDENTIFICATION DEVICE device (such as a card) connected *or* inserted into a system to identify or provide authorization for a user **Kennkarte**

piece accent *noun* floating accent **gleitender Akzent**
◊ **piece fractions** *noun* printed fractions contained in one character space **fertige Bruchzifferntypen (mit waagerechtem Bruchstrich)**

pie chart *noun* diagram where ratios are shown as slices of a circle **Kreisdiagramm**

piezoelectric *adjective (of certain crystals)* being able to change their electrical properties when a force is applied *or* to change their physical dimensions when an electrical signal is applied **piezoelektrisch**

piggyback *verb* to connect two integrated circuits in parallel, one top of the other to save space **huckepack verbinden;** *piggyback those two memory chips to boost the memory capacity;* **piggyback entry** = to gain unauthorized access to a computer system by using an authorized user's password *or* terminal **Huckepackzugang**
◊ **piggybacking** *noun* using transmitted messages to carry acknowledgements from a message which has been received earlier **Huckepackübertragung**

PILOT computer programming language that uses a text-based format and is mainly used in computer-aided learning **PILOT (Programmiersprache)**

pilot
1 *noun* used as a test, which if successful will then be expanded into a full operation **Pilotprojekt;** *the company set up a pilot project to see if the proposed manufacturing system was efficient; the pilot factory has been built to test the new production process;* **pilot system** = system constructed to see if it can be manufactured, if it works and if the end-user likes it **Pilotsystem**
2 *verb* to test **testen;** *they are piloting the new system*

PIN = PERSONAL IDENTIFICATION NUMBER unique sequence of digits that identifies the user **persönliche Identifikationsnummer**

COMMENT: the PIN is commonly used in automatic cash machines in banks, along with a card (PID) which allows the user to be identified

pin *noun*
(a) one of several short pieces of wire attached to an integrated circuit package which fits into a hole in a socket that allows the IC to be connected to a circuit board **Kontaktstift**
(b) short piece of metal, part of a plug which fits into a hole in a socket **Kontaktstift**; *use a three-pin plug to connect the printer to the mains*; **three-pin mains plug** = plug with three pins (one neutral, one live and one earthed) **Netzstecker mit drei Kontaktstiften**; **two-pin mains plug** = plug with two pins (one neutral, one live) **Netzstecker mit zwei Kontaktstiften**

◊ **pin cushion distortion** *noun* optical image distortion in which objects are seen with stretched corners due to lens aberration **Nadelkissenverzerrung**

◊ **pinfeed** *noun see* TRACTOR FEED

◊ **pin photodiode** *noun* electronic photodiode that can detect light, made up of layers of P-type, Intrinsic and N-type semiconductor **PIN-Photodiode**

pinchwheel *noun* small rubber wheel in a tape machine that holds the tape in place and prevents flutter **Andruckrad**

PIO = PARALLEL INPUT/OUTPUT *see also* PIPO, PISO

pipeline (computer)
1 *noun* CPU or ALU that is constructed in blocks and executes instructions in steps, each block dealing with one part of the instruction, so speeding up program execution **Leitung**
2 *verb*
(a) to schedule inputs to arrive at the microprocessor when nothing else is happening, so increasing apparent speed **im Pipelinesystem verarbeiten**
(b) to begin processing of a second instruction while still processing the present one to increase speed of execution of a program **im Pipelinesystem verarbeiten**

◊ **pipelining** *noun*
(a) method of scheduling inputs to arrive at the microprocessor when nothing else is happening, so increasing apparent speed **Pipelining-Methode**

(b) beginning the processing of a second instruction while still processing the present one to increase speed of execution of a program **Pipelining**

PIPO = PARALLEL INPUT/PARALLEL OUTPUT

pirate
1 *noun* person who copies a patented invention *or* a copyright work and sells it **Patenträuber, Markenpirat; Hersteller von Raubdrucken**; *the company is trying to take the software pirates to court; a pirate copy of a computer program*
2 *verb* to manufacture copies of an original copyrighted work illegally **unerlaubt nachahmen/nachbauen/nachdrucken**; *a pirated tape or a pirated design; the designs for the new system were pirated in the Far East; he used a cheap pirated disk and found the program had bugs in it*

◊ **piracy** *noun* copying of patented inventions *or* copyright works **Patentraub; Raubdruck, Raubpressung**; NOTE: no plural

COMMENT: the items most frequently pirated are programs on magnetic disks and tapes which are relatively simple to copy

PISO = PARALLEL INPUT/SERIAL OUTPUT

pitch *noun*
(a) measurement of the horizontal spacing of typed characters **Schreibdichte, Zeichen pro Zoll**
(b) actual frequency of a sound **Tonhöhe**; **pitch envelope** = shape that defines how the frequency of a sound will vary with time **Hüllkurve**
(c) satellite *or* antenna movement about the horizontal axis **Nicken**
(d) **sales pitch** = talk by a salesman to persuade someone to buy **Verkaufsgespräch**

pix *noun* picture *or* pictures **Bilder**

◊ **pix lock** *noun* synchronization of a video playback circuit by an external signal **Bildsynchronisation**

◊ **pixel** *or* **picture element** *noun* smallest single unit *or* point of a display whose colour *or* brightness can be controlled **Bildelement**

COMMENT: in high resolution display systems the colour or brightness of a single pixel can be controlled; in low resolution systems a group of pixels are controlled at the same time

PL/1 = PROGRAMMING LANGUAGE/1 high level programming language mainly used in commercial and scientific work on large computers, containing features of ALGOL, COBOL and FORTRAN **PL/1 (Programmiersprache)**

PLA = PROGRAMMABLE LOGIC ARRAY IC that can be permanently programmed to perform logic operations on data **programmierbares logisches Feld**

COMMENT: a PLA consists of a large matrix of paths between input and output pins, with logic gates and a fusible link at each connection point which can be broken or left to conduct when programming to define a function from input to output

place *noun* position of a digit within a number **Platz, Stelle**

plaintext *noun* text *or* information that has not been encrypted *or* coded **Klartext;** *the messages were sent as plaintext by telephone; enter the plaintext message into the cipher machine*

PLAN low-level programming language **PLAN (Programmiersprache)**

plan
1 *noun*
(a) organized way of doing something **Plan**
(b) drawing which shows how something is arranged *or* how something will be built **Plan; floor plan** = drawing of a floor in a building, showing where different departments are **Grundriß; street plan** *or* **town plan** = map of a town showing streets and buildings **Stadtplan**
2 *verb* to organize carefully how something should be done **planen;** NOTE: **planning - planned**

◇ **planchest** *noun* piece of furniture with wide flat drawers, in which large plans *or* artwork can be kept **Graphik-, Planschrank**

◇ **planner** *noun*
(a) software program that allows appointments and important meetings to be recorded and arranged in the most efficient way **Planprogramm**
(b) desk planner *or* **wall planner** = book *or* chart which shows days *or* weeks *or* months

so that the work of an office can be shown by diagrams **Terminplaner**

◇ **planning** *noun* organizing how something should be done **Planung;** *long-term planning or short-term planning* NOTE: no plural

planet *noun* large body in space (such as the earth), moving in orbit round the sun **Planet**

◇ **planetary camera** *noun* microfilm camera in which the film and article being photographed are stationary **(Mikrofilm)schrittkamera**

plant *verb* to store a result in memory for later use **zwischenspeichern**

plasma display *or* **gas plasma display** *noun* display screen using the electroluminescing properties of certain gases to display text **Plasmabildschirm**

COMMENT: this is a modern thin display usually used in small portable computers

QUOTE the disadvantage of using plasma technology is that it really needs mains power to work for any length of time
QUOTE the plasma panel came out of the extended use test well
Micro Decision

plastic bubble keyboard *noun* keyboard whose keys are small bubbles in a plastic sheet over a contact which when pressed completes a circuit **Plastikblasentastatur**

COMMENT: these are very solid and cheap keyboards but are not ideal for rapid typing

plate *noun*
(a) illustration in a book, usually printed separately and on better quality paper than the text **Abbildung, Tafel**
(b) etched *or* patterned printing surface that carries the ink to the paper **Platte, Druckform**
(c) photographic image using a sheet of glass as the backing material **Platte; plate camera** = camera which takes pictures on glass plates **Plattenkamera**

COMMENT: photographic plates are now used mainly in high quality, large-format professional cameras while the most popular backing material is still plastic as in a film

platen *noun*
(a) roller which supports the paper in a printer *or* typewriter **Walze; platen press** =

printing press where the paper passes under a flat printing plate **Tiegeldruckpresse** (b) device that keeps film in a camera in the correct position **Filmandruckplatte**

play back *verb* to read data *or* a signal from a recording medium **abspielen, wiedergeben;** *after you have recorded the music, press this button to play back the tape and hear what it sounds like*
◊ **playback head** *noun* transducer that reads signals recorded on a storage medium and usually converts them to an electrical signal **Hör-/Lesekopf;** *disk playback head; tape playback head*

player missile graphics *see* SPRITES

PLD = PROGRAMMABLE LOGIC DEVICE

plex database *noun* database structure in which data items can be linked together **komplexe Datenbank**
◊ **plex structure** *noun* network structure *or* data structure in which each node is connected to all the others **komplexe Netzwerkstruktur**

PL/M = PROGRAMMING LANGUAGE FOR MICROPROCESSORS high level programming language derived from PL/1 for use on microprocessors **PL/M (Programmiersprache)**

plot
1 *noun* graph *or* map **Zeichnung**
2 *verb* to draw an image (especially a graph) based on information supplied as a series of coordinates **graphisch darstellen; plotting mode** = ability of some word-processors to produce graphs by printing a number of closely spaced characters rather than individual pixels (this results in a broad low-resolution line) **Graphikmodus**
◊ **plotter** *noun* computer peripheral that draws straight lines between two coordinates **Kurvenschreiber, Plotter; plotter driver** = dedicated software that converts simple instructions issued by a user into complex control instructions to direct the plotter **Plottertreiber; plotter pen** = instrument used in a plotter to mark the paper with ink as it moves over the paper **Plotterschreibkopf; digital plotter** = plotter which receives the coordinates to plot to in a digital form **Digitalplotter; drum plotter** = computer output device that consists of a movable pen and a piece of paper wrapped around a drum that rotates, creating patterns and text **Trommelplotter; incremental plotter** = plotter which receives positional data as increments to its current

position rather than separate coordinates **Stufenform-Plotter; printer-plotter** = high-resolution printer that is able to mimic a plotter and produce low-resolution plots **Drucker-Plotter; x-y plotter** *or* **graph plotter** = plotter which plots to coordinates supplied, by moving the pen in two planes while the paper remains stationary **Plotter, Kurvenzeichner**

COMMENT: plotters are used for graph and diagram plotting and can plot curved lines as a number of short straight lines

plug
1 *noun*
(a) connector with protruding pins that is inserted into a socket to provide an electrical connection **Stecker;** *the printer is supplied with a plug;* **adapter plug** = plug which allows devices with different plugs (two-pin, three-pin, etc.) to be fitted into the same socket **Zwischenstecker; plug-compatible** = equipment manufactured to operate with another system when connected to it by a connector *or* cable **steckerkompatibel;** *this new plug-compatible board works much faster than any of its rivals, we can install it by simply plugging it into the expansion port*
(b) to give a plug to a new product = to publicize a new product **für ein neues Produkt die Werbetrommel rühren**
2 *verb*
(a) to plug in = to make an electrical connection by pushing a plug into a socket **einstecken;** *no wonder the computer does nothing, you have not plugged it in at the mains;* **plug-in unit** = small electronic circuit that can be simply plugged into a system to increase its power **Steckeinheit;** NOTE: opposite is **unplug**
(b) to publicize *or* to advertise **Werbung betreiben;** *they ran six commercials plugging holidays in Spain*
◊ **plugboard** *or* **patchboard** *noun* board with a number of sockets connected to devices into which plugs can be inserted to connect various other devices **Schalttafel**

QUOTE it allows room for up to 40K of RAM via plug-in memory cartridges
Which PC?
QUOTE adding memory is simply a matter of plugging a card into an expansion bus connector
Byte

plus *or* **plus sign** *noun* printed *or* written sign (+) showing that figures are added *or* showing a positive value **Pluszeichen**

PMBX = PRIVATE MANUAL BRANCH EXCHANGE small telephone exchange inside a company where all calls coming in or going out have to be placed through the switchboard **private Handvermittlungsanlage**

PMOS = P-channel METAL OXIDE SEMICONDUCTOR metal oxide semiconductor transistor that conducts via a small region of p-type semiconductor **p-Kanal-MOS**

PMR = PRIVATE MOBILE RADIO

PMT = PHOTOMECHANICAL TRANSFER

pn-junction *noun* area where regions of p-type and n-type semiconductor meet, resulting in a diode characteristic **pn-Übergang; diffused pn-junction** = practical result of doping one section of semiconductor as p-type and an adjacent section as n-type, where the doping concentration drops gradually over a short distance between the two areas **diffundierter pn-Übergang; step pn-junction** = ideal junction between p-type and n-type areas in a semiconductor where the doping changes occur suddenly **pn-Stufenübergang**
◇ **pnp transistor** *noun* layout of a bipolar transistor whose collector and emitter are of p-type semiconductor and whose base is n-type semiconductor **pnp-Transistor**

pocket *noun* **pocket calculator** *or* **pocket diary** = calculator *or* diary which can be carried in the pocket **Taschenrechner; Taschenkalender**

point
1 *noun*
(a) place *or* position **Punkt; access point** = point on a circuit board *or* in software, allowing an engineer to check signals *or* data **Zugriffspunkt; breakpoint** = symbol inserted into a program which stops its execution at that point to allow registers, variables and memory locations to be examined (used when debugging a program) **bedingter Programmstop; re-entry point** = point in a program *or* routine where it is re-entered **Wiedereinstiegspunkt; starting point** = place where something starts **Startpunkt**
(b) binary point = dot which indicates the division between the bits for the numbers' whole units and the fractional part of the binary number **Binärstelle; decimal point** = dot (in a decimal number) which indicates the division between a whole unit and its fractional parts (such as 4.25) **Dezimalstelle; percentage point** = 1 per cent **Prozentpunkt**
(c) measurement system used in typesetting (one point is equal to 0.351 mm) **(typographischer) Punkt;** *the text of the book is set in 9 point Times; if we increase the point size to 10, will the page extent increase?* NOTE: usually written **pt** after figures: **10pt Times Bold**
2 *verb* **to point out** = to show **hinweisen**
◇ **pointer** *noun*
(a) variable in a computer program that contains the address to a data item *or* instruction **Hinweisadresse;** *increment the contents of the pointer to the address of the next instruction;* **pointer file** = file of pointers referring to large amounts of stored data **Verweisungsdatei**
(b) graphical symbol used to indicate the position of a cursor on a computer display **Zeiger;** *desktop publishing on a PC is greatly helped by the use of a pointer and mouse*
◇ **point-of-sale (POS)** *noun* the place where goods in a shop are paid for **Kasse; point-of-sale material** = display material (such as posters, dump bins) to advertise a product where it is being sold **Werbematerial an der Kasse; point-of-sale terminal** *or* **POS terminal** = computer terminal at a point-of-sale, used to provide detailed product information and connected to a central computer to give immediate stock control information **Computerkasse; electronic point-of-sale (EPOS)** = system that uses a computer terminal at a point-of-sale site for electronic funds transfer, as well as for product identification and stock control **elektronische Kasse**
◇ **point to point** *noun* communications network where every point is connected to every other point **Punkt zu Punkt**

> COMMENT: this provides rapid reliable transmissions but is very expensive and wasteful in cabling

> QUOTE the arrow keys, the spacebar or the mouse are used for pointing, and the enter key or the left mouse button are to pick
> *PC User*
> QUOTE pointing with the cursor and pressing the joystick button eliminates use of the keyboard entirely
> *Soft*

poke *noun* computer instruction that modifies an entry in a memory by writing a number to an address in memory **POKE-Anweisung (Übertragung eines Byte an eine bestimmte Stelle im aktuellen Arbeitsspeichersegment);** *poke 1423,74 will write the data 74 into location 1423; compare with* PEEK

POL = PROBLEM-ORIENTATED LANGUAGE

polar *adjective* referring to poles **polar; polar coordinates** = system of defining positions as an angle and distance from the origin **Polarkoordinaten;** *compare with* CARTESIAN COORDINATES; **polar diagram** = graphical representation of polar coordinates **Polardiagramm; polar orbit** = satellite flight path that flies over the earth's poles **polare Umlaufbahn; polar signal** = signal that uses positive and negative voltage levels **Doppelstromsignal; unipolar signal** = signal that uses only positive voltage levels **Einfachstrom-Signal**

◊ **polarity** *noun* definition of direction of flow of flux *or* current in an object **Polarität; electrical polarity** = definition of whether an electrical signal is positive *or* negative, indicating if a point is a source or collector of electrical current (positive polarity terminals are usually marked red, negative are black) **elektrische Polarität; magnetic polarity** = method of indicating if a point is a source *or* collector of magnetic flux patterns **magnetische Polarität; polarity test** = check to see which electrical terminal is positive and which negative **Polaritätsprüfung; reverse polarity** = situation where positive and negative terminals have been confused, resulting in the equipment not functioning **umgekehrte Polarität (durch Umpolung)**

◊ **polarized** *adjective*
(a) broadcast signal waveforms are all aligned in one plane **polarisiert; vertically polarized** = signal whose waveforms travel horizontally while alternating vertically **vertikal polarisiert**
(b) polarized plug = plug which has a feature (usually a peg *or* a special shape) so that it can only be inserted into a socket in one way **polarisierter Stecker; polarized edge connector** = edge connector that has a hole or key to prevent it being plugged in the wrong way round **polarisierter Randstecker**

polaroid filter *noun* photographic filter that only allows light in one plane, vertical *or* horizontal, to be transmitted **Polaroidfilter**

COMMENT: often used to remove glare by placing in front of a camera lens or as glasses in front of a person's eyes

Polish notation *see* REVERSE

poll *verb (of computer)* to determine the state of a peripheral in a network **abrufen; polled interrupt** = interrupt signal determined by a polling device **Unterbrechung auf Abruf**

◊ **polling** *noun* system of communication between a controlling computer and a number of networked terminals (the computer checks each terminal in turn to see if it is ready to receive *or* transmit data,

and takes the required action) **Sendeaufruf; polling characters** = special sequence of characters for each terminal to be polled (when a terminal recognises its sequence, it responds) **Sendeabrufzeichen; polling interval** = period of time between two polling operations **Sendeaufrufintervall; polling list** = order in which terminals are to be polled by a computer **Aufrufliste; polling overhead** = amount of time spent by a computer in calling and checking each terminal in a network **Aufrufzeitaufwand**

COMMENT: the polling system differs from other communications systems in that the computer asks the terminals to transmit *or* receive, not the other way round

polynomial code *noun* error detection system that uses a set of mathematical rules applied to the message before it is transmitted and again when it is received to reproduce the original message **Polynomcode**

POP 2 high level programming language used for list processing applications **POP 2 (Programmiersprache)**

pop *verb* (instruction to a computer) to read and remove the last piece of data from a stack **letzten Eintrag lesen und löschen; pop-down menu** *or* **pop-up menu** = menu that can be displayed on the screen at any time by pressing the appropriate key, usually displayed over material already on the screen **Hervorholmenü, Pulldown-Menü; to pop off** *or* **pop on** = to remove *or* add suddenly an image *or* section of image from a frame **wegnehmen; hervorholen;** *this is the last frame of the film so pop on the titles*

◊ **pop filter** *noun* electronic circuit used when recording voices to attenuate signals caused by wind *or* breathing **Pop-Filter;** *every time you say a 'p' you overload the tape recorder, so put this pop filter in to stop it*

QUOTE you can use a mouse to access pop-up menus and a keyboard for word processing
Byte

porch *see* FRONT PORCH

port *noun* socket *or* physical connection allowing data transfer between a computer's internal communications channel and another external device **Anschlußstelle; asynchronous port** = connection to a computer allowing asynchronous data communications **Asynchronanschlußstelle; input port** = circuit *or* connector that allows a computer to receive data from other external devices **Eingabeanschluß; joystick port** = socket and interfacing circuit into which a joystick can be plugged **Joystickanschlußstelle; output port** = circuit *or* connector that allows a computer to output *or* transmit data to another machine *or* device **Ausgabeanschluß; parallel port** = circuit and connector that allows parallel data to be received *or* transmitted **Parallelanschlußstelle; printer port** = output port of a computer with a standard connector to which a printer is connected to receive character data (either serial *or* parallel) **Druckeranschluß; serial port** = circuit that converts parallel data in a computer to and from a serial form, allowing serial data access **serielle Anschlußstelle; port selector** = switch that allows the user to choose which peripheral a computer (via its o/p port) is connected to **Anschlußwahlschalter; port sharing** = device that is placed between one I/O port and a number of peripherals, allowing the computer access to all of them **Gemeinschaftsanschluß**

QUOTE the 40 Mbyte hard disk model is provided with eight terminal ports
Micro Decision

portable

1 *noun* compact self-contained computer that can be carried around and used either with a battery pack *or* mains power supply **tragbarer Computer, Aktentaschencomputer**
2 *adjective* (any hardware *or* software *or* data files) that can be used on a range of different computers **übertragbar, kompatibel; portable software** *or* **portable programs** = programs that can be run on several different computer systems **übertragbare Programme**

◊ **portability** *noun* extent to which software *or* hardware can be used on several systems **Übertragbarkeit**

QUOTE although portability between machines is there in theory, in practice it just isn't that simple
Personal Computer World

POS = POINT-OF-SALE place in a shop where goods are paid for **Kasse; EPOS** = ELECTRONIC POINT-OF-SALE system that uses a computer terminal at a point-of-sale site for electronic fund transfer *or* stock control as well as product pricing, etc. **elektronische Kasse**

position

1 *noun* place where something is **Stelle, Position;** *this is the position of that chip on the PCB*

2 *verb* to place something in a special place **setzen;** *the VDU should not be positioned in front of a window; position this photograph at the top right-hand corner of the page;* **positioning time** = amount of time required to access data stored in a disk drive *or* tape machine, including all mechanical movements of the read head and arm **Einstellzeit**

◊ **positional** *adjective* referring to position; in a certain position **Stellen-, stellen-**

positive *adjective*

(a) meaning "yes" **positiv; positive response** = communication signal that indicates correct reception of a message **positive Antwort; positive terminal** = connection to a power supply source that is at a higher electrical potential than ground and supplies current to a component **positive Klemme**
(b) (image) which shows objects as they are seen **Positiv; positive display** = (screen) where the text and graphics are shown as black on a white background to imitate a printed page **schwarz auf weiß Anzeige; positive presentation** = screen image which is coloured on a white background **farbig auf weiß Anzeige;** *compare* NEGATIVE
(c) electrical voltage greater than zero **positive Spannung; positive logic** = logic system in which a logical one is represented by a positive voltage level, and a logical zero represented by a zero or negative voltage level **positive Logik**

◊ **positive feedback** *noun* part of an output signal that is added into the input of a device **positive Rückkopplung;** *make sure the microphone is not too close to the loudspeaker or positive feedback will occur and you will overload the amplifier*

COMMENT: positive feedback is often accidental, resulting in a stronger output which provides a bigger positive feedback signal which rapidly overloads the system

post

1 *verb* to enter data into a record in a file **eintragen**
2 *prefix* action that occurs after another **nachträglich, Nach-, nach-; post-editing** = editing and modifying text after it has been compiled *or* translated by a machine **nachträgliches Modifizieren von Daten; post-formatted** = (text) arranged at printing time rather than on screen **nachträglich bearbeitet; post mortem** = examination of a computer program *or* piece of hardware after it has failed to try to find out why the failure took place **Post-Mortem-Fehlersuche**

◇ **postbyte** *noun* in a program instruction, the data byte following the op code that defines the register to be used **Postbyte**

◇ **postfix** *noun* word *or* letter written after another **Postfix; postfix notation =** mathematical operations written in a logical way, so that the operator appears after the operands, this removes the need for brackets **Postfixschreibweise;** *normal notation: (x-y) + z, but using postfix notation: xy - z+* NOTE: often referred to as reverse Polish notation

◇ **postprocessor** *noun*
a) microprocessor that handles semi-processed data from another device **Postprozessor**
b) program that processes data from another program, which has already been processed **Postprozessorprogramm**

poster *noun* large printed sheet, used to advertise something **Plakat**

pot = POTENTIOMETER

potential *noun* ability of energy to carry out work (by transformation) **Potential, Spannung; potential difference =** voltage difference between two points in a circuit **Potentialunterschied**

◇ **potentiometer** *noun* mechanical variable resistance component consisting of a spindle which is turned to move a contact across a resistance track to vary the resistance of the potentiometer **Potentiometer;** *see also* VARIABLE RESISTOR ◇ APPENDIX

power *noun*
a) unit of energy in electronics equal to the product of voltage and current, measured in Watts **(Netz)strom, Leistung; automatic power off =** equipment that will switch itself off if it has not been used for a certain time **automatische Stromabschaltung; power dump =** to remove all power from a computer **den Strom abschalten; power failure =** stoppage of the electrical power supply (for a long *or* very short period of time) which will cause electrical equipment to stop working or malfunction, unless they are battery backed **Stromausfall; power loss =** amount of power lost (in transmission *or* due to connection equipment) **Spannungsverlust; "power off" =** switching off *or* disconnecting an electrical device from its power supply **Netz aus; "power on" =** indication that a voltage is being applied to a piece of electrical equipment **Netz ein; power-on reset =** automatic reset of CPU to a known initial state immediately after power is applied (some CPUs will not automatically start with clear registers, etc., but might contain garbage) **Netz Ein-Grundstellung; power pack =** self-contained box that will provide a voltage and current supply for a circuit **Netzteil; power supply** *or* **power supply unit (PSU) =** electrical circuit that provides certain direct current voltage and current levels from an alternating current source for use in other electrical circuits (a PSU will regulate, smooth and reduce the mains voltage level for use in low power electronic circuits) **Stromversorgungseinheit; power up =** to switch on *or* apply a voltage to a electrical device **den Strom einschalten; uninterruptable power supply (UPS) =** power supply that can continue to provide a regulated supply to equipment even after mains power failure **unterbrechungslose Stromversorgungsanlage (UPS)**
(b) mathematical term describing the number of times a number is to be multiplied by itself **Potenz;** *5 to the power 2 is equal to 25* NOTE: written as small figures in superscript: 10^5 : say: "ten to the power five"

◇ **powered** *adjective* driven by a type of energy **angetrieben**

PPM = PULSE POSITION MODULATION pulse modulation method that varies the time between pulses in relation to the magnitude of an input signal **Pulslagenmodulation;** *see also* PULSE MODULATION

ppm = PAGES PER MINUTE

PR = PUBLIC RELATIONS *a PR firm is handling all our publicity; he is working in PR; the PR people gave away 100,000 leaflets*

pre- *prefix* meaning before **vorher, prä-; pre-agreed =** which has been agreed in advance **vorher abgesprochen; pre-allocation =** execution of a process which does not begin until all memory and peripheral requirements are free for use **Vorab-Zuordnung; pre-fetch =** instructions read and stored in a short temporary queue with a CPU that contains the next few instructions to be processed, increasing the speed of execution **Befehlsvorauslese**

◇ **pre-amplifier** *noun* low noise electronic circuit that increases the magnitude of very small signals, used before a power amplifier **Vorverstärker**

precede *verb* to come before **vorangehen;** *instruction which cancels the instruction which precedes it*

◇ **precedence** *noun* computational rules defining the order in which mathematical operations are calculated (usually multiplications are done first, then divisions, additions, and subtractions last) **Vorrang; operator precedence** = order in which a number of mathematical operations will be carried out **Bedienungsreihenfolge**

precise *adjective* very exact **genau, präzis;** *the atomic clock will give the precise time of starting the process*

◊ **precision** *noun* being very accurate **Genauigkeit, Präzision; double precision** = using two data words to store a number, providing greater precision **doppelte Genauigkeit; multiple precision** = using more than one byte of data for number storage to increase possible precision **Mehrfachgenauigkeit; precision of a number** = number of digits in a number **Zahlengenauigkeit; single precision** = number stored in one word **einfache Genauigkeit;** *compare with* MULTIPLE, DOUBLE

precompiled code *noun* code that is output from a compiler, ready to be executed **vorkompilierter Code**

precondition *verb* to condition data before it is processed **Vorbedingung**

predefined *adjective* which has been defined in advance **vordefiniert**

◊ **predesigned** *adjective* (graphic material) provided to the customer already designed **vorher entworfen;** *a wide selection of predesigned layouts help you automatically format typical business and technical documents*

◊ **predetermined** *adjective* which has already been determined **vorherbestimmt**

predicate *noun* function *or* statement used in rule-based programs such as expert systems **Prädikat**

QUOTE we should stick to systems which we know are formally sound, such as predicate logic
Personal Computer World

pre-edit *verb* to change text before it is run through a machine to make sure it is compatible **vorher bearbeiten**

◊ **pre-emphasise** *verb* to boost certain frequencies of a signal before transmission *or* processing to minimize noise (signals are de-emphasised on reception) **vorverzerren, anheben**

prefix *noun*
(a) code *or* instruction *or* character at the beginning of a message *or* instruction **Vorspann**
(b) word attached to the beginning of another word to give it a special meaning **Präfix, Vorsilbe**

◊ **prefix notation** *noun* mathematical operations written in a logical way, so that the operator appears before the operands; this removes the need for brackets **Präfixschreibweise**

preformatted *adjective* which has been formatted already **vorformatiert;** *a preformatted disk*

premix *noun* combination of a number of signals before they have been processed in any way **Vormischung**

preparation *noun* getting something ready **Erstellung, Vorbereitung, Programmodifikation; data preparation** = conversion of data into a machine-readable form (usually by keyboarding) before data entry **Datenaufbereitung**

preprinted *adjective* already printed *or* printed in advance **vorgedruckt; preprinted form** = paper used for printing databases *or* applications programs that already contain some information printed **vorgedrucktes Formular; preprinted stationery** = computer stationery (such as invoices) which has already been printed with the company's logo and address as well as the blank columns, etc. **Vordruck**

preprocessor *noun*
(a) software that partly processes *or* prepares data before it is compiled *or* translated **Vorkompilierer**
(b) small computer that carries out some initial processing of raw data before passing it to the main computer **Vorprozessor**

◊ **preprocess** *verb* to carry out initial organization and simple processing of data **vorübersetzen**

QUOTE the C preprocessor is in the first stage of converting a written program into machine instructions
QUOTE the preprocessor can be directed to read in another file before completion, perhaps because the same information is needed in each module of the program
Personal Computer World

preproduction *noun* organization of the filming *or* recording of a video *or* compact disk, taking the form of diagrams and scene descriptions **Vorproduktion**

reprogrammed *adjective* (chip) which as been programmed in the factory to erform one function **vorprogrammiert**

rerecord
verb to record something which will be layed back later *or* to record sound effects hat are added to a film at a later date **oraufzeichnen**; *the answerphone plays a rerecorded message*
noun section of text stored in a word-processor system which will be used as the asis for a form letter **Voraufzeichnung**

resentation layer *noun* ISO/OSI tandard network layer that agrees on ormats, codes and requests for start and nd of a connection **Darstellungsschicht**; *see lso* ISO/OSI, LAYER

reset *verb* to set something in advance **oreinstellen**; *the printer was preset with new age parameters*
OTE: **presetting - preset**

ress
noun
a) newspapers and magazines **Presse; the ocal press** = newspapers which are sold in small area of the country **die Lokalpresse; he national press** = newspapers which sell n all parts of the country **die überregionale resse**; *the new car has been advertised in he national press; we plan to give the roduct a lot of press publicity; there was no nention of the new product in the press;* **ress conference** = meeting where reporters rom newspapers are invited to hear news f a new product *or* of a takeover bid, etc. **ressekonferenz; press coverage** = reports bout something in the press **Pressebericht;** *e were very disappointed by the press overage of the new car;* **press cutting** = iece cut out of a newspaper *or* magazine, vhich refers to an item which you find nteresting **Zeitungsausschnitt;** *we have kept file of press cuttings about the new oftware package;* **press release** = advance ublicity material about a new product iven out to newspapers and other media **resseverlautbarung;** *the company sent out a ress release about the launch of the new canner* NOTE: no plural
b) printing press = machine which prints **ruckerpresse; the book is on the press** = he ook is being printed **das Buch ist im Druck**
verb to push with the fingers **drücken;** *to nd the program press ESCAPE*

ressure pad *noun* transducer that onverts pressure changes into an electrical ignal **Druckumwandler;** *the pressure pad*

under the carpet will set off the burglar alarm if anyone steps on it

prestore *verb* to store data in memory before it is processed **vorweg speichern**

presumptive address *noun* initial address in a program, used as a reference for others **unmodifizierte Adresse**
◇ **presumptive instruction** *noun* unmodified program instruction which is processed to obtain the instruction to be executed **unmodifizierter Befehl**

prevent *verb* to stop something happening **verhindern;** *the police prevented anyone from leaving the building; we have changed the passwords to prevent hackers getting into the database*
◇ **preventive** *or* **preventative** *adjective* which tries to stop something happening **vorbeugend; preventive maintenance** = regular checks on equipment to correct and repair any small faults before they cause a major problem **vorbeugende Wartung;** *we have a preventive maintenance contract for the system*
◇ **prevention** *noun* preventing something happening **Vorbeugung**

preview *verb* to display text *or* graphics on a screen as it will appear when it is printed out **das Layout kontrollieren**
◇ **previewer** *noun* feature that allows a user to see on screen what a page will look like when printed **Layoutkontrolle;** *the built-in previewer allows the user to check for mistakes*

previous *adjective* which happens earlier **vorherig;** *copy data into the present workspace from the previous file*
◇ **previously** *adverb* happening earlier **vorherig;** *the data is copied onto previously formatted disks*

primary *adjective* first *or* basic *or* most important **Primär-, primär-, Haupt-, haupt-; primary colours** = colours (red, yellow and blue) from which all other colours can be derived **Grundfarben; primary group** = number of signals that are merged into one signal (which may be merged with others) prior to transmission **Primärgruppe; primary key** = unique identifying word that selects one entry from a database **Primärschlüssel; primary memory** *or* **store** *or* **main memory** = (i) small fast-access internal memory of a computer system (whose main memory is slower secondary storage) which stores the program currently being used; (ii) main internal memory of a computer system

**(i) primärer Speicher; (ii) Hauptspeicher;
primary station** = the single station in a
data network that can select a path and
transmit the primary station status is
temporary and is transferred from one
station to another **Primärstation**
◊ **primarily** *adverb* mainly **hauptsächlich**

prime
1 *adjective* very important **Haupt-, haupt-;
prime attribute** = most important feature *or*
design of a system **Hauptattribut; prime time**
= (i) time when there are the greatest
number of TV viewers; (ii) most expensive
advertising time for TV commercials **(i) &
(ii) Hauptsendezeit (Sendezeit mit den
höchsten Einschaltquoten);** *we are putting out
a series of prime-time commercials*
2 *noun* number that can only be divided by
itself and by one **Primzahl;** *the number seven
is a prime*

primer *noun* manual *or* simple instruction
book with instructions and examples to
show how a new program *or* system
operates **Elementarbuch**

primitive *noun* basic unit **Basiseinheit**

print
1 *noun*
(a) image produced using an etched
printing plate **Druck;** *he collects 18th century
prints; the office is decorated with Japanese
prints*
(b) positive photographic image in which
black is black and white is white **Abzug;**
compare with NEGATIVE; **print contrast
ratio** = difference between the brightest and
darkest areas of an image **Kontrastverhältnis
(c)** characters made in ink on paper
Gedrucktes; *he was very pleased to see his
book in print; the print from the daisy-wheel
printer is clearer than that from the line
printer;* **print control character** = special
character sent to a printer that directs it to
perform an action *or* function (such as
change font), rather than print a character
Drucksteuerzeichen; print format = way in
which text is arranged when printed out,
according to embedded codes, etc., used to
set the margins, headers, etc. **Druckformat;
print hammer** = moving arm in a daisy-
wheel printer that presses the metal
character form onto the printer ribbon
leaving a mark on the paper **Druckhammer;
print life** = number of characters a
component can print before needing to be
replaced **Druckerlebensdauer;** *the printhead
has a print life of over 400 million
characters;* **print modifiers** = codes in a
document that cause a printer to change
mode, i.e. from bold to italic

Druckanweisungen; print pause =
temporarily stopping a printer while
printing (to change paper, etc.) **Druckpause
print spooling** = automatic printing of a
number of different documents in a queue
at the normal speed of the printer, while
the computer is doing some other task
SPOOL-Funktion; print style = typeface used
on a certain printer *or* for a certain
document **Drucktype, Schriftart**
2 *verb*
(a) to put letters *or* figures in ink on paper
drucken; *printed agreement; printed
regulations; the printer prints at 60
characters per second*
(b) to put letters *or* illustrations onto sheets
of paper so that they form a book **drucken;**
*the book was printed in Hong Kong; the
book is printing at the moment, so we will
have bound copies at the end of the month*
(c) to write in capital letters **in Druckschrift
schreiben;** *please print your name and
address on the top of the form*
◊ **printed circuit** *or* **printed circuit board
(PCB)** *noun* flat insulating material that has
conducting tracks of metal printed *or*
etched onto its surface which complete a
circuit when components are mounted on
it **gedruckte Schaltkarte**
◊ **printer** *noun*
(a) device that converts input data in an
electrical form into a printed readable form
Drucker; computer printer *or* **line printer** =
machine which prints information from a
computer, printing one line at a time
Zeilendrucker; barrel printer = type of
printer where characters are located
around a rotating barrel
Typenwalzendrucker; bi-directional printer =
printer which is able to print characters
from left to right *or* from right to left as the
head moves backwards and forwards
across the paper **Zweirichtungsdrucker; chain
printer** = printer whose characters are
located on a continuous belt **Kettendrucker;
daisy-wheel printer** = printer with
characters arranged on interchangeable
daisy-wheels **Typenraddrucker; dot-matrix
printer** = printer which forms characters
from a series of tiny dots printed close
together **Matrixdrucker, Nadeldrucker; impact
printer** = printer that prints text and
symbols by striking an inked ribbon onto
paper with a metal character
**Anschlagdrucker, mechanischer Drucker; ink-
jet printer** = printer that produces
characters by sending a stream of tiny
drops of electrically charged ink onto the
paper (the movement of the ink drops is
controlled by an electric field)
Tintenstrahldrucker; laser printer = high-
resolution printer that uses a laser source to
print high quality dot-matrix characters
Laserdrucker; line printer = printer which

prints draft-quality information at high speed (typical output is 200 - 3000 lines per minute) **Zeilendrucker; page printer =** printer which composes one page of text, then prints it rapidly **Seitendrucker, Blattschreiber; thermal printer =** printer where the character is formed on thermal paper with a printhead containing a matrix of small heating elements **Thermodrucker; printer buffer =** temporary store for character data waiting to be printed (used to free the computer before the printing is completed making the operation faster) **Druckerpuffer; printer control characters =** command characters in a text which transmit printing commands to a printer **Druckersteuerzeichen; printer driver =** dedicated software that converts and formats users' commands ready for a printer **Drucker-Treiber; printer-plotter =** high resolution printer that is able to operate as a low resolution plotter **Drucker-Plotter; printer port =** output port of a computer to which a printer is connected to receive character data (either parallel or serial) **Druckeranschlußstelle; printer quality =** standard of printed text from a particular printer (high resolution dot-matrix printers produce near letter-quality, daisy-wheel printers produce letter-quality text) **Druckqualität; printer ribbon =** roll of inked material which passes between a printhead and the paper **Farbband**
(b) company which prints books *or* newspapers **Druckerei;** *the book will be sent to the printer next week; we are using Japanese printers for some of our magazines*

◇ **printhead** *noun* (i) row of needles in a dot-matrix printer that produce characters as a series of dots; (ii) metal form of a character that is pressed onto an inked ribbon to print the character on paper **(i) Druckerkopf; (ii) Typenkopf**

◇ **printing** *noun* action of printing **Drucken**

◇ **print out** *verb* to print information stored in a computer with a printer **ausdrucken**

◇ **printout** *noun* **computer printout =** printed copy of information from a computer **Computerausdruck;** *the sales director asked for a printout of the agents' commissions*

◇ **printrun** *noun* number of copies of a book which are printed at one time **Auflage**

◇ **print shop** *noun* shop where jobbing printing takes place **Akzidenzdruckerei**

◇ **printwheel** *noun* daisy-wheel *or* the wheel made up of a number of arms, with a character shape at the end of each arm, used in a daisy-wheel printer **Typenrad**

prior *adjective* happening before **zuvor; prior to =** before **bevor;** *the password has to be keyed in prior to accessing the system*

◇ **priority** *noun* importance of a device *or* software routine in a computer system **Vorrang, Priorität;** *the operating system has priority over the application when disk space is allocated; the disk drive is more important than the printer, so it has a higher priority;* **job priority =** importance of a job compared to others **Jobvorrangigkeit; priority interrupt =** signal to a computer that takes precedence over any other task **Vorrangunterbrechung;** *see also* INTERRUPT, NON-MASKABLE INTERRUPT; **priority interrupt table =** list of peripherals and their priority when they send an interrupt signal (used instead of a hardware priority scheduler) **Vorrangunterbrechungstabelle; priority sequence =** the order in which various devices that have sent an interrupt signal are processed, according to their importance or urgency (a disk drive will usually come before a printer in a priority sequence) **Prioritätsreihenfolge; priority scheduler =** system that organizes tasks into correct processing priority (to improve performance) **Prioritätsplaner**

privacy *noun* the right of an individual to limit the extent of and control the access to the data that is stored about him **(Daten)schutz; privacy of data =** rule that data is secret and must not be accessed by users who have not been authorized **Datenschutz; privacy of information =** rule that unauthorized users cannot obtain data about private individuals from databases *or* that each individual has the right to know what information is being held about him *or* her on a database **Informationsschutz; privacy transformation =** encryption of messages *or* data to ensure that it remains private **Schutzverschlüsselung**

private *adjective* belonging to an individual *or* to a company, not to the public **privat; private address space =** memory address range that is reserved for a single user, not for public access **privater Adreßbereich; private automatic branch exchange (PABX) =** small telephone exchange in a company that handles all internal and external calls to the main public network **Nebenstellenanlage; private automatic exchange (PAX) =** small telephone exchange in a company that only allows internal calls within the company to be made **private Fernsprechvermittlung; private branch exchange (PBX) =** small manual *or* automatic exchange in a company that can handle internal *or* external calls **private Vermittlungsanlage;**

private dial port = unlisted telephone number that connects one user to a packet network system **privater Wählanschluß; private line** = special telephone line, rented from the telephone company and used only by the user **Privatleitung; private manual branch exchange (PMBX)** = small telephone exchange inside a company where all telephone calls coming in *or* going out have to be placed through a switchboard **private Handvermittlungsanlage; private mobile radio (PMR)** *see* MOBILE; **private telephone system** = telephone system in a company that cannot be accessed from a public telephone system **privates Telefonsystem**

privilege *noun* status of a user referring to the type of program he can run and the resources he can use **Zugriffsrecht; privileged account** = computer account that allows special programs *or* access to sensitive system data **bevorrechtigter Bereich;** *the system manager can access anyone else's account from his privileged account;* **privileged instructions** = computer commands which can only be executed via a privileged account, such as delete another account *or* set up a new user *or* examine passwords **bevorrechtigte Befehle**

problem *noun*
(a) question to which it is difficult to find an answer **Problem; to solve a problem** = to find an answer to a problem **ein Problem lösen; problem definition** = the clear explanation, in logical steps, of a problem that is to be solved **Problemdarstellung; problem-orientated language (POL)** = high-level programming language that allows certain problems to be expressed easily **problemorientierte Programmiersprache**
(b) malfunction *or* fault with hardware or software **Fehler; problem diagnosis** = finding the cause and method of repairing a fault *or* error **Fehlererkennung**

procedure *noun*
(a) small section of computer instruction code that provides a frequently used function and can be called upon from a main program **Prozedur;** *this procedure sorts all the files into alphabetic order, you can call it from the main program by the instruction SORT; see also* SUBROUTINE
(b) method *or* route used when solving a problem **Vorgehensweise;** *you should use this procedure to retrieve lost files; the procedure is given in the manual;* **procedure-orientated language** = high-level programming language that allows procedures to be programmed easily **verfahrensorientierte Programmiersprache**

◇ **procedural** *adjective* using a procedure (to solve a problem) **Prozedur-, prozedur-, prozedural; procedural language** = high-level programming language in which the programmer enters the actions required to achieve the result wanted **verfahrensorientierte Programmiersprache**

proceed *verb* to move forward **fortfahren;** *after spellchecking the text, you can proceed to the printing stage*

process
1 *noun* a number of tasks that must be carried out to achieve a goal **Verfahren, Prozeß;** *the process of setting up the computer takes a long time; there are five stages in the process;* **process bound** = program that spends more time executing instructions and using the CPU than in I/O operations **prozeßgebunden; process camera** = camera designed for the stages required in printing, such as tone and colour separation **Reprokamera; process chart** = diagram that shows each step of the computer procedures needed in a system **Verfahrensdiagramm; process control** = automatic control of a process by a computer **Prozeßsteuerung; process control computer** = dedicated computer that controls and manages a process **Prozeßrechner; process control system** = complete input, output modules, a CPU with memory and a program (usually stored in ROM) and control and feedback devices such as A/D and D/A converters that completely monitors, manages and regulates a process **Prozeß-Steuersystem**
2 *verb* to carry out a number of tasks to produce a result (such as sorting data *or* finding the solution to a problem) **verarbeiten;** *we processed the new data; processing all the information will take a long time*

◇ **processing** *noun* sorting of information; using a computer to solve a problem *or* organize data **Verarbeitung;** *page processing time depends on the complexity of a given page; see also* CPU; **batch processing** = computer system, where information is collected into batches before being loaded into the computer **Stapelverarbeitung, Batch-Betrieb; data processing** *or* **information processing** = selecting and examining data in a computer to produce information in a special form **Datenverarbeitung, Informationsverarbeitung (EDV); image processing** = analysis of information contained in an image (usually by electronic means or by using a computer to provide the analysis or for recognition of objects in the image) **Abbildungsverarbeitung; immediate**

processing = processing data when it appears, rather than waiting for a certain clock pulse or time **unmittelbare Verarbeitung; off-line processing** = processing by devices not under the control of a central computer **Verarbeitung unabhängug von der DV-Anlage; on-line processing** = processing by devices connected to and under the control of the central computer (the user remains in contact with the central computer while processing) **Verarbeitung abhängig von der DV-Anlage; query processing** = processing of queries, either by extracting information from a database *or* translating query commands from a query language **Anfrageverarbeitung; real-time processing** = processing operations that take a time of the same order of magnitude as the problem to be solved **Echtzeitbetrieb; serial processing** = executing one instruction at a time **Serienverarbeitung;** *compare with* PARALLEL PROCESSING; **word-processing** *or* **text processing** = working with words, using a computer to produce, check and change texts, reports, letters, etc. **Textverarbeitung;** NOTE: no plural

COMMENT: the central processing unit is a hardware device that allows a computer to manipulate and modify data; a compiler is a software language processor that translates data and instructions in one language into another form

processor *noun* hardware *or* software device that is able to manipulate *or* modify data according to instructions **Prozessor; array processor** = computer that can act upon several arrays of data simultaneously for very fast mathematical applications **Vektorenrechner, Array-Prozessor; associative processor** = processor that uses associative storage **Assoziativprozessor; attached processor** = separate microprocessor in a system that performs certain functions under the control of a central processor **Anschlußprozessor; auxiliary processor** = extra, specialized processor, such as an array or numerical processor, that can work with a main processor to improve performance **Hilfsprozessor; back-end processor** = special purpose auxiliary processor **Nachschaltrechner; bit-slice processor** = construction of a large word size CPU by joining a number of smaller word size blocks **Slice-Prozessor, Bitscheibenprozessor; distributed processor** = using many small computers at different workstations instead of one central computer **verteilte Verarbeitung; front-end processor (FEP)** = processor placed between an input source and the central computer, whose function is to preprocess

received data to reduce the main computer's workload **Vorschaltrechner; input/output processor** = processor that handles data communications, including DMA and error correcting functions **Ein-/Ausgabeprozessor; language processor** = program that translates from one language to machine code (there are three type of translator: (i) assembler; (ii) compiler; (iii) interpreter) **(i) Assemblierer; (ii) Kompilierer; (iii) Übersetzer; network processor** = signal multiplexer controlled by a microprocessor in a network **Netzwerkprozessor;** *(in a multiprocessor system)* **order code processor** = a processor which decodes and performs the arithmetic and logical operations according to the program code **Anweisungscodeprozessor; processor controlled keying** = data entry by an operator which is prompted and controlled by a computer **prozessorgesteuerte Eingabe; processor interrupt** = to send an interrupt signal to a processor requesting attention, that will usually cause it to stop what it is doing and attend to the calling device **Prozessorabbruchsignal; processor status word (PSW)** = word which contains a number of status bits, such as carry flag, zero flag and overflow flag **Prozessor-Statuswort; processor-limited** = (operation *or* execution time) that is set by the speed of the processor rather than a peripheral **durch den Prozessor begrenzt; dual processor** = computer system with two processors for faster program execution **Computer mit zwei Prozessoren; image processor** = electronic *or* computer system used for image processing **Image-Prozessor; word-processor** = small computer which is used for working with words, to produce texts, reports, letters, etc. **Textverarbeitungscomputer**

QUOTE each chip will contain 128 processors and one million transistors
Computer News

produce *verb* to make *or* manufacture **herstellen**

◇ **producer** *noun*
(a) person *or* company *or* country which manufactures **Hersteller;** *country which is a producer of high quality computer equipment; the company is a major magnetic tape producer*
(b) person who is in charge of a film *or* TV show, who has the idea for the show, and organizes the filming, the actors, etc **Produzent**

◇ **producing** *adjective* which produces **produzierend; producing capacity** = capacity to produce **Produktionskapazität**

product *noun*
(a) item which is made *or* manufactured

Produkt, Erzeugnis; **basic product** = main product made from a raw material **Ausgangsprodukt; end product** or **final product** or **finished product** = product made at the end of a production process **Endprodukt**
(b) manufactured item for sale **Produkt, Erzeugnis; product advertising** = advertising a particular named product, not the company which makes it **Produktwerbung; product analysis** = examining each separate product in a company's range to see why it sells or who buys it, etc. **Produktanalyse; product design** = design of consumer products **Produktdesign, Produktgestaltung; product development** = improving an existing product line to meet the needs of the market **Produktentwicklung; product engineer** = engineer in charge of the equipment for making a product **Fertigungsingenieur; product line** or **product range** = series of different products made by the same company which form a group (such as printers in different models or different colours, etc.) **Produktgruppe, Sortiment; product management** = directing the making and selling of a product as an independent item **Produktmanagement; product mix** = group of quite different products made by the same company **Warenmischung, Produktmix**
(c) result after multiplication **Produkt**

◊ **production** noun making or manufacturing of goods for sale **Produktion, Herstellung;** *production will probably be held up by industrial action; we are hoping to speed up production by installing new machinery;* **batch production** = production in batches **Stapelherstellung, Serienfertigung; mass production** = manufacturing of large quantities of goods **Massenproduktion;** *mass production of monitors or of calculators;* **rate of production** or **production rate** = speed at which items are made **Produktionsrate; production control** = control of the manufacturing of a product (using computers) **Fertigungssteuerung; production cost** = cost of making a product **Produktionskosten; production department** = section of a company which deals with the making of the company's products **Fertigungsabteilung; production line** = system of making a product, where each item (such as a TV set) moves slowly through the factory with new sections added to it as it goes along **Fließband;** *he works on the production line; she is a production line worker; a typical use of an image processor includes production line control;* **production manager** = person in charge of the production department **Produktionsleiter; production run** = manufacturing a product or running a program, as opposed to a test run

Produktionslauf; **production unit** = separate small group of workers producing a certain product **Produktionseinheit**
NOTE: no plural

◊ **productive** adjective during or in which something useful is produced **produktiv; productive time** = period of time during which a computer can run error-free tasks **Bearbeitungszeit**

program

1 noun complete set of instructions which direct a computer to carry out a particular task **Programm; assembly program** = number of assembly code instructions which perform a task **Assemblerprogramm; background program** = computer program with a very low priority **Hintergrundprogramm; blue-ribbon program** = perfect program that runs first time with no errors **erstklassiges Programm; control program/monitor** or **control program for microcomputers (CP/M)** = popular operating system for microcomputers **Steuerprogramm (CP/M); diagnostic program** = software that helps find faults in a computer system **Diagnostikprogramm; executive program** = master program in a computer system that controls the execution of other programs **Organisationsprogramm; foreground program** = high priority program in a multitasking system **Vordergrundprogramm, Prioritäts-, Vorrangprogramm; hardwired program** = computer program built into the hardware (and which cannot be changed) **festverdrahtetes Programm; job control program** = short program of job control instructions loaded before a particular application is run, that sets up the system as required by the application **Jobsteuerprogramm; library program** = (i) number of specially written or relevant software routines, which a user can insert into his own program, saving time and effort; (ii) group of functions which a computer needs to refer to often, but which are not stored in main memory **(i) & (ii) Bibliotheksprogramm; linear program** = computer program that contains no loops or branches **lineares Programm; user program** = program written by a user (often in a high-level language) **Benutzerprogramm; program address counter** = register in a CPU that contains the location of the next instruction to be processed **Adreßregister; program branch** = one or more paths that can be followed after a conditional statement **Programmzweig; program cards** = punched cards that contain the instructions that make up a program **Programmkarten; program coding sheet** =

specially preprinted form on which computer instructions can be written, simplifying program writing **Programmierblatt; program compatibility** = ability of two pieces of software to function correctly together **Programmkompatibilität; program compilation** = translation of an encoded source program into machine code **Programmübersetzung; program counter (PC)** *or* **instruction address register (IAR)** = register in a CPU that contains the location of the next instruction to be processed **Programmzähler; Befehlsadreßregister;** *see also* INSTRUCTION ADDRESS REGISTER; SEQUENCE CONTROL REGISTER; **program crash** = unexpected failure of a program due to a programming error *or* a hardware fault **Programmabsturz;** *I forgot to insert an important instruction which caused a program to crash, erasing all the files on the disk!;* **program design language (PDL)** = programming language used to design the structure of a program **Programmentwurfssprache; program development** = all the operations involved in creating a computer program from first ideas to initial writing, debugging and the final product **Programmentwicklung; program development system** = all the hardware and software needed for program development on a system **Programmentwicklungssystem; program documentation** = set of instruction notes, examples and tips on how to use a program **Programmunterlagen;** *see also* MANUAL; **program editor** = software that allows the user to alter, delete and add instructions to a program file **Programm-Editor; program execution** = instructing a processor to execute in sequence the instructions in a program **Programmausführung; program file** = file containing a program rather than data **Programmdatei; program flowchart** = diagram that graphically describes the various steps in a program **Programmablaufplan; program generator** = software that allows users to write complex programs using a few simple instructions **Programmgenerator; program instruction** = single word *or* expression that represents one operation (in a high level program each program instruction can consist of a number of low level machine code instructions) **Programmbefehl; program library** = collection of useful procedures and programs which can be used for various purposes and included into new software **Programmbibliothek; program line** = one row of commands *or* arguments in a computer program **Programmzeile; program line number** = number that refers to a line of program code in a computer program **Zeilennummer; program listing** = list of the

set of instructions that make up a program (program listings are displayed in an ordered manner, BASIC listings by line number, assembly listings by memory location; they do not necessarily represent the order in which the program will be executed, since there could be jumps *or* subroutines) **Programmauflistung; program maintenance** = keeping a program free of errors and up to date **Programmwartung; program name** = identification name for a stored program file **Programmname; program origin** = address at which the first instruction of a program is stored **Programmbeginn; program register** = register in a CPU that contains an instruction during decoding and execution operations **Programmregister; program relocation** = moving a stored program from one area of memory to another **Programmverschiebung; program report generator** = software that allows users to create reports from files, databases and other stored data **Programmlistengenerator; program run** = executing (in correct order) the instructions in a program **Programmlauf; program segment** = section of a main program that can be executed in its own right, without the rest of the main program being required **Programmabschnitt;** *see also* OVERLAY; **program specification** = document that contains details on all the functions and abilities of a computer program **Programmbeschreibung; program stack** = section of memory reserved for storing temporary system *or* program data **Programmkellerspeicher; program statement** = high level program instruction that is made up of a number of machine code instructions **Programmanweisung; program step** = one operation within a program, usually a single instruction **Programmschritt; program storage** = section of main memory in which programs (rather than operating system *or* data) can be stored **Programmspeicher; program structure** = the way in which sections of program code are interlinked and operate **Programmstruktur; program testing** = testing a new program with test data to ensure that it functions correctly **Programmprüfung; program verification** = number of tests and checks performed to ensure that a program functions correctly **Programmprüfung**

2 *verb* to write *or* prepare a set of instructions which direct a computer to perform a certain task **programmieren; programmed halt** = instruction within a program that when executed, halts the processor (to restart the CPU a reset action is required) **programmierter Stop; programmed learning** = using educational software which allows a learner to follow a

course of instruction **programmiertes Lernen;**
NOTE: **programs - programming - programmed**

◇ **programmable** *adjective (& noun)*
(device) that can accept and store
instructions then execute them
programmierbar; programmable calculator =
small calculator which can hold certain
basic mathematical calculating programs
**programmierbarer Rechner; programmable
logic array (PLA)** *or* **programmable logic
device (PLD) =** integrated circuit that can
be permanently programmed to perform
logic operations on data using a matrix of
links between input and output pins
**programmierbares logisches Feld /Gerät;
programmable interrupt controller =** circuit
or chip which can be programmed to ignore
certain interrupts, accept only high priority
interrupts and select the priority of
interrupts **programmierte
Unterbrechungssteuerung; programmable
key =** special key on a computer terminal
keyboard that can be programmed with
various functions *or* characters
**programmierbare Taste; programmable
memory (PROM) =** electronic device in
which data can be stored **programmierbarer
Speicher;** *see also* EAROM; EEPROM;
EPROM; ROM; **programmable read only
memory (PROM) =** memory integrated
circuit that can be programmed with data
by a user (some PROMs provide
permanent storage, others such as
EPROMs are erasable) **programmierbarer
Festwertspeicher; hand-held programmable
=** very small computer, which can be held
in the hand, used for inputting information
when a larger terminal is not available (as
by a salesman on a call) **Handcomputer**

◇ **programmer** *noun*
(a) person who is capable of designing and
writing a working program **Programmierer/-
in;** *the programmer is still working on the
new software;* **applications programmer =**
programmer who writes applications
software **Anwendungsprogrammierer;
systems programmer =** programmer who
specializes in writing systems software
Systemprogrammierer
(b) device that allows data to be written
into a programmable read only memory
Programmiergerät

◇ **programming** *noun*
(a) writing programs for computers
Programmieren; programming in logic =
PROLOG; **programming language =**
software that allows a user to write a series
of instructions to define a particular task,
which will then be translated to a form that
is understood by the computer
**Programmiersprache; programming
standards =** rules to which programs must
conform to produce compatible code
Programmiernormen

(b) writing data into a PROM device
Programmieren

COMMENT: programming languages are
grouped into different levels: the high-
level languages such as BASIC and
PASCAL are easy to understand and use,
but offer slow execution time since each
instruction is made up of a number of
machine code instructions; low-level
languages such as assembler are more
complex to read and program in but offer
faster execution time

QUOTE we've included some useful program
tools to make your job easier. Like the symbolic
debugger
Personal Computer World
QUOTE the other two for the socket is to program
2, 4, 8 or 16Kbyte EPROMS
Electronics & Wireless World
QUOTE each of the 16 programmable function
keys has two modes normal and shift - giving 32
possible functions
Micro Decision

programme *or (US)* **program** *noun* TV *o*
radio broadcast which is separate from
other broadcasts, and has its own producer
director, etc **Programm, Sendung;** *they wer*
filming a wild life programme; children'.
programmes are scheduled for early evening
viewing

project
1 *noun* planned task **Projekt;** *his lates*
project is computerizing the sales team; th
design project was entirely worked out o
computer; CAD is essential for accurat
project design
2 *verb* to forecast future figures from a se
of data **vorausplanen, projektieren;** *th*
projected sales of the new PC
◇ **projection** *noun*
(a) forecast of a situation from a set of dat
Vorausplanung; *the projection indicates tha*
sales will increase
(b) showing pictures on a screen **Projektion
projection room =** room in a cinema wher*
the projectors which show the films ar*
housed **Vorführraum**
◇ **projector** *noun* **film projector** *or* **slid*
projector = mechanical device that display
films *or* slides on a screen **Filmprojekto**
Diaprojektor; *see also* OVERHEAD

PROLOG = PROGRAMMING IN LOGIC
high-level programming language usin
logical operations for artificial intelligenc
and data retrieval applications **PROLO**
(Programmiersprache)

PROM
(a) = PROGRAMMABLE READ-ONL*
MEMORY read-only memory which can b

rogrammed by the user (as opposed to ROM, which is programmed by the manufacturer) **PROM (programmierbarer estwertspeicher); PROM burner** or **rogrammer** = electronic device used to program a PROM **PROM-Programmiergerät;** *ee also* EPROM

) = PROGRAMMABLE MEMORY lectronic memory in which data can be tored **programmierbarer Speicher**

rompt *noun* message *or* character isplayed to inform the user that an input s expected **Eingabeaufforderung;** *the prompt READY indicates that the system is vailable to receive instructions;* **command rompt** = symbol displayed to indicate a ommand is expected **Befehlsaufforderung**

roof
noun printed matter from a printer that as to be checked and corrected **orrekturabzug; galley proofs** = proofs in the orm of long pieces of text, not divided into ages, printed on long pieces of paper **orrekturfahnen; page proofs** = proofs which re divided into pages, but may not have age numbers *or* headings inserted mbruchfahnen, **Bogenkorrekturen**
verb to produce proofs of a text **einen orrekturabzug anfertigen**

> proofer *noun* printer which produces roofs, as opposed to finished printed ages **Andruckpresse;** *output devices such as ser proofers and typesetters*

> proofing *noun* producing proofs of text hich have to be read and corrected nfertigung von **Korrekturabzügen**

> proofread *verb* to correct spelling and rinting errors in a printed text **Korrektur sen;** *has all the text been proofread yet?*

> proofreader *noun* person who reads and orrects proofs **Korrektor, Korrekturenleser**

COMMENT: the stages of full proofing are galley proofs, page on galley (where the pages are indicated, but the proofs are still printed on long pieces of paper), and page proofs. It is usual to miss out some of these stages, and many books are proofed in pages from the start

ropagate *verb* to travel *or* spread **sich usbreiten; propagated error** = one error in a rocess that has affected later operations **itgelaufener Fehler; propagating error** = an rror that occurs in one place *or* operation nd affects another operation *or* process **itlaufender Fehler**

propagation delay *noun* time taken for signal to travel through a circuit; time ken for an output to appear in a logic gate

after the input is applied **Schaltverzögerung;** *propagation delay in the transmission path causes signal distortion*

proportion *noun* size of something as compared to others **Proportion**

◊ proportional spacing *noun* printing system where each letter takes a space proportional to the character width ('i' taking less space than 'm') **Proportionalschrittschaltung (Schriftart, bei der die Drucktypen verschiedene Dicke haben);** *compare* MONOSPACING

protect *verb* to stop something being damaged **schützen; protected location** = memory location that cannot be altered *or* cannot be accessed without authorization **geschützter Speicherplatz; protected storage** = section of memory that cannot be altered **geschützter Speicher; copy protect** = switch used to prevent copies of a disk being made **Kopierschutz;** *all the disks are copy protected;* **crash-protected** = (disk) which uses a head protection *or* data corruption protection system **absturzgesichert;** *if the disk is crash protected, you will never lose your work*

◊ protection *noun* action of protecting **Schutz; protection key** = signal checked to see if a program can access a section of memory **Speicherschutzschlüssel; protection master** = spare copy of a master film *or* tape **Schutzkopie; copy protection** = preventing copies being made **Kopierschutz;** *a hard disk may crash because of faulty copy protection; the new product will come without copy protection;* **data protection** = making sure that data is not copied by an unauthorized user **Datenschutz; Data Protection Act** = act which prevents confidential data about people being copied without authority (also every organization that keeps information subject to the act on a computer, must protect it adequately) **Datenschutzgesetz**

◊ protective *adjective* which protects **Schutz-, schutz-;** *the disks are housed in hard protective cases*

protocol *noun* pre-agreed signals, codes and rules to be used for data exchange between systems **Leistungsprozedur, Protokoll; protocol converter** = device used for converting protocols from one computer system to another, such as for converting data from a micro to a phototypesetter **Protokollumsetzer; protocol standards** = standards laid down to allow data exchange between any computer systems conforming to the standard **Leistungsprozedurnormen**

QUOTE there is a very simple protocol that
would exclude hackers from computer networks
using the telephone system
Practical Computing

prototype *noun* first working model of a
device *or* program, which is then tested and
adapted to improve it **Prototyp**

◊ **prototyping** *noun* making a prototype
Herstellung eines Prototyps

provider *noun* **information provider (ip)** =
company *or* user that provides an
information source for use in a videotext
system (such as the company providing
weather information *or* stock exchange
reports) **jd, der Informationen zur Verfügung
stellt**

ps = PICOSECOND

PSA = PUBLIC SERVICE
ANNOUNCEMENT advertisement for a
public service *or* charity, which is shown on
TV, but for which the TV company is not
paid **kostenlose Werbeansage zur Information
der Öffentlichkeit/für gemeinnützige
Institutionen**

pseudo- *prefix* meaning similar to
something, but not genuine **Pseudo-,
pseudo-**

◊ **pseudo-code** *noun* English sentence
structures, used to describe program
instructions which are translated at a later
date into machine code **Pseudocode**

◊ **pseudo-digital** *adjective* (modulated
analog signals) produced by a modem and
transmitted over telephone lines
pseudodigital

◊ **pseudo-instruction** *noun* label (in an
assembly language program) that
represents a number of instructions
Pseudobefehl

◊ **pseudo-operation** *noun* command in an
assembler program that controls the
assembler rather than producing machine
code **Pseudooperation**

◊ **pseudo-random** *adjective* generated
sequence that appears random but is
repeated over a long period **pseudozufällig;
pseudo-random number generator** =
hardware *or* software that produces pseudo-
random numbers
Pseudozufallszahlengenerator

PSN = PACKET SWITCHED NETWORK

PSTN = PUBLIC SWITCHED TELEPHONE
NETWORK

PSU = POWER SUPPLY UNIT electric
circuit that provides certain direct curren
voltage and current levels from a
alternating current source to othe
electrical circuits **Stromversorgungseinheit**

COMMENT: a PSU will regulate, smooth
and step down a higher voltage supply for
use in small electronic equipment

PSW = PROCESSOR STATUS WORD

PTR = PAPER TAPE READER

p-type semiconductor *nou*
semiconductor material that has bee
doped with a chemical to provide ext
holes (positive charge carriers), giving it a
overall positive potential compared
intrinsic semiconductor **p-Halbleiter;** *se*
also HOLES, INTRINSIC SEMICONDUCTO

public *adjective* open to anyone to us
made for the use of everyone **öffentlic
public address system (PA)** = microphon
amplifier and loudspeaker set up to allo
one person to be heard by a group of peop
Lautsprecheranlage; public data network
data transmission service for the publ
öffentliches Datennetz; public dial port = po
connecting a packet network to a publ
telephone system **öffentlicher Wählanschlu
public domain (PD)** = documents *or* text
program that has no copyright and can b
copied by anyone **Gemeingut; Public Doma
Software (ohne Kopierschutz); public ke
cipher system** = cipher that uses a publ
key to encrypt messages and a secret key
decrypt them (conventional cipher system
use one secret key to encrypt and decry
messages) **Verschlüsselungssystem m
bekanntem Chiffrierschlüssel;** *see* *al*
CIPHER, KEY; **public switched telephor
network (PSTN)** = national telephor
system *or* country and world-wic
exchanges, lines and telephone sets that a
all interconnected and can be used by th
public **öffentliches Telefonnetz**

publication *noun*
(a) making something publ
Veröffentlichung; *the publication of t*
report on data protection; the publicatio
date of the book is November 15th
(b) printed book *or* leaflet, etc. which is so
to the public *or* which is given awa
Veröffentlichung; *government publicatio*
can be bought at special shops; the compar
specializes in publications for the busine
reader

publicity *noun* attracting the attention of the public to products *or* services by mentioning them in the media *or* by advertising them **Werbung, Publicity; publicity bureau** = office which organizes publicity for companies **Werbebüro, Werbeagentur; publicity campaign** = period when planned publicity takes place **Werbekampagne; publicity department** = department in a company which organizes the publicity for the company's products **Werbeabteilung; publicity matter** = leaflets *or* posters, etc., which publicize a product *or* service **Werbematerial**

◇ **publicize** *verb* to attract people's attention to a product *or* service **bekannt machen, Werbung durchführen;** *they are publicizing their low prices for computer stationery; the new PC has been publicized in the press*

publish *verb* to print a text (such as a book *or* newspaper *or* catalogue) and then sell *or* give it to the public **veröffentlichen;** *the institute has published a list of sales figures for differenthome computers; the company specializes in publishing referencebooks*

◇ **publisher** *noun* company which prints books *or* newspapers and sells *or* gives them to the public **Verlag**

◇ **publishing** *noun* the business of printing books *or* newspapers and selling them *or* giving them to the public **Verlagswesen; desktop publishing (DTP)** = design, layout and printing of documents using special software, a small computer and a printer **Desktop Publishing; electronic publishing** = (i) use of desktop publishing packages and laser printers to produce printed matter; (ii) using computers to write and display information (such as viewdata) **(i) elektronisches Publizieren; (ii) Bildschirmtextverfahren; professional publishing** = publishing books on law, accountancy, and other professions **Verlegen von Fachliteratur**

QUOTE desktop publishing or the ability to produce high-quality publications using a minicomputer, essentially boils down to combining words and images on pages
Byte

pull *verb* to remove data from a stack **herausnehmen;** *compare with* PUSH

pull-down *or* **pull-up menu** *noun* menu that can be displayed on screen at any time by pressing an appropriate key, usually displayed over the material already on screen **Pulldown-Menü**

◇ **pull up** *verb* **to pull up a line** = to connect *or* set a line to a voltage level **eine Leitung**

unter **Spannung setzen;** *pull up the input line to a logic one by connecting it to 5 volts*

QUOTE the gated inputs lower the standby current and also eliminate the need for input pull-up or pull-down resistors
Electronics & Power

pulse
1 *noun* short rush of electricity; short period of a voltage level **Impuls** ▷ APPENDIX **pulse amplitude modulation (PAM)** = pulse modulation where the height of the pulse depends on the input signal **(Im)pulsamplitudenmodulation; pulse code modulation (PCM)** = pulse stream that carries data about a signal in binary form **Pulscodemodulation (PCM); pulse duration modulation (PDM)** = pulse modulation where the pulse width depends on the input signal **(Im)pulsdauermodulation; pulse generator** = electronic test equipment used to produce different size pulses **Zeichengeber; pulse modulation** = use of a series of short pulses which are modified by an input signal, to carry information **(Im)pulsmodulation; pulse position modulation (PPM)** = pulse modulation where the time between pulses depends on the input signal **Pulslagenmodulation; pulse stream** = continuous series of similar pulses **Impulsstrom; pulse width modulation (PWM)** = pulse modulation where the pulse width depends on the input signal **(Im)pulsbreitenmodulation**
2 *verb* to apply a short-duration voltage level to a circuit **einen Impuls geben;** *we pulsed the input but it still would not work*

COMMENT: electric pulse can be used to transmit information, as the binary digits 0 and 1 correspond to 'no pulse' and 'pulse' (the voltage level used to distinguish the binary digits 0 and 1, is often zero and 5 or 12 volts, with the pulse width depending on transmission rate)

punch
1 *noun* device for making holes in punched cards **Locher**
2 *verb* to make a hole **lochen; punch** *or* **punched card** = small piece of card which contains holes which represent various instructions *or* data **Lochkarte; punched card reader** = device that transforms data on a punched card to a form that can be recognized by a computer **Lochkartenleser; punched tag** = card attached to a product in a shop, with punched holes containing data about the product **gelochtes Etikett; punched (paper) tape** = strip of paper tape that contains holes to represent data **Lochstreifen**

punctuation **mark** *noun* printing symbol, which cannot be spoken, but which helps to understand the text **Satzzeichen**

> COMMENT: the main punctuation marks are the question mark and exclamation mark; inverted commas (which show the type of text being written); the comma, full stop, colon and semicolon (which show how the words are broken up into sequences); the apostrophe (which shows that a letter or word is missing); the dash and hyphen and brackets (which separate or link words)

pure *adjective* clean *or* not mixed with other things **rein; pure code** = code that does not modify itself during execution **reiner Code; pure semiconductor** = semiconductor material that has not had extra doping substances added **reiner Halbleiter;** *see also* INTRINSIC; **pure tone** = single frequency containing no harmonics **reiner Ton**

purge *verb* to remove unnecessary *or* out of date data from a file **löschen**

push *verb* to press something *or* to move something by pressing on it **drücken; push-down list** *or* **stack** = temporary storage queue system where the last item added is at the top of the list **Umkehrliste; Umkehrstapel;** *see also* LIFO; **push instruction** *or* **operation** = computer instruction that stores data on a LIFO list *or* stack **Befehl zur Speicherung nach dem LIFO-Prinzip; push-up list** *or* **stack** = temporary storage queue system where the last item added is at the bottom of the list **Eingangsfolgeliste;** *see also* FIFO

◇ **pushbutton** *adjective* which works by pressing on a button **Drucktasten-; pushbutton dialling** = using buttons rather than a dial on a telephone to dial a number **Drucktastenwählen; pushbutton telephone** = telephone operated with buttons rather than a dial **Drucktastentelefon**

put *verb* to push *or* place data onto a stack **schreiben**

PWM = PULSE WIDTH MODULATION

Qq

QBE = QUERY BY EXAMPLE

QISAM = QUEUED INDEXED SEQUENTIAL ACCESS METHOD indexed sequential file that is read item by item into a buffer **QISAM (erweiterte indizierte Zugriffsmöglichkeit für sequentielle Dateien)**

QSAM = QUEUED SEQUENTIAL ACCESS METHOD queue of blocks that are waiting to be processed, retrieved using a sequential access method **QSAM (erweiterte Zugriffsmöglichkeit für sequentielle Dateien)**

QL = QUERY LANGUAGE

quad *noun*
(a) sheet of paper four times as large as a basic sheet **Quartblatt**
(b) meaning four times **vierfach; quad density** = four bits of data stored in the usual place of one **vierfache Schreibdichte**
(c) em quad = space printed that is equal in size to an em **Geviert (in der Größe eines m); en quad** = space that is half the width of an em quad space **Halbgeviert (in der Größe eines n)**
◇ **quadding** *noun* insertion of spaces into text to fill out a line **Zeilenfüllen; Ausschließen**

> QUOTE in this case, interfacing is done by a single quad-wide adapter
> *Minicomputer News*

quadr- *prefix* meaning four **quadro-**
◇ **quadrophonic** *adjective* (audio music system) using four speakers **quadrophon**
◇ **quadruplex** *noun* four signals combined into a single one **Quadruplex**
◇ **quadruplicate** *noun* **in quadruplicate** = with the original and three copies **in vierfacher Ausfertigung;** *the statements are printed in quadruplicate*
NOTE: no plural

quadrature *noun* video quality error due to the heads being wrongly aligned to the edge of the tape **Quadratur**

quality *noun* what something is like *or* how good or bad something is **Qualität;** *there is a market for good quality secondhand computers;* **high quality** *or* **top quality** = very best quality **beste Qualität, Spitzenqualität;** *the store specializes in high quality imported items;* **printer quality** = standard of printed text from a particular printer (high-resolution dot-matrix printers produce near-letter quality, daisy-wheel printers produce letter-quality text) **Druckqualität;** *see also* LETTER, NEAR LETTER, DRAFT; **quality control** = checking that the quality of a product is good

Qualitätskontrolle; quality controller = person who checks the quality of a product **Qualitätsprüfer;** NOTE: no plural

QUOTE the computer operates at 120cps in draft quality mode and 30cps in near letter-quality mode
Minicomputer News

quantify *verb* to quantify the effect of something = to show the effect of something in figures **die Auswirkungen von etwas in Zahlen ausdrücken;** *it is impossible to quantify the effect of the new computer system on our production*

◇ **quantifiable** *adjective* which can be quantified **in Zahlen ausdrückbar;** *the effect of the change in the pricing structure is not quantifiable*

◇ **quantifier** *noun* sign *or* symbol which indicates the quantity *or* range of a predicate **Quantor**

quantity *noun*
a) amount *or* number of items **Menge;** *a small quantity of illegal copies of the program have been imported; he bought a large quantity of spare parts*
b) large amount **große Menge;** *the company offers a discount for quantity purchases*

quantize *verb* to convert an analog signal into a numerical representation **quantisieren;** *the input signal is quantized by an analog to digital converter;* **quantizing noise** = noise on a signal due to inaccuracies in the quantizing process **Quantisierungsgeräusch**

◇ **quantizer** *noun* device used to convert an analog input signal to a numerical form, that can be processed by a computer **Quantisierer, Größenwandler**

◇ **quantization** *noun* conversion of an analog signal to a numerical representation **Quantisierung; quantization error** = error in converting an analog signal into a numerical form due to limited accuracy *or* rapidly changing signal **Quantisierungsfehler;** *see also* A/D

quantum *noun* smallest unit of energy of an electromagnetic radiation at a certain frequency **Quant**

quartile *noun* one of three figures below which 25%, 50% *or* 75% of a total falls **Quartil**

quarto *noun* paper size, made when a sheet is folded twice to make eight pages **Quarto**

quartz (crystal) clock *noun* small slice of quartz crystal which vibrates at a certain frequency when an electrical voltage is supplied, used as a very accurate clock signal for computers and other high precision timing applications **Quarzuhr**

quasi- *prefix* almost *or* which seems like **quasi-; quasi-instruction** = label (in an assembly program) that represents a number of instructions **Quasi-Befehl**

quaternary *adjective* referring to four bits *or* levels *or* objects **quaternär**

query
1 *noun* question **Abfrage; query by example (QBE)** = way of finding information in a database by stating the items that are to be found **Abfrage mittels Beispiel; query facility** = program (usually a database *or* retrieval system) that allows the user to ask questions and receive answers *or* access certain information according to the query **Abfragemöglichkeit; query language (QL)** = language in a database management system, that allows a database to be searched and queried easily **Abfragesprache, Datenbanksprache; query processing** = processing of queries, either by extracting information from a database *or* by translating query commands from a query language **Abfragebearbeitung**
2 *verb* to ask a question about something *or* to suggest that something may be wrong **in Frage stellen, bezweifeln**

question
1 *noun*
(a) words which need an answer **Frage;** *the managing director refused to answer questions about faulty keyboards; the market research team prepared a series of questions to test the public's reactions to colour and price*
(b) problem **Frage;** *he raised the question of moving to less expensive offices; the main question is that of cost; the board discussed the question of launching a new business computer*
2 *verb*
(a) to ask questions **(be)fragen;** *the police questioned the accounts staff for four hours; she questioned the chairman on the company's sales in the Far East*
(b) to query *or* to suggest that something may be wrong **bezweifeln;** *we all question how accurate the computer printout is*

◇ **questionnaire** *noun* printed list of questions, especially used in market research **Fragebogen;** *to send out a questionnaire to test the opinions of users of* *the system; to answer or to fill in a questionnaire about holidays abroad*

queue
1 *noun*
(a) line of people waiting one behind the other **(Warte)schlange;** *to form a queue or to join a queue*
(b) list of data *or* tasks that are waiting to be processed; series of documents (such as orders, application forms) which are dealt with in order **Warteschlange; channel queue** = (i) queue of requests to use a channel; (ii) queue of data that has yet to be sent over a channel **(i) & (ii) Kanalwarteschlange; file queue** = number of files temporarily stored in order before being processed **Dateiwarteschlange;** *output devices such as laser printers are connected on-line with an automatic file queue;* **job queue** = number of tasks arranged in order waiting to be processed in a batch system **Jobwarteschlange; his order went to the end of the queue** = his order was dealt with last **sein Auftrag kam ans Ende der Warteschlange; queue discipline** = method used as the queue structure, either LIFO or FIFO **Warteschlangenstruktur; queue management** *or* **queue manager** = software which orders tasks to be processed **Warteschlangenverwaltung;** *this is a new software spooler with a built-in queue management*
2 *verb* to add more data *or* tasks to the end of a queue **in die Warteschlange einreihen; queued indexed sequential access method (QISAM)** = indexed sequential file that is read item by item into a buffer **erweiterte indizierte Zugriffsmöglichkeit für sequentielle Dateien (QISAM); queued sequential access method (QSAM)** = queue of blocks that are waiting to be processed, retrieved using a sequential access method **erweiterte Zugriffsmöglichkeit für sequentielle Dateien (QSAM); queuing time** = period of time messages have to wait before they can be processed *or* transmitted **Wartezeit**

quick *adjective* fast *or* not taking any time **schnell;** *the company made a quick recovery; he is looking for a quick return on his investment; we are hoping for a quick sale*

◊ **quickly** *adverb* without taking much time **schnell**

◊ **quicksort** *noun* very rapid file sorting and ordering method **Quicksort, Schnellsortierer**

quiescent *adjective* state of a process *or* circuit *or* device when no input signal is applied **ruhig**

quiet *adjective* not making very muc noise **leise;** *laser printers are much quiete than dot-matrix*

quintet *noun* byte made up of five bi **Fünf-Bit-Byte**

quit *verb* to leave a system *or* a progran **beenden;** *do not forget to save your tex before you quit the system*
NOTE: **quitting - quit**

quote
1 *verb*
(a) to repeat words used by someone else to repeat a reference number **zitieren;** *quoted figures from the newspaper report; i reply please quote this number; whe making a complaint please quote the batc number printed on the computer case; h replied, quoting the number of the accoun*
(b) to estimate *or* to say what costs may b **einen Preis angeben/nennen;** *to quote a pric for supplying stationery; their prices ar always quoted in dollars; he quoted me price of £1,026; can you quote for supplyin 20,000 envelopes?*
2 *noun* **quotes** = quotation marks inverted commas **Anführungszeichen; sing**l **quotes** = single inverted commas **einfach Anführungszeichen; double quotes** = doub**l** inverted commas **(doppelte Anführungszeichen;** *the name of th company should be put in double quotes*

◊ **quotation marks** *noun* inverted comma *or* signs printed at the beginning and end c text to show that it has been quoted fron another source **Anführungszeichen**

quotient *noun* result of one numbe divided by another **Quotient**

COMMENT: when two numbers are divided, the answer is made up of a quotient and a remainder (the fractiona**l** part), 16 divided by 4 is equal to a quotient of 4 and zero remainder, 16 divided by 5 is equal to a quotient of 3 and a remainder of 1

QWERTY *noun* **QWERTY keyboard** English language keyboard for a typewrit**e** *or* computer, where the top line of lette are Q-W-E-R-T-Y **QWERTY-Tastatur;** *th computer has a normal QWERT keyboard; see also* AZERTY

QUOTE the keyboard does not have a QWERTY layout but is easy to use
Micro Decisior

Rr

R & D = RESEARCH AND DEVELOPMENT; **R & D department** = department in a company that investigates new products, discoveries and techniques **Forschungs- und Entwicklungsabteilung**

race *noun* error condition in a digital circuit, in which the state *or* output of the circuit is very dependent on the exact timing between the input signals (faulty output is due to unequal propagation delays on the separate input signals at a gate) **Zeitbedingung**

rack *noun*
(a) frame to hold items for display **Ständer;** *a display rack; a rack for holding mag tapes*
(b) metal supporting frame for electronic circuit boards and peripheral devices such as disk drives **Rahmen; rack mounted** = system consisting of removable circuit boards in a supporting frame **Konsole**

radar *noun* method of finding the position of objects such as aircraft, by transmitting radio waves which are reflected back if they hit an object and are displayed on a screen **Radar**

radial transfer *noun* data transfer between two peripherals *or* programs that are on different layers of a structured system (such as an ISO/OSI system) **Radialübertragung**

radiant *adjective* which radiates **strahlend, Strahlungs-, strahlungs-; radiant energy** = amount of energy radiated by an aerial **Strahlungsenergie**
◇ **radiate** *verb*
(a) to go out in all directions from a central point **ausstrahlen**
(b) (i) to send out rays; (ii) to convert electrical signals into travelling electromagnetic waves **(i) ausstrahlen; (ii) aussenden; radiating element** = single basic unit of an antenna that radiates signals **Primärstrahler**
◇ **radiator** *noun* single basic unit of an antenna *or* any device that radiates signals **Radiator**
◇ **radiation** *noun* (i) sending out of waves of energy from certain substances; (ii) conversion of electrical signals in an antenna into travelling electromagnetic waves **(i) Strahlung; (ii) Ausstrahlung**

radio *noun* medium used for the transmission of speech, sound and data over long distances by radio frequency electromagnetic waves **Funk; radio frequency (RF)** = range of electromagnetic waves used for radiocommunications **Hochfrequenz, Funkfrequenz;** *the radio frequency range extends from a few hertz to hundreds of gigahertz;* **radio microphone** = audio microphone with a small radio transmitter attached allowing the transmission of sound signals without wires **Funkmikrophon; radio pager** *or* **radio paging device** = small pocket receiver that responds to a certain unique transmitted code to alert the user **Piepser, Mobilfunk;** *you could contact your salesman if he had a radio pager;* **radio paging** = calling someone by transmitting a code to their radio pager **über einen Piepser aufrufen; radio phone** *or* **radio telephone** = mobile two-way radio communications system that can access the public telephone network **Funktelefon; radio receiver** = device that can receive signals broadcast on one radio frequency and convert them into their original audio form **Empfangsgerät; radio spectrum** = range of radio frequencies **Funkspektrum; radio telegraphy** = telegraph codes transmitted via radio **Funktelegraphie; radio transmission of data** = sending data by radio **Datenübertragung per Funk; radio waves** = electromagnetic radiation waves **Funkwellen**
◇ **radiocommunications** *noun* transmission and reception of sound and data by radio waves **Funkverkehr**

radix *noun* the value of the base of the number system being used **Basis, Radix;** *the hexadecimal number has a radix of 16;* **radix complement** *see* TEN'S, TWO'S COMPLEMENT; **radix notation** = numbers represented to a certain radix **Radixschreibweise;** *see also* BASE (e); **radix point** = dot which indicates the division between a whole unit and its fractional parts **Radixpunkt**

ragged *adjective* not straight *or* with an uneven edge **ausgefranst; ragged left** = printed text with a flush right-hand margin and uneven left-hand margin **rechtsbündiger Flattersatz; ragged right** = printed text with a flush left-hand margin and uneven right-hand margin **linksbündiger Flattersatz; ragged text** = unjustified text, text with a ragged right margin **Text im Flattersatz**

RAM = RANDOM ACCESS MEMORY memory that allows access to any location in any order, without having to access the rest first **Direktzugriffsspeicher, RAM;** *compare* SEQUENTIAL ACCESS MEMORY; **partial RAM** = RAM chip in which only a certain area of the chip functions correctly, usually in newly released chips (partial RAM's can be used by employing more than one to make up the capacity of one fully functional chip) **Teil-RAM; RAM chip** = chip which stores data, allowing random access **RAM-Chip; RAM disk** = section of RAM that is made to look like and behave as a high-speed disk drive (using special software) **RAM-Platte; RAM loader** = routine that will transfer a program from external backing store into RAM **RAM-Lader; RAM refresh** = signals used to update the contents of dynamic RAM chips every few thousandths of a second, involving reading and rewriting the contents, needed to retain data **RAM-Regenerierer; RAM refresh rate** = number of times every second that the data in a dynamic RAM chip has to be read and rewritten **RAM-Regenerationsgeschwindigkeit; self-refreshing RAM** = dynamic RAM chip that has built-in circuitry to generate refresh signals, allowing data to be retained when the power is off by using a battery **selbstregenerierender RAM; dynamic RAM** = most common RAM ICs, which use capacititive charge to retain data but which must be refreshed (read from and rewritten to) every few thousandths of a second **dynamischer RAM; static RAM** = RAM ICs that do not have to be refreshed but cannot store as much data per chip as dynamic RAM **statischer RAM;** *see also* CHIP, ROM NOTE: there is no plural for RAM, and it often has no article: **512K of RAM; the file is stored in RAM**

COMMENT: dynamic RAM which uses a capacitor to store a bit of data (as a charge) needs to have each location refreshed from time to time to retain the data, but is very fast and can contain more data per unit area than static RAM which uses a latch to store the state of a bit, and has the advantage of not requiring to be refreshed to retain its data, and will keep data for as long as power is supplied

QUOTE in addition the board features 512K of video RAM, expandable up to a massive 1MB
PC Business World
QUOTE fast memory is RAM that does not have to share bus access with the chip that manages the video display
Byte

random *adjective* (event) that cannot be anticipated **zufällig, willkürlich; pseudo-random** = generated sequence that appears random but is repeated over a long period **pseudozufällig; random number** = number that cannot be predicted **Zufallsnummer;**

random number generator = program whic generates random numbers (used i lotteries, games, etc.) **Zufallszahlgenerato random process** = system whose outpu cannot be related to its input *or* interna structure **unkalkulierbarer Vorgang**

◇ **random access** *noun* direct acces ability to access immediately memor locations in any order **wahlfreier Zugriff;** *dis drives are random access, magnetic tape sequential access memory;* **random acces device** = device whose access time t retrieve data is not dependent on th location or type of data **Vorrichtung fü wahlfreien Zugriff; random access files** = fil in which each item *or* record can b immediately accessed by its addres without searching through the rest of th file, and is not dependent on the previou location **Direktzugriffsdatei; random acces memory (RAM)** = memory that allow access to any location in any order, usuall in the form of ICs **Direktzugriffsspeiche (RAM); random access storage** = storag medium that allows access to any locatio in any order **Direktzugriffsspeicher**

◇ **random processing** *noun* processing o data in the order required rather than th order in which it is stored **wahlfrei Verarbeitung**

range

1 *noun*
(a) series of items from which the custome can choose **Bereich, Auswahl;** *a wide range products; the catalogue lists a wide range computer stationery*
(b) set of allowed values between maximum and minimum **Wertebereich;** *th telephone channel can accept signals in th frequency range 300 - 3400Hz; magneti tape is stable within a temperature range 0° to 40°C;* **number range** = set of allowabl values **Wertebereich; frequency range** range of allowable frequencies, betwee two limits **Frequenzbereich**
2 *verb*
(a) to vary *or* to be different **sich beweger rangieren;** *the company's products rang from a cheap lapheld micro to multistation mainframe*
(b) to put text in order to one sid **ausrichten, verschieben; range left** = mov text to align it to the left margin; to mov the contents of a word to the left edge **link ausrichten, nach links verschieben**

rank *verb* to sort data into an order usually according to size *or* importanc **ordnen, einstufen**

rapid *adjective* fast **schnell; rapid access** device *or* memory whose access time is ver short **Schnellzugriff(sspeicher); rapid access memory** or **fast access memory (FAM)** = storage locations that can be read from or written to very quickly **Schnellzugriffsspeicher**

raster noun system of scanning the whole of a CRT screen with a picture beam by sweeping across it horizontally, moving down one pixel or line at a time **Raster; raster graphics** = graphics where the picture is built up in lines across the screen or page **Rastergraphik; raster image processor** = raster which translates software instructions into an image or complete page which is then printed by the printer **Rasterbildverarbeiter;** an electronic page can be converted to a printer-readable video image by an on-board raster image processor; **raster scan** = one sweep of the picture beam horizontally across the front of a CRT screen **Zeilenabtastung**

rate
1 noun quantity of data or tasks that can be processed in a set time **Rate;** the processor's instruction execution rate is better than the older version; **error rate** = number of errors that occur within a certain time **Fehlerrate; information rate** = amount of information content per character multiplied by the number of characters transmitted per second **mittlerer Informationsfluß**
2 verb to evaluate how good something is or how large something is **abschätzen; rated throughput** = maximum throughput of a device that will still meet original specifications **Nenndurchlauf**
◊ **ratings** noun calculation of how many people are watching a TV programme **Einschaltquote; ratings battle** or **war** = fight between two TV companies to increase their share of the market **Kampf um die Einschaltquote**

ratio noun proportion of one number to another **Verhältnis;** the ratio of 10 to 5 is 2:1; the ratio of corrupt bits per transmitted message is falling with new technology
◊ **rational number** noun number that can be written as the ratio of two whole numbers **rationale Zahl;** 24 over 7 is a rational number; 0.333 can be written as the rational number 1/3

raw adjective in the original state or not processed **roh, unbearbeitet; raw data** = (i) pieces of information that have not yet been input into a computer system; (ii) data in a database which has to be processed to provide information to the user **(i) Ausgangsdaten; (ii) Ursprungsdaten;** this small computer collects raw data from the sensors, converts it and transmits it to the mainframe

ray noun one line of light or radiation in a beam or from a source **Strahl;** the rays of light pass down the optical fibre

react verb **to react to something** = to act in response to something **auf etwas reagieren; to react with something** = to change because a substance is present **mit etwas reagieren**
◊ **reactance** noun impedance associated with a component (capacitor or inductor) **Reaktanz, Blindwiderstand**
◊ **reaction** noun action which takes place because of something which has happened earlier **Reaktion**
◊ **reactive mode** noun computer operating mode in which each entry by the user causes something to happen but does not provide an immediate response **Reaktionsmodus;** compare with INTERACTIVE; BATCH

read verb
(a) to look at printed words and understand them **lesen;** conditions of sale are printed in such small characters that they are difficult to read; can the OCR read typeset characters?
(b) to retrieve data from a storage medium **lesen;** this instruction reads the first record of a file; access time can be the time taken to read from a record; **destructive read** = read operation in which the stored data is erased as it is retrieved **löschendes Lesen; read back check** = system to ensure that data was correctly received, in which the transmitted data is sent back and checked against the original for any errors **Leseprüfung; read cycle** = period of time between address data being sent to a storage device and the data being returned **Lesezyklus; read head** = transducer that reads signals stored on a magnetic medium and converts them back to their original electrical form **Lesekopf; read only** = device or circuit whose stored data cannot be changed **nur zum Lesen; read only memory (ROM)** = memory device that has had data written into it at the time of manufacture, and now its contents can only be read **Festwertspeicher;** the manufacturer provided the monitor program in two ROM chips; **read rate** = number of bytes or bits that a reader can read in a certain time **Lesegeschwindigkeit; read/write channel** = channel that can carry signals travelling in two directions **Lese-/Schreibkanal; read/write cycle** = sequence of events used to retrieve and store data **Lese-/Schreibzyklus; read/write head** = transducer

that can read *or* write data from the surface of a magnetic storage medium, such as a floppy disk **Lese-/Schreibkopf; read/write memory** = storage medium that can be written to and read from **Lese-/Schreibspeicher;** *compare with* READ ONLY

◇ **readable** *adjective* that can be read *or* understood by someone *or* an electronic device **lesbar;** *the electronic page is converted to a printer-readable video image;* **machine readable** = (commands *or* data) stored on a medium that can be directly input to the computer **maschinenlesbar**

◇ **reader** *noun* device that reads data stored on one medium and converts it into another form **Leser; card reader** = device that transforms data on a punched card to a form that can be recognized by the computer **Lochkartenleser; tape reader** = machine that reads punched holes in paper tape *or* signals on magnetic tape **Magnetbandleser;** *see also* OPTICAL

◇ **read-in** *or* **read in** *verb* to transfer data from an external source to main memory **einlesen;** *the computer automatically read-in thirty values from the A/D converter*

◇ **reading** *noun* note taken of figures *or* degrees, especially of degrees on a scale **Ablesewert**

◇ **readout** *noun* display of data **Anzeige;** *the readout displayed the time; the clock had a digital readout;* **destructive readout** = display device that erases previous characters when displaying new ones **löschendes Lesen; readout device** = device that allows information (numbers *or* characters) to be displayed **Anzeigevorrichtung**

> QUOTE some OCR programs can be taught to read typefaces that are not in their library
> *Publish*
> QUOTE the machine easily reads in text from typewriters and daisy-wheel printers
> *PC Business World*

ready *adjective* fit to be used *or* sold; (equipment) that is waiting and able to be used **bereit;** *the green light indicates the system is ready for another program; the programming will not be ready until next week; the maintenance people hope that the system will be ready for use in 24 hours;* **ready state** = communications line *or* device that is waiting to accept data **Bereitzustand**

real memory *noun* actual physical memory that can be addressed by a CPU **Realspeicher;** *compare with* VIRTUAL MEMORY

◇ **real number** *noun (in computing)* number that is represented with a fractional part (sometimes refers to numbers represented in a floating-point form) **reelle Zahl**

◇ **real time** *noun* actions *or* processing time that is of the same order of magnitude a the problem to be solved (i.e. the processing time is within the same time a the problem to be solved, so that the resul can influence the source of the data **Echtzeit, Real-time;** *a navigation system needs to be able to process the position of ship in real time and take suitable actio before it hits a rock; (US)* **program shown i real time** = TV program which is broadcas live **Live-Sendung; real-time clock** = clock i a computer that provides the correct tim of day **Uhrzeitgeber;** *compare* RELATIVE TIME CLOCK; **real-time input** = data inpu to a system as it happens *or* is require **Echtzeiteingabe; real-time multi-tasking** = executing several real-time task simultaneously without slowing th execution of any of the processes **Echtzei Multitasking; real-time processing** = processing operation that takes a time o the same order of magnitude as th problem to be solved **Echtzeitbetrieb; real time simulation** = computer model of process where each process is executed in similar time to the real proces **Echtzeitsimulation**

◇ **real-time system** *noun* system whose processing time is within that of the problem, so that it can influence the sourc of the data **Echtzeitsystem;** *in a real-tim system, as you move the joystick left, th image on the screen moves left. If there is pause for processing it is not a true real-tim system*

> QUOTE a real-time process is one which interacts with a real external activity and respects deadlines imposed by that activity
> *.EXE*
> QUOTE define a real-time system as any system which is expected to interact with its environment within certain timing constraints
> *British Telecom Technology Journal*

reboot *verb* to reload an operating system during a computing session **erneut laden;** *we rebooted and the files reappeared; see also* BOOT

recall

1 *noun* bringing back text *or* files from store **Aufruf**

2 *verb* to bring back text *or* files from store for editing **aufrufen**

> QUOTE automatic recall provides the facility to recall the last twenty commands and to edit and re-use them
> *Practical Computing*

receive *verb* to accept data from a communications link **empfangen;** *the computer received data via the telephone line;* **receive only** = computer terminal that can only accept and display data (but not transmit) **Empfänger**

◇ **receiver** *noun* electronic device that can detect transmitted signals and present them in a suitable form **Empfänger; radio receiver** = device that detects signals broadcast on one radio frequency and converts them into their original audio form **Empfangsgerät;** *the radio receiver picked up your signal very strongly;* **receiver register** = temporary storage register for data inputs, before processing **Empfangsregister**

reception *noun* quality of a radio *or* TV signal received **Empfang;** *signal reception is bad with that aerial*

re-chargeable *adjective* (battery) which can be charged again with electricity when it is flat **wiederaufladbar**

recode *verb* to code a program which has been coded for one system, so that it will work on another **umcodieren**

recognition *noun* (i) being able to recognize something; (ii) process that allows something to be recognized, such as letters on a printed text *or* bars on a bar codes, etc. **(i) & (ii) (Wieder)erkennung; recognition logic** = logical software used in OCR, AI, etc. **Erkennungslogik; optical character recognition** = process that allows printed *or* written characters to be recognized optically (using an optical character reader), and converted into a form that can be input into a computer **optische Zeichenerkennung; optical mark recognition** = process that allows certain marks *or* lines *or* patterns to be recognized optically (using an optical character reader), and converted into a form that can be input into a computer **optische Markierungserkennung**

◇ **recognize** *verb* to see something and remember that it has been seen before **(wieder)erkennen;** *the scanner will recognize most character fonts*

◇ **recognizable** *adjective* which can be recognized **erkennbar**

recompile *verb* to compile a source program again, usually after changes *or* debugging **neu kompilieren**

reconfigure *verb* to alter the structure of data in a system **rekonfigurieren**

◇ **reconfiguration** *noun* altering the structure of data in a system **Rekonfiguration;** *I reconfigured the field structure in the file; this program allows us to reconfigure the system to our own requirements; see also* CONFIGURE, SET UP

reconnect *verb* to connect again **wiederanschließen;** *the telephone engineers are trying to reconnect the telephone*

reconstitute *verb* to return a file to a previous state, usually to restore a file after a crash *or* corruption **rekonstituieren, wiederherstellen**

record
1 *noun*
(a) set of items of related data **(Daten)satz;** *your record contains several fields that have been grouped together under the one heading; this record contains all their personal details;* **chained record** = data record in a chained file **geketteter Satz; change** *or* **transaction record** = record containing new data which is to be used to update a master record **Änderungssatz; logical record** = number of items of related data that are held in temporary memory ready to be processed **logischer Satz; physical record** = record and control data combination stored on a backing device **physischer Satz; record count** = number of records within a stored file **Satzanzahl; record format** *or* **layout** = organization and length of separate fields in a record **Satzformat; record length** = quantity of data in a record **Satzlänge; records management/manager** = program which maintains records and can access and process them to provide information **Satzverwaltungsprogramm**
(b) plastic disk on the surface of which music *or* other sounds are recorded **Schallplatte**
2 *verb* to store data *or* signals on tape *or* on disk *or* in a computer **aufzeichnen;** *record the results in this column; this device records signals onto magnetic tape; digitally recorded data are used to generate images;* **record button** = key pressed on a recorder when ready to record signals onto a medium **Aufnahmetaste; record gap** *see* BLOCK GAP; **record head** *or* **write head** = transducer that converts an electrical signal into a magnetic field to write the data onto a magnetic medium **Schreibkopf**

QUOTE you can echo the previous record if a lot of replication is involved
QUOTE records may be sorted before the report is created, using up to nine sort fields
Byte
QUOTE file and record-locking procedures have to be implemented to make sure that files cannot be corrupted when two users try to read or write to the same record simultaneously
Micro Decision

recorder *noun* equipment able to transfer input signals onto a storage medium **Aufnahmegerät; magnetic tape recorder** = device with a motor, read/write head and circuitry to allow electrical signals to be recorded onto *or* played back from magnetic tape **Magnetbandgerät**

COMMENT: the signal recorded is not always in the same form as the input signal: many recorders record a modulated carrier signal for better quality. A recorder is usually combined with a suitable playback circuit since the read and write heads are often the same physical device

recording *noun*
(a) action of storing signals *or* data on tape *or* in a computer **Aufzeichnen; recording density** = number of bits of data that can be stored in a unit area on a magnetic disk *or* tape **Zeichendichte; recording trunk** = telephone line between a local and long distance exchange for operator use **Verbindungsleitung**
(b) signal (especially music) which has been recorded on tape *or* disk **Aufnahme;** *a new recording of Beethoven's quartets*

QUOTE file and record-locking procedures have to be implemented to make sure that files cannot be corrupted when two users try to read or write to the same record simultaneously
Micro Decision

recover *verb* to get back something which has been lost **wiederherstellen;** *it is possible to recover the data but it can take a long time*
◊ **recoverable error** *noun* error type that allows program execution to be continued after it has occurred **wiederherstellbarer Fehler**
◊ **recovery** *noun*
(a) returning to normal operating after a fault **Wiederaufnahme; automatic recovery program** = software that is automatically run when a piece of equipment fails, to ensure that the system continues to operate **automatisches Wiederanlaufprogramm; failure recovery** = resuming a process *or* program after a failure has occurred and has been corrected **Wiederaufnahme nach Abbruch; fall back recovery** = resuming a program after a

fault has been fixed, from a point at which the fall back routines were called **Programmwiederaufnahme; sense recovery time** = time that a RAM device takes to switch from read to write mode **Lese-Erholzeit; recovery procedure** = processes required to return a system to normal operation after an error **Wiederanlaufverfahren**
(b) getting back something which has been lost **Zurückgewinnung;** *the recovery of lost files can be carried out using the recovery procedure*

rectangular waveguide *noun* microwave channel that is rectangular in cross section **rechteckige Wellenleitung**

rectify *verb*
(a) to correct something *or* to make something right **berichtigen;** *they had to rectify the error at the printout stage*
(b) to remove the positive *or* negative sections of a signal so that it is unipolar **gleichrichten**
◊ **rectifier** *noun* electronic circuit that converts an alternating current supply into a direct current supply **Gleichrichter**

recto *noun* right hand page of a book (usually given an odd number) **Rekto**

recursion *or* **recursive routine** *noun* subroutine in a program that calls itself during execution **Rekursion; rekursives Unterprogramm; recursive call** = subroutine that calls itself when it is run **rekursiver Aufruf**

redefine *verb* to change the function *or* value assigned to a variable *or* object **neu definieren;** *we redefined the initial parameters;* **to redefine a key** = to change the function of a programmable key **eine Taste neu definieren;** *I have redefined this key to display the figure five when pressed*
◊ **redefinable** *adjective* which can be redefined **neu definierbar**

QUOTE the idea of the packages is that they enable you to redefine the keyboard
Practical Computing
QUOTE one especially useful command lets you redefine the printer's character-translation table
Byte

red, green, blue (RGB) *noun*
(a) high-definition monitor system that uses three separate input signals controlling red, green and blue colour picture beams **Rot-Grün-Blau-System**
(b) the three colour picture beams used in a colour TV **Rot-Grün-Blau**

COMMENT: there are three colour guns producing red, green and blue beams acting on groups of three phosphor dots at each pixel location

redirect *verb* to send a message to its destination by another route **umleiten**
◇ **redirection** *noun* sending a message to its destination by another route **Umleiten;** *call forwarding is automatic redirection of calls*

redo *verb* to do something again **neu anfangen; redo from start** = start again from the beginning **nochmals von vorne anfangen**

redraw *verb* to draw again **erneut zeichnen;** *can the computer redraw the graphics showing the product from the top view?*

reduce *verb*
(a) to make smaller **verringern**
(b) to convert raw data into a more compact form which can then be easily processed **reduzieren**
◇ **reduced instruction set computer (RISC)** *noun* CPU design whose instruction set contains a small number of simple fast-executing instructions, that makes program writing more complex, but increases speed **Computer mit reduziertem Befehlsvorrat;** *compare with* WISC
◇ **reduction** *noun* act of reducing; proportion by which something is made smaller **Verringerung;** *we need a 25% reduction to fit the halftone in the space*

redundant *adjective*
(a) (data) that can be removed without losing any information **überflüssig, redundant;** *the parity bits on the received data are redundant and can be removed;* **redundant character** = character added to a block of characters for error detection or protocol purposes, and carries no information **redundantes Zeichen; redundant code** = check bit or data added to a block of data for error detection purposes, and carries no information **redundanter Code**
(b) (extra piece of equipment) kept ready for a task in case of faults **redundant**
◇ **redundancy** *noun* providing extra components in a system in case there is a breakdown **Redundanz; longitudinal redundancy check** = check on received blocks of data to detect any errors **Blockprüfung; network redundancy** = extra links between points allowing continued operation in the event of one failing **Netzwerkredundanz; vertical redundancy check** = (odd) parity check on each

character of a block received, to detect any errors **Querprüfung; redundancy checking** = checking of received data for correct redundant codes to detect any errors **Redundanzprüfung**

reel *noun* holder round which a tape is rolled **Spule;** *he dropped the reel on the floor and the tape unwound itself;* **pick-up reel** = empty reel used to store tape as it is played from a full reel **Leerspule**
◇ **reel to reel** *noun* copying one tape of data onto another magnetic tape **von Band auf Band (kopieren); reel to reel recorder** = magnetic tape recording machine that uses tape held on one reel and feeds it to a pick-up reel **Magnetbandgerät mit zwei Rollen**

re-entrant program *or* **code** *or* **routine** *noun* one program or code shared by many users in a multi-user system (it can be interrupted or called again by another user before it has finished its previous run, and returns to the point at which it was interrupted when it has finished that run) **wiederverwendbares Programm; wiederverwendbarer Code**
◇ **re-entry** *noun* calling a routine from within that routine; running a program from within that program **Rücksprung; re-entry point** = point in a program or routine where it is re-entered **Rücksprungstelle**

refer *verb* to mention or to deal with or to write about something **sich beziehen auf;** *the manual refers to the serial port, but I cannot find it*
◇ **reference**
1 *noun*
(a) value used as a starting point for other values, often zero **Bezugspunkt; reference address** = initial address in a program used as an origin or base for others **Bezugsadresse; reference level** = signal level to which all others are calibrated **Bezugspegel**
(b) mentioning or dealing with something **Bezug; reference file** = file of data which is kept so that it can be referred to **Zuordnungsdatei; reference instruction** = command that provides access to sorted or stored data **Zuordnungsbefehl; reference list** = list of routines or instructions and their location within a program **Verweisliste; reference mark** = printed symbol to indicate the presence of a note or reference not in the text **Verweiszeichen; reference retrieval system** = index which provides a reference to a document **Wiederauffindungssystem; reference table** = list of ordered items **Bezugstabelle; reference time** = point in time that is used

as an origin for further timings *or* measurements **Bezugszeit**
2 *verb* to access a location in memory **zugreifen auf;** *the access time taken to reference an item in memory is short*

> QUOTE a referencing function dynamically links all references throughout a document
>
> *Byte*

reflect *verb* to send back (light *or* image) from a surface **reflektieren;** *in a reflex camera, the image is reflected by an inbuilt mirror*

◊ **reflected code** *noun* coding system in which the binary representation of decimal numbers changes by only one bit at a time from one number to the next **Gray-Verschlüsselung**

◊ **reflectance** *noun* difference between the amount of light *or* signal incident and the amount that is reflected back from a surface **Remission, Reflexionsgrad;** NOTE: the opposite is **absorptance**

◊ **reflection** *noun* light *or* image which is reflected **Reflexion, Spiegelung; signal reflection** = amount of transmitted signal that is reflected at the receiver due to an impedance mismatch *or* fault **Signalreflexion**

◊ **reflective disk** *noun* video disk that uses a reflected laser beam to read the data etched into the surface **reflektierende Platte**

reflex (camera) *noun* camera with an optical mirror that allows a scene to be viewed through the camera lens so that the user sees what he is photographing **Spiegelreflexkamera**

reformat *verb* to format a disk that already contains data, and erasing the data by doing so **neu formatieren;** *do not reformat your hard disk unless you can't do anything else*

◊ **reformatting** *noun* act of formatting a disk which already contains data **Neuformatierung;** *reformatting destroys all the data on a disk; see also* FORMAT

refract *verb* to change the direction of light as it passes through a material (such as water *or* glass) **brechen**

◊ **refraction** *noun* change in direction of light rays as they pass through a material **Brechung**

◊ **refractive index** *noun* measure of the angle that light is refracted by, as it passes through a material **Brechungsindex**

refresh *verb*
(a) to update regularly the contents of dynamic RAM by reading and rewriting

stored data to ensure data is retained **wiederauffrischen;** *memory refresh signal;* **RAM refresh rate** = number of times every second that the data in a dynamic RAM chip has to be read and rewritten **RAM-Regenerationsgeschwindigkeit;** **self-refreshing RAM** = dynamic RAM chip that has built-in circuitry to generate refresh signals, allowing data to be retained when the power is off, using a battery backup **selbstregenerierender RAM**
(b) screen refresh = to update regularly the images on a CRT screen by scanning each pixel with a picture beam to make sure the image is still visible **Bildwiederholung; refresh rate** = number of times every second that the image on a CRT is redrawn **Bildwiederholfrequenz**

regenerate *verb* (i) to redraw an image on a screen many times a second so that it remains visible; (ii) to receive distorted signals, process and error check them, then retransmit the same data **(i) & (ii) regenerieren**

◊ **regeneration** *noun* process of regenerating a signal **Regeneration**

◊ **regenerative memory** *noun* storage medium whose contents need to be regularly refreshed to retain its contents **Regenerationsspeicher;** *dynamic RAM is regenerative memory - it needs to be refreshed every 250ns; the CRT display can be thought of as regenerative memory, it requires regular refresh picture scans to prevent flicker;* **regenerative reading** = reading operation that automatically regenerates and rewrites the data back into memory **regeneratives Lesen**

region *noun* special *or* reserved area of memory or program **Region, Bereich**

◊ **regional breakpoint** *noun* breakpoint that can be inserted anywhere within a program that is being debugged **regionaler Programmstop;** *see also* BREAKPOINT, DEBUGGING

register
1 *noun*
(a) (i) special location within a CPU (usually one or two words wide) that is used to hold data and addresses to be processed in a machine code operation; (ii) reserved memory location used for special storage purposes **(i) & (ii) Register; accumulator register** = most important internal storage register in a CPU, containing the data to be processed **Akkumulatorregister; address register** = register in a computer that is able to store all the bits of an address which can then be processed as a single unit **Adreßregister; base register** = register in a

CPU (not usually in small computers) that contains the address of the start of a program **Basisregister; buffer register** = temporary storage for data being written to *or* read from memory **Pufferregister; circulating register** = shift register whose output is fed back into its input (to form a closed loop) **Ringschieberegister; control register** = storage location for control data **Steuerregister; data register** = area within a CPU used to store data temporarily before it is processed **Datenregister; external register** = registers which are located outside the main CPU, in locations within main memory, allowing the user to access them easily **externes Register; index register** = computer address register that is added to a reference address to provide the location to be accessed **Indexregister; input/output register** = temporary storage for data received from memory before being transferred to an I/O device *or* data from an I/O device waiting to be stored in main memory or to be processed **Ein-/Ausgaberegister; instruction register** = temporary storage for the instruction that is being executed **Befehlsregister; instruction address register (IAR)** = register in a CPU that stores the location of the next instruction to be processed **Befehlsadreßregister; memory address register (MAR)** = register within the CPU that contains the address of the next location to be accessed **Speicheradreßregister; next instruction register** = register in the CPU that contains the address of the next instruction to be processed **Befehlsfolgeregister; program status word register (PSW register)** = register which contains a number of status bits, such as carry flag, zero flag, overflow flag **Programmstatuswortregister (PSW-Register); sequence control register (SCR)** = CPU register that contains the address of the next instruction to be processed **Befehlsfolgeregister;** *see also* NEXT INSTRUCTION REGISTER; **shift register** = temporary storage into which data can be shifted **Schieberegister; register addressing** = instruction whose address field contains the register in which the operand is stored **Registeradressierung; register file** = number of registers used for temporary storage **Registerdatei; register length** = size (in bits) of a register **Registerlänge;** *in this small micro, the data register is eight bits wide, an address register is sixteen bits wide;* **register map** = display of the contents of all the registers **Registerinhaltsverzeichnis**

(b) superimposing two images correctly **Register; the two colours are out of register** = the colours are not correctly printed one on top of the other **die zwei Farben halten nicht Register**

2 *verb*
(a) to react to a stimulus **ansprechen auf;** *light-sensitive films register light intensity*
(b) to correctly superimpose two images **Register halten; register marks** = marks at the corners of a film used to help in lining up two images **Paßmarken**

regulate *verb* to control a process (usually using sensors and a feedback mechanism) **regeln; regulated power supply** = constant, controlled voltage *or* current source whose output will not vary with input supply variation **Konstantstromversorgung**

COMMENT: a regulated power supply is required for all computers where components cannot withstand voltage variations

rehyphenation *noun* changing the hyphenation of words in a text after it has been put into a new page format *or* line width **erneute Worttrennung**

reject *verb* to refuse to accept something **zurückweisen;** *the computer rejects all incoming data from incompatible sources*
◊ **rejection** *noun* refusing to accept something **Zurückweisung; rejection error** = error by a scanner which cannot read a character and so leaves a blank **Zurückweisungsfehler**

relational database *noun* set of data where all the items are related **relationale Datenbank; relational operator** *or* **logical operator** symbol that compares two items **Vergleichsoperator; relational query** = database query that contains relational operators **kombinierte Abfrage;** *the relational query 'find all men under 35 years old' will not work on this system*
◊ **relationship** *noun* way in which two similar things are connected **Beziehung**

relative *adjective* which is compared to something **relativ; relative address** = location specified in relation to a reference address **relative Adresse; relative coding** = writing a program using relative address instructions **relative Codierung; relative coordinates** = positional information given in relation to a reference point **relative Koordinaten; relative data** = data that gives new coordinate information relative to previous coordinates **relative Daten; relative error** = difference between a number and its correct value (caused by rounding off) **relativer Fehler; relative-time clock** = regular pulses that allow software in a computer to calculate the real time **Relativzeitgeber**

relay *noun* electromagnetically controlled switch **Relais;** *there is a relay in the circuit; it is relay-rated at 5 Amps;* **microwave relay** = radiocommunications equipment used to receive microwave signals, then boost and retransmit them **Mikrowellenrelais**
2 *verb* to receive data from one source and then retransmit it to another point **(weiter)übertragen;** *all messages are relayed through this small micro*

release
1 *noun*
(a) version of a product **Version;** *the latest software is release 5; see also* VERSION
(b) putting a new product on the market **Freigabe; new releases** = new records put on the market **Neuerscheinungen; on general release** = (i) available to the public; (ii) (film) shown at many cinemas **(i) allgemein zugänglich; (ii) überall angelaufen**
(c) press release = sheet giving news about a news item which is sent to newspapers and TV and radio stations so that they can use the information in it **Presseverlautbarung**
2 *verb* to put a new product on the market **auf den Markt bringen; freigeben; veröffentlichen**

relevant *adjective* which has an important connection **relevant, sachdienlich**
◊ **relevance** *noun* (i) way in which something has a connection with something else; (ii) importance of something in a situation *or* process **(i) & (ii) Relevanz**

reliability *noun* the ability of a device to function as intended, efficiently and without failure **Zuverlässigkeit;** *it has an excellent reliability record; the product has passed its reliability tests*
◊ **reliable** *adjective* which can be trusted to work properly **zuverlässig;** *the early versions of the software were not completely reliable*

relief printing *noun* printing process in which the ink is held on a raised image **Hochdruckverfahren, Reliefdruck**

reload *verb* to load again **neu laden;** *we reloaded the program after the crash; see also* LOAD

relocate *verb* to move data from one area of storage to another **verschieben;** *the data is relocated during execution;* **self-relocating program** = program that can be loaded into

any part of memory (that will modify its addresses depending on the program origin address) **selbstverschiebliches Programm**

◊ **relocatable** *adjective* which can be moved to another area of memory without affecting its operation **verschiebbar; relocatable program** = computer program that can be loaded into and executed from any area of memory **relativierbares Programm;** *the operating system can load and run a relocatable program from any area of memory*

◊ **relocation** *noun* moving to another area in memory **Verschiebung; dynamic relocation** = moving data *or* coding *or* assigning absolute locations during a program execution **dynamische Verschiebung; relocation constant** = quantity added to all addresses to move them to another section of memory, (equal to the new base address) **Verschiebungskonstante; static relocation** = moving data *or* coding *or* assigning absolute locations before a program is run **statische Verschiebung**

REM = REMARK statement in a BASIC program that is ignored by the interpreter, allowing the programmer to write explanatory notes **REM (Bemerkung)**

remainder
1 *noun* number equal to the dividend minus the product of the quotient and divider **Rest;** *7 divided by 3 is equal to 2 remainder 1; compare with* QUOTIENT
2 *verb* to sell products below cost price **verramschen;** *this computer model is out of date so we have to remainder the rest of the stock*

remedial maintenance *noun* maintenance to repair faults which have developed in a system **Bedarfswartung**

remote *adjective* (communications) with a computer at a distance from the systems centre **entfernt, fern-, Fern-;** *users can print reports on remote printers;* **remote console** *or* **device** = input/output device located away from the computer (sending data to it by line *or* modem) **Außenstelle; remote control** = control of a process *or* machine from a distance **Fernsteuerung;** *the video recorder has a remote control facility;* **remote job entry (RJE)** = batch processing system where instructions are transmitted to the computer from a remote terminal **Jobferneingabe; remote station** = communications station that can be controlled by a central computer **Gegenstelle; remote terminal** = computer terminal connected to a distant computer system **entfernt stehende Datenstation**

remove *verb* to take away *or* to move to another place **entfernen;** *the file entry was removed from the floppy disk directory*
◊ **removable** *adjective* which can be removed **auswechselbar;** *a removable hard disk*
◊ **removal** *noun* taking away **Beseitigung;** *the removal of this instruction could solve the problem*

rename *verb* to give a new name to a file **neu benennen;** *save the file and rename it CUSTOM*

renumber *noun* feature of some computer languages that allows the programmer to allocate new values to all *or* some of a program's line numbers **neu numerieren;** *see also* LINE NUMBER

reorganize *verb* to organize again **neu organisieren;** *wait while the spelling checker database is being reorganized*

repaginate *verb* to renumber or change the lengths of pages of text **mit neuen Seitenzahlen versehen, neu paginieren;** *the dtp package allows simple repagination; the text was repaginated with a new line width*

repeat *verb* to do an action again **wiederholen; repeat counter** = register that holds the number of times a routine *or* task has been repeated **Wiederholungszähler; repeat key** = key on a keyboard which repeats the character pressed **Dauertaste**
◊ **repeater** *noun* device that receives a signal, amplifies it, then retransmits it (sometimes regenerating the received signal) **Verstärker(station);** *this cheap repeater does not regenerate the signals*
◊ **repeating group** *noun* pattern of data that is duplicated in a bit stream **Wiederholungsgruppe**

reperforator *noun* machine that punches paper tape according to ,received signals **Lochstreifenempfänger; reperforator transmitter** = reperforator and a punched tape transmitter connected together **Lochstreifensender mit Empfangslocher**

repertoire *noun* the range of functions of a device *or* software **Repertoire;** *the manual describes the full repertoire;* **character repertoire** = list of all the characters that can be displayed *or* printed **Zeichenvorrat; instruction repertoire** = all the commands

that a system can recognise and execute **Befehlsvorrat;** *see also* RESERVED WORD

QUOTE the only omissions in the editing repertoire are dump, to list variables currently in use, and find
Computing Today

repetitive letter *noun* form letter *or* standard letter into which the details of each addressee (such as name and address) are inserted **Formbrief**

replace *verb*
(a) to put something back where it was before; to put something in the place of something else **ersetzen;** *the printer ribbons need replacing after several thousand characters*
(b) instruction to a computer to find a certain item of data and put another in its place **austauschen;** *see also* SEARCH AND REPLACE

replay
1 *noun*
(a) playback *or* reading back data *or* a signal from a recording **Wiedergabe**
(b) repeating a short section of filmed action, usually in slow motion **Wiederholung;** *the replay clearly showed the winner; this video recorder has a replay feature;* **instant replay** = feature of video recording systems that allows an action that has just been recorded to be viewed immediately **sofortige Wiedergabe**
2 *verb* to play back (something which has been recorded) **wiedergeben;** *he replayed the tape; she recorded the TV programme on video tape and replayed it the next evening*

replenish *verb* to charge a battery with electricity again **wiederaufladen**

replicate *verb* to copy **wiederholen;** *the routine will replicate your results with very little effort*
◊ **replication** *noun* (i) extra components in a system in case there is a breakdown *or* fault in one; (ii) copying a record *or* data to another location **(i) Replikation; (ii) Kopie**

report generator *noun* software that allows data from database files to be merged with a document (in the form of graphs or tables) to provide a complete report **Listengenerator**
◊ **report program generator (RPG)** *noun* programming language used mainly on personal computers for the preparation of business reports, allowing data in files, databases, etc., to be included **Listenprogrammgenerator**

represent *verb*
(a) to act as a symbol for something **darstellen;** *the hash sign is used to represent a number in a series*
(b) to act as a salesman for a product **repräsentieren, vertreten**

◇ **representation** *noun* action of representing something **Darstellung; character representation** = combination of bits used for each character code **Zeichendarstellung**

◇ **representative**
1 *adjective* typical example of something **repräsentativ**
2 *noun* salesman who represents a company **Vertreter, Beauftragter;** *the representative called yesterday about the order*

reprint
1 *verb* to print more copies of a document *or* book **nachdrucken**
2 *noun* printing of copies of a book after the first printing **Nachdruck, Neuauflage;** *we ordered a 10,000 copy reprint*

repro *noun* *(informal)* finished artwork *or* camera-ready copy, ready for filming and printing **Repro; repro proof** = perfect proof ready to be reproduced **Reproabzug**

reproduce *verb* to copy data *or* text from one material *or* medium to another similar one **kopieren**

◇ **reproduction** *noun* action of copying **Kopieren**

reprogram *verb* to alter a program so that it can be run on another type of computer **neu programmieren**

request
1 *noun* thing which someone asks for **Anforderung; request to send signal (RTS)** = signal sent by a transmitter to a receiver asking if the receiver is ready to accept data (used in the RS232C serial connection) **Sendeanforderung**
2 *verb* to ask for something **anfordern**

require *verb* to need something *or* to demand something **erfordern;** *delicate computer systems require careful handling*

◇ **required hyphen** *or* **hard hyphen** *noun* hyphen which is always in a word, even if the word is not split (as in co-administrator) **unveränderlicher Bindestrich;** *see also* SOFT

◇ **requirements** *noun* things which are needed **Erfordernisse, Voraussetzungen;** *memory requirements depend on the application software in use*

re-route *verb* to send by a different route **umsteuern;** *the call diverter re-routes a call*

rerun *verb* to run a program *or* a printing job again **wiederholen; rerun point** = place in the program from where to start a running again after a crash *or* halt **Wiederanlaufpunkt**

res *see* RESOLUTION; **hi-res** = HIGH RESOLUTION; **lo-res** = LOW RESOLUTION

resave *verb* to save again **nochmals abspeichern;** *it automatically resaves the text*

rescue dump *noun* data saved on disk automatically when a computer fault occurs (it describes the state of the system at that time, used to help in debugging) **Notspeicherauszug**

research *noun* scientific investigation to learn new facts about a field of study **Forschung; research and development (R & D)** = investigation of new products, discoveries and techniques **Forschung und Entwicklung;** *the company has spent millions of dollars on R & D*

reserved sector *noun* area of disk space that is used only for control data storage **reservierter Sektor; reserved word** = word *or* phrase used as an identifier in a programming language (it performs a particular operation *or* instruction and so cannot be used for other uses by the programmer *or* user) **festgelegtes Wort**

> QUOTE sometimes a process will demand cache space when the only free cache space is reserved for higher priority processes
> *.EXE*

reset *verb*
(a) to return a system to its initial state, to allow a program *or* process to be started again **zurückstellen; reset button** *or* **key** = switch that allows a program to be terminated and reset manually **Rückstelltaste; hard reset** = electrical signal that usually returns the system to its initial state when it was switched on, requiring a reboot **harte Rückstellung; soft reset** = instruction that terminates any program execution and returns the user to the monitor *or* BIOS **weiche Rückstellung**
(b) to set a register *or* counter to its initial state **in Grundstellung bringen;** *when it reaches 999 this counter resets to zero*
(c) to set data equal to zero **auf Null stellen**

COMMENT: hard reset is similar to soft reset but with a few important differences: it is a switch that directly signals the CPU, while soft reset signals the operating system; hard reset clears all memory contents; a soft reset does not affect memory contents; hard reset should always reset the system, a soft reset does not always work (if, for example, you have really upset the operating system a soft reset will not work)

resident *adjective* (data *or* program) that is always in a computer **ständig vorhanden, resident; resident engineer** = engineer who works permanently for one company **fest angestellter Ingenieur; resident software** *or* **memory-resident software** = program that is held permanently in memory (whilst the machine is on) **speicherresidentes Programm**

residual *adjective* which remains behind **Rest-, rest-; residual error rate** = ratio between incorrect and undetected received data and total data transmitted **Restfehlerhäufigkeit**

◇ **residue check** *noun* error detection check in which the received data is divided by a set number and the remainder is checked against the required remainder **Modulo-N-Prüfung**

resist
1 *verb* to fight against something *or* to refuse to do something **Widerstand leisten**
2 *noun* substance used to protect a pattern of tracks on a PCB, that is not affected by etching chemicals **Abdeckmittel;** *see also* PHOTORESIST

◇ **resistance** *noun* measure of the voltage drop across a component with a current flowing through it **Widerstand;** *see also* OHM'S LAW

◇ **resistor** *noun* electronic component that provides a known resistance **Widerstand** ▷ APPENDIX **resistor transistor logic (RTL)** = circuit design method using transistors and resistors **Widerstand-Transistor-Logik; variable resistor** = component whose resistance can be changed by turning a knob **Regelwiderstand**

resolution *noun* number of pixels that a screen *or* printer can display per unit area **Auflösungsvermögen;** *the resolution of most personal computer screens is not much more than 70 dpi (dots per inch);* **graphic display resolution** = number of pixels that a computer is able to display on the screen **Auflösungsvermögen eines Graphikbildschirms; high resolution (hi-res)** = ability to display *or* detect a very large

number of pixels per unit area **hohe Auflösung;** *the high resolution screen can display 640 by 450 pixels;* **limiting resolution** = maximum number of lines that make up an image on a CRT screen **Auflösungsgrenze; low resolution (low-res)** = ability of a display system to control a number of pixels at a time rather than individual pixels **niedrige Auflösung**

QUOTE the resolution is 300 dots per inch and the throughput is up to eight pages per minute
Practical Computing

resolving power *noun* measurement of the ability of an optical system to detect fine black lines on a white background (given as the number of lines per millimetre) **Auflösungsvermögen**

resonance *noun* situation where a frequency applied to a body being the same as its natural frequency, causes it to oscillate with a very large amplitude **Resonanz**

resource *noun* products *or* programs which are useful **Betriebsmittel; resource allocation** = dividing available resources in a system between jobs **Betriebsmittelzuteilung; resource sharing** = the use of one resource in a network *or* system by several users **gemeinsame Betriebsmittelbenutzung**

respond *verb* to reply *or* to react because of something **beantworten**

◇ **response** *noun* reaction caused by something **Antwort; response frame** = page in a videotext system that allows a user to enter data **Antwortrahmen; response position** = area of a form that is to be used for optical mark reading data **Markierungsstelle; response time** = (i) time which passes between the user starting an action (by pressing a key) and the result appearing on the screen; (ii) speed with which a system responds to a stimulus **(i) Beantwortungszeit; (ii) Antwortzeit;** *the response time of this flight simulator is very good*

restart *verb* to start again **wiederanlaufen;** *first try to restart your system*

restore *verb* to put back into an earlier state **rückstellen**

QUOTE first you have to restore the directory that contains the list of deleted files
Personal Computer World

restrict *verb* to keep something within a certain limit; to allow only certain people to access information **einschränken;** *the document is restricted, and cannot be placed on open access*

◇ **restriction** *noun* something which restricts (data flow *or* access) **Einschränkung**

result *noun* answer *or* outcome of an arithmetic *or* logical operation **Ergebnis**

resume *verb* to restart the program from the point where it was left, without changing any data **wiederaufnehmen**

retain *verb* to keep **festhalten**

◇ **retention** *noun* keeping **Zurückhalten; image retention** = time taken for a TV image to disappear after it has been displayed, caused by long persistence phosphor **Bildkonservierung**

retouch *verb* to change a print *or* photograph slightly by hand, to make it clearer *or* to remove any blemishes **retuschieren;** *I retouched the scratch mark on the last print; the artwork for the line drawings needs retouching in places*

retransmit *verb* to transmit again (a received signal) **erneut übertragen**

◇ **retransmission** *noun* signal *or* data that has been retransmitted **nochmalige Übertragung**

retrieval *noun* the process of searching, locating and recovering information from a file *or* storage device **Wiederauffinden; information retrieval** = locating quantities of data stored in a database and producing information from the data **Informationswiedergewinnung; information retrieval centre** = research system, providing specific information from a database for a user **Datenbankzentrale; text retrieval** = information retrieval system that allows the user to examine complete documents rather than just a reference to a document **Wiederauffinden eines Textes**

◇ **retrieve** *verb* to extract information from a file *or* storage device **herausfinden;** *these are the records retrieved in that search; this command will retrieve all names beginning with S*

retro- *prefix* meaning going back; progress backwards **Rück-, rück-; retrofit** = device *or* accessory added to a system to upgrade it **Nachrüstung**

retrospective parallel running *noun* running a new computer system with old

data to check if it is accurate **rückweisender Parallellauf**

◇ **retrospective search** *noun* search of documents on a certain subject since a certain date **rückwärtsgerichtete Suche**

return *noun*
(a) instruction that causes program execution to return to the main program from a subroutine **Rücksprung;** *the program is not working because you missed out the return instruction at the end of the subroutine;* **return address** = address to be returned to after a called routine finishes **Rücksprungadresse**
(b) key on a keyboard used to indicate that all the required data has been entered **Eingabetaste;** *you type in your name and code number then press return*
(c) indication of an end of line (in printing) **Zeilenbruch; carriage return (CR)** = code *or* key to indicate the end of an input line and to move the cursor to the start of the next line **Rücklauftaste**

◇ **return to zero signal** recording reference mark taken as the level of unmagnetized tape **Rückkehr-nach-Null-Signal;** NOTE: opposite is **non return to zero**

> COMMENT: the return address is put on the stack by the call instruction and provides the address of the instruction after the call, which is to be returned to after the called routine has finished

reveal *verb* to display previously hidden information once a condition has been met **aufdecken**

reverse
1 *adjective* going in the opposite direction **rückwärts; reverse channel** = low speed control data channel between a receiver and transmitter **Rückkanal, Hilfskanal; reverse characters** = characters which are displayed in the opposite way to other characters for emphasis (as black on white *or* white on black, when other characters are the opposite) **invertierte Zeichen, umgekehrte Schrift; reverse index** = movement of a printer head up half a line to print superscripts **rückläufiger Index; reverse interrupt** = signal sent by a receiver to request the termination of transmissions **Betriebsunterbrechungsanfrage; reverse polarity** = situation where the positive and negative terminals have been confused, resulting in the equipment not functioning **umgekehrte Polarität (durch Umpolung); reverse Polish notation (RPN)** = mathematical operations written in a logical way, so that the operator appears after the numbers to be acted upon, this

removes the need for brackets **Postfixschreibweise;** *three plus four, minus two is written in RPN as 3 4 + 2 - = 5; normal notation: (x-y) + z, but using RPN: xy - z+; same as* POSTFIX NOTATION; **reverse video** = screen display mode where white and black are reversed (colours are complemented) **invertierte Darstellung**
2 *verb* to go *or* travel in the opposite direction; to send (control) data from a receiver to a transmitter **umkehren**

QUOTE the options are listed on the left side of the screen, with active options shown at the top left in reverse video
PC User

revert *verb* to return to a normal state **zurückfallen in;** *after the rush order, we reverted back to our normal speed;* **revert command** = command (in text) that returns a formatted page to its original state **Rücknahmebefehl**

review *verb* to see again *or* replay and check **überprüfen;** *the program allows the user to review all wrongly spelled words*

revise *verb* to update *or* correct a version of a document *or* file **überarbeiten, revidieren;** *the revised version has no mistakes*

rewind *verb* to return a tape *or* film *or* counter to its starting point **zurückspulen;** *the tape rewinds onto the spool automatically*

rewrite
1 *verb* to write something again **neu schreiben;** *see also* REGENERATE
2 *noun* act of writing something again **erneuter Schreibvorgang;** *the program is in its second rewrite*

RF = RADIO FREQUENCY; **RF modulator** *or* **radio frequency modulator** = electronic circuit that modulates a high frequency carrier signal with a video signal to enable it to be displayed on a domestic TV **Hochfrequenzmodulator**

RGB = RED, GREEN, BLUE high-definition monitor system that uses three separate input signals controlling red, green and blue colour picture beams **Rot-Grün-Blau-System**

COMMENT: there are three colour guns producing red, green and blue beams acting on groups of three phosphor dots at each pixel location

rheostat *noun* resistance with a movable wiper that will provide a variable output voltage **Regelwiderstand, Rheostat**
NOTE: also called **variable potential divider**

RI = RING INDICATOR

ribbon *noun* long thin flat piece of material **Band; printer ribbon** = roll of inked material which passes between a printhead and the paper **Farbband; ribbon cable** = number of insulated conductors arranged next to each other forming a flat cable **Bandkabel**

right *adjective* not left **rechts; right justify** = to align the right margin so that the text is straight **rechts ausrichten; right justification** = aligning the text and spacing characters so that the right margin is straight **Rechtsausrichtung; right shift** = to move a section of data one bit to the right **nach rechts verschieben;** *see also* LOGICAL SHIFT, ARITHMETIC SHIFT

rigid *adjective* hard *or* which cannot bend **starr**

ring
1 *noun* data list whose last entry points back to the first entry **Ring; ring (data) network** = type of network where each terminal is connected one after the other in a circle **Ringnetz;** *see also* CHAINED LIST
2 *verb* to telephone **anrufen; ring back system** = remote computer system in which a user attempting to access it phones once, allows it to ring a number of times, disconnects, waits a moment, then redials (usually in a bulletin board system) **Rückrufsystem; ring down** = to call a number of users in a telephone network **einen Rundruf machen; ring indicator (RI)** = signal from a line answering device that it has detected a call to the DTE and has answered by going into an off-hook state **Anrufsignal**
◇ **ring counter** *noun* electronic counter in which any overflow from the last digit is fed into the input **Ringzählwerk**
◇ **ring shift** *noun* data movement to the left *or* right in a word, the bits falling outside the word boundary are discarded, the free positions are filled with zeros **Ringverschiebung**

RIP = REST IN PROPORTION printing instruction to indicate that all the material is to be reduced *or* enlarged in the same proportion **RIP (Druckeranweisung für proportionale Vergrößerung bzw. Verkleinerung)**

ripple *noun* small alternating current voltage apparent on a badly regulated direct current output supply **Brummspannung**

◊ **ripple-through carry** *noun* one operation producing a carry out from a sum and a carry in **Schnellübertrag**

RISC REDUCED INSTRUCTION SET COMPUTER CPU design whose instruction set contains a small number of simple fast-executing instructions, that makes program writing more complex, but increases speed **Computer mit reduziertem Befehlsvorrat;** *see also* WISC

rise time *noun* time taken for a voltage to increase its amplitude (from 10 to 90 per cent or zero to RMS value of its final amplitude) **Anlaufzeit; the circuit has a fast rise time** = electronic circuit that is able to handle rapidly changing signals such as very high frequency signals **der Schaltkreis hat eine schnelle Anlaufzeit**

RJE = REMOTE JOB ENTRY batch processing system where instructions are transmitted to the computer from a remote terminal **Jobferneingabe**

RMS = ROOT MEAN SQUARE; **RMS line current** = the root mean square of the electrical current on a line **Effektivstrom**

RO = RECEIVE ONLY computer terminal that can only accept and display data, not transmit **Empfänger**

robot *noun* device which can be programmed to carry out certain manufacturing tasks which are similar to tasks carried out by people **Roboter**

◊ **robotics** *noun* study of artificial intelligence, programming and building involved with robot construction **Robotik**

QUOTE so far no robot sensor has been devised which can operate quickly enough to halt the robot if a human being is in its path of work
IEE News

robust *adjective* solid *or* (system) which can resume working after a fault **robust, widerstandsfähig;** *this hard disk is not very robust*

◊ **robustness** *noun*
(a) strength of a system's casing and its ability to be knocked *or* dropped **Widerstandsfähigkeit**
(b) system's ability to continue functioning even with errors *or* faults during a program execution **Gutmütigkeit**

rogue indicator *noun* special code used only for control applications such as end of file marker **Endmarke**

◊ **rogue value** *or* **terminator** *noun* item in a list of data, which shows that the list is terminated **Endmarke**

role indicator *noun* symbol used to show the role of a index entry in its particular context **Funktionsanzeiger**

roll
1 *noun* length of film *or* tape wound around itself **Rolle;** *he put a new roll of film into the camera*
2 *verb*
(a) to rotate a device about its axis **rollen**
(b) to start filming **die Kameras laufen lassen; roll in/roll out** = the transfer of one process (in a multiprogramming system) from storage to processor then back once it has had its allocated processing time **ein-/ausspeichern**

◊ **rollback** *noun* reloading software after the master software has been corrupted **Neuladen**

◊ **roll-in** *verb* to transfer data from backing store into main memory **einspeichern**

◊ **rolling headers** *noun* titles *or* headers of (teletext) pages displayed as they are received **rollende Kopfzeilen**

◊ **roll-out** *verb* to save the contents of main memory onto backing store **ausspeichern**

◊ **rollover** *noun* keyboard with a small temporary buffer so that it can still transmit correct data when several keys are pressed at once **Tastatur mit überlappender Eingabe; key rollover** = use of a buffer between the keyboard and computer to provide rapid keystroke storage for fast typists **Tastenüberlappungspuffer**

◊ **roll scroll** *verb* displayed text that moves up *or* down the computer screen one line at a time **zeilenweises Blättern**

ROM = READ ONLY MEMORY; **CD-ROM** *or* **compact disk-ROM** = compact disk-ROM small plastic disk that is used as a high capacity ROM device, data is stored in binary form as holes etched on the surface which are then read by a laser **CD-Festspeicher, CD-ROM; ROM cartridge** = software stored in a ROM mounted in a cartridge that can be easily plugged into a computer **ROM-Kassette;** NOTE: there is no plural for ROM, and it is often used without the article: **the file is stored in ROM**

◊ **romware** *noun* software which is stored in ROM **ROM-Software**

roman *noun* ordinary typeface, neither italic nor bold **Antiqua;** *the text is set in Times Roman*

◇ **Roman numerals** *noun* figures written I, II, III, IV, etc. (as opposed to Arabic numerals such as 1, 2, 3, 4, etc.) **römische Zahlen**

root *noun*
(a) starting node from which all paths branch in a data tree structure **Wurzel**
(b) fractional power of a number **Wurzel; square root** = number raised to the power one half **Quadratwurzel;** *the square root of 25 is 5;* **root mean square (RMS)** = measure of the amplitude of a signal (equal to the square root of the mean value of the signal) **Effektivwert;** *the root mean square of the pure sinusoidal signal is 0.7071 of its amplitude*

rotary *adjective* which works by turning **rotierend, Dreh-; rotary camera** = camera able to photograph microfilm as it is moved in front of the lens by moving the film at the same time **Rotationskamera; rotary press** = printing press whose printing plate is cylindrical **Rotationspresse**

◇ **rotate** *verb* to move data within a storage location in a circular manner **rotieren**

◇ **rotation** *noun* amount by which an object has been rotated **Rotation; bit rotation** *or* **rotate operation** = shifting a pattern of bits in a word to the left or right, the old last bit moving to the new first bit position **Rotationsoperation; matrix rotation** = swapping the rows with the columns in an array (equal to rotating by 90 degrees) **Matrixdrehung;** *see also* SHIFT (CYCLIC)

round
(a) *adjective* which goes in a circle **rund; round robin** = way of organizing the use of a computer by several users, who each use it for a time and then pass it on the next in turn **Ringmodell, Reihum-Methode**
(b) *verb* to round down = to approximate a number to a slightly lower one of lower precision **abrunden;** *we can round down 2.651 to 2.65;* **to round off** = to approximate a number to a slightly larger *or* smaller one of lower precision **auf-, abrunden;** *round off 23.456 to 23.46;* **round off errors** = inaccuracies in numbers due to rounding off **Auf-, Abrundungsfehler; to round up** = to approximate a number to a slightly larger one of lower precision **aufrunden;** *we can round up 2.647 to 2.65*

◇ **rounding** *noun*
(a) approximation of a number to a slightly larger *or* smaller one of lower precision **runden; rounding error** = error in a result caused by rounding off the number **Rundungsfehler**
(b) giving graphics a smoother look **Abrundung; character rounding** = making a displayed character more pleasant to look at (within the limits of pixel size) by making sharp corners and edges smooth **Zeichenrundungen**

route *noun* path taken by a message between a transmitter and receiver in a network **Leitweg;** *the route taken was not the most direct since a lot of nodes were busy*

◇ **routing** *noun* determining a suitable route for a message through a network **Wegewahl;** *there is a new way of routing data to the central computer;* **routing overheads** = actions that have to be taken when routing messages **Maßnahmen zur Leitwegbestimmung;** *the information transfer rate is very much less once routing overheads have been accommodated;* **routing page** = videotext page describing the routes to other pages **Leitwegseite; routing table** = list of preferred choices for a route for a message **Leitwegtabelle**

routine *noun* a number of instructions that perform a particular task, but are not a complete program; they are included as part of a program **Programm, Routine;** *the routine copies the screen display onto a printer; the RETURN instruction at the end of the routine sends control back to the main program;* **closed routine** *or* **closed subroutine** = one section of code at a location, that is used by all calls to the routine **geschlossenes Programm; abgeschlossenes Unterprogramm; fall back routines** = routines that are called *or* processes which are executed by a user when a machine *or* system has failed **Wiederanlaufroutine; floating-point routines** = set of routines that allow floating-point numbers to be handled and processed **Gleitkommaprogramm; input routine** = short section of code that accepts data from an external device, such as reading an entry from a keyboard **Eingabeprogramm; open routine** *or* **open subroutine** = set of instructions in a routine, that are copied to whichever part of the program requires them **offenes Programm; offenes Unterprogramm; packing routine** = program which packs data into a small storage area **Verdichtungsprogramm;** *see also* CALL, RETURN

COMMENT: routines are usually called from a main program to perform a task, control is then returned to the part of the main program from which the routine was called once that task is complete

row *noun*
(a) (i) line of printed *or* displayed characters; (ii) horizontal line on a punched card **(i) Zeile; (ii) Lochzeile;** *the figures are presented in rows, not in columns; each entry is separated by a row of dots*
(b) horizontal set of data elements in an array *or* matrix **Sprosse**

RPG = REPORT PROGRAM GENERATOR

RS-232C EIA approved standard used in serial data transmission, covering voltage and control signals **RS-232C**

COMMENT: the RS232C has now been superceeded by the RS423 and RS422 interface standards, similar to the RS232, but allowing higher transmission rates

RSA cipher system the Rivest, Shamir and Adleman public key cipher system **Kryptosystem RSA**

RS-flip-flop = RESET-SET FLIP-FLOP electronic bistable device whose output can be changed according to the Reset and Set inputs **RS-Kippstufe;** *see also* FLIP-FLOP

RTE = REAL TIME EXECUTION

RTL = RESISTOR-TRANSISTOR LOGIC

RTS = REQUEST TO SEND SIGNAL

rubber banding *see* ELASTIC BANDING

rubout *see* ERASE

rubric *noun* printed headings of a book chapter *or* section **Rubrik, Überschrift**

rule *noun*
(a) set of conditions that describe a function **Regel;** *the rule states that you wait for the clear signal before transmitting;* **rule-based system** = software that applies the rules and knowledge defined by experts in a particular field to a user's data to solve a problem **auf Regeln beruhendes System**
(b) thin line in printing **Linie; em rule** = dash as long as an em, used to show that words are separated **Trennstrich (in der Größe eines m); en rule** = dash as long as an en, used to show that words are joined **Bindestrich (in der Größe eines n)**
◊ **ruler** *noun* graduated line, displaying the horizontal position of text *or* distance **Lineal**

run
1 *noun* execution by a computer of a set o instructions *or* programs *or* procedure **Ablauf;** *the next invoice run will be o Friday;* **program run** = executing (in correc order) the instructions in a progran **Programmablauf; run indicator** = indicato bit *or* LED that shows that a computer i currently executing a progran **Ablaufanzeiger**
2 *verb* to be in operation **in Betrieb sein;** *th computer has been running ten hours a da do not interrupt the spelling checker while is running; the new package runs on our PC* **parallel running** = running old and nev computer systems together to allow th new system to be checked before becomes the only system used **Parallellauf run around** = to fit text around an image o a printed page **umlaufen; run in** = to operat a system at a lower capacity for a time i case of any faults **mit reduzierter Kraft laufe**
◊ **runaway** *noun* uncontrolled operatio of a device *or* computer (due to malfunction *or* error) **Weglaufen**
◊ **running head** *noun* title line of each pag in a document **lebender Kolumnentitel**
◊ **run on** *verb*
◊ **run on** *verb*
(a) to make text continue without a brea **ohne Absatz drucken;** *the line can run on t the next without any space*
(b) to print more copies to add to a prin run **fortdrucken;** *we decided to run on 3,00 copies to the first printing;* **run-on price** price of extra copies printed after a fixe print run **Preis für zusätzliche Auflagen**
◊ **run-time** *or* **run-duration**
1 *noun*
(a) period of a time a program takes to ru **Durchlaufzeit**
(b) time during which a computer executing a program **Laufzeit**
2 *adjective* (operation) carried out onl when a program is running **Laufzeit-; rur time error** = fault only detected when program is run *or* error made while program is running **Laufzeitfehler;** *see als* EXECUTION ERROR; **run-time system** software that is required in main storag while a program is running (to execut instructions to peripherals, etc **Laufzeitsystem**

R/W = READ/WRITE
◊ **R/W cycle** = READ/WRITE CYCL sequence of events used to retrieve *or* stor data **Lese-/Schreibzyklus**
◊ **R/W head** = READ/WRITE HEA electromagnetic device that allows data be read from *or* written to a storag medium **Lese-/Schreibkopf**

RX = RECEIVE, RECEIVER *the RXed signal needs to be amplified*

Ss

S100 bus *or* **S-100 bus** *noun* IEEE-696 standard bus, a popular 8 and 16 bit microcomputer bus using 100 lines and a 100-pin connector **S-100-Bus**; *see also* BUS NOTE: say "S one hundred bus"

SAFE = SIGNATURE ANALYSIS USING FUNCTIONAL ANALYSIS signature validation technique **Unterschriftsbestätigungsmethode (mit Hilfe von Funktionsanalyse)**

safe area *noun* area of a TV image that will be seen on a standard television set **Rahmen**

◇ **safety net** *noun* software *or* hardware device that protects the system *or* files from excessive damage in the event of a system crash **Sicherheitsvorrichtung;** *if there is a power failure, we have a safety net in the form of a UPS*

salami technique *noun* computer fraud involving many separate small transactions that are difficult to detect and trace **Salamitechnik**

SAM = SERIAL ACCESS MEMORY storage where a particular data item can only be accessed by reading through all the previous items in the list (as opposed to random access) **serieller Zugriffsspeicher**

COMMENT: magnetic tape is a form of SAM; you have to go through the whole tape to access one item, while disks provide random access to stored data

sample
1 *noun* measurement of a signal at a point in time **Stichprobe;** *the sample at three seconds showed an increase;* **sample and hold circuit** = circuit that freezes an analog input signal for long enough for an A/D converter to produce a stable output **Abtast- und Haltekreis**
2 *verb* to obtain a number of measurements of a signal that can be used to provide information about the signal **abtasten; sampling interval** = time period between two consecutive samples **Abtastintervall; sampling rate** = number of measurements

of a signal recorded every second **Abtastgeschwindigkeit;** *see also* ANALOG/DIGITAL CONVERSION, QUANTIZE

◇ **sampler** *noun*
(a) electronic circuit that takes many samples of a signal and stores them for future analysis **Abtaster**
(b) electronic circuit used to record audio signals in digital form and store them to allow future playback **Abfrageschalter**

COMMENT: if the sampling is on a music signal and the sampling frequency is great enough, digitally stored signals sound like the original analog signal. For analog signals, a sampling rate of at least two times the greatest frequency is required to provide adequate detail

sans serif *noun* typeface whose letters have no serifs **serifenlose Schrift, Groteskschrift**

sapphire *noun* blue-coloured precious stone used as a substrate for certain chips **Saphir**

SAR = STORE ADDRESS REGISTER register within the CPU that contains the address of the next location to be accessed **Speicheradreßregister**

satellite *noun*
(a) device that orbits the earth receiving, processing and transmitting signals *or* generating images *or* data to be transmitted back to earth, such as weather pictures **Satellit; communications satellite** = satellite that relays radio *or* TV signals from one point on the earth's surface to another **Nachrichtensatellit; direct broadcast satellite (DBS)** = TV and radio signal broadcast over a wide area from an earth station via a satellite to homes (received with a dish aerial) **direktstrahlender Satellit; weather satellite** = device that orbits the earth, transmitting images of the weather systems above the earth's surface **Wettersatellit; satellite broadcasting** = sending public radio and TV signals from one part of the earth to another, using a communications satellite **Satellitenrundfunk; satellite link** = use of a satellite to allow the transmission of data from one point on earth to another **Satellitenstrecke; satellite network** = series of satellites which provide wide coverage of an area **Satellitennetz**
(b) small system that is part of a larger system **Satellit; satellite computer** = computer doing various tasks under the control of another computer **Satellitenrechner; satellite terminal** =

computer terminal that is outside the main network **Satellitendatenstation**

> COMMENT: in a network the floppy disk units are called 'satellites' and the hard disk unit the 'server'. In a star network each satellite is linked individually to a central server

saturation *noun* point where a material cannot be further magnetized **Sättigung; saturation noise** = errors due to saturation of a magnetic storage medium **Sättigungsstörung; saturation testing** = testing a communications network, by transmitting large quantities of data and messages over it **Sättigungstesten**

save *verb* to store data *or* a program on an auxiliary storage device **speichern, sichern;** *this WP saves the text every 15 minutes in case of a fault; don't forget to save the file before switching off;* **save area** = temporary storage area of main memory, used for registers and control data **Zwischenspeicherbereich**

sawtooth waveform *noun* waveform that regularly rises to a maximum and drops to a minimum in a linear way **Sägezahnschwingung**

SBC = SINGLE BOARD COMPUTER computer whose main components such as processor, input/output and memory are all contained on one PCB **Einplatinenrechner**

S-box *noun* matrix transformation process used in certain cipher systems **S-Box-Verfahren**

scalar *noun* variable that has a single value assigned to it **Skalar;** *a scalar has a single magnitude value, a vector has two or more positional values*

◇ **scale**
1 *noun* ratio of two values **Maßstab; large scale** *or* **small scale** = working with large *or* small amounts of data **im großen/kleinen Maßstab; large scale integration (LSI)** = integrated circuit with 500 - 10,000 components **Großintegration; medium scale integration (MSI)** = integrated circuit with 10 - 500 components **mittlere Integration; small scale integration (SSI)** = integrated circuit with 1 - 10 components **Kleinintegration; super large scale integration (SLSI)** = integrated circuit with more than 100,000 components **Größtintegration; very large scale integration (VLSI)** = integrated circuit with 10,000 - 100,000 components **Übergroßintegration**

2 *verb* **to scale down** *or* **scale up** = to lower *or* increase in proportion **verkleinern, vergrößern**

scan
1 *noun* examination of an image *or* object *or* list of items to obtain data **Abtastung;** *the heat scan of the computer quickly showed which component was overheating; the scan revealed which records were now out of date;* **raster scan** = one sweep of the picture beam horizontally across the front of the CRT screen **Rasterabtastung**
2 *verb* to examine and produce data from the shape *or* state of an object *or* drawing *or* file *or* list of items **abtasten, durchsuchen;** *he scanned the map for Teddington; the facsimile machine scans the picture and converts this to digital form before transmission; the machine scans at up to 300 dpi resolution;* **scan area** = section of an image read by a scanner **Abtastbereich; scan length** = number of items in a file *or* list that are examined in a scan **Abtastlänge**

◇ **scanner** *noun* device that scans **Abtaster, Scanner;** *a scanner reads the bar-code on the product label using a laser beam and photodiode;* **scanner memory** = memory area allocated to store images which have been scanned **Abtastspeicherbereich; image scanner** = input device that converts documents *or* drawings *or* photographs into digitized machine-readable form **Bildabtaster; optical scanner** = equipment that converts an image into electrical signals which can be stored in and displayed on a computer **optisches Abtastgerät**

> COMMENT: a scanner can be a device using photoelectric cells as in an image digitizer, or a device that samples data from a process

scanning *noun* action of examining and producing data from the shape of an object *or* drawing **Abtasten; scanning device** = device that allows micrographic images to be selected rapidly from a reel of film **Abtastgerät; scanning error** = error introduced while scanning an image **Abtastfehler; scanning radio receiver** = radio receiver that can check a range of frequencies to find a strong signal *or* a particular station **abtastender Funkempfänger; scanning line** = path traced on a CRT screen by the picture beam **Abtastzeile; scanning rate** = time taken to scan one line of a CRT image **Abtastgeschwindigkeit; scanning resolution** = ability of a scanner to distinguish between small points (usual resolution is 300 dpi) **Abtastauflösungsvermögen; scanning**

software = dedicated program that controls a scanner and allows certain operations (rotate *or* edit *or* store, etc.) to be performed on a scanned image **Scanner-Programm; scanning speed** = how fast a line *or* image is scanned **Abtastgeschwindigkeit;** *throughput is 1.3 inches per second scanning speed; its scanning speed is 9.9 seconds for an 8.5inch by 11inch document; (of modem)* **scanning** *or* **auto-baud sensing** = circuit that can automatically sense and select the correct baud rate for a line **automatischer Baudratenabfühler**

> COMMENT: a modem with auto-baud scanning can automatically sense which baud rate to operate on and switches automatically to that baud rate

◇ **scanning spot** *noun*
(a) small area of an image that is being read by a facsimile machine that moves over the whole image **Abtastfleck**
(b) small area covered by the picture beam on a TV screen that moves to follow a scanning line to write the whole of an image onto the screen **Abtastfleck; scanning spot beam** = satellite transmission to a number of areas, as the satellite passes over them **punktförmige Abtastung**

> QUOTE scanning time per page ranged from about 30 seconds to three minutes
> *PC Business World*

scatter *noun* part of a beam that is deflected *or* refracted **Streuung; scatter graph** = individual points *or* values plotted on a two axis graph **Korrelationsdiagramm; scatter proofs** = proofs showing several illustrations, not arranged in any order, prior to PMT **gemischte Fahnen mit Illustrationen;** *see also* BACKSCATTER
◇ **scatter load** *verb* to load sequential data into various (non-continuous) locations in memory **gestreut laden; scatter read** = to access and read sequential data stored in various (non-continuous) locations **gestreut lesen**

scavenge *verb* to search through and access database material without permission **unerlaubt durchsuchen**

schedule *noun*
1 *noun* order in which tasks are to be done *or* order in which CPU time will be allocated to processes in a multi-user system **(Zeit)plan**
2 *verb* to organize the broadcasting of TV *or* radio programmes at certain times **(zeitlich) planen**
◇ **scheduled circuits** *noun* telephone lines *or* data communications only **Datenübertragungsleitungen**

◇ **scheduler** *noun* program which organizes use of a CPU *or* of peripherals which are shared by several users **Zeitplanungsprogramm**
◇ **scheduling** *noun*
(a) method of working which allows several users to share the use of a CPU **Zeitablaufplanung; job scheduling** = arranging the order in which jobs are to be processed **Joborganisation**
(b) programme scheduling = organizing the broadcasting of radio *or* TV programmes at certain times **Programmplanung**

schema *noun* graphical description of a process *or* database structure **Schema**
◇ **schematic** *adjective & noun* (diagram) showing system components and how they are connected **schematisch; Schema**

scientific *adjective* referring to science **wissenschaftlich; scientific calculator** = specially adapted calculator which has several scientific functions built into it **technisch-wissenschaftlicher Rechner**

scissor *verb* to remove the areas of text *or* graphics that lie outside a page's limits **beschneiden**

SCR = SEQUENCE CONTROL REGISTER

scramble *verb* to code speech *or* data which is transmitted in such a way that it cannot be understood unless it is decoded **verwürfeln**
◇ **scrambler** *noun*
(a) device that codes a data stream into a pseudorandom form before transmission to eliminate any series of one's or zero's *or* alternate one's and zero's that would cause synchronization problems at the receiver and produce unwanted harmonics **Verwürfler**
(b) device that codes speech *or* other signals prior to transmission so that someone who is listening in without authorization cannot understand what is being transmitted (the scrambled signals are de-scrambled on reception to provide the original signals) **Verwürfler, Scrambler;** *he called the President on the scrambler telephone*

scratch
1 *noun* mark on a disk *or* on a film **Kratzer**
2 *verb* to delete *or* move an area of memory to provide room for other data **löschen**
◇ **scratch file** *or* **work file** *noun* work area which is being used for current work **Arbeitsdatei, ungeschützte Datei; scratch tape** = magnetic tape used for a scratch file **Arbeitsband**

◇ **scratchpad** *noun* workspace *or* area of high speed memory that is used for temporary storage of data currently in use **Notizblockspeicher**

screen

1 *noun*
(a) display device capable of showing a quantity of information, such as a CRT *or* VDU **Bildschirm**; *see also* READOUT; **screen border** = margin around text displayed on a screen **Bildschirmrand; screen buffer** = temporary storage area for characters *or* graphics before they are displayed **Bildschirmpuffer; screen dump** = outputting the text *or* graphics displayed on a screen to a printer **Bildschirmausdruck; screen editor** *or* **text editor** = software that allows the user to edit text on-screen, with one complete screen of information being displayed at a time **Bildschirmtexteditor; screen format** = way in which a screen is laid out **Bildschirmanzeigeformat; screen grab** = digitizing a single frame from a display *or* television **Herausgreifen eines Bildes; screen memory** = in a memory-mapped screen, the area of memory that represents the whole screen, usually with one byte representing one *or* a number of pixels **Bildschirmspeicher; on-screen** = information displayed on a screen **am Bildschirm**; *the dtp package offers on-screen font display;* **text screen** = area of a computer screen that has been set up to display text **Textbereich; touch screen** = computer display that allows the user to control the cursor position by touching the screen **Tast-Bildschirm**
(b) thing which protects **Schirm; magnetic screen** = metal screen to prevent stray magnetic fields affecting electronic components **magnetische Abschirmung**; *without the metal screen over the power supply unit, the computer just produced garbage*
2 *verb*
(a) to protect something with a screen **abschirmen**; *the PSU is screened against interference*
(b) to display *or* show information **vorführen**; *the film is now being screened*
(c) to select **aussortieren**

◇ **screenful** *noun* complete frame of information displayed on a screen **Bildschirminhalt**

script *noun* text which will be spoken by actors in a film *or* TV programme **Drehbuch**

◇ **scriptwriter** *noun* person who writes film *or* TV scripts **Drehbuchautor**

scroll *verb* to move displayed text vertically up *or* down the screen, one line *or* pixel at a time **auf-, abrollen, blättern; roll scroll** = displayed text that moves up *or* down the screen one line at a time **zeilenweises Blättern; smooth scroll** = text that is moved up a screen pixel by pixel rather than line by line, which gives a smoother movement **punktweises Blättern; scroll mode** = terminal mode that transmits every key press and displays what is received **Bilddurchlaufmodus**

scrub *verb* to wipe information off a disk *or* remove data from store **löschen**; *scrub all files with the .BAK extension*

SCSI = SMALL COMPUTER SYSTEM INTERFACE

SD = SINGLE DENSITY (DISK)

SDI = SELECTIVE DISSEMINATION OF INFORMATION

SDLC = SYNCHRONOUS DATA LINK CONTROL

SDR = STORE DATA REGISTER register in a CPU which holds data before it is processed *or* moved to memory location **Speicherdatenregister**

seal *verb* to close something tightly so that it cannot be opened **versiegeln**; *the hard disk is in a sealed case*

search

1 *noun* process of looking for and identifying a character *or* word *or* section of data in a document *or* file **Suche; chaining search** = searching a file of elements arranged as a chained list **Suche in verknüpfter Liste; linear search** = search method which compares each item in a list with the search key until the correct entry is found (starting with the first item and working sequentially towards the end) **lineare Suche; retrospective search** = search of documents on a certain subject since a certain date **rückwärtsgerichtete Suche; search key** = (i) word *or* phrase that is to be found in a text; (ii) field and other data used to select various records in a database

(i) **Suchbegriff**; (ii) **Suchkriterium**; **search memory** = method of data retrieval that uses part of the data rather than an address to locate the data **Suchraum bezogen auf Datenbereiche**; **search and replace** = feature on some word processors that allows the user to find certain words *or* phrases, then replace them with another word *or* phrase **Suchen und Ersetzen**; **global search and replace** = word-processor search and replace function covering a complete file *or* document **globales Suchen und Ersetzen** **2** *verb* to look for an item of data **suchen**

◊ **searching storage** *noun* method of data retrieval that uses part of the data rather than an address to locate the data **Suchraum bezogen auf Datenbereiche**

QUOTE a linear search of 1,000 items takes 500 comparisons to find the target, and 1,000 to report that it isn't present. A binary search of the same set of items takes roughly ten divisions either to find or not to find the target
Personal Computer World

SECAM SEQUENTIEL A MEMOIRE

COMMENT: standard which defines TV and video formats in France, the USSR and Saudi Arabia. It is similar to PAL, and uses 625 horizontal scan lines and 50 frames per second

second *adjective* (thing) which comes after the first **zweite(r,s)**; *we have two computers, the second one being used if the first is being repaired;* **second generation computers** = computer which used transistors instead of valves **Computer der zweiten Generation**; **second-level addressing** = instruction that contains an address at which the operand is stored **indirekte Adressierung**; **second sourcing** = granting of a licence to another manufacturer to produce an electronic item *or* component when production capacity is not great enough to meet demand **einen Zweitlieferanten ernennen**; **second user** *or* **second hand** = (old equipment) that has already been used and is to be sold again **Gebrauchtgerät**

◊ **secondary** *adjective* second in importance *or* less important than the first **zweitrangig, Sekundär-, sekundär-**; **secondary channel** = second channel containing control information transmitted at the same time as data **Zweitkanal**; **secondary colour** = colour produced from two primary colours **Sekundärfarbe**; **secondary station** = temporary status of a station that is receiving data **Folgestation**; **secondary storage** = any data storage medium (such as magnetic tape *or* floppy disk) that is not the main, high-speed computer storage (RAM) **Sekundärspeicher**

COMMENT: this type of storage is usually of a higher capacity, lower cost and slower access time than main memory

section *noun* part of a main program that can be executed in its own right, without the rest of the main program being required **Abschnitt**

sector
1 *noun* smallest area on a magnetic disk that can be addressed by a computer **(Platten)sektor**
2 *verb* to divide a disk into a series of sectors **sektorieren**; **(disk) sector formatting** = dividing a disk into a series of addressable sectors (a table of their addresses is also formed, allowing each sector to be accessed) **(Platten)sektorformatierung**; **sectoring hole** = hole in the edge of a disk to indicate where the first sector is located **Sektorierungsloch**; **hard-sectored** = disk with sector start locations described by holes *or* other physical marks on the disk, which are set when the disk is manufactured **hartsektoriert**; **soft-sectored** = disk where sectors are described by an address and start code data written onto it when the disk is formatted **weichsektoriert**; *see also* FORMAT

COMMENT: a disk is divided into many tracks, each of which is then divided into a number of sectors which can hold a certain number of bits

secure system *noun* system that cannot be accessed without authorization **Sicherheitssystem**

◊ **secured** *adjective* (file) that is protected against accidental writing *or* deletion *or* against unauthorized access **gesichert**

◊ **security** *noun* being protected *or* being secret **Sicherheit**; *the system has been designed to assure the security of the stored data;* **security backup** = copy of a disk *or* tape *or* file kept in a safe place in case the working copy is lost *or* damaged **Sicherheitskopie**; **security check** = identification of authorized users (by a password) before granting access **Sicherheitsprüfung**

seek *verb* to try to find **suchen**; **seek area** = section of memory that is to be searched for a particular item of data *or* a word **Suchbereich**; **seek time** = time taken by a read/write head to find the right track on a disk **Positionierzeit**; *the new hard disk drive has a seek time of just 35mS*

segment

1 *noun* section of a main program that can be executed in its own right, without the rest of the main program being required **(Programm)segment**

2 *verb* to divide a long program into shorter sections which can then be called up when required **in Abschnitte unterteilen;** *see also* OVERLAY

QUOTE you can also write in smaller program segments. This simplifies debugging and testing
Personal Computer World

select *verb* to find and retrieve specific information from a database **auswählen; chip select (CS)** = single line on a chip that will enable it to function when a signal is present (often ICs do not function even when power is applied, until a CS signal is provided) **Bausteinauswahl**

◇ **selectable** *adjective* which can be selected **auswählbar; jumper-selectable** = circuit *or* device whose options can be selected by positioning various wire connections **Brückenauswahlschaltung; selectable attributes** = the function *or* attributes of a device which can be chosen by the user **Auswahlfunktion; user-selectable** = which can be chosen or selected by the user **vom Benutzer auswählbar; this modem has user-selectable baud rates** = the receive and transmit baud rates of the modem can be chosen by the user, and are not preset **dieses Modem hat vom Benutzer wählbare Schrittgeschwindigkeiten**

◇ **selection** *noun* action of selecting **Auswählen;** *selection of information from a large database may take some time*

◇ **selective** *adjective* which chooses certain items **wahlweise, selektiv; trennscharf; selective calling** = calling a remote station from a main site **selektiver Abruf; selective dump** = display *or* printout of a selected area of memory **selektiver Speicherauszug; selective sort** = sorting a section of data items into order **Auswahlsortierung**

◇ **selectivity** *noun* ability of a radio receiver to distinguish between two nearby carrier frequencies **Trennschärfe**

◇ **selector** *noun* mechanical device that allows a user to choose an option *or* function **Selektor, Wähler;** *the selector knob for the amplification is located there; turn the selector control;* **selector channel** = communications link that operates with only one transmitter/receiver at a time **Selektorkanal**

self- *prefix* referring to oneself **Selbst-, selbst-; self-adapting system** = system that can adapt itself to various tasks

selbstanpassendes System; self-checking system = system that carries out diagnostic tests on itself usually at switch on **automatisches Prüfungssystem; self-checking code** = character coding system that can detect an error *or* bad character but not correct it **Fehlererkennungscode; self-correcting code** = character coding system that can detect and correct an error *or* bad character **selbstkorrigierender Code; self-diagnostic** = computer that runs a series of diagnostic programs (usually when it is switched on) to ensure that it is all working correctly, often memory, peripherals and disk drives are tested **selbstdiagnostisch; self-documenting program** = computer program that provides the user with operating instructions as it runs **selbstdarstellendes Programm; self-learning** = (expert system) that adds each new piece of information or rule to its database, improving its knowledge, expertise and performance as it is used **selbstlernendes (Computer)system; self-refreshing RAM** = dynamic RAM chip that has built in circuitry to generate refresh signals, allowing data to be retained when the power is off, using battery back-up **selbstregenerierender RAM; self-relocating program** = program that can be loaded into any part of memory (that will modify its addresses depending on the program origin address) **selbstverschiebliches Programm; self-resetting** *or* **self-restoring loop** = loop that returns any locations *or* registers accessed during its execution to the state they were in **selbstrücksetzende Schleife**

semantics *noun* (i) part of language which deals with the meaning of words, parts of words or combinations of words; (ii) (in computing) meanings of words or symbols used in programs **(i) & (ii) Semantik; semantic error** = error due to use of an incorrect symbol within a program instruction **Semantikfehler**

semaphore *noun*
(a) coordination of two jobs and appropriate handshaking to prevent lockouts *or* other problems when both require a peripheral *or* function **Semaphor**
(b) signalling system that uses two flags held in different positions by two mechanical *or* human arms **Winkeralphabet, Semaphor**

semi- *prefix* meaning half *or* partly **Semi-, semi-, Halb-, halb-; semi-processed data** = raw data which has had some processing carried out, such as sorting, recording, error detection, etc. **halbverarbeitete Daten**

semicolon *noun* printing sign (;) which indicates a separation between parts of a sentence *or* marks the end of a program line *or* statement in some languages (such as C and Pascal) **Strichpunkt**

semicompiled *adjective* (object code) program converted from a source code program, but not containing the code for functions from libraries, etc., that were used in the source code **halbkompiliert**

semiconductor *noun* material that has conductive properties between those of a conductor (such as a metal) and an insulator **Halbleiter; semiconductor device =** electronic component that is constructed on a small piece of semiconductor (the components on the device are constructed using patterns of insulator *or* conductor *or* semiconductor material whose properties have been changed by doping) **Halbleiterbauelement; semiconductor memory =** storage using capacitors (dynamic memory) *or* latches and bistables (static memory) constructed as a semiconductor device to store bits of data **Halbleiterspeicher; semiconductor** *or* **solid-tate laser =** piece of semiconductor bar that has a polished end, and a semi-silvered mirror, generating pulses of photons that reflect inside the bar until they have enough power to leave via the semi-silvered end **Halbleiterlaser; Festkörperlaser**

COMMENT: semiconductor material (such as silicon) is used as a base for manufacturing integrated circuits and other solidstate components, usually by depositing various types of doping substances on *or* into its surface

sender *noun* person who sends a message **Absender**

send-only device *noun* device such as a terminal which cannot receive data, only transmit it **Sendegerät**

sense *verb* to examine the state of a device *or* electronic component **prüfen;** *the condition of the switch was sensed by the program; this device senses the holes punched in a paper tape;* **auto-baud sensing** *see* SCANNING; **sense recovery time =** time that a RAM takes to switch from read to write mode **Lese-Erholzeit; sense switch =** switch on a computer front panel whose state can by examined by the computer **Programmschalter**

sensitive *adjective* which can sense even small changes **sensibel, empfindlich;** *the computer is sensitive even to very slight changes in current; light-sensitive film changes when exposed to light*

◊ **sensitivity** *noun* being sensitive to something **Empfindlichkeit;** *the scanner's sensitivity to small objects*

◊ **sensor** *noun* electronic device that produces an output dependent upon the condition *or* physical state of a process **Meßwertgeber, Sensor;** *see also* TRANSDUCER *the sensor's output varies with temperature; the process is monitored by a bank of sensors;* **image sensor =** photoelectric device that produces a signal related to the amount of light falling on it **Lichtsensor**

sentinel *noun* (i) marker *or* pointer to a special section of data; (ii) a flag that reports the status of a register after a mathematical *or* logical operation **(i) & (ii) Markierung**

separate
1 *adjective* not together **getrennt; separate channel signalling =** use of independent communications channel *or* bands in a multichannel system to send the control data and messages **getrennte Kanalsignalisierung**
2 *verb* to divide **trennen; separated graphics** = displayed characters that do not take up the whole of a character matrix, resulting in spaces between them **einzeln gestellte Zeichen**

◊ **separation** *noun* act of separating **Trennung; colour separation =** process by which colours are separated into primary colours **Farbauszug, Farbseparation; colour separations =** different artwork *or* film for the various colours to be used in multicolour printing **Farbauszüge**

◊ **separator** *noun* symbol used to distinguish parts of an instruction line in a program, such as command and argument **Trennzeichen;** *see also* DELIMITER

septet *noun* word made up of seven bits **Sieben-Bit-Byte**

sequence *noun* number of items *or* data arranged as a logical, ordered list **Folge, Sequenz;** *the sequence of names is arranged alphabetically; the program instructions are arranged in sequence according to line numbers;* **binary sequence =** series of binary digits **Binärsequenz; control sequence =** (series of) codes containing a control character and various arguments, used to carry out a process *or* change mode in a device **Steuerzeichenfolge; sequence check =** check to ensure that sorted data is in the correct order **Folgekontrolle; sequence**

control register (SCR) *or* **sequence counter** *or* **sequence register** *or* **instruction address register** = CPU register that contains the address of the next instruction to be processed **Befehlsfolgeregister; Adreßfolgeregister; logon sequence** = order in which user number, password and other authorization codes are to be entered when attempting to access a system **Anmeldesequenz**

◇ **sequencer** *noun* section within a bit-slice microprocessor that contains the next microprogram address **Ablaufsteuerung**

◇ **sequential** *adjective* arranged in an ordered manner **sequentiell, aufeinanderfolgend; queued indexed sequential access method (QISAM)** = indexed sequential file that is read item by item into a buffer **erweiterte indizierte Zugriffsmöglichkeit für sequentielle Dateien (QISAM); queued sequential access method (QSAM)** = queue of blocks waiting to be processed, retrieved using a sequential access method **erweiterte Zugriffsmöglichkeit für sequentielle Dateien (QSAM); sequential batch processing** = completing one job in a batch before the next can be started **sequentielle Stapelverarbeitung; sequential computer** = type of computer, for which each instruction must be completed before the next is started, and so cannot handle parallel processing **sequentieller Computer; sequential file** *or* **serial file** = stored file whose records are accessed sequentially **sequentielle Datei; sequential logic** = logical circuit whose output depends on the logic state of the previous inputs **sequentielle Logik;** *if the input sequence to the sequential logic circuit is 1101 the output will always be zero (0); compare with* COMBINATIONAL CIRCUIT; **sequential mode** = each instruction in a program is stored in consecutive locations **sequentieller Modus; sequential operation** = operations executed one after the other **sequentielle Arbeitsweise; sequential processing** = data *or* instructions processed sequentially, in the same order as they are accessed **sequentielle Verarbeitung;** *see also* INDEXED; **sequential search** = each item in a list (starting at the beginning) is checked until the required one is found **sequentielle Suche**

◇ **sequentially** *adverb* (done) one after the other, in sequence **sequentiell**

◇ **sequential access** *noun* method of retrieving data from a storage device by starting at the beginning of the medium (such as tape) and reading each record until the required data is found **sequentieller Zugriff; sequential access storage** = storage medium in which the data is accessed sequentially **Speicher mit sequentiellem Zugriff**

COMMENT: a tape storage system uses sequential access, since the tape has to be played through until the section required is found. The access time of sequential access storage is dependent on the position in the file of the data, compared with random access that has the same access time for any piece of data in a list

Séquentiel à Mémoire (SECAM standards that define TV and vide formats, mainly in France, USSR an Saudi Arabia, using 625 horizontal sca lines and 50 frames per second (similar PAL) **SECAM**

serial *adjective* (data *or* instructions ordered sequentially (one after the othe and not in parallel **seriell, in Reihe; seria access** = one item of the data accessed b reading through all the data in a list unt the correct one is found (as on a tap **serieller Zugriff; serial-access memor (SAM)** = storage where a particular da item can only be accessed by reading all th previous items in the list (as opposed t random access) **Speicher mit seriellem Zugrif serial adder** = addition circuit that acts o one digit at a time from a larger numbe **Serienaddierer; serial computer** = compute system that has a single ALU and carrie out instructions one at a time **serielle Computer;** *see also* SEQUENTIA COMPUTER; **serial data transmission** transmission of the separate bits that mak up data words, one at a time down a singl line **serielle Datenübertragung; serial file** stored file whose records are accesse sequentially **serielle Datei; seria input/output (SIO)** *see* SERIA TRANSMISSION; **serial input/parallel outp (SIPO)** *or* **serial to parallel converter** device that can accept serial data an transmit parallel data **seriel Eingabe/parallele Ausgabe; Serien-Paralle Umsetzer; serial input/serial output (SISO** = *see* SERIAL TRANSMISSION; **seria interface** *or* **port** = circuit that conver parallel data in a computer to and from serial form that allows serial data to b transmitted and received from othe equipment (the most common form is th RS232C interface) **serielle Schnittstell** *parallel connections are usually less troubl to set up and use than serial interfaces, b are usually limited to 20 feet in lengt* **serial memory** = memory in which data stored sequentially, only allowin sequential access **serieller Speicher; seria operation** = device that acts on data in sequential manner **serielle Arbeitsweis serial printer** = printer that prin characters one at a time **Seriendrucke**

Zeichendrucker; **serial processing** = data or instructions processed sequentially, in the same order as they are retrieved **serielle Verarbeitung; serial storage** = storage which only allows sequential access **Serienspeicher; serial to parallel converter** = electronic device that converts data from a serial form to a parallel form **Serien-Parallel-Umsetzer; serial transmission** or **serial input/output** = data transmitted one bit at a time (this is the normal method of transmission over long distances, since although slower it uses fewer lines and so is cheaper than parallel transmission) **serielle Übertragung; serielle Ein-/Ausgabe; word serial** = data words transmitted one after the other, along a parallel bus **Wortserie**

◊ **serially** adverb one after the other or in a series **seriell, in Reihe;** their transmission rate is 64,000 bits per second through a parallel connection or 19,200 serially

◊ **series** noun group of related items ordered sequentially **Reihe, Serie; series circuit** = circuit in which the components are connected serially **Reihenschaltung**

COMMENT: in a series circuit the same current flows through each component; in a parallel circuit the current flow is dependent upon the component impedance

serif noun small decorative line attached to parts of characters in certain typefaces **Serife; sans serif** = typeface without serifs **serifenlose Schrift**

server noun dedicated computer or peripheral that provides a function to a network **Server; file server** = small microcomputer and large backing storage device that is used for the management and storage of users' files in a network **Dateiserver, Controller für Speicherzugriff; LAN server** = dedicated computer and backing storage used by terminals and operators in a LAN **Lokalnetzserver**

COMMENT: in a network the hard disk machine is called the 'server' and the floppy disk units the 'satellites'. In a star network each satellite is linked individually to a central server

service verb to check or repair or maintain a system **warten, instandhalten;** the disk drives were serviced yesterday and are working well; **service bit** = transmitted bit that is used for control rather than data **Hilfsbit; service contract** = agreement that an engineer will service equipment if it goes wrong **Wartungsvertrag; service program** = useful program that is used for routine

activities such as file searching, copying, sorting, debugging, etc. **Wartungsprogramm**

servo or **servomechanism** noun mechanical device whose position or state can be accurately controlled **Folgesteuerungsmechanismus**

session noun period of work **Arbeitsabschnitt; session key** = cipher key used for a particular session **Verschlüsselung für einen bestimmten Arbeitsabschnitt; session layer** = layer in the ISO/OSI standard model that makes the connection/disconnection between transmitter and receiver **Sitzungsschicht**

set
1 noun
(a) number of related data items **Gruppe, Satz; character set** = all the characters that can be displayed or printed **Zeichensatz; set theory** = mathematics related to numerical sets **Mengenlehre**
(b) width of a printed typeface **Set; set size** = measurement of horizontal dimensions in sets (one set equals one point) **Set-Maß; set width** = width of the body of a printed character **Kegelbreite**
(c) radio or television receiver **Radio-, Fernsehgerät; set-top converter** = device that converts TV signals from a network or satellite into a form that can be displayed **Kopfumsetzer**
(d) physical layout of a stage or filming studio including props and background **Bühnenbild; Filmkulisse**
2 verb
(a) (i) to make one variable equal to a value; (ii) to define a parameter value **(i) setzen; (ii) einstellen;** we set the right-hand margin at 80 characters; **set breakpoints** = to define the position of breakpoints within a program being debugged **Unterbrechungspunkte setzen**
(b) to give a bit the value of 1 **setzen**
(c) to compose a text into typeset characters **setzen;** the page is set in 12 point Times Roman; see also TYPESET
◊ **setting** noun
(a) action of fixing or arranging something **Einstellung; brightness setting** = TV brightness control position **Helligkeitseinstellung; contrast setting** = TV contrast control position **Kontrasteinstellung**
(b) action of composing text into typeset characters **Setzen;** the MS has been sent to the typesetter for setting; **setting charges** have increased since last year; **computer setting** = typesetting using a computerized typesetting machine **Computersatz**
◊ **set up** verb to initialize or define or start an application or system **aufbauen,**

einstellen; *the new computer worked well as soon as the engineer had set it up;* **set-up option** = the choices available when setting up a system **Wahlmöglichkeiten beim Einstellen; set-up time** = period of time between a signal to start an operation and the start **Rüstzeit**

sexadecimal *see* HEXADECIMAL
◊ **sextet** *noun* byte made up of six bits **Sechs-Bit-Byte, Sextett**

sf signalling = SINGLE FREQUENCY SIGNALLING

shade *noun* (i) variation in a printed colour due to added black; (ii) quantity of black added to a colour to make it darker **(i) Schattierung, Farbtönung; (ii) Bildschwarz**
◊ **shading** *noun* showing darker sections of a line drawing by adding dark colour *or* by drawing criss-cross lines **Schraffur, Schattierung**

shadow *noun* area where broadcast signals cannot be received because of an obstacle that blocks the transmission medium **Schatten;** *the mountain casts a shadow over those houses, so they cannot receive any radio broadcasts*
◊ **shadowmask** *noun* sheet with holes placed just behind the front of a colour monitor screen to separate the three-colour picture beams **Lochmaske**
◊ **shadow memory** *or* **page** *noun* duplicate memory locations accessed by a special code **Schattenspeicher; shadow page table** = conversion table that lists real memory locations with their equivalent shadow memory locations **Seitentabelle für Schattenspeicher;** *see also* VIRTUAL
◊ **shadow ROM** *noun* read-only shadow memory **Schatten-ROM**

shannon *noun* measure of the information content of a transmission **Shannon**
◊ **Shannon's Law** *noun* law defining the maximum information carrying capacity of a transmission line **Shannonsches Gesetz**

COMMENT: Shannon's Law is defined as B lg(1 + S/N) where B = Bandwidth, lg is logarithm to the base two and S/N is Signal to Noise ratio

share *verb* to own *or* use something together with someone else **gemeinsam benutzen;** *the facility is shared by several independent companies;* **shared access** = computer *or* peripheral used by more than one person *or* system **gemeinsam benutzter**

Zugang; *see also* TIME-SHARING SYSTEM MULTI-USER; **shared bus** = one bus used (usually) for address and data transfer between the CPU and a peripheral **Gemeinschaftsbus; shared file** = stored file that can be accessed by more than one user *or* system **Gemeinschaftsdatei; shared line** *or* **party line** = one telephone line shared by a number of subscriber **Gemeinschaftsleitung; shared logic system** = one computer and backing storage device used by a number of people in a network for an application **zentralisiertes System shared logic text processor** = word processing available to a number of users on a shared logic system **gemeinsam benutzte Textverarbeitungssystem; shared memory** = memory that can be accessed by more than one CPU **Gemeinschaftsspeicher; shared resources system** = system where one peripheral *or* backing storage device *or* other resource is used by a number of user **Mehrplatzsystem; time-sharing** = computer system that allows several independent users to use it *or* be on-line at the same time **Gemeinschaftsbetrieb**
◊ **shareware** *noun* software that i available free to try, but if kept the user i expected to pay a fee to the writer (often confused with public domain software which is completely free) **Shareware**

sheet *noun* large piece of paper **Blatt sheet feed** = paper feed system that put single sheets of paper into a printer, one a a time **Blattzuführung; sheet feed attachmen** = device which can be attached to a printe to allow single sheets of paper to be fed i automatically **Einzelblattzuführung**

shelf life *noun* maximum storage time o a product before it is no longer guaranteed good to use **Dauer der Lagerfähigkeit;** *th developer has a shelf life of one year*

shell sort *noun* algorithm for sortin data items, in which items can be move more than one position per sort action „Shell"-Sortierung

SHF = SUPER HIGH FREQUENCY

shield
1 *noun* metal screen connected to earth that prevents harmful voltages interference reaching sensitive electroni equipment **Abschirmung**
2 *verb* to protect a signal *or* device from external interference *or* harmful voltage **abschirmen; shielded cable** = cable made u of a conductive core surrounded by a insulator, then a conductive layer t

protect the transmitted signal against interference **Isolierkabel**

shift *verb*
(a) to move a bit *or* word of data left or right by a certain amount (usually one bit) **verschieben; arithmetic shift** = word *or* data moved one bit to the right *or* left inside a register, losing the bit shifted off the end **arithmetische Stellenverschiebung; cyclic shift** = rotation of bits in a word with the previous last bit inserted in the first bit position **zyklische Stellenverschiebung; logical shift** = data movement to the left *or* right in a word, the bits falling outside the free word boundary are discarded, the free positions are filled with zeros **logische Stellenverschiebung; shift instruction** = computer command to shift the contents of a register to the left or right **Verschiebebefehl; shift left** = left arithmetic shift of data in a word (the number is doubled for each left shift) **Linksverschiebung;** *0110 left shifted once is 1100;* **shift register** = temporary storage into which data can be shifted **Verschieberegister; shift right** = right arithmetic shift of data in a word (the number is halved for each right shift) **Rechtsverschiebung**
(b) to change from one character set to another, allowing other characters (such as capitals) to be used **umschalten; shift character** = transmitted character code that indicates that the following code is to be shifted **Umschaltzeichen; shift code** = method of increasing total possible bit combinations by using a number of bits to indicate the following code is to be shifted **Umschaltcode**

◇ **shift key** *noun* key on a keyboard that switches secondary functions for keys, such as another character set, by changing the output to upper case **Umschalttaste**

shoot *verb* to take a film **aufnehmen, drehen;** *they shot hundreds of feet of film, but none of it was any good; the programme was shot on location in Spain*
NOTE: **shooting - shot**

short *adjective* not long **kurz; short card** = add-on expansion board that is shorter than a standard size **Kurzlochkarte; short haul modem** = modem used to transmit data over short distances (often within a building), usually without using a carrier **Nahbereichsmodem**

short circuit
1 *noun* electrical connection of very low resistance between two points **Kurzschluß**

2 *verb* to connect two points together with a (very low resistance) link **kurzschließen; short-circuited** = two points that are electrically connected, usually accidentally **kurzgeschlossen**

COMMENT: short circuits can be accidental, due to bad circuit design or used as a protective measure

shorten *verb* to make shorter **kürzen;** *we had to shorten the file to be able to save it on one floppy*

short-run *adjective* with a printrun of only a few hundred copies **kleine Auflage;** *a printer specializing in short-run printing; the laser printer is good for short-run leaflets*

short wave (SW) *noun* radio communications frequency below 60 metres **Kurzwelle; short-wave receiver** = radio receiver able to pick up broadcasts on the short wave bands **Kurzwellenempfänger**

shotgun microphone *noun* long, highly directional microphone **besonders empfindliches Richtmikrophon**

show-through *noun* text printed on one side of a piece of paper that can be seen from the other **durchscheinender Druck**

shrink *verb* to become smaller **schrumpfen;** *the drawing was shrunk to fit the space*
NOTE: **shrinks - shrank - has shrunk**

shut down *verb* to switch off and stop the functions of a machine *or* system **abschalten**
◇ **shut-off mechanism** *noun* device which stops a process in case of fault **Abschaltmechanismus**

COMMENT: most hard disks have an automatic shut-off mechanism to pull the head back from the read position when the power is turned off

shutter *noun* device on a camera which opens and shuts rapidly allowing light from an object to fall on the film **Verschluß**

SI units = SYSTEME INTERNATIONAL UNITS international measurement units such as candela, lumen, and ampere **internationale Maßeinheiten;** *see also* MKS ⇨ APPENDIX

sibilance *noun* excess signal recorded when certain letters such as 's' are spoken **Zischen**

sideband *noun* frequency band of a modulated signal, a little above or below the carrier frequency **Seitenband;** *upper sideband; lower sideband;* **double sideband** = modulation technique whose frequency spectrum contains two modulated signals above and below the unmodulated carrier frequency **Zweiseitenbandübertragung; double sideband suppressed carrier (DSBSC)** = modulation technique that uses two modulated signal sidebands, but no carrier signal **Zweiseitenbandübertragung mit unterdrückter Trägerwelle; single sideband** = modulated signal filtered to leave just one sideband, usually the upper (this is very economical on bandwidth but requires more complex circuitry) **Einseitenband**

side lobe *noun* side sections of an aerial's response pattern **Nebenzipfel**

sideways ROM *noun* software which allows selection of a particular memory bank *or* ROM device **Seiten-ROM-Programm**

sign
1 *noun* polarity of a number *or* signal (whether it is positive *or* negative) **Vorzeichen; sign and modulus** = way of representing numbers, where one bit shows if the number is positive *or* negative (usually 0 = positive, 1 = negative) **Absolutzahl mit Vorzeichen(ziffer); sign bit** *or* **sign indicator** = single bit that indicates if a binary number is positive *or* negative (usually 0 = positive, 1 = negative) **Vorzeichenbit; sign digit** = one digit that indicates if a number is positive *or* negative **Vorzeichenziffer; sign and magnitude** *or* **signed magnitude** = number representation in which the most significant bit indicates the sign of the number, the rest of the bits its value **Größendarstellung mit Vorzeichen; sign position** = digit *or* bit position that contains the sign bit *or* digit **Vorzeichenposition; signed field** = storage field which can contain a number and a sign bit **Speicherfeld mit Vorzeichen**
2 *verb* to identify oneself to a computer using a personalized signature **unterschreiben; to sign off** = to logoff a system **sich abmelden; to sign on** = to logon to a system **sich anmelden**

signal
1 *noun* (i) generated analog *or* digital waveform used to carry information; (ii) short message used to carry control codes **(i) & (ii) Signal;** *the signal received from the computer contained the answer;* **interrupt signal** = voltage pulse from a peripheral sent to the CPU requesting attention

Unterbrechungssignal; signal conditioning = converting *or* translating a signal into form that is accepted by a device **Signalaufbereitung; signal conversion** = processing, changing or modulating signal **Signalumwandlung; signal converter** = device that converts signals from one format to another, usually from UHF to VHF for TV signals **Signalumsetzer; signal distance** = number of bit positions with different contents in two data word **Hamming-Abstand;** *see also* HAMMING; **signal element** = smallest basic unit used when transmitting digital data **Schritt;** *the signal element in this system is a short voltage pulse, indicating a binary one; the signal elements for the radio transmission system are 10mS of 40KHz and 10mS of 60KHz for binary 0 and 1 respectively;* **signal generator** = device that can produce various signal of varying amplitude, frequency and shape **Zeichengeber; signal to noise ratio (S/N)** = ratio of the amplitude of the transmitted signal to the noise on the received signal **Rauschabstand; signal processing** = processing of signals to extract the information contained **Signalverarbeitung;** *the system is used by students doing research on signal processing techniques; the message was recovered by carrier signal processing*
2 *verb* to send a radio signal *or* a message to a computer **melden;** *signal to the network that we are busy*

◇ **signalling** *noun* (i) method used by transmitter to warn a receiver that message is to be sent; (ii) communication to the transmitter about the state of the receiver **(i) & (ii) Signalisierung; in band signalling** = use of a normal voice grade channel for data transmission **Imband Signalisierung**

signature *noun*
(a) name written in a special way by someone **Unterschrift;** *do you recognize the signature on the cheque?*
(b) series of printed and folded pages in book (usually 8, 16 or 32 pages) **Signatur**
(c) special authentication code, such as password, which a user gives prior to access to a system *or* prior to the execution of task (to prove identity) **Signatur**

COMMENT: in some systems this can be written by the user or determined from the user in some way (such as fingerprint or eye scan: these are very advanced and secure systems)

signify *verb* to mean **bedeuten;** *a carriage return code signifies the end of an input line*

◇ **significance** *noun* special meaning **Bedeutung**

◇ **significant** *adjective* which has a special meaning **bedeutsam; significant digit codes** *or* **faceted codes** = codes which indicate various details of an item, by assigning each one a value **bedeutsame Zifferncodes, Facettencodes**

silicon *noun* element with semiconductor properties, used in crystal form as a base for IC manufacture **Silizium; silicon chip** = small piece of silicon in and on the surface of which a complete circuit *or* logic function has been produced (by depositing other substances *or* by doping) **Silizium-Chip; silicon disk** *or* **RAM disk** = section of RAM that is made to look and behave like a high speed disk drive **Siliziumplatte; silicon foundry** = works where pure silicon crystals are grown, sliced into wafers and cleaned ready for use **Siliziumerzeugungsanlage; silicon gate** = type of MOS transistor gate that uses doped silicon regions instead of a metal oxide to provide the function **Siliziumgatter;** *see also* MOS, GATE; **silicon on sapphire (SOS)** = manufacturing technique that allows MOS devices to be constructed onto a sapphire substrate for high speed operation **Silizium-Saphir-Technologie; Silicon Glen** = area of Scotland where many Scottish IT companies are based **Silicon Glen; silicon transistor** = microelectronic transistor manufactured on a silicon semiconductor base **Siliziumtransistor; Silicon Valley** = area in California where many US semiconductor device manufacturers are based **Silicon Valley; silicon wafer** = thin slice of a pure silicon crystal, usually around 4 inches in diameter on which integrated circuits are produced (these are then cut out of the wafer to produce individual chips) **Siliziumscheibe**

COMMENT: silicon is used in the electronics industry as a base material for integrated circuits. It is grown as a long crystal which is then sliced into wafers before being etched or treated, producing several hundred chips per wafer. Other materials, such as germanium or gallium arsenide, are also used as a base for ICs

silk *noun* fine white material used to diffuse light when photographing a subject **Seide**

SIMD = SINGLE INSTRUCTION STREAM MULTIPLE DATA STREAM

simple *adjective* not complicated, not difficult **einfach; simple to use** = (machine *or* software) easy to use and operate **einfach zu benutzen**

simplex *noun* data transmission in only one direction **Simplex** NOTE: opposite is **duplex**

simplify *verb* to make something simpler **vereinfachen;** *function keys simplify program operation*

simulate *verb* to copy the behaviour of a system *or* device with another **nachvollziehen, simulieren;** *this software simulates the action of an aeroplane*

◇ **simulator** *noun* device that simulates another system **Simulator; flight simulator** = computer program which allows a user to pilot a simulated plane, showing a realistic control panel and moving scenes (either as training programme *or* computer game) **Flugsimulator**

◇ **simulation** *noun* operation where a computer is made to imitate a real life situation *or* a machine, and shows how something works *or* will work in the future **Nachahmung, Simulation;** *simulation techniques have reached a high degree of sophistication*

simultaneity *adjective* in which the CPU and the I/O sections of a computer can handle different data *or* tasks at the same time **Gleichzeitigkeit**

simultaneous *adjective* which takes place at the same time as something else **gleichzeitig, Simultan-, simultan-; simultaneous processing** = two or more processes executed at the same time **Simultanverarbeitung; simultaneous transmission** = transmission of data *or* control codes in two directions at the same time **Simultanübertragung;** NOTE: same as **duplex**

◇ **simultaneously** *adverb* at the same time **gleichzeitig, simultan**

COMMENT: true simultaneous processing requires two processors, but can be imitated by switching rapidly between two tasks with a single processor

sin *or* **sine** *noun* mathematical function defined as: the sine of an angle (in a right-angled triangle) is equal to the ratio of opposite to hypotenuse sides **Sinus**

◇ **sine wave** *noun* waveform that is the sine function with time (classic wave shape, changing between a maximum and minimum with a value of zero at zero time) **Sinuswelle**

COMMENT: sine waves are usually the basic carrier waveform shape in modulation systems

single *adjective* only one **einfach, einzeln; single address code** *or* **instruction** = machine code instruction that contains one operator and one address **Einadreßcode; single address message** = message with a single destination **Einfachadresse; single board computer (SBC)** = micro *or* mini computer whose components are all contained on a single printed circuit board **Einplatinenrechner; single density disk (SD)** = standard magnetic disk and drive able to store data **Platte mit einfacher Schreibdichte; single frequency signalling** *or* **sf signalling** = use of various frequency signals to represent different control codes **Einfrequenztonwahl; single function software** = applications program that can only be used for one kind of task **auf einen Anwendungsbereich beschränktes Programm; single instruction stream multiple data stream (SIMD)** = architecture of a parallel computer that has a number of ALUs and data buses with one control unit **SIMD-Rechner (Parallelrechner); single instruction stream single data stream (SISD)** = architecture of a serial computer, that has one ALU and data bus, with one control unit **SISD-Rechner (serieller Rechner); single key response** = software that requires only one key to be pressed (no CR required) to select an option **Einzelanschlag-Programm; single length precision** = number stored in one word **einfache Genauigkeit;** *compare with* DOUBLE, MULTIPLE ; **single length working** = using numbers that can be stored within a single word **Arbeiten mit einfacher Wortlänge; single line display** = small screen which displays a single line of characters at a time **Einzeilenanzeige; single operand instruction** *see* SINGLE ADDRESS INSTRUCTION; **single operation** = communications system that allows data to travel in only one direction at a time (controlled by codes S/O = send only, R/O = receive only, S/R = send or receive) **Einzeloperation;** *see also* SIMPLEX; **single pass operation** = software that produces the required result *or* carries out a task after one run **Einschrittoperation; single pole** = switch that connects two points **einseitiger Schalter; single precision** = number stored in one word **einfache Genauigkeit; single scan non segmented** = video tape system that allows freeze framing by recording one complete television picture field at a time **(Halb)bildabtastung; single sheet feed** = device attached to a printer to allow single sheets of paper to be used instead of continuous stationery **Einzelblatteinzug;**

single sideband = modulated signal filtere◖ to leave just one sideband, usually th◖ upper (this is very economical o bandwidth, but needs more circuitr◣ **Einseitenband; single-sided disk (SSD)** floppy disk that can only be used to stor data on one side, because of the way it ◣ manufactured *or* formatted **Diskette m◣ einfacher Schreibdichte; single step** = th◣ execution of a program one instruction at time **Einzelschritt; single-strike ribbon** printer ribbon which can only be used onc **Einmal-Farbband;** *compare* MULTI-STRIKE **single-user system** = computer syster which can only be used by a single user at time (as opposed to a multi-user system **Einzelplatzsystem**

sink *noun* receiving end of communications line **(Nachrichten)senke◣ heat sink** = metal device used to conduc heat away from an electronic component t prevent damage **Wärmeableitung, Kühlkörpe◣ sink tree** = description in a routing table c all the paths in a network to a destinatio **Baumdiagramm;** NOTE: the opposite of sink ◣ **source**

sinusoidal *adjective* waveform *or* motio◣ that is similar to a sine wave **sinusförmig;** *t◣ carrier has a sinusoidal waveform*

SIO = SERIAL INPUT/OUTPUT

siphoning *noun* transmission of a direc broadcast TV programme over a cabl◣ network **Hebern**

SIPO = SERIAL INPUT/PARALLE◣ OUTPUT

SISD = SINGLE INSTRUCTION STREAM SINGLE DATA STREAM

SISO = SERIAL INPUT/SERIAL OUTPUT

site *noun* place where something is base◣ **Gelände**
◇ **site poll** *verb* to poll all the terminals ◣ devices in a particular location *or* are◣ **global aufrufen;** *see also* POLLING

sixteen-bit *adjective* (microcompute◣ system *or* CPU) that handles data in sixtee◣ bit words, providing much faster operatio◣ than older eight bit systems **16-Bit-CPU**

sixteenmo *or* **16mo** *noun* size of a boo◣ page, where the sheet of paper has bee◣ folded four times to make a signature of 3◣ pages **Sedezformat**

size

1 *noun* physical dimensions of an image *or* object *or* page **Größe;** *the size of the print has been increased to make it easier to read;* **page size** = physical dimensions of a printed page **Seitengröße;** *our page sizes vary from 220 x 110 to 360 x 220;* **screen size** = (i) number of characters a computer display can show horizontally and vertically; (ii) size of a monitor screen based on international paper sizes **(i) Bildschirmformat; (ii) Bildschirmgröße**
2 *verb* to calculate the resources available, and those required to carry out a particular job **abschätzen**
◇ **sizing** *noun* reducing *or* enlarging a picture to fit **Einpassen, Skalieren;** *photographs can be edited by cropping, sizing, etc*

skeletal code *noun* program which is not complete, with the basic structure coded **Rahmencodierung**

sketch

1 *noun* rough drawing made rapidly **Skizze**
2 *verb* to make a rough rapid drawing **skizzieren**

skew *noun* image scanned *or* drawn whose horizontal *or* vertical lines are not straight **Schrägstellung**

skip *verb*

(a) to transmit radio waves over an abnormally long distance due to the reflective properties of the atmosphere **(eine Strecke) überspringen**
(b) to ignore an instruction in a sequence of instructions **überspringen;** *the printer skipped the next three lines of text;* **skip capability** = feature of certain word-processors to allow the user to jump backwards *or* forwards by a quantity of text in a document **Überspringfähigkeit; skip instruction** = null computer command which directs the CPU to the next instruction **Überspringbefehl; high-speed skip** = rapid movement of paper in a printer, ignoring the normal line advance **schneller Papiervorschub**

slash *or* **oblique stroke** *noun* printing sign (/) like a stroke sloping to the right **Schrägstrich**
◇ **slashed zero** *noun* a printed *or* written sign (Ø) to distinguish a zero from the letter O **durchgestrichene Null**

slave *noun* remote secondary computer *or* terminal controlled by a central computer **Nebencomputer; bus slave** = data sink which receives data from a bus master **untergeordneter Bus; slave cache** *or* **store** = section of high-speed memory which stores data that the CPU can access quickly **Nebenspeicher; slave processor** = dedicated processor that is controlled by a master processor **untergeordneter Prozessor; slave terminal** = terminal controlled by a main computer *or* terminal **untergeordnete Datenstation; slave tube** = second CRT display connected to another so that it shows exactly the same information **Zweiröhre**

sleep *noun* system that is waiting for a signal (log-on) before doing anything **bereitstehendes System;** *see also* WAKE-UP

sleeve *noun* cover for a magnetic disk *or* for a record **Schutzhülle**

slew *noun* rapid movement of paper in a printer, ignoring the normal line advance **schneller Papiervorschub**

slice *noun* section *or* piece of something **Scheibe, Slice; bit-slice architecture** = construction of a large word size CPU by joining a number of smaller word size blocks **(Bit-)Slice-Aufbau;** *the bit-slice design uses four four-bit word processors to make a sixteen-bit processor;* **time slice** = period of time allocated for a user *or* program *or* job within a multitasking system; amount of time allowed for a single task in a time-sharing system *or* in multiprogramming **Zeitscheibe**
◇ **slicing** *noun* cutting thin round wafers from a bar of silicon crystal **In-Scheiben-Schneiden**

slide

1 *noun* positive transparent photographic image **Dia(positiv); slide projector** = device that projects slide images onto a screen **Diaprojektor; slide/sync recorder** = audio tape recorder that can control a slide projector in sync with music *or* commentary **Diaprojektor mit Tonspur**
2 *verb* to move smoothly across a surface **gleiten;** *the disk cover slides on and off easily*

slip pages *or* **slip proofs** *noun* proofs, where each page of text is printed on a separate piece of paper **Bogenkorrekturen**

slot

1 *noun*
(a) long thin hole **Schlitz;** *the system disk should be inserted into the left-hand slot on the front of the computer;* **expansion slot** = expansion connector available on a

computer's backplane *or* motherboard, into which an expansion board can be plugged **Erweiterungsposition;** *there are two free slots in the micro, you only need one for the add-on board*
(b) message slot = number of bits that can hold a message which circulates round a ring network **Nachrichtenschlitz**
2 *verb* to insert an object into a hole **hineinstecken;** *the disk slots into one of the floppy drive apertures*

slow motion *noun* playing back of a video tape *or* disk sequence slower than recorded **Zeitlupe;** *the film switched to slow motion; play the film again in slow motion*
◇ **slow scan television** *noun* television images transmitted line by line over a transmission link at a slow rate **Schmalbandfernsehen**

SLSI = SUPER LARGE SCALE INTEGRATION

slug *noun* line of metal type, cast in hot metal setting **Zeilenguß**

slur *noun* (i) printed image which is blurred because of movement during printing; (ii) distortion of voice during transmission **(i) Schmitz; (ii) Verzerrung**

small *adjective* not large **klein; small caps** = printing style, with capital letters which are the same size as ordinary letters **Kapitälchen; small scale integration (SSI)** = integrated circuit with 1 to 10 components **Kleinintegration**

smart *adjective* intelligent **intelligent; smart card** = plastic card with a memory and microprocessor embedded in it, so that it can be used for direct money transfer *or* for identification of the user **Chipkarte;** *see also* PID; **smart terminal** *or* **intelligent terminal** = computer terminal that is able to process information **intelligente Datenstation**

smog *noun* **electronic smog** = excessive stray electromagnetic fields and static electricity generated by large numbers of electronic equipment (this can damage equipment and a person's health) **elektronischer Smog**

smoke test *noun (informal)* casual test that indicates that the machine must be working if no smoke appears when it is switched on **Feuerprobe**

SNA = SYSTEMS NETWORK ARCHITECTURE

snapshot *noun* (i) recording of all the states of a computer at a particular instant; (ii) storing in main memory the contents of a screen full of information at an instant **(i) selektives Protokollprogramm; (ii) selektives Bildschirmspeichern; snapshot dump** = printout of all the registers and a section of memory at a particular instant, used when debugging a program **dynamischer Speicherauszug**

SNOBOL = STRING ORIENTATED SYMBOLIC LANGUAGE high-level programming language that uses string processing methods **SNOBOL (Programmiersprache)**

snow *noun* television image distortion in the form of random moving white dots due to a low quality signal **Schnee**

s/n ratio = SIGNAL TO NOISE RATIO ratio of the amplitude of the transmitted signal to the noise on the received signal **Rauschabstand**

soak *verb* to run a program *or* device continuously for a period of time to make sure it functions correctly **ununterbrochen laufen lassen;** *the device was soak-tested prior to delivery*

socket *noun* device with a set of holes into which a plug fits **Steckdose; female socket** = hole into which a pin *or* plug can be inserted to make an electrical connection **Steckdose**

QUOTE the mouse and keyboard sockets are the same, and could lead to the kind of confusion that arose with the early PCs when the keyboard could be connected to the tape socket
PC User

soft *adjective*
(a) (material) that loses its magnetic effect when removed from a magnetic field **weich soft**
(b) (data) that is not permanently stored in hardware (soft usually refers to data stored on magnetic medium) **weich; soft copy** = text listed on screen (as opposed to hard copy on paper) **Bildschirmaufzeichnung; soft error** = random error caused by software or data errors (this type of error is very difficult to trace and identify since it only appears under certain conditions) **Fehler durch Fremdkörpereinwirkung;** *compare with* HARD ERROR; **soft-fail** = system that is still partly operational even after a part of the

system has failed **Soft-Fail, weicher Fehler; soft hyphen** = hyphen which is inserted when a word is split at the end of a line, but is not present when the word is written normally **weiche Trennfuge; soft keys** = keys which can be changed by means of a program **frei belegbare Funktionstasten; soft keyboard** = keyboard where the functions of the keys can be changed by programs **frei belegbare Tastatur; soft-reset** = instruction that terminates any program execution and returns the user to the monitor program *or* BIOS **Weichrückstellung;** *compare with* HARD RESET; **soft-sectored disk** = disk where the sectors are described by an address and start code data written onto it when the disk is formatted **weichsektorierte Platte; soft zone** = text area to the left of the right margin in a word-processed document, where if a word does not fit completely, a hyphen is automatically inserted **Bereich um die weiche Trennfuge; Ausschließzone**

software *noun* any program *or* group of programs which instructs the hardware on how it should perform, including operating systems, word processors and applications programs **Software, Programmausrüstung; applications software** = programs which are used by the user to perform a certain task **Anwendungssoftware; bundled software** = software which is included in the price of the system **im Preis eingeschlossene Software; common software** = useful routines that can be used by any program **Allgemeinsoftware; network software** = software which is used to establish the link between a users' program and a network **Netzsoftware; pirate software** = illegal copy of a software package **Raubkopie; system software** = programs which direct the basic functions, input-output control, etc., of a computer **Systemsoftware; unbundled software** = software which is not included in the price of a system **im Preis nicht eingeschlossene Software; user-friendly software** = program that is easy for a non-expert to use and interact with **benutzerfreundliche Software; software compatible** = (computer) that will load and run programs written for another computer **Software-kompatibel; software development** = processes required to produce working programs from an initial idea **Software-Entwicklung; software documentation** = information, notes and diagrams that describe the function, use and operation of a piece of software **Software-Dokumentation; software engineer** = person who can write working software to fit an application **Software-Ingenieur; software engineering** = field of study covering all software-related

subjects **Software-Engineering; software house** = company which develops and sells computer programs **Software-Haus; software interrupt** = high priority program generated signal, requesting the use of the central processor **Software-Unterbrechung; software library** = number of specially written routines, stored in a library file which can be inserted into a program, saving time and effort **Software-Bibliothek; software licence** = agreement between a user and a software house, giving details of the rights of the user to use *or* copy the software **Software-Lizenz; software life cycle** = period of time when a piece of software exists, from its initial design to the moment when it becomes out of date **Lebensdauer einer Software; software maintenance** = carrying out updates and modifications to a software package to make sure the program is up to date **Software-Wartung; software package** = complete set of programs (and the manual) that allow a certain task to be performed **Software-Paket; software piracy** = illegal copying of software for sale **Software-Piraterie; software quality assurance (SQA)** = making sure that software will perform as intended **Software-Qualitätssicherung; software reliability** = ability of a piece of software to perform the task required correctly **Software-Zuverlässigkeit; software specification** = detailed information about a piece of software's abilities, functions and methods **Software-Spezifikation; software system** = all the programs required for one or more tasks **Software-System; software tool** = program used in the development of other programs **Programmentwicklungswerkzeug**
NOTE: no plural for **software;** for the plural say **pieces of software**

solar *adjective* referring to the sun **solar, Sonnen-, sonnen-; solar cell** = component that converts the light of the sun into electrical energy **Solarzelle; solar power** = (electrical) power derived from the sun **Sonnenenergie; solar-powered calculator** = calculator with a battery powered by light **Solarrechner**

solder
1 *noun* soft lead which, when melted, forms a solid electrical connection to join wires, pins and metal components **Lötmetall;** NOTE: no plural
2 *verb* to join two pieces of metal with molten solder **löten**

◇ **solderless** *adjective* which does not use solder; (board, such as a breadboard) which does not need solder **lötstellenfrei**

solenoid *noun* mechanical device operated by an electromagnetic field **Solenoid**

solid *adjective* (printed text) with no spaces between the lines **kompreß; solid error** = error that is always present when certain equipment is used **bleibender Fehler; solid font printer** = printer which uses a whole character shape to print in one movement, such as a daisy wheel printer **Festzeichendrucker**

◊ **solid-state** *adjective* referring to semiconductor devices **Halbleiter-, Festkörper-; solid-state device** = electronic device that operates by using the effects of electrical *or* magnetic signals in a solid semiconductor material **Halbleiterbauteil; solid-state memory device** = solid-state memory storage device (usually in the form of RAM or ROM chips) **Festkörperspeicher**

solve *verb* to find the answer to a problem **lösen**

◊ **solution** *noun*
(a) answer to a problem **Lösung**
(b) liquid in which certain chemicals have been dissolved **Lösung**

son file *noun* latest working version of a file **Sohndatei;** *compare with* FATHER FILE, GRANDFATHER FILE

sonar *noun* device that uses sound waves to determine the state and depth of water **Echolot**

◊ **sonic** *adjective* referring to sound; (sound signals) within the human hearing range (20 - 20,000Hz) **akustisch; ultrasonic** = (sound pressure waves) at a frequency above the audio band (above 20kHz) **Ultraschall-**

sophisticated *adjective* technically advanced **hochentwickelt;** *a sophisticated desktop publishing program*

◊ **sophistication** *noun* being technically advanced **hoher Entwicklungsstand;** *the sophistication of the new package is remarkable*

sort *verb* to put data into order, according to a system, on the instructions of the user **sortieren;** *to sort addresses into alphabetical order; to sort orders according to account numbers;* **bubble sort** = sorting method which repeatedly exchanges various pairs of data items until they are in order **Bubblesort, Blasensortierung; shell sort** = algorithm for sorting data items, in which items can be moved more than position per

sort action „**Shell**"**-Sortierung; sort/merge** program which allows new files to be sorte and then merged in correct order in existing files **Sortier-/Mischprogramm; tr selection sort** = rapid form of selectic where the information from the first so pass is used in the second pass to speed u selection **Auswahlsortierverfahren**

◊ **sortkey** *or* **sort field** *noun* field in stored file that is used to sort the fi **Sortierschlüssel; Sortierfeld;** *the orders we sorted according to dates by assigning th date field as the sortkey*

SOS = SILICON ON SAPPHIRE

sound *noun* noise *or* something which ca be heard **Geräusch; sound advance** distance between a film frame and i sound track on a film due to the differenc in position of the sound head and camer aperture **Vorrücken der Tonspur; sound chip** electronic device that can generate soun signals **Ton-Chip; sound effects** = artificiall produced sounds used when recording t give the impression of real soun **Klangeffekte, Geräuschkulisse;** *all the soun effects for the film were produce electronically;* **sound head** = device tha converts to or from a magnetic sign stored on tape **Tonkopf; sound pressure lev (SPL)** = measurement of the magnitude the pressure wave conveying soun **Schalldruckpegel; sound synthesizer** device able to produce complex real soun by the combination of various generate signals **Synthesizer; sound track** = track on film on which the sound is recorde **Tonspur**

◊ **soundproof** *adjective* which does n allow sound to pass through **schalldicht;** *th telephone is installed in a soundproof boo*

source *noun*
(a) point where a transmitted signal enter a network **Quelle;** NOTE: opposite is **sink**
(b) name of a terminal on a FET devic **Quelle** �▷ APPENDIX
(c) original *or* initial point **Ursprung(spunkt source code** = set of codes written by th programmer which cannot be directl executed by the computer, but has to b translated into an object code program by compiler *or* interpreter **Ausgangscod source deck** *or* **pack** = set of punched car that contain the source code for a progra **Ursprungskartensatz; source document** form *or* document from which data extracted prior to entering it into database **Originaldokument; source editor** software that allows the user to alter, dele or add instructions in a program source fi **Ursprungsdatei-Editor; source file** = progra

written in source language, which is then converted to machine code by a compiler **Ursprungsdatei; source language** = programming language in which the source program is written **Ursprungssprache; source listing** = (i) listing of a text in its original form; (ii) listing of a source program **(i) Auflistung des Originaltextes; (ii) Auflistung des Ursprungsprogramms; source machine** = computer which can compile source code **Übersetzungsanlage;** *compare with* OBJECT MACHINE; **source program** = program, prior to translation, written in a programming language by a programmer **Quellprogramm**

◊ **source language** *noun* (i) language in which a program is originally written; (ii) language of a program prior to translation **(i) & (ii) Ursprungssprache;** NOTE: opposite is **object** *or* **target language**

SP = STACK POINTER

space

1 *noun*

(a) gap (printed *or* displayed in text) **Zwischenraum; space character** = character code that prints a space **Leerzeichen; space bar** = long bar at the bottom of a keyboard, which inserts a space into the text when pressed **Leertaste**

(b) transmitted signal representing a binary zero **Leerzeichen;** NOTE: opposite is **mark**

(c) region extending out and around from the earth's atmosphere **Weltraum; space craft** = vehicle that travels in space **Raumfahrzeug; space station** = space craft which remains in orbit for a long time, and can be visited by other space vehicles **Weltraumstation**

2 *verb* to spread out text **spationieren;** *the line of characters was evenly spaced out across the page*

◊ **spacer** *noun* **intelligent spacer** = facility on a word-processing system used to prevent words from being hyphenated *or* separated at the wrong point **intelligentes Trennprogramm**

◊ **spacing** *noun* way in which spaces are inserted in a printed text **Wortabstände (einrichten);** *the spacing on some lines is very uneven*

span *noun* set of allowed values between a maximum and minimum **Bereich**

spark printer *noun* thermal printer which produces characters on thermal paper by electric sparks **Funkendrucker**

sparse array *noun* data matrix structure containing mainly zero *or* null entries **schwach besetzte Matrix**

speaker *see* LOUDSPEAKER

spec *informal* = SPECIFICATION; **high-spec** = high specification **hochspezifiziert**

special *adjective* which is different *or* not usual **speziell, Sonder-, sonder-; special character** = character which is not a normal one in a certain font (such as a certain accent *or* a symbol) **Sonderzeichen; special effects** = way of making strange things happen in films (such as monsters *or* explosions, etc.) **Tricks, optische Effekte; special sort** = extra printing character not in the standard font range **Sonderzeichen**

◊ **specialize** *verb* to study and be an expert in a subject **sich spezialisieren;** *he specializes in the design of CAD systems*

◊ **specialist** *noun* expert in a certain field of study **Spezialist/-in, Fachmann;** *you need a specialist programmer to help devise a new word-processing program*

specify *verb* to state clearly what is needed **angeben**

◊ **specification** *noun* detailed information about what is to be supplied *or* about a job to be done **Spezifikation; to work to standard specifications** = to work to specifications which are accepted anywhere in the same industry **nach anerkannten Normen arbeiten; the work is not up to specification** *or* **does not meet the customer's specifications** = the product was not manufactured in the way which was detailed in the specifications **die Arbeit entspricht nicht den vorgegebenen Normen; high specification** *or* **high spec** = high degree of accuracy *or* large number of features **hoher Qualitätsmaßstab;** *high spec cabling needs to be very carefully handled;* **program specification** = detailed information about a program's abilities, features and methods **Programmspezifizierung**

specific address *noun* storage address that directly, without any modification, accesses a location *or* device **absolute Adresse**

◊ **specific code** *noun* binary code which directly operates the central processing unit, using only absolute addresses and values **absoluter Code; specific coding** = program code that has been written so that it only uses absolute addresses and values **absolute Adressierung**

◊ **specificity** *noun* ratio of non-relevant entries not retrieved to the total number of non-relevant entries contained in a file, database or library **Spezifität**

spectrum *noun* range of frequencies; range of colours **Spektrum; spectrum analyzer** = electronic test equipment that displays the amplitudes of a number of frequencies in a signal **Spektralanalysator**

speech *noun* speaking *or* making words with the voice **Sprache; speech chip** = integrated circuit that generates sounds (usually phonemes) which when played together sound like human speech **Sprach-Chip; speech plus** = method of transmitting a bandlimited speech signal and a number of low speed data signals in a voice grade channel **Einlagerungstelegraphie; speech processor** = device that alters speech, such as a scrambler **Sprachprozessor; speech recognition** = analysing spoken words in such a way that a computer can recognize spoken words and commands **Spracherkennung; speech signal** = signal which transmits spoken words **Sprachsignal; speech synthesis** = production of spoken words by a speech synthesizer **Sprachsynthese; speech synthesizer** = device which takes data from a computer and outputs it as spoken words **Sprachsynthesizer**

QUOTE speech conveys information, and the primary task of computer speech processing is the transmission and reception of that information
Personal Computer World

speed *noun*
(a) measure of the sensitivity of a photographic material (film *or* paper) to light **Lichtempfindlichkeit;** *high speed film is very sensitive to light*
(b) time taken for a movement divided by the distance travelled **Geschwindigkeit; speed of loop** = method of benchmarking a computer by measuring the number of loops executed in a certain time **Schleifendurchgangsgeschwindigkeit; playback speed** = rate at which tape travels past a playback head **Wiedergabegeschwindigkeit**

spellcheck *verb* to check the spelling in a text by comparing it with a dictionary held in the computer **auf Schreibfehler prüfen**

◊ **spellchecker** *or* **spelling checker** *noun* dictionary of correctly spelled words, held in a computer, and used to check the spelling of a text **Orthographie-, Rechtschreibprüfprogramm;** *the program will be upgraded with a word-processor and a spelling checker*

spherical aberration *noun* optical distortion causing lines to appear curved **sphärische Aberration**

spike *noun* very short duration voltage pulse **Überschwingspitze**

spillage *noun* situation when too much data is being processed and cannot be contained in a buffer **Überlauf**

spin *verb* to turn round fast **sich (schnell) drehen;** *the disk was spun by the drive; the disk drive motor spins at a constant velocity* NOTE: spinning - span - spun

spindle *noun* object which grips and spins a disk in the centre hole **(Antriebs)spindel**
◊ **spindling** *noun* turning a disk by hand **Umdrehen**

spine *noun* back edge of the book which is covered by the binding **Rücken;** *the author's name and the title usually are shown on the spine as well as on the front cover*

spirit duplication *noun* short-run printing method using spirit to transfer ink onto the paper **Umdruckverfahren, Hektographieren**

SPL = SOUND PRESSURE LEVEL

splice *verb* to join two lengths of magnetic tape *or* film, forming a continuous length **verspleißen, zusammenkleben;** *you can use glue or splicing tape to splice the ends;* **splicing block** = device used to correctly position the ends of two lengths of tape *or* film that are to be spliced **Klebeeinrichtung; splicing tape** = non-magnetic tape which is applied to the back of the two ends of tape to be spliced **Klebeband**

split screen *noun* system where more than one text file can appear on the screen at the same time (such as the text being worked on and another text from memory for comparison) **geteilter Bildschirm**
◊ **splitter** *noun* device which allows a number of other devices to be plugged into one supply *or* line **Verteiler; beam splitter** = optical device to redirect part of a light beam **Strahlteiler**

spool
1 *noun* reel on which a tape *or* printer ribbon is wound **Spule**
2 *verb* to transfer data from a disk to a tape **spulen**
◊ **spooler** *or* **spooling device** *noun* device which holds a tape and which receives

information from a disk for storage **Spulgerät**

◊ **spooling** *noun* transferring data to a disk from which it can be printed at the normal speed of the printer, leaving the computer available to do something else **Spulbetrieb, SPOOL-Betrieb**

sporadic fault *noun* error that occurs occasionally **sporadischer Fehler**

spot *noun* point on a CRT screen that is illuminated by the electron beam **Punkt, Spurelement**

◊ **spot beam** *noun* narrow (satellite) antenna coverage of a select region (on earth) **scharfbündelnde Antenne**

spreadsheet *noun* (i) program which allows calculations to be carried out on several columns of numbers; (ii) printout of calculations on wide computer stationary (i) **elektronische Kalkulationstabelle**; (ii) **Kalkulations-Tabellendruck**

sprite *noun* object which moves round the screen in computer graphics **Kobold**

sprocket *or* **sprocket wheel** *noun* wheel with teeth round it which fit into holes in continuous stationery *or* punched tape **Stachelradwalze**

◊ **sprocket feed** *noun* paper feed, where the printer pulls the paper by turning sprocket wheels which fit into a series of holes along each edge of the sheet **Stachelbandführung**; *see also* TRACTOR FEED

◊ **sprocket holes** *noun* series of small holes on each edge of continuous stationery, which allow the sheet to be pulled through the printer **Führungslöcher**

spur *noun* connection point into a network **Netzanschlußpunkt**

SPX = SIMPLEX

SQA = SOFTWARE QUALITY ASSURANCE

square wave *noun* waveform with a square shape **Rechteckwelle**

SS = SINGLE-SIDED

SSBSC = SINGLE SIDEBAND SUPPRESSED CARRIER

SSD = SINGLE-SIDED DISK

SSI = SMALL SCALE INTEGRATION

stable *adjective* not moving *or* not changing **stabil**; **stable state** = the state of a system when no external signals are applied **Ruhezustand, Grundzustand**

◊ **stability** *noun* being stable **Stabilität**; **image stability** = ability of a display screen to provide a flicker-free picture **Bildstabilität**

stack *noun* temporary storage for data, registers *or* tasks where items are added and retrieved from the same end of the list **Kellerspeicher**; *see also* LIFO; **pushdown stack** *or* **pushdown list** = method of storing data, where the last item stored is always at the same location, the rest of the list being pushed down by one address **Rückstellstapel**; **virtual memory stack** = temporary store for pages in a virtual memory system **virtueller Matrixblock**; **stack address** = location pointed to by the stack pointer **Stapeladresse**; **stack base** = address of the origin *or* base of a stack **Anfangsadresse**; **stack job processing** = storing a number of jobs to be processed in a stack and automatically executing one after the other **Stapeljobverarbeitung**; **stack pointer (SP)** = address register containing the location of the most recently stored item of data *or* the location of the next item of data to be retrieved **Stapelzeiger**

stage *noun* one of several points in a process **Stufe**; *the text is ready for the printing stage; we are in the first stage of running in the new computer system*

◊ **staged** *adjective* carried out in stages, one after the other **Schritt für Schritt**; **staged change-over** = change between an old and a new system in a series of stages **schrittweises Überwechseln**

stand-alone *or* **standalone** *adjective* & *noun* (device *or* system) which can operate without the need of any other devices **selbständig(es), autonom(es) System**; *the workstations have been networked together rather than used as stand-alone systems*; **stand-alone terminal** = computer terminal with a processor and memory which can be directly connected to a modem, without being a member of a network *or* cluster **autonome Datenstation**

standard *adjective* normal *or* usual **standardmäßig**; **standard document** *or* **standard form** *or* **standard paragraph** *or* **standard text** = normal printed document *or* form *or* paragraph which is used many times (with different names and addresses often inserted - as in a form letter)

Standardtext; Standardformular; standard function = special feature included as normal in a computer system **Standardfunktion; standard interface** = interface between two or more systems that conforms to pre-defined standards **Standardschnittstelle; standard letter** = letter which is sent without any change to the main text, but being personalised by inserting the names and addresses of different people **Standard-, Formbrief; standard subroutine** = routine which carries out an often used function, such as keyboard input or screen display **Standard-Unterprogramm**

◊ **standardize** verb to make a series of things conform to a standard **normalisieren, standardisieren;** the standardized control of transmission links

◊ **standards** noun normal quality or normal conditions which are used to judge other things **Normen; production standards** = quality of production **Produktionsnormen, Produktionsstandards; up to standard** = of an acceptable quality **den Anforderungen entsprechend;** this batch of disks is not up to standard; **standards converter** = device to convert received signals conforming to one standard into a different standard **Normenumsetzer;** the standards converter allows us to watch US television broadcasts on our UK standards set; **video standards** see VIDEO; **modem standards** = rules defining transmitting frequencies, etc., which allow different modems to communicate **Modem-Normen**

COMMENT: modem standards are set by the CCITT in the UK, the Commonwealth and most of Europe, while the USA and part of South America use modem standards set by Bell

standby noun **standby equipment** = secondary system identical to the main system, to be used if the main system breaks down **Reserveausrüstung; cold standby** = backup system that will allow the equipment to continue running but with the loss of any volatile data **Cold-Standby-System; hot standby** = backup equipment that is kept operational at all times in case of system failure **Hot-Standby-System (mitlaufendes Reservesystem)**

QUOTE before fault-tolerant systems, users had to rely on the cold standby, that is switching on a second machine when the first developed a fault; the alternative was the hot standby, where a second computer was kept running continuously
Computer News

star network noun network of several machines where each terminal or floppy

disk unit or satellite is linked individually to a central hard disk machine or server **Sternnetz;** compare BUS NETWORK, RING NETWORK

◊ **star program** noun perfect program that runs (first time) with no errors or bugs **fehlerloses Programm**

start adjective beginning or first part **Start; cold start** = switching on a computer or to run a program from its original start point **Kaltstart; start bit** or **element** = transmitted bit used (in asynchronous communications) to indicate the start of a character **Startbit;** NOTE: opposite is **stop bit** **warm start** = restarting a program which has stopped, without losing any data **Warmstart; start of header** = transmitted code indicating the start of header (address or destination) information for a following message **Anfang des Kopfes; start of text (SOT** or **STX)** = transmitted code indicating the end of control or address information and the start of the message **Textanfang**

stat informal = PHOTOSTAT

state noun the way something is **Zustand, Status; active state** = state in which an action can or does occur **aktiver Status; steady state** = circuit or device or program state in which no action is occurring but can accept an input **Dauerbetrieb**

statement noun (i) expression used to convey an instruction or define a process; (ii) instruction in a source language which is translated into several machine code instructions **(i) & (ii) Anweisung; conditional statement** = program instruction that will redirect program control according to the outcome of an event **bedingte Anweisung; control statement** = (i) program instruction that directs a program (to another branch, etc.); (ii) program instruction that directs a CPU to provide controlling actions or controls the actions of the CPU **(i) & (ii) Steueranweisung; directive statement** = program instruction used to control the language translator, compiler, etc. **Übersetzungsanweisung; input statement** = computer programming command that waits for data entry from a port or keyboard **Eingabeanweisung; multi-statement line** = line from a computer program that contains more than one instruction or statement **Mehrfachanweisungszeile; narrative statement** = statement which sets variables and allocates storage **erklärende Festlegung, Setzanweisung; statement number** = number assigned (in a sequential way) to a series of instruction statements **Anweisungsnummer;** *see also* LINE NUMBER

state-of-the-art *adjective* very modern *or* technically as advanced as possible **auf dem neuesten Stand der Technik**

QUOTE the main PCB is decidedly non-state-of-the-art

Personal Computer World

static

1 *noun*

(a) (i) loud background noise *or* interference in a radio broadcast due to atmospheric conditions; (ii) background noise in a recorded signal **(i) atmosphärische Störungen; (ii) Rauschen**

(b) charge that does not flow **Reibungselektrizität, statische Aufladung;** NOTE: no plural

2 *adjective* (i) (data) which does not change with time; (ii) (system) that is not dynamic **(i) fest; (ii) statisch; static dump** = printout of the state of a system when it has finished a process **statischer Speicherauszug; static memory** = non-volatile memory that does not require refreshing **statischer Speicher; static RAM** = RAM which retains data for as long as the power supply is on, and where the data does not have to be refreshed **statischer RAM;** *compare with* DYNAMIC RAM; **static subroutine** = subroutine that uses no variables apart from the operand addresses **statisches Unterprogramm**

COMMENT: static RAM uses bistable devices such as flip-flops to store data; these take up more space on a chip than the capacititive storage method of dynamic RAM but do not require refreshing

station *noun*

(a) point in a network *or* communications system that contains devices to control the input and output of messages, allowing it to be used as a sink *or* source **Station; secondary station** = temporary status of the station that is receiving data **Sekundärstation; workstation** = desk with computer, keyboard, monitor, printers, etc., where a person works **Arbeitsplatz**

(b) earth station = dish antenna and circuitry used to communicate with a satellite **Erdfunkstelle; radio station** = broadcast signal booster *or* relay point consisting of a receiver and transmitter linked with ancillary equipment **Funkstation;** *the signal from this radio station is very weak; we are trying to jam the signals from that station*

stationary *adjective* not moving **stationär; geostationary orbit** = orbit of a satellite which keeps it above the same part of the earth **geostationäre Umlaufbahn**

stationery *noun* office supplies for writing, especially paper, envelopes, labels, etc. **Büromaterial, Schreibwaren; computer stationery** = paper specially made for use in a computer printer **Computerdruckerpapier; continuous stationery** = printer stationery which takes the form of a single long sheet **Endlospapier; preprinted stationery** = computer stationery (such as invoices) which is preprinted with the company heading and form layout onto which the details will be printed by the computer **vorgedrucktes Briefpapier, Vordruck** NOTE: no plural

statistics *noun* (study of) facts in the form of figures **Statistik**

◇ **statistical** *adjective* based on statistics **statistisch; statistical time division multiplexing (STDM)** = time division multiplexing system that allocates time slots when they are required, allowing greater flexibility and a greater number of devices to transmit **statistische Zeitmultiplexmethode;** *see also* TIME DIVISION MULTIPLEXING

◇ **statistician** *noun* person who analyses statistics **Statistiker/-in**

status *noun* importance *or* position **Status, Zustand; status bit** = single bit in a word used to provide information about the state *or* result of an operation **Zustandsbit; status line** = line at the top *or* bottom of a screen which gives information about the task currently being worked on (number of lines, number of columns, filename, time, etc.) **Statuszeile; status poll** = signal from a computer requesting information on the current status of a terminal **Statusabfrage; status register** = register containing information on the status of a peripheral device **Statusregister; program status word (PSW)** = word which contains a number of status bits, such as carry flag, zero flag, overflow bit, etc. **Programmstatuswort**

STD = SUBSCRIBER TRUNK DIALLING

STDM = STATISTICAL TIME DIVISION MULTIPLEXING

steady state *noun* circuit *or* device *or* program state in which no action is occurring but can accept an input **Dauerbetrieb**

stencil *noun* material with component shapes and symbols already cut out, allowing designers to draw components and other symbols rapidly **Schablone;** *the stencil has all the electronic components on it; the schematic looks much neater if you use a stencil;* **flowchart stencil** *or* **template** = plastic sheet with template symbols cut out, to allow flowcharts to be quickly and clearly drawn **Zeichenschablone**

step
1 *noun* a single unit **Schritt; single step** = executing a computer program one instruction at a time, used for debugging **Einzelschritt**
2 *verb* to move forwards *or* backwards by one unit **(einen Schritt vorwärts) gehen;** *we stepped forward through the file one record at a time; we stepped forward the film one frame at a time*
◊ **stepper motor** *or* **stepping motor** *noun* motor which turns in small steps as instructed by a computer (used in printers, disk drives and robots) **Schrittmotor**

steradian *noun* unit of solid angle **Sterad(iant)** ⇨ APPENDIX

stereo *informal* = STEREOPHONIC

stereophonic *adjective* using two audio signals recorded from slightly different positions to provide a three-dimensional sound effect when replayed through two separate loudspeakers **stereophon, Stereo-, stereo-; stereophonic microphone** = one device containing two microphones allowing stereo signals to be recorded **Stereomikrophon; stereophonic recorder** = tape recorder that records two audio signals onto magnetic tape **Stereorekorder**

still frame *noun* one single video *or* film frame displayed by itself **Stillstandprojektion**

stochastic model *noun* mathematical representation of a system that includes the effects of random actions **Zufallsmodell**

stock control program *noun* software designed to help manage stock in a business **Programm zur Lagerbestandsführung**

stop *verb* not doing any action **anhalten; stop and wait protocol** = communications protocol in which the transmitter waits for a signal from the receiver that the message was correctly received before transmitting further data **Anhalt- und Warteprotokoll; tab stop** = preset point along a line, where the printing head *or* cursor will stop for each tabulation command **Tabulatorstop**

◊ **stop bit** *or* **stop element** *noun* transmitted bit used in asynchronous communications to indicate the end of a character **Stopbit; stop code** = instruction that temporarily stops a process to allow the user to enter data **Haltecode; stop instruction** = computer programming instruction that stops program execution **Haltebefehl; stop list** = list of words that are not to be used *or* are not significant for a file *or* library search **Stopliste; stop time** = time taken for a spinning disk to come to a stop after it is no longer powered **Abbremszeit**

storage *noun* memory *or* part of the computer system in which data *or* programs are kept for further use **Speicher; archive storage** = storage of data for a long period of time **Archivspeicherung; auxiliary storage** = any data storage medium (such as magnetic tape *or* disk) that is not the main, high speed memory **Zusatzspeicher, peripherer Speicher; dynamic storage** *or* **memory** = memory that requires its contents to be updated regularly **dynamischer Speicher; external storage** = storage device which is located outside the main computer system but which can be accessed by the CPU **externer Speicher; information storage** = storing data in a form which allows it to be processed at a later date **Informationsspeicherung; instruction storage** = section of memory that is used to store instructions **Befehlsspeicher; intermediate storage** = temporary area of memory for items that are currently being processed **Zwischenspeicher; mass storage system** = data storage that can hold more than one million million bits of data **Großspeicher; nonerasable storage** = storage medium that cannot be erased and re-used **nicht löschbarer Speicher; primary storage** = (i) small fast-access internal memory of a system which contains the data currently being executed; (ii) main internal memory of a system **(i) & (ii) Hauptspeicher, Primärspeicher; secondary storage** = any data storage medium (such as magnetic tape *or* floppy disk) that is not the main high-speed computer storage **Zusatzspeicher; static storage** = non-volatile memory that does not require refreshing **statischer Speicher; temporary storage** = storage which is not permanent **Zwischenspeicher; volatile storage** = memory *or* storage medium that loses data stored when the power supply is switched off **flüchtiger Speicher; storage allocation** = how memory is allocated for different uses such as programs, variables, data, etc **Speicherplatzzuteilung; storage capacity** =

amount of space available for storage of data **Speicherkapazität; storage density =** number of bits that can be recorded per unit area of storage medium **Aufzeichnungsdichte; storage device =** any device that can store data and then allow it to be retrieved when required **Speicher; storage disk =** disk used to store data **Speicherplatte; storage dump =** printout of all the contents of an area of storage space **Speicherauszug; storage media =** various materials which are able to store data **Speichermedien, Datenträger; storage tube =** special CRT used for computer graphics that retains an image on screen without the need for refresh actions **Speicherröhre;** *see also* REFRESH

◇ **store**
1 *noun* memory *or* part of the computer system in which data *or* programs are kept for further use **Speicher; store address register (SAR) =** register in a CPU that contains the address of the next location to be accessed **Speicheradreßregister; store data register (SDR) =** register in a CPU which holds data before it is proceesed *or* moved to a memory location **Speicherdatenregister; store location** *or* **cell =** unit in a computer system which can store information **Speicherzelle**
2 *verb* to save data, which can then be used again as necessary **speichern;** *storing a page of high resolution graphics can require 3Mb;* **store and forward =** communications system that stores a number of messages before retransmitting them **speichern und übermitteln; stored program =** computer program that is stored in memory (if it is stored in dynamic RAM it will be lost when the machine is switched off, if stored on disk or tape (backing store) it will be permanently retained) **gespeichertes Programm; stored program signalling =** system of storing communications control signals on computer in the form of a program **speicherprogrammgesteuertes Signal**

COMMENT: storage devices include hard and floppy disk, RAM, punched paper tape and magnetic tape

straight-line coding *noun* program written to avoid the use of loops and branches, providing a faster execution time **lineare Codierung**

stray *adjective* lost *or* wandering; (something) which has avoided being stopped **vereinzelt, verstreut, verirrt;** *the metal screen protects the CPU against stray electromagnetic effects from the PSU*

streaking *noun* horizontal television picture distortion **Nachzieheffekt, Fahnen**

stream *noun* long flow of serial data **Strom; job stream =** number of tasks arranged in order waiting to be processed in a batch system **Jobfolge, Programmablauffolge**

◇ **streamer** *noun* **tape streamer** *or* **streaming tape drive =** (device containing a) continuous loop of tape, used as backing storage **Magnetbandstreamer**

QUOTE the product has 16Mb of memory, 45Mb of Winchester disk storage and 95Mb streaming tape storage
Minicomputer News

string *noun* any series of consecutive alphanumeric characters *or* words that are manipulated and treated as a single unit by the computer **Zeichenfolge, Zeichenkette; alphanumeric** *or* **character string =** storage allocated for a series of alphanumeric characters **alphanumerische Zeichenfolge; numeric string =** string which contains only numbers **numerische Zeichenfolge; null** *or* **blank string =** string that contains nothing **Null-String, Zeichenfolge der Länge Null; string area =** section of memory in which strings of alphanumeric characters are stored **String-Bereich; string concatenation =** linking a series of strings together **Zeichenfolgenverkettung; string function =** program operation which can act on strings **Zeichenfolgenfunktion; string length =** the number of characters in a string **Länge der Zeichenfolge, String-Länge; string name =** identification label assigned to a string **Name der Zeichenfolge, String-Name; string orientated symbolic language (SNOBOL) =** high-level programming language that uses string processing methods **SNOBOL (Programmiersprache); string variable =** variables used in a computer language that can contain alphanumeric characters as well as numbers **String-Variable**

◇ **stringy floppy** *or* **tape streamer** *noun* continuous loop of tape, used for backing storage **Magnetbandstreamer**

strip
1 *noun* long thin piece of material **Streifen; strip window =** display which shows a single line of text **Einzeilenfenster; magnetic strip =** layer of magnetic material on the surface of a plastic card, used for recording data **Magnetstreifen**
2 *verb* to remove the control data from a received message, leaving only the relevant information **strippen**

stripe *noun* long thin line of colour **Streifen; balance stripe** = thin magnetic strip on a cine film on the opposite side to the sound track, so that the whole film will lie flat when played back **Ausgleichsstreifen**

strobe *verb* to send a pulse (usually on the selection line) of an electronic circuit **einen Impuls geben; address strobe** = signal indicating that a valid address is on the address bus **Adreßimpulseingang; data strobe** = signal indicating that valid data is on the data bus **Datenimpulseingang**

◊ **stroboscope** *or* **strobe** *noun* light source which produces flashes of light **Stroboskop**

stroke *noun* basic curved *or* straight line that makes up a character **Strich**

strowger exchange *noun* telephone exchange worked by electromechanical switches **Strowgersches Fernsprechamt**

structure
1 *noun* way in which something is organized *or* formed **Struktur; network structure** = data structure that allows each node to be connected to any of the others **Netzwerkstruktur**
2 *verb* to organize *or* to arrange in a certain way **strukturieren;** *you first structure a document to meet your requirements and then fill in the blanks;* **structured design** = problem solved by a number of interconnected modules **strukturierte Entwicklung; structured programming** = well-ordered and logical technique of assembling programs **strukturierte Programmierung**

studio *noun* place where a designer draws; place where recordings take place; place where films are made **Studio**

STX = START OF TEXT

style sheet *noun* (i) sheet giving the style which should be followed by an editor; (ii) template that can be preformatted to generate automatically the style *or* layout of a document such a a manual, a book, a newsletter, etc. **(i) Merkblatt zur Manuskriptgestaltung; (ii) Schablone**

stylus *noun*
(a) (transducer) needle which converts signals on an audio record into electrical signals **Stift, Abspielnadel**
(b) pen-like device that is used in computer graphics systems to dictate cursor position

on the screen **(Licht)stift;** *use the stylus on the graphics tablet to draw*
(c) (transducer) that detects data stored or a video disk **Anzeigenadel; stylus printer** *see* DOT MATRIX PRINTER

sub- *prefix* meaning less (important) than *or* lower than **Unter-, unter-; subaddress** = peripheral identification code, used to access one peripheral (this is then followed by address data to access a location within the peripheral's memory) **Sub-Adresse; subaudio frequencies** = frequencies below the audio range (below 20Hz) **Frequenzen unterhalb des Hörbereichs; subclass** = number of data items to do with one item in a master class **Unterklasse; subbing** *or* **sub editing** = editing of a manuscript before it is sent for typesetting **redigieren; subrange** = below the normal range **unterhalb der normalen Reichweite**

subdirectory *noun* directory of disk *o* tape contents contained within the main directory **Unterverzeichnis**

> QUOTE if you delete a file and then delete the subdirectory where it was located, you cannot restore the file because the directory does not exist
>
> *Personal Computer World*

subprogram *noun* (i) subroutine in a program; (ii) program called up by a main program **(i) & (ii) Unterprogramm**

subroutine *noun* section of a program which performs a required function and that can be called upon at any time from inside the main program **Unterprogramm; subroutine call** = computer programming instruction that directs control to a subroutine **Aufruf eines Unterprogramms; closed** *or* **linked subroutine** = number of computer instructions in a program that can be called at any time, with control being returned on completion to the next instruction after the call **abgeschlossenes/verbundenes Unterprogramm; open subroutine** = code for a subroutine which is copied into memory whenever a call instruction is found **offenes Unterprogramm; static subroutine** = subroutine that uses no variables apart from the operand addresses **statisches Unterprogramm; two-level subroutine** = subroutine containing another subroutine **zweistufiges Unterprogramm; subroutine call** = computer programming instruction that directs control to a subroutine **Aufruf eines Unterprogramms**

COMMENT: a subroutine is executed by a call instruction which directs the processor to its address; when finished it returns to the instruction after the call instruction in the main program

subscriber *noun* (i) person who has a telephone; (ii) person who pays for access to a service such as a BBS **(i) & (ii) Teilnehmer/-in; subscriber trunk dialling (STD)** = system where a person can dial direct from one telephone to another, without referring to the operator **Selbstwählferndienst**

subscript *noun* small character which is printed below the line of other characters **(tiefstehender) Index;** *see also* SUPERSCRIPT (NOTE: used in chemical formulae: CO_2) **subscripted variable** = element in an array, which is identified by a subscript **indizierte Variable**

◊ **subset** *noun* small set of data items which forms part of another larger set **Untermenge**

◊ **subsegment** *noun* small section of a segment **Sub-Segment**

substance *noun* any matter whose properties can be described **Materie, Substanz**

substitute *verb* to put something in the place of something else **ersetzen; substitute character** = character that is displayed if a received character is not recognized **Ersatzzeichen;** NOTE: you substitute one thing **for** another

◊ **substitution** *noun* replacing something by something else **Austausch, Substitution; substitution error** = error made by a scanner which mistakes one character *or* letter for another **Substitutionsfehler; substitution table** = list of characters *or* codes that are to be inserted instead of received codes **Substitutionstabelle**

substrate *noun* base material on which an integrated circuit is constructed **Trägermaterial;** *see also* INTEGRATED CIRCUIT

subsystem *noun* one smaller part of a large system **Teilsystem**

◊ **subtotal** *noun* total at the end of a column, which when added to others makes the grand total **Zwischensumme**

subtraction *noun* taking one number away from another **Subtraktion**

◊ **subtrahend** *noun* in a subtraction operation, the number to be subtracted from the minuend **Subtrahend**

subvoice grade channel *noun* communications channel using frequencies (240 - 300Hz) below a voice channel, used for low speed data transmission **Nachrichtenkanal für Frequenzen zwischen 240Hz und 300Hz**

successive *adjective* which follow one after the other **aufeinanderfolgend;** *each successive operation adds further characters to the string*

suffix notation *noun* mathematical operations written in a logical way, so that the symbol appears after the numbers to be acted upon **Suffix-Schreibweise;** *see also* POSTFIX NOTATION

suite of programs *noun* (i) group of programs which run one after the other; (ii) number of programs used for a particular task **(i) Programmfolge; (ii) Programmgruppe;** *the word-processing system uses a suite of three programs, editor, spelling checker and printing controller*

sum *noun* total of a number of items added together **Summe**

◊ **summation check** *noun* error detection check performed by adding together the characters received and comparing with the required total **Summenprüfung**

sun outage *noun* length of time during which a satellite does not operate due to the position of the moon *or* earth, causing a shadow over the satellite's solar cells **Ausfallzeit mangels Sonnenlicht**

super- *prefix* meaning very good *or* very powerful **besonders gut/groß; supercomputer** = very powerful mainframe computer used for high speed mathematical tasks **Größtrechner; supergroup** = a number (60) of voice channels collected together into five adjacent channels for simultaneous transmission **Übergruppe, Sekundärgruppe**

◊ **super high frequency (SHF)** *noun* frequency range between 3 - 30GHz **Frequenz zwischen 3GHz und 30GHz**

◊ **super large scale integration (SLSI)** *noun* integrated circuit with more than 100,000 components **Größtintegration**

◊ **super master group** *noun* collection of 900 voice channels **Quartärgruppe**

superheterodyne radio *noun* radio receiver that converts a received signal by means of a heterodyne process to an intermediate frequency for easier processing **Superüberlagerungsfunkempfänger**

superimpose *verb* to place something on top of something else **überlagern**

superior number *noun* superscript figure **Hochzahl, Index**

superscript *noun* small character printed higher than the normal line of characters **hochgestelltes Zeichen, Index;** *compare with* SUBSCRIPT
NOTE: used often in mathematics: 10^5 (say: ten to the power five)

supersede *verb* to take the place of something which is older *or* less useful **ablösen;** *the new program supersedes the earlier one, and is much faster*

superstation *noun* (US) TV system, where a single TV station broadcasts many programmes simultaneously via satellite and cable **Superstation**

supervise *verb* to watch carefully to see if work is well done **überwachen;** *the manufacture of circuit boards is very carefully supervised*

◇ **supervision** *noun* being supervised **Überwachung**

◇ **supervisor** *noun* (i) person who makes sure that equipment is always working correctly; (ii) section of a computer operating system that regulates the use of peripherals and the operations undertaken by the CPU **(i) Aufsichtsperson; (ii) Supervisor**

◇ **supervisory** *adjective* as a supervisor **Überwachungs-, überwachungs-; supervisory program** *or* **executive program** = master program in a computer system that controls the execution of other programs **Überwachungsprogramm, Supervisor; supervisory sequence** = combination of control codes that perform a controlling function in a data communications network **Steuerzeichenfolge; supervisory signal** = (i) signal that indicates if a circuit is busy; (ii) signal that provides an indication of the state of a device **(i) & (ii) Überwachungssignal**

supply
1 *noun* providing goods *or* products *or* services **Versorgung;** *the electricity supply has failed; they signed a contract for the supply of computer stationery*
2 *verb* to provide something which is needed (for which someone will pay) **versorgen;** *the computer was supplied by a recognized dealer; they have signed a contract to supply on-line information*

◇ **supplier** *noun* company which supplies **Lieferant;** *a supplier of computer parts; a supplier of disk drives or a disk drive supplier; Japanese suppliers have set up warehouses in the country*

support *verb* to give help to *or* to help to run **unterstützen;** *the main computer supports six workstations;* **support chip** = dedicated IC that works with a CPU, and carries out an additional function *or* a standard function very rapidly, so speeding up the processing time **Unterstützungschip;** *the maths support chip can be plugged in here*

QUOTE enhanced screen and I/O handling, and supporting up to 80 screens
PC User

suppress *verb* to remove **unterdrücken;** *the filter is used to suppress the noise due to static interference;* **suppressed carrier modulation** = modulated waveform where the carrier signal has been suppressed prior to transmission, leaving only the modulated sidebands **Modulation mit unterdrückter Trägerwelle; double sideband suppressed carrier (DSBSC)** = amplitude modulation that has a suppressed carrier, leaving only two sidebands **Zweiseitenbandübertragung mit unterdrückter Trägerwelle; single sideband suppressed carrier (SSBSC)** = amplitude modulation that has a suppressed carrier, and only one sideband for data transmission **Einseitenbandübertragung mit unterdrückter Trägerwelle**

COMMENT: single sideband suppressed carrier modulation allows a greater number of channels in a frequency range, since each one is narrower

◇ **suppression** *noun* act of suppressing **Unterdrückung**

◇ **suppressor** *noun* device which suppresses interference **Unterdrücker; echo suppressor** = device used on long-distance speech lines to prevent echoing effects **Echosperre**

surge *noun* sudden increase in electrical power in a system, due to a fault *or* noise *or* component failure **Stromstoß; surge protector** = electronic device that cuts off the power supply to sensitive equipment if it detects a power surge that could cause damage **Überspannungsableiter**

COMMENT: power surges can burn out circuits before you have time to pull the plug; a surge protector between your computer and the wall outlet will help prevent damage

sustain *verb* to keep a voltage at a certain level for a period of time **(Spannung) aufrechterhalten**

SW = SHORT WAVE

swap
1 *noun* = SWAPPING
2 *verb* to stop using one program, put it into store temporarily, run another program, and when that is finished, return to the first one **austauschen**

◇ **swapping** *or* **swap** *noun* system where a program is moved to backing storage while another program is being used **wechselndes Heraus- und Hereinholen**

sweep *noun* movement of the electron beam over the area of a television screen in regular horizontal and vertical steps, producing the image **Hin- und Rücklauf, Zeitablenkung**

swim *noun* computer graphics that move slightly due to a faulty display unit **Schwimmen**

switch
1 *noun*
(a) point in a computer program where control can be passed to one of a number of choices **Verzweigung**
(b) mechanical *or* solid state device that can electrically connect *or* isolate two or more lines **Verteiler; switch train** = series of switches between a caller and a receiver in a telephone network **Schaltfolge**
2 *verb* to connect *or* disconnect two lines by activating a switch **schalten; to switch on** = to start to provide power to a system by using a switch to connect the power supply lines to the circuit **einschalten; to switch off** = to disconnect the power supply to a device **ausschalten; to switch over** = to start using an alternative device when the primary one becomes faulty **umschalten; switched network backup** = user's choice of a secondary route through a network if the first is busy **Wählleitungsausweichverfahren; switched star** = cable television distribution system **sternförmiges Verteilungssystem; switched virtual call** = connection between two devices in a

network that is only made when required, after a request signal **Verbindung auf Anfrage**

◇ **switchboard** *noun* central point in a telephone system, where the lines from various telephone handsets meet, where calls can be directed to any other telephone **Telefonzentrale, Vermittlung; switchboard operator** = person who works a central telephone switchboard, by connecting incoming and outgoing calls to various lines **Telefonist/-in**

◇ **switching** *noun* constant update of connections between changing sinks and sources in a network **Vermittlung; switching centre** = point in a communications network where messages can be switched to and from the various lines and circuits that end there **Vermittlungszentrale; switching circuit** = electronic circuit that can direct messages from one line *or* circuit to another in a switching centre **Umschaltnetzwerk; line switching** = communication line and circuit established on demand and held until no longer required **Durchschaltetechnik**

symbol *noun* sign *or* picture which represents something **Symbol;** *this language uses the symbol ? to represent the print command;* **logic symbol** = graphical symbol used to represent a type of logic function in a diagram **logisches Symbol; symbol table** *or* **library** = list of labels *or* names in a compiler *or* assembler, which relate to their addresses in the machine code program **Symboltabelle**

◇ **symbolic** *adjective* which acts as a symbol *or* which uses a symbol name *or* label **symbolisch; symbolic address** = address represented by a symbol *or* name **symbolische Adresse; symbolic code** *or* **instruction** = instruction that is in mnemonic form rather than a binary number **symbolischer Code/Befehl; symbolic debugging** = debugger that allows symbolic representation of variables *or* locations **symbolische Austestung; symbolic language** = (i) any computer language where locations are represented by names; (ii) any language used to write source code **(i) & (ii) symbolische Programmiersprache; symbolic logic** = study of reasoning and thought (formal logic) **mathematische Logik; symbolic name** = name used as a label for a variable *or* location **(symbolischer) Name; symbolic programming** = writing a program in a source language **symbolisches Programmieren**

symmetric difference *noun* logical function whose output is true if either (of 2) inputs is true, and false if both inputs are the same **Antivalenz**

sync *noun* *(informal)* = SYNCHRONIZATION; **sync bit** = transmitted bit used to synchronize devices **Synchronisierungsbit; sync character** = transmitted character used to synchronize devices **Synchronisierungszeichen; sync** *or* **synchronization pulses** = transmitted pulses used to make sure that the receiver is synchronized with the transmitter **Synchronisierungsimpulse; in sync** = synchronized **synchronisiert; the two devices are out of sync** = the two devices are not properly synchronized **die beiden Geräte sind nicht synchronisiert**

◇ **synchronization** *noun* action of synchronizing two or more devices **Synchronisieren**

◇ **synchronize** *verb* to make sure that two or more devices *or* processes are coordinated in time or action **synchronisieren**

◇ **synchronizer** *noun* device that will perform a function when it receives a signal from another device **Synchronisierer**

◇ **synchronous** *adjective* which runs in sync with something else (such as a main clock) **synchron; synchronous computer** = computer in which each action can only take place when a timing pulse arrives **Synchronrechner; synchronous data link control (SDLC)** = protocol and rules used to define the way in which synchronous data is transmitted *or* received **synchrone Datenübertragungssteuerung; synchronous data network** = communications network in which all the actions throughout the network are controlled by a single timing signal **synchrones Datennetz; synchronous detection** = method of obtaining the signal from an amplitude modulation carrier **Synchronisationsdemodulation; synchronous idle character** = character transmitted by a DTE to ensure correct synchronization when no other character is being transmitted **Synchronisierungszeichen; synchronous mode** = system mode in which operations and events are synchronized with a clock signal **Synchronverfahren; synchronous network** = network in which all the links are synchronized with a single timing signal **Synchronnetz; synchronous system** = system in which all devices are synchronized to a main clock signal **Synchronsystem; synchronous transmission** = transmission of data from one device to another, where both devices are controlled by the same clock, and the transmitted data is synchronized with the clock signal **Synchronübertragung**

synonym *noun* word which means the same thing as another word **Synonym**

◇ **synonymous** *adjective* meaning the same **synonym;** *the words "error" and "mistake" are synonymous*

syntactic error *noun* programming error in which the program statement does not follow the syntax of the language **syntaktischer Fehler**

syntax *noun* grammatical rules that apply to a programming language **Syntax; syntax analysis** = stage in compilation where statements are checked to see if they obey the rules of syntax **Syntaxanalyse; syntax error** = programming error in which the program statement does not follow the syntax of the language **Syntaxfehler**

synthesis *noun* producing something artificially (from a number of smaller elements) **Synthese**

◇ **synthesize** *verb* to produce something artificially (from a number of smaller elements) **synthetisieren**

◇ **synthesizer** *noun* device which generates something (signals *or* sound *or* speech) **Synthesizer, Synthetisator; music synthesizer** = device which makes musical notes which are similar to those made by musical instruments **Musik-Synthesizer; speech synthesizer** = device which generates sounds which are similar to the human voice **Sprach-Synthetisator**

◇ **synthetic address** *noun* location used by a program that has been produced by instructions within the program **errechnete Adresse; synthetic language** = programming language in which the source program is written **synthetische Sprache**

QUOTE despite the fact that speech can now be synthesized with very acceptable quality, all it conveys is linguistic information
Personal Computer World

sysgen = SYSTEM GENERATION

system *noun* any group of hardware *or* software *or* peripherals, etc., which work together **System; adaptive system** = system which is able to alter its responses and processes according to inputs *or* situations **anpassungsfähiges System; computer system** = central processor with storage and associated peripherals which make up a working computer **Computersystem; information system** = computer system which provides information according to a user's requests **Informationssystem; interactive system** = system which provides an immediate response to the user's commands *or* programs *or* data **interaktives System; operating system (op sys)** = basic software that controls the running of the hardware and the management of data files, without the user having to operate it **Betriebssystem; secure system** = system that cannot be accessed without authorization **Sicherheitssystem; system check** = running diagnostic routines to ensure that there are no problems **Systemprüfung; system control panel** = main computer system control switches and status indicators **Bedienungspult; system crash** = situation where the operating system stops working and has to be restarted **Systemabsturz; system design** = identifying and investigating possible solutions to a problem, and deciding upon the most appropriate system to solve the problem **Systemplanung; system diagnostics** = tests, features and messages that help find hardware or software faults **Systemdiagnose; system disk** = disk which holds the system software **Systemplatte; system firmware** = basic operating system functions and routines in a ROM device **im Festspeicher implementierte Systemsoftware; system flowchart** = diagram that shows each step of the computer procedures needed in a system **Systemablaufplan; system generation or sysgen** = process of producing an optimum operating system for a particular task **Systemgenerierung; system library** = stored files that hold the various parts of a computer's operating system **Systembibliothek; system life cycle** = time when a system exists, between its initial design and its becoming out of date **Lebensdauer eines Systems; system log** = record of computer processor operations **Systemprotokoll; system security** = measures, such as password, priority protection, authorization codes, etc., designed to stop browsing and hackers **Systemsicherheit; system software** = software which makes applications run on hardware **Systemsoftware; system specifications** = details of hardware and software required to perform certain tasks **Pflichtenheft; system support** = group of people that maintain and operate a system **Einsatzunterstützung**

◇ **systems analysis** noun (i) analysing a process or system to see if it could be more efficiently carried out by a computer; (ii) examining an existing system with the aim of improving or replacing it **(i) & (ii) Systemanalyse; systems analyst** = person who undertakes system analysis **Systemanalytiker; systems program** = program which controls the way in which a computer system works **Systemprogramm; systems programmer** = person who writes system software **Systemprogrammierer**

Tt

T junction noun connection at right angles with a main signal or power carrying cable **T-Verbindung**

◇ **T network** noun simple circuit network with three electronic components connected in the shape of a letter T **T-Netz**

TAB = TABULATE

tab verb to tabulate or to arrange text in columns with the cursor automatically running from one column to the next in keyboarding **tabellieren**; *the list was neatly lined up by tabbing to column 10 at the start of each new line;* **tab memory** = ability of a editing program (usually a word-processor) to store details about various tab settings **Tabulatorspeicher; tab rack or ruler line** = graduated scale, displayed on the screen, showing the position of tabulation columns **Tabulatorraster**; *the tab rack shows you the left and right margins;* **tab stop** = preset points along a line, where the printing head or cursor will stop for each tabulation command **Tabulatorstop**

◇ **tabbing** noun movement of the cursor in a word-processing program from one tab stop to the next **Tabellieren**; *tabbing can be done from inside the program;* **decimal tabbing** = adjusting a column of numbers so that the decimal points are aligned vertically **mit Dezimaltabulator einrichten**

table noun list of data in columns and rows on a printed page or on the screen **Tabelle; decision table** = list of all possible events or states that could happen and the actions taken (sometimes used instead of a flowchart) **Entscheidungstabelle; look-up table** = collection of stored results that can be accessed very rapidly **Nachschlagetabelle**; *this is the value of the key pressed, use a look-up table to find its ASCII value;* **table lookup** = using one known value to select one entry in a table, providing a secondary value **Tabellensuchen; reference program table** = list produced by a compiler or system of the location, size and type of the variables, routines and macros within a program **Referenzprogrammtabelle; symbol table** = list of all the symbols that are accepted by a

table 298 **tape**

language _or_ compiler and their object code translation **Symboltabelle; table of contents** = list of the contents of a book, usually printed at the beginning **Inhaltsverzeichnis**

tablet _noun_ **graphics tablet** = graphics pad _or_ flat device that allows a user to input graphical information into a computer by drawing on its surface **Graphiktablett** _it is much easier to draw accurately with a tablet than with a mouse_

tabulate _verb_ to arrange text in columns, with the cursor moving to each new column automatically as the text is keyboarded **tabellieren**

◊ **tabular** _adjective_ **in tabular form** = arranged in a table **in Tabellenform**

◊ **tabulating** _noun_ processing punched cards, such as a sorting operation **Tabellieren**

◊ **tabulation** _noun_ (i) arrangement of a table of figures; (ii) moving a printing head _or_ cursor a preset distance along a line **(i) tabellarische Aufstellung; (ii) Tabulieren; tabulation markers** = symbols displayed to indicate the position of tabulation stops **Tabulatormarkierer; tabulation stop** = preset point along a line at which a printing head _or_ cursor will stop for each tabulation command **Tabulatorstop**

◊ **tabulator** _noun_ part of a typewriter _or_ word-processor which automatically sets words _or_ figures into columns **Tabulator**

TACS = TOTAL ACCESS COMMUNICATION SYSTEM UK standard for cellular radio systems **Nachrichtensystem**

tactile _adjective_ using the sense of touch **fühlbar; tactile feedback** = information provided by using the sense of touch **taktile Information; tactile keyboard** = keyboard that provides some indication that a key has been pressed, such as a beep **taktile Tastatur**

tag _noun_
(a) one section of a computer instruction **Tag**
(b) identifying characters attached to a file _or_ item (of data) **Identifizierungskennzeichen;** _each file has a three letter tag for rapid identification_

tail _noun_
(a) data recognized as the end of a list of data **Schluß**
(b) control code used to signal the end of a message **Endcode**

takedown _verb_ to remove paper _or_ disk _or_ tape from a peripheral after one job and prepare it for the next **entfernen; takedown time** = amount of time required to takedown a peripheral ready for another job **Vorbereitungszeit**

take-up reel _noun_ reel onto which magnetic tape is collected **Aufwickelspule** _put the full reel on this spindle, and feed the tape into the take-up reel on the other spindle_

talk _verb_ to speak _or_ to communicate **sprechen**

◊ **talkback** _noun_ speech communication between a control room and a studio **Anweisungen im Hintergrund**

QUOTE a variety of technologies exist which allow computers to talk to one another
Which PC?

tandem _noun_ **working in tandem** = situation where two things are working together **im Gespann arbeiten; tandem switching** = one switch controlling another switch in the same exchange by means of a secondary switch **Durchgangsvermittlung**

tape _noun_ long thin flat piece of material **Band; cassette tape** = tape stored on two small reels protected by a solid casing **Kassettenband;** _cassette tape is mainly used with home computers;_ **(magnetic) tape** = narrow length of thin plastic coated with a magnetic material used to store signals magnetically **Magnetband; master tape** = magnetic tape which contains all the vital operating system routines, loaded by the initial program loader once when the computer is switched on _or_ hard reset **Hauptband; (paper) tape** _or_ **punched tape** = strip of paper on which information can be recorded in the form of punched holes **Lochstreifen; (video cassette) tape** = magnetic tape used in a video recorder to store pictures and sound **Videoband; open reel tape** = tape on a reel which is not enclosed in a cassette _or_ cartridge **Wickelrolle; streaming tape drive** = device containing a continuous loop of tape, used as backing store **Endlosbandbetrieb; tape back-up** = use (usually magnetic) tape as a medium for storing back-ups from faster main _or_ secondary storage (such as RAM _or_ hard disk) **Sicherung auf Band; tape cable** _or_ **ribbon cable** = number of insulated conductors arranged next to each other forming a flat cable **Bandkabel; tape cartridge** = cassette box containing magnetic tape (on a reel) **Magnetbandkassette; tape cassette** = small box containing a reel of magnetic tape and a pickup reel **(Magnetband)kassette; tape code** = coding system used for punched data representation on paper tape **Bandcode; tape counter** = indication (on a tape recorder) of the amount of tape that has been used **Bandzählwerk; tape deck** = device which plays back and records data onto magnetic tape **Magnetbandgerät; tape drive** = mechanism which controls magnetic tape movement over the tape heads **Magnetbandlaufwerk;** *our new product has a 96Mb streaming tape drive;* **tape format** = way in which blocks of data, control codes and location data is stored on tape **Bandformat; tape guide** = method by which the tape is correctly positioned over the tape head **Bandführung;** *the tape is out of alignment because one of the tape guides has broken;* **tape head** = transducer that can read and write signals onto the surface of magnetic tape **Bandlese-/schreibkopf; tape header** = identification information at the beginning of a tape **Vorspann; tape label** = tape header and trailer containing information about the contents of a tape **Bandkennzeichnung; tape library** = (i) secure area for the storage of computer data tapes; (ii) series of computer tapes kept in store for reference **(i) & (ii) Bandbibliothek; tape loadpoint** = position on a magnetic tape at which reading should commence to load a file **Bandladepunkt; tape punch** = machine that punches holes into paper tape **Streifenlocher; tape reader** = machine that reads punched holes in paper tape *or* signals on magnetic tape **Lochstreifenleser; tape recorder** = machine that records data and signals onto magnetic tape **Magnetbandgerät; tape streamer** = continuous loop of tape used for backing storage **Magnetbandstreamer; tape timer** = device that displays the total time left *or* amount of playing time used on a reel of magnetic tape **Bandzeitgeber; tape to card converter** = device that reads data from magnetic tape and stores it on punched cards **Lochstreifen-in-Lochkarte-Umsetzer; tape transmitter** = device that reads data from paper tape and transmits it to another point **Magnetband für Datenfernverarbeitung; tape trailer** = identification information at the beginning of a tape **Vorsatz; tape transport** = method (in a magnetic tape recorder) by which the tape is moved smoothly from reel to reel over the magnetic heads **Bandtransport; tape unit** = device with tape deck, amplifier, circuitry, etc. for recording and playing back tapes **Bandgerät**

COMMENT: cassettes *or* reels of tape are easy to use and cheaper than disks, the cassette casing usually conforms to a standard size. They are less adaptable and only provide sequential access, usually being used for master copies *or* making back-ups

target *noun* goal which you aim to achieve **Ziel; target computer** = computer which software is to be run on (but not necessarily written on, e.g. using a cross-assembler) **Zielcomputer; target language** = language into which a language will be translated from its source language **Objektsprache;** *the target language for this PASCAL program is machine code*

◇ **target level** = interpretive processing mode for program execution **Zielebene; target** *or* **run phase** = period of time during which the target program is run **Bearbeitungszeit; target program** = object program *or* computer program in object code form, produced by a compiler **Zielprogramm**

QUOTE the target board is connected to the machine through the in-circuit emulator cable
Electronics & Wireless World

tariff *noun* charge incurred by a user of a communications *or* computer system **Gebühr;** *there is a set tariff for logging on, then a rate for every minute of computer time used*

TASI = TIME ASSIGNED SPEECH INTERPOLATION method of using a voice channel for other signals during the gaps and pauses in a normal conversation **TASI (Verfahren zur Mehrfachausnutzung von Sprachkanälen bei Transatlantikkabeln)**

task *noun* job which is to be carried out by a computer **Aufgabe; multitasking** = ability of a computer system to run two or more programs at the same time **Multitasking;** *this operating system provides a multitasking environment, but not a multi-user one;* **task management** = system software that controls the use and allocation of resources to programs **Aufgabensteuerung, Tasksteuerung; task queue** = temporary storage of jobs waiting to be processed **Task-Warteschlange**

TAT = TURNAROUND TIME

TDM = TIME DIVISION MULTIPLEXING

TDS = TRANSACTION-DRIVEN SYSTEM computer system that will normally run batch processing tasks until interrupted by a new transaction, at which point it allocates resources to the new transaction **vorganggesteuertes System**

tearing *noun* distortion of a television image due to bad sweep synchronization **Zerreißen, Zeilenausreißen**

technical *adjective* referring to a particular machine *or* process **technisch;** *the document gives all the technical details on the new computer*

◇ **technician** *noun* person who is specialized in industrial work **Techniker/-in;** *the computer technicians installed the new system;* **laboratory technician** = person who deals with practical work in a laboratory **Labortechniker/-in**

◇ **technique** *noun* skilled way of doing a job **Technik;** *the company has developed a new technique for processing customers' disks; he has a special technique for answering complaints from users of the software*

technology *noun* applying scientific knowledge to industrial processes **Technologie; information technology (IT)** = technology involved in acquiring, storing, processing, and distributing information by electronic means (including radio, TV, telephone and computers) **Informationstechnik; the introduction of new technology** = putting new electronic equipment into a business *or* industry **die Einführung neuer Technologien**

◇ **technological** *adjective* referring to technology **technologisch; the technological revolution** = changing of industrial methods by introducing new technology **die technologische Revolution**

tel = TELEPHONE

tele- *prefix* (i) meaning long distance; (ii) referring to television **(i) Fern-, (ii) Tele-; telebanking** = system by which an account holder can carry out transactions with his bank via a terminal and communications network **Home-Banking; telecine** = method of displaying a cine film on television **Film-Fernsehbetrieb-Methode; telecommunications** = technology of passing and receiving messages over a distance (as in radio, telephone, telegram, satellite broadcast, etc.) **Fernmeldewesen; teleconference** *or* **teleconferencing** = several people in different places using a communications network to talk together **Telekonferenz; telecontrol** = control of a remote device by a telecommunications

link   **Nachrichtenübertragungssteuerung telegram** = message sent to another countr by telegraph **Telegramm;** *to send a international telegram*

telegraph
1 *noun* message transmitted using telegraphy system **Telegramm; telegrap office** = office from which telegrams can b sent **Telegraphenamt**
2 *verb* to send a telegram to another person to send printed *or* written *or* drawn materia by long-distance telegraphy **telegraphiere** *they telegraphed their agreement; th photographs were telegraphed to New Yor*

◇ **telegraphic** *adjective* referring to telegraph system **telegraphisch; telegraph address** = short address to which a telegra is sent **Telegrammadresse**

◇ **telegraphy** *noun* system of sendin messages along wires using direct curren pulses **Telegraphie; carrier telegraphy** system of transmitting telegraph signals vi a carrier signal **Trägerfrequenztelegraphie**

teleinformatic services *noun* an data only service, such as telex, facsimil which uses telecommunication **Datenfernübertragungsservice**

telematics *noun* interaction of all dat processing and communications device (computers, networks, etc.) **Telematik**

telemessage *noun (GB)* message ser by telephone, and delivered as a car **Fernnachricht**

telemetry *noun* data from remot measuring devices transmitted over telecommunications link **Fernmessung**

teleordering *noun* book orderin system, in which the bookseller's orders ar entered into a computer which then pu the order through to the distributor at th end of the day **Bestellelektronik**

telephone
1 *noun* machine used for speaking someone over a long distance **Telefon;** *had a new telephone system installed la week;* **to be on the telephone** = to b speaking to someone using the telephor **telefonieren;** *the managing director is on th telephone to Hong Kong; she has been o the telephone all day;* **by telephone** = usir the telephone **über das Telefon, per Telefo** *to place an order by telephone; to reserve room by telephone;* **conference telephone** telephone specially made to be used in teleconference **Konferenztelefon; hous**

telephone or internal telephone = telephone for calling from one room to another in an office or hotel **Haustelefon**; **telephone answering machine** = device that answers a telephone, plays a prerecorded message and records any response **automatischer Anrufbeantworter**; **telephone book** or **telephone directory** = book which lists people and businesses in alphabetical order with their telephone numbers **Telefonbuch**; *he looked up the number of the company in the telephone book*; **telephone call** = speaking to someone on the telephone **Telefonanruf**; **to make a telephone call** = to dial a number and speak to someone on the telephone **telefonieren**; **to answer the telephone** or **to take a telephone call** = to speak in reply to a call on the telephone **das Telefon abnehmen**; **ein Telefongespräch annehmen**; **telephone as a data carrier** = using a modem to send binary data as sound signals over a telephone line **Telefon als Datenträger**; **telephone exchange** = central office where the telephones of a whole district are linked **Fernsprechamt**; **telephone number** = set of figures for a particular telephone subscriber **Telefonnummer**; *can you give me your telephone number?*; **telephone operator** = person who operates a telephone switchboard **Telefonist/-in**; **telephone orders** = orders received by telephone **telefonische Bestellungen**; *since we mailed the catalogue we have received a large number of telephone orders*; **telephone repeater** = receiver, transmitter and associated circuits that boost a telephone signal **Telefonsignalverstärker**; **telephone subscriber** = person who has a telephone connected to the main network **Teilnehmer/-in**; **telephone switchboard** = central point in a private telephone system where all internal and external lines meet **(Telefon)zentrale**
2 *verb* **to telephone a person** = to call a person by telephone **jemanden anrufen**; *his secretary telephoned to say he would be late*; **he telephoned the order through to the warehouse** = he telephoned the warehouse to place an order **er hat die Bestellung ans Lager durchtelefoniert**; **to telephone about something** = to make a telephone call to speak about something **wegen etwas anrufen**; *he telephoned about the order for computer stationery;* **to telephone for something** = to make a telephone call to ask for something **wegen etwas anrufen, etwas telefonisch bestellen**; *he telephoned for a taxi*

◊ **telephonist** *noun* person who works a telephone switchboard **Telefonist/-in**

◊ **telephony** *noun* data or signal transmission over a telephone using audio frequencies **Fernsprechwesen**

teleprinter *noun* device that is capable of sending and receiving data from a distant point by means of a telegraphic circuit, and printing out the message on a printer **Fernschreiber**; *you can drive a teleprinter from this modified serial port;* **teleprinter interface** = terminal interface or hardware and software combination required to control the functions of a terminal **Fernschreiberschnittstelle**; **teleprinter roll** = roll of paper onto which messages are printed **Fernschreiberpapier**

teleprocessing (TP) *noun* processing of data at a distance (as on a central computer from outside terminals) **Datenfernverarbeitung**

telesales *noun* sales made by telephone **telefonischer Verkauf**

◊ **teleshopping** *noun* use of a telephone-based data service such as viewdata to order products from a shop **Teleshopping**

telesoftware (TSW) *noun* software which is received from a viewdata or teletext service **Bildschirmtextsystem**; *the telesoftware was downloaded yesterday*

teletext *noun* method of transmitting text and information with a normal television signal, usually as a serial bit stream that can be displayed using a special decoder **Teletext**

teletype (TTY) *noun* term used for teleprinter equipment **Fernschreiber**

◊ **teletypewriter** *noun* keyboard and printer attached to a computer system which can input data either direct or by making punched paper tape **Fernschreiber**

◊ **teletypesetting** *noun* typesetter operated from a punched paper tape **Fernsatz**

television (TV) *noun* (i) system for broadcasting pictures and sound using high-frequency radio waves, captured by a receiver and shown on a screen; (ii) device that can receive (modulated) video signals from a computer or broadcast signals with an aerial and display images on a CRT screen with sound **(i) Fernsehen**; **(ii) Fernsehgerät**; **television camera** = optical lenses in front of an electronic device which can convert images into electronic signals in a form that can be transmitted or displayed on a TV **Fernsehkamera**; **television monitor** = device able to display signals from a computer without sound, but not broadcast signals (this is usually because there is no demodulator device which is needed for broadcast signals) **Fernsehmonitor; television projector** = device that projects a TV image onto a large screen **Fernsehprojektor; television receiver** = device able to display with sound, broadcast signals *or* other modulated signals (such as signals from a video recorder) **Fernsehempfänger; television receiver/monitor** = device able to act as a TV receiver *or* monitor **Fernsehempfänger/-monitor; television scan** = horizontal movement of the picture beam over the screen, producing one line of an image **Abtastung; television tube** = CRT with electronic devices that provide the line by line horizontal and vertical scanning movement of the picture beam **Fernsehröhre;** *see also* CRT, RGB

> COMMENT: in a colour TV there are three electron guns corresponding to red, green and blue signals. In the UK the TV screen has 625 lines to be scanned; this is normally done in two sweeps of alternate lines, providing a flicker-free image

telex
1 *noun*
(a) system for sending messages using telephone lines, which are printed out at the receiving end on a special printer **Telex;** *to send information by telex; the order came by telex;* **telex line** = wire linking a telex machine to the telex system **Telexverbindung;** *we cannot communicate with our Nigerian office because of the breakdown of the telex lines;* **telex operator** = person who operates a telex machine **Telex-Operator; telex subscriber** = company which has a telex **Telex-Teilnehmer**
(b) a telex = (i) a machine for sending and receiving telex messages; (ii) a message sent by telex **(i) ein Fernschreiber; (ii) ein Telex;** *he sent a telex to his head office; we received his telex this morning*
2 *verb* to send a message using a teleprinter **ein Telex schicken;** *can you telex the Canadian office before they open? he telexed the details of the contract to New York*

template *noun* (i) plastic *or* metal sheet with cut-out symbols to help the drawing of flowcharts and circuit diagrams; (ii); *(in text processing)* standard text (such as a standard letter *or* invoice) into which specific details (company address *or* prices *or* quantities) can be added **(i) & (ii) Schablone; template command** = command that allows functions *or* other commands to be easily set **Schablonenbefehl;** *a template paragraph command enables the user to specify the number of spaces each*

paragraph should be indented; see also STANDARD, FORM LETTER

temporary storage *noun* storage which is not permanent **Zwischenspeicher; temporary register** = register used for temporary storage for the results of an ALU operation **Zwischenregister**
◊ **temporarily** *adverb* for a certain time *or* not permanently **vorübergehend**

ten's complement *noun* formed by adding one to the nine's complement of a decimal number **Zehnerkomplement**

tera- *prefix* one million million (ten to the power 12) **Tera-, terahertz** = frequency of one million million hertz **Terahertz** �▷ APPENDIX

terminal
1 *noun*
(a) device usually made up of a display unit and a keyboard which allows entry and display of information when on-line to a central computer system **Datenstation, Terminal; addressable terminal** = terminal that will only accept data if it has the correct address and identification data in the message header **adressierbare Datenstation;** *all the messages go to all the terminals since none are addressable terminals;* **applications terminal** = terminal (such as at a sales desk) which is specifically configured to carry out certain tasks **Anwendungsterminal; dumb terminal** = peripheral that can only receive and transmit data, and is not capable of processing data **nicht programmierbarer Terminal (zum Drucken-Sichern-Kopieren); central terminal** = terminal which controls communications between a central *or* host computer and remote terminals **Zentraldatenstation; intelligent terminal** *or* **smart terminal** = computer terminal which contains a CPU and memory, allowing basic data processing to be carried out, usually with the facility to allow the user to program it independently of the host computer **intelligente Datenstation;** *the new intelligent terminal has a built-in text editor;* **master terminal** = one terminal in a network that has priority over any other, used by the system manager to set-up the system *or* carry out privileged commands **Hauptbedienerstation;** *the system manager uses the master terminal to restart the system;* **remote terminal** = computer terminal connected to a distant computer system **entfernt aufgestellte Datenstation; slave terminal** = terminal controlled by a main computer *or* terminal **abhängige/untergeordnete Datenstation;**

terminal area = part of a printer circuit board at which edge connectors can be connected **Anschlußstelle für eine Datenstation; terminal character set** = range of characters available for a particular type of terminal, these might include graphics or customized characters **Zeichensatz einer Datenstation; terminal controller** = hardware device or IC that controls a terminal including data communications and display **Terminalsteuerelement; terminal identity** = unique code transmitted by a viewdata terminal to provide identification and authorization of a user **Stationsidentifikationscode; terminal interface** = hardware and software combination required to control the functions of a terminal from a computer **Geräteschnittstelle;** *the network controller has 16 terminal interfaces; (slang)* **terminal junky (TJ)** = person (a hacker) who is obsessed with computers **Computerfreak;** *my son has turned into a real terminal junky;* **terminal keyboard** = standard QWERTY or special keyboard allowing input at a terminal **Tastatur einer Datenstation**

(b) an electrical connection point; **terminal block** = strip of insulated connection points for wires **Anschlußblock**

(c) point in a network where a message can be transmitted or received **Netzstation;** *see also* SOURCE, SINK

2 *adjective* fatal or which cannot be repaired **endgültig;** *the computer has a terminal fault*

COMMENT: computer terminals can be intelligent, smart or dumb according to the inbuilt processing capabilities

terminate *verb* to end **abbrechen, beenden**

◇ **termination** *noun* ending or stopping **Abbruch; abnormal termination** = unexpected stoppage of a program which is being run, caused by a fault or power failure **abnormaler Abbruch**

◇ **terminator** *or* **rogue value** *noun* item in a list of data, which indicates the end of a list **Endmarke**

ternary *adjective* (number system) with three possible states **ternär**

test

1 *noun* action carried out on a device or program to establish whether it is working correctly, and if not, which component or instruction is not working **Prüfung, Test; test bed** = (software) environment used to test programs **Testumgebung; test data** = data with known results prepared to allow a new program to be tested **Prüfdaten; test equipment** = special equipment which tests

hardware or software **Prüfgerät;** *the engineer has special test equipment for this model;* **test numeric** = check to ensure that numerical information is numerical **Prüfung auf numerisch; test pattern** = graphical pattern displayed on a TV screen to test its colour, balance, horizontal and vertical linearity and contrast **Testmuster;** *see also* BENCHMARK; **test run** = program run with test data to ensure that the software is working correctly **Testlauf;** *a test run will soon show up any errors*

2 *verb* to carry out an examination of a device or program to see if it is working correctly **prüfen, testen; saturation testing** = testing a communications network by transmitting large quantities of data and messages over it **Sättigungsprüfung**

text *noun* alphanumeric characters that convey information **Text; ragged text** = unjustified text, text with a ragged right margin **Flattersatz; start-of-text (SOT** *or* **STX)** = transmitted code indicating the end of control and address information and the start of the message **Anfang des Textes; text compression** = reducing the space required by a section of text, by using one code to represent more than one character, by removing spaces and punctuation marks, etc. **Textkomprimierung; text-editing facilities** = word-processing system that allows the user to add, delete, move, insert and correct sections of text **Textverarbeitungssystem, Editierprogramm; text-editing function** = option in a program that provides text-editing facilities **Textverarbeitungs-, Editierfunktion;** *the program includes a built-in text-editing function;* **text editor** = piece of software that provides the user with text-editing facilities **Text-Editor;** *the text editor will only read files smaller than 64Kbytes long;* **text file** = stored file on a computer that contains text rather than digits or data **Textdatei; text formatter** = program that arranges a text file according to preset rules, such as line width and page size **Textformatierer;** *people use the text formatter as a basic desk-top publishing program;* **text management** = facilities that allow text to be written, stored, retrieved, edited and printed **Textanwendungen; text manipulation** = facilities that allow text editing, changing, inserting and deleting **Textbearbeitung; text processing** = word-processing or using a computer to keyboard, edit and output text, in the forms of letters, labels, etc. **Textverarbeitung; text register** = temporary computer storage register for text characters only **Textregister; text retrieval** = information retrieval system that allows the user to examine complete documents rather than just a reference to one

Textretrieval, Textwiederauffindung; text screen = area of computer screen that has been set up to display text **Textbereich; text-to-speech converter** = electronic device that uses a speech synthesizer to produce the spoken equivalent of a piece of text that has been entered **Text-in-Sprache-Umwandler**

◊ **textual** *adjective* referring to text **Text-;** *the editors made several textual changes before the proofs were sent back for correction*

thermal *adjective* referring to heat **Thermo-; thermal paper** = special paper whose coating turns black when heated, allowing characters to be printed by using a matrix of small heating elements **Thermopapier, wärmeempfindliches Spezialpapier; thermal printer** = type of printer where the character is formed on thermal paper with a printhead containing a matrix of small heating elements **Thermodrucker**

COMMENT: this type of printer is very quiet in operation since the printing head does not strike the paper

◊ **thermal transfer** *noun* method of printing where the ink is attached to the paper by heating **Thermodrucken;** *a thermal transfer printer; colour ink-jet technology and thermal transfer technology compete with each other*

thermistor *noun* electronic device whose resistance changes with temperature **Thermistor (temperaturabhängiger Widerstand)**

thermo-sensitive *adjective* which is sensitive to heat **wärmeempfindlich**

thesaurus *noun* collection of words, not in alphabetical order like a dictionary *or* encyclopaedia, but under certain headings **Thesaurus**

thick *adjective* with a large distance between two surfaces **dick; thick film** = miniature electronic circuit design in which miniature components are mounted on an insulating base, then connected as required **Dickschicht**

COMMENT: this provides a package that is larger but cheaper for short runs than chips

thimble printer *noun* computer printer using a printing head similar to a daisy wheel but shaped like a thimble **Fingerhutdrucker**

thin *adjective* with only a small distance between two surfaces **dünn; thin film** = method of constructing integrated circuits by depositing in a vacuum very thin patterns of various materials onto a substrate to form the required interconnected components **Dünnschicht;** *see also* CHIP, SUBSTRATE; **thin film memory** = high-speed access RAM device using a matrix of magnetic cells and a matrix of read/write heads to access them **Dünnschichtspeicher; thin window** = single line display window **Einzeilenfenster**

third *adjective* **third generation computers** = range of computers where integrated circuits were used instead of transistors **Computer der dritten Generation; third party** = company which supplies items *or* services for a system sold by one party (the seller) to another (the buyer) **Fremdhersteller**

COMMENT: a third party might supply computer maintenance *or* might write programs, etc.

QUOTE they expect third party developers to enhance the operating systems by adding their own libraries
PC Business World

thirty-two bit system *noun* microcomputer system *or* CPU that handles data in thirty-two bit words **32-Bit-System**

thrashing *noun* computer program design fault that results in the CPU wasting time moving pages of data between main memory and backing store **Überlastung**

thread *noun* program that consists of many independent smaller sections or beads **gekettetes Programm; threaded file** = file in which an entry will contain data and an address to the next entry that has the same data content (allowing rapid retrieval of all identical records) **gekettete Datei; threaded language** = programming language that allows many small sections of code to be written then used by a main program **gekettete Programmiersprache; threaded tree** = structure in which each node contains a pointer to other nodes **gekettete Baumstruktur**

three-address instruction *noun* instruction which contains the addresses of two operands and the location where the result is to be stored **Dreiadreßbefehl**

◊ **three-dimensional** *or* **3D** *adjective* (image) which has three dimensions (width, breadth and depth), and therefore gives the impression of being solid **dreidimensional; 3D**

◊ **three input adder** *see* FULL ADDER

three-pin plug *noun* standard plug with three connections, to connect an electric device to the mains electricity supply **Stecker mit drei Kontaktstiften**

COMMENT: the three pins are for the live, neutral and earth connections

three state logic *noun* logic gate *or* IC that has three possible output states (rather than the usual two): logic high, logic low and high impedance **Dreizustandslogik, Tri-State-Logik**

throughput *noun* rate of production by a machine *or* system, measured as total useful information processed in a set period of time **Datendurchlauf**; *for this machine throughput is 1.3 inches per second (ips) scanning speed;* **rated throughput** = maximum throughput of a device that will still meet original specifications **maximale Durchsatzrate**

thyristor *noun* semiconductor device that will allow the control of an AC voltage according to an input signal **Thyristor**

tie line *or* **tie trunk** *noun* communications link between switchboards *or* PBX systems **Querverbindungsleitung**

tilde *noun* printed accent, commonly used over the letter "ñ" in Spanish, vowels in Portuguese, etc. **Tilde**

tilt and swivel *adjective* (monitor) which is mounted on a pivot so that it can be moved to point in the most convenient direction for the operator **kippbar und schwenkbar**

time

1 *noun* period expressed in hours, minutes, seconds, etc. **Zeit; addition time** = time an adder takes to carry out an addition operation **Additionszeit; cycle time** = time between start and stop of an operation, especially between addressing a memory location and receiving the data **Zykluszeit; queuing time** = period of time messages have to wait before they are processed *or* transmitted **Wartezeit; real time** = actions *or* processing time that is of the same order of magnitude as the problem to be solved (i.e. the processing time is within the same time as the problem to be solved, so that the result can influence the source of the data)

Echtzeit; response time = (i) time which passes between the user starting an action (by pressing a key) and the result appearing on the screen; (ii) speed with which a system responds to a stimulus **(i) Beantwortungszeit; (ii) Antwortzeit; stop time** = time taken for a spinning disk to come to rest after it is no longer powered **Stopzeit; time address code** = signal recorded on a video tape to display time elapsed when editing **Zeitadreßcode; time base** = (i) signal used as a basis for timing purposes; (ii) regular sawtooth signal used in an oscilloscope to sweep the beam across the screen **(i) & (ii) Zeitbasis; time coded page** = teletext page that contains additional text which is displayed after a period of time **zeitcodierte Seite; time derived channel** = communications channel using time division multiplexing techniques **Zeitmultiplexkanal; time display** = digits *or* dial which show the current time **Zeitanzeige; time division multiple access** = time division multiplexing system that allocates time slots to various users according to demand **zeitmultiplexe Zugriffsmethode; time division multiplexing (TDM)** = multiplexing system that allows a number of signals to be transmitted down a single line by sending a sample of the first signal for a short period, then the second, and so on **Zeitmultiplexmethode; time division switching** = moving data from one time slot to another **Zeitmultiplexdurchschaltung; time domain analysis** = signal analysis as it varies with time **Zeitbereichsanalyse; time shift viewing** = use of a video recorder to record programs which are then replayed at a more convenient time **zeitversetztes Anschauen; time slice** = amount of time allowed for a single task in a time-sharing system *or* in multiprogramming; period of time allocated for a user *or* program *or* job within a multitasking system **Zeitscheibe; time slot** = period of time that contains an amount of data about one signal in a time division multiplexing system **Zeitkanal**

2 *verb* to measure the time taken by an operation **die Zeit messen; microprocessor timing** = correct selection of system clock frequency to allow for slower peripherals etc. **Zeitberechnung mit Mikroprozessoren; network timing** = signals that correctly synchronize the transmission of data **Netzsynchronisation; timing loop** = computer program loop that is repeated a number of times to produce a certain time delay **Taktschleife; timing master** = clock signal that synchronizes all the components in a system **Haupttaktgeber**

◊ **timeout** *noun* (i) logoff procedure carried out if no data is entered on an on-line terminal; (ii) period of time reserved for an operation (i) **Zeitsperre**; (ii) **Zeitauslösung**

◊ **timer** *noun* device which records the time taken for an operation to be completed **Zeitnehmer**

◊ **time-sharing** *noun* computer system that allows several independent users to use it *or* be on-line at the same time **Gemeinschaftsbetrieb, Timesharing**

COMMENT: in time-sharing, each user appears to be using the computer all the time, when in fact each is using the CPU for a short time slice only; the CPU processing one user for a short time then moving on to the next

title *noun* identification name given to a file *or* program *or* disk **(externer) Name; title of disk** = identification of a disk, referring to its contents **Plattenname; title page** = first main page of a book, with the title, the name of the author and the name of the publisher **Titelseite**

toggle *verb* to switch between two states **kippen; toggle switch** = electrical switch that has only two positions **Kippschalter**

QUOTE the symbols can be toggled on or off the display
Micro Decision

token *noun* internal code which replaces a reserved word *or* program statement in a high-level language **Kennzeichen, Token; token ring network** = network in which a device can transmit data by taking one free token which circulates and inserting the message after it **Tokenring-Netzwerk; control token** = special sequence of bits transmitted over a LAN to provide control actions **Steuertoken**

tomo- *prefix* meaning a cutting *or* section **Tomo-**

◊ **tomogram** *noun* picture of part of the body taken by tomography **Tomogramm**

◊ **tomography** *noun* scanning of a particular part of the body using X-rays *or* ultrasound **Tomographie; computerized axial tomography (CAT)** = X-ray examination where a computer creates a picture of a section of a patient's body **Computertomographie**

tone *noun*
(a) sound at one single frequency **Ton; dialling tone** = sound made by a telephone to show that it is ready for the number to be dialled **Freizeichen; engaged tone** = sound made by a telephone showing that the number dialled is busy **Besetztzeichen; tone**

dialling = telephone dialling system that uses different frequency tones to represent the dialled number **Tonwählsystem; tone signalling** = tones used in a telephone network to convey control *or* address signals **Tonsignalsystem**
(b) shade of a colour **Farbton, Schattierung** *the graphics package can give several tones of blue*

◊ **toner** *noun* liquid put into a photocopier *or* photographic device to develop the image **Toner; toner cartridge** = sealed cartridge containing toner, which can be easily replaced in a photocopier **Tonerbehälter, Tonerpatrone;** *change toner and toner cartridge according to the manual; the toner cartridge and the imaging drum can be replaced as one unit when the toner runs out*

toolbox *noun* box containing instruments needed to repair *or* maintain *or* install equipment **Werkzeugkasten**

◊ **toolkit** *noun* series of functions which help a programmer write *or* debug programs **Werkzeug(ausrüstung)**

◊ **tools** *noun* set of utility programs (backup, format, etc.) in a computer system **Hilfsprogramme**

top *noun* part which is the highest point of something **Spitze; top down programming = structured programming** = method of writing programs where a complete system is divided into simple blocks *or* tasks, each block unit is written and tested before proceeding with the next one **strukturierte Programmierung; top of stack** = the newest data item added to a stack **Spitze des Stapels; top space** = number of blank lines left at the top of a printed text **Durchschuss am oberen Rand**

topology *noun* way in which the various elements in a network are interconnected **Topologie; network topology** = layout of machines in a network (such as a star network *or* a ring network *or* a bus network) which will determine what cabling and interfaces are needed and what possibilities the network can offer **Netzwerktopologie**

torn tape *noun* communication switching method, in which the received message is punched onto a paper tape which is fed by hand into the appropriate tape reader for transmission to the required destination **Lochstreifen**

total *noun* **hash total** = total of a number of hashed entries, used for error detection **Kontrollsumme**

touch *verb* to make contact with something with the fingers **berühren; touch pad** = flat device that can sense where on its surface and when it is touched, used to control a cursor position *or* switch a device on or off **Cursor-Steuerungsfeld; touch screen** = computer display that has a grid of infrared transmitters and receivers, positioned on either side of the screen used to control a cursor position (when a user wants to make a selection *or* move the cursor, he points to the screen, breaking two of the beams, which gives the position of his finger) **Sensor-Bildschirm**

◊ **touch up** *verb* to remove scratches *or* other marks from a photograph *or* image **retuschieren**

TP = TELEPROCESSING, TRANSACTION PROCESSING

TPI = TRACKS PER INCH

trace *noun* method of verifying that a program is functioning correctly, in which the current status and contents of the registers and variables used are displayed after each instruction step **Programmablaufverfolgung; trace program** = diagnostic program that executes a program that is being debugged, one instruction at a time, displaying the states and registers **Programm zur Programmablaufverfolgung; trace trap** = selective breakpoint where a tracing program stops, allowing registers to be examined **Unterbrechung während einer Ablaufverfolgung**

track

1 *noun* one of a series of thin concentric rings on a magnetic disk *or* thin lines on a tape, which the read/write head accesses and along which the data is stored in separate sectors **(Magnet)spur; address track** = track on a magnetic disk containing the address of files, etc., stored on the other tracks **Adressenspur; track address** = location of a particular track on a magnetic disk **Spuradresse; tracks per inch (TPI)** = number of concentric data tracks on a disk surface per inch **Spuren pro Inch**
2 *verb* to follow a path *or* track correctly **spurgenau laufen;** *the read head is not tracking the recorded track correctly*

COMMENT: the first track on a tape is along the edge and the tape may have up to nine different tracks on it, while a disk has many concentric tracks around the central hub; the track and sector addresses are set-up during formatting

trackball *noun* device used to move a cursor on-screen, which is controlled by turning a ball contained in a case **Steuerungsball, Maus**

tractor feed *noun* method of feeding paper into a printer, where sprocket wheels on the printer connect with the sprocket holes on either edge of the paper to pull the paper through **Stachelbandführung**

QUOTE the printer is fairly standard with both tractor and cut sheet feed system
Which PC?

traffic *noun* term covering all the messages and other signals processed by a system **Datenverkehr; traffic analysis** = study of the times, types and quantities of messages and signals being processed by a system **Datenverkehrsanalyse; traffic density** = number of messages and data transmitted over a network *or* system in a period of time **Datenverkehrsdichte; traffic intensity** = ratio of messages entering a queue against those leaving the queue within a certain time **Datenverkehrsquote; incoming traffic** = data and messages received **eingehende Daten**
NOTE: no plural

trail *noun* line followed by something **Spur; audit trail** = recording details of the use made of a system by noting transactions carried out (used for checking on illegal use *or* malfunction) **Prüfprotokoll**

◊ **trailer** *noun*
(a) leader *or* piece of non magnetic tape to the start of a reel of magnetic tape to make loading easier **Vorspannband**
(b) final byte of a file containing control *or* file characteristics **Nachsatz; trailer record** = last record in a file containing control *or* file characteristics **Nachsatz**

transaction *noun* one single action which affects a database (a sale, a change of address, a new customer, etc.) **Datenbewegung, Transaktion; transaction-driven system (TDS)** = computer system that will normally run batch processing tasks until interrupted by a new transaction, at which point it allocates resources to the transaction **bewegungsgesteuertes System; transaction file** *or* **change file** *or* **detail file** *or* **movement file** = file containing recent changes *or* transactions to records which is then used to update a master file **Bewegungsdatei; transaction processing (TP)** = interactive processing in which a user enters commands and data on a terminal which is linked to a central computer, with results being displayed on-screen **Transaktionsverarbeitung; transaction record** or **change record** = record containing new data which is to be used to update a master record **Bewegungssatz**

transborder data flow noun passing of data from one country to another using communications links such as satellites or land lines **grenzüberschreitender Datenfluß**

transceiver noun transmitter and receiver or device which can both transmit and receive signals (such as a terminal or modem) **Fernkopierer-Sender/Empfänger; radio transceiver** = radio transmitter and receiver in a single housing **Funkgerät**

transcoder noun electronic device used to convert television signal standards **Umwandler;** use the transcoder to convert PAL to SECAM

transcribe verb to copy data from one backing storage unit or medium to another **umschreiben**
◊ **transcription** noun action of transcribing data **Umschreibung**

transducer noun electronic device which converts signals in one form into signals in another **Meßwertwandler;** the pressure transducer converts physical pressure signals into electrical signals

transfer verb
(a) to change command or control **übertragen;** all processing activities have been transferred to the mainframe; **conditional transfer** = programming instruction that provides a jump to a section of a program if a certain condition is met **bedingte Übertragung; radial transfer** = data transfer between two peripherals or programs that are on different layers of a structured system (such as an OSI/ISO system) **radiale Übertragung; transfer check** = check that a data transfer is correct according to a set of rules **Übertragungskontrolle; transfer command** = instruction that directs processor control from one part of a program to another **Übertragungsbefehl;** see also JUMP, CALL; **transfer control** = when a branch or jump instruction within a program is executed, control is transferred to another point in the program **Übertragungssteuerung**
(b) to copy a section of memory to another location **übertragen; transfer rate** = speed at which data is transferred from backing store to main memory **Übertragungsgeschwindigkeit; transfer time** =

time taken to transfer data between device or locations **Übertragungszeit**

transform verb to change somethin from one state to another **umwandel transformieren**
◊ **transformation** noun action of changin **Umwandlung, Transformation**
◊ **transformational rules** noun set of rule that are applied to data that is to b transformed into coded forr **Transformationsregeln**
◊ **transformer** noun device which change the voltage or current amplitude of an A(signal **Transformator**

COMMENT: a transformer consists of two electrically insulated coils of wire; the AC signal in one induces a similar signal in the other which can be a different amplitude according to the ratio of the turns in the coils of wire

transient
1 adjective state or signal which is presen for a short period of time **kurzzeiti(Übergangs-; power transient** = very sho duration voltage pulse or spik **Übergangsstrom; transient suppressor** device which suppresses voltage transien **Spannungssprungunterdrücker; transient are** = section of memory for user programs an data **Übergangsbereich; transient error** temporary error which occurs for a sho period of time **kurzzeitiger Fehler**
2 noun **line transient** or **voltage transient** spike of voltage that is caused by a tim delay in two devices switching or noise o the line **(Netz)spannungssprung**

transistor noun electroni semiconductor device which can contro the current flow in a circuit (there are tw main types of transistors: bipolar an unipolar) **Transistor; bipolar (junctior transistor (BJT)** = transistor constructed c three layers of alternating types of dope semiconductor (p-n-p or n-p-n), each laye has a terminal labelled emitter, base an collector, usually the base controls th current flow between emitter and collect(**bipolarer Sperrschichttransistor; field effe(transistor (FET)** = electronic device tha can act as a variable current flow contr((an external signal varies the resistance c the device and current flow by changing th width of a conducting channel by means c a field. It has three terminals: source, ga and drain) **Feldeffekttransistor (FET transistor-resistor logic (TRL)** = early log gate design method using bipol transistors and resistors **Aufbau v(Schaltelementen durch Transistoren ur**

Widerstände; transistor-transistor logic (TTL) = most common family of logic gates and high-speed transistor circuit design, in which the bipolar transistors are directly connected (usually collector to base) to provide the logic function **Aufbau von Schaltelementen durch Transistoren (TTL);** unipolar transistor = FIELD EFFECT TRANSISTOR

transition *noun* change from one state to another **Übergang; transition point =** point in a program *or* system where a transition occurs **Übergangsstelle**

translate *verb* to convert data from one form into another **übersetzen**

◊ **translation tables** *or* **conversion tables** *noun* lookup tables *or* collection of stored results that can be accessed very rapidly by a process without the need to calculate each result when needed **Übersetzungstabellen**

◊ **translator (program)** *noun* program that translates a high level language program into another language (usually machine code) **Übersetzerprogramm;** *see also* INTERPRETER, COMPILER

transmit *verb* to send information from one device to another, using any medium, such as radio, cable, wire link, etc. **senden**

◊ **transmission** *noun* sending of signals from one device to another **Übertragung; neutral transmission =** (transmission) in which a voltage pulse and zero volts represent the binary digits 1 and 0 **neutrale Übertragung; parallel transmission =** number of data lines carrying all the bits of a data word simultaneously **Parallelübertragung; serial transmission =** data transmission one bit at a time (this is the normal method of transmission over longer distances, since although slower, it uses fewer lines and so is cheaper than parallel) **serielle Übertragung; synchronous transmission =** transmission of data from one device to another, where both devices are controlled by the same clock, and the transmitted data is synchronized with the clock signal **Synchronübertragung; transmission channel =** physical connection between two points that allows data to be transmitted (such as a link between a CPU and a peripheral) **Übertragungskanal; transmission errors =** errors due to noise on the line **Übertragungsfehler; transmission media =** means by which data can be transmitted, such as radio, light, etc. **Übertragungsmedien; transmission rate =** measure of the amount of data transmitted in a certain time

Übertragungsgeschwindigkeit; *their average transmission is 64,000 bits per second (bps) through a parallel connection or 19,200 bps through a serial connection;* **transmission window =** narrow range of wavelengths to which a fibre optic cable is most transparent **Übertragungsfenster**

◊ **transmissive disk** *noun* optical data storage disk in which the reading laser beam shines through the disk to a detector below **Übertragungsplatte;** *compare with* REFLECTIVE DISK

◊ **transmittance** *noun* amount of light transmitted through a material in ratio to the total light incident on the surface of the material **Transmittanz, (Licht)durchlaßgrad**

◊ **transmitter (TX)** *noun* device that will take an input signal, process it (modulate *or* convert to sound, etc.) then transmit it by some medium (radio, light, etc.) **Sender**

QUOTE an X-ray picture can be digitized and transmitted from one hospital to a specialist at another for diagnosis
Electronics & Business World
QUOTE modern high-power transmitters are much reduced in size and a simple and uncluttered appearance
Electronics & Power

transparent *noun*
(a) computer program which is not obvious to the user *or* which cannot be seen by the user when it is running **transparent; transparent interrupt =** mode in which, if an interrupt occurs, all program and machine states are saved, the interrupt is serviced and then the system is restored to its previous states **transparente Unterbrechung; transparent paging =** software that allows the user to access any memory location in a paged memory system as if it were not paged **Transparentpaginierung**
(b) device *or* network that allows signals to pass through it without being altered in any way **durchsichtiges System**

◊ **transparency** *noun* transparent positive film, which can be projected onto a screen *or* to make film for printing **Diapositiv, Transparentkopie**

transphasor *noun* optical transistor, that is constructed from a crystal which is able to switch a main beam of light according to a smaller input signal **Transphasor**

COMMENT: this is used in the latest research for an optical computer which could run at very high speeds, i.e., at the speed of light

transponder *noun* communications device that receives and retransmits signals **Transponder**

transport *verb* to carry from one place to another **befördern, transportieren; transport layer** = layer in the ISO/OSI standard that checks and controls the quality of the connection **Transportschicht;** *see also* LAYER
◊ **transportable** *adjective* which can be carried **transportierbar;** *a transportable computer is not as small as a portable or a laptop*

transposition *noun* changing the order of a series of characters (as "comuter" for "computer" *or* "1898" for "1988" **Umstellung, Vertauschung;** *a series of transposition errors caused faulty results*

transputer *noun* single large very powerful chip containing a 32-bit microprocessor running at around 10 MIPS, that can be connected together to form a parallel processing system (running OCCAM) **Transputer**

transverse mode noise *noun* interference which is apparent between power supply lines **Rauschen durch transversale Eigenschwingung**
◊ **transverse scan** *noun* method of reading data from a video tape in which the playback head is at right angles to the tape **Querabtastung**

trap *noun* device, software or hardware that will catch something, such as a variable, fault or value **Fangstelle; trace trap** = selective breakpoint where a tracing program stops, allowing registers to be examined **Unterbrechung während einer Ablaufverfolgung**
◊ **trapdoor** *noun* way of getting into a system to change data *or* browse *or* hack **Fangstelle**

tree *noun* tree (structure) = data structure system where each item of data is linked to several others by branches (as opposed to a line system where each item leads on to the next) **Baum(struktur); tree and branch network system** = system of networking where data is transmitted along a single output line, from which other lines branch out, forming a tree structure that feeds individual stations **Baumnetzsystem; tree selection sort** = rapid form of selection where the information from the first sort pass is used in the second pass to speed up selection **Auswahlsortierverfahren; binary**

tree = data system where each item of data *or* node has only two branches **binärer Baum**

tremendously high frequency (THF) *noun* radio frequency between 300GHz and 3000GHz **Frequenz zwischen 300GHZ und 3000GHz**

triad *noun* (i) three elements *or* characters *or* bits; (ii) triangular shaped grouping of the red, green and blue colour phosphor spots at each pixel location on the screen of a colour RGB monitor **(i) Triade; (ii) Dreier**

trial *noun* test for new equipment to see if it works **Probe; trials engineer** = person who designs, runs and analyses trials of new equipment **Ingenieur in der Versuchsabteilung**

tributary station *noun* any station on a multilink network other than the main control station **Außenstelle**

trim *verb* to cut off the edge of something **beschneiden;** *the printed pages are trimmed to 198 x 129mm; you will need to trim the top part of the photograph to make it fit*

TRL = TRANSISTOR-RESISTOR LOGIC

Trojan Horse *noun* program inserted into a system by a hacker that will perform a harmless function while copying information in a classified file into a file with a low priority, which the hacker can then access without the authorized user knowing **Trojanisches Pferd**

troposphere *noun* region of space extending up to six miles above the earth's surface, causing radio wave scatter **Troposphäre;** *see also* IONOSPHERE

troubleshoot *verb* (i) to debug computer software; (ii) to locate and repair faults in hardware **(i) Softwarefehler bereinigen; (ii) Hardwarefehler suchen und beseitigen**
◊ **troubleshooter** *noun* person who troubleshoots hardware *or* software **jd, der Computerfehler beseitigt**

trough *noun* lowest point in a waveform **(Wellen)tal;** *compare* PEAK

TRUE *noun* logical condition (representing binary one) **WAHR;** *compare* FALSE

truncate *verb*
(a) to cut short **abschneiden**

(b) to give an approximate value to a number by reducing it to a certain number of digits **abstreichen**

◊ **truncation** *noun* removal of digits from a number so that it is a certain length **Abschneiden;** *3.5678 truncated to 3.56;* **truncation error** = error caused when a number is truncated **Abschneidefehler**

trunk *noun* bus *or* communication link consisting of wires *or* leads, which connect different parts of a hardware system **Fernverbindungskabel**

◊ **trunk call** *noun (GB)* long-distance telephone call **Ferngespräch**

◊ **trunk exchange** *noun (GB)* telephone exchange that only handles trunk calls **Fernvermittlungsstelle**

truth table *noun* method of defining a logic function as the output state for all possible inputs **Wahrheitstabelle; truth value** = two values (true *or* false, T *or* F, 1 *or* 0) used in Boolean algebra **Wahrheitswert**

TSW = TELESOFTWARE

TTL = TRANSISTOR-TRANSISTOR LOGIC most common family of logic gates and high-speed transistor circuit design in which the bipolar transistors are directly connected (usually collector to base) **TTL (Aufbau von Schaltelementen durch Transistoren); TTL compatible** = MOS or other electronic circuits *or* components that can directly connect to and drive TTL circuits **TTL-kompatibel; TTL logic** = use of TTL design and components to implement logic circuits and gates **TTL-Logik**

TTY = TELETYPE

tune *verb*
(a) to set a system at its optimum point by careful adjustment **optimal einstellen; to fine tune** = to adjust by small amounts the parameters of hardware *or* software to improve performance **feineinstellen**
(b) (i) to adjust a radio receiver's frequency until the required station is received clearly; (ii) to adjust a transmitter to the correct frequency **(i) einstellen; (ii) abstimmen**

Turing machine *noun* mathematical model of a device that could read and write data to a controllable tape storage while altering its internal states **Turing-Maschine**

◊ **Turing test** *noun* test to decide if a computer is "intelligent" **Turing-Test**

turn off *verb* to switch off *or* to disconnect the power supply to a machine **ausschalten;** *turn off the power before unplugging the monitor*

◊ **turn on** *verb* to switch on *or* to connect the power supply to a machine **einschalten**

◊ **turnaround document** *noun* document which is printed out from a computer, sent to a user and returned by the user with new notes *or* information written on it, which can be read by a document reader **Kreisverkehrdokument**

◊ **turnaround time (TAT)** *noun*
(a) length of time it takes to switch data flow direction in a half duplex system **Verweilzeit**
(b) time taken for a product to be constructed and delivered after an order has been received **Fertigungs- und Lieferzeit**
(c) *(US)* time taken to activate a program and produce the result which the user has asked for **Durchlaufzeit**

◊ **turnkey system** *noun* complete system which is designed to a customer's needs and is ready to use (to operate it, the user only has to switch it on or turn a key) **schlüsselfertiges System**

turtle *noun* device whose movement and position are controllable, which is used to draw graphics (with instructions in the computer language LOGO), either a device which works on a flat surface (floor turtle) *or* which draws on a VDU screen (screen turtle), used as a teaching aid **Schildkröte; turtle graphics** = graphic images created using a turtle and a series of commands **Schildkrötengraphik;** *the charts were prepared using turtle graphics*

TV = TELEVISION

tweeter *noun (informal)* small loudspeaker used for high frequency sounds only **Hochtonlautsprecher;** *compare* WOOFER

twisted pair cable *noun* cheap cable for telephones, with two wires twisted round each other (as opposed to co-axial cable), to provide some protection against interference and minimize inductive and capacitive effects of the wires **Torsionskabel**

two-address instruction *noun* instruction format containing the location of two operands, the result being stored in one of the operand locations **Eins-plus-Eins-Adreßbefehl; two-plus-one instruction** = instruction containing the locations of two

operands and an address for the result
Zwei-plus-Eins-Adreßbefehl

◇ **two-dimensional** *adjective* which has
two dimensions (that is, flat, with no
depth) **zweidimensional; two-dimensional
array** = array which locates items both
vertically and horizontally
zweidimensionale Feldgruppe

◇ **two input adder** *see* HALF ADDER

◇ **two-level subroutine** *noun* subroutine
containing another subroutine
zweischichtiges Unterprogramm

◇ **two-part** *noun* paper (for computers *or*
typewriters) with a top sheet for the
original and a second sheet for a copy
zweilagiges Papier; *two-part invoices; two-
part stationery*

◇ **two-pass assembler** *noun* assembler
that converts an assembly language
program into machine code in two passes -
the first pass stores symbolic addresses, the
second converts them to absolute addresses
Assemblierer in zwei Durchgängen

two's complement *noun* formed by
adding one to the one's complement of a
binary number, often used to represent
negative binary numbers **Zweierkomplement**

two way cable *noun (US)* system of
cable TV, where the viewer can take which
programmes he wants by selecting them *or*
where the viewer can respond to broadcast
questions by sending his response down the
cable **Gegenkabelfernsehbetrieb**

two way radio *noun* radio transmitter
and receiver in a single housing, allowing
duplex communication with another user
Gegenradiobetrieb

two wire circuit *noun* two insulated
wires used to carry transmitted and
received messages independently
Zweidrahtleitung

TX = TRANSMITTER

type
1 *noun*
(a) metal bars with a raised characters used
for printing **Type**
(b) characters used in printing *or* characters
which appear in printed form **Buchstaben,
Schrift;** *they switched to italic type for the
heading*
(c) definition of the processes *or* sorts of
data which a variable in a computer can
contain (this can be numbers, text only,
etc.) **Typ; variable data type** = variable that
can contain any sort of data, such as
numerical, text, etc. **variabler Datentyp;**

string type = variable that can contain
alphanumeric characters only **Typ de
Zeichenfolge**
2 *verb* to write with a typewrite
maschineschreiben, tippen; *he can type quite
fast; all his reports are typed on his portable
typewriter*

typeface *or* **typestyle** *or* **font** *noun* se
of characters designed in a certain style
Schriftbild; Schriftart

typescript *noun* copy of a text written by
an author on a typewriter **Typoskript**
compare MANUSCRIPT

typeset *verb* to set text in type fo
printing **setzen;** *in desktop publishing, the
finished work should look almost as if it had
been typeset*

◇ **typesetter** *noun* company which
typesets **Setzerei;** *the text is ready to be sent
to the typesetter*

◇ **typesetting** *noun* action of setting tex
in type **Setzen;** *typesetting costs can be
reduced by supplying the typesetter with
prekeyed disks; see also*
PHOTOTYPESETTING

typesize *noun* size of type, calculated ir
"points" which refer to the height of the
character, but not its width **Schriftgrad**

typewriter *noun* machine which prints
letters *or* figures on a piece of paper when a
key is pressed by striking an inked ribbon
onto the paper with a character type
Schreibmaschine; *she wrote the letter on he
portable typewriter; he makes fewe
mistakes now he is using an electronic
typewriter;* **typewriter faces** = spacing, size
and font of characters available on a
typewriter **Schrifttypen der Schreibmaschine**

◇ **typewritten** *adjective* written on a
typewriter **maschinengeschrieben;** *he sent in
a typewritten job application*

◇ **typing** *noun* writing letters with a
typewriter **Maschineschreiben; typing erro**
= mistake made when using a typewrite
Tippfehler; *the secretary must have made a
typing error;* **typing pool** = group of typists
working together in a company, offering a
secretarial service to several department
zentraler Schreibdienst; copy typing = typing
documents from originals, not from
dictation **Abtippen von Dokumenten;** NOTE: n
plural

◇ **typist** *noun* person whose job is to write
letters using a typewriter **Schreibkraft; copy
typist** = person who types documents from
originals, not from dictation **Schreibkra**
(ohne Diktat) shorthand typist = typist who

akes dictation in shorthand and then types ≀ **Stenotypist/-in**

typo *noun (informal)* typographical error which is made while typesetting **typographischer Fehler**

◊ **typographer** *noun* person who designs a ypeface *or* text to be printed **Typograph**

◊ **typographic** *or* **typographical** *adjective* referring to typography *or* to typesetting **typographisch;** *no typographical skills are required for this job; a typographical error made while typesetting is called a "typo";* **typographical error** = mistake made while typesetting **typographischer Fehler**

◊ **typography** *noun* art and methods used in working with type **Typographie**

Uu

UART = UNIVERSAL ASYNCHRONOUS RECEIVER/TRANSMITTER chip which converts asynchronous serial bit streams to a parallel form *or* parallel data to a serial bit stream **UART (universelle Schnittstelle für die Umsetzung von bitparalleler in bitserielle Übertragung und umgekehrt im asynchronverfahren); UART controller** = circuit that uses a UART to convert (serial) data from a terminal into a parallel form, then transmits it over a network **UART-steuereinheit;** *see also* USART

UBC = UNIVERSAL BLOCK CHANNEL

UHF = ULTRA HIGH FREQUENCY

ULA = UNCOMMITTED LOGIC ARRAY chip containing a number of unconnected logic circuits and gates which can then be connected by a customer to provide a required function **nicht festgeschriebene logische Anordnung**

Ultra- *prefix* meaning very large *or* further than **ultra-; ultra high frequency (UHF)** = very high frequency range between 500MHz and 3GHz **Ultrahochfrequenz (UHF), Dezimeterwellenbereich; ultrafiche** = microfiche with images that have been reduced by more than ninety times **Ultramikrofiche; ultrasonic** = sound pressure waves at a frequency above the audio band, above 20KHz **Ultraschallwellen; ultrasound** = sound emitted at a frequency above the audio band **Ultraschall; ultraviolet (UV)**

light = electromagnetic radiation with wavelength just greater than the visible spectrum, from 200 to 4000 angstroms **Ultraviolettstrahlung; ultraviolet erasable PROM** = EPROM whose contents are erased by exposing to UV light **mit Ultraviolett löschbarer Festwertspeicher**

umlaut *noun* accent consisting of two dots over a German a, o or u **Umlaut**

un- *prefix* meaning not **un-; unallowable digit** = illegal combination of bits in a word, according to predefined rules **unerlaubte Ziffer; unauthorized** = which has not been authorized **unbefugt;** *the use of a password is to prevent unauthorized access to the data;* **uncut** = (pages of a book) whose edges have not been cut **unbeschnitten**

unary operation *noun* computing operation on only one operand, such as the logical NOT operation **einstellige Operation**

unattended operation *noun* system that can operate without the need for a person to supervise **automatischer Betrieb**

unbundled software *noun* software which is not included in the price of the equipment **im Kaufpreis nicht inbegriffene Software**

unclocked *adjective* electronic circuit *or* flip-flop that changes state as soon as an input changes, not with a clock signal **ohne Taktgeber**

uncommitted logic array (ULA) *noun* chip containing a number of unconnected logic circuits and gates which can then be connected by a customer to provide a required function **nicht festgeschriebenes logisches Feld; uncommitted storage list** = table of the areas of memory in a system that are free *or* have not been allocated **nicht festgeschriebene Speicherliste**

unconditional *adjective* which does not depend on any condition being met **unbedingt; unconditional branch** *or* **jump** *or* **transfer** = instruction which transfers control from one point in the program to another, without depending on any condition being met **unbedingte Verzweigung; unbedingter Sprungbefehl; unbedingte Übertragung**
NOTE: opposite is **conditional**

underexposed *adjective* (photograph) that is too dark because it did not receive a long enough exposure **unterbelichtet**

underflow *noun* result of a numerical operation that is too small to be represented with the given accuracy of a computer **Unterlauf**

underline *or* **underscore**
1 *noun* line drawn *or* printed under a piece of text **Unterstreichung;** *the chapter headings are given a double underline and the paragraphs a single underline*
2 *verb* to print *or* write a line under a piece of text **unterstreichen; underlining** = word-processing command which underlines text **Unterstreichen**

undertake *verb* to agree to do something **übernehmen;** *he has undertaken to reprogram the whole system*
NOTE: **undertaking - undertaken - undertook**

undetected *adjective* which has not been detected **unentdeckt;** *the programming error was undetected for some time*

unedited *adjective* which has not been edited **nicht redigiert, unediert, unredigiert;** *the unedited text is with the publisher for editing*

unformatted *adjective* (disk) which has not been formatted **unformatiert;** *it is impossible to copy to an unformatted disk; the cartridge drive provides 12.7Mbyte of unformatted storage*

uni- *prefix* meaning one *or* single **Ein-, ein-**
◊ **unidirectional microphone** *noun* microphone that is most sensitive in one direction only **Richtmikrophon;** *compare with* OMNIDIRECTIONAL
◊ **union** *noun* logical function that produces a true output if any input is true **Union**
◊ **unipolar** *adjective*
(a) (transistor) that can act as a variable current flow control an external signal varies the resistance of the device **unipolar;** *see also* FET, TRANSISTOR
(b) (transmission system) in which a positive voltage pulse and zero volts represents the binary bits 1 and 0 **unipolar;** *compare with* POLAR; **unipolar signal** = signal that uses only positive voltage levels **unipolares Signal**

uninterruptable power supply (UPS) *noun* power supply that can continue to provide a regulated supply t equipment even after a mains powe failure (using a battery) **unterbrechungslos Stromversorgungsanlage**

unique *adjective* which is different fror everything else **eindeutig, einzigartig;** *eac separate memory byte has its own uniqu address*

unit *noun*
(a) smallest element **Einheit; unit buffer** buffer that is one character lon **Einheitenpuffer;** (NOTE: usually used to mean tha there are no buffering facilities) **unit record** single record of information **einzelne (Daten)satz**
(b) single machine (possibly with man different parts) **einzelne Maschine arithmetic and logic unit (ALU)** = section c the CPU that performs all th mathematical and logical functior **Rechenwerk; central processing unit (CPU** = group of circuits which perform the basi functions of a computer, made up of thre main parts: the control unit, the arithmeti and logic unit and the input/output un **CPU, Zentraleinheit; control unit** = section c the CPU that selects and execute instructions **Steuereinheit; desk top unit** computer that will fit onto a des **Tischcomputer; input/output unit** *or* **device** peripheral (such as a terminal i workstation) which can be used both fc inputting and outputting data to processor **Ein-/Ausgabeeinheit**

universal *adjective* which applie everywhere *or* which can be use everywhere *or* for a number of task **allgemein, universell; universal asynchronou receiver/transmitter (UART)** = chip whic converts an asynchronous serial bit strear to a parallel form *or* parallel data to a seri. bit stream **universelle Schnittstelle für di Umsetzung von bitparalleler in bitseriell Übertragung und umgekehrt ir Asynchronverfahren; universal block channe (UBC)** = communications channe allowing high speed transfer of blocks c data to and from high speed periphera **universeller Blockkanal; universal device** = (UART; (ii) USRT; (iii) USART **(i) UART; (i USRT; (iii) USART; universal product cod (UPC)** = standard printed bar codir system used to identify products in a sho (using a bar code reader *or* at a EPO! **Balkencode;** *see also* EAN; **univers: programming** = writing a program that not specific to one machine, so that it ca run on several machines **universelle Programmieren; universal set** = complete s. of elements that conform to a set of rule

universeller Satz; *the universal set of prime numbers less than ten and greater than two is 3,5,7;* **universal synchronous asynchronous receiver-transmitter (USART)** = chip that can be instructed by a CPU to communicate with asynchronous or synchronous bit streams or data lines **universelle Schnittstelle für die Umsetzung von bitparalleler in bitserielle Übertragung und umgekehrt im Synchronverfahren und im Asynchronverfahren (USART); universal synchronous receiver/transmitter (USRT)** = single integrated circuit that can carry out all the serial to parallel and interfacing operations required between a computer and transmission line **universelle Schnittstelle für die Umsetzung von bitparalleler in bitserielle Übertragung und umgekehrt im Synchronverfahren (USRT)**

Unix *noun* popular operating system for small micros and large mainframes **Unix (Betriebssystem)**

unjustified *adjective* (text) which has not been justified **im Flattersatz, nicht ausgerichtet; unjustified tape** *or* **idiot tape** = tape containing unformatted text, which cannot be printed until formatting data (such as justification, line width and page size) has been added by a computer **nicht-justiertes Band**

unmodified instruction *noun* program instruction which is directly processed without modification to obtain the operation to be performed **unmodifizierter Befehl**

unmodulated *adjective* (signal) which has not been modulated **unmoduliert;** *see also* BASE BAND

unpack *verb* to remove packed data from storage and expand it to its former state **auspacken;** *this routine unpacks the archived file*

unplug *verb* to take a plug out of a socket **den Stecker herausziehen;** *do not move the system without unplugging it; simply unplug the old drive and plug-in a new one*

unprotected *adjective* (data) that can be modified and is not protected by a security measure **ungeschützt; unprotected field** = section of a computer display that a user can modify **ungeschütztes Feld**

unrecoverable error *noun* computer hardware *or* software error that causes a program to crash **nicht korrigierbarer Fehler**

unsigned *adjective* (number system) that does not represent negative numbers **ohne Vorzeichen**

unsorted *adjective* (data) which has not been sorted **unsortiert;** *it took four times as long to search the unsorted file*

unwanted *adjective* which is not needed **unerwünscht, störend;** *use the global delete command to remove large areas of unwanted text*

up *adverb* (of computer or program) working *or* running **laufend;** *they must have found the fault - the computer is finally up and running;* **up time** *or* **uptime** = time during which a device is operational and error free **Nutzeit**
NOTE: opposite is **down**

◊ **up and down propagation time** *noun* total length of time that a transmission takes to travel from earth to a satellite and back to an earth station **Gesamtlaufzeit**

UPC = UNIVERSAL PRODUCT CODE

update
1 *noun* (i) master file which has been made up-to-date by adding new material; (ii) printed information which is an up-to-date revision of earlier information; (iii) new version of a system which is sent to users of the existing system **(i) aktuelle Datei; (ii) aktuelle Information; (iii) neueste Version; update file** *or* **transaction file** = file containing recent changes or transactions to records which is used to update the master file **Fortschreibungsdatei**
2 *verb* to change *or* add to specific data in a master file so as to make the information up-to-date **auf den neuesten Stand bringen;** *he has the original and updated documents on disks*

QUOTE it means that any item of data stored in the system need be updated only once
Which PC?

up/down counter *noun* electronic counter that can increment *or* decrement a counter with each input pulse **Auf-/Abzähler**

upgrade *verb* to make (a system) more powerful *or* more up-to-date by adding new equipment **aufrüsten, verbessern;** *they can upgrade the printer; the single processor with 2Mbytes of memory can be upgraded to 4Mbytes; all three models have an on-site upgrade facility*

upkeep *noun* keeping data up-to-date; keeping devices in working order **Instandhaltung;** *the upkeep of the files means reviewing them every six months*

upload *verb* to transfer data files *or* programs from a small computer to a main CPU **hochladen;** *the user can upload PC data to update mainframe applications* NOTE: the opposite is **download**

◇ **uploading** *noun* action of transferring files to a main CPU **Hochladen;** *the image can be manipulated before uploading to the host computer*

upper case *noun* series of capital letters and other symbols on a typewriter *or* keyboard, which are accessed by pressing the shift key **Großbuchstaben, Versalien**

UPS = UNINTERRUPTABLE POWER SUPPLY power supply that can continue to provide a regulated supply to equipment even after a mains power failure (using a battery) **unterbrechungslose Stromversorgungsanlage**

uptime *noun* time when a computer is functioning correctly (as opposed to downtime) **Nutzzeit**

upwards compatible *or (US)* **upward compatible** *adjective* (hardware *or* software) designed to be compatible either with earlier models *or* with future models which have not yet been invented **aufwärts kompatibel**

usable *adjective* which can be used *or* which is available for use **nutzbar;** *the PC has 512K of usable memory;* **maximum usable frequency** = highest signal frequency which can be used in a circuit without distortion **höchste Nutzfrequenz**

USART = UNIVERSAL SYNCHRONOUS ASYNCHRONOUS RECEIVER-TRANSMITTER chip that can be instructed by a CPU to communicate with asynchronous *or* synchronous bit streams or parallel data lines **universelle Schnittstelle für die Umsetzung von bitparalleler in bitserielle Übertragung und umgekehrt im Synchronverfahren und im Asynchronverfahren (USART)**

USASCII *(US)* = USA STANDARD CODE FOR INFORMATION INTERCHANGE *se* ASCII

use
1 *noun*
(a) way in which something can be used **Benutzung, Gebrauch;** *the printer has been i use for the last two hours; the use of the tha file is restricted;* **to make use of something** to use something **etwas benutzen**
(b) value; being useful **Nutzen;** *what use an extra disk drive? it's no use, I cannot fin the error;* **in use** = already in operation **Betrieb/Gebrauch;** *sorry, the printer already in use*
2 *verb*
(a) to operate something **benutzen verwenden;** *if you use the computer fo processing the labels, it will be muc quicker; the computer is used too often b the sales staff*
(b) to consume heat, light, etc. **verbraucher** *it's using too much electricity*

◇ **used** *adjective* which is not new **benutz gebraucht;** *special offer on used terminals*

user *noun* (i) person who uses a compute *or* machine *or* software; (ii) especially, keyboard operator **(i) & (ii) Benutzer; use area** = part of the memory which available for the user, and does not contai the operating system **Benutzerspeiche user-definable** = feature *or* section of program that a user can customize a required **benutzerdefinierbar;** *the style shee contains 125 user-definable symbols;* **user defined characters** = characters which ai created by the user and added to th standard character set **benutzerdefiniert Zeichen; user documentation** documentation provided with a progra which helps the user run **Benutzerdokumentation;** *using the packag was easy with the excellent us documentation;* **user group** = association club of users of a particular system computer **Benutzergruppe;** *I found how t solve the problem by asking people at th user group meeting;* **user guide** = manua describing how to use a software package system **Benutzerhandbuch; user ID** = uniqu identification code that allows a compute to recognize a user **Benutzerkennzeichen;** *you forget your user ID, you will not be abl to logon;* **user interface** = hardware software designed to make it easier for user to communicate with the machin **Benutzerschnittstelle; user-operate language** = high-level programmin language that allows certain problems procedures to be easily expresse **benutzerorientierte Programmiersprache; use**

port = socket which allows peripherals to be connected to a computer **Benutzeranschluß; user's program** = computer software written by a user rather than a manufacturer **Benutzerprogramm; user-selectable** = which can be chosen *or* selected by the user **vom Benutzer auswählbar;** *the video resolution of 640 by 300, 240 or 200 pixels is user-selectable*

◇ **user-friendly** *adjective* (language *or* system *or* program) that is easy to use and interact with **benutzerfreundlich;** *it's such a user-friendly machine; compared with the previous version this one is very user-friendly*

QUOTE the user's guides are designed for people who have never seen a computer, but some sections have been spoiled by careless checking
PC User

QUOTE the first popular microcomputer to have a user-friendly interface built into its operating system
Micro Decision

USRT = UNIVERSAL SYNCHRONOUS RECEIVER/TRANSMITTER

utility (program) *noun* useful program that is concerned with such routine activities as file searching, copying files, file directories, sorting and debugging and various mathematical functions **Dienstprogramm;** *a lost file cannot be found without a file-recovery utility; on the disk is a utility for backing up a hard disk*

UV light = ULTRAVIOLET LIGHT

Vv

V = VOLTAGE

V & V = VERIFICATION AND VALIDATION

V format *noun* data organization, in which variable length records are stored with a header which contains their length **V-Format, variables Format**

V series *noun* CCITT (UK-European) standards for data transmission using a modem **V-Serie (Steckernorm)**
NOTE: **V.21** = 300 baud transmit and receive, full duplex **V.22** = 1200 baud transmit and receive, half duplex **V.22 BIS** = 1200 baud transmit and receive full duplex **V.23** = 75 baud transmit, 1200 baud receive, half duplex

vacuum *noun* state with no air **Vakuum;** *there is a vacuum in the sealed CRT;* **vacuum tube** = electronic current flow control device consisting of a heated cathode and an anode in a sealed glass tube with a vacuum inside it **Vakuumröhre**

COMMENT: used in the first generation of computers, now replaced by solid state current control devices such as the transistor

valid *adjective* correct, according to a set of rules **gültig; valid memory address** = signal on control bus indicating that an address is available on the address bus **gültige Speicheradresse**

◇ **validate** *verb* to check that an input *or* data is correct according to a set of rules **für gültig erklären**

◇ **validation** *noun* check performed to validate data **Gültigkeitsprüfung**

◇ **validity** *noun* correctness of an instruction *or* password **Gültigkeit; validity check** = check that data *or* results are realistic **Gültigkeitsprüfung**

value *noun* what something is worth (either in money *or* as a quantity) **Wert; absolute value** = value of a number regardless of its sign **Absolutwert;** *the absolute value of -62.34 is 62.34;* **initial value** = starting point (usually zero) set when initializing variables at the beginning of a program **Anfangswert**

◇ **value added network (VAN)** *noun* network where the transmission lines are leased from a public utility such as the telephone service, but where the user can add on private equipment **Netz mit erweiterten Übertragungsmöglichkeiten**

◇ **value added reseller (VAR)** *noun* retailer who sells equipment and systems which are specially tailored to certain types of operation **Vertriebsfirma, die Standardprodukte durch eigene Spezialentwicklungen ergänzt**

valve *noun* electronic current flow control device consisting of a heated cathode and an anode in a sealed glass vacuum tube **Ventil**

COMMENT: used in the first generation of computers, now replaced by solid state current control devices such as a transistor

VAN = VALUE ADDED NETWORK

vapourware *noun (informal)* products which exist in name only **nur auf dem Papier existierende Ware**

VAR = VALUE ADDED RESELLER

variable

1 *adjective* able to change **veränderlich, variabel; variable data** = data which can be modified, and is not write-protected **variable Daten; variable length record** = record which can be of any length **Satz mit variabler Länge; variable word length computer** = computer in which the number of bits which make up a word is variable, and varies according to the type of data **Computer mit variabler Wortlänge**

2 *noun* (computer program identifier for a) register *or* storage location which can contain any number *or* characters and which may vary during the program run **Variable; global variable** = number that can be accessed by any routine *or* structure in a program **globale Variable; local variable** = number which can only be accessed by certain routines in a certain section of a computer program **lokale Variable**

◊ **vary** *verb* to change **sich verändern;** *the clarity of the signal can vary with the power supply*

VCR = VIDEO CASSETTE RECORDER

VDT *or* **VDU** = VISUAL DISPLAY TERMINAL, VISUAL DISPLAY UNIT terminal with a screen and a keyboard, on which text *or* graphics can be viewed and information entered **Bildschirmgerät; Datensicht-, Videoterminal**

QUOTE it normally consists of a keyboard to input information and either a printing terminal or a VDU screen to display messages and results
Practical Computing
QUOTE a VDU is a device used with a computer that displays information in the form of characters and drawings on a screen
Electronics & Power

vector *noun*

(a) address which directs a computer to a new memory location **Vektor**

(b) coordinate that consists of a magnitude and direction **Vektor; vector graphics** *or* **vector image** *or* **vector scan** = computer drawing system that uses line length and direction from an origin to plot lines **Vektorbild; vector processor** = coprocessor that operates on one row or column of an array at a time **Vektorprozessor**

◊ **vectored interrupt** *noun* interrupt signal which directs the processor to a routine at a particular address **zeigergesteuerte Unterbrechung**

QUOTE the great advantage of the vector-scan display is that it requires little memory to store a picture
Electronics & Power

Veitch diagram *noun* graphical representation of a truth table **Veitch-Diagramm**

velocity *noun* speed **Geschwindigkeit;** *the disk drive motor spins at a constant velocity*

Venn diagram *noun* graphical representation of the relationships between the states in a system *or* circuit **Venn-Diagramm**

verify *verb* to check that data recorded *or* entered is correct **überprüfen, bestätigen**

◊ **verification** *noun* checking that data has been keyboarded correctly *or* that data transferred from one medium to another has been transferred correctly **Verifikation; keystroke verification** = check made on each key pressed to make sure it is valid for a particular application **Tastenanschlagsprüfung; verification and validation (V & V)** = testing a system to check that it is functioning correctly and that it is suitable for the tasks intended **Funktions- und Eignungsprüfung**

◊ **verifier** *noun* special device for verifying input data **Prüfer**

version *noun* copy *or* program *or* statement which is slightly different from others **Version;** *the latest version of the software includes an improved graphics routine*

verso *noun* left hand page of a book (usually given an even number) **Rückseite, Verso**

vertical *adjective* at right angles to the horizontal **vertikal, senkrecht; vertical blanking interval** *see* RASTER; **vertical format unit (VFU)** = part of the control system of a printer which governs the vertical format of the document to be printed (such as vertical spacing, page length) **vertikale Formatsteuerungseinheit; vertical justification** = adjustment of the spacing between lines of text to fit a section of text into a page **vertikale Texteinrichtung, vertikaler Zeilenausgleich; vertical parity check** = error detection test in which the bits of a word are added and compared with a correct total **Querparitätsprüfung; vertical redundancy check (VRC)** = (odd) parity check on each character of a block received, to detect any errors **Querprüfung; vertical scrolling** = displaying text so that it moves up or down the computer screen one line at a time **vertikale blättern; vertical tab** = number of lines that should be skipped before printing starts again **Vertikaltabulator**

◇ **vertically** *adverb* from top to bottom *or* going up and down at right angles to the horizontal **vertikal**; *the page has been justified vertically;* **vertically polarized signal** = signal whose waveforms are all aligned in one vertical plane **vertikal polarisiertes Signal**

very high frequency (VHF) *noun* range of radio frequencies between 30-300 MHz **Ultrakurzwellenbereich**

very large scale integration (VLSI) *noun* integrated circuit with 10,000 to 100,000 components **Übergroßintegration**

very low frequency (VLF) *noun* range of radio frequencies between 3-30 KHz **Niederfrequenz**

vestigial sideband *noun* single sideband transmission with a small part of the other sideband kept to provide synchronization data, often used in TV transmissions **Restseitenband**

vf band = VOICE FREQUENCY BAND

VFU = VERTICAL FORMAT UNIT

VHD = VERY HIGH DENSITY video disk able to store very large quantities of data **VHD**

VHF = VERY HIGH FREQUENCY radio frequency between 30MHz and 300MHZ (used for broadcasting radio and TV programmes) **Ultrakurzwellenbereich**

via *preposition* going through something *or* using something to get to a destination **über, via**; *the signals have reached us via satellite; you can download the data to the CPU via a modem*

video *noun* text *or* images *or* graphics viewed on television *or* a monitor **Video**; **video bandwidth** = frequency range required to carry TV images **Videobandbreite**; **video camera** = optical lenses in front of an electronic device that can convert images into electronic signals in a form that can be displayed on a TV **Videokamera**; **infrared video camera** = video camera sensitive to infrared light **Infrarot-Videokamera**; *some instructors monitor their trainees with infrared video cameras;* **video cassette** = cassette with video tape in it (either blank for recording, or with a prerecorded film) **Videokassette**; **video cassette recorder (VCR)** = device attached

to a TV set, which can be programmed to record TV programmes on videotape and play them back at another time **Videorekorder**; **video compressor** = device that reduces the bandwidth of a TV signal allowing it to be transmitted over a (telephone), using a video expander at the receiving end **Videokompressor**; **video conference** = conference system where two or more people can talk to and see each other using satellite TV links **Videokonferenz**; **videodisk** = read-only optical disk able to store TV pictures and sound in binary form, also capable of storing large amounts of computer data **Video-, Bildplatte**; **video display** = device which can display text *or* graphical information, such as a CRT **Sicht-, Bildschirmgerät**; **video expander** = device that stores one frame of a video image as it is slowly received over a voice grade communications link, with a video compressor used at the transmitting end **Videoexpander**; **video frame** = single image on a video tape *or* TV **Videovollbild**; *with an image processor you can freeze a video frame;* **video game** = game played on a computer, with action shown on a video display **Videospiel**; **video image** = single frame from a video tape *or* TV **Videobild**; *a printer-readable video image can be sent to a basic laser printer through a video port;* **video interface chip** = chip that controls a video display allowing information stored in a computer (text, graphics) to be displayed **Videoschnittstellenchip**; **video memory** *or* **video RAM (VRAM)** = high speed random access memory used to store computer-generated *or* digitized images **Video-RAM**; **video monitor** = device able to display, without sound, signals from a computer **Video-, Sichtmonitor**; *(informal)* **video nasties** = horror films available on video cassette **Videohorrorfilme**; **video phone** = two way voice and image transmission **Bildschirmtelefon**; **video player** = device that can play back video recordings but cannot record **Videoabspielgerät**; **video port** = connection on a video recorder allowing the data read from the tape to be used in other ways, such as being stored in a computer **Videoanschluß**; **video recorder** = device for recording TV images and sound onto video tape **Videorekorder**; **video signal** = signal which provides line picture information and synchronization pulses **BAS-Signal**; **video scanner** = device which allows images of objects *or* pictures to be entered into a computer **Bildabtaster**; *new video scanners are designed to scan three-dimensional objects;* **video standards** = protocols defining video signal format (there are three main international video standards: NTSC, PAL and SECAM)

Fernsehsysteme; **videotape** = magnetic tape used in a video recorder, for storing TV pictures and sound information **Videoband; videotape recorder** = device that can record and playback TV images and sound on video tape **Video(band)rekorder; video terminal** = keyboard with a monitor **Videoterminal, Datensichtgerät**

◊ **videotext** *or* **videotex** *noun* system for transmitting text and displaying it on a screen **Bildschirm-, Videotext**

COMMENT: this covers information transmitted either by TV signals (teletext) *or* by signals sent down telephone lines (viewdata)

view *verb* to look at something, especially something displayed on a screen **einsehen, ansehen;** *the user has to pay a charge for viewing pages on a bulletin board*

◊ **viewdata** *noun* interactive system for transmitting text *or* graphics from a database to a user's terminal by telephone lines, providing facilities for information retrieval, transactions, education, games and recreation **Bildschirmtextsystem**

COMMENT: the user calls up the page of information required, using the telephone and a modem, as opposed to teletext, where the pages of information are repeated one after the other automatically

◊ **viewer** *noun*
(a) person who watches television **Zuschauer**
(b) device with an eyepiece through which a person can look at film *or* transparencies **Leuchtkasten, Dia-, Bildbetrachter, Gucki**

◊ **viewfinder** *noun* eyepiece in a camera that allows a user to see what is being filmed **Sucher; electronic viewfinder** = miniature cathode ray tube in a television *or* video camera, that allows the camera operator to see the images being recorded **elektronischer Sucher**

virgin *adjective* (tape) that has not been recorded on before **unbespielt**

virtual *adjective* feature *or* device which does not actually exist but which is simulated by a computer and can be used by a user as if it did exist **virtuell; virtual address** = an address referring to virtual storage **virtuelle Adresse; virtual circuit** = link established between a source and sink (in a packet-switching network) for the duration of the call **virtuelle Verbindung; virtual disk** = section of RAM used with a short controlling program as if it were a fast disk storage system **virtuelle Platte; virtual machine** = simulated machine and its

operations **virtuelle Maschine; virtual memory** *or* **virtual storage (VS)** = large imaginary main memory made available by loading smaller pages from a backing store into the available main memory only as and when they are required **virtueller Speicher; virtual terminal** = ideal terminal specifications used as a model by a real terminal **virtueller Terminal**

virus *noun* short hidden routine that corrupts all data and files and spreads from computer to computer when disks are exchanged **(Computer)virus**

visible *adjective* which can be seen **sichtbar; visible light** = range of light colours that can be seen with the human eye **sichtbares Licht**

visual
1 *adjective* which can be seen *or* which is used by sight **visuell; visual programming** = method of programming a computer by showing it or taking it through the processes of what it has to do rather than writing a series of instructions **visuelles Programmieren**
2 *noun* **visuals** = graphics *or* photographs *or* illustrations, used as part of a printed output **Abbildungen, Bildmaterial**

◊ **visual display terminal (VDT)** *or* **visual display unit (VDU)** *noun* terminal with a screen and a keyboard, on which text *or* graphics can be viewed and information entered **Bildschirmgerät; Datensicht-, Videoterminal**

◊ **visualize** *verb* to imagine how something will appear, even before it has been created **sich vorstellen**

VLF = VERY LOW FREQUENCY radio frequency between 30Hz and 30KHz **Niederfrequenz**

VLSI = VERY LARGE SCALE INTEGRATION system with between 10,000 and 100,000 components on a single IC **Übergroßintegration**

voice *noun* sound of human speech **Stimme; voice answer back** = computerized response service using a synthesized voice to answer enquiries **Sprachantwort; voice band** = minimum bandwidth required for recognizable transmission of speech (usually 300 - 3400Hz) **Sprechfrequenzband; voice data entry** *or* **input** = input of information into a computer using a speech recognition system and the user's voice **Spracheingabedaten; voice grade channel** = communications channel (bandwidth usually equal to voice band), able to carry speech and some data (such as facsimile) **Sprechkanal; voice messaging** = device for recording a caller's spoken message if the number he calls does not reply **Anrufaufzeichnung; voice output** = production of sounds which sound like human speech, made as a result of voice synthesis **Sprachausgabe; voice print** = identification of a person by registering tones and signals in that person's speech **Stimmabdruck; voice recognition** = ability of a computer to recognize certain words in a human voice and provide a suitable response **Spracherkennung; voice response** = VOICE OUTPUT; **voice synthesis** = reproduction of sounds similar to those of the human voice **Sprachsynthese; voice synthesizer** = device which generates sounds which are similar to the human voice **Sprachsynthesizer**

◇ **voice-over** *noun* spoken commentary by an actor who does not appear on the screen (as the text of a TV commercial) **Hintergrundkommentar**

◇ **voice unit** *noun* unit of signal measurement equal to a one millivolt signal across a 600 ohm resistance **Sprecheinheit**

QUOTE the technology of voice output is reasonably difficult, but the technology of voice recognition is much more complex
Personal Computer World

volatile memory *or* **volatile store** *or* **volatile dynamic storage** *noun* memory *or* storage medium which loses data stored in it when the power supply is switched off **flüchtiger Speicher;** NOTE: opposite is **non-volatile memory**

◇ **volatility** *noun* number of records that are added *or* deleted from a computer system compared to the total number in store **Flüchtigkeit**

volt *noun* SI unit of electrical potential, defined as voltage across a one ohm resistance when one amp is flowing **Volt**

◇ **voltage** *noun* electromotive force expressed in volts **elektrische Spannung; voltage dip** *or* **dip in voltage** = sudden fall in voltage which may last only a very short while, but which can affect the operation of a computer system **Spannungsabfall; voltage regulator** = device which provides a steady output voltage even if the input supply varies **Spannungsregler; voltage transient** = spike of voltage that is caused by a time delay in two devices switching *or* by noise on the line **Übergangsspannung**

COMMENT: electricity supply can have peaks and troughs of current, depending on the users in the area. Fluctuations in voltage can affect computers; a voltage regulator will provide a steady supply of electricity

volume *noun*
(a) total space occupied by data in a storage system **Volumen, Gesamtraum**
(b) measure of sound pressure **(Klang)volumen, Lautstärke; volume control** = knob which turns to increase the volume from a radio, TV or amplifier **Lautstärkeregler**

VRAM = VIDEO RANDOM ACCESS MEMORY high speed random access memory used to store computer-generated *or* digitized images **Video-RAM**

VRC = VERTICAL REDUNDANCY CHECK (odd) parity check on each character of a block received, to detect any errors **Querparitätsprüfung**

VS = VIRTUAL STORAGE

V series series of CCITT recommendations for data communications **V-Serie**

VTR = VIDEO TAPE RECORDER

VU = VOICE UNIT

Ww

wafer *noun* thin round slice of a large single crystal of silicon onto which hundreds of individual integrated circuits are constructed, before being cut into individual chips **Halbleiterscheibe**

◇ **wafer scale integration** *noun* one large chip, the size of a wafer, made up of smaller integrated circuits connected together (these are still in the research stage) **Integrationstechnikplättchen**

wait condition *or* **state** *noun* state where a processor is not active, but waiting for input from peripherals **Wartestatus**

◇ **wait loop** *noun* processor that repeats one loop of program until some action occurs **Warteschleife**

◊ **wait time** *noun* time delay between the moment when an instruction is given and the execution of the instruction *or* return of a result (such as the delay between a request for data and the data being transferred from memory) **Wartezeit**

◊ **waiting list** *noun see* QUEUE

◊ **waiting state** *noun* computer state, in which a program requires an input *or* signal before continuing execution **Wartestatus**

wake up *verb* to switch on *or* start *or* initiate **einschalten**; **wake up a system** = code entered at a remote terminal to indicate to the central computer that someone is trying to log-on at that location **Wake-up-Code**

walk through *verb* to examine each step of a piece of software **durchgehen**

WAN = WIDE AREA NETWORK

wand *noun* bar code reader *or* optical device which is held in the hand to read bar codes on products in a store **Lesestift**

warm standby *noun* secondary backup device that can be switched into action a short time after the main system fails **Warm-Standby-System**; *compare with* COLD STANDBY, HOT STANDBY

◊ **warm start** *noun* restarting a programme which has stopped, but without losing any data **Warmstart**; *compare* COLD START

◊ **warm up** *verb* to allow a machine to stand idle for a time after switching on, to reach the optimum operating conditions **anwärmen**

> QUOTE warm-up time measures how long each printer takes to get ready to begin printing
> *Byte*

warn *verb* to say that something dangerous is about to happen; to say that there is a possible danger **warnen**; *he warned the keyboarders that the system might become overloaded* NOTE: you warn someone **of** something, or **that** something may happen

◊ **warning** *noun* notice of possible danger **Warnung**; *to issue a warning; warning notices were put up around the high powered laser;* **warning light** = (small light) which lights up to show that something dangerous may happen **Warnlicht**; *when the warning light on the front panel comes on, switch off the system*

warrant *verb* to guarantee **garantieren**; *all the spare parts are warranted*

◊ **warrantee** *noun* person who is given warranty **Garantieinhaber, Garantieempfänge**

◊ **warrantor** *noun* person who gives warranty **Garantiegeber, Garant**

◊ **warranty** *noun*
(a) guarantee *or* legal document whic promises that a machine will work properl *or* that an item is of good quality **Garanti** *the printer is sold with a twelve-mont warranty; the warranty covers spare part but not labour costs*
(b) promise in a contract **Gewähr; breach c warranty** = failing to do something which i a part of a contract **Verletzung de Gewährleistungspflicht**

wash PROM *verb* to erase the data fror a PROM **einen Festwertspeicher löschen**

waste instruction *noun* instructio that does not carry out any action (excep increasing the program counter to th location of next instruction) **leer Anweisung**

Watt *noun* SI unit of measurement c electrical power, defined as powe produced when one amp of current flow through a load that has one volt of voltag across it **Watt**

wave *noun* signal motion that rises an falls periodically as it travels through medium **Welle; microwave** = hig frequency, short wavelength signals use for communication links, such as an eart station to satellite link **Mikrowelle; soun wave** = pressure wave that carries soun **Schallwelle**

◊ **waveform** *noun* shape of a wav **Schwingungsverlauf, Wellenform; waveforr digitization** = conversion and storing waveform in numerical form using an A/I converter **Wellenformdigitalisierung**

◊ **waveguide** *noun* physical system use to direct waves in a particular directio (usually metal tubes for microwave signa *or* optical fibres for light signals) **Hohlleite**

◊ **wavelength** *noun* distance between tw corresponding points of adjacent waves i a periodic waveform; defined as the spee of the wave divided by the frequenc **Wellenlänge**

WBFM = WIDEBAND FREQUENC MODULATION

weigh *verb*
(a) to measure how heavy something i **wiegen (lassen)**; *he weighed the packet at th post office*

(b) to have a certain weight **wiegen;** *the packet weighs twenty-five grams*

◇ **weighing machine** *noun* machine which measures how heavy a thing *or* a person is **Waage**

◇ **weight** *noun* measurement of how heavy something is **Gewicht; gross weight** = weight of both the container and its contents **Bruttogewicht; net weight** = weight of goods after deducting the packing material and container **Nettogewicht; paper weight** = amount which a certain quantity of paper weighs **Papiergewicht;** *our paper weight is 70 - 90 gsm*

◇ **weighted** *adjective* sorted according to importance *or* priority **gewichtet; weighted average** = average calculated taking several factors into account, giving some more value than others **gewichteter Durchschnitt, Bewertungsdurchschnitt; weighted bit** = each bit having a different value depending on its position in a word **gewichtetes Bit**

◇ **weighting** *noun*
(a) sorting of users, programs or data by their importance or priority **Gewichtung**
(b) additional salary *or* wages paid to compensate for living in an expensive part of the country **Zulage;** *salary plus a London weighting*

well-behaved *adjective* (program) that does not make any non-standard system calls, using only the standard BIOS input/output calls rather than directly addressing peripherals *or* memory **gut funktionierend(es Programm)**

COMMENT: if well-behaved, the software should work on all machines using the same operating system

wetware *noun (US) informal* the human brain *or* intelligence which writes software to be used with hardware **Wetware**

What-You-See-Is-All-You-Get (WYSIAYG) *noun* program where the output on screen cannot be printed out in any other form (that is, it cannot contain hidden print *or* formatting commands) **Was-man-sieht-ist-alles-was-man-bekommen-kann (WYSIAYG)**

What-You-See-Is-What-You-Get (WYSIWYG) *noun* program where the output on the screen is exactly the same as the output on printout, including graphics and special fonts **Was-man-sieht-ist-was-man-bekommt (WYSIWYG)**

while-loop *noun* conditional program instructions that carries out a loop while a condition is true **WHILE-Schleife**

white *adjective & noun* the colour of snow **weiß, das Weiße; white flag** = signal indicating a new frame on a video disk **Signal, das ein neues Videovollbild anzeigt; white level** = maximum TV signal strength corresponding to maximum brightness on the screen **Weißpegel; white noise** = random noise that is of equal power at all frequencies **weißes Rauschen; white writer** = laser printer which directs its laser beam on the points that are not printed **spezieller Laserdrucker;** NOTE: the opposite is **black writer**

COMMENT: with a white writer, the black areas are printed evenly but edges and borders are not so sharp

wide-angle lens *noun* lens which has a large acceptance angle **Weitwinkelobjektiv**

◇ **wide area network (WAN)** *noun* network where the various terminals are far apart and linked by radio, satellite and cable **Weitverkehrsnetz, Breitnetz;** *compare with* LAN

COMMENT: WANs use modems, radio and other long distance transmission methods; LANs use cables or optical fibre links

wideband *noun* transmission with a bandwidth greater than that of a voice channel **Breitband; wideband frequency modulation (WBFM)** = frequency modulation that uses a large frequency bandwidth and has more than one pair of sidebands **Breitbandfrequenzmodulation**

widow *noun* first line of a paragraph which is printed by itself at the bottom of a column **Hurenkind;** *compare* ORPHAN

width *noun* size of something from edge to edge **Breite; page width** *or* **line width** = number of characters across a page *or* line **Seitenbreite; Zeilenbreite**

wild card *noun* symbol that represents all files *or* names used when searching for data **beliebig verwendbares Symbol;** *a wild card can be used to find all files names beginning DIC*

WIMP = WINDOW, ICON, MOUSE, POINTERS description of an integrated software system that is entirely operated using windows, icons and a mouse controlled pointer **WIMP (Fenster, Ikon, Maus, Zeiger);** *see also* ENVIRONMENT

Winchester disk *or* **drive** *noun* compact high-capacity hard disk which is usually built into a computer system and cannot be removed **Winchesterplatte, Festplatte; removable Winchester** = small hard disk in a sealed unit, which can be detached from a computer when full *or* when not required **herausnehmbare Winchesterplatte**

window

1 *noun* (i) reserved section of screen used to display special information, that can be selected and looked at at any time and which overwrites information already on the screen; (ii) part of a document currently displayed on a screen; (iii) area of memory *or* access to a storage device **(i) & (ii) Fenster; (iii) Ausschnitt;** *several remote stations are connected to the network and each has its own window onto the hard disk; the operating system will allow other programs to be displayed on-screen at the same time in different windows;* **active window** = area of the display screen where the operator is currently working **aktives Fenster; command window** = area of the screen that always displays the range of commands available **Befehlsfenster;** *the command window is a single line at the bottom of the screen;* **edit window** = area of the screen in which the user can display and edit text *or* graphics **Editier-, Aufbereitungsfenster; text window** = window in a graphics system, where the text is held in a small space on the screen before being allocated to a final area **Textfenster; window, icon, mouse, pointer (WIMP)** = description of an integrated software system that is entirely operated using windows, icons and a mouse controlled pointer **Fenster, Ikon, Maus, Zeiger (WIMP)**

2 *verb* to set up a section of screen by defining the coordinates of its corners, that allows information to be temporarily displayed, overwriting previous information but without altering information in the workspace **ein Fenster definieren**

◊ **windowing** *noun* (i) action of setting up a window to show information on the screen; (ii) displaying *or* accessing information via a window **(i) & (ii) Fenstertechnik**

QUOTE when an output window overlaps another, the interpreter does not save the contents of the obscured window
Personal Computer World
QUOTE windowing facilities make use of virtual screens as well as physical screens
Byte
QUOTE you can connect more satellites to the network, each having its own window onto the hard disk
PC Plus
QUOTE the network system uses the latest windowing techniques
Desktop Publishing
QUOTE the functions are integrated via a windowing system with pull-down menus used to select different operations
Byte

wipe *verb* to clean data from a disk **löschen;** *by reformatting you will wipe the disk clean*

◊ **wiper** *noun* movable arm in a potentiometer, a variable resistor *or* selector switch that can be turned to select a new resistance *or* function **Abstreifer**

wire

1 *noun*
(a) thin metal conductor **Draht; wire printer** = dot-matrix printer; *Nadeldrucker* **wire wrap** = simple method of electrically connecting component terminals together using thin insulated wire wrapped around each terminal which is then soldered into place, usually used for prototype systems **Drahtwickeln**

2 *verb* to install wiring **verkabeln;** *the studio is wired for sound;* **wired** *or* **hardwired program computer** = computer with a program built into the hardware which cannot be changed **verbindungsprogrammierter Computer;** *see also* HARDWIRED

◊ **wireless**
1 *noun* (old use) device that can receive radio broadcasts **Radio**
2 *adjective* communication system that does not require wires to carry signals **drahtlos; wireless microphone** = audio microphone with a small transmitter attached allowing the transmission of signals without interconnecting wires **drahtloses Mikrophon**

◊ **wire tap** *noun* unauthorized connection to a private communications line in order to listen to conversations *or* obtain private data **Abhöranlage**

◊ **wiring** *noun* series of wires **elektrische Leitungen;** *the wiring in the system had to be replaced*

WISC = WRITABLE INSTRUCTION SET COMPUTER CPU design that allows a programmer to add extra machine code instructions using microcode, to customize the instruction set **beschreibbare CPU**

woofer *noun (informal)* large loudspeaker used to produce low frequency sounds **Tieftonlautsprecher** *compare* TWEETER

word *noun*
(a) separate item of language, which is used with others to form speech *or* writing which can be understood **Wort; words per minute (wpm** *or* **WPM)** = method of measuring the speed of a printer **Wörter pro Minute; word break** = division of a word at the end of a line, where part of the word is left on one line with a hyphen, and the rest of the word is taken over to begin the next line **Worttrennung; word count** = number of words in a file *or* text **Wortzahl; word wrap** *or* **wraparound** = system in word processing where the operator does not have to indicate the line endings, but can keyboard continuously, leaving the program to insert word breaks and to continue the text on the next line **Umlaufsystem**
(b) separate item of data on a computer, formed of a group of bits, stored in a single location in a memory **Wort; word length** = length of a computer word, counted as the number of bits **Wortlänge; word mark** = symbol indicating the start of a word in a variable word length machine **Wortmarke; word serial** = data words transmitted along a parallel bus one after the other **Wortserie; word time** = time taken to transfer a word from one memory area *or* device to another **Wort(takt)zeit**

◇ **word-process** *verb* to edit, store and manipulate text using a computer **Text verarbeiten;** *it is quite easy to read word-processed files*

◇ **word-processing (WP)** *noun* using a computer to keyboard, edit, and output text, in the form of letters, labels, address lists, etc. **Textverarbeitung (TV);** *load the word-processing program before you start keyboarding;* **word-processing bureau** = office which specializes in word-processing for other companies **Textverarbeitungsbüro;** NOTE: no plural

◇ **word-processor** *noun*
(a) small computer *or* typewriter with a computer in it, used for word-processing text and documents **Textverarbeitungscomputer**
(b) word-processing package *or* program for a computer which allows the editing and manipulation and output of text, such as letters, labels, address lists, etc. **Textverarbeitungssystem**

work
1 *noun* things done using the hands *or* brain

Arbeit; work area = memory space which is being used by an operator **Arbeitsbereich; work disk** = disk on which current work is stored **Arbeitsplatte; work file** *or* **scratch file** temporary work area which is being used for current work **Arbeitsdatei, ungeschützte Datei; working store** *or* **scratch pad** = area of high-speed memory used for temporary storage of data in current use **Arbeitsspeicher; Notizblockspeicher;** NOTE: no plural
2 *verb* to function **arbeiten, funktionieren;** *the computer system has never worked properly since it was installed*

◇ **working** *adjective* (something) which is operating correctly **funktionierend, in Betrieb**

◇ **workload** *noun* amount of work which a person *or* computer has to do **Arbeitsbelastung;** *he has difficulty in dealing with his heavy workload*

◇ **workplace** *noun* place where you work **Arbeitsplatz**

◇ **work-sharing** *noun* system where two part-timers share one job **Arbeitsteilung**

◇ **workspace** *noun* space in memory, which is available for use *or* is being used currently by an operator **Arbeitsbereich**

◇ **workstation** *noun* place where a computer user works, with a terminal, printer, modem, etc. **Arbeitsplatz;** *the system includes five workstations linked together in a ring network; the archive storage has a total capacity of 1200 Mb between seven workstations*

> QUOTE an image processing workstation must provide three basic facilities: the means to digitize, display and manipulate the image data
> *Byte*

WORM = WRITE ONCE READ MANY TIMES MEMORY

wow *noun* fluctuation of the frequency of a recorded signal at playback, (usually caused by uneven tape movement) **Gleichlaufschwankung, Jaulen**

WP = WORD-PROCESSING

WPM *or* **wpm** = WORDS PER MINUTE

wrap *noun* **omega wrap** = system of threading video tape round a video head (the tape passes over most of the circular head and is held in place by two small rollers **Omega-Wicklung**

◇ **wraparound** *or* **word wrap** *noun* system in word-processing where the operator does not have to indicate the line endings, but can keyboard continuously, leaving the program to insert word breaks and to continue the text on the next line **Umlaufsystem; horizontal wraparound** = movement of a cursor on a computer display from the end of one line to the beginning of the next **Zeilenumlauf**

write *verb*
(a) to put words *or* figures on to paper **schreiben;** *she wrote a letter of complaint to the manager; the telephone number is written at the bottom of the notepaper*
(b) to put text *or* data onto a disk *or* tape **schreiben;** *access time is the time taken to read from or write to a location in memory;* **write head** = transducer that can write data onto a magnetic medium **Schreibkopf; write once, read many times memory (WORM)** = optical disk storage system that allows one writing action but many reading actions in its life **einmal beschreibbarer, mehrfach lesbarer Speicher; writing pad** = special device which allows a computer to read in handwritten characters which have been written onto a special pad **Sensor(schreib)block;** *see* OCR; **write time** = time between requesting data transfer to a storage location and it being written **Schreibzeit;** NOTE: you write data **to** a file. Note also: **writing - wrote - has written**

◇ **writable instruction set computer (WISC)** *noun* CPU design that allows a programmer to add extra machine code instructions using microcode, to customize the instruction set **beschreibbare CPU**

◇ **write-permit ring** *noun* ring on a reel of magnetic tape which allows the tape to be overwritten *or* erased **Schreiberring**

◇ **write protect** *verb* to make it impossible to write to a floppy disk *or* tape by moving a special write-protect tab **einen Schreibschutz anbringen; write-protect tab** = tab on a floppy disk which if moved, prevents any writing to *or* erasing from the disk **Schreibschutzetikett**

◇ **writer** *noun see* BLACK, WHITE

◇ **writing** *noun* something which has been written **Schrift;** *to put the agreement in writing; he has difficulty in reading my writing*
NOTE: no plural

WYSIAYG = WHAT YOU SEE IS ALL YOU GET

WYSIWYG = WHAT YOU SEE IS WHAT YOU GET

Xx

X = EXTENSION

X-axis *noun* horizontal axis of a graph **x-Achse, Abszisse(nachse)**

◇ **X-coordinate** *noun* horizontal axis position coordinate **x-Koordinate, Abszisse**

◇ **X direction** *noun* movement horizontally **x-Richtung**

◇ **X distance** *noun* distance along an X-axis from an origin **Entfernung auf der x-Achse**

xerographic printer printer (such as a photocopier) where charged ink is attracted to areas of a charged picture **xerographischer Drucker**

◇ **xerography** *noun* copying method that relies on ink being attracted to dark regions of a charged picture **Xerographie**

Xerox
1 *noun*
(a) trademark for a type of photocopier **Xerox (Xerokopiergerät);** *to make a xerox copy of a letter; we must order some more xerox paper for the copier; we are having a new xerox machine installed tomorrow*
(b) photocopy made with a xerox machine **Xerokopie;** *to send the other party a xerox of the contract; we have sent xeroxes to each of the agents*
2 *verb* to make a photocopy with a xerox machine **xerokopieren;** *to xerox a document; she xeroxed all the files*

x punch *noun* card punch for column 11, often used to represent a negative number **x-Lochung**

X-ray *noun*
(a) ray with a very short length, which is invisible, but can go through soft tissue and register as a photograph on a film **Röntgenstrahl; X-ray imaging** = showing images of the inside of a body using X-rays **Röntgen**
(b) photograph taken using X-rays **Röntgenbild;** *the medical text is illustrated with X-ray photographs*

X-series *noun* recommendations for data communications over public data networks **x-Serie**

X-Y *noun* coordinates for drawing a graph, where X is the vertical and Y the horizontal value **x/y-Koordinaten; X-Y plotter** = device for drawing lines on paper between given coordinates **Koordinatenschreiber, Plotter**

Yy

yaw *noun* rotation of satellite about a vertical axis with the earth **Gieren**

Y-axis *noun* vertical axis of a graph **y-Achse, Ordinate(nachse)**

◇ **Y-coordinate** *noun* vertical axis position coordinate **y-Koordinate, Ordinate**

◇ **Y-direction** *noun* vertical movement **y-Richtung**

Y-distance *noun* distance along an Y-axis from an origin **Entfernung auf der y-Achse**

yoke *noun* **deflection yoke** = magnetic coils around a TV tube used to control the position of the picture beam **Ablenkjoch**

y punch *noun* card punch for column 12 (often used to indicate a positive number) **y-Lochung**

Zz

Z = IMPEDANCE

zap *verb* to wipe off all data currently in the workspace **löschen**; *he pressed CONTROL Z and zapped all the text*

z-axis *noun* axis for depth in a three-dimensional graph *or* plot **z-Achse**

zero
1 *noun* (i) the digit 0; (ii) equivalent of logical off or false state **(i) & (ii) Null**; *the code for international calls is zero one zero (010)*; **jump on zero** = conditional jump executed if a flag *or* register is zero **Sprungbefehl bei Null; zero compression** *or* **zero suppression** = shortening of a file by the removal of unnecessary zeros **Nullenunterdrückung; zero**

flag = indicator that the contents of a register *or* result is zero **Nullkennzeichnung**; *the jump on zero instruction tests the zero flag;* **zero-level address** *or* **immediate address** = instruction in which the address is the operand **virtuelle Adresse**
2 *verb* to erase *or* clear a file **löschen; to zero a device** = to erase the contents of a programmable device **einen Zusatz löschen; to zero fill** = to fill a section of memory with zero values **mit Nullen auffüllen**

◇ **zero insertion force (ZIF)** *noun* chip socket that has movable connection terminals, allowing the chip to be inserted with no force, then a small lever is turned to grip the legs of the chip **Nullkraftstecker**

ZIF = ZERO INSERTION FORCE

zip code *noun* (*US*) numbers used to indicate a postal delivery area in an address on an envelope **Postleitzahl**
NOTE: the GB English for this is **post code**

zone *noun* region *or* part of a screen defined for specialized printing **Zone; hot zone** = text area to the left of the right margin in a word-processed document, if a word does not fit completely into the line, a hyphen is automatically inserted **Ausschließzone, Bereich um die weiche Trennfuge**

zoom *verb* (i) to change the focal length of a lens to enlarge (or reduce) the object in the viewfinder; (ii) to enlarge an area of text (to make it easier to work on) **(i) zoomen; (ii) vergrößern**

◇ **zooming** *noun* enlarging an area of text *or* graphics **Vergrößern**; *variable zooming from 25% to 400% of actual size*

◇ **zoom lens** *noun* lens whose focal length can be varied to make an object larger in the viewfinder **Zoom(objektiv)**

QUOTE there are many options to allow you to zoom into an area for precision work
Electronics & Wireless World
QUOTE any window can be zoomed to full-screen size by pressing the F-5 function key
Byte

Deutsch-Englisches
Register

Aa

abändern: *alter; modify*

Abänderung: *modification*

Abbild: *image; map*

abbilden: *map*

Abbildung: *chart; figure; plate*

Abbildungen: *visuals*

Abbildungsverarbeitung: *image processing*

abblenden: *fade out*

abbrechen: *abort; cancel; terminate*

Abbremszeit: *stop time*

Abbruch: *hangup; termination* anormaler ~ *abnormal end or abend or abnormal termination*

Abbruchfehler: unkorrigierbarer ~ *fatal error*

Abbruchmaske: *interrupt mask*

Abdeckhaube: *dustcover*

Abdeckmittel: *resist*

Abenteuerspiel: *adventure game*

Aberration: *aberration* sphärische ~ *spherical aberration*

Abfall: *decrease; garbage*

abfallen: *decay; drop*

Abfrage: *inquiry; interrogation; query* kombinierte ~ *relational query*

Abfragebearbeitung: *query processing*

Abfragemethode: binäre ~ *binary look-up*

Abfrage mittels Beispiel: *query by example (QBE)*

Abfragemöglichkeit: *query facility*

Abfrageschalter: *sampler*

Abfragesprache: *query language (QL)*

Abfragestation: *inquiry station*

abgerundet: *in round figures*

abgeschlossen: *complete*

abgleichen: *match*

Abgrenzung: *delimiter; demarcation*

abhängig: *dependent*

Abhöranlage: *wire tap*

Abkürzung: *abbreviation*

Ablage: *filing*

Ablagekorb: *filing basket or filing tray*

Ablagesystem: *filing system* elektronisches ~ *electronic filing*

Ablauf: *expiration; run* überwachter ~ *attended operation*

Ablaufanzeiger: *run indicator*

ablaufen: *expire; pass*

Ablauflinie: *flowline*

Ablaufrichtung: *flow direction*

Ablaufsteuerung: *sequencer*

ablegen: *deposit*

Ablegesatz: *dead matter*

ableiten: sich ~ von *derive*

Ableitungsgraph: *derivation graph*

ablenken: *deflect*

Ablenkjoch: *deflection yoke*

Ablesewert: *reading*

ablösen: *supersede*

Abmachung: *deal*

Abmelden: *logging off*

abmelden: sich ~ *to log off or log out; to sign off*

Abnahme: *acceptance*

Abnahmeprüfung: *acceptance test or testing*

abnehmen: *decay; decrease*

abrollen: *scroll*

Abruf: *attention; fetch* selektiver ~ *selective calling*

Abruf auf Anforderung: *demand fetching*

Abruf-Ausführ-Zyklus: *fetch-execute cycle*

Abrufbefehl: *fetch instruction*

abrufen: *call up; poll*

Abrufphase: *fetch phase*

Abrufsignal: *fetch signal*

Abruftaste: *attention key*

Abrufunterbrechung: *attention interruption*

Abrufzyklus: *fetch cycle*

abrunden: *to round down; to round off*

Abrundung: *rounding*

Abrundungsfehler: *round off errors*

Absatz: ohne ~ drucken *run on*

abschalten: *disconnect; shut down*

Abschaltmechanismus: *shut-off mechanism*

abschätzen: *rate; size*

abschießen: *launch*

abschirmen: *screen; shield*

Abschirmung: *shield* magnetische ~ *magnetic screen*

abschließen: *finish*

Abschluß: *completion; ending* unplanmäßiger ~ *disorderly close-down*

Abschneidefehler: *truncation error*

Abschneiden: *truncation*

abschneiden: *cut off; perform; truncate*

Abschnitt: *section*

Abschnitte: in ~ unterteilen *segment*

Abschuß: *launch*

abschwächen: *attenuate*

Abschwächung: *attenuation*

Absender: *sender*

Absicht: *objective*

Absolutwert: *absolute value*

Absolutzahl mit Vorzeichenziffer: *sign and modulus*

absorbieren: *absorb*

Absorption: *absorption* atmosphärische ~ *atmospheric absorption*

Absorptionsfilter: *absorption filter*

Absorptionskonstante: *absorptance*

Absorptionsverlust: *ground absorption*

abspielen: *play back*

Abspielnadel: *stylus*

Abstand: halber ~ *half space*

abstimmen: *adjust; tune*

Abstimmung: *adjustment* geräuschfreie ~ *interstation muting*

abstreichen: *truncate*
Abstreifer: *wiper*
Abstrich: *down stroke*
Absturz: *crash*
abstürzen: *bomb (informal); crash*
absturzgesichert: *crash-protected*
Abszisse: *X-coordinate*
Abszissenachse: *horizontal axis; X-axis*
Abtastauflösungsvermögen: *scanning resolution*
Abtastbereich: *scan area*
Abtasten: *scanning*
abtasten: *sample; scan*
Abtaster: *sampler; scanner* optischer ~ *bar-code reader or optical scanner*
Abtastfehler: *scanning error*
Abtastfleck: *scanning spot*
Abtastgerät: *scanning device* optisches ~ *optical scanner*
Abtastgeschwindigkeit: *sampling or scanning rate; scanning speed*
Abtastintervall: *sampling interval*
Abtastlänge: *scan length*
Abtastspeicherbereich: *scanner memory*
Abtast- und Haltekreis: *sample and hold circuit*
Abtastung: *scan; television scan* punktförmige ~ *scanning spot beam*
Abtastzeile: *scanning line*
Abtippen von Dokumenten: *copy typing*
Abtretende(r): *assignor*
Abtretung: *assignment*
Abwanderung: *drift*
abwärts: *downward*
Abwärtskompatibilität: *downward compatibility*
abwechselnd: *alternate; alternately*
Abweichung: *divergence* chromatische ~ *chromatic aberration*
abziehen: *deduct*
Abzug: *print*
achromatisch: *achromatic*
Achse: *axis*
Acht-Bit-Byte: *eight-bit byte or octet*
Achtung Unterbrechung: *attention interruption*
Ackermann-Funktion: *Ackerman's function*
ADA: *ADA*
Adapter: *adapter or adaptor*
Adapter zum Hauptrechner: *host adapter*
Addiereinrichtung: *adder*
addieren: *add*
Addierer: binärer ~ *binary adder*
Addierer mit Parallelübertrag: *carry look ahead*
Addition: *addition* löschende ~ *destructive addition*
Addition ohne Übertrag: *addition without carry*
Additionsregister: *add register*
Additionszeit: *add time; addition time*
Administrator: *administrator*
Adreßabbild: *address mapping*
Adreßänderung: *address modification*

Adressat: *addressee*
Adreßbereich: privater ~ *private address space*
Adreßbuch: *directory; street directory*
Adreßbus: *address bus*
Adreßbusleitung: *bus address lines*
Adresse: *address* absolute ~ *absolute or actual or explicit or machine or specific address* aktuelle ~ *current address* direkte ~ *one-level address* effektive ~ *effective address* errechnete ~ *generated or synthetic address* indizierte ~ *indexed address* relative ~ *relative address* symbolische ~ *floating or floating symbolic or symbolic address* tatsächliche ~ *actual or absolute address* unmodifizierte ~ *presumptive address* virtuelle ~ *virtual or zero-level or immediate address*
Adressendecodierer: *address decoder*
Adressenende: *end of address (EOA)*
Adressenliste: *address list*
Adressenregister: *address register*
Adressenspur: *address track*
Adressenvielfachleitung: *address highway*
Adressenzugriffszeit: *address access time*
Adreßfeld: *address field*
Adreßfolgeregister: *sequence control register (SCR) or sequence counter or sequence register or instruction address register*
Adreßformat: *address format*
adressierbar: *addressable*
Adressierbarkeit: *addressability*
Adressierebene: *addressing level*
adressieren: *address*
Adressierkapazität: *addressing capacity*
Adressiermaschine: *addressing machine*
Adressiermethode: *addressing method*
Adressierung: *addressing* absolute ~ *absolute addressing* ausgesetzte ~ *deferred addressing* direkte ~ *direct addressing* erweiterte ~ *augmented addressing* indirekte ~ *indirect addressing; deferred addressing; second-level addressing* indizierte ~ *indexed addressing* relative ~ *base addressing* unmittelbare ~ *immediate addressing*
Adressierungsart: *addressing mode*
Adreßimpulseingang: *address strobe*
Adreßliste: *mailing list* eine ~ erwerben *to buy a mailing list*
Adreßmarke: *address mark*
Adreßmodifikation: *address modification*
Adreßraum: *address space*
Adreßrechnung: *address computation*
Adreßregister: *program address counter; address register* aktuelles ~ *current address register (CAR)*
Adreßwort: *address word*
affirmativ: *affirmative*
Akkumulator(register): *accumulator or AC (register)*
akkurat: *accurate(ly)*
Akronym: *acronym*
Akte: *file*
Aktendeckel: *folder*

Aktenkopie: *file copy*
Aktenordner: *file* **kastenförmiger** ~ *box file*
Aktenschrank: *filing cabinet*
Aktentaschencomputer: *lapheld computer or laptop computer; portable*
Aktion: *action*
Aktionsfeld: *action field*
Aktionsnachricht: *action message*
Aktionsrahmen: *action frame*
Aktionszyklus: *action cycle*
aktiv: *active* **nicht** ~ *inactive*
aktivieren: *activate; enable; execute*
Aktivität: *activity*
Aktivvorrichtung: *active device*
aktuell: *current*
Akustik: *acoustics*
Akustikkoppler: *acoustic coupler*
akustisch: *acoustic; audible; sonic*
Akut: *acute accent*
Akzent: *accent* **gleitender** ~ *floating accent; piece accent* **mit** ~ *accented*
akzeptabel: *acceptable*
akzeptieren: *accept*
Akzidenzdrucker: *jobbing printer*
Akzidenzdruckerei: *print shop*
Albumin: *albumen plate*
Algebra: *algebra*
algorithmisch: *algorithmic*
Algorithmus: *algorithm*
Alleinvertretungsvereinbarung: *exclusive agreement*
allgemein: *general; universal*
Allgemeinsoftware: *common software*
allgemein zugänglich: *on general release*
allmählich einführen: *to phase in*
Allophon: *allophone*
Alphabet: *alphabet*
Alpha-Beta-Technik: *alpha beta technique*
alphabetisch: *alphabetically*
alphabetisch ordnen: *alphabetize; alphasort*
alphafotografisch: *alphaphotographic*
alphageometrisch: *alphageometric*
Alphamosaik-: *alphamosaic*
Alphawindung: *alpha wrap*
alternativ: *alternative*
Alternative: *alternative*
Alternativmodus: *alternate mode*
Alternativweg: *alternate route*
alternieren: *alternate*
alternierend: *alternate(ly)*
A-MAC: *A-MAC*
Ampere: *amp or ampere (A)*
Amplitude: *amplitude*
Amplitudenmodulation: *amplitude modulation (AM)*
Amplituden-Quantisierung: *amplitude quantization*
Amplitudenverzerrung: *amplitude distortion*

Amtswahl: *direct outward dialling*
Analog-: *analog or analogue*
Analogaufzeichnung: *analog recording*
Analogdarstellung: *analog representation*
Analog-Digital-Umsetzer: *analog to digital converter (ADC or A to D converter)*
Analog-Digital-Umwandlung: *analog to digital (A to D or A/D)*
Analogkanal: *analog channel*
Analogmultimeter: *analog multimeter (AMM)*
Analogrechner: *analog computer*
Analogschaltelement: *analog gate*
analphabetisch: *illiterate*
Analysator: *analyzer*
Analyse: *analysis* **lexikalische** ~ *lexical analysis* **numerische** ~ *numerical analysis*
analysieren: *analyse or analyze*
Analytiker: *analyst*
Anbieter: **steckerkompatibler** ~ *PCM*
andauernd: *continuous*
ändern: *alter*
anders: *alien; different*
Änderung: *alteration*
Änderungsband: *change tape*
Änderungsdatei: *change file*
Änderungssatz: *amendment record; change record; change or transaction record*
andeuten: *to block in*
Andruckposition: *imprint position*
Andruckpresse: *proofer*
Andruckrad: *pinchwheel*
Anerkennung: *acknowledgements*
Anerkennungsurkunde: *certificate of approval*
Anfang: *beginning; head; origin*
Anfang des Kopfes: *start of header*
Anfang des Textes: *start-of-text (SOT or STX)*
anfangen: **neu** ~ *redo*
Anfangs-: *initial*
Anfangsadresse: *initial address; stack base*
Anfangsadressierung: *inherent addressing*
Anfangsbedingung: *initial condition*
Anfangsbuchstabe: *initial*
Anfangsfehler: *initial error*
Anfangskennsatz: *header; header label*
Anfangskurve: *attack envelope*
Anfangssatz: *home record*
Anfangswert: *initial value*
Anfertigung: *origination*
Anfertigung von Korrekturabzügen: *proofing*
anfordern: *request*
Anforderung: *enquiry; request*
Anforderungen: **den** ~ **entsprechend** *up to standard*
Anfrage: *inquiry*
Anfragecode: *inquiry character (ENQ)*
Anfrageverarbeitung: *query processing*
anfügen: *append*
anführen: *head*

Anführungszeichen: *inverted comma(s); quotes; double quotes; quotation marks* **einfache** ~ *single quotes*

angeben: *specify*

angegeben: wie ~ *as per specification*

angegliedert: *affiliated*

Angelegenheit: *matter*

Angestellte(r): leitende(r) ~ *executive*

angetrieben: *driven; powered*

Angleichung: *adjustment*

angliedern: *affiliate*

angrenzend: *adjacent; contiguous*

Angström: *angstrom*

anhalten: *halt; hold; stop*

Anhalt- und Warteprotokoll: *stop and wait protocol*

Anhang: *appendix*

anhängen: *append*

anhäufen: *accumulate*

anheben: *boost; pre-emphasise*

Anheber: *lifter*

Animation: *animation*

animieren: *animate*

ankommend: *incoming*

Anlage: *equipment; installation*

Anlaufzeit: *acceleration time; rise time*

anlegen: *lay in*

Anmelden: *logging on*

anmelden: sich ~ *to log in or log on; to sign on*

Anmeldesequenz: *logon sequence*

Anmeldung: automatische ~ *auto-login or auto-logon; automatic log on*

Anmerkung: *annotation*

annähernd: *approximate(ly); approximating*

Annäherungswert: *approximation*

annehmbar: *acceptable*

annehmen: *accept*

Anode: *anode*

anordnen: *format*

Anordnung: *array* **chronologische** ~ *chronological order* **lexikographische** ~ *lexicographical order*

Anordnung einer Zeichenkette: *string array*

anormal: *abnormal; abnormally*

anpassen: *adapt; interface*

Anpassungsfähigkeit: *adaptation*

Anpassungstransformator: *matching transformer*

Anreiz: *event*

anreizgesteuert: *event-driven*

Anruf: *call; calling*

Anrufablenker: *call diverter*

Anrufaufzeichner: *call logger*

Anrufaufzeichnung: *call logging; voice messaging* **automatische** ~ *automatic message accounting*

Anrufbeantworter: automatischer ~ *answering machine; answerphone; telephone answering machine*

Anrufbeantworterbüro: *answering service*

Anrufbeantwortung: automatische ~ *auto-answer*

Anrufdauer: *call duration*

Anrufe aufzeichnen: *to log calls*

Anrufeinrichtung: automatische ~ *automatic calling unit (ACU)*

anrufen: *call; call in; ring*

Anrufer: *caller*

Anrufsignal: *ring indicator (RI)*

Anrufumleiter: *call diverter*

Anrufumleitung: *call forwarding*

Anschauen: zeitversetztes ~ *time shift viewing*

Anschlagbestätigung: *keystroke verification*

Anschlagdrucker: *impact printer*

anschlagen: *hit*

Anschlagetafel: *notice board*

Anschlagsklicken: *key click*

Anschlagzahl: *keystroke count*

anschließen: *attach*

Anschluß: *attachment; connector; continuity*

Anschlußblock: *terminal block*

Anschlußbuchse: *female connector*

Anschlußgerät: *peripheral; peripheral unit*

Anschlußgeräte: *peripheral equipment*

Anschlußkarte: *adapter card*

Anschlußleitung: *access line*

Anschlußprozessor: *attached processor*

Anschlußstecker: *connector*

Anschlußstelle: port serielle ~ *serial port*

Anschlußstifte: gereihte ~ *inline*

Anschlußteil: *interfacing*

Anschlußwahlschalter: *port selector*

Anschlußwerte-Meßmethode: *kiloVolt-ampere output rating (KVA)*

ansehen: *view*

Ansicht: zur ~ *on approval*

ANSI-Tastatur: *ANSI keyboard*

ansprechen auf: *register*

Ansprechzeit: *access time*

Ansteckmikrophon: *lapel microphone*

Anstellung: *staff appointment*

Anstieg: prozentualer ~ *percentage increase*

Antenne: *aerial; antenna* **raumfeste** ~ *de-spun antenna* **scharfbündelnde** ~ *spot beam*

Antennengruppierung: *antenna array*

Antennenverstärkung: *antenna gain*

anti-: *anti-*

Antiqua: *roman*

Antivalenz: *symmetric difference*

Antivalenzfunktion: *non-equivalence function (NEQ)*

Antivalenzglied: *anticoincidence circuit or function; non-equivalence gate*

Antrag: *application*

Antragsformular: *application form*

antreiben: *drive*

Antriebsspindel: *spindle*

Antwort: *answer; answer back; response* **positive ~** *positive response*

antworten: *answer*

Antwortrahmen: *response frame*

Antwortzeit: *response time*

anwählen: *dial into*

Anwählen: blindes ~ *blind dialling*

anwärmen: *warm up*

anweisen: *assign; order*

Anweiser: *assignor*

Anweisung: *order; statement* **bedingte ~** *conditional statement* **leere ~** *blank or null or dummy or waste instruction* **nicht ausführbare ~** *non-operable instruction* **zusammengesetzte ~** *compound statement*

Anweisungen: bedingte ~ *control*

Anweisungen im Hintergrund: *talkback*

Anweisung ohne Adresse: *no-address operation*

Anweisungscodeprozessor: *order code processor*

Anweisungsnummer: *statement number*

Anwendung: *application*

Anwendungsprogramm: *applications software or applications program*

Anwendungsprogrammierer: *applications programmer*

Anwendungsprogrammpaket: *applications package*

Anwendungsschicht: *application layer*

Anwendungssoftware: *applications software*

Anwendungssoftwarepaket: *applications package*

Anwendungsterminal: *applications terminal*

anwesend sein: *attend*

Anzeige: *readout* **alphanumerische ~** *alphanumeric display* **wandernde ~** *marching display*

Anzeigebit: *indicator flag*

Anzeigeformat: *display format*

Anzeigelicht: *indicator light*

Anzeigemodus: *display mode*

anzeigen: *display; indicate*

Anzeigenadel: *stylus*

Anzeiger: *flag; indicator*

Anzeigerdiagramm: *indicator chart*

Anzeigeregister: *condition code register; display register*

Anzeigetafel: elektronische ~ *electronic blackboard*

Anzeigevorrichtung: *readout device*

Apertur: effektive ~ *effective aperture*

Aperturflächenausleuchtung: *aperture illumination*

Apogäum: *apogee*

Apostroph: *apostrophe*

Äquator: *equator*

Äquivalenz: *equivalence*

Äquivalenz-Funktion: *equivalence function or operation*

Äquivalenzglied: *equivalence gate*

Arbeit: *work*

arbeiten: *operate; work*

Arbeitgeberverband: *employers' organization*

Arbeitsabschnitt: *session*

Arbeitsauftrag: *job*

Arbeitsband: *scratch tape*

Arbeitsbelastung: *work load; workload*

Arbeitsbereich: *work area; workspace*

Arbeitsdatei: *scratch file or work file*

Arbeitsgang: *operation; pass*

Arbeitsgangpriorität: *operation priority*

Arbeitsplatte: *work disk*

Arbeitsplatz: *workstation; workplace*

Arbeitsspeicher: *working store or scratch pad*

Arbeitsspeicherbereich: *partition*

Arbeitsteilung: *work-sharing*

Arbeitsweise: sequentielle ~ *sequential operation* **serielle ~** *serial operation*

Arbeitswiederholung: *duplication of work*

Arbeitswissenschaft: *ergonomics*

Arbeitszeit: gleitende ~ *flexible working hours*

Archetyp: *archetype*

Architektur: *architecture*

Archiv: *archive*

Archivdatei: *archive file*

archivieren: *archive*

Archivierungsqualität: *archival quality*

Archivkopie: *archived copy*

Archivspeicherung: *archive storage*

argumentieren: *argue*

Arithmetik: *arithmetic*

Array-Prozessor: *array processor*

Art der Schaltungstechnik: *logic*

Artikel: *article*

Art und Weise: *mode*

ASA: *ASA*

ASCII-Code: *American Standard Code for Information Interchange (ASCII)*

ASCII-Datei: *ASCII file*

ASCII-Tastatur: *ASCII keyboard*

ASCII-Zeichen: *ASCII character*

Aspekt: *aspect*

Aspektkarte: *aspect card*

Aspektsystem: *aspect system*

ASR-Tastatur: *ASR keyboard*

Assemblerliste: *assembly listing*

Assemblerprogramm: *assembler; assembly (language) program*

assemblieren: *assemble*

Assemblierer: *language processor* **absoluter ~** *absolute assembler*

Assemblierer-Fehlermeldungen: *assembler error messages*

Assemblersprache: *assembly language or assembler language; base language*

Assistent: *assistant* **persönlicher ~** *personal assistant*

assistieren: *assist*

Assoziativadressierung: *associative addressing or content-addressable addressing*

Assoziativdatei: *content-addressable file or location*

Assoziativprozessor: *associative processor*

Assoziativschnitt: *associational editing*

Assoziativspeicher: *associative memory or storage; content-addressable memory (CAM)*

Assoziativspeicherregister: *associative storage register*

assoziiert: *associate*

Astigmatismus: *astigmatism*

α-Strahlen: *alpha radiation*

asynchron: *asynchronous*

Asynchronanschlußstelle: *asynchronous port*

Asynchronrechner: *asynchronous computer*

Asynchronübertragung: *asynchronous mode*

α-Teilchen: *alpha-particle*

Atmosphäre: *atmosphere*

atmosphärisch: *atmospheric*

Atom: *atom*

Atom-: *atomic*

Atomuhr: *atomic clock*

Attrappe: *mock-up*

Attribut: *attribute*

ätzen: *etch*

Ätztype: *etch type*

audio-: *audio*

audioaktiv: *audio active*

audiovisuell: *audiovisual (AV)*

Auf-/Abzähler: *up/down counter*

Aufbau: *architecture; layout* **objektorientierter ~** *object or object-orientated architecture*

aufbauen: *set up*

aufbereiten: *edit*

Aufbereitungsfenster: *edit window*

Aufbereitungslauf: *editing run*

Aufbereitungssymbol: *editing symbol*

aufdecken: *detect; reveal*

aufeinander abstimmen: *coordinate*

aufeinanderfolgend: *consecutive(ly); sequential; successive*

aufeinander wirken: *interact*

auffächern: *fan*

Auffächerung: *fan*

auffordern: *invite*

Aufforderung: *enquiry*

auffüllen: *fill; pad*

Auffüllen: *padding*

Auffüllzeichen: *pad character*

Aufgabe: *assignment; load; task*

Aufgabe niedriger Priorität: *low-priority work*

Aufgabensteuerung: *task management*

aufgerundet: *in round figures*

aufhalten: *block; delay*

aufhängen: *hang*

Aufkleber: *external label*

aufladbar: *chargeable*

Aufladung: statische ~ *static*

Auflage: *circulation; edition; impression; printrun* **kleine ~** *short-run*

Auflagenziffer: *circulation*

auflegen: *hang up*

auflisten: *list*

Auflistung: *listing*

Auflistung des Originaltextes: *source listing*

Auflistung des Ursprungsprogramms: *source listing*

Auflösung: *definition* **digitale ~** *digital resolution* **hohe ~** *high resolution (hi-res)* **niedrige ~** *low resolution (low-res)*

Auflösungsgrenze: *limiting resolution*

Auflösungsvermögen: *resolution; resolving power*

Auflösungsvermögen eines Graphikbildschirms: *graphic display resolution*

Aufmerksamkeit: *attention*

Aufnahme: *recording* **digitalisierte photographische ~** *digitized photograph*

Aufnahmegerät: *recorder*

Aufnahmespule: *pickup reel*

Aufnahmetaste: *record button*

aufnehmen: *shoot*

Aufprojektion: *front projection; matt or matte*

aufrechnen: *accumulate*

aufrechterhalten: *sustain*

aufrollen: *scroll*

Aufruf: *cue; invitation; recall* **rekursiver ~** *recursive call*

Aufrufbefehl: *call instruction*

Aufruf eines Unterprogramms: *subroutine call*

aufrufen: *call; contact bounce; invite; invoke; recall*

Aufruffolge von Unterprogrammen: *calling sequence*

Aufrufliste: *polling list*

Aufrufzeitaufwand: *polling overhead*

aufrunden: *to round off; to round up*

Aufrundungsfehler: *round off errors*

aufrüsten: *upgrade*

aufsaugen: *absorb*

aufschließen: *close up*

Aufschwung: *boom* **einen ~ nehmen** *boom*

Aufschwungindustrie: *boom industry*

Aufsichtsperson: *supervisor*

Aufsichtsrat: *board; board of directors*

Aufstellung: tabellarische ~ *tabulation*

aufteilen: *partition*

Aufteilung in Speicherseiten: *paging*

Auftreffen: *impact*

Auftreten von Fahnen: *hangover*

Auftrieb: *boost*

aufwärts kompatibel: *upwards compatible or upward compatible (US)*

Aufwendungen: außerordentliche ~ *below-the-line expenditure*

Aufwickelspule: *take-up reel*

Aufzeichnen: *logging; recording*
aufzeichnen: *record*
Aufzeichnung: detaillierte ~ *detailed account* **magnetische ~** *magnetic recording* **digitale optische ~** *digital optical recording (DOR)*
Aufzeichnungsdichte: *packing density; storage density*
Augend: *augend*
aural: *aural*
ausbalancieren: *balance*
Ausblendbefehl: *extract instruction*
ausblenden: *cross fade*
ausbreiten: sich ~ *propagate*
Ausbrennen: *burn out*
ausdenken: sich ~ *devise*
Ausdruck: *hard copy; expression* **logischer ~** *logical expression*
ausdrucken: *print out*
ausdrücken: *express*
Auseinandersetzung: *argument*
Ausfall: *breakdown; drop out; failure; outage* **induzierter ~** *induced failure*
Ausfallabstand: mittlerer ~ *mean time between failures (MTBF)*
ausfallen: *break down; fail*
Ausfallrate: *failure rate*
Ausfallzeit: *down time; fault time*
Ausfallzeit mangels Sonnenlicht: *sun outage*
Ausfertigung: in doppelter ~ *in duplicate* **in vierfacher ~** *in quadruplicate*
ausführen: *execute; perform* **immer wieder ~** *cycle*
Ausführung: *execution* **gefahrfreie ~** *hazard-free implementation*
Ausführungsadresse: *execution address*
Ausführungsbefehl: *executive instruction*
Ausführungsbestimmung: *execute statement*
Ausführungsfehler: *execution error*
Ausführungsmodus: *execute mode*
Ausführungsphase: *execute phase; run phase*
Ausführungssignal: *execute signal*
Ausführungszeit: *execution time*
Ausführungszyklus: *execute cycle; execution cycle*
ausfüllen: *fill*
Ausgabe: *copy; output (o/p or O/P)* **alte ~** *back number*
Ausgabeanschlußpunkt: *output port*
Ausgabe auf Mikrofilm: *computer output on microfilm (COM); electron beam recording (EBR)*
Ausgabebereich: *output area or block*
Ausgabedatei: *output file*
Ausgabeformatierer: *output formatter*
ausgabegebunden: *output bound or limited*
Ausgabegerät: *output device*
Ausgabekarte: analoge ~ *analog output card*
Ausgabemodus: *output mode*
Ausgabe-Pufferregister: *output buffer register*
Ausgaberegister: *output register*

Ausgabestrom: *output stream*
Ausgang: *outlet*
Ausgangscode: *source code*
Ausgangsdaten: *raw data*
Ausgangslastfaktor: *fan-out*
Ausgangsprodukt: *basic product*
Ausgangsstelle: *exit point*
Ausgangsstellung: *home*
ausgeben: *output (o/p or O/P)*
ausgefallen: *down*
ausgefranst: *ragged*
Ausgeglichenheit: *balance*
ausgehend von: *based on*
ausgenommen: *excluding*
ausgerichtet: nicht ~ *unjustified*
Ausgewogenheit: *balance*
ausgleichen: *balance; equalize*
Ausgleichsstreifen: *balance stripe*
Ausgleichszahl: *offset*
Auslandsvorwahl: *international dialling code*
Auslassungszeichen: *caret mark or sign*
auslaufen: *finish*
auslaufen lassen: *to phase out*
Auslesen: löschendes ~ *destructive readout; DRO* **nichtlöschendes ~** *non-destructive readout (NDR)*
Ausleuchtung: *aperture illumination*
Auslöschung: *destructive interference*
Ausmaß: *dimension; magnitude*
Ausmerzung von Softwarefehlern: *bug patches*
Ausnahme: *exception*
Ausnahmebericht: *exception report*
Ausnahmelexikon: *exception dictionary*
auspacken: *unpack*
ausrichten: *align; range*
Ausrichtung: *alignment*
Ausrichtungsnadel: *alignment pin*
Ausrichtungstransportbahn: *aligner*
ausrücken: *outdent*
Ausrufezeichen: *exclamation mark*
Aussagewahrscheinlichkeit: *confidence level*
ausschalten: *disable; switch off; turn off*
ausschlagen: *peg*
ausschließen: *bar; eliminate; exclude; justify*
Ausschließen: quadding **das ~ verbieten** *justify inhibit*
ausschließlich: *exclusive*
ausschließlich zugeordnet: *dedicated*
Ausschließung: *exclusion*
Ausschließzone: *hot zone; soft zone*
Ausschluß: *exclusion*
Ausschlußklausel: *exclusion clause*
ausschneiden: *clip*
Ausschnitt: *window*
Aussehen: *aspect; finish*
Außenarbeit: *field work*
Außenaufnahmen: *location shots*

aussenden: *emit; radiate*
Außendienst: im ~ *in the field* **technischer ~** *customer engineering*
Außendiensttechniker: *field engineer*
Außendienstverkaufsleiter: *field sales manager*
Außenstation: aufgabenorientierte ~ *job orientated terminal*
Außenstelle: *remote console or device; tributary station*
außer: *except; excluding*
Außerbandsignalisierung: *out of band signalling*
außergewöhnich: *exceptional*
außerhalb: *external*
äußerst: *extremely*
aussortieren: *screen*
ausspeichern: *roll-out*
Aussperrung: *lockout*
ausstatten: *equip*
Ausstattung: *equipment*
Ausstellungsmaterial: *display material*
Aussteuerbereich: *dynamic range*
Aussteuerungsautomatik: *automatic gain control (AGC)*
ausstrahlen: *broadcast; emit; radiate*
Ausstrahlung: *radiation*
Austasten: *blanking*
Austastlücke: *blanking interval*
Austausch: *exchange; interchange; substitution*
austauschbar: *exchangeable; interchangeable*
austauschen: *change; exchange; interchange; replace; swap*
Austauschfunktion: globale ~ *global exchange*
Austestung: symbolische ~ *symbolic debugging*
Auswahl: *menu selection; range*
auswählbar: *generic; selectable*
auswählen: *select*
Auswählen: *selection*
Auswahlfunktion: *selectable attributes*
Auswahlmöglichkeit: *option*
Auswahlsortierung: *selective sort*
Auswahlsortierverfahren: *tree selection sort*
auswechselbar: *exchangeable; removable*
Ausweichleitweg: *alternate route*
Ausweichmodus: *alternate mode*
Ausweichmöglichkeit: *alternative*
Ausweisleser: *badge reader*
auswerten: *evaluate; interpret*
Auswertung: *evaluation*
auswirken: sich ~ auf *affect*
Auswirkung: *impact*
auszeichnen: *mark up*
authentifizieren: *authenticate*
Authentifizierung: *authentication*
authentisch: *authentic*
auto-: *auto*
Automat: *automatic; automatic vending machine; dispenser*
automatisch: *auto; automatic; automatically*

automatisieren: *automate*
Automatisierung: *automation*
autonom: *stand-alone or standalone*
Autor: *author*
autorisieren: *authorize*
autorisiert: *authorized*
Autotypieverfahren: *halftone process or halftoning*
Avalanche-Diode: *avalanche photodiode (APD)*
AZERTY-Tastatur: *azerty or AZERTY keyboard*
Azetat: *acetate*
Azimut: *azimuth*

Bb

B1-Komplement: *diminished radix complement*
Backus-Naur-Form: *Backus-Naur-Form (BNF)* **erweiterte ~** *extended BNF (EBNF)*
Balken: *bar*
Balkencode: *bar code; universal product code (UPC)*
Balkencodeleser: *bar-code reader; optical bar reader or optical wand*
Balkendiagramm: *bar chart or bar graph*
Balkenüberschrift: *banner*
Band: *band; floppy tape or tape streamer; ribbon tape* **leeres ~** *blank tape or blank disk* **nicht justiertes ~** *unjustified tape or idiot tape*
Bandanfangsmarke: *beginning of tape (bot) marker*
bandbegrenzt: *bandlimited*
Bandbibliothek: *tape library*
Bandbreite: effektive ~ *effective bandwidth*
Bandcode: *tape code*
Banddrucker: *band printer*
Bandende: *end of tape*
Bandfilter: *bandpass filter*
Bandformat: *tape format*
Bandführung: *tape guide*
Bandgerät: *tape unit*
Bandkabel: *tape cable or ribbon cable*
Bandkennzeichnung: *tape label*
Bandkopf: *tape head*
Bandladepunkt: *tape loadpoint*
Bandlaufwerk: *tape deck; tape drive*
Bandlese-/schreibkopf: *tape head*
Bandmaß: *tape measure*
Bandpaß: *bandpass filter*
Bandtransport: *tape transport*
Bandvorsatz: *tape header*
Bandzählwerk: *tape counter*
Bandzeitgeber: *tape timer*
Bandzuteilung: *band allocation*
Bank: *bank*
Bankauswahl: *bank switching*
Bankpostpapier: *bond paper*

Bargeldautomat: *cash dispenser*

Bargeldkarte: *cash card*

Barytpapier: *baryta paper*

BASIC: *Beginner's All-Purpose Symbolic Instruction Code (BASIC)*

BASIC-Version: *integer BASIC*

Basis: *base; basis; radix*

Basisadresse: *base address*

Basisband: *base band*

Basisbandnetz: *base band local area network*

Basisdateien: *base*

Basiseinheit: *primitive*

Basisgewicht: *basic weight*

Basisregister: *base register*

Baß: *bass*

BAS-Signal: *video signal*

Baßlautsprecher: *bass driver or speaker*

Baßsignal: *bass signal*

Baßwiedergabe: *bass response*

Batchbetrieb: *batch mode or batch processing*

Batchdatei: *batch file*

Batchregion: *batch region*

Batterie: *battery* mit ~ abgesichert *battery-backed* wiederaufladbare ~ *re-chargeable battery*

Batterieaufladen: *battery charging*

Batteriesicherung: *battery backup*

batterieunterstützt: *battery-backed*

Baud-Abtastung: automatische ~ *auto-baud scanning*

Baudot-Code: *baudot code*

Baudrate: *baud or baud rate* geteilte ~ *split baud rate*

Baudratenabfühler: automatischer ~ *auto-baud scanning or auto-baud sensing*

Baudratengenerator: *baud rate generator*

Bauelement: *device* integriertes ~ *integrated device*

Baukastenprinzip: nach dem ~ *modular*

Baum: *tree (structure)* binärer ~ *binary tree; heap*

Baumdiagramm: *sink tree*

Baumnetzsystem: *tree and branch network system*

Baumstruktur: *tree (structure)* gekettete ~ *threaded tree*

Baustein: *building block; module*

Bausteinauswahl: *chip select (CS)*

BCPL: *BCPL*

Beachtung schenken: *attend to*

beantragen: etwas ~ *apply*

beantworten: *answer; respond*

Beantwortungszeit: *answer time; response time*

bearbeiten: *manipulate*

Bearbeitung: *manipulation*

Bearbeitungsnummer: *batch number*

Bearbeitungszeit: *productive time; target or run phase*

Beauftragte(r): *representative*

bebildern: *illustrate*

Bedarfswartung: *remedial maintenance*

bedeuten: *mean; signify*

bedeutsam: *significant*

Bedeutung: *significance*

bedienen: *operate*

Bediener: *operator*

Bedienerkonsole: *control panel; operating console; operator's console*

Bedienung: *shop assistant*

Bedienungsanweisung: *operating instructions*

Bedienungspult: *system control panel*

Bedienungsreihenfolge: *operator precedence*

bedingt: *conditional*

Bedingung: *condition*

Bedingungen: atmosphärische ~ *atmospheric conditions*

beeinflussen: *affect*

beenden: *complete; end; exit; finish; quit; terminate*

befangen: *biased*

befassen: sich ~ mit *to deal with*

Befehl: *command; instruction; order* eingebetteter ~ *embedded command* endgültiger ~ *effective instruction* indizierter ~ *indexed instruction* symbolischer ~ *symbolic instruction* unmodifizierter ~ *presumptive instruction; unmodified instruction* unzulässiger ~ *illegal instruction*

Befehle: bevorrechtigte ~ *privileged instructions*

befehlen: *instruct*

Befehl „keine Operation": *no-op instruction*

Befehlsablauf: *instruction cycle*

Befehlsablaufzeit: *instruction cycle time*

Befehlsadresse: *instruction address*

Befehlsadreßregister: *instruction address register (IAR)*

Befehlsänderung: *instruction modification*

Befehlsaufforderung: *command prompt*

Befehlsausführungszeit: *instruction execution time*

Befehlsbereich: *code area; instruction area*

Befehlscode: *command code; order code*

Befehlscodeprozessor: *order code processor (OCP)*

Befehlsdatei: *command file*

Befehlsdateiprozessor: *command file processor*

Befehlsdecodierer: *instruction decoder*

Befehlseingabeformat: *command prompt*

Befehlsfenster: *command window*

Befehlsfolgeregister: *next instruction register; sequence control register (SCR)*

Befehlsformat: *instruction format*

Befehlskette: *command chain*

Befehlsprozessor: *instruction processor*

Befehlsregister: *command register; instruction register (IR)* aktuelles ~ *current instruction register (CIR)*

Befehlsschnellspeicher: *instruction cache*

Befehlsspeicher: *instruction storage*

Befehlsspeicherbereich: *instruction area*
Befehlssprache: *command language*
Befehlssteuersprache: *command control language*
Befehlsstruktur: *instruction format*
Befehlsvorauslese: *pre-fetch*
Befehlsvorrat: *instruction repertoire or set*
Befehlswort: *instruction word*
Befehlszähler: *instruction counter*
Befehlszeichen: *instruction character*
Befehlszeile: *command line*
befestigen: *attach; mount*
befinden: *sich ~ locate*
befördern: *transport*
befragen: *question*
Befugnis: *authority*
Begleitkarte: *inlay card*
begrenzen: *delimit*
Begrenzer: *limiter*
Begrenzungssymbol: *delimiter*
Behauptung: *assertion*
beherrschen: *master*
beidohrig: *binaural*
beilegen: *enclose*
Beirat: *board*
bejahend: *affirmative*
bekannt machen: *publicize*
Bel: *bel*
belasten: *load*
Belastung: *load* **angepaßte ~** *matched load*
Belastungsverteilung: *load sharing*
belaufen: *sich ~ auf to amount to*
beleben: *animate*
Beleg: *document*
Belegbearbeitung: *document processing*
Belegleser: *document reader*
belegt: *busy*
Belegwiederherstellung: *document recovery*
beleuchten: *illuminate*
Beleuchtung: *illumination*
Beleuchtungsstärke: *illuminance*
Beleuchtungstechniker: *lighting director*
Belichtungsreihe: *bracketing*
Bemerkung: *annotation*
benachbart: *adjacent*
benennen: *declare* **neu ~** *rename*
benutzen: *use* **etwas ~** *to make use of something*
Benutzer: *user* **berechtigter ~** *authorized user* **vom ~ auswählbar** *user-selectable*
Benutzeranschluß: *user port*
benutzerbestimmbar: *discretionary*
Benutzerdatei: *authority file or list*
benutzerdefinierbar: *user-definable*
Benutzerdokumentation: *user documentation*
benutzerfreundlich: *user-friendly*
Benutzergruppe: *user group*
Benutzerhandbuch: *user's manual; user guide*

Benutzerkennzeichen: *user ID*
Benutzerkreis: **geschlossener ~** *closed user grou.* *(CUG)*
Benutzerprogramm: *user program; user': program*
Benutzerschnittstelle: *user interface*
Benutzerspeicher: *user area*
Benutzerzahl: **höchstmögliche ~** *maximum users*
Benutzerzeit: **verfügbare ~** *available time*
benutzt: *used*
Benutzung: *use*
beratend: *consulting*
Berater: *consultant*
Beratung: *consultancy*
berechenbar: *computable*
berechnen: *calculate; compute*
Berechnung: *calculation; computation* **grobe ~** *rough calculation*
berechtigen: *authorize*
berechtigt: *authorized*
Berechtigung: *authority; authorization; clearanc·*
Berechtigungscode: *authorization code*
Bereich: *area; range; region; span* **bevorrechtigte·** *~ privileged account* **leerer ~** *empty or null or voi·* *set*
Bereiche freimachen: *blast*
Bereichssuche: *area search*
bereinigen: *debug*
bereit: *idle; ready*
bereit-Signal: *O.K.*
Bereitzustand: *ready state*
Berichterstattung: *press coverage or medi·* *coverage* **elektronische ~** *electronic new· gathering (ENG)*
berichtigen: *rectify*
Bernoulli-Box: *Bernoulli box*
berühren: *touch*
beschädigen: *damage*
beschädigt: *damaged*
beschäftigt: *busy*
beschichten: *coat; laminate*
Beschichtung: *emulsion*
Beschleunigungszeit: *acceleration time*
Beschneiden: *cropping*
beschneiden: *scissor; trim*
Beschnitt: *off-cut*
beschreiben: *describe; document*
Beschreiber: *descriptor*
Beschreibung: *description*
Beseitigung: *removal*
besetzt: *busy*
Besetztzeichen: *line busy tone; engaged tone*
Besetztzustand: *congestion*
Besetzungsdirektor: *casting director*
besonders: *extremely*
Besprechung: *conference*
bestätigen: *acknowledge; authenticate; verify*

Bestätigung: *authentication*
Bestätigungsschaltstück: *actuator*
Bestellelektronik: *teleordering*
Bestellung: auf ~ angefertigt *custom-built*
Bestellungen: telefonische ~ *telephone orders*
Best Fit: *best fit*
Bestimmungsort: *destination*
Bestzeitcode: *optimum code or minimum access code or minimum delay code*
Beteiligungsgesellschaft: *associate company*
Beteuerung: *assertion*
betont: *accented*
betragen: *to amount to*
betreffen: *apply; involve*
Betrieb: automatischer ~ *unattended operation* **in ~ in use; working in ~ sein** *run* **stationärer ~** *on local; local mode*
Betriebsanlage: *facility (US)*
Betriebsart: *mode*
Betriebsbereitschaftssignal: *data set ready (DSR) or data terminal ready (DTR); enabling signal*
Betriebsinformation: *operational information*
Betriebsmittel: *resource* **kritische ~** *critical resource*
Betriebsmittelbenutzung: gemeinsame ~ *resource sharing*
Betriebsmittelzuteilung: *resource allocation*
Betriebssystem: *disk operating system (DOS); operating system (OS)*
Betriebssystemplatte: *master disk*
Betriebsunterbrechungsanfrage: *reverse interrupt*
Betriebsuntersuchung: *operation trial*
Betriebszeit: *operating time*
Betrug: *fraud*
Beutel: *bag*
bevor: *prior to*
bewältigen: zu ~ *manageable*
bewegen: *move* **sich ~** *range*
beweglich: *mobile; movable*
Bewegung: *action; movement*
Bewegungen: *activities*
Bewegungsdatei: *transaction or change or detail or movement file*
Bewegungshäufigkeit: *activity ratio*
Bewegungshäufigkeit der Dateien: *file activity ratio*
Bewegungssatz: *transaction record or change record*
Beweis: *induction*
beweisen: *induce*
bewerben: sich ~ *apply*
bewerten: *evaluate*
Bewertungsdurchschnitt: *weighted average*
Bezeichnen: *labelling*
bezeichnen: *label*
Bezeichnung: *label*
beziehen: sich ~ auf *refer*

Beziehung: *relationship*
Bezug: *reference*
Bezugsadresse: *base address; reference address* **direkte ~** *direct reference address*
Bezugspegel: *reference level*
Bezugspunkt: *reference*
Bezugsregister: *base register*
Bezugstabelle: *reference table*
Bezugszeit: *reference time*
bezweifeln: *query; question*
Bibliographie: *bibliography*
bibliographisch: *bibliographic or bibliographical*
Bibliothek: *library*
Bibliothekar: *librarian*
Bibliotheksfunktion: *library function*
Bibliotheksprogramm: *library program*
Bibliotheksroutine: *library routine*
Bibliotheksunterprogramm: *library subroutine*
Bild: *picture* **einfarbiges ~** *monochrome* **latentes ~** *latent image* **verschwommenes ~** *blur*
Bildabtaster: *image scanner; video scanner*
Bildabtastung: *field sweep; single scan non segmented*
Bildanordnung: *film assembly*
Bildaustastung: *field blanking*
Bildbereich: *image area*
Bildbeständigkeit: *image stability*
Bildbetrachter: *viewer*
Bilddurchlaufmodus: *scroll mode*
Bildelement: *picture element or pixel*
bilden: *form*
Bilder: *pix*
Bilderläuterung: *caption*
Bilder pro Sekunde: *frames per second (fps)*
Bildfrequenz: *frame frequency*
Bildfunk: *facsimile transmission (FAX)*
Bildgestaltungstechnik: *imaging*
Bild-Grabber: *frame grabber*
Bildkonservierung: *image retention*
Bildlageeinstellung: *framing*
Bildmaterial: *visuals*
Bildplatte: *videodisk*
Bildröhre: *cathode ray tube (CRT)*
Bildröhrenspeicher: *cathode ray tube storage*
Bildrücklauf: *field flyback*
Bildschirm: *display; display screen; display unit; monitor; screen* **am ~ on-screen geteilter ~** *split screen* **graphischer ~** *graphic display*
Bildschirmanschluß: *display adapter*
Bildschirmanzeigeformat: *screen format*
Bildschirmattribute: *screen attributes*
Bildschirmauflösung: *display resolution*
Bildschirmaufzeichnung: *soft copy*
Bildschirmausdruck: *screen dump*
Bildschirmblättern: *display scrolling*
Bildschirmfarbe: *display colour*
Bildschirmformat: *display format; screen size*
Bildschirmgerät: *VDT or VDU; video display*

Bildschirmgröße: *display size; screen size*
Bildschirminhalt: *screenful*
Bildschirmnotizblock: *screen notepad*
Bildschirmprozessor: *display processor*
Bildschirmpuffer: *screen buffer*
Bildschirmrand: *screen border*
Bildschirmregler: *display controller*
Bildschirmreinigungsausrüstung: *screen cleaning kit*
Bildschirms: außerhalb des ~ *off screen*
Bildschirmspeicher: *screen memory*
Bildschirmspeichern: selektives ~ *snapshot*
Bildschirmsteuereinheit: *display controller*
Bildschirmtelefon: *video phone*
Bildschirmtext: *videotext or videotex*
Bildschirmtexteditor: *screen editor or text editor*
Bildschirmtextsystem: *interactive videotext; telesoftware (TSW); viewdata*
Bildschirmtextverfahren: *electronic publishing*
Bildschirmvariable: *display attribute*
Bildschwarz: *shade*
Bildsensor: *image sensor*
Bildspeicher: *frame store; image table*
Bildspeicherplatz: *image storage space*
Bildstabilität: *image stability*
Bildsynchronisation: *pix lock*
Bildsynchronisierpuls: *field sync pulse*
Bildtelefon: *picture phone*
Bildtelegraphie: *facsimile transmission (FAX); phototelegraphy*
Bildträger: *image carrier*
Bildüberschrift: *caption*
Bildübertragung: *picture transmission*
Bildungs-: *educational*
Bildungsprogramm: *educational TV*
Bildunterschrift: *caption*
Bildverarbeiter: *image processor*
Bildverarbeitung: *image processing; picture processing* **computergestützte ~** *computer image processing*
Bildverschlechterung: *image degradation*
Bildverzerrung: *image distortion*
Bildwiederholfrequenz: *refresh rate*
Bildwiederholung: *screen refresh*
Bildwiederholungsspeicher: *image table*
Bildzeile: *display line*
billigen: *to approve of*
Billigung: *approval*
Bimmeln: *jingle*
binär: *binary*
Binärarithmetik: *binary arithmetic*
Binärcode: *binary code*
Binär-dezimal-Umwandlung: *binary-to-decimal conversion*
Binärexponent: *binary exponent*
Binärkomma: *binary point*
Binärlader: *binary loader*
Binäroperation: *binary operation*

Binärschreibweise: *binary notation*
Binärsequenz: *binary sequence*
Binärskala: *binary scale*
Binärstelle: *binary point*
Binärsystem: *binary system*
Binärzahl: *binary number*
Binärzähler: *binary counter*
Binärzeichen: *bit*
Binärziffer: *binary digit or bit*
binaural: *binaural*
Bindelader: *linking loader*
Binden: *binding*
binden: *bind*
Binderprogramm: *linkage editing*
Bindestrich: *en dash or en rule; hyphen* **mit ~ geschrieben** *hyphenated* **unveränderlicher ~** *required hyphen or hard hyphen*
Bindewort: *connective*
Binnenmarkt: *domestic market*
Binnenproduktion: *domestic production*
BIOS: *basic input/output operating system (BIOS)*
Biosensor: *biosensor*
bipolar: *bipolar*
Biquinärcode: *biquinary code*
bistabil: *bistable*
Bit: *bit* **binärer ~** *binary bit* **gewichtetes ~** *weighted bit* **niederwertiges ~** *low-order digit* **niederwertigstes ~** *least significant bit (LSB)* **wichtigstes ~** *most significant bit or msb or MSB*
Bitadressierung: *bit addressing*
Bitbearbeitung: *bit handling*
16-Bit-CPU: *sixteen-bit*
Bitdichte: *bit density*
Bit-Füllung: *bit stuffing*
Bitmuster: *bit pattern*
Bitposition: *bit position*
Bitreihe: *bit stream*
Bitscheibenaufbau: *bit slice design*
Bitscheibenprozessor: *bit-slice processor*
Bit-Slice-Aufbau: *bit-slice architecture*
Bits pro Inch: *bits per inch; BPI or bpi*
Bits pro Sekunde: *bits per second; BPS or bps*
Bitspur: *bit track*
Bitstelle: *bit position*
8-Bit-System: *eight-bit (system)*
32-Bit-System: *thirty-two bit system*
Bitte: *demand*
Bitübertragungsgeschwindigkeit: *debit*
Bitübertragungsschicht: *physical layer*
Bitverarbeitung: *bit manipulation*
Bitverschiebung: zyklische ~ *cyclic shift*
Black Box: *black box*
Blasensortierung: *bubble sort*
Blasenspeicher: *bubble memory*
Blasenspeicherkassette: *bubble memory cassette*
Blatt: *leaf; page; sheet* **einseitig bedrucktes ~** *broadsheet*

blättern: *scroll*
Blättern: punktweises ~ smooth scroll zeilenweises ~ roll scroll
Blattschreiber: *page printer*
Blattzuführung: *sheet feed*
Blaupause: *blueprint*
Bleisatz: *hot type*
Blende: *lens stop*
Blendenöffnungsverhältnis: *f-number*
Blendung: *glare*
blind: *blind*
Blindenschrift: *Braille*
Blindwiderstand: *reactance*
Blinken: *blinking*
blinken: *flash*
Block: *block; pad*
Blockade: *block* **kreisförmige ~** *bullet*
Blockbegrenzung: *flag sequence*
Blockbewegungsbefehl: *move block*
Blockcode: *block code*
Blockdatenprüfung: *BCC*
Blockdiagramm: *block diagram*
Blockdiagrammsymbol: Entscheidung: *decision box*
Blockeingabeverarbeitung: *block input processing*
Blöcken: zwischen ~ *interblock*
Blockende: *end of block (EOB)*
Blockfehlerhäufigkeit: *block error rate*
blockieren: *block*
Blockignorierungszeichen: *block ignore character*
Blockkanal: universeller ~ *universal block channel (UBC)*
Blockkopf: *block header*
Blocklänge: *block length*
Blockliste: *block list*
Blockmarke: *block mark*
Blockmarkierungszeichen: *block markers*
Blockmarkierungszeichen setzen: *mark block*
Blockoperation: *block operation*
Blockparitätsprüfung: *block parity*
Blockprüfung: zyklische ~ *cyclic redundancy check (CRC)*
Blocks: kopieren eines ~ *block copy*
Blockschrift: *block capitals or block letters*
Blocksynchronisierung: *block synchronization*
Blocktransfer: *block transfer*
Blockübertragung: *block transfer*
Blockungsfaktor: *blocking factor*
Blockzeichenprüfung: *block character check (BCC)*
Blockzugriff: *block retrieval*
Blockzwischenraum: *block or interblock gap (IBG)*
Bocksprungtest: *leap-frog test*
Boden: *ground*
Bodenfunkstelle: *ground station*

Bodenstation: *earth station*
Bogenkorrekturen: *page proofs; slip pages or slip proofs*
Bondpapier: *bond paper*
Boolesche: dyadische ~ Operation *dyadic Boolean operation*
Boolesche Algebra: *Boolean algebra or logic*
Boolesche Operation: *Boolean operation*
Boolescher Operator: *Boolean connective; Boolean operator*
Boolescher Wert: *Boolean value*
Boolesche Variable: *Boolean variable*
Boom: *boom*
borgen: *borrow*
BOS: *basic operating system (BOS)*
Bose-Chandhuri-Hocquenghem-Code: *Bose-Chandhuri-Hocquenghem code (BCH)*
Bottom-Up-Verfahren: *bottom up method*
Branchenverzeichnis: *classified directory*
brandneu: *brand new*
brechen: *break; refract*
Brechung: *refraction*
Brechungsindex: *refractive index*
B-Register: *B box; B register*
Breitband: *broadband; wideband*
Breitbandfrequenzmodulation: *wideband frequency modulation (WBFM)*
Breitbandradio: *broadband radio*
Breite: *width*
Breitnetz: *wide area network (WAN)*
Brennelement: *element*
Brenner: *burner*
Brennweite: *focal length*
Brennzahl: *f-number*
Brettschaltung: *breadboard*
Bridgeware: *bridgeware*
Brief: letter einen ~ beantworten *to answer a letter* **einen ~ kopieren** *to duplicate a letter*
Briefkasten: *letter box or mail box or mailbox* **elektronischer ~** *electronic mailbox*
Briefkopf: *letterhead*
Briefpapier: vorgedrucktes ~ *preprinted stationery*
Briefschreiben: automatisches ~ *automatic letter writing*
Briefschreiber: *correspondent*
Briefumschlag: *envelope*
brilliant: *brilliant*
Brillianz: *brilliance*
Britisches Normeninstitut: *British Standards Institute (BSI)*
Bromidsilberdruck: *bromide or bromide print*
Bromidsilberplatte: *bromide or bromide print*
broschiert: *paperbound*
Broschüre: *booklet; brochure*
Bruch: *fraction* **binärer ~** *binary fraction*
Bruch-: *fractional*
Bruchzifferntypen: fertige ~ *piece fractions*

Brücke: *bridge or bridging product; jumper* **wählbare ~** *jumper-selectable*
Brückenauswahlschaltung: *jumper-selectable*
Brummen: *hum*
Brummspannung: *ripple*
Bruttogewicht: *gross weight*
BTAM-Zugriffsmethode: *basic telecommunications access method (BTAM)*
Btx-Anbieter: *ip*
Btx-Datenstation: *ip terminal*
Bubblesort: *bubble sort*
Buch: *book* **fest gebundenes ~** *cased book*
Buchbinder: *binder*
Buchbinderei: *binder; bindery*
Buchdecke: *case*
Buchdeckenmaschine: *case-making machine*
buchen: *book*
Bücherstand: *bookstall*
Buchführungsarbeit: *bookwork*
Buchhändler: *bookseller*
Buchhandlung: *bookshop; bookstore (US)*
Buchproduktion: *bookwork*
Buchse: *jack*
Buchstabe: *alphabetic character (set); letter*
Buchstaben: *type*
Buchstabenkette: *alphabetic string*
Buchungskontrolle: *audit trail*
Bühnenarbeiter: *grip*
Bühnenbild: *set*
Bündel: *bundle* **kohärentes ~** *coherent bundle*
Bundsteg: *gutter*
Büro: *bureau; office* **automatisiertes ~** *automated office* **computerisiertes ~** *paperless office* **elektronisches ~** *electronic office*
Büroausstattung: *business equipment; office equipment*
Büroautomatisierung: *office automation (OA)*
Bürocomputer: *office computer*
Büro der Zukunft: *office of the future*
Bürokopierer: *office copier*
Büromaterial: *stationery*
Bus: *bus* **untergeordneter ~** *bus slave*
Busdatenübertragungsleitung: *bus data lines*
Bushauptkontrolle: *bus master*
Buskarte: *bus board*
Busnebenstelle: *bus slave*
Busnetzwerk: *bus network*
Busplatine: *bus board*
Bussteuerungsleitung: *bus control lines*
Busstruktur: *bus structure* **verkettete ~** *daisy chain bus*
Bustreiber: *bus driver*
Buszuteilung: *bus arbitration*
Büttenrand: *deckle edge*
Byte: *byte*
Byteadresse: *byte address*
Bytemanipulation: *byte manipulation*
Byte-Modus: *byte mode*

Cc

Cache-Speicher: *cache memory*
Callier-Effekt: *callier effect*
Cambridge-Netz: *Cambridge ring*
Candela: *candela*
Capstan: *capstan*
Caret-Zeichen: *caret mark or sign*
Cartridge-Laufwerk: *cartridge drive*
C-Band: *C band*
CB Citizen-Band: *CB*
CCP: *command console processor (CCP)*
CD: *compact disk (CD)*
CD-Festspeicher: *CD-ROM or compact disk ROM*
CD-ROM: *CD-ROM or compact disk-ROM*
CD-Spieler: *compact disk player*
Cedille: *cedilla*
Centronics-Schnittstelle: *Centronics interface*
CEPT-Norm: *CEPT standard*
charakteristisch: *characteristic*
Chefredakteur: *editor*
Chemikalie: *chemical*
chemisch: *chemical*
Chiffrieralgorithmus: *cryptographic algorithm*
Chiffrierschlüssel: *cipher key; cryptographic key*
Chip: *chip* **auf dem ~** *on-chip*
Chip-Anzahl: *chip count*
Chip-Architektur: *chip architecture*
Chip-Karte: *smart card; chip card*
Chip-Satz: *chip set*
Chip-Verbindungsstelle: *chip select line*
chromatisch: *chromatic*
Chromatizität: *chromaticity*
CIM: *CIM*
Cinematographie: *cinematography*
Citizen-Band: *citizens band radio (CB)*
Clip: *clip*
C-MAC: *C-MAC*
CMOS: *CMOS*
CNC: *CNC*
COBOL: *COBOL*
Code: *code* **absoluter ~** *absolute or actual or specific code* **eingebetteter ~** *embedded code* **geketteter ~** *chain code* **gleichgewichteter ~** *constant ratio code* **redundanter ~** *redundant code* **reiner ~** *pure code* **selbstkorrigierender ~** *self correcting code* **symbolischer ~** *symbolic code* **vorkompilierter ~** *precompiled code* **wiederverwendbarer ~** *re-entrant code* **zyklischer ~** *cyclic code*
Codeelement: *code element*
Codes: maschinenlesbare ~ *machine-readable codes*
Codeumschaltung: *escape character*
Codeumschaltungstaste: *escape key*
Codeumsetzer: *encoder*
Codeumsetzung: *code conversion*

Codieren: *coding*
codieren: *code; encode*
Codierer: *coder*
Codierer/Decodierer: *CODEC*
Codiersystem: *M out of N code*
Codierung: bipolare ~ *bipolar coding* **direkte** ~ *direct coding* **lineare** ~ *straight-line coding* **magnetische** ~ *magnetic encoding* **optimale** ~ *optimum code* **relative** ~ *relative coding*
Codierungsformat: *encoding format*
Codierzeile: *code line*
Cold-Standby-System: *cold standby*
COM: *COM*
COMAL: *COMAL*
Computer: *computer* **dedizierter** ~ *dedicated computer* **gebrauchsfertiger** ~ *appliance computer* **sequentieller** ~ *sequential computer* **serieller** ~ *serial computer* **tragbarer** ~ *portable computer* **verbindungsprogrammierter** ~ *wired or hardwired program computer*
Computerabteilung: *computer department*
Computeranimation: *computer animation*
Computeranlage: *installation*
Computeranwendungen: *computer applications*
Computerarchitektur: *computer architecture*
Computerauflistung: *computer listing*
Computerausdruck: *hard copy; computer printout*
Computerausgabe: *computer output*
Computerbediener: *computer operator*
Computerbüro: *computer bureau*
Computerbürosystem: *computer office system*
Computercode: *computer code*
Computerdatei: *computer file*
Computerdruckerpapier: *computer stationery*
Computerfachkenntnis: *computer literacy*
Computerfehler: *computer error*
Computerfreak: *terminal junky (TJ) (slang)*
Computergenerationen: *computer generations*
computergeneriert: *computer-generated*
computergestützt: *computer-aided or computer-assisted*
Computergraphik: *computer graphics*
Computeringenieur: *computer engineer*
computerisieren: *computerize*
Computerisierung: *computerization*
Computerkasse: *point-of-sale terminal or POS terminal*
Computerkonferenz: *computer conferencing*
Computerkriminalität: *computer crime; computer fraud*
Computerlauf: *machine run*
Computerleistung: *computer power*
computerlesbar: *computer-readable*
Computerlogik: *computer logic*
Computernetz: *computer network* **dezentralisiertes** ~ *decentralized computer network* **hierarchisches** ~ *hierarchical computer network* **homogenes** ~ *homogeneous computer network* **zentrales** ~ *centralized computer network*

Computeroperator: *computer operator*
Computerprogramm: *computer program*
Computer-Programmlauf: *computer run*
computersachverständig: *computer-literate*
Computersatz: *computer setting*
Computerservice: *computer services*
Computerspiel: *computer game* **öffentliches** ~ *arcade game*
Computerstärke: *computer power*
Computersystem: *computer system* **selbstlernendes** ~ *self-learning system*
Computertomographie: *computerized axial tomography (CAT)*
Computerübersetzung: *language translation*
Computerverwalter: *computer manager*
Computervirus: *virus*
Computing: *computing*
Controller für Speicherzugriff: *file server*
Coprozessor: *coprocessor*
CORAL: *CORAL*
co-resident: *coresident*
Co-Routine: *coroutine*
Coulomb: *coulomb*
CPM: *critical path method (CPM)*
CPU: *central processing unit (CPU)* **beschreibbare** ~ *writable instruction set computer (WISC)*
CPU-Quittungsbetrieb: *CPU handshaking*
CPU-Teile: *CPU elements*
CPU-Zeit: *CPU time*
CPU-Zyklus: *CPU cycle*
Crawl-Effekt: *crawl*
CRC-Prüfung: *cyclic redundancy check (CRC)*
CSM: *combined symbol matching (CSM)*
CSMA/CD: *carrier sense multiple access - collision detection (CSMA-CD)*
CTRL-Taste: *control; CTR or CTRL*
Cursor: *cursor* **adressierbarer** ~ *addressable cursor* **löschender** ~ *destructive cursor* **nichtlöschender** ~ *non-destructive cursor*
Cursorausgangsstellung: *cursor home*
Cursor-Steuerungsfeld: *touch pad*
Cursortasten: *cursor control keys; cursor pad*

Dd

3D: *three-dimensional or 3D*
dämpfen: *attenuate; deaden*
Dämpfung: *attenuation; loss*
Danksagung: *acknowledgements*
darlegen: *deposit*
darstellen: *represent*
Darstellung: *representation* **digitale** ~ *digital representation* **hexadezimale** ~ *hex dump* **invertierte** ~ *reverse video* **logarithmische** ~ *logarithmic graph*
Darstellungsfläche: *display space*
Darstellungsschicht: *presentation layer*

Datagramm: *datagram*

Datanbanksystem: verteiltes ~ *distributed database system*

Datei: *file; data file* **aktive ~** *active file* **aktuelle ~** *update* **angrenzende ~** *contiguous file* **eine ~ löschen** *to junk a file* **eine ~ sperren** *to lock a file* **erweiterbare serielle ~** *extending serial file* **externe ~** *external data file* **gekettete ~** *chained or threaded file* **indizierte ~** *indexed file* **invertierte ~** *inverted file* **permanente ~** *permanent file* **sequentielle ~** *sequential file* **serielle ~** *serial file* **ungeschützte ~** *scratch or work file* **untergliederte ~** *partitioned file* **versteckte ~** *hidden file*

Dateiabfrage: *file interrogation*

Dateianfang: *beginning of file (bof)*

Dateiaufbau: *file layout*

Dateibeschreibung: *file descriptor*

Dateien: verborgene ~ *hidden files* **verkettete ~** *concatenated data set*

Dateiende: *end of file (EOF)*

Dateien verschmelzen: *link files*

Dateien zusammenfügen: *join files*

Dateieröffnungsroutine: *open routine*

Dateierstellung: *file creation*

Datei-Index: *file index*

Dateikennsatz: *file label*

Dateikopie: *file copy*

Dateilänge: *file length*

Datei löschen: *kill file*

Dateilöschung: *file deletion; file purge*

Dateimanager: *file manager*

Dateimenge: *file set*

Dateiname: *file identification; file name; filename* **uneindeutiger ~** *ambiguous filename*

Dateiprüfung: *file validation*

Dateisäuberung: *file cleanup*

Datei schließen: *close file*

Dateischutz: *file protection; file security*

Dateiserver: *file server*

Dateisortierung: *file collating; file sort*

Dateispeicher: *file store*

Dateispeicherung: *file storage*

Dateistruktur: *file structure*

Dateisystem: verteiltes ~ *distributed file system*

Dateitransfer: *file transfer*

Dateiumfang: *file extent*

Dateiumsetzung: *file conversion*

Dateiverarbeitung: *file processing*

Dateiverfallsdatum: *expiration date*

Dateiverwalter: *file manager*

Dateiverwaltung: *file management*

Dateiverwaltungsblock: *file control block*

Dateiverwaltungsroutine: *file handling routine*

Dateiverwaltungssystem: *file management system*

Dateiverzeichnis: *file directory*

Dateivorfahre: *ancestral file*

Dateiwarteschlange: *file queue*

Dateiwartung: *file maintenance*

Dateiwiederherstellungsprogramm: *file-recover utility*

Dateizwischenraum: *file gap*

Daten: *data* **alphanumerische ~** *alphanumer data* **digitale ~** *digital data* **eingehende ~** *incoming traffic* **graphische ~** *graphic da* **halbverarbeitete ~** *semi-processed data* **relative ~** *relative data* **tendenziöse ~** *biased data* **variable ~** *variable data*

Datenadapter: *data adapter unit*

Datenadreßkettung: *data chaining*

Datenanalyse: *data analysis*

Datenanordnung: verdichtete ~ *packed format*

Datenanschlußeinheit: *data adapter unit*

Datenaufbereitung: *data preparation*

Datenaufzeichnung: automatische ~ *automat. data capture*

Datenaustausch: *data communications*

Datenaustauschgerät: *data communicatior equipment (DCE)*

Datenaustauschpuffer: *data communicatior buffer*

Datenaustauschvermittlung: *data switchir exchange*

Datenauswertung: *data analysis*

Datenbank: *databank; database* **hierarchische ~** *hierarchical database* **integrierte ~** *integrate database* **komplexe ~** *plex database* **physische ~** *physical database* **relationale ~** *relation database*

Datenbankaufgliederung: *database mapping*

Datenbankmaschine: *database machine*

Datenbank mit Direktanschluß: *on-line databas*

Datenbanknetz: *information network; networ database*

Datenbankschema: *database schema*

Datenbanksprache: *database language; quer language (QL)*

Datenbanksystem: *database system*

Datenbankverwalter: *database administratc (DBA)*

Datenbankverwaltungssystem: *databas management system (DBMS) or databas manager*

Datenbankzentrale: *information retrieval centr*

Datenbegrenzungszeichen: *data delimiter*

Datenbehandlungssprache: *data manipulatic language (DML)*

Datenbereich: *data area*

Datenbeschreibungssprache: *data descriptio language (DDL)*

Datenbewegung: *data transaction*

Datenblock: *data block*

Datendurchlauf: *throughput*

Datenebene: *data level*

Dateneingabe: *data entry; data input* **direkte ~** *direct data entry (DDE)*

Dateneingabebus: *data input bus (DIB)*

Dateneingabe von Mikrofilm: *computer inp from microfilm (CIM)*

Dateneingeber: *keyboarder*

Dateneinheit: *entity*
Datenelementkette: *data element chain*
Datenempfangssignal: *data carrier detect (DCD)*
Datenende: *end of data (EOD)*
Datenendeinrichtung: *data terminal equipment (DTE)*
Daten erfassen: *capture*
Datenerfassung: *data acquisition; data capture; data collection; data logging*
Datenerfassungsstation: *data collection platform*
Datenerstellung: *data origination*
Datenfehler: *data error*
Datenfeld: *data field; data item*
Datenfernübertragungsservice: *teleinformatic services*
Datenfernverarbeitung: *data communications; teleprocessing (TP)*
Datenfluß: *data flow* **grenzüberschreitender ~** *transborder data flow*
Datenflußdiagramm: *data flow diagram (DFD)*
Datenflußplan: *data flowchart*
Datenformat: *data format*
datengesteuert: *data-driven*
Datengruppierung: *data aggregate*
Datenhierarchie: *data hierarchy*
Datenimpulseingang: *data strobe*
Datenkanal: *data channel*
Datenkassette: *data cassette*
Datenkettung: *data chaining*
Datenkommunikationsnetzwerk: *data communications network*
Datenkomprimierung: *data compacting*
Datenkonzentrator: *data concentrator*
Datenkorrektur: *data cleaning*
Datenkorruption: *data corruption*
Datenleitung: *dataline*
Datenleitungssteuerung: *data link control*
Datenleitweg: *data routing*
Datenmultiplexmethode: *dataplex*
Datenname: *data name*
Datennetz: *data network* **öffentliches ~** *public data network* **synchrones ~** *synchronous data network*
Datenpaket: *packet*
Datenpaketvermittlung: *packet switching*
Datenpflege: *data management*
Datenprüfung: *data check; data validation; data vetting*
Datenpuffer: *data buffer*
Datenquelle: *data source*
Datenregister: *data cartridge; data register*
Datenreinigung: *data cleaning*
Datensatz: *data record* **einzelner ~** *unit record*
Datenschutz: *privacy; privacy of data; data protection*
Datenschutzgesetz: *Data Protection Act*
Datenschwingungsträger: *data carrier*
Datensenke: *data sink*

Datenservice: *data services* **paketweiser ~** *packet switched data service*
Datensicherheit: *data integrity*
Datensicherung: *data protection; data security*
Datensicherungsplatte: *backup disk*
Datensicherungsprozedur: *backup procedure*
Datensichtgerät: *display*
Datensichtterminal: *visual display terminal (VDT) or visual display unit (VDU)*
Datensignale: *data signals*
Datenspeicher: *data storage*
Datenstation: *data station; data terminal;* terminal **abhängige ~** *slave terminal* **adressierbare ~** *addressable terminal* **anwendungsorientierte ~** *applications terminal* **autonome ~** *stand-alone terminal* **dialogfähige ~** *interactive terminal* **entfernt aufgestellte ~** *or* **entfernt stehende ~** *remote terminal* **frei programmierbare ~** *or* **intelligente ~** *smart or intelligent terminal* **nichtprogrammierbare ~** *dumb terminal* **untergeordnete ~** *slave terminal*
Datenstation der Firmenleitung: *executive terminal*
Datenstrobe: *data strobe*
Datenstrom: *data stream* **kontinuierlicher ~** *continuous data stream*
Datenstruktur: *data structure* **dynamische ~** *dynamic data structure*
Datenteil: *data division*
Datenträger: *data carrier; data medium; storage medium* **unbeschrifteter ~** *empty medium*
Datenträgerende: *end of medium (EM)*
Datentyp: *data type* **variabler ~** *variable data type*
Datenübermittlung: **wechselseitige ~** *either-way operation*
Datenübertragung: *data transmission* **parallele ~** *parallel data transmission* **serielle ~** *serial data transmission*
Datenübertragung auf Sprachfrequenz: *data in voice (DIV)*
Datenübertragung per Funk: *radio transmission of data*
Datenübertragungsabschnitt: *data link*
Datenübertragungsblock: *frame*
Datenübertragungseinrichtung: *data communications equipment (DCE)*
Datenübertragungsgeschwindigkeit: *data rate; data signalling rate; data transfer rate*
Datenübertragungsleitungen: *scheduled circuits*
Datenübertragungsmaschine: *milking machine*
Datenübertragungsmethode: **paketvermittelte ~** *flooding*
Datenübertragungsplatte: *milk disk*
Datenübertragungssteuerung: **synchrone ~** *synchronous data link control (SDLC)*
Datenübertragungsweg: *data highway*
Datenübertragung über Sprachfrequenz: *data above voice (DAV)*
Datenübertragung unter Sprachfrequenz: *data under voice (DUV)*
Datenumlagerung: *data migration*

Datenumsetzung: *data translation*
Datenunabhängigkeit: *data independence*
Datenunterbrechung: *data break*
Datenverarbeitung: *data processing (DP or dp); information processing* **automatische** ~ *automatic data processing (ADP)* **dezentralisierte** ~ *decentralized data processing* **elektronische** ~ *electronic data processing (EDP)* **integrierte** ~ *integrated data processing (IDP)* **manuelle** ~ *manual data processing* **verteilte** ~ *distributed data processing (DDP)* **zentrale** ~ *centralized data processing*
Datenverarbeitungsmanager: *data processing manager*
Datenverbindung: *data circuit; data connection* **optische** ~ *optical data link*
Datenverbund: *data aggregate*
Datenverdichtung: *data compacting; data compression; data reduction*
Datenverfälschung: *data corruption*
Datenverkehr: *traffic* **elektronischer** ~ *electronic traffic*
Datenverkehrsanalyse: *traffic analysis*
Datenverkehrsdichte: *traffic density*
Datenverkehrsquote: *traffic intensity*
Datenverlust: unerklärlicher ~ *line gremlin*
Datenverschlüsselung: *data encryption*
Datenverschlüsselungsnorm: *data encryption standard (DES)*
Datenverwalter: *data administrator*
Datenvielfachleitung: *data highway*
Datenvorbereitung: *data preparation*
Datenweg: *data path*
Datenwiedergewinnung: *data retrieval*
Datenwort: *data word*
Datenwörterbuch: *data dictionary/directory (DD/D)*
Datenwortlänge: *data word length*
Datenzeiger: *data pointer*
Datenzugriffsverwaltung: *data access management*
Datenzuverlässigkeit: *data reliability*
datieren: *date*
Datum: *date*
Dauer: *duration*
Dauerbetrieb: *steady state*
Dauer der Lagerfähigkeit: *shelf life*
Dauer der Verbindung: *connect time*
Dauerfunktion: *auto repeat; automatic repeat*
dauerhaft: *durable; permanent(ly)*
Dauerkennzeichen: *continuous signal*
Dauerschleife: *continuous loop*
Dauerspeicher: *permanent memory* **dynamischer** ~ *permanent dynamic memory*
Dauertaste: *repeat key*
Debugger: *debugger*
Decodierer: *decoder; de-scrambler*
dediziert: *dedicated*
defekt: *defective*
Defektelektron: *hole*

definierbar: neu ~ *redefinable*
definieren: *define* **neu** ~ *redefine*
defokussieren: *defocus*
Dekade: *decade*
Dekadenzähler: *decade counter*
Dekrement: *decrement*
Delta-Delta-Verbindung: *delta-delta*
Deltamodulation: *delta modulation*
Delta-Uhr: *delta clock*
Demarkationsstreifen: *demarcation strip*
Demodulation: *demodulation*
Demodulator: *demodulator*
Demostrationsmodell: *demonstration model*
Densitometer: *densitometer*
desaktivieren: *disarm*
Desaktivierung: *disarmed state*
Designabteilung: *design department*
Designer: *designer*
Designparameter: *design parameters*
Designstudio: *design studio*
Deskriptor: *descriptor*
Desktop Publishing: *desktop publishing (DTP)*
Detail: im ~ *in detail; detailed*
Detaildatei: *detail file*
Detektor: *detector*
deterministisch: *deterministic*
Deweysche Dezimalklassifikation: *Dewe decimal classification*
Dezi-: *deci-*
Dezibel: *decibel*
Dezibelmeter: *decibel meter*
Dezile: *decile*
Dezimal-binär-Umwandlung: *decimal-to-binar conversion*
Dezimalcode: zyklischer ~ *cyclic decimal code*
Dezimaldarstellung: *denary notation*
Dezimale: natürliche binärcodierte ~ *natur binary coded decimal (NBCD)*
dezimalisieren: *decimalize*
Dezimalisierung: *decimalization*
Dezimalschreibweise: *decimal notation*
Dezimalstelle: *decimal point*
Dezimalstellenausrichtung: automatische *automatic decimal adjustment*
Dezimalsystem: *decimal system*
Dezimaltabulator: mit ~ **einrichten** *decim tabbing*
Dezimaltabulatortaste: *decimal tab key*
Dezimalzahl: binär codierte ~ *binary code decimal (BCD)* **gepackte** ~ *packed decimal*
Dezimeterwellenbereich: *ultra high frequenc (UHF)*
D-Flipflop: *D-flip-flop*
DFV: *communications; data communications*
DFV-Abtaster: *communications scanner*
DFV-Anschluß: *communications port*
DFV-Hauptsteuerprogramm: *communicatior executive*

DFV-Netz: *communications network*
DFV-Netz-Prozessor: *communications network processor*
DFV-Puffer: *(data) communications buffer*
DFV-Satellit: *communications satellite*
DFV-Schnittstellenanschluß: *communications interface adapter*
DFV-Verbindungsweg: *communications link*
Dia: *slide*
Diabetrachter: *hand viewer; viewer*
Diade: *doublet or diad*
Diagnose: *diagnosis*
Diagnosechip: *diagnostic chip*
Diagnosehilfsmittel: *diagnostic aid*
Diagnosemeldung: *diagnostic message*
Diagnoseprogramm: *checking program; diagnostic program*
Diagnosetest: *diagnostic test*
Diagnostik: *diagnostics*
Diagnostikhilfe: *diagnostic aid*
Diagnostikprogramm: *diagnostic routine; diagnostic program*
diagnostizieren: *diagnose*
Diagramm: *chart; diagram; graph* **logisches ~** *logical chart*
diagrammatisch: *in diagrammatic form; diagramatically*
Dialekt: *dialect*
Dialog: *dialogue*
Dialogbetrieb: *conversational (mode); interactive mode or processing; on-line system* **im ~** *interactive; on-line*
Dialogprogramm: *interactive routine*
Dialogsystem: *interactive system*
Dialogtestsystem: **integriertes ~** *interactive debugging system*
DIANE: *direct information access network for Europe (DIANE)*
Diapositiv: *diapositive; slide; transparency*
Diapositiv mit Tonspur: *audio slide*
Diaprojektor: *diascope; film projector or slide projector*
Diaprojektor mit Tonspur: *slide/sync recorder*
Diazokopie: *diazo (process)*
Dibit: *dibit*
Dichroise: *dichroic*
Dichte: *density*
Dichtemesser: *densitometer*
dick: *thick*
Dickschicht: *thick film*
Dielektrikum: *dielectric; electret*
Dienstprogramm: *utility (program)*
Dienstweg: **den ~ gehen** *to go through the official channels*
Differentialpulscodemodulation: *differential PCM*
Differenz: **symmetrische ~** *symmetric difference*
diffundieren: *diffuse*
diffundierter pn-Übergang: *diffused pn-junction*

Diffusion: *diffusion*
digital: *digital; digitally*
Digital-Analog-Umsetzer: *digital to analog converter (DAC or D to A converter) or D/A converter*
Digitalaufnahme: *digital recording*
Digitalausgabe: *digital output*
Digitalisierblock: *digitizing pad*
digitalisieren: *digitize*
Digitalisierer: *digitizer*
Digitalkassette: *digital cassette*
Digitalmultimeter: *digital multimeter (DMM)*
Digitalnetz: **integriertes ~** *integrated digital network*
Digitalplotter: *digital plotter*
Digitalrechner: *digital computer* **elektronischer ~** *electronic digital computer*
Digitalschaltung: *digital circuit*
Digitalsteuerung: **direkte ~** *direct digital control (DDC)*
Digitalsystem: *digital system*
Digitaluhr: *digital clock*
Digitalzugriff: **integrierter ~** *integrated digital access (IDA)*
Diktat: *dictation* **ein ~ aufnehmen** *to take dictation*
diktieren: *dictate*
Diktiergerät: *dictating machine*
Diktiertempo: *dictation speed*
DIL-Gehäuse: *dual-in-line package (DIL or DIP)*
Dimension: *dimension*
Dimensionierung: *dimensioning*
DIN: *DIN*
Diode: *diode* **lichtaussendende ~** *light-emitting diode (LED)*
Dioptrie: *diopter or dioptre*
Diplex: *diplex*
Dipol: *dipole*
Dipolantenne: *dipole*
Dipolzeilenantenne: *linear array*
direkt: *direct; directly*
Direktanschluß: *direct connect*
Direktanweisung: *direct instruction*
Direktbefehl: *immediate instruction*
Direktcode: *direct or one-level or specific code*
Direktmodus: *direct mode; immediate mode*
Direktoperand: *immediate operand*
Direktor: **geschäftsführender ~** *managing director* **technischer ~** *technical director*
Direktsatz: *direct impression*
Direktübertragung: *direct transfer*
Direktumschaltung: *direct change-over*
Direktversand: *direct mail*
Direktwerbung: *direct-mail advertising; direct mailing*
Direktzugriff: *direct access*
Direktzugriffsdatei: *random access files*

Direktzugriffsspeicher: *direct access storage device (DASD); random access memory (RAM); random access storage*

Disassembler: *disassembler*

Disjunktion: *disjunction*

Diskette: *diskette; floppy disk or floppy or FD* **anders formatierte** ~ *alien disk* **umzudrehende** ~ *flippy*

Diskettenlaufwerk: *floppy disk drive or unit*

Diskettensektor: *floppy disk sector*

Diskettensteuerelemente: *floppy disk controller (FDC)*

diskret: *discrete*

diskutieren: *argue*

Dispersion: *dispersion* **chromatische** ~ *chromatic dispersion*

Distanz(adresse): *displacement*

Dittographie: *dittogram*

Divergenz: *divergence*

Divident: *dividend*

Division: *division*

Divisor: *divisor*

DMA-Zyklusraub: *DMA cycle stealing*

Dokumentation: *documentation*

Dokumente ablegen: *to file documents*

Dollarzeichen: *dollar sign*

Dongle: *dongle*

Doppelbelichtung: *double exposure*

Doppelbild: *double document*

Doppelkreuz: *double dagger*

Doppelpunkt: *colon*

Doppelreihe: *dual column*

Doppelreihengehäuse: *dual-in-line package (DIL or DIP)*

Doppelstromsignal: *polar signal*

Doppelsystem: *dual systems*

doppelt: *double; dual*

Doppelwort: *double word*

DOS: *disk operating system (DOS)*

dotieren: *dope*

dotiert: *doped*

Dotierung: *doping*

Dotierungsstoff: *dopant*

Doublette: *double document*

Download-Fonts: *downloadable fonts*

Draht: *wire*

Drahtführungskamm: *fanning strip*

drahtlos: *wireless*

Drahtwickeln: *wire wrap (Nadeldrucker)*

Drain(strom): *drain*

Dreh-: *rotary*

Dreharbeiten: *filming*

Drehbuch: *script*

Drehbuchautor: *scriptwriter*

Drehen: *filming*

drehen: *shoot* **sich** ~ *spin*

Dreiadreßbefehl: *three-address instruction*

dreidimensional: *three-dimensional or 3D*

Dreieckschaltung: *delta*

Dreiecksleitweg: *delta routing*

Dreier: *triad*

Dreizustandslogik: *three state logic*

Drift: *drift*

Druck: *print* **durchscheinender** ~ *show-through*

Druckanweisungen: *print modifiers*

Druckanweisungscodes: *non-printing codes*

Drucken: *printing* **elektrosensitives** ~ *electrosensitive printing* **halbfettes** ~ *emboldening*

drucken: *print*

drücken: *click; press; push*

Drucken ohne Restbogen: *even working*

Drucker: *printer* **elektrostatischer** ~ *electrostatic printer* **logischer** ~ *logic-seeking printer* **mechanischer** ~ *impact printer* **nicht-mechanischer** ~ *non-impact printer* **xerographischer** ~ *xerographic printer*

Druckeranschlußstelle: *printer port*

Druckerei: *printer*

Druckerkopf: *printhead*

Druckerlebensdauer: *print life*

Drucker-Plotter: *printer-plotter*

Druckerpresse: *printing press*

Druckerpuffer: *printer buffer*

Druckerregler: *printer's controller*

Druckerschnittstelle: *hard copy interface*

Druckersteuerzeichen: *printer control characters*

Drucker-Treiber: *printer driver*

Druckfehler: *erratum; literal*

Druckform: *form; plate*

Druckformat: *print format*

Druckformatierer: *print formatter*

Druckgang: *machining*

Druckhammer: *print hammer*

Druckpause: *print pause*

Druckqualität: *printer quality*

Drucksache: *printed matter*

Druckschrift: in ~ **schreiben** *print*

Drucksteuerzeichen: *print control character*

Drucktasten-: *pushbutton*

Drucktastentelefon: *pushbutton telephone*

Drucktastenwählen: *pushbutton dialling*

Drucktype: *print style*

Druckumwandler: *pressure pad*

Druckzylinder: *impression cylinder*

D-Schicht der Ionosphäre: *D-region*

dual: *binary*

Dualkartenverarbeitung: *card image*

Dual-Port-Speicher: *dual port memory*

Dualprozessor(system): *dual processor*

Dualschreibweise: *binary notation or representation*

Dualzahl: *binary number*

Dunkelkammer: *darkroom*

Dunkelschriftröhre: *dark trace tube*

Dunkelstrom: *dark current*

dünn: *thin*

Dünnschicht: *thin film*
Dünnschichtspeicher: *magnetic thin film storage; thin film memory*
Duodezimalsystem: *duodecimal number system*
Duplex: *fd or FD; full duplex*
Duplexbetrieb: *duplex operation*
Duplexpapier: *duplex*
Duplexsystem: *duplex computer*
Duplexübertragung: *duplex*
Duplikat: *duplicate*
durchbrennen: *fuse*
Durchführbarkeit: *feasibility*
Durchführbarkeitsbericht: *feasibility report*
durchführen: *perform*
Durchgangsvermittlung: *tandem switching*
durchgehen: *walk through*
Durchlaßgrad: *transmittance*
Durchlässigkeit: magnetische ~ *permeability*
Durchlauf: *pass*
Durchlaufbetrieb: freier ~ *free running mode*
Durchlaufzeit: *run-time or run-duration; turnaround time (TAT) (US)*
Durchmesser: *diameter*
durchnumerieren: *number*
Durchprüfung: sprungweise ~ *leap-frog test*
Durchsatzrate: maximale ~ *rated throughput*
Durchschaltevermittlungstechnik: *line switching*
Durchschaltnetz: *circuit switched network*
Durchschießen: *interleaving*
Durchschlag: *carbon; carbon copy*
Durchschnitt: *average; mean* **den** ~ **ermitteln** *to average* **gewichteter** ~ *weighted average*
durchschnittlich: *on an average; average; mean*
durchschnittlich betragen: *average out*
durchschossen: *interleaved*
Durchschuß: *lead; leading*
durchsickern: etwas ~ **lassen** *leak*
durchsuchen: *browse; scan*
Durchwahl: direct inward dialling **internationale** ~ *international direct dialling (IDD)*
durchwählen: *to dial direct*
Durchwählen: *direct dialling*
DV: *dp or DP*
dynamisch: *dynamic*

Ee

EAN: *EAN*
EAPROM: *electrically alterable, programmable read-only memory (EAPROM)*
EAROM: *electrically alterable read-only memory (EAROM)*
EBCDIC-Code: *extended binary coded decimal interchange code (EBCDIC)*
eben: *flat*
Ebene: auf gleicher ~ *flush*

EBNF: *EBNF*
Echo: *echo*
echofrei: *anechoic*
Echolot: *sonar*
Echoprüfung: *echo check*
Echosperre: *echo suppressor*
echt: *authentic; genuine*
Echtheitsbestätigung von Meldungen: *authentication of messages*
Echtzeit: *real time*
Echtzeitbetrieb: *real-time processing*
Echtzeiteingabe: *real-time input*
Echtzeit-Multitasking: *real-time multitasking*
Echtzeitsimulation: *real-time simulation*
Echtzeitsystem: *real-time system*
edieren: *edit*
EDIT-Befehle: *edit commands; editing terms*
EDIT-Fenster: *edit window*
Editierfenster: *edit window*
Editierfunktion: *text-editing function*
Editierprogramm: *text-editing facilities*
Editor: *editor*
EDITOR: *editor program*
EDIT-Taste: *edit key*
EDV: *EDP* **auf** ~ **umstellen** *computerize*
EDV-Personal: *liveware*
EEPROM: *electrically erasable programmable read-only memory (EEPROM)*
EEROM: *electrically erasable read-only memory (EEROM)*
Effekt: elektrooptischer ~ *electro-optic effect*
Effekte: optische ~ *special effects*
effektiv: *effective*
Effektivstrom: *RMS line current*
Effektivwert: *root mean square (RMS)*
EGA: *EGA*
EGA-Bildschirm: *enhanced graphics adapter screen*
EIA-Schnittstelle: *EIA interface*
Eichung: *calibration*
Eigentum: öffentliches ~ *public domain*
Ein-: *mono-; uni-*
Einadreßbefehl: *one address instruction*
Einadreßcode: *single address code*
Einadreßcomputer: *one address computer*
Ein-/Ausgabe: *input/output (I/O)* **parallele** ~ *parallel input/output (PIO)* **serielle** ~ *serial input/output* **speicherorientierte** ~ *memory-mapped I/O* **zwischengespeicherte** ~ *buffered input/output*
ein-/ausgabeabhängig: *I/O bound*
Ein-/Ausgabeadressierung: *I/O mapping*
Ein-/Ausgabeanschlußstelle: *I/O port*
Ein-/Ausgabebefehl: *I/O instruction*
Ein-/Ausgabebus: *I/O bus*
Ein-/Ausgabe-Chip: paralleler ~ *parallel input/output chip*
Ein-/Ausgabedatei: *I/O file*

Ein-/Ausgabedatenbus: *input/output data bus (I/O bus)*

Ein-/Ausgabeeinheit: *input/output unit*

Ein-/Ausgabegerät: *I/O device*

Ein-/Ausgabekanal: *I/O channel*

Ein-/Ausgabemapping: *I/O mapping*

Ein-/Ausgabeprozessor: *input/output processor*

Ein-/Ausgabepuffer: *I/O buffer*

Ein-/Ausgabequittungsbetrieb: *handshake I/O control*

Ein-/Ausgaberegister: *input/output register*

ein-/ausspeichern: *roll in/roll out*

Einband: *binding* **fester** ~ *case binding*

einbauen: *house*

Einbaumodem: *integrated modem*

Einblattdruck: *broadsheet*

Einbrennen: *burn-in*

einbrennen: *blast; burn in*

Einchip-Mikrocontroller: *single-chip microcontroller*

eindeutig: *unique*

Einerkomplement: *one's complement*

einfach: *simple; single*

Einfachadresse: *single address message*

Einfachstrom-Signal: *unipolar signal*

einfach zu benutzen: *easy-to-use; simple to use*

Einfangwinkel: *acceptance angle*

einfarbig: *monochrome*

Einfrequenztonwahl: *single frequency signalling or sf signalling*

einfrieren: *to freeze (frame)*

Einfügemodus: *insert mode*

einfügen: *insert*

Einfügungsdämpfung: *insertion loss*

Einfügungsmodus: *insert mode*

einführen: *introduce; launch*

Einführung: *launch*

Einführungsseite: *lead in page*

Eingabe: *entering; entry; input (i/p or I/P)* **prozessorgesteuerte** ~ *processor controlled keying*

Eingabeanschluß: *input port*

Eingabeanweisung: *input statement*

Eingabeaufforderung: *prompt*

Eingabebedingung: *entry condition*

eingabebegrenzt: *input-bound or limited*

Eingabebereich: *input area*

Eingabeeinheit: *input unit*

Eingabegerät: *input device*

Eingabekarte: **analoge** ~ *analog input card*

Eingabemodus: *input mode*

Eingabeprogramm: *input routine; input section*

Eingabepufferregister: *input buffer register*

Eingaberegister: *input register*

Eingabespeicherbereich: *input area; input section*

Eingabetaste: *enter key; return*

Eingabewarteschlange: *input work queue*

Eingabezeit: *entry time*

Eingang: *entry; input (i/p or I/P)*

Eingangs-: *front-end*

Eingangsfolgeliste: *push-up list or stack*

Eingangslastfaktor: *fan-in*

Eingangssoftware: **benutzerfreundliche** ~ *manager*

eingebaut: *built-in; inbuilt; integral*

Eingebeblock: *input block*

Eingeben: *input (i/p or I/P); keyboarding*

eingeben: *capture; enter; input (i/p or I/P); key in; keyboard*

Eingeben von Hand: *manual entry or manual input*

eingeklammert: *bracketed*

Eingriff: *intervention*

Einheit: *unit* **eingebaute** ~ *integral* **mobile** ~ *mobile unit*

Einheitenpuffer: *unit buffer*

Einheitenstatuswort: *device status word (DSW)*

Einheitenvorrangliste: *device priority*

einklammern: *bracket together*

Einkleben eines Einsteckbogens: *guarding*

Einlagerungstelegraphie: *speech plus*

einlesen: *read-in or read in*

Einmal-Farbband: *single-strike ribbon*

einohrig: *monoaural*

Einpassen: *sizing*

Einplatinenrechner: *single board computer (SBC)*

Einprogrammsystem: *monoprogramming system*

einrahmen: *box in*

einrichten: *adjust*

Einrichten des Zeilenabstands: *interlinear spacing*

Einrichtung: *equipment; feature*

Einrichtungen: *facilities*

einrücken: *to indent*

Einrücken: *indenation*

Einrückung: *indent*

Einsatz: *attack*

Einsatzort: am ~ *on-site*

Einsatzunterstützung: *system support*

einschalten: *activate; enable; switch on; turn on; wake up*

Einschaltquote: *audience rating; ratings*

einschränken: *restrict*

Einschränkung: *restriction*

Einschrittoperation: *single pass operation*

einsehen: *view*

Einseitenband: *single sideband*

Einspeichern: bedarfsmäßiges ~ *demand staging*

einspeichern: *roll-in*

Eins-plus-Eins-Adreßbefehl: *two-address instruction*

Eins-plus-Eins-Adresse: *one-plus-one address*

Einsprungbefehl: *entry instruction*

Einsprungstelle: *entry point*

einstecken: *to plug in*

einstellen: *adjust; appoint; set; set up; tune*

einstellen auf: *to lock onto*
Einstellung: *framing; setting*
Einstellzeit: *positioning time*
Einstichverfahren: *dichotomizing search*
einstufen: *rank*
Eins-zu-Null-Verhältnis: *one to zero ratio*
Einteilung: hierarchische ~ *hierarchical classification*
Eintrag: *attribute; entry* **sekundärer** ~ *or* **zusätzlicher** ~ *added entry*
eintragen: *post*
Einverständnis: *approval*
Einwählmodem: *dial-in modem*
Einweggleichrichter: *half wave rectifier*
Einwegverpackung: *non-returnable packing*
Einzeilenanzeige: *single line display*
Einzeilenfenster: *strip window; thin window*
Einzelanschlag-Programm: *single key response*
Einzelbild: *frame*
Einzelblatteinzug: *single sheet feed* **automatischer** ~ *cut sheet feeder*
Einzelblattzuführung: *sheet feed attachment*
Einzelchipcomputer: *single chip computer*
einzeln: *single*
Einzeloperation: *single operation*
Einzelperson: *individual*
Einzelplatinencomputer: *single board computer (sbc)*
Einzelplatinenmikrocomputer: *single-board microcomputer*
Einzelplatzsystem: *single-user system*
Einzelschritt: *single step*
einzigartig: *unique*
Einzug: *indent*
Eisenoxid: *ferric oxide or ferrite*
Elektretmikrophon: *electret microphone*
elektrisch: *electric; electrical(ly)*
Elektrizität: *electricity*
Elektrode: *electrode*
Elektrofotografie: *electrophotography*
elektrolumineszent: *electroluminescent*
Elektrolumineszenz: *electroluminescence*
Elektrolumineszenzanzeige: *electroluminescent display*
elektrolumineszierend: *electroluminescing*
Elektromagnet: *electromagnet*
elektromagnetisch: *electromagnetic(ally)*
Elektron: *electron*
Elektronenkanone: *electron gun*
Elektronenstrahl: *electron beam*
Elektronenstrahlaufzeichnung: *electron beam recording (EBR)*
Elektronik: *electronics*
Elektronikbaustein: ladungsgekoppelter ~ *charge-coupled device (CCD)*
Elektronikingenieur: *electronic engineer*
elektronisch: *electronic; electronically*
elektrostatisch: *electrostatic; electrostatically*

Element: *element; item* **eingliedriges** ~ *one element* **logisches** ~ *logic element* **zusammengesetztes logisches** ~ *compound logical element*
elementar: *elementary*
Elementarbuch: *primer*
eliminieren: *eliminate*
Eliminierung: *elimination*
Eliminierungsfaktor: *elimination factor*
Elite: *elite*
Ellipse: *ellipse*
ELSE-Regel: *else rule*
Em: *em*
E-Mail: *electronic mail or email or e-mail*
Emission: *emission*
Emitter: *emitter*
Empfang: *reception*
empfangen: *receive*
Empfänger: *addressee; receive only or RO; receiver*
Empfangsbereich: *earth coverage*
Empfangscharakteristik: herzförmige ~ *cardioid response*
Empfangsgerät: *radio receiver*
Empfangsregister: *receiver register*
Empfangssignal eines Datenschwingungsträgers: *data carrier detect (DCD)*
empfindlich: *sensitive*
Empfindlichkeit: *sensitivity*
Empfindlichkeit für α-Teilchen: *alpha-particle sensitivity*
Ems pro Stunde: *ems per hour*
Em-Strich: *em dash or em rule*
Emulation: *emulation*
Emulationsfähigkeit: *emulation facility*
Emulator: *emulator* **integrierter** ~ *integrated emulator*
emulieren: *emulate*
Emulsion: *emulsion*
En: *en*
Endcode: *tail*
Ende: *end; ending; finish* **abnormales** ~ *abend*
Ende der Laufroutine: *end of run routine*
Ende des (Datenübertragungs)blocks: *end of block (EOB)*
enden: *finish*
endgültig: *terminal*
endlos: *endless*
Endlosbandbetrieb: *streaming tape drive*
Endlosfilm: *loop film*
Endlospapier: *continuous stationery; listing paper*
Endlospapiereinzug: *continuous feed*
Endlosschleife: *endless loop; infinite loop*
Endmarke: *rogue indicator; rogue value or terminator*
Endprodukt: *end or final or finished product*
Endübertrag: *end about carry*
Endverbraucher: *end user*
Energie: *energy*

energiesparend: *energy-saving*
En-Strich: *en dash or en rule*
entblocken: *deblock*
entfernen: *remove; takedown*
entfernt: *distant; remote*
Entfernung verdeckter Linien: *hidden line removal*
enthalten: *contain*
enthüllen: *disclose*
entleihen: *borrow*
Entleiher: *borrower*
entmagnetisieren: *degauss; demagnetize*
Entmagnetisierer: *demagnetizer*
Entmagnetisierungsgerät: *degausser*
entmultiplexieren: *demultiplex*
Entmultiplexor: *demultiplexor*
entprellen: *de-bounce*
Entprellungsstromkreis: *de-bounce circuit*
Entscheidung: *decision* logische ~ *decision or discrimination instruction; logical decision*
Entscheidungsbaum: *decision tree*
Entscheidungsschaltung: *decision circuit*
Entscheidungstabelle: *decision table*
Entscheidungsunterstützungssystem: *decision support system*
Entschluß: *decision*
entschlüsseln: *decipher; decode; decrypt; descramble*
Entschlüsselung: *decoding; decryption*
entsprechen: *conform*
Entsprechung: *analog or analogue; correspondence*
entweichen: *leak*
entwenden: *abstract*
entwerfen: *design; draft; lay out; map out*
entwickeln: *develop*
Entwickler: *developer*
Entwicklerflüssigkeit: *developer*
Entwicklung: *development* strukturierte ~ *structured design*
Entwicklungsstand: hoher ~ *sophistication*
Entwicklungszeit: *development time*
Entwurf: *design; draft; layout* einen ~ machen *to draft*
Entzerrer: *equalizer*
Entzerrung: *equalization*
Enveloppe: *envelope*
EOF: *end of file (EOF)*
Epidiaskop: *episcope; opaque projector*
Epitaxie: *epitaxy*
Erde: *earth; GND; ground*
erden: *earth*
Erdfunkstelle: *earth station*
Erdstation: mobile ~ *mobile earth terminal*
Erdung: *earth wire*
Ereignis: *event*
ereignisgesteuert: *event-driven*
erfassen: *collect*

Erfassungsbereich: *coverage; footprint*
erfordern: *require*
Erfordernisse: *requirements*
Ergänzung: *appendix*
Ergebnis: *result*
Ergonom: *ergonomist*
Ergonomie: *ergonomics*
erhalten: *gain; obtain*
erinnern: sich ~ *memorize*
erkennbar: *recognizable*
erkennen: *detect; recognize*
Erkennung: *detection; recognition*
Erkennungslogik: *recognition logic*
Erkennungsteil: *identification division*
Erklärung: *docket (US); narrative* lokale ~ *local declaration*
Erklärungsliste: *description list*
erlauben: *enable*
erledigen: *deal with*
ermächtigen: *authorize*
Ernannte(r): *appointee*
ernennen: *appoint*
Ernennung: *appointment*
Ernennungsschreiben: *letter of appointment*
erneut laden: *reboot*
erneut übertragen: *retransmit*
erneut zeichnen: *redraw*
eröffnen: *open*
Erratum: *erratum*
erreichen: *achieve*
errichten: *construct*
Errichtung: *construction*
Ersatzteil: *spare part*
Ersatz- und Ergänzungsblatt: *cancel page*
Ersatzzeichen: *substitute character*
Erscheinung: *aspect*
Erschließer: *property developer*
ersetzen: *replace; substitute*
Erstadresse: *first-level address*
erstellen: *create; construct*
Erstellen von Computermodellen: *modelling*
Erstellung: *preparation; construction*
erweisen: *establish*
erweiterbar: *extensible*
Erweiterer: *enhancer*
erweitern: *augment; enhance; extend*
Erweiterung: *enhancement; extension*
Erweiterungsplatine: *daughter board; expansion board or add on board*
Erweiterungsposition: *expansion slot*
Erwerb: *acquisition*
erzeugen: *generate*
Erzeugnis: *product*
Erziehungs-: *educational*
ESC-Codes: *escape codes*
E-Schicht der Ionosphäre: *E-region or Heaviside-Kennelly layer*

ESC-Taste: *ESC; escape key*
ESC-Zeichen: *escape character*
Etikett: *external label* **gelochtes** ~ *punched tag*
Euronet: *Euronet*
Exemplar: *copy*
exklusiv-NOR-Funktion: *exclusive NOR (EXNOR)*
exklusiv-NOR-Gatter: *exclusive NOR gate; EXNOR gate*
exklusiv-ODER-Funktion: *exclusive OR (EXOR); exjunction*
exklusiv-ODER-Gatter: *except gate; exclusive OR gate; EXOR gate*
Exklusivvertrag: *exclusive agreement*
expandierbar: *expandable*
expandieren: *expand*
Experte: *expert*
Expertensystem: *expert system*
Expertin: *expert*
Exponent: *exponent* **binärer** ~ *binary exponent* **kodierter** ~ *biased exponent*
Extension beim Dateinamen: *filename extension*
extern: *external*
Extracode: *extracode*
Extrapolation: *extrapolation*

Ff

Fabrik: *factory*
Fabrikpreis: *factory price*
Facette: *facet*
Facettencode: *faceted code*
-fach: *-fold*
Fachausstellung: anwendungsorientierte ~ *business efficiency exhibition*
Fächerantenne: *fan antenna*
Fachmann: *specialist*
Fachzeitschrift: *learned journal*
Fähigkeit: arithmetische ~ *arithmetic capability*
Fahnen: *streaking*
Fahrzeug: computergesteuertes ~ *buggy*
Faksimile: *facsimile*
Faksimilezeichengenerator: *facsimile character generator*
Faktor: entscheidender ~ *deciding factor*
Faktoren: in ~ **zerlegen** *factorize*
Faktotum: *gofer (informal)*
Fakultät: *factorial*
falsch: *false; inaccurate; incorrect*
FALSE-Code: *false code*
falten: *fold*
Falzmaschine: *folding machine*
Familie: *family*
Fangstelle: *trap; trapdoor*
Faraday: *farad (F)*
Faradaykäfig: *Faraday cage*

Farbaberration *or* **Farbabweichung:** *chromatic aberration*
Farbabstimmung: *colour balance*
Farbauszug: *colour separation*
Farbband: *printer ribbon* **mehrfach benutzbares** ~ *multi-strike printer ribbon*
Farbbildschirm: *colour display*
Farbcodierer: *colour encoder*
Farbdecodierer: *colour decoder*
Farbdetektor: *chroma detector*
Farbdia: *colour transparency*
Farbe: *colour*
Farbenreinheit *or* **Farbenintensität:** *chroma*
Farberkennungssignal: *colour burst*
Farbgraphikadapter: *colour graphics adapter (CGA)*
Farbkontrolle: *chroma control*
Farbmischen: additives ~ *additive colour mixing*
Farbmischsignal: *composite video signal*
Farbmonitor: *colour monitor*
Farbsättigung: *colour saturation*
Farbseparation: *colour separation*
Farbsignal: *chrominance signal*
Farbtemperatur: *colour temperature*
Farbton: *tone*
Farbtonänderung: *hangover*
Farbtönung: *shade*
Farbumsetzer: *colour encoder*
Farbverschiebung: *colour shift*
Farbzelle: *colour cell*
Faseroptik: *fibre optics*
Fax: *fax or FAX*
faxen: *to fax or FAX*
Fazilität: *facility*
Fehlanpassung: *mismatch*
Fehler: *defect; error; fault; inaccuracy; problem* **andauernder** ~ *hard error* **bewußter** ~ *conscious error* **bleibender** ~ *solid error* **dauerhafter** ~ *permanent error* **erkannter** ~ *detected error* **generierter** ~ *generated error* **kurzzeitiger** ~ *transient error* **logischer** ~ *logical error* **mitgelaufener** ~ *propagated error* **mitgeschleppter** ~ *inherited error* **mitlaufender** ~ *propagating error* **nicht korrigierbarer** ~ *unrecoverable error* **relativer** ~ *relative error* **schlimmer** ~ *catastrophic error* **sporadischer** ~ *sporadic fault* **ständiger** ~ *permanent error* **symmetrischer** ~ *balanced error* **syntaktischer** ~ *syntactic error* **typographischer** ~ *typo (informal); typographical error* **unentdeckter** ~ *undetected error* **weicher** ~ *soft-fail* **wiederherstellbarer** ~ *recoverable error* **zeitweise auftretender** ~ *intermittent error*
Fehlerbedingung: *error condition*
Fehlerbehebung: *error handling or management; error recovery; error trapping*
Fehlerbereich: asymmetrischer ~ *bias*
Fehlercode: *error code*
Fehlerdiagnose: *error diagnosis; fault diagnosis*
Fehlerdiagnostik: *error diagnostics*
Fehler durch Fremdkörpereinwirkung: *soft error*

Fehlerentdeckung: *fault detection*
Fehlererfassung: *error logging*
Fehlererkennung: *error detection; problem diagnosis* **automatische** *~ automatic error detection*
Fehlererkennungscode: *error detecting code; self-checking code*
Fehlererkennungsroutine: *malfunction routine*
Fehlererkennung und -korrektur: *error detection and correction (EDAC)*
Fehlerfortpflanzung: *error propagation*
fehlerfrei: *perfect(ly)*
fehlerhaft: *corrupt; faulty*
Fehlerhäufigkeit: *error rate*
Fehlerhäufung: *error burst*
Fehlerkorrektur: *error correction* **automatische** *~ automatic error correction* **rückwärtige** *~ backward error correction*
Fehlerkorrekturcode: *error correcting code*
Fehlerlokalisierungsprogramm: *fault location program*
Fehler löschen: *bloop*
Fehlermeldung: *error message* **diagnostische** *~ diagnostic error message* **falsche** *~ false error*
Fehlerprotokoll: *fault trace*
Fehlerprüfcode: *error checking code*
Fehlerprüfung: zyklische *~ cyclic check*
Fehlerprüfung und -korrektur: *ERCC*
Fehlerquote *or* **Fehlerrate:** *error rate*
Fehlerroutine: *error routine*
Fehlersignalisierung: *alarm*
Fehlerspanne *or* **Fehlerspielraum:** *margin of error*
Fehlersuchprogramm: *debugger*
fehlertolerant: *fault-tolerant*
Fehlertoleranz: *fault tolerance*
Fehlerüberwachung: *error control*
Fehlerunterbrechungen: *error interrupts*
Fehlerwiederherstellung: *failure recovery*
fein: *fine*
feineinstellen: *fine tune*
Feinlinierung: *feint*
Feld: *field* **festes** *~ fixed field* **geschütztes** *~ protected field* **programmierbares logisches** *~ programmable logic array (PLA)* **ungeschütztes** *~ unprotected field*
Feldanordnung: *fielding*
Feldeffekttransistor: *field effect transistor (FET)*
Feldeffekttransistor mit Metalloxid-Halbleiteraufbau: *metal oxide semiconductor field effect transistor (MOSFET)*
Feldforschung: *field work*
Feldfrequenz: *field frequency*
Feldgröße: *item size*
Feldgruppe: *array* **alphanumerische** *~ alphanumeric array* **flexible** *~ flexible array* **mehrdimensionale** *~ multidimensional array* **zweidimensionale** *~ two-dimensional array*
Feldkennung: *field label*
Feldlänge: *field length*

Feldmarkierungszeichen: *field marker or separator*
Feldnamenerklärung: *data dictionary/directory (DD/D)*
Feldprogrammierung: *field programming*
Feldstärke: *field strength*
Femto-: *femto- (f)*
Femtosekunde: *femto second*
Fenster: *window* **aktives** *~ active window*
Fenstertechnik: *windowing*
Fensterumschlag: *window envelope*
Fern-: *remote; tele-*
Ferndatensteuereinheit: *data adapter unit*
Ferngespräch: *long-distance call; trunk call (GB)*
fernladbar: *downloadable*
fernladen: *download*
Fernleihe: *inter-library loan (ILL)*
Fernmeldesatellit: internationaler *~ INTELSAT*
Fernmeldewesen: *telecommunications*
Fernmessung: *telemetry*
Fernnachricht: *telemessage (GB)*
Fernsatz: *teletypesetting*
Fernschreiber: *teleprinter; teletype (TTY); teletypewriter; telex*
Fernschreiberpapier: *teleprinter roll*
Fernschreiberschnittstelle: *teleprinter interface*
Fernsehempfänger: *television receiver*
Fernsehen: *television (TV)*
Fernsehen mit Extragebühr: *pay TV*
Fernsehgerät: *set; television (TV)*
Fernsehkamera: *television camera*
Fernsehmonitor: *television monitor*
Fernsehprogramm: vernetztes *~ networked TV programme*
Fernsehprojektor: *television projector*
Fernsehröhre: *television tube*
Fernsehsignalverstärker: *launch amplifier*
Fernsehsysteme: *video standards*
Fernsprechamt: *telephone exchange* **computergesteuertes** *~ automatic telephone exchange*
Fernsprechvermittlung: private *~ private automatic exchange (PAX)*
Fernsprechwesen: *telephony*
Fernsteuerung: *remote control*
Fernverbindungskabel: *trunk*
Fernvermittlungsstelle: *trunk exchange (GB)*
Ferritkern: *ferrite core*
Ferrodielektrikum: *electret*
fertig: *complete; finished*
Fertigerzeugnisse: *finished goods*
fertig sein: *finish*
Fertigung: computergestützte *~ computer-aided or -assisted manufacture (CAM)* **computerintegrierte** *~ computer-integrated manufacturing (CIM)* **maschinelle** *~ machining*
Fertigungsabteilung: *production department*
Fertigungsingenieur: *product engineer*
Fertigungssteuerung: *production control*

Fertigungssystem: flexibles ~ *flexible manufacturing system (FMS)*
Fertigungs- und Lieferzeit: *turnaround time (TAT)*
fest: *static*
fest binden: *case*
Festdaten: *fixed data*
fest eingebaut: *built into*
festhalten: *retain*
Festkommarechnung: *fixed-point arithmetic*
Festkommaschreibweise: *fixed-point notation*
Festkopf: *disk head*
Festkörper-: *solid-state*
Festkörperlaser: *solid-state laser*
Festkörperspeicher: *solid-state memory device*
Festlegung: erklärende ~ *narrative statement*
Festplatte: *fixed disk; hard disk; Winchester disk or drive*
Festplattenlaufwerk: *hard disk drive*
Festplattenlaufwerksplatine: *hard card*
Festplattenmodell: *hard disk model*
Festplattenspeicher: *fixed disk storage*
Festprogrammcomputer: *fixed program computer*
festsetzen: *establish; fix*
Festspeichermonitorprogramm: residentes ~ *firmware monitor*
Feststelltaste: *caps lock*
Fest(wert)speicher: *read only memory (ROM)* **maskierter ~** *masked ROM* **einen ~ löschen** *wash PROM* **einen ~ programmieren** *blow*
Festzeichendrucker: *solid font printer*
fett: *bold face*
Fettdruck: *bold face*
Feuerprobe: *smoke test*
FIFO-Speichermethode: *FIFO memory or first in first out memory*
FIFO-Warteschlange: *FIFO queue*
Film: *film; motion picture* **fotografischer ~** *photographic film* **lithographischer ~** *lith film* **orthochromatischer ~** *ortho or orthochromatic film*
Film-: *cine-*
Filmabtaster: *film pickup*
Filmandruckplatte: *platen*
Filmebene: *image plane*
Filmempfindlichkeitsangabe: *ASA exposure index*
Filmen: *cinematography* **das ~** *the cinema*
Film-Fernsehbetrieb-Methode: *telecine*
Filmkamera: *camera; cine camera*
Filmleseeinheit: optische ~ *film optical scanning device for input into computers (FOSDIC)*
Filmlochkarte: *aperture card*
Filmprojektor: *film projector*
Filmstreifen: *film strip*
Filmträger: *film base*
Filmtransport(hebel): *film advance*
Filmvorführaggregat: *film chain*

Filter: *filter*
finden: *find*
Fingerhutdrucker: *thimble printer*
Finish: *finish*
Firma: *house*
Firmeninformationsblatt: *company newsletter*
Firmenname: *corporate name*
Firmenverzeichnis: *commercial or trade directory*
Firmenvorstand: *board*
Firmware: *firmware*
First Fit: *first fit*
Fischauge: *fisheye lens*
fixieren: *fix*
Fixierung: *fix*
Flachbettgerät: *flatbed*
Flachbettplotter: *flatbed plotter*
Flachbettpresse: *flatbed press*
Flachbettscanner: *flatbed transmitter*
Flachdatei: *flat file*
Flächenmaß: *square measure*
Flachgehäuse: *flat pack*
flackern: *flicker*
Flag: *flag*
Flattermarken: *collating marks*
Flattern: *jitter*
Flattersatz: ragged text im ~ *unjustified* **linksbündiger ~** *ragged right* **rechtsbündiger ~** *ragged left*
Fleisch: *beard*
flexibel: *flexible*
Flexibilität: *flexibility*
Flickschusterei: *kludge or kluge (informal)*
fliegen: *fly*
fliegend: *on the fly*
Fließband: *production line*
fließen: *flow*
fließend: *floating*
Fließkommaarithmetik: *floating point arithmetic*
Fließkommabetriebsart: *noisy mode*
Fließkommaoperation: *floating point operation (FLOP)*
Fließkommaprozessor: *floating point processor*
Fließkommarechnungen pro Sekunde: *FLOPs per second*
Fließkommaschreibweise: *floating point (notation)*
Fließkommazahl: *floating point number*
flimmerfrei: *flicker-free*
flimmern: *flicker*
Flipflop: *flip-flop (FF)*
Flippy: *flippy*
Flüchtigkeit: *volatility*
Flugblatt: *broadside (US)*
Flugsimulator: *flight simulator*
Fluß: *flow* **magnetischer ~** *magnetic flux*
Flußdiagramm: *flowchart; flow diagram* **logisches ~** *logic(al) flowchart*

Flüssigkristallanzeige: *liquid crystal display (LCD)*

Flußsteuerung: *flow control*

Fokussierung: magnetische ~ *magnetic focusing*

Folge: *sequence*

Folgekontrolle: *sequence check*

Folgeseite: *continuation page*

Folgestation: *secondary station*

Folgesteuerungsmechanismus: *servo or servomechanism*

Folientastatur: *touch sensitive keyboard*

Font: *font or fount*

Förderband: *conveyor*

fordern: *demand*

Forderung: *demand*

Form: ausführbare ~ *executable form*

Format: *format* **gepacktes** ~ *packed format* **internes** ~ *internal format* **variables** ~ *variable format; V format*

formatieren: *to format a disk* **neu** ~ *reformat*

Formatierung: *disk formatting*

Formatisierungsprogramm: *formatter*

Formatmodus: *format mode*

Formatsteuerungseinheit: vertikale ~ *vertical format unit (VFU)*

Formbrief: *form letter; repetitive letter; standard letter*

Formel: *formula*

Formmaske *or* **Formschablone:** *form overlay*

Formular: *form* **vorgedrucktes** ~ *preprinted form*

Formulareinblendung: *form flash*

Formulare mit Kohlepapier: *carbon set*

Formularmodus: *form mode*

Formularseite: *form*

Formularvorschub: *form feed*

FOR-NEXT-Schleife: *for-next loop*

Forschung: *research*

Forschungs- und Entwicklungsabteilung: *R & D department*

Forschung und Entwicklung: *research and development (R & D)*

fortdrucken: *run on*

fortfahren: *proceed*

fortgeschritten: *advanced*

FORTH: *FORTH*

FORTRAN: *FORTRAN*

Fortschaltungsadressierung: *implied addressing*

Fortschreibung: *file maintenance; file update*

Fortschreibungsdatei: *update file or transaction file*

fortsetzen: *continue*

Fortsetzung: *continuation*

Fortsetzungsseite: *continuation page*

Foto-: *photo*

Fotoapparat: *camera*

Fotografie: *photograph; photography*

fotografieren: *film*

fotografisch: *photographic; photographically*

Fotogravüre: *photogravure*

Fotokopie: *photocopy; photostat*

Fotokopierbüro: *photocopying bureau*

Fotokopieren: *photocopying*

fotokopieren: *photocopy; photostat*

Fotokopierer: *photocopier*

Fotolithographie: *photolithography*

Fotoresist *or* **Fotolack:** *photoresist*

Fotoresistverfahren: positives ~ *positive photoresist*

Fotosatz: *filmsetting; photocomposition; phototext; phototypesetting*

Fotosetzer: *phototypesetter*

Fourier-Serie: *Fourier series*

Frage: *interrogation; question* **in** ~ **stellen** *to query*

Frage-Antwort-System: *inquiry/response*

Fragebogen: *questionnaire*

fragen: *question*

Fragmentierung: *fragmentation*

frei: *free; freely*

Freigabe: *release*

freigeben: *clear; deallocate; release*

freihalten: *assign*

Freiheit: *freedom*

Freilaufprotokoll: *free wheeling*

Freiraumdämpfung: *free space loss*

Freispeicher: *heap*

Freizeichen: *dial tone; dialling tone*

Freizeichensignal: *mark hold*

Freizeichnungsklausel: *exclusion clause*

fremd: *alien*

Fremdhersteller: *original equipment manufacturer (OEM); third party*

Fremdsprache: *foreign language*

Fremdübernahme: *importation*

Frequenz: *frequency* **extremhohe** ~ *extremely high frequency (EHF)* **zugeordnete** ~ *assigned frequency*

Frequenzanalysator: *frequency analyzer*

Frequenzbandaufteilung: *beam diversity*

Frequenzbereich: *frequency range*

Frequenzebene: *frequency domain*

Frequenzentzerrer: *frequency equalizer*

Frequenzgang: *frequency response*

Frequenzmodulation: *frequency modulation (FM)* **modifizierte** ~ *modified frequency modulation*

Frequenz-Multiplexmethode: *frequency division multiplexing (FDM)*

Frequenzteiler: *frequency divider*

Frequenzumtastung: *frequency shift keying (FSK)*

Frequenzvariation: *frequency variation*

Frequenzverschieber: *frequency changer*

Friktionsantrieb: *friction feed*

FROM: *fusible read only memory (FROM)*

Front: *front*

Frontplatte: *fascia plate*

F-Schicht der Ionosphäre: *F-region*

fühlbar: *tactile*

Führungskante: *aligning edge; leading edge*

Führungskraft: *executive*

Führungslöcher: *sprocket holes; feed holes*

Führungspunkte: *leader*

füllen: *fill*

Füllzeichen: *fill character; gap character*

Füllziffer: *gap digit*

Fünf-Bit-Byte: *quintet*

Funk: *radio*

Funkamateur: *radio ham*

Funkempfänger: abtastender ~ *scanning radio receiver* **mobiler** ~ *mobile (informal)*

Funkendrucker: *spark printer*

Funkfeld: *hop*

Funkfrequenz: *radio frequency (RF)*

Funkgerät: *radio transceiver*

Funkmikrophon: *radio microphone*

Funk- od Fernsehnetz: *radio or television network*

Funkspektrum: *radio spectrum*

Funkstation: *radio station*

Funkstörung: *garbage*

Funktelefon: *radio phone or radio telephone* **mobiles** ~ *mobile radiophone*

Funktelegraphie: *radio telegraphy*

Funktion: *function* **lineare** ~ *linear function*

Funktionen: arithmetische ~ *arithmetic functions*

funktionieren: *function; work*

funktionierend: *working* **gut** ~ *well-behaved*

Funktions-: *functional*

Funktionsanzeiger: *role indicator*

Funktionsbeschreibung: *functional specification*

Funktionscode: *function code*

Funktionsdiagramm: *functional diagram*

Funktionseinheit: *functional unit*

funktionsfähig: *operational*

Funktionsnetz: *nomogram or nomograph*

Funktionsstörung: technische ~ *man-made noise*

Funktionstabelle: *function table*

Funktionstaste: *function key*

Funktionstasten: frei belegbare ~ *soft keys*

Funktions- und Eignungsprüfung: *verification and validation (V & V)*

Funkübertragungssystem: *gap*

Funkverkehr: *radiocommunications*

Funkwellen: *radio waves*

Fusion: *fusion*

Fusionsfrequenz: kritische ~ *critical fusion frequency*

Fuß: *foot*

Fußkerze: *foot candle*

Fußnote: *footnote*

Fußsteg: *bottom space*

Fußzeile: *footer or footing*

Gg

GaAs: *gallium arsenide (GaAs)*

Gabelung: *bifurcation*

Galgen: *boom*

Gamma: *gamma*

Gangzahl: *cycle count*

Garant: *warrantor*

Garantie: *guarantee; warranty*

Garantieempfänger: *warrantee*

Garantiegeber: *warrantor*

Garantieinhaber: *warrantee*

garantieren: *warrant*

Gatter: *gate*

Gatteranordnung: *gate array*

Gebiet: *area*

Gebietsleiter: *area manager*

Gebrauch: *use*

Gebrauchsanweisung: *directions for use*

gebraucht: *used*

Gebrauchtgerät: *second user or second hand equipment*

gebrochen: *fractional*

Gebühr: *tariff*

Gedankenstrich: *dash; em dash or em rule*

Gedrucktes: *print*

Gefahr: *hazard*

gegen-: *anti-; counter-*

Gegenkabelfernsehbetrieb: *two way cable (US)*

Gegenprobe: *cross-check*

Gegenradiobetrieb: *two way radio*

Gegensprechanlage: *intercom*

Gegenstelle: *remote station*

Gegenteil: *inverse*

gegenüberstellen: *contrast*

Gegenverkehrsverbindung: *duplex circuit*

Gehalt: *content*

Gehäuse: *case; casing; chassis; enclosure; housing* **nichtgeerdetes** ~ *hot chassis*

Geisterbild: *ghost*

Gelände: *site*

Geldausgabeautomat: *automated teller machine (ATM); automatic telling machine or automatic teller machine (US)*

Geldkassette: *cash box*

gemäß: *as per*

Gemeingut: *public domain*

gemeinsam: *common*

gemeinsam benutzen: *share*

Gemeinschaft: *community*

Gemeinschaftsanschluß: *port sharing*

Gemeinschaftsantennenanlage: *master antenna television system (MATV)*

Gemeinschaftsbetrieb: *time-sharing*

Gemeinschaftsbus: *shared bus*

Gemeinschaftscomputersystem: *multiple base page*

Gemeinschaftsdatei: *shared file*

Gemeinschaftsleitung: *party line or shared line*

Gemeinschaftsspeicher: *shared memory*

genau: *accurate; precise*

genau auflisten: *detail*

Genauigkeit: *accuracy; precision* **doppelte ~** *double precision* **~ single precision**

genehmigen: *authorize*

Genehmigungszertifikat: *certificate of approval*

Generalindex: *main index*

Generation: *generation* **erste ~** *first generation*

Generator: *generator*

generieren: *generate*

Generierung: *generation*

Generierungsprogramm: *generator*

geordnet: *order*

gerade: *even*

Gerät: *appliance; device* **intelligentes ~** *intelligent device*

Geräteanordnung: *hardware configuration*

Geräteanzeiger: *device flag*

Gerätefehler: *equipment failure*

Gerätekennung: *device code*

Geräteschnittstelle: *terminal interface*

Gerätesteuerprogramm: *peripheral software driver*

Gerätesteuerzeichen: *device control character*

Gerätetreiber: *device driver*

geräteunabhängig: *device independent*

Gerätezeichensteuerung: *device character control*

Geräusch: *sound*

Geräuschkulisse: *sound effects*

gereinigt: *clean*

gerichtet: *directional*

Germanium: *germanium*

Gesamtausfall: *blackout or black out*

Gesamtindex: *dense index*

Gesamtlaufzeit: *up and down propagation time*

Gesamtraum: *volume*

Gesamtverarbeitungszeit: *elapsed time*

Geschäft: *business; deal*

Geschäftsadresse: *business address*

Geschäftscomputer: *business computer*

Geschäftskorrespondenz: *business correspondence*

Geschäftsleute am Ort: *the local business community*

Geschäftsname als Markenbezeichnung: *own brand*

geschehen: *occur*

geschichtet: *layered*

Geschlechtsumwandler: *gender changer (informal)*

Geschwindigkeit: *speed; velocity* **mittlere ~** *medium speed*

gesichert: *secured*

gesondert verarbeiten: *cache*

Gespann: **im ~ arbeiten** *work in tandem*

gestreut laden: *scatter load*

gestreut lesen: *scatter read*

getrennt: *separate*

Geviert: *em quad*

Gewähr: *warranty*

gewartet: **gut ~** *well maintained*

Gewebeband: *fibre ribbon*

Gewicht: *weight*

gewichtet: *weighted*

Gewichtung: *weighting*

GHz: *GHz*

Gieren: *yaw*

Gießmaschine: *caster machine*

Gigabyte: *gigabyte*

Gigahertz: *gigahertz*

Giga *or* **G:** *giga- or G*

GIGO: *garbage in garbage out (GIGO)*

GINO: *GINO*

Glanz-: *glossy*

glänzend: *glossy*

Glasfaser: *optical fibre*

glatt beschnitten: *flush*

glätten: *filter*

gleich: *equal; equally*

Gleichheit: *equality; equivalence; parity*

gleichkommen: *equal*

Gleichlaufschwankung: *flutter; wow*

gleichmachen: *equalize*

gleichrichten: *rectify*

Gleichrichter: *rectifier*

gleichsetzen: *equate*

Gleichstrom: *direct current (DC)*

Gleichstromsignal: *DC signalling*

Gleichstromumrichter: *inverter*

Gleichung: *equation*

Gleichwertigkeit: *equivalence*

gleichwertig sein: *to be equivalent to*

gleichzeitig: *simultaneous; simultaneously*

gleichzeitig ablaufend: *concurrent; concurrently*

Gleichzeitigkeit: *simultaneity*

gleiten: *slide*

Gleitkommaprogramm: *floating-point routines*

Gleitpunktexponent: *characteristic*

Glied: *member*

Gliederung: *outline*

Gliederungsdiagramm: *outline flowchart*

global: *global*

global aufrufen: *site poll*

Goldkontakte: *gold contacts*

Grad: *grade*

Grafikerbüro: *design studio*

Gramm: *gram or gramme*

Grammatik: *grammar*

Gramm pro Quadratmeter: *gsm or g/m^2*

Graph: *graph*

Graphik: *graphics* **zusammenhängende ~** *contiguous graphics*
Graphikbibliothek: *graphics library*
Graphikblock: *graphics pad*
Graphik-Coprozessor: *graphics coprocessor*
Graphikkarte: erweiterte ~ *enhanced graphics adapter (EGA)*
Graphikkernsystem: *graphics kernel system (GKS)*
Graphikmodus: *graphics mode; plotting mode*
Graphikprozessor: *graphics processor*
Graphikschrank: *planchest*
Graphiksoftware: *graphics software*
Graphiktablett: *graphics tablet*
Graphikterminal: *graphics terminal*
Graphikterminal für Fotosatz: *graphics art terminal*
Graphik-VDU: *graphics VDU*
Graphikverarbeitung: dialogfähige ~ *interactive graphics*
graphisch: *graphic; graphical; graphically*
graphisch darstellen: *plot*
Grauschleier: *fog*
Grauskala *or* **Grauwerte:** *grey scale*
Gravis: *grave accent*
Gray-Verschlüsselung: *Gray code; reflected code*
greifen: *grab; grip*
Grenzauflösung: *limiting resolution*
Grenzen: *boundary; bounds* **elastische ~** *elastic banding*
Grenzen der Strukturgröße: *array bounds*
Grenzenregister: *boundary register*
Grenzenschutz: *boundary protection*
Grenzfrequenz: *cutoff frequency*
Grenzmarkierung: *boundary punctuation*
Grenzwerte: *limits*
Großbuchstabe: *majuscule*
Großbuchstaben: *block capitals or block letters; capitals or caps (informal); upper case*
Größe: *size*
Größendarstellung mit Vorzeichen: *sign and magnitude or signed magnitude*
Größenwandler: *quantizer*
Großintegration: *large-scale integration (LSI)*
Großrechner: *mainframe (computer); supercomputer; large-scale computer*
Großrechnerzugang: *mainframe access*
Großspeicher: *mass storage system*
Größtintegration: *super large scale integration (SLSI)*
Größtrechner: *supercomputer*
Großvaterdatei: *grandfather file*
Großvaterzyklus: *grandfather cycle*
Groteskschrift: *sans serif*
Grundadresse: *base address*
Grundbefehl: *basic instruction*
Grundcode: *basic code*
Grunde: im ~ *basically*
Grundfarben: *primary colours*

Grundfrequenz: *fundamental frequency*
grundlegend: *basic*
Grundlinie: *base line*
Grundplatine: *motherboard*
Grundposition: *base*
Grundriß: *floor plan*
Grundschrift: *body type*
Grundstellung: in ~ bringen *reset*
Grundstruktur: *framework*
Grundzustand: *stable state*
Gruppe: *group; set*
Gruppenabruf *or* **Gruppenaufruf:** *group poll*
Gruppenmarke: *group mark or marker*
Gruppenschalter: *ganged switch*
Gruppensteuereinheit: *cluster controller*
gruppieren: *group*
gruppiert: *ganged*
Gruppierung: *clustering*
Gucki: *(hand) viewer*
gültig: *legal; valid* **für ~ erklären** *validate*
Gültigkeit: *validity*
Gültigkeitsprüfung: *validation; validity check*
Gummituchzylinder: *blanket cylinder*
Güteklasse: *grade*
gutheißen: *to approve of*
Gutmütigkeit: *robustness*

Hh

Hacker: *hacker*
Halbaddierer: *half adder or two input adder* **binärer ~** *binary half adder*
Halbbild: *field*
Halbbildabtastung: *field sweep*
Halbbildaustastung: *field blanking*
Halbduplexmodem: *half-duplex modem*
Halbduplex(übertragung): *half duplex; HD*
Halbgeviert: *en quad*
Halbierungsverfahren: *binary search or chop*
halbkompiliert: *semicompiled*
Halbleiter: *semiconductor* **reiner ~** *pure semiconductor*
Halbleiterbauelement: *semiconductor device*
Halbleiterbauteil: *solid-state device*
Halbleiterlaser: *semiconductor laser*
Halbleiterscheibe: *wafer*
Halbleiterspeicher: *semiconductor memory*
Halbton(bild): *halftone or half-tone*
Halbwort: *half word*
Hälfte: *half*
Halleffekt: *hall effect*
Halleffektschalter: *hall effect switch*
Hallraum: *echo chamber*
Halogenid: *halide*
Halt: programmierter ~ *programmed halt*
Haltbedingung: *halt condition*

Haltbefehl: *halt instruction*
Haltebefehl: *stop instruction*
Haltecode: *stop code*
Halteimpuls: *hold*
Haltelinie: *holding line*
Haltestrom: *hold current*
Haltezeit: *holding time*
‚Hammer': *howler*
Hamming-Abstand: *Hamming distance*
Hamming-Code: *Hamming code*
Hand: von ~ *manually*
Handbuch: *manual*
Handbuch mit Anweisungen: *instruction manual*
Handcomputer: *hand-held programmable*
Handelsadreßbuch: *commercial or trade directory*
handgeschrieben: *handwritten*
Händler: *dealer*
Handschrift: *handwriting*
Handvermittlungsanlage: private ~ *private manual branch exchange (PMBX)*
Handzettel: *flier; leaflet*
Hardcover: *hardcover*
Hardware: *hardware*
Hardware-Fehler: *hard failure*
Hardwarekompatibilität: *hardware compatibility*
hardwarenah: *machine intimate*
Hardwaresicherheit: *hardware security*
Hardwareteil: *external device*
Hardwareunterbrechung: *hardware interrupt*
hart: *hard*
Hartbleisatz: gegossener ~ *hot metal composition*
Hartformatierung: *hard-sectoring*
Hartkopie: *hard copy*
Hartley: *hartley*
hartsektoriert: *hard-sectored*
Hash-Code: *hash code*
Hash-Code-System: *hash-code system*
Hash-Funktion Algorithmus: *hashing function*
Hash-Index: *hash index*
Hash-Tabelle: *hash table*
Hash-Wert: *hash value*
Hash-Zeichen: *hashmark or hash mark*
Haube: *hood*
häufig: *common; frequent*
Haupt-: *central; main; master; primary; prime*
Hauptattribut: *prime attribute*
Hauptband: *master tape*
Hauptbedienerstation: *master terminal*
Hauptbelastungszeit: *peak period*
Hauptbüro: *general office*
Hauptdaten: *master data*
Hauptdatenstation: *key terminal*
Haupteinrichtung: *key feature*
Haupteintrag: *main entry*
Hauptmenü: *main menu*
Hauptplatine: *motherboard*

Hauptplatte: *master disk*
Hauptprogramm: *main routine*
Hauptprogrammdatei: *master program file*
Hauptquartier: *base*
Hauptrechner: *host computer; master computer*
hauptsächlich: *primarily*
Hauptspeicher: *core memory or store; mai memory or storage; primary memory or store c storage*
Hauptspeicherabbild: *memory map*
Hauptstrahl: *main beam*
Haupttaktgeber: *main clock; master clock; timin master*
Hauptterminal: *central terminal*
Hauptübertragungsweg: *A-bus*
Hauptverbindung: *bus*
Hauptvermittlungskanal: *forward channel*
Hauptverteiler: *main distributing frame*
Hauptzyklus: *major cycle*
Hauskorrekturen: *house corrections*
Hausstil: *house style*
Haustelefon: *house (tele)phone or interna (tele)phone*
HD-Videosystem: *HDVS*
Hebern: *siphoning*
heften: *clip*
Heimcomputer: *home computer*
Heiratsvermittlung: computerisierte ~ *compute dating*
Hektographieren: *spirit duplication*
helfen: *aid; assist*
Heliogravüre: *photogravure*
hell: *light*
Hell-auf-dunkel-Bild: *cameo*
Helligkeit: *brightness*
Helligkeitsbereich: *brightness range*
Helligkeitseinstellung: *brightness setting*
herausfiltrieren: *filter*
herausfinden: *retrieve*
Herausgeber: *editor*
Herausgreifen eines Bildes: *screen grab*
herausnehmen: *extract; pull*
herstellen: *manufacture; produce*
Hersteller: *manufacturer; producer*
Hersteller von Fremdfabrikaten: *OEM*
Hersteller von Raubdrucken: *pirate*
Herstellung: *origination; production*
Herstellung eines Prototyps: *prototyping*
Herstellung eines Schriftsatzes: *boilerplating*
Hertz: *Hertz*
hervorheben: *to highlight*
Hervorhebungen: *highlights*
hervorholen: *to pop on*
Hervorholmenü: *pop-down or pop-up menu*
heuristisch: *heuristic*
Hexadezimalschreibweise: *hex or hexadecima notation*
Hidden-Line-Algorithmus: *hidden line algorithr*

Hierarchie: *hierarchy*
Hi-Fi: *hi fi or hifi*
Hi-Fi-Anlage: *hi fi system*
High-Fidelity: *high fidelity*
Hilfe: *aid; assistance; help*
HILFE-Funktion: *help*
Hilfsbit: *service bit*
Hilfsgeräte: *auxiliary equipment*
Hilfskanal: *backward channel; reverse channel*
Hilfsmittel: audiovisuelle ~ *audiovisual aids*
Hilfsprogramme: *tools*
Hilfsprozessor: *auxiliary processor*
Hilfsspeicher: *auxiliary storage or memory or store; backing store or storage or memory*
Hilfszugriffsspeicher: *intermediate access memory (IAM)*
hineinstecken: *insert; slot*
Hintergrund: *background* **im ~** *ambient*
Hintergrundfarbe: *background colour*
Hintergrundgeräusch: *ambient noise level*
Hintergrundjob: *background job*
Hintergrundkommentar: *voice-over*
Hintergrundprogramm: *background program*
Hintergrundprogrammbetrieb: *background*
Hintergrundprojektion: *background or back projection*
Hintergrundtask: *background task*
Hintergrundverarbeitung: *background processing*
hinübertragen: *carry*
Hin- und Rücklauf: *sweep*
hinunterfallen: *drop*
hinunterladbar: *downloadable*
hinunterladen: *download*
Hinweisadresse: *pointer*
hinweisen: *point out*
Hinweisschildchen: *label*
Hinweisspur: *library track*
hinzufügen: *add*
Histogramm: *histogram*
Hochdruckverfahren: *relief printing*
hochentwickelt: *sophisticated*
Hochfrequenz: *HF; high frequency; radio frequency (RF)*
Hochfrequenzmodulator: *RF modulator or radio frequency modulator*
Hochgeschwindigkeits-: *high-speed*
Hochgeschwindigkeits-analog-digital-Umsetzer: *flash A/D*
Hochgeschwindigkeitskopierer: *high-speed duplicator*
Hochglänzenden: die ~ *the glossies (informal)*
Hochladen: *uploading*
hochladen: *upload*
Hochleistung: *high performance*
Hochleistungsausrüstung: *high performance equipment*
Hochpaßfilter: *high pass filter*
Hochrechnung: *extrapolation*

hochspezifiziert: *high-spec (informal)*
Höchstleistung: *peak output*
Höchstleistungsgrenze: *maximum capacity*
höchstpassend: *best fit*
Höchststand: den ~ erreichen *to peak*
Hochtonlautsprecher: *tweeter (informal)*
Hochzahl: *superior number*
hochzählen: *increment*
Höhen: gemischte ~ *mixed highs*
Hohlleiter: *waveguide*
Holanweisung: *get*
Hollerith-Code: *Hollerith code*
Hologramm: *hologram; holographic image*
Holographie: *holography*
Holographum: *holograph*
Holzschliffpapier: *mechanical paper*
Home-Banking: *home banking; telebanking*
Hör-: *aural*
hörbar: *audible*
Hörer abgehoben: *off hook*
Hörer aufgelegt: *on hook*
horizontal: *horizontal*
Horizontalprüfung: *horizontal check*
Horizontalsynchronisationsimpuls: *horizontal synchronization pulse*
Hörkopf: *playback head*
Hornstrahler: *horn*
Hörschärfe: *acuity*
Hot-Standby-System: *hot standby*
Huckepackübertragung: *piggybacking*
huckepack verbinden: *piggyback*
Huckepackzugang: *piggyback entry*
Huffman-Code: *huffman code*
Hülle: *hood; jacket*
Hüllkurve: *envelope; pitch envelope*
Hüllkurvengleichrichtung: *envelope detection*
Hurenkind: *widow*
Hybridanlage: *hybrid system*
Hybridrechner: *hybrid computer*
Hybridschaltung: *hybrid circuit*
Hybridschnittstelle: *hybrid interface*
Hybridstation: *combined station*
Hypo: *hypo*

Ii

ideal: *ideal*
Idealformat: *ideal format*
Identifikation: *identification*
Identifikationsnummer: persönliche ~ *personal identification number (PIN)*
Identifikationszeichen: *identification character*
identifizieren: *identify*
Identifizierungscode: *ID code*
Identifizierungskennzeichen: *tag*
identisch: *identical*

Identität: *identity*
Identitätsblock: *identity burst*
Identitätsfunktion: *identity operation*
Identitätsgatter: *identity gate*
Identitätsvergleich: *logical comparison*
IEC-Bus: *general purpose interface bus (GPIB)*
IEEE-488-Norm: *IEEE-488 (USA)*
IEEE-Bus: *IEEE bus (USA)*
IF-Anweisung: *IF statement*
IF-THEN-ELSE-Anweisung: *IF-THEN-ELSE*
Il-Logik: *integrated injection logic (IIL)*
Ikon: *icon*
illegal: *illegal; illegally*
Illustration: *illustration*
illustrieren: *illustrate*
Image Master: *image master*
Image-Prozessor: *image processor*
Imband-Signalisierung: *in-band signalling*
Immobilienmakler: *property developer*
Impedanz: *impedance*
implantieren: *implant*
implementieren: *implement*
Implementierung: *implementation*
Implikation: *implication*
importieren: *import*
Impressum: *imprint*
Impuls: *impulse; pulse* **einen ~ geben** *pulse; strobe* **elektronischer ~** *electronic pulse*
Impulsamplitudenmodulation: *pulse amplitude modulation (PAM)*
Impulsbreitenmodulation: *pulse width modulation (PWM)*
Impulsdauermodulation: *pulse duration modulation (PDM)*
impulsiv: *impulsive*
Impulsmodulation: *pulse modulation*
Impulsstörung: *impulsive noise*
Impulsstrom: *pulse stream*
Inäquivalenz-Funktion: *inequivalence; NEQ function*
Inäquivalenz-Gatter: *NEQ gate*
Inches pro Sekunde: *inches-per-second (ips)*
Index: *index; subscript; superscript* **rückläufiger ~** *reverse index*
Indexbuchstabe: *index letter*
Indexerstellung: *index build*
Indexkarte: *flash card*
Indexloch: *index hole*
Indexregister: *B box; index register*
Indexschlüssel: *index key*
Indexseite: *index page*
Indexwert: *index value*
Indexzahl: *index number*
indirekt: *indirect*
individuell: *individual*
individuell anfertigen: *personalize*
individuell anpassen: *customize*
Individuum: *individual*

Indizieren: *indexing*
indizieren: *index*
Indiziersprache: *indexing language*
Indizierung: **abgeleitete ~** *derived indexing* **freie ~** *free indexing*
Induktion: *induction*
Induktionsspule: *induction coil*
Induktivität: *inductance*
Industriedesign: *industrial design*
induzieren: *induce*
ineinandergreifen: *interlace*
inert: *inert*
Inferenz: *inference*
Inferenzkontrolle: *inference control*
Infixschreibweise: *infix notation*
Informatik: *computer science; informatics*
Information: *information* **aktuelle ~** *update* **bibliographische ~** *bibliographical information* **taktile ~** *tactile feedback*
Informationsanbieter: *information provider (IP)*
Informationsanfangsmarke: *beginning of information mark (BIM)*
Informationsausgabe: *information output*
Informationsbüro: *information bureau; common carrier*
Informationseingabe: *information input*
Informationsfluß: **mittlerer ~** *information rate*
Informationsfreiheit: *freedom of information*
Informationsgehalt: *information content*
Informationsnetz: *information network*
Informationsschutz: *privacy of information*
Informationsspeicherung: *information storage*
Informationsspeicherung und wiederauffindung: *information storage and retrieval (ISR)*
Informationssystem: *information system*
Informationstechnik: *information technology (IT)*
Informationstheorie: *information theory*
Informationsträgerkanal: *information bearer channel*
Informationsverarbeitung: *information processing*
Informationsverwaltungssystem: *information management system*
Informationswiedergewinnung: *information retrieval*
Informationszeile: *information line*
infrarot: *infrared*
Infrarotdetektor: *infrared detector*
Infrarotfotografie: *infrared photography*
Infrarotlicht: *infrared light (IR light)*
Infrarotnachrichtenübermittlung: *infrared communications*
Infrarotsichtgeräte: *infrared sights*
Infrarot-Videokamera: *infrared video camera*
Infraschallfrequenz: *infrasonic frequency*
Infrastruktur: *infrastructure*
Ingenieur: **fest angestellter ~** *resident engineer*
Inhalt: *content; contents*

Inhaltsverzeichnis: *table of contents*
Initiale: *initial*
initialisieren: *initialize*
Initialisierung: *initialization*
Injektionslaser: *injection laser*
Inklusion: *inclusion*
inklusiv: *inclusive*
Inkrement: *increment*
Inkrementalrechner: *incremental computer*
Inkrementdaten: *incremental data*
inkrementieren: *increment*
Inlands-: *domestic*
Inlandskonsum: *domestic consumption*
Innenkennung: *interior label*
Innenschleife: *inner loop*
innerbetrieblich: *in-house*
In-Scheiben-Schneiden: *slicing*
Installationsfläche: *footprint*
Installationshandbuch: *installation manual*
installieren: *install*
instandhalten: *service*
Instandhaltung: *maintenance; upkeep*
Instrumentierung: *instrumentation*
Integration: *integration* **mittlere** ∼ *medium scale integration (MSI)*
Integrationstechnikplättchen: *wafer scale integration*
integriert: *integrated*
Integrität: *integrity*
intelligent: *intelligent; smart*
Intelligenz: *intelligence* **künstliche** ∼ *artificial intelligence (AI); machine intelligence* **verteilte** ∼ *distributed intelligence*
Intensität: *intensity* **halbe** ∼ *half-intensity*
Intensivanzeige: *display highlights*
Interaktion: *interaction*
interaktiv: *interactive*
Interferenzbild: *interference pattern*
Interferenzschwund: *interference fading*
intern: *internal*
international: *international*
Internationale Vorwahl: *international dialling code*
Interpolierung: *interpolation*
Interpretiercode: *interpretative code*
Interpretierer: *interpreter*
Interpretierprogramm: *interpretative program*
Inverter: *inverter*
Ion: *ion*
Ionosphäre: *ionosphere*
ISBN: *international standard book number (ISBN)*
Isolation: *isolation*
Isolationseinrichtung für Kanäle: *channel isolation*
Isolator: *insulator; isolator*
isolieren: *insulate; isolate*
Isolierkabel: *shielded cable*
Isoliermaterial: *insulation material*

Isoliersteg: *barrier box*
ISO-Norm: *International Standards Organization Open System Interconnection (ISO/OSI)*
isotrop: *isotropic*
ISSN: *international standard serial number (ISSN)*
Iteration: *iteration*
Iterationsschleife: *iterate or iterative routine*

Jj

Jahr: pro ∼ *per year*
Jargon: *buzzword (informal)*
Jaulen: *flutter; wow*
Jedermannfunk: *citizens band radio (CB)*
jemanden anrufen: *to phone someone; to telephone a person*
jemanden ausrufen lassen: *to page someone*
Jingle: *jingle*
JK-Flipflop: *JK-flip-flop*
Job: *job*
Jobanweisungssteuerung: *job statement control*
Jobbearbeitung: sequentielle ∼ *stacked job control*
Jobbetriebssprache: *job control language (JCL)*
Jobdatei: *job file*
Jobende: *end of job (EOJ)*
Jobferneingabe: *remote job entry (RJE)*
Jobfolge: *job stream*
Jobkontrolldatei: *job control file*
Jobkontrollsprache: *job control language (JCL)*
Jobmischung: *job mix*
Jobnummer: *job number*
Joborganisation: *job scheduling*
Jobpriorität: *job priority*
Jobschritt: *job step*
Jobsteuerprogramm: *job control program*
Jobsteuerungssprache: *control language*
Jobverarbeitung: *job processing*
Jobvorrangigkeit: *job priority*
Jobwarteschlange: *job queue*
Journalist: *journalist*
Joystick: *joystick*
Jumbochip: *jumbo chip*
justieren: *adjust; align*
Justieren des Richtungswinkels: *azimuth alignment*
Justierschiene: *aligner*
Justiervorrichtung: *gate*

Kk

Kabel: *cable; cabling; cord; flex* **ausgegossenes** ∼ *filled cable*

Kabelausschnitt: elementarer ~ *elementary cable section*

Kabelfernsehen: *cable television or cable TV; CATV; community antenna television (CATV)* **dialogfähiges ~** *interactive cable television*

Kabelfernsehen mit Extragebühr: *paycable (US)*

Kabelkanal: *duct*

Kabelrohr: *conduit*

Kabeltreiber: *line driver*

Kabine: *booth*

Kalkulation: *calculation*

Kalkulationstabelle: elektronische ~ *spreadsheet*

Kalkulations-Tabellendruck: *spreadsheet*

kalkulieren: *calculate*

Kalligraphie: *calligraphy*

Kaltfehler: *cold fault*

Kaltstart: *cold start*

Kameraaggregat: *camera chain*

Kamerateam: *camera crew*

Kanal: *channel* **dedizierter ~** *dedicated channel* **logischer ~** *logical channel*

Kanalanschluß: *channel adapter*

Kanalbank: *channel bank*

Kanalbefehl: *channel command*

Kanalgruppe: *channel group*

Kanalisierung: *channelling*

Kanalkapazität: *channel capacity*

Kanalsignalisierung: getrennte ~ *separate channel signalling*

Kanalsynchronisierer: *channel synchronizer*

Kanalüberlastung: *channel overload*

Kanalwarteschlange: *channel queue*

Kanal-zu-Kanal-Verbindung: *channel-to-channel connection*

Kanalzuordnung: adaptive ~ *adaptive channel allocation*

Kante: *edge*

Kanzleipapier: *foolscap*

Kapazität: *capacitance; capacity*

Kapazitätsausweitung: *expansion*

Kapazitätsüberschreitung: *overflow or OV*

kapazitiv: *capacitative or capacititive*

Kapitälchen: *small caps*

Kapitel: *chapter*

Kapitelende: *chapter stop*

Kapitelüberschrift: *chapter heading*

kappen: *clip*

Karbonband: *carbon ribbon*

Karnaugh-Diagramm: *Karnaugh map*

Karte: *card*

Kartei: *card index*

Karteikarte: *filing card; index card*

Kartenchassis: *card frame or card chassis*

Kartenformat: *card format*

Kartenhäuschen: *ticket booth*

Kartenlader: *card loader*

Kartenlocher: *card punch (CP)*

Kartenmagazin: *hopper*

Kartenmischer: *collator*

Kartenrandverbindung: *card edge connector*

Kartentelefon: *card phone*

Kartenzeile: *card row*

Kartenzuführung: *card feed*

Karton: *card; cardboard*

Kaskadensteuerung: *cascade control*

Kaskadenübertrag: *cascade carry*

Kaskadenverbindung: *cascade connection*

Kasse: *point-of-sale (POS)* **elektronische ~** *electronic funds transfer point of sale (EFTPOS); electronic point-of-sale (EPOS)*

Kassette: *cartridge; cassette*

Kassettenband: *cassette tape*

Kassettenfarbband: *cartridge ribbon*

Kassettenrekorder: *cassette recorder*

Kasten: *box*

Katalog: *catalogue*

Katalogdatei: *card-index file*

katalogisieren: *card-index; catalogue*

Katalogisierer: *cataloguer*

Katalogisierung: *card-indexing*

Katastrophe: *catastrophe*

Kathode: *cathode*

Kathodenstrahlröhre: *cathode ray tube (CRT)*

Kb: *Kb*

Kegelbreite: *set width*

Keller: *cellar*

Kellerspeicher: *stack*

Kennbit: *dirty bit*

Kennkarte: *ID card; personal identification device (PID)*

Kennsatz: *label record*

Kenntnis: globale ~ *global knowledge*

Kennnummer: *identity number*

Kennung: *label*

Kennungsfeld: *label field*

Kennwort: *identifier word; keyword; password*

Kennzeichen: *identifier; token*

Kennzeichenregister: *flag register*

kennzeichnen: *mark*

Keramikkondensatoren: *ceramic capacitors*

keramisch: *ceramic*

Kerblochkarte: *edge notched card*

Kern: *core*

Kerning: *kerning*

Kernprogramm: *core program*

Kernroutine: *kernel*

Kernspeicher: *core memory or primary memory*

Kernspintomographie: *magnetic resonance imaging*

Kerze: neue ~ *candela*

Kette: *catena; chain*

Ketten: *chaining*

ketten: *append; chain*

Kettenbefehl: *chain*

Kettencode: *chain code*

Kettendrucker: *chain printer*
Kettenliefermethode: *chain delivery mechanism*
Keule: *lobe*
Key: *dongle*
KHz: *kHz*
Kilobaud: *kilobaud*
Kilobit: *kilobit or Kb*
Kilobyte: *kilobyte or KB or Kbyte*
Kilohertz: *kilohertz or KHz*
Kiloohm: *kilo-ohm*
Kilowatt: *kilowatt or kW*
Kilowort: *kiloword or KW*
Kimball-Etikett: *kimball tag*
Kino: *cinema*
kippbar und schwenkbar: *tilt and swivel*
kippen: *toggle*
Kippschalter: *toggle switch*
Kippschaltung: bistabile ~ *bistable circuit or multivibrator*
Kiste: *case; packing case*
Klammern: eckige ~ *square brackets* **runde** ~ *round brackets*
Klangeffekte: *sound effects*
Klangtreue: *fidelity; high fidelity or hifi or hi fi*
Klangvolumen: *volume*
Klarheit: *clarity*
klar machen: *convey*
Klartext: *plaintext*
klar verständlich: *clear*
Klasse: *grade*
klassifizieren: *classify*
Klassifizierung: *classification*
Klatsch: *key plate*
Klebeband: *splicing tape*
Klebebindung: *perfect binding* **mit** ~ *perfect bound*
Klebeeinrichtung: *splicing block*
Kleinbuchstabe: *minuscule*
Kleinbuchstaben: *lower case*
Kleingerätschnittstelle: erweiterte ~ *enhanced small device interface (ESDI)*
Kleinintegration: *small scale integration (SSI)*
Kleinstbaum: *minimal tree*
Klemme: positive ~ *positive terminal*
klemmen: *clamp*
Klicken: *click*
Klingel: *bell character*
Klirrverzerrung: *harmonic distortion*
Klon: *clone*
knacken: *break*
Knopf: *knob*
Koaxialkabel: *co-axial cable*
Kobold: *sprite*
Koerzitivkraft: *coercivity*
Koffercomputer: *luggable (informal)*
Kofferradio: *hand receiver*
kohärent: *coherent*

Kohlemikrophon: *carbon microphone*
Kohlepapier: *carbon paper*
Koinzidenzgatter: *coincidence gate*
Koinzidenzschaltung: *coincidence circuit or element*
Kollationierungsfolge: *collating sequence*
Kollege: *associate*
Kolumne: *column*
Kolumnentitel: lebender ~ *running head*
Kolumnenzentimeter: *column-centimetre*
Koma: *coma*
Kombination: *combination*
Kombinatorik: *combinational logic*
Komma: *comma*
Kommandoschnittstelle: *command interface*
Kommandosprache: *command language*
Kommandozeile: *command line*
Kommentar: *comment; commentary*
Kommentarfeld: *comment field*
Kommission: *board*
Kommunikation offener Systeme: *Open System Interconnection (OSI)*
Kommunikationsschnittstellenanschluß: asynchroner ~ *asynchronous communications interface adapter (ACIA)*
Kommunikationssystem: hierarchisches ~ *hierarchical communications system*
kommunizieren: *communicate*
kompakt: *compact*
Kompaktcode: *compact code*
Kompaktkassette: *compact cassette*
Kompandierer: *compandor*
Kompandierung: *companding*
kompatibel: *compatible; portable* **nicht** ~ *incompatible*
Kompatibilität: *compatibility* **fehlende** ~ *noncompatibility*
kompilieren: *compile* **neu** ~ *recompile*
kompilieren und verarbeiten: *compile and go*
Kompilierer: *compiler (program); language processor*
Kompiliererdiagnostik: *compiler diagnostics*
Kompilierersprache: *compiler language*
Kompilierfehler: *compilation error*
Kompilierphase: *compile phase*
Kompilierung: *compilation*
Kompilierzeit: *compilation time*
Komplement: *complement*
komplementär: *complementary*
Komplementärfarben: *complementary colours*
Komplementbildung: *complementation*
komplementieren: *complement*
komplementiert: *complemented*
komplex: *complex*
Komplexität: *complexity*
Komplexitätsmaß: *complexity measure*
kompliziert: *complicated*
Komponente: *component*

Komponentendichte: *component density*
Komponentenfehler: *component error*
kompreß: *solid*
Kompression: *crushing*
komprimieren: *compact; compress; concentrate*
Komprimierung: *compression*
Komprimierungsalgorithmus: *compacting algorithm*
Kondensatoren: elektrolytische ~ *electrolytic capacitors* **nicht-elektrolytische** ~ *non-electrolytic capacitors* **variable** ~ *variable capacitors*
Kondensatormikrophon: *capacitor microphone*
Kondensatorspeicher: *capacitor storage*
Konferenz: *conference*
Konferenzraum: *conference room*
Konferenzschaltung: *conference call*
Konferenztelefon: *conference telephone*
Konfiguration: *configuration*
Konfigurationszustand: *configuration state*
konfigurieren: *configure*
konfiguriert: *configured-in* **nicht** ~ *configured-off or configured out*
Konkurrenzbetrieb: *contention*
Konkurrenzbus: *contention bus*
Konkurrenzprogramm: ein ~ **senden** *counterprogramm(ing)*
Konsole: *console; paddle; panel*
Konstante: *constant*
Konstantstromversorgung: *regulated power supply*
Konstruieren: computergestütztes ~ *computer-aided or assisted engineering (CAE)*
Kontakt: *contact* **trockener** ~ *dry contact*
Kontaktdruck: *contact printing*
Kontaktstift: *pin*
Kontaktstreifen: *contact negative*
Kontern: *lateral reversal*
Kontext: *context*
kontinuierlich: *continuous*
Kontinuität: *continuity*
Kontrast: *contrast*
kontrastarm: *flat*
Kontrasteinstellung: *contrast; contrast setting*
Kontrastgrad: *gamma*
kontrastieren: *contrast*
kontrastierend: *contrasting*
kontrastreich: *hard*
Kontrastverhältnis: *print contrast ratio*
Kontrastverstärkungsfilter: *contrast enhancement filter*
Kontrollautsprecher: *monitor*
Kontrolle: *control* **außer** ~ *out of control*
Kontrollfeld: *control field*
kontrollgesteuert: *control driven*
Kontrollgruppe: *control group*
kontrollierbar: *controllable*
Kontrollrechner: *control computer*
Kontrollschirm: *monitor*

Kontrollsprache: *control language*
Kontrollsumme: *checksum or check total; control total*
Kontrollsysteme: *control systems*
Konturplatte: *key plate*
Konus: *cone*
Konvention: *convention*
Konverter: *converter or convertor*
konvertierbar: *convertible*
Konvertierbarkeit: *convertibility*
konvertieren: *convert*
Konvertierungsprogramm: *conversion program*
Konzentrator: *concentrator*
konzentrieren: *concentrate*
Koordinaten: *coordinates* **kartesische** ~ *cartesian coordinates* **rechtwinklige** ~ *rectangular coordinates* **relative** ~ *relative coordinates*
Koordinatenachse: *axis*
Koordinatenbild: *coordinate graph*
Koordinatennetz: *grid*
Koordinatenschreiber: *X-Y plotter*
koordinieren: *coordinate*
Koordinierung: *coordination*
Kopf: *head* **fliegender** ~ *flying head*
Kopfausrichtung: *head alignment*
Kopfentmagnetisierer: *head demagnetizer*
Kopfhörer: *headset or headphones*
Kopfparken: *head park*
Kopfrad: *head wheel*
Kopfreinigungsdiskette: *head cleaning disk*
Kopfstelle: *head end*
Kopfumsetzer: *set-top converter*
Kopfzeile: *header; heading*
Kopfzeilen: rollende ~ *rolling headers*
Kopie: *copy; duplicate; facsimile copy; replication* **erste** ~ *first generation image*
Kopieren: *duplicating; reproduction*
kopieren: *copy; dump; duplicate; reproduce*
Kopierer: *duplicating machine*
Kopiergenehmigung: *authorization to copy (ATC)*
Kopiergerät: *copier or copying machine or duplicating machine*
kopiergeschützt: *copy protect*
Kopierpapier: *duplicating paper*
Kopierschutz: *copy protect; copy protection*
koppeln: *couple*
Koppler: *coupler*
Korn: *grain*
Körnung: *granularity*
Korrektor: *proofreader*
Korrektur: *correction; patch*
Korrekturabzug: *proof*
Korrekturbogen mit Preßrevision: *master proof*
Korrekturenleser: *proofreader*
Korrekturfahne: *galley proof or slip*
Korrektur lesen: *proofread*
Korrekturzeichen: *proof correction marks*

Korrelationsdiagramm: *scatter graph*
Korrespondent: *correspondent*
Korrespondenz: *correspondence*
Korrespondenzfähigkeit: *correspondence print quality*
korrespondieren: mit jdm ~ *to correspond with someone*
korrigieren: *correct; debug*
Kostenanalyse: *cost analysis*
Kraft: *force* **elektromotorische ~** *electromotive force (EMF)* **in ~ treten** *to come into force*
Kratzer: *scratch*
Kredit: *credit*
Kreditkarte: *charge card; credit card*
Kreisblattschreiber: *chart recorder*
Kreisdiagramm: *pie chart*
kreisen: *circulate*
kreisförmig: *circular*
Kreislaufregister: *circulating register*
Kreisliste: *circular list*
Kreisumlaufbahn: *circular orbit*
Kreisverkehrdokument: *turnaround document*
Kreuz: *dagger*
Kreuzassemblierer: *cross-assembler*
Kreuzkompilierer: *cross-compiler*
Kristall: *crystal*
Kriterium: *criterion*
kritisch untersuchen: *analyse or analyze*
Kryptoanalyse: *cryptanalysis*
Kryptographie: *cryptography*
kryptographisch: *cryptographic*
Kryptosystem RSA: *RSA cipher system*
KSR: *keyboard send/receive (KSR)*
Kugelantenne: *isotropic radiator*
Kugelcharakteristik: mit ~ *omnidirectional*
Kugelkopf: *golf-ball*
Kugelkopfdrucker: *golf-ball printer*
Kühlkörper: *heat-sink; heat sink*
kummern: sich ~ um *attend to*
Kumulativindex: *cumulative index*
Kunde: *customer*
Kundendienst(abteilung): *customer service department*
Kundenkredit: *customer credit*
kundenspezifisch: *custom-built*
Kundin: *customer*
künstlich: *man-made*
Kunststoffe: *synthetic materials*
Kupfer: *copper*
Kupferdruck: *copperplate printing*
kursiv: *italic*
Kursive: *italic*
Kursivschrift: *italics*
Kurve: charakteristische ~ *characteristic curve*
Kurvenschreiber *or* **Kurvenzeichner:** *x-y plotter or graph plotter*
Kurzadressierung: *abbreviated addressing or abb. add.*

Kurzdarstellung: *abstract* **gewertete ~** *evaluative abstract*
kürzen: *cut; shorten*
kurzgeschlossen: *short-circuited*
Kurzlochkarte: *short card*
kurzschließen: *to short circuit*
Kurzschluß: *short circuit*
Kürzung: *cut*
Kurzunterbrechung: *check*
Kurzwelle: *short wave (SW)*
Kurzwellenempfänger: *short-wave receiver*
kurzzeitig: *transient*
Kurzzeit-Nachleuchten: *lag*
KWAC-Index: *keyword and context (KWAC)*
KWIC-Index: *keyword in context (KWIC)*
KWOC-Index: *keyword out of context (KWOC)*
KWort: *kiloword or KW*
Kybernetik: *cybernetics*

Ll

Labor: *laboratory*
Labortechniker: *laboratory technician*
Laden: *boot up or booting; loading*
laden: *boot; charge; load* **neu ~** *reload*
Ladeprogramm: *loader* **automatisches ~** *automatic loader* **binäres ~** *binary loader*
Ladepunkt: *load point*
Ladung: *charge* **elektrische ~** *electric charge*
Lagercode: *stock code*
LAN: *LAN or lan*
lancieren: *launch*
Lancierung: *launch*
Länge: *length*
Länge der Zeichenfolge: *string length*
Länge des Dateinamens: *length of filename*
Längen- und Seitenverhältnis: *aspect ratio*
LAN-Server: *LAN server*
Laptop-Computer: *lapheld computer or laptop computer*
Laser: *laser*
Laserbildplatte: *laser disk*
Laserdrucker: *laser printer; non-impact printer* **spezieller ~** *black writer; white writer*
Laserplatte: *optical disk; optical memory*
Laserspeicher: *photodigital memory*
Laserstrahlaufzeichnung: *laser beam recording (LBR)*
Laserstrahlkommunikation: *laser beam communications*
laufend: *up*
Laufwerk: *drive* **halbhohes ~** *half-height drive*
Laufzeit: *run-time or run-duration*
Laufzeitentzerrer: *delay equalizer*
Laufzeitfehler: *run-time error*
Laufzeitspeicher: *delay line store*

Laufzeitsystem: *run-time system*

Laufzeitverzerrung: *delay distortion*

Läuten: dezimonisches ~ *decimonic ringing*

Lautsprecher: *loudspeaker* **elektrostatischer** ~ *electrostatic speaker*

Lautsprecheranlage: *public address system (PA)*

Lautstärke: *loudness; volume*

Lautstärkeregler: *volume control*

Lautstärkeumfang: *dynamic range*

Lawine: *avalanche*

Lawinendiode: *avalanche photodiode (APD)*

Layout: *area composition* **das** ~ **kontrollieren** *preview*

Layoutkontrolle: *previewer*

LCD-Anzeige: *LCD*

LC-Oszillator: *LC circuit*

Leasing-Vertrag: *lease*

Lebensdauer: mittlere ~ *mean time to failure (MTF)*

Lebensdauer bei Belastung: *load life*

Lebensdauer einer Software: *software life cycle*

Lebensdauer eines Kopfes: *headlife*

Lebensdauer eines Systems: *system life cycle*

Leck: *leak; leakage*

LED: *light emitting diode (LED)*

leer: *blank; empty*

Leerbefehl: *do-nothing (instruction)*

Leerimpuls: *blanking pulse*

Leerlaufzeit: *idle time*

Leerliste: *empty or null list*

Leerspule: *pick-up reel*

Leerstring: *empty or null string*

Leertaste: *space bar*

Leerzeichen: *blank character; idle character; space character; space*

Leerzeichenfüllung: *character stuffing*

Lehr-: *educational*

leichtgewichtig: *lightweight*

leise: *quiet*

leisten: *achieve*

Leistung: *performance; power*

Leistungen eines Datenverarbeitungssystems: *electronic data processing capability*

leistungsfähig: *capable; efficient*

Leistungsfähigkeit: *capability; efficiency*

Leistungsliste: *capability list*

Leistungsniveau: *performance*

Leistungsprozedur: *protocol*

Leistungsprozedurnormen: *protocol standards*

Leistungsrückgang: kontrollierter ~ *graceful degradation*

Leistungsvergleichsaufgabe: *benchmark problem*

Leistungsvermögen: *capacity*

Leistungsvermögen eines Stromkreises: *circuit capacity*

Leitartikel: *editorial*

Leitdaten: *master data*

leiten: *channel; conduct; direct; manage*

Leiter: *conductor; director; manager* **technischer** ~ *technical director*

leitfähig: *conductive*

Leitfähigkeit: *conduction*

Leitkarte: *header card; master card*

Leitlinien: *guide bars*

Leitrechner: *host computer*

Leitrechnersystem: *master computer system*

Leitung: *direction; line; management* **festgeschaltete** ~ *dedicated line* **symmetrische** ~ *balanced line*

Leitungen: elektrische ~ *wiring*

Leitungsbelastung: *line load*

Leitungsbündel: *bundle*

Leitungsgeräuschpegel: *circuit noise level*

Leitungsimpedanz: *line impedance*

Leitungsstufe: *line level*

Leitungsvermittlung: *circuit switching*

Leitweg: *route* **adaptiver** ~ *adaptive routing*

Leitwegseite: *routing page*

Leitwegtabelle: *routing table*

Lernen: computergestütztes ~ *computer-based learning (CBL); computer-managed learning (CML); computer-aided or assisted learning (CAL)* **programmiertes** ~ *programmed learning*

Lernkurve: *learning curve*

Lernsystem: intelligentes ~ *intelligent tutoring system*

lesbar: *legible; readable*

Lesbarkeit: *legibility*

Lese-Erholzeit: *sense recovery time*

Lesefehler: transienter ~ *transient read error*

Lesegeschwindigkeit: *read rate*

Lesekopf: *read head* **fliegender** ~ *flying head*

Lesen: digitales optisches ~ *DOR* **löschendes** ~ *destructive read; destructive readout* **nur zum** ~ *read only* **regeneratives** ~ *regenerative reading* **unmittelbares** ~ *demand reading*

lesen: *read*

Leseprüfung: *read back check*

Leser: optischer ~ *bar-code reader or optical scanner; OCR*

Lese-/Schreibkanal: *read/write channel*

Lese-/Schreibkopf: *read/write head; R/W head*

Lese-/Schreibspeicher: *read/write memory*

Lese-/Schreibzyklus: *read/write cycle; R/W cycle*

Lesesperre: *fetch protect*

Lesestift: *wand*

Lesezyklus: *read cycle*

Leuchtdichte: *luminance*

Leuchtdichtsignal: *luminance signal*

Leuchtkasten: *viewer*

Licht: *light* **aktinisches** ~ *actinic light* **kohärentes** ~ *coherent light* **sichtbares** ~ *visible light* **ultraviolettes** ~ *ultra-violet light (UV light)* **vorhandenes** ~ *available light*

Lichtdurchlaßgrad: *transmittance*

lichtempfindlich: *light-sensitive*

Lichtempfindlichkeit: *speed*
Lichtfleck: intensiver ~ *hot spot*
Lichtgriffel: *electronic pen or stylus or wand*
Lichthof: *halo*
Lichthofbildung: *halation*
Lichthofschutzschicht: *matt or matte*
Lichtleitung: *light conduit*
Lichtmaschine: *alternator*
Lichtpunktabtastung: *flying spot scan*
Lichtreflexe: *flare*
Lichtsensor: *image sensor*
lichtstark: *fast*
Lichtstift: *electronic pen or stylus or wand; light pen* **graphischer** ~ *graphics light pen*
Lichtundurchlässigkeit: *opacity*
Lichtwellenleiter: *light guide*
Lichtwellenleiterkabel: *fibre optic cable or connection*
Lieferant: *supplier*
LIFO: *last in first out (LIFO)*
Ligatur: *ligature*
Lineal: *ruler*
linear: *linear*
Linie: *line; rule*
Linien: versteckte ~ *hidden lines*
Linienanhebungsfilter: *character enhancement filter*
Linkage Editierung: *linkage editing*
links: nach ~ **verschieben** *range left*
Linksausrichtung: *left justification*
linksbündig ausrichten: *left justify*
Linksbündigkeit: *left justification*
Linksverschiebung: *left shift; shift left*
Linse: *lens* **anastigmatische** ~ *anastigmat* **apochromatische** ~ *apochromatic lens* **konkave** ~ *concave lens* **konvexe** ~ *convex lens* **mittlere** ~ *medium lens*
LISP: *LISP*
LISP (Programmiersprache): *list processing*
Liste: *list* **gekettete** ~ *chain list; chained list* **geordnete** ~ *ordered list* **lineare** ~ *linear list* **verbundene** ~ *linked list* **vollständige** ~ *dense list*
Liste freier Speicherplätze: *available list*
Listenbearbeitung: *list processing*
Listengenerator: *report generator*
Listenprogrammgenerator: *report program generator (RPG)*
Literal: *literal*
Literaturverzeichnis: *bibliography*
lithographisch: *lithographic*
Live-Sendung: *program shown in real time (US)*
Lizenz: *licence*
Loch: *hole*
lochen: *punch*
Locher: *perforator; punch*
Lochkarte: *punch(ed) card*
Lochkartencode: *card code; punched code*
Lochkartenfeld: *card field*

Lochkartenformat: *card format*
Lochkartenleser: *punch(ed) card reader*
Lochkartensatz: *deck*
Lochkartenspalte: *card column*
Lochmaske: *shadowmask*
Lochstreifen: *paper tape; perforated tape; punched (paper) tape; torn tape*
Lochstreifenempfänger: *reperforator*
Lochstreifen-in-Lochkarte-Umsetzer: *tape to card converter*
Lochstreifenleser: *paper tape reader*
Lochstreifensender mit Empfangslocher: *reperforator transmitter*
Lochstreifenstanzer: *paper tape punch*
Lochstreifenzuführung: *paper tape feed*
Lochung: numerische ~ *numeric punch*
Lochzeile: *row*
logarithmisch: *logarithmic*
Logarithmus: *logarithm*
Logik: *logic* **dedizierte** ~ *dedicated logic* **digitale** ~ *digital logic* **emittergekoppelte** ~ *emitter-coupled logic (ECL)* **festverdrahtete** ~ *hardwired logic* **formale** ~ *formal logic* **mathematische** ~ *symbolic logic* **negative** ~ *negative-true logic* **n-stufige** ~ *n-level logic* **positive** ~ *positive logic* **sequentielle** ~ *sequential logic*
Logikanalysator: *logic state analyzer*
Logikpegel: *logic level*
Logikplan: *logical chart*
logisch: *logical; logic-seeking*
LOGO: *LOGO*
Logo: *logo*
lokalisieren: *locate*
Lokalnetz: *local area network (LAN or lan)*
Lokalnetzserver: *local area network server; LAN server*
Lokalpresse: die ~ *the local press*
Lokalspeicher: *local memory*
löschbar: *erasable*
Löscheinrichtung: *eraser*
löschen: *clear; delete; erase; flush; free; junk; kill; purge; scratch; scrub; wipe; zap; zero*
Löschkopf: *erase head*
Löschsatz: *deletion record*
Löschzeichen: *delete character*
lösen: *solve*
Lösung: *solution*
löten: *solder*
Lötmetall: *solder*
lötstellenfrei: *solderless*
LQ: *letter-quality*
LRU-Algorithmus: *least recently used algorithm*
LRU-Speichermethode: *activity loading*
LSI: *LSI*
Lücke: *blank*
Luft: mit ~ **kühlen** *fan*
Luftansicht or Luftbild: *aerial image*
Luftkabel: *aerial cable*
Luftpostumschlag: *air mail envelope*

Luftschalter: *air circuit breaker*
Luftspalt: *air or head gap*
Lumen: *lumen*
Lux: *lux*

Mm

mA: *milliampere or mA*
MAC: *multiplexed analog components (MAC)*
Mädchen für alles: *gofer (informal)*
Magazin: *magazine*
Magazinformat: *magazine format*
Magnet: *magnet*
Magnetband: *magnetic tape*
Magnetbandcodierer: *magnetic tape encoder*
Magnetband für Datenfernverarbeitung: *tape transmitter*
Magnetbandgerät: *magnetic tape recorder*
Magnetbandkassette: *magnetic tape cartridge or cassette*
Magnetbandkassettenlaufwerk: *cartridge drive*
Magnetbandlaufwerk: *tape drive*
Magnetbandleser: *magnetic tape reader*
Magnetbandstreamer: *tape streamer*
Magnetbandtransport: *magnetic tape transport*
Magnetblasenspeicher: *magnetic bubble memory*
Magnetfeld: *magnetic field*
magnetisch: *magnetic*
magnetisieren: *magnetize*
Magnetkarte: *magnetic card*
Magnetkartenleser: *magnetic card reader*
Magnetkern: *ferrite core; magnetic core*
Magnetkernspeicher: *core memory or store*
Magnetkopf: *magnetic head*
Magnetplatte: *magnetic disk*
Magnetplatteneinheit: *magnetic disk unit*
Magnetschirm: *magnetic screen*
Magnetschrift-Zeichenerkennung: *magnetic ink character recognition (MICR)*
Magnetspeicher: *magnetic memory or store*
Magnetspur: *track*
Magnetstreifen: *magnetic strip*
Magnetstreifenleser: *magnetic strip reader*
Magnettinte: *magnetic ink*
Magnetträger: *magnetic medium or material*
Magnettrommelspeicher: *magnetic drum*
Magnetzelle: *magnetic cell*
Mailer: *mailing piece*
Mailmerge: *mail-merge*
Majuskel: *majuscule*
Makroassemblierer: *macro assembler or assembly program*
Makroauflösung: *macro expansion*
Makroaufruf: *macro call* **verschachtelter ~** *nested macrocall*

Makrobefehl: *macro command or macro instruction*
Makrobibliothek: *macro library*
Makrocode: *macro code*
Makrodefinition: *macro definition*
Makroelement: *macroelement*
Makroflußdiagramm: *macro flowchart*
Makroprogrammierung: *macro programming*
Makrosprache: *macro language*
Makroumwandlung: *macro expansion*
Management-: *managerial*
Managementinformationssystem: *management information system (MIS)*
Managementtraining: *management training*
Manager: **stellvertretender ~** *assistant manager*
Mantisse: *mantissa* **binäre ~** *binary mantissa*
Mantisse (einer Fließkommazahl): *fraction*
manuell: *manual; manually*
Manuskript: *manuscript or MS* **handschriftliches ~** *holograph* **schlechtes ~** *bad copy*
Map: *map* **logische ~** *logic map*
Marginalien: eingezogene ~ *cut in notes*
Marginierung: *margination*
Marke: *brand; label; mark*
Markenartikel: *branded goods*
Markenimage or Markenprofil: *brand image*
Markenname: *brand name*
Markenpirat: *pirate*
Markieren: *flagging*
markieren: *flag; mark*
Markierstift: *marker pen*
Markierung: *flagging; marker; sentinel*
Markierungserkennung: optische ~ *optical mark recognition (OMR)*
Markierungsleser: *mark sense device or reader* **optischer ~** *optical mark reader (OMR)*
Markierungsstelle: *response position*
Markierungszeit: *marking interval*
Maschine: *machine* **einzelne ~ informationsverarbeitende** *unit information processor* **virtuelle ~** *virtual machine*
maschinenabhängig: *machine dependent*
Maschinenabzug: *machine proof*
Maschinenadresse: *machine address*
Maschinenausrüstung: *hardware*
Maschinenbefehl: *machine instruction* **endgültiger ~** *absolute instruction; actual instruction*
Maschinencode: *computer or machine code*
Maschinencodebefehl: *machine code instruction*
Maschinencodeformat: *machine code format*
maschinengeschrieben: *typewritten*
Maschinengleichung: *machine equation*
maschinenlesbar: *machine-readable*
Maschinenprüfung: *machine check*
Maschinensprache: *computer language; machine language; object language* **die ~ umsetzen** *machine language compile* **einheitliche ~** *common language*

Maschinensteuerungssystem: flexibles ~ *flexible machining system (FMS)*

Maschinenteufelchen: *gremlin (informal)*

Maschinenübersetzung: *machine translation*

maschinenunabhängig: *machine independent*

Maschinenwort: *computer word; machine word*

Maschinenzuverlässigkeit: *hardware reliability*

Maschinenzyklus: *machine cycle*

Maschinerie: *machinery*

Maschineschreiben: *typing*

maschineschreiben: *type*

Maschinist: *machinist*

Maser: *MASER*

Maske: *mask*

Maskenbit: *mask bit*

Maskenregister: *mask register*

maskierbar: *maskable*

maskieren: *mask*

Maskierung: *masking*

Maß: *measure*

Masse: *GND; ground*

Maße: *measurements*

Maßeinheiten: internationale ~ *SI units*

Maßeinteilung: mit ~ versehen *graduated*

Massenmedien: *mass media*

Massenproduktion: *mass production*

Massenspeicher: *mass storage*

Massenspeichereinheit: *mass storage device*

Massenspeichermedium: *bulk storage medium*

Massenspeichersystem: *mass storage system*

Maßnahme: *measure*

Maßnahmen zur Leitwegbestimmung: *routing overheads*

Maßstab: *measurement; scale* **im großen ~** *large scale* **im kleinen ~** *small scale*

Mast: *radio mast or TV mast*

Material: material ferromagnetisches ~ *ferromagnetic material* **magnetisierbares ~** *magnetic material or medium*

Materialsteuerung: *materials control*

Material vom N-Typ: *n-type or N-type material*

Materie: *substance*

Mathematik: *mathematics*

mathematisch: *mathematical*

Matrix: matrix dreidimensionale ~ *three-dimensional array* **numerische ~** *numeric array* **schwach besetzte ~** *sparse array* **zweidimensionale ~** *two-dimensional array*

Matrixblock: virtueller ~ *virtual memory stack*

Matrixdimension: *array dimension*

Matrixdrehung: *matrix rotation*

Matrixdrucker: *matrix printer or dot-matrix printer*

Matrixelement: *array element*

Matrixgrenzen: *array bounds*

matt: *matt or matte*

Mattaufnahme: *matt or matte*

Maus: *mouse*

mausgesteuert: *mouse-driven*

Maustreiber: *mouse driver*

maximal: *maximum*

Maximum: *maximum*

Maximumwerte: absolute ~ *absolute maximum rating*

Mbps: *Mbps*

Mbyte: *MB or Mb or Mbyte*

mechanisch: *mechanical*

Mechanismus: *mechanism*

Medien: media interaktive ~ *interactive media* **magnetische ~** *magnetic media*

Medienforschung: *media research*

Megabit: *megabit (Mb)*

Megabits pro Sekunde: absolute ~ *megabits per second (Mbps)*

Megabyte: *megabyte (MB)*

Mehradreßbefehl: *multi-address or multi-address instruction*

Mehrbussystem: *multi-bus system*

mehrdeutig: *ambiguous*

Mehrdeutigkeit: *ambiguity*

Mehrdeutigkeitsfehler: *ambiguity error*

mehrdimensional: *multidimensional*

mehrfach: *multi-; multiple*

Mehrfachanweisungszeile: *multi-statement line*

Mehrfachausstrahlung: *multicasting*

Mehrfachbefehlsstrom - Einfachdatenstrom: *multiple instruction stream - single data stream (MISD)*

Mehrfachbefehlsstrom - Mehrfachdatenstrom: *multiple instruction stream - multiple data stream (MIMD)*

Mehrfachbusarchitektur: *multiple bus architecture*

Mehrfachdatenstation: *cluster*

Mehrfachgenauigkeit: *multiple precision; multiprecision*

Mehrfachüberschreibung: *multipass overlap*

Mehrfachverbindungssystem: *multilink system*

Mehrfachzugriff: bedarfsbestimmter ~ *demand assigned multiple access (DAMA)*

Mehrfachzugriffscode: *multiple address code*

mehrfarbig: *multicolour*

Mehrfenster-Editor: *multi-window editor*

Mehrfrequenzwahlverfahren: dual tone, multifrequency (DTMF)

Mehrfunktions-: *multifunction; multifunctional*

Mehrfunktionsdatenstation: *multifunction workstation*

Mehrfunktionskarteneinheit: *multifunction card*

Mehrkanal-: *multichannel*

Mehrpfadprogramm: *multithread*

Mehrphasenprogramm: *multiphase program*

Mehrplatinencomputer: *multi-board computer*

Mehrplatten-: *multi-disk*

Mehrplatten-Leser: *multi-disk reader*

Mehrplatten-Option: *multi-disk option*

Mehrplatzsystem: *multi-user system; shared resources system*

Mehrprogrammbetrieb: *multi-programming*

Mehrprozessorenverschachtelung: *multiprocessor interleaving*

Mehrprozessorsystem: *multiprocessor*

Mehrpunkt-: *multipoint*

Mehrschichtplatine: *multilayer*

mehrstufig: *multilevel*

Mehrzweckhardware: *common hardware*

Mehrzweckregister: *general register or general purpose register (gpr)*

Mehrzweckschnittstelle: *general purpose interface adapter (GPIA)*

Mehrzweckschnittstellenbus: *general purpose interface bus (GPIB)*

Mehrzwecksoftware: *common software*

melden: *signal*

Melder: *indication*

Membran: *diaphragm*

Memomotion: *memomotion*

Menge: *amount; quantity*

Mengen: in großen ~ *in bulk*

Mengenlehre: *set theory*

Mensch-Maschine-Schnittstelle: *human-computer or human-machine interface (HMI); man machine interface (MMI)*

Menü: *menu*

Merkblatt zur Manuskriptgestaltung: *style sheet*

Merkmal: *characteristic*

messen: *gauge; measure*

Meßlehre: *gauge*

Meßwertgeber: *sensor*

Meßwertwandler: *transducer*

Metabit: *metabit*

Metakompilierung: *metacompilation*

Metalldetektor: *metal detector*

Metalloxid-Halbleiter: *metal oxide semiconductor (MOS)*

Metasprache: *metalanguage*

MHz: *MHz*

Middleware: *middleware*

mieten: *lease*

Mietleitung: *leased circuit; leased line*

Mikrobefehl: *microinstruction*

Mikrobefehlscode: *microcode*

Mikrobild: *microimage*

Mikrochip: *microchip*

Mikrocomputer: *microcomputer or micro*

Mikrocomputerarchitektur: *microcomputer architecture*

Mikrocomputerbus: *microcomputer bus*

Mikrocomputerentwicklungsbausatz: *microcomputer development kit*

Mikrocomputer-Rückwandplatine: *microcomputer backplane*

Mikrocomputing: *microcomputing*

Mikrocontroller: *microcontroller*

Mikrodiskette: *microfloppy*

Mikroelektronik: *microelectronics*

Mikrofiche: *microfiche*

Mikrofilm: *microfilm* **auf ~ aufnehmen** *to microfilm*

Mikrofilmschrittkamera: *planetary camera*

Mikroform: *microform*

Mikrofotografie: *microphotography*

Mikrogerät: *microdevice*

Mikrographie: *micrographics*

Mikrokassette: *microcassette*

Mikrometer: *micrometre*

Mikron: *micron*

Mikrophon: *microphone* **drahtloses ~** *wireless microphone* **dynamisches ~** *dynamic microphone* **piezoelektrisches ~** *crystal microphone*

Mikroprogramm: *microprogram*

Mikroprogramm-Assembliersprache: *microprogram assembly language*

Mikroprogramm-Befehlsvorrat: *microprogram instruction set*

Mikroprogrammierung: *microprogramming*

Mikroprogrammspeicher: *control memory or ROM; microprogram store*

Mikroprogrammzähler: *microprogram counter*

Mikroprozessor: *microprocessor; microprocessor unit (MPU)*

Mikroprozessor-Adreßleistungen: *microprocessor addressing capabilities*

Mikroprozessoraufbau: *microprocessor architecture*

Mikroprozessorchip: *microprocessor chip*

Mikroschaltung: *microcircuit*

Mikroschreiber: *microwriter*

Mikrosekunde: *microsecond*

Mikrosequenz: *microsequence*

Mikrowelle: *microwave*

Mikrowellenrelais: *microwave relay*

Mikrowellenübertragung: *microwave communications link; microwave transmission*

Mikrozyklus: *microcycle*

Milliampere: *milliampere or mA*

Milliarde: *billion*

milliardstel: ein ~ *nano- or n (US)*

Millimeterpapier: *graph paper*

Millisekunde: *millisecond or ms*

Miniaturisierung: *miniaturization*

Minicomputer: *minicomputer or mini*

Minidiskette: *minifloppy*

Minimax-Methode: *minmax*

minimieren: *minimize*

Minimum: *minimum*

Miniplatte: *minidisk*

Mini-Winchesterplatte: *miniwinny (slang)*

Minuend: *minuend*

Minuskel: *minuscule*

Minuszeichen: *minus or minus sign*

Mischen: *mixing*

mischen: *merge; mix*

Mischer: *mixer*

Mischsatz: *mixing*
Mischung: *mix*
Mitsprechanlage: *intrusion*
Mittel: *medium*
Mittel-: *mean; medium*
Mittelfrequenz: *medium frequency*
Mittelpunkt: *centre or center (US)*
Mittelwert: *mean*
Mittensignal: *M signal*
mks-System: *MKS*
Mnemonik: *mnemonic*
Mobilfunk: *pager; radio pager or radio paging device*
modal: *modal*
Modell: *model* **mathematisches** ~ *mathematical model*
modellhaft: *model*
Modem: *dataset (US); modem or MODEM*
Modembuchse: *data jack*
Modem-Normen: *modem standards*
Moden: *mode*
Modenstreuung: *mode dispersion*
Modifikationsschleife: *modification loop*
Modifizierer: *modifier*
modular: *modular*
Modularisierung: *modularization*
Modularität: *modularity*
Modulation: *modulation*
Modulationssignal: *modulating signal*
Modulator: *modulator*
modulieren: *modulate*
Modulo-Arithmetik: *modulo arithmetic*
Modulo N: *modulo-N*
Modulo-N-Prüfung: *modulo-N check; residue check*
Modus: sequentieller ~ *sequential mode* **verzögerter** ~ *deferred mode*
Möglichkeiten: *facilities*
Monitor: *monitor*
Monitorprogramm: *monitor program*
monochrom: *monochrome*
monolithisch: *monolithic*
Monomode-Faser: *monomode fibre*
monophon: *monophonic*
monostabil: *monostable*
Montage: *assembly; installation; layout*
Montagewerk: *assembly plant*
Monte-Carlo-Methode: *Monte Carlo method*
Morsealphabet: *Morse code*
Morsetaste: *morse key*
MOS: *MOS*
Mosaik: *mosaic*
MOS-Speicher: *MOS memory*
MOS-Transistor: *MOSFET*
Motor: *motor*
ms: *millisecond or ms*
MS-DOS: *MS disk operating system or Microsoft DOS (MS-DOS)*

M-Signal: *M signal*
MSX-Norm: *MSX*
Mucken: *bug (informal)*
Multi-Burst-Signal: *multiburst signal*
multifunktional: *multifunction(al)*
multimedial: *multimedia*
Multimeter: *multimeter* **digitales** ~ *digital multimeter (DMM)*
Multimode-Faser: *multimode fibre*
Multiplexbus: *multiplexed bus*
Multiplexing: optisches ~ *optical multiplexing*
Multiplexmethode: *multiplexing* **bedarfsmäßige** ~ *demand multiplexing* **dynamische** ~ *dynamic multiplexing* **heterogene** ~ *heterogeneous multiplexing* **homogene** ~ *homogeneous multiplexing*
Multiplexor: *multiplexor (MUX)*
Multiplikant: *multiplicand*
Multiplikation: *multiplication*
Multiplikationszeichen: *multiplication sign*
Multiplikator: *multiplier*
multiplizieren: *multiply*
Multiscan-Monitor: *multi-scan or multi-sync monitor*
Multitasking: *multitasking or multi-tasking*
Multivibrator: *multivibrator* **astabiler** *or* **instabiler** ~ *astable multivibrator*
Murray-Code: *Murray code*
Musikchip: *music chip*
Musik-Synthesizer: *music synthesizer*
Muster: *pattern* **als** ~ **speichern** *bit-map* **gemäß dem** ~ *as per sample*

Nn

Nachahmung: *simulation*
Nachdruck: *reprint*
nachdrucken: *reprint*
nachlassen: *decrease; fade*
Nachleuchtdauer: *persistence*
Nachricht: *message* **eingehende** ~ *incoming message*
Nachrichten: *news*
Nachrichtenagentur: *news agency*
Nachrichtenberechtigungscode: *MAC*
Nachrichtenende: *end of message (EOM)*
Nachrichtenformat: *message format*
Nachrichtenkopf: *message heading*
Nachrichtennetz: *communications network*
Nachrichtennumerierung: *message numbering*
Nachrichtensatellit: *communications satellite*
Nachrichtenschlitz: *message slot*
Nachrichtensenke: *sink*
Nachrichtensystem: computergestütztes ~ *computer-based message system (CBMS)*
Nachrichtentext: *message text*

Nachrichtenübertragungskanal: *information transfer channel*

Nachrichtenübertragungsleitweg: optimaler ~ *minimum weight routing*

Nachrichtenübertragungssteuerung: *telecontrol*

Nachrichtenübertragungssystem: optisches ~ *optical communication system*

Nachrichtenverbindung: *communication*

Nachrichtenverbindungen: neue ~ erschließen *to open up new channels of communication*

Nachrichtenvermitteln: *message switching*

Nachrichtenvermittlung: *message routing*

Nachrichtenveröffentlichung: *news release*

Nachrüstung: *retrofit*

Nachsatz: *trailer; trailer record*

Nachschaltrechner: *back-end processor*

Nachschlagetabelle: *look-up table or LUT*

Nachspann: *credits*

nachträglich: *post*

nachträglich bearbeitet: *post-formatted*

nachvollziehen: *simulate*

Nachzieheffekt: *streaking*

Nadel: *needle*

Nadeldrucker: *dot-matrix printer*

Nadeldruckwerk: *clapper*

Nadelkissenverzerrung: *pin cushion distortion*

Nahaufnahme: *close-up*

Nahbereichsmodem: *short haul modem*

Näherung: *approximation*

Näherungsfehler: *approximation error*

Näherungswert: *approximation*

Nahlinse: *diopter lens*

Name: *identifier; name*

Name der Zeichenfolge: *string name*

Namentabelle: *name table*

NAND-Funktion: *alternative denial; dispersion; NAND function; NOT-AND*

NAND-Gatter: *NAND gate*

nano-: *nano- or n (US)*

Nanometer: *nanometre or nm*

Nanoschaltung: *nanocircuit or nanosecond circuit*

Nanosekunde: *nanosecond or ns*

natürlich: *natural*

NC Computer: *numerical control (NC) or computer numerical control (CNC)*

Nebencomputer: *slave*

Nebeneinanderstellung: *juxtaposition*

Nebengeräusch: *background noise; hiss*

Nebenherdrucken: *background printing*

Nebenleitung: *line extender*

Nebenspeicher: *extension memory; slave cache or store*

Nebensprechen: *babble; crosstalk*

Nebenstellenanlage: *private automatic branch exchange (PABX)*

Nebenweg: *bypass*

Nebenzipfel: *side lobe*

negativ: *negative*

Negativfilm: *negative*

negieren: *negate*

Negierung: *negation*

Nenndurchlauf: *rated throughput*

Nettogewicht: *net weight*

Netz: *network* **gleichberechtigtes ~** *democratic network* **heterogenes ~** *heterogeneous network* **vermaschtes ~** *mesh network* **vollverbundenes ~** *fully connected network* **zwangssynchronisiertes ~** *despotic network*

Netzanschlußpunkt: *spur*

Netz aus: *"power off"*

Netz ein: *"power on"*

Netz Ein-Grundstellung: *power-on reset*

Netzführung: *network management*

Netz im Datenpaketbetrieb: *packet switched network (PSN)*

Netzkabel: *lead*

Netzknoten: *node*

Netzplantechnik: *network analysis*

Netzsoftware: *network software*

Netzspannungssprung: *line voltage transient*

Netzspannungsüberwachung: *power monitor*

Netzstation: *terminal*

Netzsteuerungscomputer: *communications computer*

Netzsteuerungseinheit: *communications control unit*

Netzstrom: *power*

Netzstruktur: *network structure*

Netzsynchronisation: *network timing*

Netzteil: *power pack*

Netzüberwacher: *network controller*

Netzwerk: sternförmiges ~ *active star*

Netzwerkarchitektur: *network architecture*

Netzwerkausstrahlung: *networking*

Netzwerkbetrieb: *networking*

Netzwerk-Hardware: *networking or network hardware*

Netzwerkplan: *network diagram*

Netzwerkprozessor: *network processor*

Netzwerkredundanz: *network redundancy*

Netzwerk-Software: *networking or network software*

Netzwerkspezialist: *networking specialist*

Netzwerksteuerprogramm: *network control program*

Netzwerkstruktur: *network structure* **komplexe ~** *plex structure*

Netzwerktopologie: *network topology*

Netzwerkverlegung: *networking*

Neuauflage: *reprint*

Neuerscheinungen: *new releases*

Neuerwerbungen: *accessions*

Neuformatierung: *reformatting*

Neuladen: *rollback*

Neunerkomplement: *nine's complement*

neutral: *neutral*

NEW: *new (command)*

N-Halbleiter: *n-type material or N-type material or n-type semiconductor*
NICHT-Funktion: *NOT function*
NICHT-Gatter: *negation or NOT gate*
Nichtleiter: *dielectric*
nichtlinear: *nonlinear*
nichts: *null*
Nicken: *pitch*
Niederfrequenz: *low frequency (LF)*
Niedrigstkostenplan: *least cost design*
Niveau: *grade*
N-Kanal-Metalloxidhalbleiter: *n-channel metal oxide semiconductor*
NLQ Druckmodus: *near letter-quality (NLQ) printing*
nochmals abspeichern: *resave*
Nomenklatur: *nomenclature*
Nomogramm: *nomogram or nomograph*
NOR-Funktion: *joint denial; neither-nor function; NOR function*
NOR-Gatter: *NOR gate*
Normalbereich: *normal range*
Normalformat: *normal format*
normalisieren: *normalize; standardize*
Normalisierung: *normalization*
Normen: *standards*
Normen der ECMA: *ECMA symbols*
Normenorganisation: internationale ~ *International Standards Organization (ISO)*
Normenumsetzer: *standards converter*
normieren: *normalize*
Normierungsbit: *noisy digit*
Notizblockspeicher: *scratchpad (memory); working store or scratch pad*
Notspeicherauszug: *rescue dump*
n-plus-Eins-Adreßbefehl: *n-plus-one address instruction*
n-plus-Eins-Befehl: *n-plus-one instruction*
ns: *ns*
NTSC: *National Television Standards Committee (NTSC)*
Null: *zero* auf ~ stellen *reset* durchgestrichene ~ *slashed zero* führende ~ *leading zero*
Nullanzeiger: *nil pointer*
Nullen: mit ~ auffüllen *to zero fill*
Nullenunterdrückung: *zero compression or zero suppression*
Nullkennzeichnung: *zero flag*
Nullkraftstecker: *zero insertion force (ZIF)*
Nullmodem: *null modem*
Nullsatz: *null set*
Null-String: *null or blank string*
Nullzeichen: *erase character; null character*
Numeral: *numeral*
numerieren: *number* neu ~ *renumber*
Numerierungstyp: *enumerated type*
numerisch: *numeric; numerical*
numerischer 10er-Block: *numeric (key)pad*
Nummer: internationale ~ *international number*

nutzbar: *usable*
Nutzen: *use*
Nutzflächenüberschreitung: *overscan*
Nutzfrequenz: höchste ~ *maximum usable frequency*
Nutzzeit: *up time or uptime*

Oo

Oberlänge: *ascender*
Oberschwingung: harmonische ~ *harmonic*
Objekt: *object*
Objektcode: *object code*
Objektiv: *objective*
Objektprogrammkartensatz: *object deck*
Objektsprache: *target language*
Objektvariable: *object*
OCCAM: *OCCAM*
OCP: *OCP*
OCR-Zeichensatz: *optical font or OCR font*
ODER-Funktion: *either-or operation; join; OR function*
ODER-Gatter: *OR gate*
offen: *open*
Offenlassen von Dateien: *leaving files open*
Offenlegung: *disclosure*
öffentlich: *public*
offline: *off-line*
Offline-Drucken: *off-line printing*
Offline-Verarbeitung: *off-line processing*
öffnen: *open*
Öffnung: *aperture; mouth* effektive ~ *effective aperture*
Öffnungsverhältnis: *lens speed*
Offsetdruck: *offset printing*
Offsetlithographie: *offset lithography*
Ohm: *ohm*
Ohmsches Gesetz: *Ohm's Law*
Oktalskala: *octal scale*
Oktalsystem: *octal (notation)*
Oktalziffer: *octal digit*
Oktave: *octave*
Oktett: *eight-bit byte or octet; octet*
Omega-Wicklung: *omega wrap*
One-for-one: *one for one*
online: *on-line*
Online-Datenbank: *on-line database*
Online-Informationswiedergewinnung: *on-line information retrieval*
Online-System: *on-line system*
Online-Transaktionsverarbeitung: *on-line transaction processing*
Online-Verarbeitung: *on-line processing*
opak: *opaque*
Opazität: *opacity*
Open Code: *open code*

Open-Routine: *open routine*
Operand: *operand* **aktueller** ~ *literal operand* **alphanumerischer** ~ *alphanumeric operand* **numerischer** ~ *numeric operand*
Operandenfeld: *operand field*
Operation: *operation* **adreßfreie** ~ *no-address operation* **duale** ~ *binary operation* **dyadische** ~ *dyadic operation* **einstellige** ~ *unary operation* **iterative** ~ *iterative process* **logische** ~ *logic operation* **monadische** ~ *monadic operation* **negierte** ~ *complementary operation* **unzulässige** ~ *illegal operation* **vollständige** ~ *complete operation* „**keine** ~" *no op or no operation instruction*
Operationenrangfolge: *operator precedence*
Operationscode: *op code*
Operationsfeld: *operation field*
Operationsregister: *operation register*
Operationsschlüssel: *operation code (op code)* **symbolische** ~ *assembler mnemonics or mnemonic operation codes*
Operationsschlüsselregister: *op register*
Operationsumwandler: *operation decoder*
Operationsverstärker: *operational amplifier (op amp)*
Operationszeit: *operation time*
Operationszyklus: *operation cycle*
Operator: **logischer** ~ *logical operator* **monadischer** ~ *monadic (Boolean) operator*
optimal: *optimum*
optimal einstellen: *tune*
optimieren: *optimize*
Optimierer: *optimizer*
Optimierung: *optimization*
Optimierungscode: *optimized code*
Optimum: *optimum*
Option: *option*
optisch: *optical*
optoelektrisch: *optoelectrical*
Optoelektronik: *optoelectronics*
optoelektronisch: *optoelectronic*
Ordinate: *Y-coordinate*
Ordinatenachse: *vertical axis; Y-axis*
ordnen: *rank*
Organigramm: *organization chart*
Organisation: **eine staatliche** ~ *a government organization*
Organisationsprogramm: *executive program*
Organisation und Durchführung: *organization and methods*
organisatorisch: *organizational*
organisieren: **neu** ~ *reorganize*
orientiert: *orientated*
Orientierung: *orientation*
Original: *top copy; original*
Original-: *master*
original: *original*
Originaldokument: *source document*
Originalvorlage: *original*
Ort: **vor** ~ *on location*

orthogonal: *orthogonal*
Orthographieprüfprogramm: *spellchecker or spelling checker*
Ortsgespräch: *local call*
Ortsnetzkennzahl: *area code*
Oszillator: *oscillator*
Oszilloskop: *oscilloscope*
Overlay-Systemprogramm: *overlay manager*
Oxid: *oxide*

Pp

Packager: *packager*
Packaging: *packaging*
Packen: *packing*
packen: *grab; pack*
paginieren: *folio* **neu** ~ *repaginate*
Paginierung: *pagination*
Palette: *palette*
PAL-System: *phase alternating line (PAL)*
PAM: *PAM*
Paperback: *paperback*
Papier: *paper* **elektrosensitives** ~ *electrosensitive paper* **gestrichenes** ~ *coated paper* **ohne** ~ *paperless* **selbstdurchschreibendes** ~ *carbonless paper* **zweilagiges** ~ *two-part*
Papierbehälter: *paper tray*
Papierendesensor: *form stop*
Papiergewicht: *grammage; paper weight*
Papiernachbereitungsmaschine: *form handling equipment*
Papierschneidemaschine: *guillotine*
Papiertraktor: *tractor feed*
Papiertransport: *paper feed*
Papiervorschub: **schneller** ~ *paper throw; high-speed skip; slew*
Papierzuführer: **automatischer** ~ *feeder*
Pappe: *cardboard*
Pappkarton: *cardboard box*
Parabolantenne: *dish aerial*
Paragraph: *article*
parallel: *parallel*
Parallelabfragespeicher: *parallel search storage*
Paralleladdierer: *parallel adder*
Parallelanschlußstelle: *parallel port*
Parallelbetrieb: *parallel operation*
Parallelbetriebssystem: *concurrent operating system*
Paralleldrucker: *parallel printer*
Parallellauf: *parallel running* **rückweisender** ~ *retrospective parallel running*
Parallelschaltung: *parallel connection*
Parallelübergabe: *parallel transmission*
Parallelübertrag: *carry look ahead*
Parallelübertragung: *parallel transfer; parallel transmission*
Parallelverbindung: *parallel connection*

Parallelzugriff: *parallel access*
Parameter: *argument; parameter* **physikalischer** ~ *physical parameter*
Parameterprüfung: *parameter testing*
Parameterwort: *parameter word*
Parametrisierung: *parameterization*
Parität: *parity*
Paritätsanzeiger: *parity flag*
Paritätsprüfung: *odd-even check; parity check*
Paritätsprüfungsabbruch: *parity interrupt*
Parsing: *parsing*
Partner: *associate*
PASCAL: *PASCAL*
Paßmarken: *register marks*
Paßwort: *password*
Patentraub: *piracy*
Patenträuber: *pirate*
pauschal: *flat*
Pauschalabmachung: *blanket agreement*
Pauschalangebot: *package deal*
Pauschaltarif: *flat rate*
Pause: *interval*
Pauspapier: *detail paper*
PC: *PC*
PC-kompatibel: *PC compatible*
PCM: *PCM*
p-Code: *P-code*
PDM: *PDM*
PEEK-Anweisung: *peek*
Pegel: *level* **logischer** ~ H *logical high* **logischer** ~ L *logical low*
perfekt: *perfect; perfectly*
Perfektor: *perfector*
Perforationen: *perforations*
Perigäum: *perigee*
Periodika: *periodical*
periodisch: *periodic or periodical*
peripher: *peripheral*
Peripheriegerät: *external device; peripheral (unit)* **langsames** ~ *slow peripheral* **schnelles** ~ *fast peripheral*
Peripheriegeräte: *peripheral equipment*
Perle: *bead*
Permeabilität: *permeability*
Permutation: *permutation*
Personalausweis: *ID card*
Personalcomputer: *personal computer (PC) or home computer*
persönlich: *personal*
Perzentil: *percentile*
Pfad: *path*
Pflichtenheft: *system specifications*
p-Halbleiter: *p-type semiconductor*
Phantom-ROM: *phantom ROM*
Phase: *phase*
Phasenentzerrer: *phase equalizer*
phasengleich: *in phase*
Phasenmodulation: *phase modulation*

phasenverschoben: *out of phase*
Phasenwinkel: *phase angle*
Phon: *phon*
Phonem: *phoneme*
Phonetik: *phonetics*
phonetisch: *phonetic*
Phosphor: **grüner** ~ *green phosphor* **langleuchtender** ~ *long persistence phosphor*
Phosphorbeschichtung: *phosphor coating*
Phosphoreszenz: *phosphorescence*
Phosphorpunkte: *phosphor dots*
Phosphorwirksamkeit: *phosphor efficiency*
Photodiode: *photodiode*
photoelektrisch: *photoelectric*
Photoelektrizität: *photoelectricity*
Photoemission: *photoemission*
Photoleiter: *photoconductor*
Photoleitfähigkeit: *photoconductivity*
Photometrie: *photometry*
Photon: *photon*
Photosensor: *photosensor*
Phototransistor: *phototransistor*
photovoltaisch: *photovoltaic*
Photozelle: *light-sensitive device; photocell; photoelectric cell*
physisch: *physical*
Pica: *pica*
Pico-: *pico- (p)*
Picofarad: *picofarad (pF)*
Picosekunde: *picosecond (ps)*
piepsen: *beep; bleep*
Piepser: *bleeper; pager; radio pager or radio paging device*
Piepton: *beep; bleep*
piezoelektrisch: *piezoelectric*
Pigmentpapier: *carbon tissue*
Piktogramm: *icon or ikon*
PILOT: *PILOT*
Pilotprojekt: *pilot*
Pilotsystem: *pilot system*
PIN-Photodiode: *pin photodiode*
Pipelinesystem: **im** ~ **verarbeiten** *pipeline (computer)*
Pipeline-Verarbeitung der Befehle: *instruction pipelining*
Pipelining: *pipelining*
Pipelining-Methode: *pipelining*
p-Kanal: *p-channel*
p-Kanal-MOS: *p-channel MOS; PMOS*
Plakat: *poster*
PLAN: *PLAN*
Plan: *plan; schedule*
planen: *to plan; to schedule*
Planet: *planet*
Planprogramm: *planner*
Planschrank: *planchest*
Planung: *planning*

Plasmabildschirm: *gas discharge or plasma or electroluminescent display*
Plastikblasentastatur: *plastic bubble keyboard*
Platine: *board; card* **auf der** ~ *on-board*
Platinenerweiterung: *card extender*
Platinengehäuse: *card cage*
Platte: *disk; plate* **beidseitig beschreibbare** ~ *double-sided disk* **leere** ~ *blank disk* **optische** ~ *optical disk* **reflektierende** ~ *reflective disk* **virtuelle** ~ *virtual disk* **weichsektorierte** ~ *soft-sectored disk*
Platten: **auf** ~ **basierend** *disk-based (operating system)*
Plattenabsturz: *disk crash*
Plattenbetriebssystem: *disk operating system (DOS)*
Plattendarstellung: *disk map*
Plattendatei: *disk file*
Platteneinheit: *disk unit*
Plattenformatierung: *disk formatting*
Plattenindexlöcher: *disk index holes*
Plattenkamera: *plate camera*
Plattenkassette: *disk cartridge*
Plattenlaufwerk: *disk drive* **doppelseitiges** ~ *double-sided disk drive* **externes** ~ *external disk drive*
plattenlos: *diskless*
Plattenname: *title of disk*
Plattensektor: *disk sector*
Plattensektorformatierung: *(disk) sector formatting*
Plattenspeicher: *disk storage; disk memory* **auswechselbarer** ~ *exchangeable disk storage (EDS)*
Plattenspur: *disk track*
Plattenstapel: *disk pack*
Plattensteuereinheit: *disk controller*
Plattensteuereinheitskarte: *disk-controller card*
Plattenverzeichnis: *disk catalogue or directory*
Plattenwechsler: *record changer*
Plattenzugriff: *disk access*
Plattenzugriffsarm: *access arm*
Plattenzugriffsverwaltung: *disk access management*
Platz: *place* **freier** ~ *empty slot*
Plotter: **digitaler** ~ *digital plotter*
Plotterschreibkopf: *plotter pen*
Plottertreiber: *plotter driver*
Pluszeichen: *plus or plus sign*
pnp-Transistor: *pnp transistor*
pn-Stufenübergang: *step pn-junction*
pn-Übergang: *pn-junction*
POKE-Anweisung: *poke*
polar: *polar*
Polardiagramm: *polar diagram*
polarisiert: *polarized*
Polarität: *polarity* **elektrische** ~ *electrical polarity* **magnetische** ~ *magnetic polarity* **umgekehrte** ~ *reverse polarity*

Polaritätsprüfung: *polarity test*
Polarkoordinaten: *polar coordinates*
Polaroidfilter: *polaroid filter*
Polynomcode: *polynomial code*
POP 2: *POP 2*
Pop-Filter: *pop filter*
Position: *position*
Positionierzeit: *seek time*
Positionsanzeiger: *cursor* **adressierbarer** ~ *addressable cursor*
Positiv: *positive*
positiv: *affirmative; positive*
Post: *mail* **elektronische** ~ *electronic mail or email or e-mail* **multimediale** ~ *multimedia mail*
Postbyte: *postbyte*
Postfachnummer: *box number*
Postfix: *postfix*
Postfixschreibweise: *postfix notation; reverse Polish notation (RPN)*
Postleitzahl: *post code or zip code (US)*
Postlumineszenz: *phosphorescence*
Post-Mortem-Fehlersuche: *post mortem*
Postprozessor: *postprocessor*
Postprozessorprogramm: *postprocessor*
Postwurfsendung: *mailing piece*
Postwurfsendungen: *junk mail*
Potential: *potential*
Potentialunterschied: *potential difference*
Potentiometer: *potentiometer*
Potenz: *power*
Potenzierung: *exponentiation*
prä-: *pre-*
Prädikat: *predicate*
Präfix: *prefix*
Präfixschreibweise: *prefix notation*
praxisgetestet: *field tested*
präzis: *precise*
Präzision: *precision*
Preisabsprache: *common pricing*
Preis ab Werk: *factory price or price ex factory*
Prellen: *bounce*
Presse: *press* **die überregionale** ~ *the national press*
Presseausschnittdienst: *clipping service*
Pressebericht: *press coverage*
Pressefreiheit: *freedom of the press*
Pressekonferenz: *press conference*
Presseverlautbarung: *press release*
Primärgruppe: *primary group*
Primärschlüssel: *primary key*
Primärspeicher: *primary storage*
Primärstation: *primary station*
Primärstrahler: *radiating element*
Primzahl: *prime*
Priorität: *priority*
Prioritätsaufgabe: *foreground*
Prioritätsplaner: *priority scheduler*

Prioritätsprogramm: *foreground program*
Prioritätsreihenfolge: *priority sequence*
privat: *private*
Privatadresse: *home address*
Privatleitung: *private line*
pro: *per*
Probe: *trial* **auf** ~ *on approval*
Probelauf: *desk check; dry run*
Problem: ein ~ **lösen** *to solve a problem*
Problemdarstellung: *problem definition*
Produkt: *product*
Produktanalyse: *product analysis*
Produktdesign *or* **Produktgestaltung:** *product design*
Produktentwicklung: *product development*
Produktgruppe: *product line or product range*
Produktion: *production*
Produktionseinheit: *production unit*
Produktionskapazität: *producing capacity*
Produktionskosten: *production cost*
Produktionslauf: *production run*
Produktionsleiter: *production manager*
Produktionsnormen: *production standards*
Produktionsrate: *rate of production or production rate*
produktiv: *productive*
Produktmanagement: *product management*
Produktmix: *product mix*
Produktwerbung: *product advertising*
Produzent: *producer*
produzierend: *producing*
Programm: *listings; program; routine* **absolutes** ~ *absolute program* **befehlsgetriebenes** ~ *command-driven program* **ein** ~ **auflisten** *to list a program* **erstklassiges** ~ *blue-ribbon program* **fehlerloses** ~ *star program* **festverdrahtetes** ~ *hardwired program* **gekettetes** ~ *thread* **geschlossenes** ~ *closed routine or closed subroutine* **gespeichertes** ~ *stored program* **gestrecktes** ~ *in-line program* **gut funktionierendes** ~ *well-behaved program* **intern gespeichertes** ~ *internally stored program* **korrigiertes** ~ *debugged program* **lineares** ~ *linear program* **offenes** ~ *open routine or open subroutine* **relativierbares** ~ *relocatable program* **selbstdarstellendes** ~ *self-documenting program* **selbstverschiebliches** ~ *self-relocating program* **speicherresidentes** ~ *resident software or memory-resident software* **wiederverwendbares** ~ *re-ntrant program*
Programmabbruch: *crash*
Programmablauf: *program run*
Programmablaufanlage: *object computer*
Programmablauffolge: *job stream*
Programmablaufplan: *program flowchart*
Programmablaufverfolgung: *trace*
Programmabschnitt: *program segment*
Programmabsturz: *program crash*
Programmanweisung: *program statement*
Programmauflistung: *program listing*

Programmausführung: *program execution*
Programmausrüstung: *software*
Programmbefehl: *program instruction*
Programmbeginn: *program origin*
Programmbeschreibung: *program specification*
Programmbibliothek: *program library*
Programmdatei: *program file*
Programme: übertragbare ~ *portable software or portable programs*
Programm-Editor: *program editor*
Programmeldung: *dialogue box*
Programmentwicklung: *program development*
Programmentwicklungssoftware: *development software*
Programmentwicklungssystem: *program development system*
Programmentwicklungswerkzeug: *software tool*
Programmentwurfssprache: *program design language (PDL)*
Programmfehler: bug verborgener ~ *hidden defect in a program*
Programmfolge: *suite of programs*
Programmgenerator: *program generator*
Programmgruppe: *suite of programs*
programmierbar: *programmable*
Programmierblatt: *program coding sheet*
Programmieren: *programming* **automatisches** ~ *automatic programming* **defensives** ~ *defensive computing* **elegantes** ~ *elegant programming* **symbolisches** ~ *symbolic programming* **universelles** ~ *universal programming* **visuelles** ~ *visual programming*
programmieren: *program* **neu** ~ *reprogram*
Programmieren in Maschinensprache: *machine language programming*
Programmierer: *(computer) programmer*
Programmiergerät: *programmer*
Programmiernormen: *programming standards*
Programmiersprache: *programming language* **algorithmische** ~ *ALGOL* **anwendungsorientierte** ~ *A programming language (APL)* **aufgabenorientierte** ~ *job orientated language* **benutzerorientierte** ~ *user-operated language* **computerunabhängige** ~ *computer independent language* **gekettete** ~ *threaded language* **höhere** ~ *high-level (programming) language (HLL)* **maschinenorientierte** ~ *low-level language (LLL)* **maschinenunabhängige** ~ *machine independent language* **mehrdimensionale** ~ *multidimensional language* **problemorientierte** ~ *problem-orientated language (POL)* **verfahrensorientierte** ~ *procedure-orientated language; procedural language*
Programmierung: lineare ~ *linear programming* **modulares** ~ *modular programming* **strukturierte** ~ *structured programming; top down programming*
Programmierungshilfe: *language support environment*
Programmkarten: *program cards*
Programmkellerspeicher: *program stack*
Programmkompatibilität: *program compatibility*

Programmlauf: *program run*
Programmlistengenerator: *program report generator*
Programmname: *program name*
Programmodul: *module*
Programmplanung: *programme scheduling*
Programmprüfung: *program testing or verification*
Programmregister: *program register*
Programmschalter: *sense switch*
Programmschema: *coding sheet or coding form*
Programmschritt: *program step*
Programmsegment: *segment*
Programmspeicher: *program storage*
Programmspezifizierung: *program specification*
Programmstatuswort: *program status word (PSW)*
Programmstatuswortregister: *program status word register (PSW register)*
Programmsteuerung: automatische ~ *automatic sequencing*
Programmstop: bedingter ~ *conditional breakpoint; dynamic stop* **regionaler ~** *regional breakpoint*
Programmstopsignal: *breakpoint symbol*
Programmstruktur: *program structure*
Programmübersetzung: *program compilation*
Programm- und Datennotausdruck: *disaster dump*
Programmunterbrechung: *interrupt*
Programmunterlagen: *(program) documentation*
Programmverbindung: *linking*
Programmverbindungssoftware: *linkage software*
Programmverschiebung: *program relocation*
Programmwartung: *program maintenance*
Programmwiederaufnahme: *fall back recovery*
Programmzähler: *program counter (PC)*
Programmzeile: *program line*
Programm zur Lagerbestandsführung: *stock control program*
Programm zur Programmablaufverfolgung: *trace program*
Programmzweig: *(program) branch*
Projekt: *project*
projektieren: *project*
Projektion: *projection*
Projektstudie: eine ~ durchführen *to carry out a feasibility study on a project*
PROLOG: *PROLOG*
PROM: *PROM*
PROM-Programmiergerät: *PROM burner or programmer*
Proportion: *proportion*
Proportionalschrittschaltung: *proportional spacing*
Protokoll: *audit; journal; log; protocol*
Protokolldatei: *journal file*
protokollieren: *to log*
Protokollprogramm: selektives ~ *snapshot*

Prototyp: *prototype*
Prozedur: *procedure*
prozedural: *procedural*
Prozedurvereinbarung: *procedure declaration*
Prozent: *per cent*
Prozentpunkt: *percentage point*
Prozentsatz: *percentage*
prozentual: *per cent*
Prozeß: process irreversibler ~ *irreversible process*
prozeßgebunden: *process bound*
Prozessor: *processor* **untergeordneter ~** *slave processor*
Prozessorabbruchsignal: *processor interrupt*
Prozessor-Statuswort: *processor status word (PSW)*
Prozeßrechner: *process control computer*
Prozeß-Steuersystem: *process control system*
Prozeßsteuerung: *process control*
Prüfanzeiger: *check indicator*
Prüfbit: *check bit; parity bit*
Prüfdaten: *test data*
Prüfeinrichtung: automatische ~ *automatic test equipment (ATE)*
prüfen: *check; sense; test*
Prüfen: computergestütztes ~ *computer-aided or assisted testing (CAT)*
Prüfer: *verifier*
Prüfgerät: *test equipment*
Prüfnummer: *check number*
Prüfprogramm: *checking program*
Prüfprotokoll: *audit trail*
Prüfpunkt: *check point*
Prüfregister: *check register*
Prüfspur: *parity track*
Prüfung: check; test automatische ~ *automatic checking*
Prüfung auf numerisch: *test numeric*
Prüfungssystem: automatisches ~ *self-checking system*
Prüfzahl: *check number*
Prüfzeichen: *check character; check key*
Prüfziffer: *check digit*
Pseudobefehl: *pseudo-instruction*
Pseudocode: *pseudo-code*
pseudodigital: *pseudo-digital*
Pseudooperation: *pseudo-operation*
pseudozufällig: *pseudo-random*
Pseudozufallszahlengenerator: *pseudo-random number generator*
Publicity: *publicity*
Publikum: *audience*
Publizieren: elektronisches ~ *electronic publishing*
Publizieren am Schreibtisch: *desktop publishing (DTP)*
Puffer: *buffer* **dynamische ~** *dynamic buffer* **elastischer ~** *elastic buffer*
Puffergröße: *buffer size*

Pufferlänge: *buffer length*
Pufferregister: *buffer register*
Pufferspeicher: *buffered memory*
Pufferung: doppelte ~ *double buffering*
Pulldown-Menü: *pop-up menu or pull-down menu*
Pulscodemodulation: *pulse code modulation (PCM)*
Pulslagenmodulation: *pulse position modulation (PPM)*
Punkt: *dot; element; period (US); point; spot* **benutzbarer** ~ *available point* **erdfernster** ~ *apogee* **erdnächster** ~ *perigee* **großer** ~ *bullet*
Punktbefehl: *dot command*
Punkte pro Inch: *dots per inch or d.p.i. or dpi*
Punktmatrix: verbesserte ~ *enhanced dot matrix*
Punkt zu Punkt: *point to point*

Qq

QISAM: *QISAM*
QSAM: *QSAM*
Quadratur: *quadrature*
Quadratwurzel: *square root*
quadrophon: *quadrophonic*
Quadruplex: *quadruplex*
Qualität: beste ~ *high or top quality*
Qualitätskontrolle: *quality control*
Qualitätskontrolle mittels Stichprobe: *acceptance sampling*
Qualitätsmaßstab: hoher ~ *high specification or high spec*
Qualitätsprüfer: *quality controller*
Quant: *quantum*
quantisieren: *quantize*
Quantisierer: *quantizer*
Quantisierung: *(amplitude) quantization*
Quantisierungsfehler: *quantization error*
Quantisierungsgeräusch: *quantizing noise*
Quantor: *quantifier*
Quartärgruppe: *super master group*
Quartblatt: *quad*
Quartil: *quartile*
Quarto: *quarto*
Quarzoszillator: *crystal oscillator*
Quarzuhr: *quartz (crystal) clock*
Quasi-Befehl: *quasi-instruction*
quaternär: *quaternary*
Quecksilber-Verzögerungsleitung: *mercury delay line*
Quellcode: *source code*
Quelle: *source*
Quellenfindung: *homing*
Quellprogramm: *source program*
Querabtastung: *transverse scan*
Querleitung: *high usage trunk*
Quermodulation: *cross modulation*

Querparitätsprüfung: *vertical parity check*
Querprüfung: *vertical redundancy check (VRC)*
Querschnitt: *cross-section*
Querverbindungsleitung: *tie line or tie trunk*
Querverweis: *cross-reference*
Quicksort: *quicksort*
Quittungsbetrieb: *handshake or handshaking*
Quittungsduplikat: *duplicate receipt or duplicate of a receipt*
Quittungszeichen: *acknowledge character*
Quotient: *quotient*
QWERTY-Tastatur: *QWERTY keyboard*

Rr

Radar: *radar*
Radialübertragung: *radial transfer*
Radiator: *radiator*
Radio: *wireless*
Radiogerät: *set*
Radio- und Fernsehsatellit: *domestic satellite*
Radix: *radix*
Radixpunkt: *radix point*
Radixschreibweise: *radix notation*
Rahmen: *frame; rack; safe area*
Rahmenantenne: *loop antenna*
Rahmenbit: *framing bit*
Rahmencode: *framing code*
Rahmencodierung: *skeletal code*
Rahmenfehler: *frame error*
Rahmenrücklauf: *frame flyback*
RAM: *RAM* **dynamischer** ~ *dynamic RAM* **selbstregenerierender** ~ *self-refreshing RAM* **statischer** ~ *static RAM*
RAM-Chip: *RAM chip*
RAM-Lader: *RAM loader*
RAM-Platte: *RAM disk*
RAM-Regenerationsgeschwindigkeit: *RAM refresh rate*
RAM-Regenerierer: *RAM refresh*
Rand: *edge; margin* **den** ~ **setzen** *to set the margin*
Randausgleich: *justification*
Rand ausgleichen: *justify*
Randauswertung: *edge detection*
Randschärfe: *acutance*
Randstecker: polarisierter ~ *polarized edge connector*
rangieren: *range*
Rangsystem: paralleles ~ *parallel priority system*
Raster: *grid; raster*
Rasterabtastung: *raster scan*
Rasterbildverarbeiter: *raster image processor*
Rasterfeld: *frame*
Rastergraphik: *raster graphics*
Rat: um ~ **fragen** *consult*
Rate: *rate*

Raubdruck _or_ **Raubpressung:** _piracy_
Raubkopie: _bootleg_
Raum: freier ~ _free space media_
Raumfahrzeug: _space craft_
Rauschabstand: _signal to noise ratio; s/n ratio_
Rauschen: _noise; static_ **außerirdisches** ~ _extraterrestrial noise_ **galaktisches** ~ _galactic noise_ **thermisches** ~ _thermal noise_ **weißes** ~ _white noise_
Rauschtemperatur: _noise temperature_
reagieren: auf etwas ~ _to react to something_ **mit etwas** ~ _to react with something_
Reaktanz: _reactance_
Reaktion: _feedback; reaction_ **chemische** ~ _chemical reaction_
Reaktionsmodus: _reactive mode_
reaktionsträge: _inert_
realisieren: _implement_
Realisierung: _implementation_
Realspeicher: _real memory_
Real-time: _real time_
Rechen-: _computational; computing_
Rechenbefehl: _arithmetic instruction_
Rechen-Coprozessor: _maths coprocessor_
Rechenelement: erweitertes ~ _extended arithmetic element_
Rechenfehler: _computational error_
Rechengeschwindigkeit: _computing speed_
Rechengröße: _operand_
Rechenmaschine: _calculator_
Rechenoperation: _arithmetic operation_
Rechenprüfung: _arithmetic check_
Rechenregister: _arithmetic register_
Rechenstärke: _computing power_
Rechensystem: _computer system_
Rechenvorgang: interner ~ _internal arithmetic_
Rechenwerk (im CPU): _arithmetic logic unit (ALU)_ _or arithmetic unit_
Rechenzeichen: _arithmetic operator(s)_
Rechenzeit: _computer time_
Rechenzentrumsoperator: _centre operator_
Rechner: konventioneller ~ _complex instruction set computer (CISC)_ **programmierbarer** ~ _programmable calculator_ **technisch-wissenschaftlicher** ~ _scientific calculator_
Rechnung: detaillierte ~ _detailed account_ **extern ausgeführte** ~ _external arithmetic_
Rechteckwelle: _square wave_
rechts: nach ~ **verschieben** _right shift_
Rechtsausrichtung: _right justification_
rechts(bündig) ausrichten: _right justify_
Rechtschreibprüfprogramm: _spellchecker or spelling checker_
Rechtsverschiebung: _shift right_
Redaktion: elektronische ~ _electronic editing_
redaktionell: _editorial_
Redaktions-: _editorial_
Redaktionsausschuß: _editorial board_

Redaktionstextverarbeitungszentrale: _editorial processing centre_
Redefreiheit: _freedom of speech_
redigieren: _subbing or sub-editing_
redigiert: nicht ~ _unedited_
redundant: _redundant_
Redundanz: _redundancy_
Redundanzprüfung: _redundancy checking_
reduzieren: _reduce_
Referenzprogramm: _benchmark_
Referenzprogrammtabelle: _reference program table_
reflektieren: _reflect_
reflektierend: _flared_
Reflexion: _reflection_
Reflexionsgrad: _reflectance_
Regel: _rule_
Regelkreis: geschlossener ~ _closed loop_ **offener** ~ _open loop_
regelmäßig: _periodic; periodically_
regeln: _regulate_
Regelung: direkte digitale ~ _DDC_
Regelvokabular: _controlled vocabulary_
Regelwiderstand: _variable resistor; rheostat_
Regeneration: _regeneration_
Regenerationsspeicher: _regenerative memory_
regenerieren: _regenerate_
Region: _region_
Regisseur: _director_
Register: _index; register_ **externes** ~ _external register_ **gepaartes** ~ _paired register_
Registeradressierung: _register addressing_
Registerdatei: _register file_
Registererstellung: _indexing_
Register halten: _register_
Registerinhaltsverzeichnis: _register map_
Registerlänge: _register length_
Regler: _controller_
Reibungselektrizität: _static_
Reichweite: außer ~ _out of range_
Reihe: series in ~ _serial; serially_
Reihenfolge: alphabetische ~ _alphabetical order_
Reihenfolge der Lagen: _collating sequence_
Reihenschaltung: _series circuit_
Reihum-Methode: _round robin_
rein: _intrinsic; pure_
reinigen: _clean_
Reinkopie: _clean copy; clean proof_
Reinschrift: _fair copy or final copy; finished document_
Reklamezettel: _leaflet_
Rekonfiguration: _reconfiguration_
rekonfigurieren: _reconfigure_
rekonstituieren: _reconstitute_
Rekto: _recto_
Rekursion: _recursion or recursive routine_ **verkettete** ~ _daisy chain recursion_
Relais: _relay_

Relaisstation für Kabelfernsehen: *cable TV relay station*
relativ: *relative*
Relativzeigerwert: *offset value or offset word*
Relativzeitgeber: *relative-time clock*
relevant: *relevant*
Relevanz: *relevance*
Reliefdruck: *relief printing*
REM: *REM*
Remission: *reflectance*
Reparaturdauer: mittlere ~ *mean time to repair*
reparieren: *fix*
Repertoire: *repertoire*
Replikation: *replication*
repräsentativ: *representative*
repräsentieren: *represent*
Repro: *repro (informal)*
Reproabzug: *repro proof*
Reprokamera: *process camera*
Reprovorlage: *artwork*
Reserveausrüstung: *standby equipment*
resident: *resident*
Resonanz: *resonance*
Resonanzwand: *baffle*
Rest: *modulus or MOD; remainder*
Rest-: *residual*
Restfehlerhäufigkeit: *residual error rate*
Restkapazitäten ausnutzen: *to use up spare or excess capacity*
Restseitenband: *vestigial sideband*
retuschieren: *retouch; touch up*
revidieren: *revise*
Revision: *audit*
Revolution: die technologische ~ *the technological revolution*
Rheostat: *rheostat*
Richtantenne: *directional antenna*
Richtdiagramm: *directional pattern*
richtig: *correct* **nicht** ~ **ausgerichtet** *out of alignment;* nonaligned **nicht** ~ **funktionieren** *malfunction*
richtig ausgerichtet: *in alignment*
Richt(leistungs)wirkungsgrad: *available power*
Richtlinien: *convention*
Richtmikrophon: *unidirectional microphone* **besonders empfindliches** ~ *shotgun microphone*
Richtungen: in beiden ~ *bi-directional*
Richtungswinkel: *azimuth*
Ring: *ring*
Ringmodell: *round robin*
Ringnetz: *loop network; ring (data) network*
Ringschieben: *end about shift*
Ringschieberegister: *circulating register*
Ringverschiebung: *ring shift*
Ringzählwerk: *ring counter*
RIP: *RIP*
Roboter: *robot*
Robotik: *robotics*

robust: *robust*
roh: *raw*
Rohprogramm: *rough copy*
Rolle: *coil; roll*
rollen: *roll*
Rollenbesetzungsdirektor: *casting director*
Rollenzuführung: *feed reel*
ROM: kundenspezifischer ~ *custom ROM (PROM)*
ROM-Kassette: *ROM cartridge*
ROM-Software: *romware*
Röntgen: *X-ray imaging*
Röntgenbild: *X-ray*
Röntgenstrahl: *X-ray*
Rotation: *rotation*
Rotationskamera: *rotary camera*
Rotationsoperation: *bit rotation or rotate operation*
Rotationspresse: *rotary press*
Rot-Grün-Blau(-System): *red, green, blue (RGB); RGB*
rotieren: *rotate*
rotierend: *rotary*
Routine: *routine*
RS-232C: *RS-232C*
RS-Kippstufe: *RS-flip-flop*
Rubrik: *rubric*
Rück-: *retro-*
rückassemblieren: *disassemble*
Rückassemblierer: *disassembler*
Rücken: *spine*
Rückführung: *feedback* **negative** ~ *negative feedback* **positive** ~ *positive feedback*
Rückführungskreis: *feedback control*
Rückführungsschleife: *feedback loop*
Rückgespräch: *transferred charge call or collect call (US)*
Rückinformation: *feedback*
Rückkanal: *reverse channel*
Rückkehr-nach-Null-Signal: *return to zero signal*
Rückkopplung: *feedback* **negative** ~ *negative feedback* **positive** ~ *positive feedback*
Rücklauf: *flyback*
Rücklauftaste: *carriage return (CR)*
Rückmeldung: akustische ~ *acoustical feedback* **negative** ~ *negative acknowledgement (NAK)* **positive** ~ *acknowledge; affirmative acknowledgement*
Rücknahmebefehl: *revert command*
Rückrufsystem: *ring back system*
Rucksack: *back pack*
Rückseite: *back; verso*
Rücksetzungszeichen: *backspace character*
Rücksprung: *re-entry; return*
Rücksprungadresse: *return address*
Rücksprungstelle: *re-entry point*
Rückstand: *backlog*
rückstellen: *restore*

Rückstelliste: *pushdown list*
Rückstellstapel: *pushdown stack*
Rückstelltaste: *reset button or key*
Rückstellung: harte ~ *hard reset* **weiche** ~ *soft reset*
Rückstreuung: *backscatter*
Rücktaste: *backspace key*
Rückumsetzung: *decompilation*
Rückwandplatine: *backplane*
Rückwandverdrahtung: gedruckte ~ *backplane*
rückwärts: *backward or backwards; reverse*
Rückwärtsmodus: *backward mode*
Rückwärtsschritt: *backspace*
Rückwärtssteuerung: *backwards supervision*
Rückweisungsfehler: *rejection error*
Rufannahmesignal: *call accept(ed) signal*
Ruhezustand: *stable state*
ruhig: *quiescent*
rund: *round*
Runddatei: *circular file*
Runden: *rounding*
Rundfunksatellitentechnik: *broadcast satellite technique*
Rundfunksendestelle: *broadcasting station*
Rundhohlleiter: *circular waveguide*
Rundpuffer: *circular buffer*
Rundruf: einen ~ **machen** *ring down*
Rundskala: *dial*
Rundspruch: *broadcast*
Rundspruchnetz: *broadcast network*
Rundungsfehler: *rounding error*
Rundverschiebung: *circular shift*
Rüstzeit: *set-up time*
rütteln: *joggle*

Ss

S-100-Bus: *S100 bus or S-100 bus*
sachdienlich: *relevant*
Sache: *matter*
Sachverständige(r): *expert*
Sägezahnschwingung: *sawtooth waveform*
Salamitechnik: *salami technique*
Sammelfeld: *bucket*
Sammellinse: *condenser lens*
sammeln: *gather*
sammelnd (auf)schreiben: *gather write*
sammelnd laden: *collect transfer*
Sammelschiene: *bus*
Saphir: *sapphire*
Satellit: *satellite* **direktstrahlender** ~ *direct broadcast satellite (DBS)* **geostationärer** ~ *geostationary satellite*
Satellitendatenstation: *satellite terminal*
Satellitennetz: *satellite network*
Satellitenrechner: *satellite computer*

Satellitenrundfunk: *satellite broadcasting*
Satellitenstrecke: *satellite link*
Satellit für Grundsteuerungssysteme: *basic control system satellite (BCS)*
Sättigung: *saturation*
Sättigungsprüfung: *saturation testing*
Sättigungsstörung: *saturation noise*
Sättigungstesten: *saturation testing*
Satz: *block; record; set* **einzelner** ~ *unit record* **geketteter** ~ *chained record* **logischer** ~ *logical record* **physischer** ~ *physical record* **universeller** ~ *universal set*
Satzanweisungen machen: *mark up*
Satzanzahl: *record count*
Satzbreite: *measure*
Satzende: *end of record (EOR)*
Satzformat: *record format or layout*
Satzlänge: *record length*
Satzspiegel: *type area; matter* **angeschnittener** ~ *bleed*
Satzumfang: geschätzter ~ *cast off*
Satzumfang schätzen: *to cast off*
Satzverwaltungsprogramm: *records management*
Satzverwaltungssystem: *records manager*
Satzzeichen: *punctuation mark*
Satzzwischenraum: *record gap*
sauber: *clean*
Säulendiagramm: *columnar graph*
S-Box-Verfahren: *S-box*
Scanner: *scanner*
Scanner-Programm: *scanning software*
Schablone: *mask; stencil; style sheet; template*
Schablonenbefehl: *template command*
Schablonenspeicherung: *local format storage*
Schachtel: *case*
Schaden: *damage*
Schaden erleiden: *to suffer damage*
Schaden zufügen: *to cause damage*
Schall: umgebender ~ *ambisonics*
schalldicht: *dead; soundproof*
Schalldruckpegel: *sound pressure level (SPL)*
Schallplatte: *record*
Schallschluckhaube: *acoustic hood*
schalltot: *anechoic*
Schallwelle: *sound wave*
Schaltbild: *circuit diagram*
Schaltbrücke: *communications channel*
schalten: *switch*
Schalter: einseitiger ~ *single pole* **elektronischer** ~ *latch* **federnder** ~ *momentary switch*
Schaltfolge: *switch train*
Schaltkarte: *circuit board or card* **beidseitig gedruckte** ~ *double-sided printed circuit board* **gedruckte** ~ *printed circuit board (PCB)*
Schaltkreis: *gate circuit* **integrierter optischer** ~ *integrated optical circuit* **integrierter** ~ *integrated circuit (IC)* **kombinierter** ~ *composite circuit* **logischer** ~ *logic circuit* **trockener** ~ *dry circuit*

Schaltkreisplatine: *logic card or logic board*

Schaltlogik: *circuitry*

Schaltnetz: *combinational circuit*

Schaltschritt: gleichbleibender ~ *monospacing*

Schalttafel: *plugboard or patchboard*

Schaltung: *circuit* **analoge integrierte** ~ *linear integrated circuit* **bistabile** ~ *flip-flop (FF)* **elektromechanische** ~ *electromechanical switching* **gedruckte** ~ *printed circuit* **logische** ~ *logic circuit*

Schaltungsentwurf: *circuit design*

Schaltverzögerung: *gate or propagation delay; propagation time*

scharf: *acute; hard*

Schärfe: *acuity; focus*

scharfstellen: *focus*

Schatten: *shadow*

Schattenmaske: *aperture mask*

Schatten-ROM: *shadow ROM*

Schattenschwärzung: *black crush*

Schattenspeicher: *shadow memory*

Schattierung: *shade; shading; tone*

schätzen: *calculate*

Schätzen des Satzumfangs: *casting off*

Scheckbuch: *cheque book*

Scheibe: *slice*

Scheinvariable: *dummy variable*

Scheinwiderstand: *impedance*

Scheinwiderstandsanpassung: *impedance matching* **fehlerhafte** ~ *impedance mismatch*

Schema: *schema; schematic* **externes** ~ *external schema* **kanonisches** ~ *canonical schema*

schematisch: *schematic*

Schicht: *deposit; layer* **anwendungsbezogene** ~ *application layer* **epitaxiale** ~ *epitaxial layer*

Schicht-Laserspeicher: *emulsion laser storage*

schieben: *drag*

Schieberegister: *shift register*

Schildkröte: *turtle*

Schildkrötengraphik: *turtle graphics*

Schirm: *screen* **elektrostatischer** ~ *electrostatic screen*

schlagen: *jar*

Schlagzeilen: *banner headlines*

Schlange: *queue*

Schlaufe: *loop*

Schleier: *fog*

Schleife: *loop* **selbstrücksetzende** ~ *self-resetting or self-restoring loop* **verschachtelte** ~ *nested loop*

Schleifendurchgangsgeschwindigkeit: *speed of loop*

Schleifenindex: *cycle index*

Schleifenprogramm: *loop or looping program*

Schleifenprüfung: *loop check*

Schleifenrumpf: *loop body*

Schleifenzähler: *loop counter*

Schleife ohne Ausgang: *closed loop*

schließen: *close*

Schließen: logisches ~ *inference*

schließlich: *in the end*

Schlinge: *loop*

Schlitz: *slot*

Schluß: *tail*

Schlüssel: *key*

Schlüsselfeld: *key field*

Schlüsselmatrix: *key matrix*

Schlüsselverwaltung: *key management*

Schlüsselwort: *keyword*

Schmalband: *narrow band*

Schmalbandfernsehen: *slow scan television*

Schmalbandfrequenzmodulation: *narrow band FM (NBFM)*

Schmitz: *blur; slur*

Schmutztitel: *half title*

Schnappschuß: *action shot*

Schnee: *snow*

Schneiden: *cutting*

schneiden: *cut*

Schneideraum: *cutting room*

schnell: *fast; immediate; quick; rapid*

Schnelleitung: *fast line*

Schnellsortierer: *quicksort*

Schnellspeicher: *fast core; immediate access store (IAS)*

Schnellübertrag: *high speed carry; ripple-through carry*

Schnellzugriff: *rapid access*

Schnellzugriffsplatte(nlaufwerk): *fixed head disk (drive)*

Schnellzugriffsspeicher: *rapid access memory or fast access memory (FAM)*

Schnittstellenanschluß: paralleler ~ *parallel interface or port*

Schnittliste: *editing plan*

Schnittmenge: *intersection*

Schnittstelle: *interface* **parallele** ~ *parallel interface* **serielle** ~ *serial interface*

Schnittstellenadapter: peripherer ~ *peripheral interface adapter (PIA)*

Schnittstellenkarte: *interface card*

Schnittstellenprogramm: *interface routines*

Schnittstellenprozessor: *interface processor*

Schnitzer: grober ~ *howler*

Schön- und Widerdruckmaschine: *perfector*

Schoß: *lap*

Schraffur: *shading*

Schrägschnitt: *diagonal cut*

Schrägspurverfahren: *helical scan*

Schrägstellung: *skew*

Schrägstrich: *slash or oblique stroke*

Schreibdichte: *pitch* **vierfache** ~ *quad density*

Schreibdienst: zentraler ~ *typing pool*

Schreiben: unmittelbares ~ *demand writing*

schreiben: *put; write* **neu** ~ *rewrite*

Schreiberring: *write-permit ring*

Schreibfehler: *erratum* **auf** ~ **prüfen** *spellcheck*

Schreibkopf: *record head or write head* **fliegender ~** *flying head*

Schreibkraft: *typist*

Schreibmaschine: *typewriter* **elektrische ~** *electric typewriter* **elektronische ~** *electronic typewriter*

Schreibschutz: einen ~ anbringen *to write protect*

Schreibschutzetikett: *write-protect tab*

Schreibtisch: *desk*

Schreibvorgang: erneuter ~ *rewrite*

Schreibwaren: *stationery*

Schreibwechsel: *correspondence*

Schreibweise: *notation* **hexadezimale ~** *hexadecimal notation* **oktale ~** *octal notation*

Schreibzeit: *write time*

Schrift: *type; writing* **magere ~** *light face* **serifenlose ~** *sans serif* **umgekehrte ~** *reverse characters*

Schriftart: *font or fount; print style; typeface or typestyle*

Schriftbild: *typeface or typestyle or font* **korrespondenzfähiges ~** *near letter-quality (NLQ)*

Schriftdatenplatte: *font disk*

Schriftenfamilie: *family*

Schriftenplatte: *font disk*

Schriftgrad: *typesize*

Schriftgrundlinie: *base line*

Schriftsatz: elektronischer ~ *electronic composition*

Schriftspiegel: *body size*

Schriftstück: *document* **fertiges ~** *finished document*

Schrifttypen der Schreibmaschine: *typewriter faces*

Schritt: *signal element; step*

Schritt für Schritt: *staged*

Schrittgeschwindigkeit: vorgegebene ~ *default rate*

schritthaltend: *inline*

Schrittkamera: *planetary camera*

Schrittmotor: *stepper motor or stepping motor*

Schrittschaltung: *escapement*

Schrott: *junk*

schrumpfen: *shrink*

Schrumpffolienverpackung: *blister pack*

Schuppenstreifen: *chadded or chadless tape*

Schusterjunge: *orphan (line)*

Schutz: *privacy; protection*

Schutz-: *protective*

Schutzabstand: *guard band*

Schutzbit: *guard bit*

schützen: *protect*

Schutzhülle: *sleeve*

Schutzkopie: *protection master*

Schutzverschlüsselung: *privacy transformation*

schwächer werden: *fade*

schwanken: *fluctuate*

Schwankung: *fluctuation*

Schwarzes Brett: *notice board*

Schwarzes-Brett-System: *bulletin board system (BBS)*

Schwarzpegel: *black level*

Schwarztreppe: vordere ~ *front porch*

Schwärzungsgrad: *density*

Schwärzungsskala: *density dial*

schwarz-weiß: *black and white*

Schwebspannung: *floating voltage*

Schwimmen: *swim*

Schwingung: kontinuierliche ~ *continuous wave*

Schwingungsverlauf: *waveform*

Schwund: *fading*

Scrambler: *scrambler*

SECAM: *SECAM*

Sechs-Bit-Byte: *sextet*

Sedezformat: *sixteenmo or 16mo*

Segment: *segment*

Sehschärfe: *acuity*

Seide: *silk*

Seite: *page* **angerufene ~** *called party* **numerierte ~** *folio* **zeitcodierte ~** *time coded page*

Seitenabrufmethode: *demand paging*

Seitenadressierung (speicher): *page addressing*

Seitenanzeige: *page display*

Seitenband: *sideband*

Seitenbeschreibungssprache: *page description language (PDL)*

Seitenbreite: *page width*

Seitendrucker: *page printer*

Seitenendeanzeiger: *end of page indicator*

Seitengrenze: *page boundary*

Seitengröße: *page size*

Seitenlänge: *page length*

Seiten pro Minute: *pages per minute (ppm)*

Seitenregister: direktes ~ *direct page register*

Seiten-ROM-Programm: *sideways ROM*

Seitenschutz: *page protection*

Seitentabelle: *page table*

Seitentabelle für Schattenspeicher: *shadow page table*

Seitenumbruch: *pagination* **erzwungener ~** *forced page break*

Seitenwechsel: *page break*

Sektor: *sector* **fehlerhafter ~** *bad sector; faulty sector* **reservierter ~** *reserved sector*

Sektorformatierung: *(disk) sector formatting*

sektorieren: *sector*

Sektorierungsloch: *sectoring hole*

Sekundär-: *secondary*

Sekundärfarbe: *secondary colour*

Sekundärgruppe: *supergroup*

Sekundärspeicher: *secondary storage*

Sekundärstation: *secondary station*

Selbst-: *self-*

selbständig: *stand-alone or standalone*

selbstdiagnostisch *or* **selbstdiagnostizierend:** *self-diagnostic*

selbstdurchschreibend: *carbonless*

Selbstprüfung: *auto verify; automatic checking* **automatische ~** *built-in check*
selbstwählen: *to auto-dial*
Selbstwähler: *auto-dial*
Selbstwählferndienst: *subscriber trunk dialling (STD)*
selektiv: *selective*
Selektor: *selector*
Selektorkanal: *selector channel*
Semantik: *semantics*
Semantikfehler: *semantic error*
Semaphor: *semaphore*
Sendeabrufzeichen: *polling characters*
Sendeanforderung: *request to send signal (RTS)*
Sendeaufruf: *invitation to send (ITS); polling*
Sendeaufrufintervall: *polling interval*
Sendeaufrufzeit: *polling overhead*
sendebereit: *clear to send (CTS)*
Sendegerät: *send-only device*
Senden: *dispatch or despatch*
senden: *broadcast; transmit*
Sender: *transmitter (TX)*
Senderecht: ein ~ anfordern *bid*
Sender/Empfänger: automatischer ~ *ASR*
Sender-Signalumsetzer: *modulator*
Sendung: *program*
Senke: *sink*
senkrecht: *vertical*
sensibel: *sensitive*
Sensibilität für α-Teilchen: *alpha-particle sensitivity*
Sensor: *sensor*
Sensor-Bildschirm: *touch screen*
sequentiell: *sequential; sequentially*
Sequenz: *sequence*
Sequenzmodus: *sequential mode*
Serie: *series*
seriell: *serial; serially*
Serienaddierer: *serial adder*
Seriendrucker: *serial printer*
Serienfertigung: *batch production*
Serien-Parallel-Umsetzer: *serial to parallel converter*
Serienspeicher: *serial storage*
Serienverarbeitung: *serial processing*
Serife: *serif*
Server: *server*
Servicequalität: *grade of service*
Set: *set*
Set-Maß: *set size*
Setzanweisung: *narrative statement*
Setzen: *composition; setting; typesetting*
setzen: *compose; position; set; typeset*
Setzer: *compositor*
Setzerei: *composing room; typesetter*
Setzkasten: *case*
Setzmaschine: elektronische ~ *electronic compositor*

Setzraum: *composing room*
Sextett: *sextet*
Shannon: *shannon*
Shannonsches Gesetz: *Shannon's Law*
Shareware: *shareware*
„Shell"-Sortierung: *shell sort*
Sicherheit: *security* **statistische ~** *confidence level*
Sicherheitskopie: *security backup*
Sicherheitsprüfung: *security check*
Sicherheitsspielraum: *safety margin*
Sicherheitssystem: *secure system*
Sicherheitsvorkehrungen: *safety measures*
Sicherheitsvorrichtung: *safety net*
sichern: *back up; save*
sicherstellen: *ensure*
Sicherung: *backup; fuse; fusible link*
Sicherung auf Band: *tape back-up*
Sicherungskondensatorspeicher: *memory backup capacitor*
Sicherungskopie: *backup or backup file or backup copy; dump (US)*
Sicherungsschicht: *data link layer*
Sichtanzeige: digitale ~ *digital read-out*
sichtbar: *visible*
Sichtgerät: *video display*
Sichtmonitor: *video monitor*
Sichtverbindung: *line of sight*
Sieben-Bit-Byte: *septet*
Siebfaktor: *filter factor*
Signal: *signal* **akustisches ~** *beep* **analoges ~** *analog signal* **bipolares ~** *bipolar signal* **digitales ~** *digital signal* **importiertes ~** *imported signal* **moduliertes ~** *modulated signal* **speicherprogrammgesteuertes ~** *stored program signal* **unipolares ~** *unipolar signal* **vertikal polarisiertes ~** *vertically polarized signal*
Signalabfall: *decay*
Signalabfallzeit: *decay time*
Signalaufbereitung: *signal conditioning*
Signalausfall: *drop out*
Signaldämpfung: *link loss*
Signalgeber: *annunciator*
Signalgröße: *signal magnitude*
Signalisierung: *signalling* **digitale ~** *digital signalling*
Signalreflexion: *signal reflection*
Signalumsetzer: *signal converter*
Signalumwandlung: *signal conversion*
Signalverarbeitung: *signal processing*
Signatur: *accession number; signature* **digitale ~** *digital signature* **elektronische ~** *electronic signature*
Signet: *colophon*
Silbentrennung: *hyphenation* **falsche ~** *bad break*
Silbenzahl pro Minute: *dictation speed*
Silberhalogenid: *halide*
Silicon Glen: *Silicon Glen*
Silicon Valley: *Silicon Valley*

Silizium: *silicon*
Silizium-Chip: *silicon chip*
Siliziumerzeugungsanlage: *silicon foundry*
Siliziumgatter: *silicon gate*
Siliziumplatte: *silicon disk*
Silizium-Saphir-Technologie: *silicon on sapphire (SOS)*
Siliziumscheibe: *silicon wafer*
Siliziumtransistor: *silicon transistor*
SIMD-Rechner: *single instruction stream multiple data stream (SIMD)*
Simplex: *simplex*
Simulation: *simulation*
Simulator: *simulator*
simulieren: *simulate*
simultan: *parallel; simultaneously*
Simultanrechner: *parallel computer*
Simultanübertragung: *simultaneous transmission*
Simultanverarbeitung: *parallel processing; simultaneous processing*
Simultanverarbeitungssystem: *multiprocessing system*
Sinnbild für Datenflußläufe: *flowchart symbols*
Sinus: *sin or sine*
sinusförmig: *sinusoidal*
Sinuswelle: *sine wave*
SISD-Rechner: *single instruction stream single data stream (SISD)*
Sitz: *base*
Sitzungsschicht: *session layer*
Skalar: *scalar*
Skalieren: *sizing*
Skizze: *sketch*
skizzieren: *to sketch*
Slice: *slice*
Slice-Aufbau: *bit-slice architecture*
Slice-Mikroprozessor: *bit-slice microprocessor*
Slice-Prozessor: *bit-slice processor*
Smog: elektronischer ~ *electronic smog*
SNOBOL: *string orientated symbolic language (SNOBOL)*
Sofortbildentwicklung: *in camera process*
Sofortwidergabe: *instant replay*
Sofortzugriff: *instantaneous access*
Soft-Fail: *soft-fail*
Software: *software* **benutzerfreundliche ~** *user-friendly software* **hardwaregeeichte ~** *intimate* **integrierte ~** *integrated software* **menügesteuerte ~** *menu-driven software* **parametergesteuerte ~** *parameter-driven software*
Software-Bibliothek: *software library*
Software-Dokumentation: *software documentation*
Software-Engineering: *software engineering*
Software-Entwickler: *software developer*
Software-Entwicklung: *software development*
Software-Fehler: *bug*
Software-Fehler bereinigen: *troubleshoot*

Software-Haus: *software house*
Software-Ingenieur: *software engineer*
software-kompatibel: *software compatible*
Software-Lizenz: *software licence*
Software-Paket: *software package; packaged or canned software*
Software-Piraterie: *software piracy*
Software-Qualitätssicherung: *software quality assurance (SQA)*
Software-Spezifikation: *software specification*
Software-System: *software system*
Software-Unterbrechung: *software interrupt*
Software-Version: neueste ~ *file update*
Software-Wartung: *software maintenance*
Software-Zuverlässigkeit: *software reliability*
Sohndatei: *son file*
solar: *solar*
Solarrechner: *solar-powered calculator*
Solarzelle: *solar cell*
Solenoid: *solenoid*
Sonder-: *special*
Sonderausgaben: *below-the-line expenditure*
Sonderdruck: *offprint*
Sonderposten: *exceptional items*
Sonderzeichen: *special character; special sort*
Sonnenenergie: *solar power*
Sonnenrauschen: *helios noise*
Sortieren: mischendes ~ *merge sort*
sortieren: *collate; sort*
Sortierer: *collator*
Sortierfeld: *sort field*
Sortierlauf: *sorting pass*
Sortiermethode: *exchange selection*
Sortierschlüssel: *sortkey*
Sortierung: externe ~ *external sort* **interne ~** *internal sort*
Sortiment: *product line or product range*
Spalt: *gap*
Spalte: *column*
Spalten: in ~ *columnar*
80-Spalten-Bildschirm: *eighty-column screen*
80-Spalten-Drucker: *80-column printer*
Spaltenparitätsprüfung: *column parity*
spaltenweise: *columnar*
Spannung: *potential* **elektrische ~** *voltage* **positive ~** *positive*
Spannungsabfall: *brown-out; voltage dip or dip in voltage*
Spannungsebene der Batterie: *battery voltage level*
Spannungsregler: *voltage regulator*
Spannungssprung: *line transient or voltage transient*
Spannungssprungunterdrücker: *transient suppressor*
Spannungsverlust: *power loss*
spationieren: *space*

Speicher: *memory; storage; storage device; store*
akustischer ~ *acoustic store or acoustic memory*
dynamischer ~ *dynamic storage or memory*
einschichtiger ~ *one-level store* **elektrostatischer**
~ *electrostatic storage* **externer** ~ *external
memory; external storage* **flüchtiger** ~ *volatile
memory; volatile storage* **geschützter** ~ *protected
storage* **interner** ~ *internal memory or store*
ladungsgekoppelter ~ *charge coupled device
(CCD) memory* **löschbarer** ~ *erasable storage or
erasable memory* **nichtflüchtiger** ~ *nonvolatile
memory* **nichtlöschbarer** ~ *nonerasable storage*
optischer ~ *optical storage* **peripherer** ~
peripheral memory; auxiliary storage **primärer** ~
primary memory or store or main memory
programmierbarer ~ *programmable memory*
rechnerabhängiger ~ *on-line storage* **serieller** ~
serial memory **statischer** ~ *static memory; static
storage* **supraleitender** ~ *cryogenic memory*
virtueller ~ *virtual memory or virtual storage (VS)*

Speicheradresse: gültige ~ *valid memory
address*

Speicheradreßregister: *memory address register
(MAR); store address register (SAR)*

Speicherarbeitsbereich: *memory workspace*

Speicheraufbereitung: *memory edit*

Speicherauszug: *dump (US); memory dump;
storage dump* **binärer** ~ *binary dump*
dynamischer ~ *dynamic dump; snapshot dump*
formatisierter ~ *formatted dump* **selektiver** ~
selective dump **statischer** ~ *static dump*

Speicherauszug der Änderungen: *change dump*

Speicherauszug des Programmstops: *check
point dump*

Speicherauszugspunkt: *dump point*

Speicherbank: *memory bank*

Speicherbereich: allgemeiner ~ *common storage
area*

Speicherbereinigung: *garbage collection*

Speicherbus: *memory bus*

Speicherchip: *memory chip*

Speicherdatenregister: *memory data register
(MDR); store data register (SDR)*

Speicherdiagnose: *memory diagnostic*

Speicherelement: *memory cell*

Speicherfeld mit Vorzeichen: *signed field*

Speicherhierarchie: *memory hierarchy*

speicherintensiv: *memory intensive*

Speicherkapazität: *density; memory capacity;
storage capacity* **doppelte** ~ *double density*

Speicherkondensator: *memory backup capacitor*

Speicherliste: nicht festgeschriebene ~
uncommitted storage list

Speicher löschen: *flush buffers*

Speichermedien: *storage media*

Speicher mit Laserschicht: *laser emulsion
storage*

speichern: *save; store*

speichern und übermitteln: *store and forward*

Speicherorganisation: spezielle ~
checkerboarding

speicherorientiert: *memory-mapped*

Speicherplatine: *memory board*

Speicherplatte: *storage disk*

Speicherplatz: geschützter ~ *isolated location;
protected location*

Speicherplatzzuordnung: dynamische ~
dynamic storage allocation

Speicherplatzzuteilung: *storage allocation*

Speicherpufferregister: *memory buffer register
(MBR)*

speicherresident: *memory-resident*

Speicherröhre: *storage tube*

Speicherschaltersystem: *memory switching
system*

Speicherschutz: *memory protect*

Speicherschutzschlüssel: *protection key*

Speicherseite: *memory page; page* **unveränderte**
~ *clean page*

Speicherstelle: *location*

Speicherung: holographische ~ *holographic
storage* **magnetische** ~ *magnetic encoding*

Speicherverwaltung: *memory management*

Speicherzelle: *store location or cell*

Speicherzugriff: direkter ~ *direct memory access
(DMA); cycle stealing*

Speicherzugriffskanal: direkter ~ *direct
memory access channel*

Speicherzugriffssteuerung: direkte ~ *DMA
controller*

Speicherzugriffszeit: *memory access time*

Speisehornstrahler: *feed horn*

Spektralanalysator: *spectrum analyzer*

Spektrum: *spectrum* **elektromagnetisches** ~
electromagnetic spectrum

Spender: *dispenser*

Sperre: *lock up* **elektronische** ~ *electronic lock*

Sperreingang: *inhibiting input*

Sperren: gegenseitiges ~ *deadlock*

sperren: *disable; inhibit; lock*

Sperrschichttransistor: bipolarer ~ *bipolar
junction transistor (BJT)*

Spezialindizierung: *indexing*

spezialisieren: sich ~ *specialize*

Spezialist: *specialist*

Spezialpapier: wärmeempfindliches ~ *thermal
paper*

speziell: *special*

Spezifikation: *specification* **hohe** ~ *high
specification or high spec*

spezifisch: *intrinsic*

Spezifität: *specificity*

Spiegel: *mirror*

Spiegelbild: *mirror image*

spiegeln: *mirror*

Spiegelreflexkamera: *reflex (camera)*

Spiegelung: *reflection*

Spiel: *game*

Spielkonsole: *game paddle*

Spielraum: *margin*

Spindel: *spindle*

Spitze: *peak; top*
Spitze des Stapels: *top of stack*
Spitzenbedarfszeit: *time of peak demand*
Spitzenqualität: *high quality or top quality*
Spitzmarke: *header; heading*
SPOOL-Betrieb: *spooling*
SPOOL-Funktion: *print spooling*
Sprachantwort: *voice answer back*
Sprachassemblierer: *language assembler*
Sprachausgabe: *voice output*
Sprachausgabeeinheit: *audio response unit*
Sprach-Chip: *speech chip*
Sprache: *language; speech* **algorithmische ~** *algorithmic language* **anwendungsbezogene ~** *application orientated language* **erweiterbare ~** *extensible language* **interne ~** *internal language* **natürliche ~** *natural language* **synthetische ~** *synthetic language*
Spracheingabedaten: *voice data entry or input*
Spracherkennung: *speech recognition; voice recognition*
Sprachkompilierer: *language compiler*
Sprachprozessor: *speech processor*
Sprachregeln: *language rules*
Sprachsignal: *speech signal*
Sprachsynthese: *speech synthesis; voice synthesis*
Sprachsynthesizer *or* **Sprach-Synthetisator:** *speech or voice synthesizer*
Sprachverarbeiter: *language processor*
Sprechanlage: *intercom*
Sprecheinheit: *voice unit*
Sprechfrequenzband: *speech or voice band*
sprechen: *talk*
Sprechfunkgeräte: *hand portable sets or handy talkies or HT's*
Sprechkanal: *voice grade channel*
Springen: fehlerhaftes ~ *defect skipping*
springen: *jump*
Sprosse: *row*
Sprung: schneller ~ *high-speed skip*
Sprunganweisung: *GOTO*
Sprungbefehl: *jump (instruction)* **bedingter ~** *conditional jump* **unbedingter ~** *unconditional jump*
Sprungoperation: *jump operation*
Spulbetrieb: *spooling*
Spule: *coil; inductor; reel; spool* **offene ~** *open reel*
spulen: *to spool*
Spulgerät: *spooler or spooling device*
Spur: *track; trail*
Spuradresse: *track address*
Spurelement: *spot*
Spuren pro Inch: *tracks per inch (TPI)*
spurgenau laufen: *to track*
Stabdrucker: *bar printer*
stabil: *stable*
Stabilität: *stability*
Stachelbandführung: *sprocket feed; tractor feed*
Stachelradwalze: *sprocket or sprocket wheel*

Stadtplan: *street directory; street plan or town plan*
Stammdatei: *master file*
stammen (von): *originate (from)*
Standardannahme: *default option*
Standardbrief: *standard letter*
Standardform: *normalized form*
Standardformular: *standard document or standard form*
Standardfunktion: *standard function* **eingebaute ~** *built-in function*
standardisieren: *normalize; standardize*
Standardisierung: *normalization*
Standardisierungsroutine: *normalization routine*
Standardlaufwerk: *default drive*
standardmäßig: *standard*
Standardschnittstelle: *standard interface*
Standardtext: *standard paragraph or standard text*
Standard-Unterprogramm: *standard subroutine*
Standardvorgabe: *default value*
Standardwert: *default response*
Ständer: *rack*
ständig: *continual; permanent*
ständig vorhanden: *resident*
Standort: *base*
Stanzrückstand: *chad*
Stapel: *batch; pack*
Stapeladresse: *stack address*
Stapelbetrieb: *batch mode*
Stapelherstellung: *batch production*
Stapeljobverarbeitung: *stack job processing*
stapeln: *to batch*
Stapelnummer: *batch number*
Stapelregion: *batch region*
Stapelspeicher: *nesting store*
Stapelübertragung: *batched communication*
Stapelverarbeiter: *batch processor*
Stapelverarbeitung: *batch processing* **sequentielle ~** *sequential batch processing*
Stapelverarbeitungsdatei: *batch file*
Stapelverarbeitungssystem: *batch system*
Stapelzeiger: *stack pointer (SP)*
stark: zu ~ einfärben *overink*
starr: *rigid*
Start: *start* **automatischer ~** *auto start*
Startadresse: *float factor*
Startbefehle: *initial instructions*
Startbit: *start bit or element*
Startprogramm: *initial program header*
Startpunkt: *starting point*
Startsignal: *go ahead*
Station: *station*
stationär: *stationary*
stationieren: *base*
Stationsaufforderung: *enquiry character*
statisch: *static*
Statistik: *statistics*

Statistiker: *statistician*

statistisch: *statistical*

Status: *state; status* **aktiver** ~ *active state*

Statusabfrage: *status poll*

Statusregister: *status register*

Statuszeile: *status line*

Stau: *jam*

stauen: sich ~ *to jam*

Steckdose: *(female) socket*

Steckeinheit: *plug-in unit*

Stecker: *jack; male connector; plug* **den** ~ **herausziehen** *unplug* **polarisierter** ~ *polarized plug*

steckerkompatibel: *plug-compatible*

Steckerplatz: freier ~ *empty slot*

steif gebunden: *hardbound*

Stelle: *appointment; place; position* **undichte** ~ *leak*

Stellenbesetzungsplan: *organization chart*

Stellenverschiebung: arithmetische ~ *arithmetic shift* **logische** ~ *logical shift* **zyklische** ~ *cycle or cyclic shift*

Stellenverschiebung nach links: *left justification*

Stenotypist(in): *shorthand typist*

Sterad(iant): *steradian*

Stereomikrophon: *stereophonic microphone*

stereophon: *stereophonic*

Stereorekorder: *stereophonic recorder*

Stern(chen): *asterisk*

Sternnetz: *star network*

Steueranweisung: *control statement*

Steuerbefehl: *control instruction*

Steuerblock: *control block*

Steuerbus: *control bus*

Steuerdaten: *control data*

Steuereinheit: *control unit (CU)* **periphere** ~ *peripheral control unit (PCU)*

Steuerelement: logisches ~ *logic gate*

Steuerelement für DFV-Verbindungswege: *communications link control*

Steuerkarten: *control cards*

Steuerknüppel: *game paddle; joystick*

Steuermodus: *control mode*

steuern: *to control*

Steuerprogramm: *master control program (MCP)*

Steuerprogramm CP/M: *control program/monitor or control program for microcomputers (CP/M)*

Steuerregister: *control register*

Steuertoken: *control token*

Steuerung: *control*

Steuerung des Informationsflusses: *information flow control*

Steuerungsablauf: *control sequence*

Steuerungsball: *trackball*

steuerungsgetrieben: *control driven*

Steuerungssignale: *control signals*

Steuerungssprache: *control language*

Steuerungsübergabe: *control transfer*

Steuerungsverfahren: codeunabhängiges ~ *high-level data link control (HLDLC)*

Steuerwort: *control word*

Steuerzeichen: *control character*

Steuerzeichenfolge: *control sequence; supervisory sequence*

Steuerzeichenkennzeichnung: *flag code*

Steuerzyklus: *control cycle*

Stibitz-Code: *excess-3 code*

Stichleitung: *drop line*

Stichprobe: *sample*

Stichtag: *deadline*

Stichwort: *headword*

Stichwortverzeichnis: *index*

Stift: *stylus*

Stillstandprojektion: *still frame*

Stimmabdruck: *voice print*

Stimme: *voice*

Stockung: *holdup*

Stop: *halt* **programmierter** ~ *programmed halt*

Stopbefehl: *breakpoint instruction or halt; breakpoint instruction; kill job*

Stopbit: *stop bit or stop element*

stopfen: *pad*

Stopliste: *stop list*

stoppen: *block; kill*

Stopzeit: *stop time*

Störabstand: *noise margin*

stören: *jam* **etwas** ~ *to interfere with something*

störend: *unwanted*

Störfestigkeit: *interference or noise immunity*

Störimpuls: *glitch (informal)*

Störmuster: *interference pattern*

stornieren: *cancel*

Stornierung: *cancellation*

Störsignal: *drop in*

Störstrom: *extra*

Störung: *interference; malfunction; malfunctioning; mush* **asymmetrische** ~ *common mode noise* **elektromagnetische** ~ *electromagnetic interference; EMI* **induzierte** ~ *induced interference*

Störung der Übertragungsleitung: *hit on the line*

Störungen: *noise* **atmosphärische** ~ *static*

Störungsaufzeichnung: *failure logging*

Störungsgebiet: *mush area*

Stoßbetrieb: *burst mode*

stoßen: *jar*

Strahl: *beam; ray* **indirekter** ~ *indirect ray*

Strahlenablenkung: *beam deflection*

Strahlenbreite: *beam width*

strahlend: *radiant*

Strahl(en)teiler: *beam splitter*

Strahlstrom: *picture beam*

Strahlung: *radiation* **elektromagnetische** ~ *electromagnetic radiation*

Strahlungsenergie: *radiant energy*

Strahlungskeule: *lobe*

Straßenverzeichnis: *street directory*
streichen: *delete*
Streichmasse: *coating*
Streichung: *deletion*
Streifen: *strip; stripe*
Streifencode: *bar code or bar graphics (US)*
Streifenlocher: *tape punch*
Streifenvorspann: *leader*
Streuladen: *scatter load*
Streuspeichermethode: *folding*
Streuung: *dispersion; scatter*
Strich: *bar; line; stroke*
Strichpunkt: *semi-colon; semicolon*
Strichzeichnungen: *line drawings*
String-Bereich: *string area*
String-Länge: *string length*
String-Name: *string name*
String-Variable: *string variable*
strippen: *strip*
Stroboskop: *stroboscope or strobe*
Strom: *current; power; stream* **den ~ abschalten** *power dump* **den ~ einschalten** *power up* **elektrischer ~** *electric current*
Stromabschaltung: automatische ~ *automatic power off*
Stromausfall: *power failure*
Strom entnehmen: *drain*
Stromkreis: *circuit* **ausgeglichener ~** *balanced circuit* **digitaler ~** *digital circuit* **monostabiler ~** *monostable*
Stromkreisunterbrecher: *circuit breaker*
Stromstoß: *surge*
Stromversorgungsanlage: unterbrechungslose ~ *uninterruptable power supply (UPS)*
Stromversorgungseinheit: *power supply or power supply unit (PSU)*
Strowgersches Fernsprechamt: *strowger exchange*
Struktur: *format; pattern; structure* **kartesische ~** *cartesian structure*
Strukturerkennung: *pattern recognition*
strukturieren: *structure*
strukturiert: *patterned*
Studio: *studio*
Studioleiter: *technical director*
Stufe: *level; stage*
Stufenform-Plotter: *incremental plotter*
Stufenquantisierung: quaternäre ~ *quatenary level quantization*
Stunde: pro ~ *per hour*
Sturm: (erd)magnetischer ~ *magnetic storm*
Sub-Adresse: *subaddress*
Sub-Segment: *subsegment*
Substanz: *substance*
Substitution: *substitution*
Substitutionsfehler: *substitution error*
Substitutionstabelle: *substitution table*
Subtrahend: *subtrahend*
Subtrahierwerk: *full subtractor*

Subtraktion: *subtraction*
Suchbegriff: *search key*
Suchbereich: *seek area*
Suche: *search* **disjunktive ~** *disjunctive search* **eliminierende ~** *dichotomizing search* **erschöpfende ~** *exhaustive search* **lineare ~** *linear search* **rückwärtsgerichtete ~** *retrospective search* **sequentielle ~** *sequential search*
Suchen: *find; hunting* **binäres ~** *binary search or chop*
suchen: *search; seek*
Suchen und Ersetzen: *find and replace; search and replace*
Sucher: *eyepiece; viewfinder* **elektronischer ~** *electronic viewfinder*
Suchgeschwindigkeit: tatsächliche ~ *effective search speed*
Suchkriterium: *search key*
Suchmethode: gerichtete ~ *directed scan*
Suffix-Schreibweise: *suffix notation*
Summand: *addend; augmenter* **erster ~** *augend*
Summe: *sum*
Summen: *buzz*
summen: *to buzz*
Summenprüfung: *summation check*
Summer: *buzzer; howler*
summieren: *accumulate*
Supercomputer: *number cruncher*
Superstation: *superstation (US)*
Superüberlagerungsfunkempfänger: *superheterodyne radio*
Supervisor: *executive or supervisor(y) program; supervisor*
Symbol: *symbol* **beliebig verwendbares ~** *wild card* **logisches ~** *logic symbol*
symbolisch: *symbolic*
Symboltabelle: *symbol table or library*
synchron: *synchronous*
Synchronisation: *dubbing*
Synchronisationsdemodulation: *synchronous detection*
Synchronisationszeichen: *flag bit*
Synchronisieren: *synchronization*
synchronisieren: *dub; synchronize*
Synchronisierer: *synchronizer*
synchronisiert: *in sync*
Synchronisierungsbit: *sync bit (informal)*
Synchronisierungsimpulse: *sync or synchronization pulses*
Synchronisierungsmechanismus: *interlock*
Synchronisierungsprojektor: *interlock projector*
Synchronisierungszeichen: *sync character; synchronous idle character*
Synchronnetz: *synchronous network*
Synchronrechner: *synchronous computer*
Synchronsignale: *clocked signals*
Synchronsystem: *synchronous system*
Synchronübertragung: *synchronous transmission*
Synchronverfahren: *synchronous mode*

Synonym: *synonym*

synonym: *synonymous*

Syntax: *syntax*

Syntaxanalyse: *syntax analysis*

Syntaxfehler: *syntax error; grammatical error*

Synthese: *synthesis*

Synthesizer *or* **Synthetisator:** *synthesizer*

synthetisieren: *synthesize*

System: *system* **anpassungsfähiges** ~ *adaptive system* **ausfallsicheres** ~ *fail safe system* **autonomes** ~ *stand-alone or standalone* **bereitstehendes** ~ *sleep* **bewegungsgesteuertes** ~ *transaction-driven system (TDS)* **durchsichtiges** ~ *transparent* **eingebettetes** ~ *embedded system* **expandierbares** ~ *expandable system* **interaktives** ~ *interactive system* **offenes** ~ *open system* **operatorbedientes** ~ *hands on* **schlüsselfertiges** ~ *turnkey system* **selbstanpassendes** ~ *self-adapting system* **selbstlernendes** ~ *self-learning system* **unbestimmtes** ~ *indeterminate system* **vorganggesteuertes** ~ *TDS* **wissensbasiertes** ~ *knowledge-based system* **zentralisiertes** ~ *shared logic system*

Systemablaufplan: *system flowchart*

Systemabsturz: *system crash*

Systemanalyse: *systems analysis*

Systemanalytiker: *systems analyst*

Systembibliothek: *system library*

Systemdiagnose: *system diagnostics*

Systeme: anpassungsfähige ~ *adaptive systems* **computerintegrierte** ~ *computer-integrated systems*

Systemgenerierung: *system generation or sysgen*

Systemplanung: *system design*

Systemplatte: *system disk*

Systemprogramm: *systems program*

Systemprogrammierer: *systems programmer*

Systemprotokoll: *system log*

Systemprüfung: *system check*

Systemsicherheit: *system security*

Systemsoftware: *system software*

systemunabhängig: *off-line*

System-Urband: *master tape*

Systemverwaltung: *housekeeping*

Systemverwaltungsroutine: *housekeeping routine*

System zum Dokumentenretrieval: *document retrieval system*

Tt

Tabelle: *columnar graph; table*

Tabellen: in ~ **arbeiten** *columnar working*

Tabellenform: in ~ *in tabular form*

Tabellensuchen: *table lookup*

Tabellieren: *tabbing; tabulating*

tabellieren: *tab; tabulate*

Tabulator: *tabulator*

Tabulatormarkierer: *tabulation markers*

Tabulatorraster: *tab rack or ruler line*

Tabulatorspeicher: *tab memory*

Tabulatorstop: *tab or tabulation stop*

Tabulieren: *tabulation*

Tafel: *plate*

Tag: *tag* **pro** ~ *per day*

Tageslicht: *available light*

Tageslichtprojektor: *overhead projector*

Tagesordnung: *agenda*

Tagesordnungspunkt: *agenda item*

takten: *clock*

taktflankengesteuert: *edge-triggered*

Taktfrequenz: *clock frequency*

Taktgabe: doppelte ~ *dual clocking*

Taktgeber: clock externer ~ *external clock* **ohne** ~ *unclocked*

Taktgeberrate: *clock rate*

Taktschleife: *timing loop*

Taktsignal: *clock pulse*

Taktspur: *clock track*

Taktzyklus: *clock cycle*

Tal: *trough*

Taschenbuch: *paperback*

Taschencomputer: *hand-held computer or programmable*

Taschenkalender: *pocket diary*

Taschenrechner: *pocket calculator*

TASI: *TASI*

Tasksteuerung: *task management*

Task-Warteschlange: *task queue*

Tastatur: *keyboard; keypad* **alphanumerische** ~ *alphanumeric keyboard* **elektronische** ~ *electronic keyboard* **frei belegbare** ~ *soft keyboard* **hexadezimale** ~ *hex pad; hex keypad* **interaktive** ~ *interactive keyboard* **nicht zählende** ~ *noncounting keyboard* **numerische** ~ *numeric(al) (key)pad* **taktile** ~ *tactile keyboard* **unsichtbar schreibende** ~ *blind keyboard*

Tastaturcodierer: *keyboard encoder*

Tastatur einer Datenstation: *terminal keyboard*

Tastaturkontaktprellen: *keyboard contact bounce*

Tastaturschablone: *keyboard overlay*

Tast-Bildschirm: *touch screen*

Taste: programmierbare ~ *programmable key*

Tastenabtaster: *keyboard scan*

Tastenanordnung: *keyboard layout*

Tastenanschlag: *keystroke*

Tastenanschlagsprüfung: *keystroke verification*

Tastenblock: *keypad*

Tastenerklärungsstreifen: *key strip*

Tastenmatrix: *key matrix*

Tastennummer: *key number*

Tastenschablone: *key overlay*

Tastentelefon: *digipulse telephone*

Tastenüberlappungspuffer: *key rollover*

Tastenweg: *key travel*

Tastenwiderstand: *key force*

Taster: *momentary switch*
Tastung: **überlappende** ~ *key rollover*
Tat: *action*
Tätigkeit: *activity*
Tauchspulenmikrophon: *moving coil microphone*
Team: *crew*
Technik: *technique*
Techniker: *technician*
technisch: *technical*
Technologie: *technology* **neue** ~ *new technology*
technologisch: *technological*
Teil: *part*
Teilbauelement: *component*
Teilbildunterdrückung: *horizontal blanking*
Teilchen: *particle*
Teilhaberfirma: *associate company*
Teilnehmer: *subscriber; telephone subscriber*
Teilprüfung im Bocksprungprogramm: *crippled leapfrog test*
Teil-RAM: *partial RAM*
Teilsystem: *subsystem*
Teilübertrag: *partial carry*
Telefax: *fax or FAX*
telefaxen: *to fax or FAX*
Telefon: *phone; telephone* **das** ~ **abnehmen** *to answer the (tele)phone; to take a call* **or** *to take a (tele)phone call* **drahtloses** ~ *cordless telephone* **lautverstärktes** ~ *amplified telephone* **per** ~ *by (tele)phone* **über das** ~ *by telephone*
Telefon als Datenträger: *telephone as a data carrier*
Telefonanruf: *phone call; telephone call*
Telefonbuch: *(tele)phone book; (telephone) directory*
Telefongespräch: **ein** ~ **annehmen** *to answer the telephone* **or** *to take a telephone call*
Telefonhörer: *handset*
telefonieren: *to make a (phone) call; to be on the (tele)phone; to make a telephone call*
telefonisch: **etwas** ~ **bestellen** *to (tele)phone for something*
Telefonist(in): *switchboard operator; telephone operator; telephonist*
Telefonkarte: *phonecard*
Telefonklingeln: **harmonisches** ~ *harmonic telephone ringer*
Telefonleitung: **freie** ~ *free line*
Telefonnetz: **öffentliches** ~ *public switched telephone network (PSTN)*
Telefonnummer: *(tele)phone number*
Telefonsignalverstärker: *telephone repeater*
Telefonsystem: **privates** ~ *private telephone system*
Telefonvermittlungsstelle: *area exchange*
Telefonzelle: *telephone booth; call box*
Telefonzentrale: *exchange; (telephone) switchboard*
Telegramm: *cable; cablegram; telegram; telegraph*
Telegrammadresse: *cable address; telegraphic address*

Telegraphenamt: *telegraph office*
Telegraphie: *telegraphy*
telegraphieren: *cable; telegraph*
telegraphisch: *telegraphic*
Telekommunikationsgenehmigung: **britische** ~ *BABT approval*
Telekonferenz: *teleconference or teleconferencing*
Telekonferenzschaltung: *dial conference*
Telematik: *telematics*
Tele-Objektiv: *extension tube*
Teleshopping: *electronic shopping; teleshopping*
Teletext: *teletext*
Telex: *telex*
Telex-Operator: *telex operator*
Telex-Teilnehmer: *telex subscriber*
Telexverbindung: *telex line*
Terahertz: *terahertz*
Termin: *appointment; deadline* **den** ~ **einhalten** *to meet a deadline*
Terminal: *terminal* **adressierbarer** ~ *addressable terminal* **nicht programmierbarer** ~ *dumb terminal* **virtueller** ~ *virtual terminal*
Terminalsteuerelement: *terminal controller*
Terminkalender: *appointments book; diary*
Terminplaner: *desk planner or wall planner*
Terminverwaltung: *diary management*
ternär: *ternary*
Test: *test* **nichtlöschender** ~ *non-destructive test*
testen: *pilot; test*
Testgerät: *exerciser*
Testlauf: *test run*
Testmuster: *test pattern*
Testprogramm: *benchmark*
Testumgebung: *test bed*
Text: *body; copy; matter; text* **verschlüsselter** ~ *ciphertext*
Textanfang: *start of text (SOT or STX)*
Textanwendungen: *text management*
Textaufbereitungsprogramm: *editor program*
Textbearbeitung: *text manipulation*
Textbereich: *text screen*
Textdatei: *text file*
Text-Editor: *text editor*
Texteinrichtung: **vertikale** ~ *vertical justification*
Textende: *end of text (EOT or ETX)*
Textfenster: *text window*
Textfernverarbeiter: *communicating word processor*
Textformatierer: *text formatter*
Text im Flattersatz: *ragged text*
Text-in-Sprache-Umwandler: *text-to-speech converter*
Textkomprimierung: *text compression*
Textkörper: *body*
Textlücke: *blank*
Textmarker: *marker pen*
Textregister: *text register*
Textretrieval: *text retrieval*

Textschrift: *body type*
Textumstellung: *cut and paste*
Text verarbeiten: *word-process*
Textverarbeitung: *text processing; word-processing (WP)*
Textverarbeitungsbüro: *word-processing bureau*
Textverarbeitungscomputer: *word-processor dedizierter* ~ *dedicated word processor*
Textverarbeitungsfunktion: *text-editing function*
Textverarbeitungssystem: *text-editing facilities; word-processor* **gemeinsam benutztes** ~ *shared logic text processor*
Textverwaltungssystem: *text manager*
Textwiederauffindung: *text retrieval*
Thema: *matter*
Theorie: verschwommene ~ *fuzzy logic or fuzzy theory*
Thermistor: *thermistor*
Thermodrucken: *thermal transfer*
Thermodrucker: *(electro)thermal printer*
Thermopapier: *thermal paper*
Thesaurus: *thesaurus*
Thyristor: *thyristor*
Tiefenbereich: *depth of field*
Tiefenregler: *bass control*
Tiefenschärfe: *depth of focus*
Tiefpaßfilter: *low pass filter*
Tieftonlautsprecher: *woofer (informal)*
Tiegeldruckpresse: *platen press*
Tilde: *tilde*
Timesharing: *time-sharing*
Tinte: *ink*
Tintenschreiber: *pen recorder*
Tintenstrahldrucker: *ink-jet printer*
tippen: *type*
Tippfehler: *typing error*
Tischcomputer: *desktop computer (system); desk top unit*
Titelseite: *title page*
T-Netz: *T network*
Tochterplatine: *daughter board*
Token: *token*
Tokenring-Netzwerk: *token ring network*
Tomogramm: *tomogram*
Tomographie: *tomography*
Ton: *tone* **reiner** ~ *pure tone*
Tonarm: *pickup*
Tonband: digitales ~ *digital audio tape (DAT)*
Tonbandkassette: *cassette tape*
Tonbereich: *audio range*
Ton-Chip: *sound chip*
Toneffekt: einsynchronisierter ~ *dubbed sound*
Toner: *toner*
Tonerbehälter *or* **Tonerpatrone:** *toner cartridge*
Tonfrequenz: *audio frequency*
Tonfrequenzbereich: *audio range*
Ton(frequenz)kompressor: *audio compressor*
Tonhöhe: *pitch*

Tonkassette: *audio cassette*
Tonkopf: *sound head*
Tonmischstudio: *mixing studio*
Tonne: *barrel*
Tonnenverzeichnung: *barrel distortion*
Tonplatte: digitale ~ *digital audio disk (DAD)*
Tonrolle: *capstan*
Tonsignal: monophones ~ *derived sound*
Tonsignalsystem: *tone signalling*
Tonspur: *sound track*
Tonteil: *sound chip*
Tonträger-Endabschaltung: *auto stop*
Tonverstärker: *audio amplifier*
Tonwählsystem: *tone dialling*
TOP: *agenda item*
Topologie: *topology*
Torschaltung: *gate*
Torsionskabel: *twisted pair cable*
tot: *blind; dead*
Totalausfall: *catastrophic failure*
Tottasten: *dead keys*
Totzeit: *dead time*
tragbar: *hand-held*
träge: *inert*
Träger: *carrier*
Trägerfrequenzsystem: *carrier system*
Trägerfrequenztelegraphie: *carrier telegraphy*
Trägermaterial: *substrate*
Trägerrakete: *launch vehicle*
Trägerschwingung: *carrier; carrier wave*
Trägersignal: *carrier signalling*
Training: computergestütztes ~ *computer-aided or -assisted training (CAT); computer-based training (CBT)*
Transaktion: *transaction*
Transaktionsverarbeitung: *transaction processing (TP)*
Transfergeschwindigkeit: *data transfer rate*
Transformation: *transformation*
Transformationsregeln: *transformational rules*
Transformator: *transformer*
transformieren: *transform*
Transistor: *transistor* **bipolarer** ~ *bipolar transistor*
Transmittanz: *transmittance*
transparent: *transparent*
Transparentkopie: *transparency*
Transparentpaginierung: *transparent paging*
Transphasor: *transphasor*
Transponder: *transponder*
transportierbar: *transportable*
transportieren: *transport*
Transportschicht: *transport layer*
Transportunternehmen: öffentliches ~ *common carrier*
Transputer: *transputer*
Treffer: *hit*
Treiber: *driver or handler*

Treiberroutine: *peripheral driver*
trennen: *decollate; disconnect; divide; isolate; separate*
trennen und ausgleichen: *hyphenate and justify*
Trennfuge: weiche ~ *soft hyphen*
Trennmaschine: *decollator*
Trennprogramm: intelligentes ~ *intelligent spacer*
trennscharf: *selective*
Trennschärfe: *selectivity*
Trennstrich: *em dash or em rule*
Trennübertrager: *isolation transformer*
Trennung: *division; separation*
Trennungsmarke: *group mark or marker*
Trennungszeichen: *hyphen* **weiches** ~ *discretionary or soft hyphen*
Trennung und Randausgleich: *hyphenation and justification or H & J*
Trennzeichen: *field marker or separator*
Triade: *triad*
Trichteröffnung: *mouth*
Tricks: *special effects*
Tri-State-Logik: *three state logic*
Trockenelement: *dry cell*
Trojanisches Pferd: *Trojan Horse*
Trommelplotter: *drum plotter*
Trommelspeicher: *drum*
Troposphäre: *troposphere*
TTL-kompatibel: *TTL compatible*
TTL-Logik: *TTL logic*
Turing-Maschine: *Turing machine*
Turing-Test: *Turing test*
T-Verbindung: *T junction*
Typ der Zeichenfolge: *string type*
Type: *type*
Typengröße: *composition size*
Typenkopf: *printhead*
Typenmischung: *mixing*
Typenrad: *daisy-wheel; printwheel*
Typenraddrucker: *daisy-wheel printer*
Typenradschreibmaschine: *daisy-wheel typewriter*
Typenwalzendrucker: *barrel printer*
Typograph: *typographer*
Typographie: *typography*
typographisch: *typographic or typographical*
Typoskript: *typescript*

Uu

UART: *UART*
UART-Steuereinheit: *UART controller*
über: *via*
überall angelaufen: *on general release*
Überanstrengung der Augen: *eye-strain*
überarbeiten: *revise*

Überbrückung: *bridge or bridging product; bridging*
überdecken: *overlap*
Übereignung: *assignment*
übereinstimmen: mit etwas ~ *to correspond with something*
überflüssig: *redundant*
Übergang: *transition*
Übergangsbereich: *transient area*
Übergangsspannung: *voltage transient*
Übergangsstelle: *transition point*
Übergangsstrom: *power transient*
übergeben: *hand off*
übergehen: *ignore*
Übergruppe: *supergroup*
überhitzen: *overheat*
überlagern: *superimpose*
Überlagern: *overlaying*
Überlagerung: *heterodyne; interference; overlay*
Überlagerungsbereich: *overlay region*
Überlagerungsnetz: *overlay network*
Überlagerungssegmente: *overlay segments*
Überlandleitung: *landline*
Überlandnetz: *long haul network*
überlappen: *overlap*
Überlappung: *interleaving; lap*
überlasten: *overload*
Überlastung: *congestion; thrashing*
Überlauf: *overflow or OV; spillage* **charakteristischer** ~ *characteristic overflow*
Überlaufanzeiger: *overflow flag or indicator*
Überlaufbit: *overflow bit*
überlaufen: *overrun*
Überlaufprüfung: *overflow check*
Überlochung: *overpunching*
Übermodulation: *overmodulation*
übernehmen: *undertake*
überprüfen: *review; verify*
Überprüfung: *checking*
überschreiben: *overstrike; overwrite*
Überschreibmodus: *replace mode*
Überschreibung: *destructive addition*
Überschrift: *heading; rubric*
Überschuß: *excess*
3-Überschußcode: *excess-3 code*
überschüssig: *excessive*
Überschwingspitze: *spike*
übersetzen: *compile; interpret; translate*
Übersetzer: *interpreter; language processor*
Übersetzerprogramm: *interpreter; translator (program)*
Übersetzersprache: *interpreted language*
Übersetzungsanlage: *source machine*
Übersetzungsanweisung: *directive; directive statement*
Übersetzungsprogramm: *language interpreter; language translator*
Übersetzungsrechner: *source machine*

Übersetzungstabellen: *conversion tables or translation tables*
Überspannungsableiter: *surge protector*
Überspannungsschutz: *over-voltage protection*
Überspringbefehl: *skip instruction*
überspringen: *jump; skip*
Überspringfähigkeit: *skip capability*
Überstrahlen: *bloom*
Übertrag: *carry*
übertragbar: *portable*
Übertragbarkeit: *portability*
übertragen: *communicate; despool; relay; transfer*
Übertragsanzeiger: *carry flag*
Übertragsbit: *carry bit*
Übertragszeit: *carry time*
Übertragung: *assignment; transmission* **asynchrone ~** *asynchronous communications; asynchronous transmission* **bedingte ~** *conditional transfer* **byteserielle ~** *byte serial transmission or mode* **drahtgebundene ~** *line communications* **fotomechanische ~** *photomechanical transfer (PMT)* **magnetische ~** *magnetic transfer* **neutrale ~** *neutral transmission* **nochmalige ~** *retransmission* **optische ~** *optical transmission* **periphere ~** *peripheral transfer* **radiale ~** *radial transfer* **serielle ~** *serial transmission* **unbedingte ~** *unconditional transfer* **verzerrte ~** *ANAPROP*
„Übertragung beendet"-Signal: *carry complete signal*
Übertragungsbefehl: *transfer command*
Übertragungsbereich: *frequency response*
Übertragungsblock: geschlossener ~ *burst*
Übertragungsende: *end of transmission (EOT)*
Übertragungsfehler: *transmission errors*
Übertragungsfenster: *transmission window*
Übertragungsgeschwindigkeit: *bit rate; line speed; transfer rate; transmission rate* **höchste ~** *maximum transmission rate* **normale ~** *low speed communications*
Übertragungskanal: *transmission channel*
Übertragungskontrolle: *transfer check*
Übertragungsmedien: *transmission media*
Übertragungsmöglichkeiten eines Nachrichtenkanals: *circuit grade*
Übertragungsplatte: *transmissive disk*
Übertragungssteuerung: *line control; transfer control* **binär-synchrone ~** *binary synchronous communications (BSC)*
Übertragungssystem: digitales ~ *digital transmission system*
Übertragungsweg: bus zweiseitig gerichteter ~ *bi-directional bus*
Übertragungswegsystem: doppeltes ~ *dual bus system*
Übertragungszeit: *transfer time*
Übertretung: *infringement*
überwachen: *monitor; supervise*
Überwachung: *supervision*
Überwachungsbefehl: *supervisory instruction*

Überwachungsprogramm: *supervisory or executive program*
Überwachungssignal: *supervisory signal*
Überwachungssystem: *monitor*
überwechseln: *change over*
Überwechseln: schrittweises ~ *staged change-over*
Überzug: *coating*
Überzugsverfahren: *deposition*
Uhr: *clock*
Uhrzeitgeber: *real-time clock*
Ultrahochfrequenz: *ultra high frequency (UHF)*
Ultrakurzwellenbereich: *very high frequency (VHF)*
Ultramikrofiche: *ultrafiche*
Ultraschall: *ultrasound*
Ultraschallwellen: *ultrasonic*
Ultraviolettstrahlung: *ultraviolet (UV) light*
umblätterbar: nicht ~ *non-scrollable*
umbrechen: *make up*
Umbruch: *make up or makeup; page break*
Umbruchfahnen: *page proofs*
umcodieren: *recode*
Umdrehen: *spindling*
Umdruckpapier: *duplicator paper*
Umdruckverfahren: *spirit duplication*
Umfang: *extent*
umfassend: *global*
umgeben: *enclose*
umgebend: *ambient*
Umgebung: *environment*
Umgebungstemperatur: *ambient temperature*
Umgrenzung: *border*
umkehren: *invert; reverse*
Umkehrentwicklung: *autopositive*
Umkehrfilm: *direct image film*
Umkehrliste: *push-down list*
Umkehrstapel: *push-down stack*
Umkehrung: *inverse; inversion*
umkreisen: *orbit*
umlagern: *page*
Umlauf: *circulation* **in ~ bringen** *circulate*
Umlaufbahn: *orbit* **äquatoriale ~** *equatorial orbit* **elliptische ~** *elliptical orbit* **geneigte ~** *inclined orbit* **geostationäre ~** *geostationary orbit* **polare ~** *polar orbit*
umlaufen: *run around*
Umlaufspeicher: *circulating storage*
Umlaufsystem: *word wrap or wraparound*
Umlaut: *umlaut*
Umleiten: *redirection*
umleiten: *redirect*
Umleiter: *diverter*
Umpolung: *polarity reversal*
Umrandung: *margination*
Umschaltcode: *shift code*
umschalten: *shift; switch over*
Umschaltnetzwerk: *switching circuit*

Umschalttaste: *case change; shift key*
Umschaltzeichen: *shift character*
Umschlag: *envelope; jacket* **offener** ~ *unsealed envelope* **zugeklebter** ~ *sealed envelope*
Umschlag für Kanzleipapier: *foolscap envelope*
umschreiben: *transcribe*
Umschreibung: *transcription*
umsetzen: *code; convert*
Umsetzer: *conversion equipment; converter or convertor*
Umsetzung: *conversion; encoding* **binäre** ~ *binary encoding*
Umsetzungsprogramm: *language compiler*
Umstellung: *crossover; transposition* **schrittweise** ~ *phased change-over*
Umstellung auf EDV: *computerization*
umsteuern: *re-route*
umwandeln: *assemble; transform*
Umwandler: *changer; transcoder*
Umwandlung: *assembly; transformation*
Umwandlungscode: *assembly code*
Umwandlungszeit: *assembly time*
unabhängig: *independent(ly)*
unbearbeitet: *raw*
unbedingt: *unconditional*
unbefugt: *unauthorized*
unbeschnitten: *uncut*
unbeschränkt: *freely*
unbespielt: *virgin*
UND-Funktion: *AND or coincidence function; conjunction; equivalence function or operation; intersection*
UND-Gatter: *AND gate*
UND-Schaltung: *AND or coincidence gate or circuit or element; coincidence circuit or element*
undurchsichtig: *opaque*
UND-Verknüpfung: *AND or coincidence operation*
Und-Zeichen: *ampersand*
unediert: *unedited*
uneindeutig: *ambiguous*
unendlich: *infinite*
Unendlicheinstellung *or* **Unendlichkeit:** *infinity*
unentdeckt: *undetected*
unerlaubt durchsuchen: *scavenge*
unerlaubt nachahmen/nachbauen/ nachdrucken: *pirate*
unerwünscht: *unwanted*
unformatiert: *unformatted*
Ungenauigkeit: *inaccuracy*
ungenügend: *insufficient*
ungerade: *odd*
ungeschützt: *unprotected*
Ungleichförmigkeit: *judder*
ungültig: *invalid*
Ungültigkeitszeichen: *cancel or ignore character*
ungültig werden: *expire*
Union: *union*
unipolar: *unipolar*

universal: *general*
Universalcomputer: *general purpose computer*
Universalprogramm: *general purpose program*
Universalschnittstellenbus: *general purpose interface bus (GPIB)*
universell: *universal*
Unix: *Unix*
unleserlich: *illegible*
unmoduliert: *unmodulated*
unredigiert: *unedited*
unruhig: *busy*
Unsinn: *gibberish; junk*
unsortiert: *unsorted*
unterbelichtet: *underexposed*
unterbrechen: *cut off; interrupt*
Unterbrechung: *attention; break; interrupt* **absichtliche** ~ *armed interrupt* **eine** ~ **herbeiführen** *to interrupt* **enable externe** ~ *external interrupt* **maskierbare** ~ *maskable interrupt* **nichtmaskierbare** ~ *non-maskable interrupt (NMI)* **ohne** ~ *continuously* **transparente** ~ *transparent interrupt* **unwirksame** ~ *disable interrupt* **zeigergesteuerte** ~ *vectored interrupt*
Unterbrechung auf Abruf: *polled interrupt*
Unterbrechungsanforderung: *interrupt request*
Unterbrechungsebene: *interrupt level*
Unterbrechungshalt: *dead or drop-dead halt*
Unterbrechungsleitung: *interrupt line* **verkettete** ~ *daisy chain interrupt*
Unterbrechungsmaske: *interrupt mask*
Unterbrechungsprioritäten: *interrupt priorities*
Unterbrechungspunkt: *cutoff point*
Unterbrechungsschichtung: *interrupt stacking*
Unterbrechungsservice: *interrupt servicing*
Unterbrechungssignal: *interrupt signal*
Unterbrechungssteuerung: **programmierte** ~ *programmable interrupt controller*
Unterbrechungs-Steuerungsprogramm: *interrupt handler (IH)*
Unterbrechungstaste: *attention key*
unterdrücken: *suppress*
Unterdrücker: *suppressor*
Unterdrückung: *suppression*
Unterdrückung des Telefonklingelns: *anti-tinkle suppression*
Unterklasse: *subclass*
Unterlagen: *documentation*
Unterlänge: *descender*
Unterlauf: *underflow*
Untermalung: *dubbed sound*
Untermenge: *subset*
Unterprogramm: *subprogram; subroutine* **abgeschlossenes** ~ *closed subroutine* **dynamisches** ~ *dynamic subroutine* **eingefügtes** ~ *inserted subroutine* **einstufiges** ~ *one-level subroutine* **offenes** ~ *open subroutine* **parametrisches** ~ *parametric (subroutine)* **rekursives** ~ *recursion or recursive routine* **statisches** ~ *static subroutine* **verbundenes** ~ *linked subroutine* **zweischichtiges**

~ two-level subroutine **zweistufiges** ~ two-level subroutine

Unterprogramme: mathematische ~ mathematical subroutines

Unterricht: computergestützter ~ computer-aided or assisted instruction (CAI); computer-managed instruction (CMI)

unterscheiden: distinguish **sich** ~ differ

Unterschied: difference

unterschiedlich: different

unterschreiben: sign

Unterschrift: signature

Unterschriftsbestätigungsmethode: SAFE

Unterstreichen: underlining

unterstreichen: to underline or underscore

Unterstreichung: underline or underscore

unterstützen: aid; back; back up; support

unterstützend: backup

Unterstützung: aid; assistance **finanzielle** ~ financial assistance

Unterstützungschip: support chip

Untersuchung: analysis

Unterverzeichnis: subdirectory

ununterbrochen laufen lassen: soak

unvorbereitet: cold

unzulässig: illegal; illegally

unzusammenhängend: disjointed

Urheber: copyright owner

Urheberrecht: copyright

urheberrechtlich geschützt: copyright; copyrighted

urheberrechtlich schützen: copyright

Urheberrechtsgesetz: Copyright Act

Urheberrechtsvermerk: copyright notice

Urlader: bootstrap (loader); initial program loader (IPL) **automatischer** ~ auto boot

Urladerprogrammspeicher: bootstrap memory

Ursprung: source

Ursprungsdatei: source file

Ursprungsdatei-Editor: source editor

Ursprungsdaten: raw data

Ursprungsformat: native format

Ursprungskartensatz: source deck or pack

Ursprungspunkt: source

Ursprungssprache: source language

Vv

Vakuum: vacuum

Vakuumröhre: vacuum tube

variabel: variable

Variable: variable **binäre** ~ binary variable **globale** ~ global variable **indizierte** ~ subscripted variable **lokale** ~ local variable

Variablenname: variable name

Vaterdatei: father file

Veitch-Diagramm: Veitch diagram

Vektor: vector

Vektorbild: vector graphics or vector image or vector scan

Vektorenrechner: array processor

Vektorprozessor: vector processor

Venn-Diagramm: Venn diagram

Ventil: valve

Ventilator: fan

Verabredung: appointment

veraltet: out of date

veränderbar: alterable

veränderlich: variable

verändern: change **sich** ~ vary

verarbeiten: process

Verarbeitung: execution; processing **nachrangige** ~ background processing **schritthaltende** ~ in-line processing **sequentielle** ~ sequential processing **serielle** ~ serial processing **stapelweise** ~ batch processing **unmittelbare** ~ demand processing; immediate processing **verteilte** ~ distributed processing **wahlfreie** ~ random processing

Verarbeitungsmenge: effektive ~ effective throughput

verbergen: conceal

verbessern: enhance; upgrade

verbieten: bar; forbid

verbinden: combine; connect; couple; interconnect; join; link

verbindend: combinational

Verbindung: connection; interconnection; linkage **festverdrahtete** ~ hardwired connection **trockene** ~ dry joint **virtuelle** ~ virtual circuit

Verbindung auf Anfrage: switched virtual call

Verbindungskabel: feeder cable

Verbindungsleitung: recording trunk **steckbare** ~ patchcord

Verbindungsprogramm: link

Verbindungsrechner: gateway

Verbindungssteuerungssignal: call control signal

Verbindungssteuerungsverfahren: link control procedure (LCP)

Verbindungsstrecke: link

Verbindungsüberprüfung: link trials

Verbindungsweg: facility

Verblassen: fading

verblassen or **verbleichen:** fade

verborgen: hidden

verbrauchen: use

Verbrauchsgüter: consumables

Verbund: group

verbunden: associate

Verbundsystem: distributed system

verdichten: compress; pack

Verdichter: compressor

Verdichtung: compression; packing

Verdichtungsprogramm: compressor; packing routine

Vereinbarung: *declaration* or *declarative statement*
vereinfachen: *simplify*
vereinigen: *coalesce*
vereinzelt: *stray*
Vereinzelungsmaschine: *burster*
Verfahren: *process*
Verfahren der (Daten)übertragungssteuerung: *basic mode link control*
Verfahrensdiagramm: *process chart*
Verfall: *expiration*
Verfallsdatum: *expiration date*
verfälschen: *corrupt*
Verfasser: *author*
Verfassersprache: *author language*
Verfassersystem: *authoring system*
verflechten: sich ~ *interlace*
verfügbar: *available*
Verfügbarkeit: *availability*
Vergleich: *comparison*
vergleichbar: *comparable*
vergleichen: *compare; match*
Vergleicher: *comparator*
Vergleichsgruppe: *control group*
Vergleichsoperator: *relational* or *logical operator*
Vergleichspunkt: *benchmark*
vergrößern: *augment; enlarge; expand; magnify; to scale up; zoom*
Vergrößern: *zooming*
Vergrößerung: *enlargement; magnification*
Verhältnis: *ratio*
verhindern: *prevent*
Verifikation: *verification*
verirrt: *stray*
verkabeln: *wire*
Verkauf: telefonischer ~ *telesales*
Verkäufer: *shop assistant*
Verkaufsgespräch: *sales pitch*
Verkehr: ankommender ~ *incoming traffic*
Verkehrslenkung: feste ~ *fixed routing* **isolierte adaptive ~** *isolated adaptive routing* **verteilte adaptive ~** *distributed adaptive routing*
verketten: *catenate; chain; concatenate; daisy-chain*
Verkettung: *daisy chain*
Verkleidung: *cladding*
Verkleidungsplatte: vordere ~ *front panel*
verkleinern: *to scale down*
Verkleinerung: starke ~ *high reduction*
verknüpfen: *bind*
Verknüpfung: *nexus*
Verknüpfungsglied: *decision circuit* or *element; logic element*
Verknüpfungszeit: *binding time*
Verlag: *house; publisher*
Verlagsstil: *house style*
Verlagswesen: *publishing*
verlängern: *extend*

Verlängerung: *extension*
Verlängerungskabel: *extension cable*
Verlegen von Fachliteratur: *professional publishing*
Verletzung: *breach*
Verletzung der Gewährleistung(spflicht): *breach of warranty*
Verletzung des Urheberrechts: *infringement of copyright* or *copyright infringement*
verlieren: *lose*
Verlust: *breakup; loss*
Verlustbelegung: *lost call*
Verlustzeit: *dead time; lost time*
Vermaschung: *mesh*
vermehren: *augment*
Verminderung: *decrease*
vermischen: *to mix down*
Vermißtenfaktor: *omission factor*
vermitteln: *convey*
Vermittler: *mid-user*
Vermittlung: *switchboard; switching* **digitale ~** *digital switching*
Vermittlungsanlage: private ~ *private branch exchange (PBX)*
Vermittlungsschicht: *network layer*
Vermittlungssystem: elektronisches ~ *electronic switching system*
Vermittlungszentrale: *switching centre*
vernetzen: *network*
veröffentlichen: *publish; release*
Veröffentlichung: *publication*
Verpacken: *packing*
verpackt: *boxed*
Verpackung(smaterial): *packaging; packing*
verramschen: *remainder*
verriegeln: *interlock; latch*
Verriegelung: *interlock*
verringern: *reduce*
Verringerung: *reduction*
Versagen: induziertes ~ *induced failure*
versagen: *fail*
Versalien: *upper case*
versauen: *mung up (informal)*
versäumen: *fail*
Versäumnis: *failure*
verschachteln: *nest*
Verschachtelungsgrad: *nesting level*
Verschicken: *mailing*
verschiebbar: *relocatable*
Verschiebebefehl: *shift instruction*
Verschieben: logisches ~ *logical shift*
verschieben: *drag; justify; range; relocate; shift*
Verschieberegister: *shift register*
Verschiebung: *relocation* **dynamische ~** *dynamic relocation* **statische ~** *static relocation*
Verschiebungskonstante: *relocation constant*
verschieden: *differential*
Verschlechterung: *degradation*

Verschluß: *shutter*
verschlüsseln: *encipher; encrypt*
Verschlüsselung: *cipher; encryption* **binäre** ~ *binary encoding*
Verschlüsselungssystem: *cipher system*
Verschmelzung: *fusion*
verschwommen: *fuzzy*
Versehen: aus ~ *in error or by error*
versiegeln: *seal*
Version: *release; version* **erweiterte** ~ *advanced version* **neueste** ~ *update*
Verso: *verso*
versorgen: *to supply*
Versorgung: *supply*
Versorgungsnetz: öffentliches ~ *mains electricity*
Verspätung: *delay*
verspleißen: *splice*
verstärken: *amplify; boost*
Verstärker: *amplifier* **rauscharmer** ~ *low noise amplifier*
Verstärkerklasse: *amplifier class*
Verstärkerstation: *repeater*
Verstärkung: *amplification; constructive interference*
Verstärkungsgrad: *gain*
Verstärkungsregelung: *gain control* **automatische** ~ *AGC*
versteckt: *hidden*
Verstoß: *breach*
verstreut: *stray*
verstümmeln: *corrupt*
Versuchsmuster: *dummy*
Vertauschung: *transposition*
verteilen: *distribute*
Verteiler: *splitter; switch*
Verteilerkasten: *junction box*
Verteilerservice: lokaler ~ *LDS*
Verteilung: *distribution*
Verteilungskanäle: *distribution channels or channels of distribution*
Verteilungssystem: sternförmiges ~ *switched star*
vertikal: *vertical; vertically*
vertikal blättern: *vertical scrolling*
vertikal polarisiert: *vertically polarized*
Vertikaltabulator: *vertical tab*
Vertragsbruch: *breach of contract*
vertreten: *represent*
Vertreter: *representative*
Vervielfältiger: *duplicator*
Vervielfältigung: *duplication*
vervollkommnen: *perfect*
verwackeln: *blur*
Verwacklung: *judder*
Verwalter: *administrator*
Verwaltung: *management*
verwanzen: *bug*

Verweilzeit: *turnaround time (TAT)*
Verweisgenerator: *cross-reference generator*
Verweisliste: *reference list*
Verweis nach vorne: *forward reference*
Verweisungsdatei: *pointer file*
Verweiszeichen: *reference mark*
verwenden: *use*
verwerfen: *discard*
verwürfeln: *scramble*
Verwürfler: *scrambler*
verzahnt: *interleaved*
Verzahnung: *interleaving*
Verzeichnis: *directory; dictionary* **hierarchisches** ~ *hierarchical directory*
Verzeichnisleitweg: *directory routing*
Verzeichnung: *anamorphic image*
verzerren: *distort*
Verzerrung: *distortion; slur* **lineare** ~ *geometric distortion*
Verzerrungsobjektiv: *distortion optics*
Verzögerung: *delay; holdup; lag* **mittlere** ~ *average delay*
Verzögerung durch Konkurrenzbetrieb: *contention delay*
Verzögerungsleitung: *delay line* **akustische** ~ *acoustic delay line*
Verzögerungsvektor: *delay vector*
verzweigen: *branch*
Verzweigung: *branch; switch* **unbedingte** ~ *unconditional branch*
Verzweigungsbefehl: *branch instruction*
Verzweigungseinrichtung: *distribution point*
Verzweigungspunkt: *branchpoint*
V-Format: *V format*
VHD: *VHD*
via: *via*
Video: *video*
Videoabspielgerät: *video player*
Videoanschluß: *video port*
Videoband: *(video cassette) tape; videotape*
Videobandbreite: *video bandwidth*
Videobandrekorder: *videotape recorder*
Videobild: *video image* **invertiertes** ~ *inverse video*
Videoeinzelbild: *video frame*
Videoexpander: *video expander*
Videohorrorfilme: *video nasties (informal)*
Videokamera: *video camera*
Videokassette: *video cassette*
Videokompressor: *video compressor*
Videokonferenz: *video conference*
Videomonitor: *video monitor*
Videoplatte: *videodisk*
Video-RAM: *video memory or video RAM (VRAM)*
Videorekorder: *video cassette recorder (VCR); video recorder; videotape recorder*
Videoschnittstellenchip: *video interface chip*
Videospiel: *video game*

Videosystem: hochauflösendes ~ *HDVS*
interaktives ~ *interactive video*
Videoterminal: *video terminal; visual display terminal (VDT) or visual display unit (VDU)*
Videotext: *videotext or videotex*
Videovollbild: *video frame*
vielfach ausnutzen: *multiplex*
Vielfachleitung: *highway or bus*
Vielfalt: *diversity*
Vieradreßbefehl: *four-address instruction*
Vier-Bit-Byte: *nibble or nybble (informal)*
vierfach: *four-fold; quad*
Vier-plus-eins-Adreßbefehl: *four-plus-one address*
Vierspurrekorder: *four-track recorder*
virtuell: *virtual*
Virus: *virus*
Visitenkarte: *business card*
visuell: *visual*
VLP-Bildplatte: *optical disk; optical memory*
voll: *full*
Volladdierer: *full adder or three input adder*
Vollaussteuerung: *maximum reading*
vollkommen: *perfect*
voll machen: *fill up*
Vollmacht: *authority*
Vollquittungsbetrieb: *full handshaking*
vollständig: *complete; full; fully*
Vollständigkeit: *integrity*
Vollständigkeit einer Datei: *integrity of a file*
vollständig löschen: *bulk erase*
Volltypen: *fully formed characters*
Volt: *volt*
Volumen: *volume*
Vorab-Zuordnung: *pre-allocation*
vorangehen: *precede*
voraufzeichnen: *to prerecord*
Voraufzeichnung: *prerecord*
vorausplanen: *project*
Vorausplanung: *projection*
Voraussetzungen: *requirements*
Vorbedingung: *precondition*
vorbehaltlich: *conditional*
vorbereiten: *arm*
Vorbereitung: *preparation*
Vorbereitungszeit: *make-ready time; takedown time*
vorbeugend: *preventive or preventative*
Vorbeugung: *prevention*
vorbildlich: *model*
vordefiniert: *predefined*
Vordergrund: *foreground*
Vordergrundfarbe: *foreground colour*
Verodergrundprogramm: *foreground program*
Vordergrundverarbeitung: *foreground processing or foregrounding*
Vorderseite: *front*
Vordruck: *form; preprinted stationery*

Vordrucksatz: *multi-part stationery*
voreingenommen: *biased*
voreinstellen: *preset*
vorformatiert: *preformatted*
vorführen: *demonstrate; screen*
Vorführgerät: *demonstration model; kludge or kluge (informal)*
Vorführraum: *projection room*
Vorführung: *demonstration*
Vorgabe: *default*
Vorgang: unkalkulierbarer ~ *random process*
vorgedruckt: *preprinted*
Vorgehenserklärung: *docket (US)*
Vorgehensweise: *procedure*
Vorgehensweise des Operatoren: *operator procedure*
Vorgriff: *look ahead*
vorher abgesprochen: *pre-agreed*
vorher bearbeiten: *pre-edit*
vorherbestimmt: *predetermined*
vorher entworfen: *predesigned*
vorherig: *previous; previously*
Vorkehrung: *measure*
Vorkompilierer: *preprocessor*
Vorlage: druckfertige ~ *photoprint* **reproreife** ~ *camera-ready copy (crc)*
Vorlaufsatz: *leader record*
Vormagnetisierung: *bias*
Vormischung: *premix*
Vorproduktion: *preproduction*
Vorprogramm: *interlude*
vorprogrammiert: *preprogrammed*
Vorprozessor: *preprocessor*
Vorrang: *precedence; priority*
Vorrangprogramm: *foreground program*
Vorrangunterbrechung: *priority interrupt*
Vorrangunterbrechungtabelle: *priority interrupt table*
Vorrat: solange ~ **reicht** *subject to availability*
Vorrichtung: *appliance*
Vorrücken der Tonspur: *sound advance*
Vorsatz: *header; tape trailer*
Vorsatzblock: *header block*
Vorschaltrechner: *front-end processor (FEP)*
Vorschub: *carriage*
Vorschublöcher: *centre holes*
Vorschubsteuerung: *carriage control*
Vorsilbe: *prefix*
Vorspann: *leader; prefix; tape header*
Vorspannband: *trailer*
Vorspannung: *bias*
Vorstand: *board of directors*
vorstellen: sich ~ *picture; visualize*
vorübergehend: *temporar(il)y*
vorübersetzen: *preprocess*
Vorverarbeitungssystem: *front-end system*
Vorverstärker: *pre-amplifier*

vorverzerren: *pre-emphasise*
Vorwahl: *area code; dialling code*
vorwärts: *forward*
vorwärtsbewegen: *advance*
Vorwärtsfehlerkorrektur: *forward error correction*
Vorwärtsmodus: *forward mode*
Vorwärtsstreuung: *forward scatter*
vorweg speichern: *prestore*
Vorzeichen: *sign* ohne ~ *unsigned*
Vorzeichenbit: *sign bit or sign indicator*
Vorzeichenposition: *sign position*
Vorzeichenziffer: *sign digit*
V-Serie: *V series*

Ww

Waage: *weighing machine*
Wagenrücklauf: *carriage return (CR)* automatischer ~ *automatic carriage return*
Wagenrücklauftaste: *carriage return key*
Wahl: andere ~ *alternative*
Wählanschluß: öffentlicher ~ *public dial port* privater ~ *private dial port*
wählen: *dial*
Wählen: *dialling*
Wähler: *selector*
wahlfrei: *optional*
Wählimpuls: *dial pulse*
Wählleitungsausweichverfahren: *switched network backup*
Wahlmöglichkeiten beim Einstellen: *set-up option*
Wählscheibe: *dial*
Wählton: *dial tone; dialling tone*
Wählvermittlungsstelle: elektronische ~ *electronic automatic exchange*
wahlweise: *selective*
Wählwiederholung: automatische ~ *auto-redial*
WAHR: *TRUE*
Wahrheitstabelle: *truth table*
Wahrheitswert: *truth value*
Wake-up-Code: *wake up a system*
Wald: *forest*
Walze: *platen*
Wanderwelle: *line transient*
Wanze: *bug*
Warencode: *stock code*
Warenmischung: *product mix*
Wärmeableitung: *heat sink*
wärmeempfindlich: *thermo-sensitive*
Warm-Standby-System: *warm standby*
Warmstart: *warm start*
warnen: *warn*
Warnlicht: *warning light*
Warnsignal: *alarm*

Warnung: *warning*
Wartbarkeit: *maintainability*
warten: *maintain; service*
Warteschlange: *device queue; queue*
Warteschlangenstruktur: *queue discipline*
Warteschlangenverwaltung: *queue management or queue manager*
Warteschleife: *holding loop; wait loop*
Wartestatus: *wait condition or state; waiting state*
Wartezeit: *latency; queuing time; wait time*
Wartung: *maintenance* fehlerbedingte ~ *corrective maintenance* vorbeugende ~ *preventive maintenance*
Wartungsprogramm: *service program*
Wartungsroutine: *maintenance routine*
Wartungsvertrag: *maintenance or service contract*
Was-man-sieht-ist-alles-was-man-bekommen-kann: *What-You-See-Is-All-You-Get (WYSIAYG)*
Was-man-sieht-ist-was-man-bekommt: *What-You-See-Is-What-You-Get (WYSIWYG)*
Watt: *Watt*
Wechsel: *alternation*
wechseln: *alternate*
Wechselrichter: *inverter (AC/DC)*
Wechselstrom: *alternating current or AC*
Wechselstromgenerator: *alternator*
Wechselwirkung: *interaction*
Weg: *channel*
Wegewahl: *routing*
Weglaufen: *runaway*
wegnehmen: *to pop off*
weich: *soft*
Weichrückstellung: *soft-reset*
weichsektoriert: *soft-sectored*
Weiße: das ~ *white*
weißglühend: *incandescent*
Weißglut: *incandescence*
Weißpegel: *white level*
weiterübertragen: *relay*
weitervermitteln: *forward*
Weitervermittlung: *forward clearing*
Weitverkehrsnetz: *wide area network (WAN)*
Weitwinkelobjektiv: *wide-angle lens*
Welle: *wave*
Wellenberg: *peak*
Wellenform: *waveform*
Wellenformdigitalisierung: *waveform digitization*
Wellenlänge: *wavelength*
Wellenleitung: rechteckige ~ *rectangular waveguide*
Wellental: *trough*
Weltraum: *space*
Weltraumabfall: *space junk*
Weltraumstation: *space station*
WENN-Anweisung: *IF statement*
WENN-DANN-SONST-Anweisung: *IF-THEN-ELSE*

Werbeabteilung: *design or publicity department*
Werbeagentur *or* **Werbebüro:** *publicity bureau*
Werbekampagne: *publicity campaign*
Werbematerial: *publicity matter*
Werbemelodie: *jingle*
Werbeprospekte: *mailing shot*
Werbespot: *commercial*
Werbeträger: *advertising medium*
Werbezettel: *flier*
Werbung: *commercial; publicity*
Werbung betreiben: *plug*
Werbung durchführen: *publicize*
Werdegang: *background*
Werk: urheberrechtlich geschütztes ~ *work still in copyright*
Werkzeugausrüstung: *toolkit*
Werkzeugkasten: *toolbox*
Werkzeugmaschinensteuerung: computergestützte numerische ~ *computer numeric control (CNC)*
Wert: *value* **häufigster** ~ *mode*
Werteaustauschbarkeit: *formula portability*
Wertebereich: *range; number range*
Wertigkeit: mit höchster ~ *high order*
wesentlichen: im ~ *basically*
Wettersatellit: *weather satellite*
Wetware: *wetware (informal)*
WHILE-Schleife: *while-loop*
Wickelkern: *hub*
Wickelrolle: *open reel tape*
widerhallen: *echo*
Widerstand: *resistance; resistor*
Widerstand leisten: *resist*
widerstandsfähig: *robust*
Widerstandsfähigkeit: *robustness*
Widerstand-Transistor-Logik: *resistor transistor logic (RTL)*
Wiederanlauf: automatischer ~ *auto restart*
wiederanlaufen: *to restart*
Wiederanlaufprogramm: automatisches ~ *automatic recovery program*
Wiederanlaufpunkt: *rerun point*
Wiederanlaufroutine: *fall back routines*
Wiederanlaufverfahren: *recovery procedure*
wiederanschließen: *reconnect*
wiederauffindbar: nicht ~ *irretrievable*
Wiederauffinden: *retrieval* **falsches** ~ *false drop or retrieval*
Wiederauffinden eines Textes: *text retrieval*
Wiederauffinden von Informationen: *information retrieval (IR)*
Wiederauffindungssystem: *reference retrieval system*
wiederauffrischen: *refresh*
wiederaufladbar: *re-chargeable*
wiederaufladen: *replenish*
Wiederaufnahme: *recovery*
Wiederaufnahme nach Abbruch: *failure recovery*

wiederaufnehmen: *resume*
Wiedereinstiegspunkt: *re-entry point*
wiedererkennen: *recognize*
Wiedererkennung: *recognition*
Wiedergabe: *replay* **sofortige** ~ *instant replay*
Wiedergabegeschwindigkeit: *playback speed*
wiedergeben: *play back; replay*
wiederherstellen: *reconstitute; recover*
Wiederherstellungsverfahren: *backward recovery*
wiederholen: *repeat; replicate; rerun*
Wiederholung: *replay*
Wiederholungsanlauf: *fall back*
Wiederholungsgruppe: *repeating group*
Wiederholungszähler: *repeat counter*
wiegen: *weigh*
willkürlich: *random*
WIMP: *WIMP*
Winchesterplatte: *Winchester disk; Winchester disk or drive* **herausnehmbare** ~ *removable Winchester*
Winkel: *angle*
Winkeralphabet: *semaphore*
wirksam: *active*
wirkungsvoll: *effective*
Wissen: *knowledge*
wissenschaftlich: *scientific*
Wissenstechnik: *knowledge engineering*
Woche: pro ~ *per week*
Wölbung: *buckling*
Wort: *word* **festgelegtes** ~ *reserved word*
Wortabstände: *spacing*
Wörterbuch: *dictionary*
Wörter pro Minute: *words per minute (wpm or WPM)*
Wortlänge: *word length* **feste** ~ *fixed word length*
Wortmarke: *word mark*
Wortmarkierungszeichen: *word marker*
Wortserie: *word serial*
Wort(takt)zeit: *word time*
Worttrennung: *hyphenation; word break* **erneute** ~ *rehyphenation*
Wortzahl: *word count*
Wortzwischenraum: variabler ~ *interword spacing*
Wurzel: *root*

Xx

x-Achse: *horizontal axis; X-axis*
Xerographie: *xerography*
Xerokopie: *Xerox*
xerokopieren: *to Xerox or xerox*
Xerox: *Xerox*
x-Koordinate: *X-coordinate*
x-Lochung: *x punch*

x-Richtung: *X direction*

x-Serie: *X-series*

Yy

y-Achse: *vertical axis; Y-axis*

y-Koordinate: *Y-coordinate*

y-Lochung: *y punch*

y-Richtung: *Y-direction*

Zz

z-Achse: *z-axis*

Zahl: *figure; number* **ganze ~** *integer* **negative ~** *negative number* **rationale ~** *rational number* **reelle ~** *real number*

Zahl der Kettenglieder: *catena*

Zahlen: arabische ~ *Arabic numbers or figures* **in ~ ausdrückbar** *quantifiable* **römische ~** *Roman numerals* **tiefgestellte ~** *inferior figures*

zählen: *count; meter*

Zahlenbereich: *number range*

Zahlenfressen': *number crunching*

Zahlenfresser': *number cruncher*

Zahlengenauigkeit: *precision of a number*

Zahlensystem: binäres ~ *base 2* **dezimales ~ base 10** **hexadezimales ~** *base 16* **oktales ~** *base 8*

Zähler: *counter; meter*

Zählmaschine: automatische ~ *comptometer*

Zählperforator: *counting perforator*

Zahlung: in ~ geben *part exchange*

Zahlungsverkehr: elektronischer ~ *electronic funds transfer (EFT)*

Zedent: *assignor*

Zehnerkomplement: *ten's complement*

zehnmal: *by a factor of ten*

Zehntelwert: *decile*

Zeichen: *character; mark* **alphanumerische ~** *alphanumeric characters or alphanumerics* **benutzerdefinierte ~** *user-defined characters* **binär codierte ~** *binary coded characters* **blinkendes ~** *character blink; flashing character* **diakritisches ~** *diacritic* **einzeln gestellte ~** *separated graphics* **graphisches ~** *graphics character* **hochgestelltes ~** *superscript* **ikonisches ~** *icon or ikon* **invertierte ~** *cameo; reverse characters* **mit ~ füllen** *character fill* **numerisches ~** *numeric character* **redundantes ~** *redundant character* **unzulässiges ~** *illegal character* **verbotenes ~** *forbidden character* **wichtigstes ~** *most significant character*

Zeichenanzeige: *character display*

Zeichenblock: *character block*

Zeichenbyte: *character byte*

Zeichencode: *character code* **interner ~** *internal character code*

Zeichendarstellung: *character representation*

Zeichendichte: *character or packing or recording density*

Zeichendrucker: *character printer; serial printer*

Zeichenerkennung: *character recognition* **optische ~** *optical character recognition (OCR)*

Zeichenfolge: *character string; string* **alphanumerische ~** *alphanumeric or character string* **leere ~** *blank string* **numerische ~** *numeric string*

Zeichenfolge aus Leerzeichen: *blank string*

Zeichenfolgenfunktion: *string function*

Zeichenfolgenverkettung: *string concatenation*

Zeichengabe: binäre ~ *binary signalling*

Zeichengeber *or* **Zeichengenerator:** *character or pulse or signal generator*

Zeichenkette: *string* **alphanumerische ~** *alphanumeric string*

Zeichenkombination: verbotene ~ *forbidden combination*

Zeichenleser: optischer ~ *optical character reader (OCR)*

Zeichenlochkarte: *mark sensing card*

Zeichenlücken: variable ~ *intercharacter spacing*

Zeichenmatrix: *character matrix*

Zeichenneigung: *character skew*

zeichenorientiert: *character orientated*

Zeichenpapier: *cartridge paper*

Zeichen pro Inch: *characters per inch (cpi)*

Zeichen pro Sekunde: *characters per second (cps)*

Zeichen pro Zoll: *pitch*

Zeichenprüfung: *character check*

Zeichenrasterung: *character assembly*

Zeichenrundungen: *character rounding*

Zeichensatz: *character set; font or fount*

Zeichensatzänderung: *font change*

Zeichensätze: auswechselbare ~ *cartridge fonts* **verfügbare ~** *resident fonts* **zusätzlich ladbare ~** *downloadable fonts*

Zeichensatz einer Datenstation: *terminal character set*

Zeichensätze laden: *download*

Zeichenschablone: *flowchart stencil or template*

Zeichentaste: *character key*

Zeichenumschaltung: *figures shift*

Zeichenvorrat: *character repertoire*

zeichnerisch: *graphic*

Zeichnung: *plot*

Zeiger: *pointer*

Zeile: *line; row* **oberste ~** *head of form*

Zeilenabstand: *line spacing*

Zeilenabtastung: *raster scan*

Zeilenausgleich: vertikaler ~ *vertical justification*

Zeilenausreißen: *tearing*

Zeilenaustastlücke: *line blanking interval*

Zeilenbreite: *line width*

Zeilenbruch: *return*

Zeilendrucker: *line printer*

Zeilen-Editor: *line editor*

Zeileneingabe: *line input*
Zeilen(ein)richter: *aligner*
Zeilenende: *line ending*
Zeilenfrequenz: *line frequency*
Zeilenfüllen: *quadding*
Zeilenguß: *slug*
Zeilenlänge: *line length*
Zeilennummer: *line number*
Zeilen pro Minute: *lines per minute (LPM)*
Zeilenrücklauf: *line flyback*
Zeilenschritt: *line increment*
Zeilentreibersignal: *line drive signal*
Zeilenumbruch: *line folding*
Zeilenumlauf: *horizontal wraparound*
Zeilenvorschub: *line feed (LF)* **automatischer ~** *auto advance*
Zeilenvorschubzeichen: *new line character*
Zeitablaufplanung: *scheduling*
Zeitablenkung: *sweep*
Zeitadreßcode: *time address code*
Zeitanzeige: *time display*
Zeitauslösung: *timeout*
Zeitbasis: *time base*
Zeitbedingung: *race*
Zeitberechnung mit Mikroprozessoren: *microprocessor timing*
Zeitbereichsanalyse: *time domain analysis*
Zeitbombe: programmierte ~ *logic bomb*
Zeitkanal: *time slot*
Zeitlupe: *slow motion*
Zeitmultiplexdurchschaltung: *time division switching*
Zeitmultiplexkanal: *time derived channel*
Zeitmultiplexmethode: *time division multiplexing (TDM)* **statistische ~** *statistical time division multiplexing (STDM)*
Zeitnehmer: *timer*
Zeitplan: *schedule*
Zeitplanungsprogramm: *scheduler*
Zeitraum: *period* **anomalistischer ~** *anomalistic period*
Zeitscheibe: *time slice*
Zeitschrift: *magazine; periodical*
Zeitsperre: *timeout*
Zeittaktgeber: programmgesteuerter ~ *programmable clock*
Zeitungsausschnitt: *press cutting*
Zeitungspapier: *newsprint*
Zelle: *cell* **binäre ~** *binary cell*
zellglasieren: *laminate*
Zellradio: *cellular radio*
Zellreferenzvariable: *cell reference variable*
Zelltelefon: *cell phone*
Zelltelefon-Fernsprechdienst: *cellular service*
Zentimeter: *centimetre*
zentral: *central*
Zentraldatenstation: *central terminal*
Zentrale: *telephone switchboard*

Zentraleinheit: *central processing unit (CPU) or central processor*
zentralisiert: *centralized*
Zentralspeicher: *central memory (CM)*
Zentralverarbeitungseinheit: *central processing element (CPE)*
zentrieren: *centre or center (US)*
Zentrierung: *centering*
Zerreißen: *tearing*
Zerstückelung: *fragmentation*
Zickzackfaltung: *accordion or concertina fold; fanfold*
Ziel: *goal; objective; target*
Zielcomputer: *target computer*
Zielebene: *target level*
Zielprogramm: *object program; target program*
Ziffer: *digit; numeral* **niederwertigste ~** *least significant digit (LSD)* **unerlaubte ~** *unallowable digit* **wichtigste ~** *most significant digit (MSD)*
Zifferblatt: *dial*
Ziffern: arabische ~ *Arabic numerals* **römische ~** *Roman numerals*
Zifferncodes: bedeutsame ~ *significant digit codes*
Ziffernstelle: *digit place or position*
Ziffern- und Zeichenfeld: *figures case*
zirkulierend: *circulating*
Zirkumflex: *circumflex (accent)*
Zischen: *sibilance*
zitieren: *quote*
8-Zoll-Diskette: *eight-inch disk*
8-Zoll-Laufwerk: *eight-inch drive*
Zone: *zone*
Zonenübergang: *junction*
zoomen: *zoom*
Zoom(objektiv): *zoom lens*
Zubehör(teil): *accessory*
Zubringer: *feeder*
Zubringerkabel: *feeder cable*
Zubringerspeicher: *external storage or external store*
zufällig: *accidental; random*
Zufallsmodell: *stochastic model*
Zufallsnummer: *random number*
Zufallszahlgenerator: *random number generator*
zuführen: *to feed*
Zuführung: *feed*
Zugang: *access* **gemeinsam benutzter ~** *shared access* **offener ~** *open access*
zugänglich: *accessible*
Zugangskennzahl: internatonale ~ *international prefix code*
zugehörig: *associate*
zugreifen auf: *access; reference*
Zugriff: *access* **asynchroner ~** *asynchronous access* **den ~ verwehren** *deny access* **paralleler ~** *parallel access* **sequentieller ~** *sequential access* **serieller ~** *serial access* **unmittelbarer ~**

instantaneous access **wahlfreier** ~ *random access*
zyklischer ~ *cyclic access*
Zugriffsarm: *access arm*
Zugriffsberechtigung: *authorization*
Zugriffscode: *access code*
Zugriffsgebühr: *access charge*
Zugriffskontrolle: *access control*
Zugriffsmethode: *access method*
indexsequentielle ~ *indexed sequential access method (ISAM)* **zeitmultiplexe** ~ *time division multiple access*
Zugriffspunkt: *access point*
Zugriffsrecht: *privilege*
Zugriffsspeicher: serieller ~ *SAM*
Zugriffszeit: *access time* **mittlere** ~ *average access time*
Zuhause: *home*
Zuhörer: *audience; listener(s)*
Zulage: *weighting*
zuordnen: *assign*
Zuordnung: *assignment*
Zuordnungsanweisung: *assignment statement*
Zuordnungsbefehl: *reference instruction*
Zuordnungsdatei: *reference file*
Zurichtungszeit: *make-ready time*
zurückfallen in: *revert*
Zurückgewinnung: *recovery*
Zurückhalten: *retention*
zurückladen: *import*
zurückrufen: *phone back*
zurückspulen: *rewind*
zurückstellen: *reset*
zurückverfolgen: *backtrack*
zurückweisen: *reject*
Zurückweisung: *rejection*
Zurückweisungsfehler: *rejection error*
zusammenfassen: *to abstract*
Zusammenfassung: *abstract*
zusammenfügen: *add; join*
Zusammenführung: *junction*
zusammengefaßt: *ganged*
zusammengeflickt: *kluged*
Zusammenhang: *context*
zusammenhängend: *coherent*
zusammenkleben: *splice*
zusammenschalten: *interface*
zusammensetzen: *assemble*
Zusammenstellung eines Schriftstücks: *document assembly or document merge*
Zusammenstoßerkennung: *collision detection*
zusammentragen: *collate*
Zusatz: *add-in; add-on* **einen** ~ **löschen** *to zero a device*
Zusatz-: *add-in; addition; add-on; peripheral*
Zusatzadreßregister: *B-line counter; B register*
Zusatzbit: *overhead bit*
Zusatzcode: *overhead*

Zusatzcursor: *ghost cursor*
Zusatzdatensatz: *addition record*
Zusatzgerät: *attachment*
Zusatzgeräte: *ancillary or auxiliary equipment*
zusätzlich: *addition(al); auxiliary; extra*
Zusatzprozessor: *coprocessor* **mathematischer** ~ *maths chip or coprocessor (informal)*
Zusatzspeicher: *backing store or storage or memory; auxiliary or secondary storage*
Zuschauer: *audience; viewer(s)*
zuspielen: *leak*
Zustand: *condition; state; status* **logischer** ~ *logic state*
Zustandsbit: *status bit*
zustimmen: *approve*
Zustimmung: *approval*
zuteilen: *allocate*
Zuteilung: *allocation* **dynamische** ~ *dynamic allocation*
Zuteilungsroutine: *allocation routine*
zuverlässig: *reliable*
Zuverlässigkeit: *reliability*
zuvor: *prior*
Zuwachs: *increment*
zuweisen: *define*
Zuweiser: *assignor*
Zuweisung: *definition*
Zweiadreßbefehl: *two-address-instruction*
Zwei-Bit-Byte: *doublet or diad*
Zwei-Byte-Wortgruppe: *gulp*
zweideutig: *ambiguous*
Zweideutigkeit: *ambiguity*
zweidimensional: *two-dimensional*
Zweidrahtleitung: *two wire circuit*
Zweierkomplement: *two's complement*
Zweig einer Schaltung: *leg*
Zweikanalsystem: *dual channel*
Zwei-plus-Eins-Adreßbefehl: *two-plus-one-address instruction*
Zweirichtungsdrucker: *bi-directional printer*
Zweiseitenbandübertragung: *double sideband*
zweiseitig gerichtet: *bi-directional*
Zweitkanal: *secondary channel*
zweitrangig: *secondary*
Zweitröhre: *slave tube*
Zweitschrift: *duplicate*
Zwiebelschalenarchitektur: *onion skin architecture*
Zwiebelschalensprache: *onion skin language*
zwingen: *force*
Zwischencode: *intermediate code*
Zwischendatei: *intermediate file*
Zwischenfrequenz: *intermediate frequency (IF or if)*
Zwischenmedien: *intermediate materials*
Zwischenraum: *gap; space*
Zwischenregister: *temporary register*

Zwischenspeicher: *buffer; erasable storage or erasable memory; intermediate storage; temporary storage*
Zwischenspeicherbereich: *save area*
zwischenspeichern: *buffer; plant*
Zwischenstecker: *adapter plug*
Zwischensumme: *subtotal*
Zwischensumme pro Stapel: *batch total*

Zwischenträgerrauschen: *intercarrier noise*
zyklisch: *cyclic*
Zyklus: *cycle*
Zyklusverfügbarkeit: *cycle availability*
Zykluszeit: *cycle time*
Zylinder:

Anhang

COMPUTER AND PERIPHERALS

SINGLE BUS COMPUTER

MAR: Memory Address Register
MDR: Memory Data Register
ALU: Arithmetic and Logic Unit
ACC: Accumulator
IR: Instruction Register

MULTI-USER COMPUTER SYSTEM

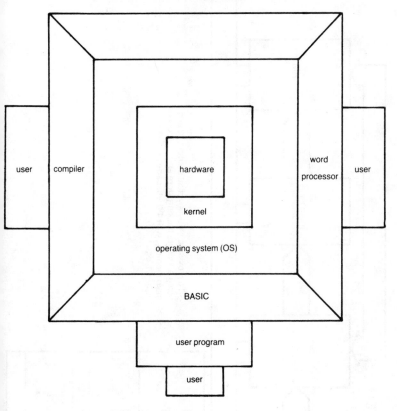

Architecture of a multi-user computer system

hardware:
the base of the system, including the CPU and
memory
kernel:
routines used by every hardware operation
(access restricted to privileged users)
operating system:
system software used by all users (access
restricted to privileged users)
applications:
a user can select applications such as a compiler
or word-processing software

VIRTUAL MEMORY SYSTEM

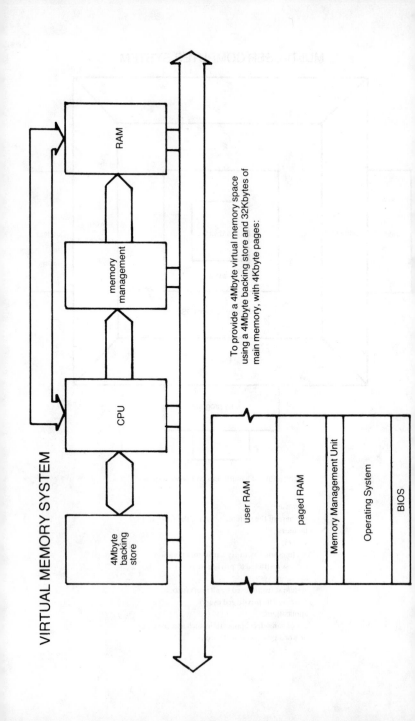

To provide a 4Mbyte virtual memory space using a 4Mbyte backing store and 32Kbytes of main memory, with 4Kbyte pages:

| 4Mbyte backing store | CPU | memory management | RAM |

| user RAM |
| paged RAM |
| Memory Management Unit |
| Operating System |
| BIOS |

HANDSHAKING

Signals ensuring correct timing for data transfer between two communicating devices.

Fully interlocked, 4 state handshaking

Half interlocked 3 state handshaking

MOST USED RS232C SIGNALS

pin	description	acronym
1	frame ground	FG
2	trasmit data to equipment	TxD
3	receive data from equipment	RxD
4	request to send	RTS
5	clear to send	CTS
6	data set ready	DSR
7	signal ground	SG
8	data carrier detect	DCD
13	secondary clear to send	(S)CTS
14	secondary transmit data	(S)TxD
15	transmitter clock	TxC
17	receiver clock	RxC
20	data terminal ready	DTR
22	ring indicator	RI
24	external transmitter clock	(TC)

IMPORTANT IEEE-488 BUS SIGNALS

line	name	comments
D101		
D102		
D103		
D104	DATA LINES	data carrying lines
D105		
D106		
D107		
D108		
DAV	DATA VALID	true if data is valid
NRFD	NOT READY FOR DATA	false when all devices are ready
NDAC	NOT DATA ACCEPTED	false when all devices have accepted data
ATN	ATTENTION	data line is carrying an address
IFC	INTERFACE CLEAR	reset signal
SRQ	SERVICE REQUEST	interrupt signal
REN	REMOTE ENABLE	
EOI	END OR IDENTIFY	end of message signal

PROGRAMMING LANGUAGES

The following demonstrates the differences in programming languages for a similar function, an input, n, is requested (the number of entries in the list) then a loop asking for the next entry and comparing it with the current biggest number is repeated n times, the biggest entry is then printed out.

ALGOL

```
begin    integer n,x,q;
         q:=0;
         read n;
         for i:=1 step 1 until n do
         begin
         B:      read x;
                 if x>00 then
                 goto A;
                 if x>q then
                     q:=x;
                 goto B;
         A:      print q;
         end;
end
```

BASIC

```
5 BIG=0
10 INPUT"How many numbers ";N
20 FOR I=1 TO N
30 INPUT X
40 IF X=0 THEN GOTO 100
50 IF X>BIG THEN BIG=X
60 NEXT I
100 PRINT BIG
110 END
```

C

```c
main()
{
        int n,i,x,big;
        scanf(%d,&n);
        (for(i = 0; i < n; i++)
        {
                scanf("%d",&x);
                if (x > big)
                        big=x;
        }
        printf("%d",big);
}
```

FORTRAN

```fortran
        INTEGER BIG
        BIG=0
        READ,N
        DO 2 I=1,N
        READ,X
   2    IF (X.GT.BIG)BIG=X
        PRINT,BIG
        STOP
        END
```

PASCAL

```pascal
program bignum(input,output);
var n,i,x,big : integer;
begin
        big := 0;
        read (n);
        for i:=1 to n do;
        begin
                read(x);
                if x > big then big:=x
        end;
        write(big)
end
```

ASCII IN DECIMAL, HEXADECIMAL

dec.	HEX	CHAR	dec.	HEX	CHAR	dec.	HEX	CHAR	dec.	HEX	CHAR
0	00	NUL	32	20	SP	64	40	@	96	60	
1	01	SOH	33	21	!	65	41	A	97	61	a
2	02	STX	34	22	"	66	42	B	98	62	b
3	03	ETX	35	23	#	67	43	C	99	63	c
4	04	EOT	36	24	$	68	44	D	100	64	d
5	05	ENQ	37	25	%	69	45	E	101	65	e
6	06	ACK	38	26	&	70	46	F	102	66	f
7	07	BEL	39	27	'	71	47	G	103	67	g
8	08	BS	40	28	(	72	48	H	104	68	h
9	09	HT	41	29	)	73	49	I	105	69	i
10	0A	LF	42	2A	*	74	4A	J	106	6A	j
11	0B	VT	43	2B	+	75	4B	K	107	6B	k
12	0C	FF	44	2C	,	76	4C	L	108	6C	l
13	0D	CR	45	2D	-	77	4D	M	109	6D	m
14	0E	SO	46	2E	.	78	4E	N	110	6E	n
15	0F	SI	47	2F	/	79	4F	O	111	6F	o
16	10	DLE	48	30	0	80	50	P	112	70	p
17	11	DC1	49	31	1	81	51	Q	113	71	q
18	12	DC2	50	32	2	82	52	R	114	72	r
19	13	DC3	51	33	3	83	53	S	115	73	s
20	14	DC4	52	34	4	84	54	T	116	74	t
21	15	NAK	53	35	5	85	55	U	117	75	u
22	16	SYN	54	36	3	86	56	V	118	76	v
23	17	ETB	55	37	7	87	57	W	119	77	w
24	18	CAN	56	38	8	88	58	X	120	78	x
25	19	EM	57	39	9	89	59	Y	121	79	y
26	1A	SUB	58	3A	:	90	5A	Z	122	7A	z
27	1B	ESC	59	3B	;	91	5B	[	123	7B	{
28	1C	FS	60	3C	<	92	5C	\	124	7C	:
29	1D	GS	61	3D	=	93	5D	]	125	7D	}
30	1E	RS	62	3E	>	94	5E	↑	126	7E	~
31	1F	US	63	3F	?	95	5F	_	127	7F	DEL

THE ASCII SYMBOLS

NUL	Null	DLE	Data Link Escape
SOH	Start of Heading	DC	Device Control
STX	Start of Text	NAK	Negative Acknowledge
ETX	End of Text	SYN	Synchronous Idle
EOT	End of Transmission	ETB	End of Transmission Block
ENQ	Enquiry	CAN	Cancel
ACK	Acknowledge	EM	End of Medium
BEL	Bell	SUB	Substitute
BS	Backspace	ESC	Escape
HT	Horizontal Tabulation	FS	File Separator
LF	Line Feed	GS	Group Separator
VT	Vertical Tabulation	RS	Record Separator
FF	Form Feed	US	Unit Separator
CR	Carriage Return	SP	Space (Blank)
SO	Shift Out	DEL	Delete
SI	Shift In		

EBCDIC code

bits 0, 1, 2, 3

bits 4,5,6,7	0	1	2	3	4	5	6	7	8	9	10	11	12	13	14	15
0	NUL	DLE			SP	&	—									0
1	SOH	DC₁					/		a	j			A	J		1
2	STX	DC₂		SYN					b	k	s		B	K	S	2
3	ETX	DC₃							c	l	t		C	L	T	3
4									d	m	u		D	M	U	4
5	HT	NL	LF						e	n	v		E	N	V	5
6	LC	BS	ETB						f	o	w		F	O	W	6
7	DEL		ESC	EOT					g	p	x		G	P	X	7
8									h	q	y		H	Q	Y	8
9									i	r	z		I	R	Z	9
10	RPT				¢	!		:								
11	VT				.	$	,	#								
12	FF	IFS		DC₄	<	★	%	@								
13	CR	IGS	ENQ	NAK	(	)	_	'								
14		IRS	ACK		+	;	>	=								
15			BEL		|	⌐	?	`								

bits 4, 5, 6, 7

LOGIC FUNCTION TABLES AND GATES

Written as	Drawn as	logic table		

A	A
0	0
1	1

A — drawn as: ——————

A	B	A*B
0	0	0
0	1	0
1	0	0
1	1	1

A AND B

A	B	A+B
0	0	0
0	1	1
1	0	1
1	1	1

A OR B

A	B	A exor B
0	0	0
0	1	1
1	0	1
1	1	0

A EXOR B

A	$\overline{A}$
0	1
1	0

NOT A

A	B	$\overline{A*B}$
0	0	1
0	1	1
1	0	1
1	1	0

A NAND B

A	B	$\overline{A+B}$
0	0	1
0	1	0
1	0	0
1	1	0

A NOR B

A	B	A exnor B
0	0	1
0	1	0
1	0	0
1	1	1

A EXNOR B

OTHER CIRCUIT SYMBOLS

buffer

inverter

JK Flip-Flop

J — Q

k — Q̄

clk

capacitor (non-polarized)

(polarized)

npn-transistor

collector
base
emitter

FETransistor

drain
gate
source

switch

battery

diode

LED

resistor

variable resistor

RESISTOR COLOUR CODING TABLES

colour	band 1 digit 1	band 2 digit 2	band 3 multiplier	band 4 tolerence
black	0	0	×1	
brown	1	1	×10	1%
red	2	2	×100	2%
orange	3	3	×1000	
yellow	4	4	×10000	
green	5	5	×100000	
blue	6	6	×1000000	
violet	7	7		
grey	8	8		
white	9	9		
gold			×0.1	5%
silver			×0.01	10%
none				20%

EXAMPLE:
brown black brown gold = 10×10 = 100 Ohms at 5%
red   green red   red = 25×100 = 2.5 KOhms at 2%

DECIMAL CONVERSION TABLES

base	Decimal 10	BCD 2	Binary 2	Octal 8	Hexadecimal 16
	00	0000 0000	0000	00	0
	01	0000 0001	0001	01	1
	02	0000 0010	0010	02	2
	03	0000 0011	0011	03	3
	04	0000 0100	0100	04	4
	05	0000 0101	0101	05	5
	06	0000 0110	0110	06	6
	07	0000 0111	0111	07	7
	08	0000 1000	1000	10	8
	09	0000 1001	1001	11	9
	10	0001 0000	1010	12	A
	11	0001 0001	1011	13	B
	12	0001 0010	1100	14	C
	13	0001 0011	1101	15	D
	14	0001 0100	1110	16	E
	15	0001 0101	1111	17	F

INTERNATIONAL STANDARD SIZES FOR PAPER

A0 = 1189 × 841 mm
A1 = 841 × 594 mm
A2 = 594 × 420 mm
A3 = 420 × 297 mm
A4 = 297 × 210 mm
A5 = 210 × 148 mm
A6 = 148 × 105 mm
A7 = 105 × 74 mm
A8 = 74 × 52 mm
A9 = 52 × 37 mm
A10 = 37 × 26 mm

SI UNITS AND ABBREVIATIONS

A	ampere	unit of electrical current
C	coulomb	unit of electrical charge (As)
cd	candela	unit of light intensity
F	farad	unit of capacitance (C/V)
H	henry	unit of inductance (Vs/A)
Hz	hertz	unit of frquency (cycles per second)
J	joule	unit of energy (kg m/s)
K	kelvin	unit of temperature
kg	kilogram	unit of mass
lm	lumen	unit of illumination (cd/sr)
lx	lux	unit of illumination density (lm/m^2)
m	metre	unit of length
mol	mole	unit of amount of substance
N	newton	unit of force (J/m)
Pa	pascal	unit of pressure
rad	radian	unit of plane angle
s	second	unit of time
sr	steradian	unit of solid angle
S	siemens	unit of electrical conductance (1/ohm)
T	tesla	unit of magnetic flux density (WB/m)
V	volt	unit of electrical potential (W/A)
W	watt	unit of power (J/s)
Wb	weber	unit of magnetic flux (Vs)
Ω	ohm	unit of electrical resistance (V/A)
C	degree Celsius	unit of temperature (K+273)

SI PREFIXES

Decimal multiples and submultiples to be used with SI units

prefix	symbol	factor	prefix	symbol	factor
tera-	T	10^{12}	centi-	c	10^{-2}
giga-	G	10^{9}	milli-	m	10^{-3}
mega-	M	10^{6}	micro-	μ	10^{-6}
kilo	k	10^{3}	nano-	n	10^{-9}
hecto-	h	10^{2}	pico-	p	10^{-12}
deda-	da	10^{1}	femto-	f	10^{-15}
deci-	d	10^{-1}	atto-	a	10^{-18}

TYPES OF MODULATION

AMPLITUDE MODULATION

ORIGINAL SIGNAL

FREQUENCY MODULATION

PULSE AMPLITUDE MODULATION

PULSE WIDTH MODULATION

BINARY DATA

FSK of binary data

PULSE POSITION MODULATION

Notizen

Notizen

Notizen

Notizen

Notizen

Notizen

Notizen

Notizen